Interpersonal Messages

Communication and Relationship Skills

Third Edition

Joseph A. DeVito

Hunter College of the City University of New York

PEARSON

Boston Columbus Indianapolis New York San Francisco Upper Saddle River
Amsterdam Cape Town Dubai London Madrid Milan Munich Paris Montréal Toronto
Delhi Mexico City São Paulo Sydney Hong Kong Seoul Singapore Taipei Tokyo

Editorial Director: Craig Campanella
Publisher: Karon Bowers
Senior Acquisitions Editor: Melissa Mashburn
Editorial Assistant: Megan Hermida
Director of Development: Sharon Geary
Senior Development Editor: Carol Alper
Director of Marketing: Brandy Dawson
Senior Marketing Manager: Blair Zoe Tuckman
Marketing Assistant: Cristina Liva
Marketing Coordinator: Theresa Graziano
Senior Managing Editor: Linda Mihatov Behrens
Project Manager: Raegan Keida Heerema
Senior Operations Supervisor: Mary Fischer
Operations Specialist: Mary Ann Gloriande
Cover Art Director: Pat Smythe
Cover Design: Ray Cruz
Cover Art: Shutterstock
Director of Digital Media: Brian Hyland
Senior Digital Media Editor: Paul DeLuca
Digital Media Editor: Lisa Dotson
Digital Media Project Manager: Michael Granger
Full-Service Project Management and Composition: Integra
Printer/Binder: Courier/Kendallville
Cover Printer: Lehigh-Phoenix Color/Hagerstown
Text Font: 10/12, Sabon LT Std

Credits and acknowledgments borrowed from other sources and reproduced, with permission, in this textbook appear on page 290.

Library of Congress Cataloging-in-Publication Data

DeVito, Joseph A.,
Interpersonal Messages: Communication and Relationship Skills/Joseph A. DeVito.—[Third Edition]
pages cm
Includes bibliographical references and index.
ISBN 978-0-205-93180-4 (student edition)—ISBN (invalid) 978-0-205-93184-2 (instructor's review copy)—
ISBN (invalid) 978-0-205-93192-7 (a la carte)
1. Interpersonal communication—Textbooks. I. Title.
BF637.C45D5 2013
158.2—dc23

2012044927

10 9 8 7 6 5 4 3 2 1

Student Edition:
ISBN-13: 978-0-205-93180-4
ISBN-10: 0-205-93180-4

Instructor's Review Copy:
ISBN-13: 978-0-205-93184-2
ISBN-10: 0-205-93184-7

À la Carte:
ISBN-13: 978-0-205-93192-7
ISBN-10: 0-205-93192-8

www.pearsonhighered.com

BRIEF CONTENTS

CONTENTS

SPECIALIZED CONTENTS

SELF-TESTS

These self-assessment tests help you analyze your own communication patterns and make plans for achieving greater interpersonal effectiveness.

ETHICAL MESSAGES

These discussions encourage you to consider the ethical implications of your interpersonal messages and will help you formulate your own code of the ethics of interpersonal communication.

SKILL BUILDING EXERCISES

These exercises help you work actively with interpersonal communication concepts and practice the many and varied interpersonal skills discussed in the text.

VIDEO CHOICE POINTS

WELCOME TO *INTERPERSONAL MESSAGES: COMMUNICATION AND RELATIONSHIP SKILLS* THIRD EDITION

It's a great pleasure to present this third edition of *Interpersonal Messages*. Although significantly revised, the book continues to emphasize its original two interrelated purposes: (1) to present you with an overview of interpersonal communication—what it is and what we know about it—and (2) to provide you with numerous ideas for improving your interpersonal communication and relationship skills. These two purposes influence everything included in the text—the topics discussed, the way each topic is presented, the specific skills highlighted, and the pedagogy incorporated.

WHAT'S NEW IN THE THIRD EDITION?

This new edition of *Interpersonal Messages* is a major revision with new features and content that we hope will make your study of interpersonal communication more satisfying and rewarding.

- Discussions throughout the book portray how **social media** is changing the way we communicate interpersonally.
- The concept that **choice** is central to all communication is integrated throughout the text as you are encouraged to consider your choices in many contexts throughout each chapter: as Video Choice Points, Interpersonal Choice Points, and Ethical Choice Points.
- The newest research on **culture** offers guidelines for improving intercultural communication.
- Expanded discussions of communication in the **workplace** offer guidelines for effective communication.
- **Learning objectives** focus on knowledge, application, and problem solving to highlight the major concepts and skills of the chapter. At the end of each major section a series of **questions** ask you to test yourself to see if you can, in fact, accomplish the objectives.
- **Messages in the Media** uses brief examples and photos from popular television programs to introduce important concepts covered in each chapter. **Messages in the Media: Wrap-Up** at the end of each chapter invites you to reconsider these media issues in light of what you learned in the chapter.
- **Viewpoints** photos and captions ask you to consider a variety of communication issues, many of which are research based and/or focus on the themes of social media, the workplace, and culture.
- **Integrated Media** icons point you to a wealth of enrichment and study tools at MyCommunicationLab (access code required).
- Each chapter now contains a **comparison table** that compares samples of effective with ineffective messages.
- **QR (Quick Response) Codes** take you to specific posts on *The Communication Blog* where you can read more about a topic, read the comments of others, and post your own comments.

CHAPTER-BY-CHAPTER UPDATES

Here, briefly, are some of the chapter-by-chapter changes. In addition to these changes, all chapters have been revised for greater clarity and less redundancy, and updated coverage of research and theory.

Part One, Preliminaries to Interpersonal Messages

Chapter 1 offers new discussions of the choice nature of interpersonal communication, workplace messages, and the nature and problems of information overload. Also new is a self-test on the forms of power. The chapter has also been rearranged for greater clarity; the section on competence now concludes the chapter. *Chapter 2* on culture includes a new table on the metaphors of culture that presents an interesting way to view culture. New sections include discussions of long- and short-term orientation (along with a new table on values in the workplace of long- and short-term-oriented executives) and indulgence and restraint. The self-test was revised to include these new cultural dimensions. *Chapter 3,* on perception and the self, includes new sections on the ways in which social networks enable and encourage social comparisons, the impostor phenomenon, a comparison table of destructive and constructive beliefs, and a new exercise on perception checking. *Chapter 4,* on listening, explains the process of listening, which is redefined to include social media message reading. Also new is a comparison table of ineffective and effective listening.

Part Two: Interpersonal Messages in Context

Chapter 5, on verbal communication, covers verbal messages and contains new sections including those on onymous and anonymous messages and immediacy. Also new are additional guidelines for appropriate use of cultural identifiers and a comparison table on confirmation and disconfirmation. *Chapter 6,* on nonverbal communication, has been reorganized around principles of nonverbal communication. The section on nonverbal competence has been reorganized around encoding and decoding skills. *Chapter 7,* on emotional messages, features a discussion of two new principles (emotions can be used strategically and emotions have consequences), along with a new visual of the model of emotions. Also new are tables on negative emotions at work, emotional happiness, verbal expressions of emotion, and a comparison table on ineffective and effective emotional expression. *Chapter 8,* on conversation messages, has been refocused to emphasize the skills involved in these interactions. Also new is a table on unsatisfying conversational partners, a new diagram explaining conversational turn taking, and a new self-test on small talk. *Chapter 9,* on interpersonal relationships, covers discussions of online relationships, relationship license, and bullying. The section on jealousy has been totally revised, and the self-test on violence has been revised to include both partners. *Chapter 10* continues the discussion of interpersonal relationships and focuses on the types of relationships and the theories explaining relationships. This chapter includes new sections on family types, online-only relationships, and romantic relationships in the workplace. *Chapter 11,* on interpersonal conflict, contains a new section on workplace conflict, a new table comparing verbal aggressiveness and argumentativeness, a new self-test on conflict management strategies, and a new exercise on I-messages.

INTERPERSONAL MESSAGES FOCUS ON CONTEMPORARY TOPICS

Discussions of contemporary topics help you communicate effectively in today's increasingly complex world.

Social Media

Interpersonal communication via **social media** is now fully integrated throughout the book. Interpersonal communication, as viewed here, incorporates the varied social media that are now an essential part of our communication lives. And so, to take just one example, the definition of listening—long defined as the reception of auditory signals—is redefined to include the reading of social media messages. The reasoning is simply that if posting on Facebook and Google+ are examples of interpersonal communication (which they surely are), then the reading of these messages must also be part of interpersonal communication and seems to fit most logically with listening. The QR (Quick Response) codes that appear throughout the text will take you to *The Communication Blog* where you can explore additional topics, read the comments of others, and comment on the posts yourself. This too is interpersonal communication and interpersonal listening.

COMMUNICATING WITH THE GRIEF STRICKEN: A SPECIAL CASE ILLUSTRATION (continued)

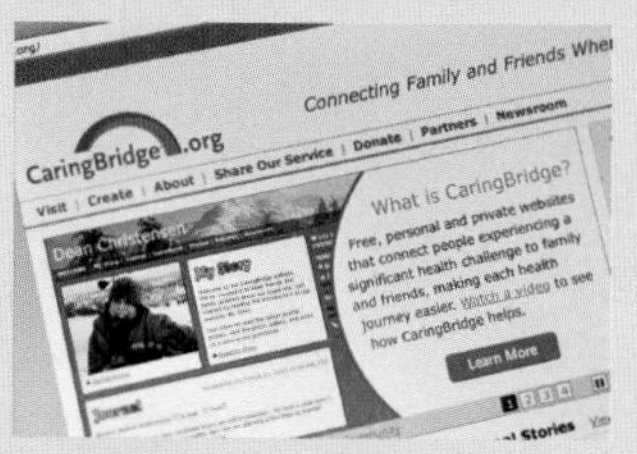

VIEWPOINTS Expressing grief

Social media websites such as CaringBridge enable people to express their caring/support/love for someone experiencing grief by writing in a guestbook that all people who are

she grieves in the ways that feel most comfortable—for example, crying or talking about old times. Don't try to change the subject or interject too often. As long as the person is talking and seems to be feeling better for it, be supportive.

- *Avoid trying to focus on the bright side.* Avoid expressions such as "You're lucky you have some vision left" or "It's better this way; Pat was suffering so much." These expressions may easily be seen as telling people that their feelings should be redirected, that they should be feeling something different.
- *Encourage the person to express feelings and talk about the loss.* Most people will welcome this opportunity. On the other hand, don't try to force people to talk about experiences or feelings they may not be willing to share.

Workplace

This third edition places additional emphasis on workplace communication and relationships with frequent examples, illustrations, and photo Viewpoints and in a variety of workplace-related topics such as workplace messages, values in the workplace as seen by long- and short-term oriented executives, emotions at work, romantic relationships in the workplace, and workplace conflict.

VIEWPOINTS Remaining mysterious

The more you reveal about yourself to others, the more areas of your life you expose to possible attack. Especially in the competitive context of work (or even romance), the more that others know about you, the more they'll be able to use against you. This simple fact has prompted power watcher Michael Korda (Korda, 1975, p. 302) to advise that you "never reveal all of yourself to other people." This advice is not to suggest that you be secretive; rather, Korda is advocating "remaining slightly mysterious, as if [you] were always capable of doing something surprising and unexpected." What's your view on this issue?

from even your closest friends and family members. Men and women who disclose that they have cheated on their relationship partner, have stolen, or are suffering from prolonged depression, for example, may find their friends and family no longer wanting to be quite as close as before.

- *Relational Risks.* Even in close and long-lasting relationships, self-disclosure can pose relational risks (Bochner, 1984). Total self-disclosure may prove threatening to a relationship by causing a decrease in mutual attraction, trust, or any of the bonds holding the individuals together. Self-disclosures concerning infidelity, romantic fantasies, past indiscretions or crimes, lies, or hidden weaknesses and fears could easily have such negative effects.
- *Professional Risks.* Revealing political views or attitudes toward different religious or racial groups may open you to professional risks and create problems on the job, as may disclosing any health problems (Fesko, 2001). Teachers who disclose former or current drug use or cohabitation with students may find themselves denied tenure, teaching at undesirable hours, and eventually falling victim to "budget cuts."

Culture

As in previous editions of *Interpersonal Messages*, the crucial role that culture plays in our communication experiences is a recurring theme. You're living in a world defined by cultural diversity, where you interact with people differing in affectional orientation, socioeconomic position, race, religion, and nationality. Culture and cultural differences are always influential in communication. For this reason, this text fully integrates culture into every chapter.

VIEWPOINTS Cultural evolution and cultural relativism

Cultural evolution (often called social Darwinism) holds that much as the human species evolved from earlier life forms to *Homo sapiens*, cultures also evolve. Under this view, some cultures may be considered advanced and others primitive. Most scholars reject this view, however, because the judgments that distinguish one culture from another have no basis in science and are instead based on individual values and preferences. **Cultural relativism**, on the other hand, holds that all cultures are different but that no culture is either superior or inferior to any other (Berry, Poortinga, Segall, & Dasen, 1992; Mosteller, 2008). What are some of the implications of these two views for intercultural communication?

ing are parts of the culture of some Latin American countries, England, and Spain, respectively, but you need not find these activities acceptable or equal to a cultural practice in which animals are treated kindly. Further, a cultural emphasis does not imply that you have to accept or follow even the practices of your own culture. For example, even if the majority in your culture holds sexist or homophobic attitudes, you need not agree with or adopt these attitudes yourself. Often, personality factors (such as your degree of assertiveness, extroversion, or optimism) will prove more influential than culture (Hatfield & Rapson, 1996). Of course, going against your culture's traditions and values is often very difficult. But it's important to realize that culture influences; it does not determine.

As demonstrated throughout this text, cultural differences exist across the interpersonal communication spectrum—from the way you use eye contact to the way you develop or dissolve a relationship (Chang & Holt, 1996). But these differences should not blind you to the great number of similarities existing among even the most widely separated cultures. Further, remember that differences are usually matters of degree. For example, most cultures value politeness, love, and honesty, but not all value these to the same degree. Also, the advances in media and technology and the widespread use of social

INTERPERSONAL MESSAGES EMPHASIZE CONTEMPORARY ISSUES

Discussions of important issues challenge students to ponder their communication decisions.

Choice

Throughout your interpersonal interactions, you'll need to make choices: between saying one thing or another, between sending an e-mail or calling on the phone, between being supportive or critical, and so on. Because of the central importance of choice, **Interpersonal Choice Points** (brief scenarios placed in the margins) invite you to analyze your choices for communicating.

In addition, a **Video Choice Point** box appears in each chapter inviting you to watch a video related to the chapter content and to examine effective and ineffective choices that the actors use in a variety of interpersonal communication situations.

VIDEO CHOICE POINT

Meet the Family

Charles will be meeting Mei Li's extended family for the first time, and both he and Mei Li are a bit nervous. They consider how the differences in their cultures may affect their relationship and their communication choices. "Meet the Family" explores the options you have for communicating in a cultural setting that is different from the one you grew up in. Illustrated here are choices that are both effective and ineffective communication among friends, romantic partners, and families. Watch to see how Charles and Mei Li's relationship is affected by their communication choices in the video "Meet the Family." Respond to the questions posed.

Watch the **Video** "Summer Internship" at **MyCommunicationLab**

INTERPERSONAL CHOICE POINT

Misusing Linguistic Privilege

You enter a group of racially similar people who are using terms normally considered offensive to refer to themselves. Trying to be one of the group, you too use such terms—but are met with extremely negative nonverbal feedback. What are some things you might say to lessen this negative reaction and to let the group know that you don't normally use such racial terms? What would you be sure not to say?

Politeness

Interpersonal communication scholars, along with business professionals throughout the world, are coming to realize the importance of politeness in our everyday communication encounters. They are finding that politeness is more than simply being a nice person; it also can help you to be a better communicator. The role that politeness plays in interpersonal interactions and the skills for polite interpersonal communication are emphasized throughout the text.

Mentoring

In a mentoring relationship, an experienced individual (mentor) helps to train a less-experienced person who is sometimes referred to as a mentee or, more often, a protégé (Ragins & Kram, 2007). An accomplished teacher, for example, might mentor a newly arrived or novice teacher. The mentor shows the new person through the "ropes," teaches the strategies and techniques for success, and otherwise communicates his or her knowledge and experience to the newcomer.

Not surprisingly, mentoring is frequently conducted online. One great advantage of e-mentoring is the flexibility it allows for communication. E-mail messages, for example, can be sent and received at times that are convenient for the individuals involved (Stewart, 2006). Further, because the individuals may be separated geographically, it's possible to have mentor–protégé relationships with people in foreign countries and in widely differing cultures, relationships that would be impossible

VIEWPOINTS Being liked at work

Among the suggestions offered by organization theorists for being liked at work are: looking and dressing the part and being positive, culturally sensitive, respectful and friendly, polite, and interested. What other qualities would make you like a workplace colleague?

Ethics

Because the messages you use have effects on others, they also have an ethical dimension. As such, ethics receives focused attention throughout the text. Chapter 1 introduces ethics as a foundation concept in all forms of interpersonal communication. In all remaining chapters, *Ethical Messages* boxes highlight a variety of ethical issues in interpersonal communication and ask you to apply ethical principles to various scenarios. We'll here consider the ethical issues that come into play in various communication situations, for example, cultural practices, lying, and ways to engage in interpersonal conflict ethically. These boxes will serve as frequent reminders that ethical considerations are an integral part of all the interpersonal communication choices/decisions you make.

ETHICAL MESSAGES

Your Obligation to Reveal Yourself

If you're in a close relationship, your influence on your partner is considerable, so you may have an obligation to reveal certain things about yourself. Conversely, you may feel that the other person—because he or she is so close to you—has an ethical obligation to reveal certain information to you.

Ethical Choice Point

Consider: At what point in a relationship—if any—do you feel you would have an ethical obligation to reveal each of the 10 items of information listed here? Visualize a relationship as existing on a continuum from initial contact at 1 to extreme intimacy at 10, and use the numbers from 1 to 10 to indicate at what point you would feel your romantic partner or close friend has a right to know each type of information about you. If you feel you would never have the obligation to reveal this information, use 0. As you respond to these items, ask yourself, what gives one person the right to know personal information about another person? What principle of ethics requires another person to disclose this information in a relationship?

At what point do you have an ethical obligation to reveal:	Romantic Partner	Friend
Age	______	______
History of family genetic disorders	______	______
HIV status	______	______
Past sexual experiences	______	______
Marital history	______	______
Annual salary and net financial worth	______	______
Affectional orientation	______	______
Attitudes toward other races and nationalities	______	______
Religious beliefs	______	______
Past criminal activity or incarceration	______	______

CONTEMPORARY PEDAGOGY HELPS YOU LEARN ABOUT INTERPERSONAL MESSAGES

Practical pedagogy helps students study and learn the concepts covered.

SKILL BUILDING EXERCISE

Explaining Your Perceptions

Complete the following table by providing a description of how you perceive the incident and how you'd go about seeking confirmation. If you have several possible explanations for the incident, describe each of these in the second column. In the third column, indicate the choices you have for seeking clarification of your initial impressions—what are your choices for asking for clarification?

Incident	Your Perceptions and Possible Interpretations or Meanings	Choices for Seeking Clarification
You've extended an invitation to a classmate to be a Facebook friend but have heard nothing back.		
Your manager at work seems to spend a lot of time with your peers but very little time with you. You're concerned about the impression you're making.		
The person you've been dating for the past several months has stopped calling for a date. The messages have become fewer and less personal.		

Skills

Interpersonal Messages continues the focused approach to skill development that was established in the first edition. Improving interpersonal communication skills is integral to all the text discussions and appears in all chapters. Twenty-three **Skill Building Exercises** appear throughout the text; completing these exercises will help you apply the material in the chapter to specific situations and thereby increase and perfect your own interpersonal skills. These exercises are practice experiences aimed at increasing your ability to formulate more effective messages. A wide variety of additional skills-related materials can be accessed at, MyCommunicationLab (access code required). The glossary also includes many skills discussed in the text, and the summaries at the ends of the chapters have special sections on skills.

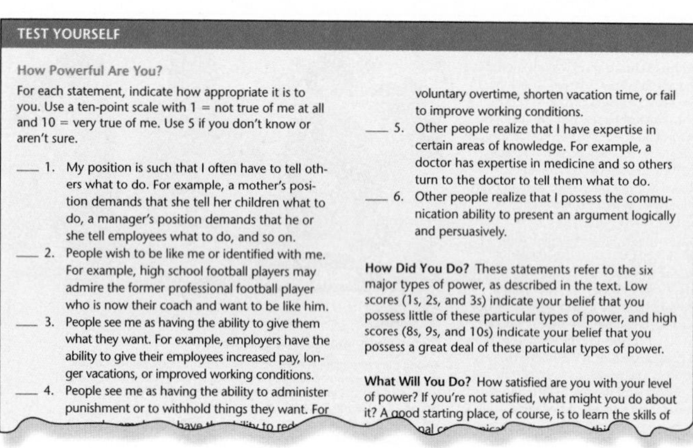
TEST YOURSELF

How Powerful Are You?

For each statement, indicate how appropriate it is to you. Use a ten-point scale with 1 = not true of me at all and 10 = very true of me. Use 5 if you don't know or aren't sure.

___ 1. My position is such that I often have to tell others what to do. For example, a mother's position demands that she tell her children what to do, a manager's position demands that he or she tell employees what to do, and so on.

___ 2. People wish to be like me or identified with me. For example, high school football players may admire the former professional football player who is now their coach and want to be like him.

___ 3. People see me as having the ability to give them what they want. For example, employers have the ability to give their employees increased pay, longer vacations, or improved working conditions.

___ 4. People see me as having the ability to administer punishment or to withhold things they want. For

voluntary overtime, shorten vacation time, or fail to improve working conditions.

___ 5. Other people realize that I have expertise in certain areas of knowledge. For example, a doctor has expertise in medicine and so others turn to the doctor to tell them what to do.

___ 6. Other people realize that I possess the communication ability to present an argument logically and persuasively.

How Did You Do? These statements refer to the six major types of power, as described in the text. Low scores (1s, 2s, and 3s) indicate your belief that you possess little of these particular types of power, and high scores (8s, 9s, and 10s) indicate your belief that you possess a great deal of these particular types of power.

What Will You Do? How satisfied are you with your level of power? If you're not satisfied, what might you do about it? A good starting place, of course, is to learn the skills of

Interactive Approach

This edition continues to provide numerous opportunities for you to interact with the material in the text in a number of ways.

Test Yourself boxes appear throughout the text and invite you to analyze your own patterns of communication and think about how you will alter your communication in the future. These tests will help you personalize the concepts and skills you'll read about in the text and improve your communication effectiveness. Additional self-tests are noted at the ends of the chapters and are available at MyCommunicationLab.

Interpersonal Choice Points appear throughout the text to encourage you to examine the choices you have available for communicating in actual real-life situations and to apply the information in the text to these situations.

Viewpoints captions, accompanying all interior photos, pose questions (mostly based on interpersonal research) designed to elicit discussion of a variety of different viewpoints.

OBJECTIVES *After reading this chapter, you should be able to:*

1. Paraphrase the eight principles of verbal messages.
2. Distinguish between disconfirmation and confirmation, and use appropriate cultural identifiers, without sexism, heterosexism, racism, and ageism.
3. Explain the ways in which language can distort thinking and apply the suggestions for greater guidelines for communicating more logically.

Learning Tools

An array of tools help you learn efficiently and study effectively.

The **learning objectives** prefacing each chapter have been totally reworked to more accurately reflect current pedagogical thinking and emphasis. These objectives highlight the major concepts and skills of the chapter. The learning objectives system used here identifies three major levels of thinking, each of which is included throughout the text (Bloom, 1956; Eggen & Kauchak, 2013; Teacher & Educational Development, 2005):

- **Knowledge** (recalling, remembering, and comprehending), introduced by such specific verbs as *define*, *paraphrase*, *describe*, and *differentiate*.
- **Application** (applying a concept to a new situation), introduced by such specific verbs as *diagram*, *illustrate*, *use*, and *give examples*.
- **Problem solving** (analyzing/breaking a concept into its parts, synthesizing/combining elements into a new whole, and evaluating/making value or appropriateness judgments), introduced by such specific verbs as *assess*, *construct*, *organize*, and *evaluate*.

At the end of each major section, a series of **questions** ask you to test yourself to see if you can, in fact, accomplish the objectives. The **Summary of Concepts and Skills,** organized by the major headings, helps you ensure you have learned the key content. Throughout the text, icons in the margins alert you to related media components (including videos, exercises, and audio segments) that you will find at MyCommunicationLab to enhance your learning.

Blog Post

Interpersonal Time

In this connection take a look at "Interpersonal Time" at tcbdevito.blogspot.com for a consideration of the varied ways time is used in interpersonal interactions.

INSTRUCTOR AND STUDENT RESOURCES

Key instructor resources include:

- Instructor's Manual and Test Bank (ISBN 0205931812)
- PowerPoint Presentation Package (ISBN 0205931944)

These supplements are available at www.pearsonhighered.com/irc (access code required). MyTest online test-generating software (ISBN 0205931839) is available at www.pearsonmytest.com (access code required). For a complete listing of the instructor and student resources available with this text, please visit the *Interpersonal Messages* 3/e e-Catalog page at www.pearsonhighered.com/communication.

MyCommunicationLab

MyCommunicationLab is an online homework, tutorial, and assessment program that truly engages students in learning. It helps students better prepare for class, quizzes, and exams—resulting in better performance in the course—and provides educators a dynamic set of tools for gauging individual and class progress. And, MyCommunicationLab comes from Pearson, your partner in providing the best digital learning experiences: www.mycommunicationlab.com

MyCommunicationLab Highlights

- **MediaShare:** This comprehensive file upload tool allows students to post speeches, outlines, visual aids, video assignments, role plays, group projects, and more in a variety of file formats. Uploaded files are available for viewing, commenting, and grading by instructors and class members in face-to-face and online course settings. Integrated video capture functionality allows students to record video directly from a webcam and allows instructors to record videos via webcam, in class or in a lab, and attach them directly to a specific student and/or assignment. The MediaShare app is available via iTunes at no additional charge for those who have purchased MediaShare or MyCommunicationLab access.
- **The Pearson eText:** Identical in content and design to the printed text, the Pearson eText lets students access their textbook anytime, anywhere, and any way they want—including downloading to an iPad. Students can take notes and highlight, just like a traditional text.
- **Videos and Video Quizzes:** Videos provide students with the opportunity to watch and evaluate chapter-related multimedia. Many videos include automatically graded quiz questions.
- **PersonalityProfile:** PersonalityProfile is Pearson's online library for self-assessment and analysis. Online resources provide students with opportunities to evaluate their own and others' communication styles. Instructors can use these tools to show learning and growth over the duration of the course.
- **Study Plan:** A personalized study plan guides students to focus directly on what they need to know, helping them succeed in the course and beyond.
- **Class Preparation Tool:** Finding, organizing, and presenting your instructor resources is fast and easy with Pearson's class preparation tool. This fully searchable database contains hundreds of resources such as lecture launchers, discussion topics, activities, assignments, and video clips. Instructors can search or browse by topic and sort the results by type. Personalized folders can be created to organize and store content or download resources, as well as upload your own content.

ACKNOWLEDGMENTS

I want to thank those who reviewed the text at the various stages of revision; they gave generously of their time and expertise, and I am, as always, in their debt.

Don Center, Arapahoe Community College
Keri Moe, El Paso Community College
Gail Hankins, Wake Technical Community College
Patrick Luster, McNeese State University
Sherry Rhodes, Collin College
Mary Tripp, Wisconsin Indianhead Technical College
Dan Wirth, Northeastern Illinois University

I also want to thank the many people who worked so hard to turn a manuscript into this book. I'm especially grateful to the people at Pearson who make revisions so enjoyable, especially communication editor Melissa Mashburn for her good spirit and always helpful ideas, development editor Carol Alper who made valuable suggestions on just about every aspect of this revision, marketing manager Blair Zoe Tuckman who skillfully handled the marketing program, and Kate Cebik who coordinated the ancillaries. Additional thank-yous go to senior digital editor Paul DeLuca, digital editor Lisa Dotson, editorial assistant Megan Hermida, production manager Raegan Heerema, and project managers Allison Campbell and Kristin Jobe and the staff at Integra.

Joseph A. DeVito
jadevito@earthlink.net
www.pearsonhighered.com/devito
http://tcbdevito.blogspot.com

CHAPTER

1

Foundations of Interpersonal Communication

MESSAGES IN THE MEDIA

In *Community* you see a group of community college students interact in a wide variety of situations. Most of the time, their communication patterns get them into trouble—not unlike people in real life. Clearly they could use a good course in interpersonal communication. This first chapter introduces this most important form of communication.

OBJECTIVES *After reading this chapter, you should be able to:*

1. Explain the personal and professional benefits to be derived from the study of interpersonal communication.
2. Define *interpersonal communication.*
3. Diagram a model of communication containing source–receiver, messages, channel, noise, and context, and define each of these elements.
4. Explain the principles of interpersonal communication, and give examples of each.
5. Define and illustrate the four essential interpersonal communication competencies.

Explore the **Exercise** "I'd Prefer to Be" at **MyCommunicationLab**

WHY STUDY INTERPERSONAL COMMUNICATION

Fair questions to ask at the beginning of this text and this course are "What will I get out of this?" and "Why should I study interpersonal communication?" As with any worthwhile study, we can identify two major benefits: personal/social and professional.

Personal and Social Success

Your personal success and happiness depend largely on your effectiveness as an interpersonal communicator. Your close friendships and romantic relationships are made, maintained, and sometimes destroyed largely through your interpersonal interactions. In fact, the success of your family relationships depends heavily on the interpersonal communication among members. For example, in a survey of 1,001 people over 18 years of age, 53 percent felt that a lack of effective communication was the major cause of marriage failure, significantly greater than money (38 percent) and in-law interference (14 percent) (Roper Starch, 1999).

Likewise, your social success in interacting with neighbors, acquaintances, and people you meet every day depends on your ability to engage in satisfying conversation—conversation that's comfortable and enjoyable.

INTERPERSONAL CHOICE POINT

Choices and Interpersonal Communication

Throughout this book. you'll find marginal items labeled *Interpersonal Choice Points*. These items are designed to encourage you to apply the material discussed in the text to specific interpersonal situations by first analyzing your available choices and then making a communication decision.

Professional Success

The ability to communicate interpersonally is widely recognized as crucial to professional success (Morreale & Pearson, 2008). From the initial interview at a college job fair to interning to participating in and then leading meetings, your skills at interpersonal communication will largely determine your success.

One study, for example, found that among the 23 attributes ranked as "very important" in hiring decisions, "communication and interpersonal skills" was at the top of the list, noted by 89 percent of the recruiters. This was a far higher percentage of recruiters than noted "content of the core curriculum" (34 percent) or "overall value for the money invested in the recruiting effort" (33 percent) (Alsop, 2004). Interpersonal skills play an important role in preventing workplace violence (Parker, 2004) and in reducing medical mishaps and improving doctor–patient communication (Epstein & Hundert, 2002; Smith, 2004; Sutcliffe, Lewton, & Rosenthal, 2004). In a survey of employers who were asked what colleges should place more emphasis on, 89 percent identified "the ability to effectively communicate orally and in writing," the highest of any skills listed (Hart Research Associates, 2010). The importance of interpersonal communication skills extends over the entire spectrum of professions.

As a preface to an area of study that will be enlightening, exciting, and extremely practical, examine your assumptions about interpersonal communication by taking the accompanying self-test.

VIEWPOINTS To communicate

Women often report that an essential quality—perhaps the most important quality—in a partner is one who can communicate. How important, compared to all the other factors you might take into consideration in choosing a partner, is the ability to communicate? What specific interpersonal communication skills would you consider "extremely important" in a life partner?

Can you explain why learning about interpersonal communication is beneficial to your personal and professional life?

TEST YOURSELF

What Do You Believe About Interpersonal Communication?

Respond to each of the following statements with T (true) if you believe the statement is usually true or F (false) if you believe the statement is usually false.

____ 1. Good communicators are born, not made.
____ 2. The more you communicate, the better at communicating you will be.
____ 3. In your interpersonal communications, a good guide to follow is to be as open, empathic, and supportive as you can be.
____ 4. In intercultural communication, it's best to ignore differences and communicate just as you would with members of your own culture.
____ 5. When there is conflict, your relationship is in trouble.

How Did You Do? As you probably figured out, all five statements are generally false. As you read this text, you'll discover not only why these beliefs are false but also the trouble you can get into when you assume they're true. For now and in brief, here are some of the reasons why each statement is (generally) false: (1) Effective communication is learned; all of us can improve our abilities and become more effective communicators. (2) It isn't the amount of communication that matters, it's the quality. If you practice bad habits, you're more likely to grow less effective than more effective. (3) Because each interpersonal situation is unique, the type of communication appropriate in one situation may not be appropriate in another. (4) Ignoring differences will often create problems; people from different cultures may, for example, follow different rules for what is and what is not appropriate in interpersonal communication. (5) All meaningful relationships experience conflict; the trick is to manage it effectively.

What Will You Do? This is a good place to start practicing the critical-thinking skill of questioning commonly held assumptions—about communication and about yourself as a communicator. Do you hold beliefs that may limit your thinking about communication? For example, do you believe that certain kinds of communication are beyond your capabilities? Do you impose limits on how you see yourself as a communicator?

THE NATURE OF INTERPERSONAL COMMUNICATION

Although this entire book is in a sense a definition of interpersonal communication, a working definition is useful at the start. **Interpersonal communication** is the verbal and nonverbal interaction between two interdependent people (sometimes more). This relatively simple definition implies a variety of characteristics.

Explore the **Exercise** "Analyzing an Interaction" at **MyCommunicationLab**

Blog Post

The Communication Blog

Throughout the text, you will find invitations to visit The Communication Blog at tcbdevito.blogspot.com for additional coverage of a topic and relevant websites. Read the comments of others and comment as you wish.

Interpersonal Communication Involves Interdependent Individuals

Interpersonal communication is the communication that takes place between people who are in some way "connected." Interpersonal communication would thus include what takes place between a son and his father, an employer and an employee, two sisters, a teacher and a student, two lovers, two friends, and so on. Although largely dyadic in nature, interpersonal communication is often extended to include small intimate groups such as the family. Even within a family, however, the communication that takes place is often dyadic—mother to child, sister to sister, and so on.

Not only are the individuals simply "connected," they are also *interdependent*: What one person does has an effect on the other person. The actions of one person have consequences for the other person. In a family, for example, a child's trouble with the police will affect the parents, other siblings, extended family members, and perhaps friends and neighbors.

Interpersonal Communication Is Inherently Relational

Because of this interdependency, interpersonal communication is inevitably and essentially relational in nature. Interpersonal communication takes place in a relationship, it affects the relationship, it defines the relationship. The way you communicate is determined in great part by the kind of relationship that exists between you and the other person. You interact differently with your interpersonal communication instructor and your best friend; you interact with a sibling in ways very different from the ways you interact with a neighbor, a work colleague, or a casual acquaintance.

But notice also that the way you communicate will influence the kind of relationship you have. If you interact in friendly ways, you're likely to develop a friendship. If you regularly exchange hateful and hurtful messages, you're likely to develop an antagonistic relationship. If you each regularly express respect and support for each other, a respectful and supportive relationship is likely to develop. This is surely one of the most obvious observations you can make about interpersonal communication. And yet so many seem not to appreciate this very clear relationship between what you say and the relationship that develops (or deteriorates).

Interpersonal Communication Exists on a Continuum

Interpersonal communication exists along a continuum (see Figure 1.1), ranging from relatively impersonal at one end to highly personal at the other (Miller, 1978, 1990). At the impersonal end of the continuum, you have simple conversation between people who, we'd say, really don't know each other—the server and the customer, for example. At the highly personal end is the communication that takes place between people who are intimately interconnected—a father and son, two longtime lovers, or best friends, for example. A few characteristics distinguish the impersonal from the personal forms of communication and are presented in Table 1.1 (Miller, 1978).

Interpersonal Communication Involves Verbal and Nonverbal Messages

The interpersonal interaction involves the exchange of verbal and nonverbal messages. The words you use as well as your facial expressions—your eye contact and your body posture, for example—send messages. Likewise, you receive messages through your sense of hearing as well as through your other senses, especially visual and touch. Even silence sends messages. These messages, as you'll see throughout this course, will vary greatly depending on the other factors involved in the interaction. You don't talk to a best friend in the same way you talk to your college professor or your parents.

One of the great myths in communication is that nonverbal communication accounts for more than 90 percent of the meaning of any message. Actually, it depends. In some situations, the nonverbal signals will carry more of your meaning than the words

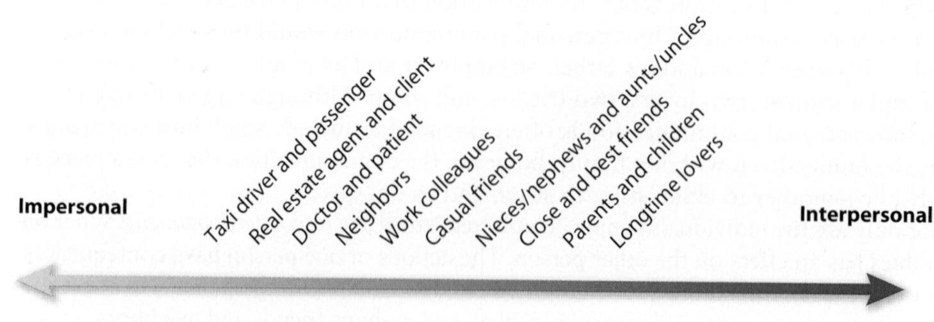

FIGURE 1.1
An Interpersonal Continuum
Here is one possible interpersonal continuum. Other people would position the relationships differently. You may want to try constructing an interpersonal continuum of your own relationships.

TABLE 1.1

IMPERSONAL AND INTERPERSONAL COMMUNICATION

Impersonal Communication	Interpersonal Communication
Social role information: You interact largely on the basis of the social roles you occupy; for example, server and customer, cab driver and passenger.	**Personal information:** You interact largely on the basis of personal roles; for example, friends, lovers, parents and children, cousins.
Social rules: You interact according to the social rules defining your interaction; for example, as a server, you would greet the customers, hand them menus, and ask if there was anything else you could do.	**Personal rules:** You interact according to the rules you both have established rather than to any societal rules; the mother and daughter follow the rules they themselves have established over the years.
Social messages: You exchange messages in a narrow range of topics—you talk to the server about food and service, not about your parents' divorce—with little emotion and little self-disclosure.	**Personal messages:** You exchange messages on a broad range of topics—you talk about food and also about your parents' divorce—with much emotion and self-disclosure.

you use. In other situations, the verbal signals will communicate more information. Most often, of course, they work together, and, rather than focusing on which channel communicates the greater percentage of meaning, it's more important to focus on the ways in which verbal and nonverbal messages occur together.

Interpersonal Communication Exists in Varied Forms

Often, interpersonal communication takes place face to face: talking with other students before class, interacting with family or friends over dinner, trading secrets with intimates. This is the type of interaction that probably comes to mind when you think of interpersonal communication. But, of course, much conversation takes place online. Online communication is a major part of people's interpersonal experience throughout the world. Such communications are important personally, socially, and professionally.

The major online types of conversation differ from one another and from face-to-face interaction in important ways. A few of the major similarities and differences are pointed out here (also see Table 1.2).

Some computer-mediated communication (for example, e-mail, tweets, or posts on Facebook) is **asynchronous**, meaning that it does not take place in real time. You may send your message today, but the receiver may not read it for a week and may take another week to respond. Consequently, much of the spontaneity created by real-time communication is lost here. You may, for example, be very enthusiastic about a topic when you send your e-mail but practically forget it by the time someone responds. E-mail is also virtually inerasable, a feature that has important consequences and that we discuss later in this chapter.

Through instant messaging, you interact online in (essentially) real time; the communication messages are **synchronous**—they occur at the same time and are similar to phone communication except that IM is text-based rather than voice-based. Through IM you can also play games, share files, listen to music, send messages to cell phones, announce company meetings, and do a great deal else with short, abbreviated messages. Among college students, as you probably know, the major purpose of IM seems to be to maintain "social connectedness" (Kindred & Roper, 2004).

TABLE 1.2

Face-to-Face and Computer-Mediated Communication

Throughout this text, face-to-face and computer-mediated communication are discussed, compared, and contrasted. Here is a brief summary of just some communication concepts and some of the ways in which these two forms of communication are similar and different.

Human Communication Element	Face-to-Face Communication	Computer-Mediated Communication
Source		
Presentation of self and impression management	Personal characteristics are open to visual inspection; disguise is difficult.	Personal characteristics are revealed when you want to reveal them; disguise is easy.
Speaking turn	You compete for speaker time with others; you can be interrupted.	It's always your turn; speaker time is unlimited; you can't be interrupted.
Receiver		
Number	One or a few who are in your visual field.	Virtually unlimited.
Opportunity for interaction	Limited to those who have the opportunity to meet.	Unlimited.
Third parties	Messages can be repeated to third parties but not with complete accuracy.	Messages can be retrieved by others or forwarded verbatim to anyone.
Impression formation	Impressions are based on the verbal and nonverbal cues the receiver perceives.	Impressions are based on text messages and posted photos and videos.
Context		
Physical	Essentially the same physical space.	Can be in the next cubicle or separated by miles.
Temporal	Communication is synchronous; messages are exchanged at the same (real) time.	Communication may be synchronous (as in chat rooms) or asynchronous (as in e-mail).
Channel		
	All senses participate in sending and receiving messages.	Visual (for text, photos, and videos) and auditory.
Message		
Verbal and nonverbal	Words, gestures, eye contact, accent, vocal cues, spatial relationships, touching, clothing, hair, etc.	Words, photos, videos, and audio messages.
Permanence	Temporary unless recorded; speech signals fade rapidly.	Messages are relatively permanent.

In chat rooms and social networking groups, you often communicate synchronously, when you and a friend are online at the same time, and asychronously, when you're sending a message or writing on the wall of a friend who isn't online while you're writing. Social networking sites give you the great advantage of enabling you to communicate with people you would never meet or interact with otherwise. Because many of these groups are international, they provide excellent exposure to other cultures, other ideas, and other ways of communicating, and they are a good introduction to intercultural communication.

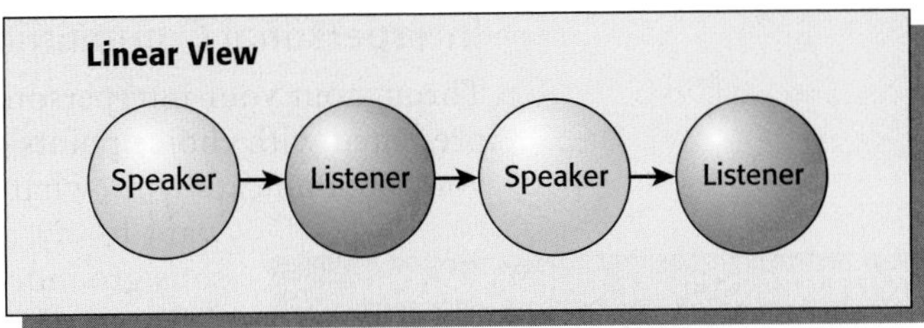

FIGURE 1.2
The Linear View of Interpersonal Communication
This figure represents a linear view of communication, in which the speaker speaks and the listener listens.

Interpersonal Communication Is Transactional

Some early theories viewed the communication process as linear (see Figure 1.2). In this linear view of communication, the speaker spoke and the listener listened; after the speaker finished speaking, the listener would speak. Communication was seen as proceeding in a relatively straight line. Speaking and listening were seen as taking place at different times—when you spoke, you didn't listen, and when you listened, you didn't speak. A more satisfying view (Figure 1.3), and the one currently held, sees communication as a transactional process in which each person serves simultaneously as speaker and listener. According to the transactional view, at the same time that you send messages, you're also receiving messages from your own communications and from the reactions of the other person. And at the same time that you're listening, you're also sending messages. In a transactional view, each person is seen as both speaker and listener, as simultaneously communicating and receiving messages.

Explore the **Exercise** "Models of Interpersonal Communication" at **MyCommunicationLab**

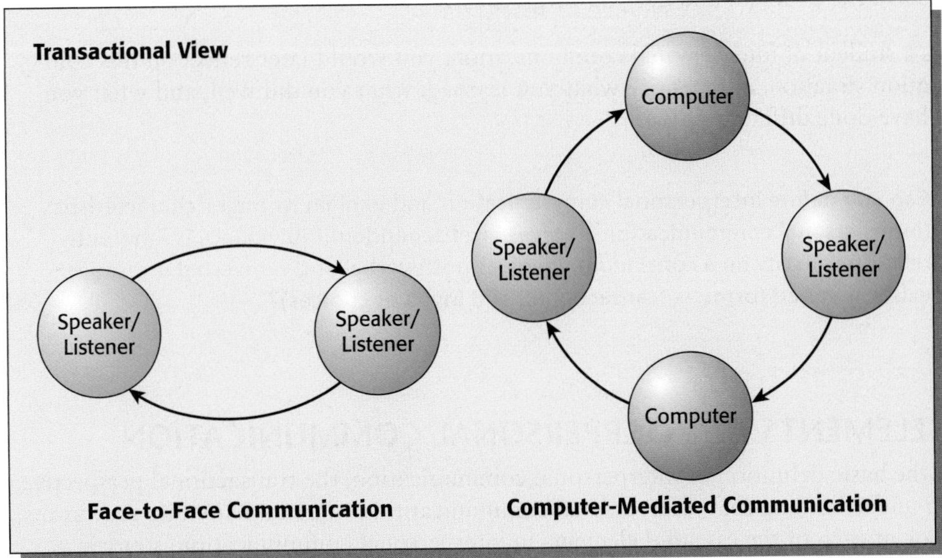

FIGURE 1.3
The Transactional View of Interpersonal Communication
This figure represents a transactional view, in which each person serves simultaneously as speaker and listener; at the same time that you send messages, you also receive messages from your own communications as well as from the reactions of the other person(s).

Interpersonal Communication Involves Choices

Throughout your interpersonal life and in each interpersonal interaction, you're presented with **choice points**—moments when you have to make a choice as to who you communicate with, what you say, what you don't say, how you phrase what you want to say, and so on. This course and this text aim to give you reasons grounded in interpersonal communication theory and research discussed throughout the text for the varied choices you'll be called upon to make in your interpersonal interactions. The course also aims to give you the skills you'll need to execute these well-reasoned choices.

INTERPERSONAL CHOICE POINT

Communicating an Image

A new position is opening at work, and you want it. Your immediate supervisor is likely the one to make the final decision. What are some of your options for making yourself look especially good so you can secure this new position?

You can look at the process of choice in terms of John Dewey's (1910) steps in reflective thinking, a model used by contemporary theorists for explaining small group problem solving and conflict resolution. It can also be used to explain the notion of choice in five steps.

- *Step 1: The problem.* View a communication interaction as a problem to be resolved, as a situation to be addressed. Here you try to understand the nature of the communication situation, what elements are involved, and, in the words of one communication model, who did what to whom with what effect. Let's say that your "problem" is that you said something you shouldn't have and it's created a problem between you and your friend, romantic partner, or family member. You need to resolve this problem.
- *Step 2: The criteria.* Here you ask yourself what your specific communication goal is. What do you want your message to accomplish? For example, you want to admit your mistake, apologize, and be forgiven.
- *Step 3: The possible solutions.* Here you ask yourself what some of your communication choices are. What are some of the messages you might communicate?
- *Step 4: The analysis.* Here you identify the advantages and disadvantages of each communication choice.
- *Step 5: The selection and execution.* Here you communicate what you hope will resolve the problem and get you forgiveness.

Explore the **Exercise** "Applying the Axioms" at **MyCommunicationLab**

As a student of interpersonal communication, you would later reflect on this communication situation and identify what you learned, what you did well, and what you could have done differently.

Can you define interpersonal communication and explain its major characteristics (interpersonal communication involves interdependent individuals, is inherently relational, exists on a continuum, involves both verbal and nonverbal messages, exists in varied forms, is transactional, and involves choices)?

THE ELEMENTS OF INTERPERSONAL COMMUNICATION

Given the basic definition of interpersonal communication, the transactional perspective, and an understanding that interpersonal communication occurs in many different forms, let's look at each of the essential elements in interpersonal communication: source–receiver, messages, feedback, feedforward, channel, noise, context, and competence (see Figure 1.4). Along with this discussion, you may wish to visit the websites of some of the major communication organizations to see how they discuss communication. See, for example, the websites of the National Communication Association, the International Communication Association, and the Association for Education in Journalism and Mass Communication for three major academic associations in communication. URLs for the major communication association are also given on The Communication Blog at http://tcbdevito.blogspot.com.

Source–Receiver

Interpersonal communication involves at least two persons. Each functions as a **source** (formulates and sends messages) and operates as a **receiver** (receives and understands messages). The linked term *source–receiver* emphasizes that each person is both source and receiver.

By putting your meanings into sound waves and gestures, facial expressions, or body movements, you're putting your thoughts and feelings into a **code**, or a set of symbols—a process called *en*coding. When you translate those symbols into ideas, you're taking them out of the code they're in, a process called *de*coding. So we can call speakers (or, more generally, senders) **encoders**: those who put their meanings *into* a code. And we can call listeners (or, more generally, receivers) **decoders**: those who take meanings *out of* a code. Since encoding and decoding activities are combined in each person, the term *encoding–decoding* is used to emphasize this inevitable dual function.

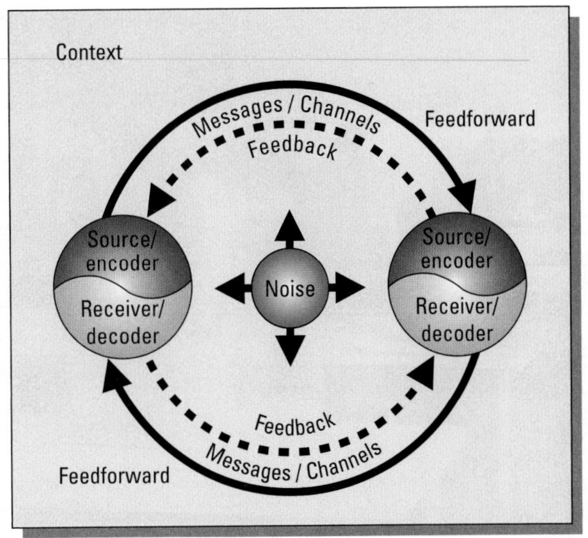

FIGURE 1.4
The Process of Interpersonal Communication
This model puts into visual form the various elements of the interpersonal communication process. How would you diagram the interpersonal communication process?

Usually you encode an idea into a code that the other person understands; for example, you use words and gestures for which both you and the other person have similar meanings. At times, however, you may want to exclude others; so, for example, you might speak in a language that only one of your listeners knows or use jargon to prevent others from understanding. At other times, you may assume incorrectly that the other person knows your code and unknowingly use words or gestures the other person simply doesn't understand. For interpersonal communication to occur, then, meanings must be both encoded and decoded. If Jamie has his eyes closed and is wearing stereo headphones as his dad is speaking to him, interpersonal communication is not taking place—simply because the messages—both verbal and nonverbal—are not being received.

Messages

For interpersonal communication to exist, **messages** that express your thoughts and feelings must be sent and received. Interpersonal communication may be verbal or nonverbal, but it's usually a combination of both. You communicate interpersonally with words as well as with gestures, emoticons, varied fonts, touch, photos, videos, and audio, for example. Everything about you has the potential to send interpersonal messages, and every message has an **effect**, or outcome. In face-to-face communication, your messages are both verbal and nonverbal; you supplement your words with facial expressions, body movements, and variations in vocal volume and rate. When you communicate through a keyboard, your message is communicated with words as well as with photos and videos, for example.

Four important types of messages need to be mentioned here: workplace, metamessages, feedback, and feedforward.

WORKPLACE MESSAGES In the workplace, messages are often classified in terms of their direction.

- **Upward communication** consists of messages sent from the lower levels of a hierarchy to the upper levels—for example, line worker to manager or faculty member to dean. This type of communication usually is concerned with job-related activities and problems; ideas for change and suggestions for improvement; and feelings about the organization, work, other workers, or similar issues.
- **Downward communication** consists of messages sent from the higher levels to the lower levels of the hierarchy; for example, messages sent by managers to workers. Common forms of downward communication include orders; explanations of procedures, goals, and changes; and appraisals of workers.

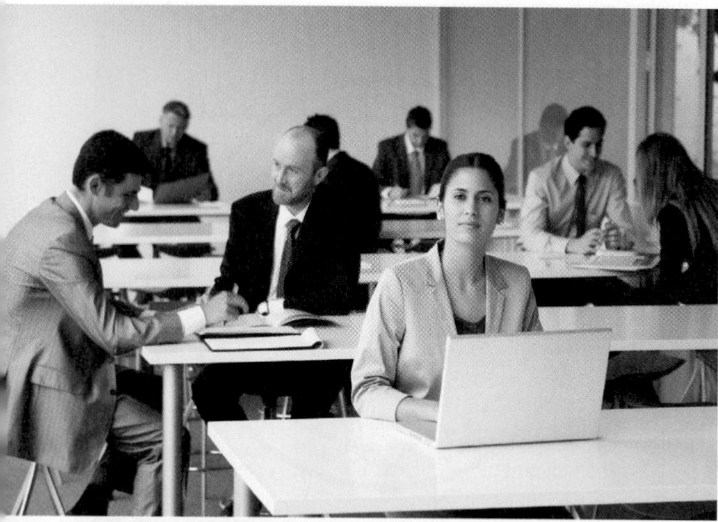

VIEWPOINTS Interpersonal communication in the workplace

Managers and employment interviewers routinely list interpersonal skills among the most important job-related skills in a desirable employee. In what ways do you see interpersonal communication skills being important in your current or future work life?

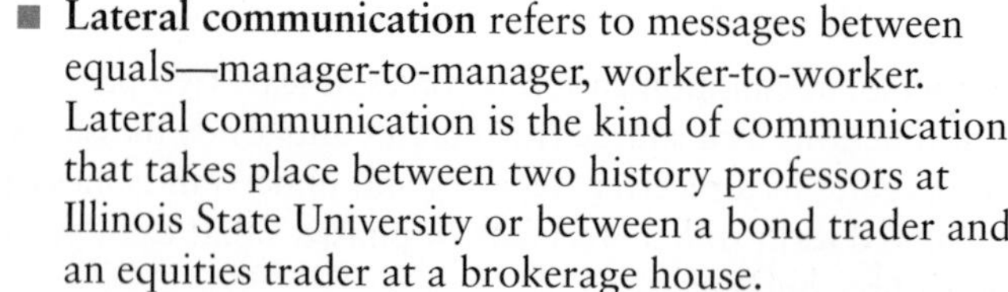

- **Lateral communication** refers to messages between equals—manager-to-manager, worker-to-worker. Lateral communication is the kind of communication that takes place between two history professors at Illinois State University or between a bond trader and an equities trader at a brokerage house.
- **Grapevine communication** messages don't follow the formal lines of communication established in an organization. Grapevine messages concern job-related issues that you want to discuss in a more interpersonal setting; for example, organizational issues that have not yet been made public, the real relationship among the regional managers, or possible changes that are being considered but not yet finalized.

METAMESSAGES One very special type of message is the **metamessage**. This type of message refers to other messages; it's a message about a message. Both verbal and nonverbal messages can be metacommunicational. Verbally, you can convey metamessages such as "Do you understand what I'm saying?" Nonverbally, you can wink to communicate that you're lying or being sarcastic. Your interpersonal effectiveness will often hinge on your competence in metacommunication. For example, in conflict situations, it's often helpful to talk about the way you argue or what your raised voice means. In romantic relationships, it may be helpful to talk about what each of you means by "exclusive" or "love." On the job, it's often necessary to talk about the ways people delegate orders or express criticism.

Explore the **Exercise** "How Would You Give Feedback?" at **MyCommunicationLab**

FEEDBACK MESSAGES **Feedback** is a special type of message that conveys information about the messages you send. When you send a spoken or written message to another person or post on a social media site, you get feedback from your own message: You hear what you say, you feel the way you move, you see what you write. On the basis of this information, you may correct yourself, rephrase something, or perhaps smile at a clever turn of phrase.

You also get feedback from others. The person with whom you're communicating is constantly sending you messages that indicate how he or she is receiving and responding to your messages. Nods of agreement, smiles, puzzled looks, likes, and questions asking for clarification are all examples of feedback. In fact, it would not be much of an exaggeration to say that one of the main purposes of posting to social media sites is to get positive feedback from others—likes, +1s, thumbs up, blog comments, and retweets, for example.

Notice that in face-to-face communication you can monitor the feedback of the other person as you're speaking. In much online communication, however, that feedback will often come much later and thus is likely to be more clearly thought out and perhaps more closely monitored. Also, when you give feedback on social media sites such as Facebook by hitting the "like" button, your feedback is not limited to the person whose post you like; your feedback goes on your page and is visible to everyone who looks at your site.

VIEWPOINTS Feedback

What effect do you think feedback has in establishing and maintaining satisfying friendships or romantic relationships? How would you characterize ideal relationship feedback?

Feedforward Messages Much as feedback contains information about messages already sent, **feedforward** conveys information about messages before you send them. For example, you might use feedforward to express your wanting to chat a bit and say something like, "Hey, I haven't seen you the entire week; what's been going on?" Or you might give a brief preview of your main message and say something like, "You'd better sit down for this; you're going to be shocked." Or you might send someone a complimentary note before asking them to be your "friend." Or you might ask others to hear you out before they judge you. The subject heading on your e-mail, the tag line after your name on your social media site, and the phone numbers and names that come up on your cell phone are likewise clear examples of feedforward. These messages tell the listener something about the messages to come or about the way you'd like the listener to respond. Nonverbally, you give feedforward by your facial expressions, eye contact, and physical posture; with these nonverbal messages, you tell the other person something about the messages you'll be sending. A smile may signal a pleasant message; eye avoidance may signal that the message to come is difficult and perhaps uncomfortable to express.

INTERPERSONAL CHOICE POINT

Giving Feedforward

The grades were just posted for a course, and you see that your dorm mate failed. You got an A. Your dorm mate asks you about the grades. You feel you want to preface your remarks. What kind of feedforward might you give in this case?

Explore the **Exercise** "How to Give Feedforward Messages" at **MyCommunicationLab**

Channel

The communication **channel** is the medium through which message signals pass. The channel works like a bridge connecting source and receiver. Normally, two, three, or four channels are used simultaneously. For example, in face-to-face speech interactions, you speak and listen, using the vocal–auditory channel. You also, however, make gestures and receive these signals visually, using the visual channel. Similarly, you emit odors and smell those of others (using the chemical channel). Often you touch one another, and this too communicates (using the tactile channel).

Another way to classify channels is by the means of communication. Thus, face-to-face contact, telephones, e-mail, movies, television, smoke signals, and telegraph would be types of channels. Of most relevance today, of course, is the difference between face-to-face and computer-mediated interpersonal communication: interaction through e-mail, social network sites, instant messaging, news postings, film, television, radio, or fax.

INTERPERSONAL CHOICE POINT

Channels

You want to ask someone out on a date and are considering how you might go about this. What are your choices among channels? Which channel would be the most effective? Which channel would provoke the least anxiety?

In many of today's organizations (and increasingly in many private lives), workers/people are experiencing **information overload**, which occurs when you have to deal with an excessive amount of information and when much of that information is ambiguous or complex. As you can easily appreciate, advances in information technology have led to increasingly greater information overload. Having hundreds of friends who post hundreds of messages, photos, and videos create information overload in even the youngest social media users.

One of the problems with information overload is that it absorbs an enormous amount of time for workers at all levels of an organization. The more messages you have to deal with, the less time you have for those messages or tasks that are central to your functions. Research finds that when you're overloaded, you're more likely to respond to simpler messages and to generate simpler messages, which may not always be appropriate (Jones, Ravid, & Rafaeli, 2004). Similarly,

"I used to call people, then I got into e-mailing, then texting, and now I just ignore everyone."

Alex Gregory/The New Yorker Collection/ www.cartoonbank.com

errors become more likely simply because you cannot devote the needed time to any one item. Information overload has even been linked to health problems in more than one-third of managers (Lee, 2000). *Technostress* is a new term that denotes the anxiety and stress resulting from a feeling of being controlled by the overwhelming amount of information and from the inability to manage the information in the time available.

Noise

Noise is anything that interferes with your receiving a message. Just as messages may be auditory or visual, noise, too, comes in both auditory and visual forms. Four types of noise are especially relevant:

- *Physical noise* is interference that is external to both speaker and listener; it hampers the physical transmission of the signal or message and includes impediments such as the screeching of passing cars, the hum of a computer, sunglasses, extraneous messages, illegible handwriting, blurred type or fonts that are too small or difficult to read, misspellings and poor grammar, and pop-up ads.
- *Physiological noise* is created by barriers within the sender or receiver and includes impairments such as loss of vision, hearing loss, articulation problems, and memory loss.
- *Psychological noise* is mental interference in speaker or listener and includes preconceived ideas, wandering thoughts, biases and prejudices, closed-mindedness, and extreme emotionalism.
- *Semantic noise* is interference created when the speaker and listener have different meaning systems; types of semantic noise include linguistic or dialectical differences, the use of jargon or overly complex terms, and ambiguous or overly abstract terms whose meanings can be easily misinterpreted.

Blog Post

Noise

Noise of a somewhat different type is discussed in "The Chain Letter as Dysfunctional Communication" at tcbdevito.blogspot.com. What's your opinion of the chain letter? Are there some chain letters that you view more positively than others?

A useful concept in understanding noise and its importance in communication is **signal-to-noise ratio.** In this phrase, the term *signal* refers to information that you'd find useful; *noise* refers to information that is useless (to you). So, for example, mailing lists or blogs that contain lots of useful information would be high on signal and low on noise; those that contain lots of useless information would be high on noise and low on signal.

All communications contain noise. Noise cannot be totally eliminated, but its effects can be reduced. Making your language more precise, sharpening your skills for sending and receiving nonverbal messages, and improving your listening and feedback skills are some ways to combat the influence of noise.

INTERPERSONAL CHOICE POINT

Noise Reduction

Looking around your classroom (or your room, if you're taking the course online), what are some of the things you can do to reduce physical noise?

Context

Communication always takes place within a context: an environment that influences the form and the content of communication. At times, this context is so natural that you ignore it, like street noise. At other times, the context stands out, and the ways in which it restricts or stimulates your communications are obvious. Think, for example, of the different ways you'd talk at a funeral, in a quiet restaurant, and at a rock concert. And consider how the same "How are you?" will have very different meanings depending on the context: Said to a passing acquaintance, it means "Hello," whereas said to a sick friend in the hospital, it means "How are you feeling?"

The **context of communication** has at least four dimensions: physical, social–psychological, temporal, and cultural.

- *Physical dimension.* The room, workplace, or outdoor space in which communication takes place—the tangible or concrete environment—is the physical dimension. When you communicate with someone face to face, you're both in essentially the same physical environment. In computer-mediated communication, you may be in drastically different environments; one of you may be on a beach in San Juan, and the other may be in a Wall Street office.

- *Social–psychological dimension.* This includes, for example, the status relationships among the participants: distinctions such as employer versus the employee or the salesperson versus the store owner. The formality or informality, the friendliness or hostility, the cooperativeness or competitiveness of the interaction are also part of the social–psychological dimension.
- *Temporal or time dimension.* This dimension has to do with where a particular message fits into a sequence of communication events. For example, if you tell a joke about sickness immediately after your friend tells you she is sick, the joke will be perceived differently from the same joke told as one of a series of similar jokes to your friends in the locker room of the gym.
- *Cultural dimension.* The cultural dimension consists of the rules, norms, beliefs, and attitudes of the people communicating that are passed from one generation to another. For example, in some cultures, it's considered polite to talk to strangers; in others, that is something to be avoided.

VIDEO CHOICE POINT

Summer Internship

Margo, a student mentor at an entertainment magazine publisher, wants to say the right thing in her mentoring discussions with a group of interns. Margo's immediate problem is that she just learned that the interns have done questionable things on Facebook—posted inappropriate pictures, used biased language, and in general portrayed themselves as not serious professionals. She wants to make them aware of how damaging this could be in their career, but wonders how she should communicate it to them. She considers the topics covered in this chapter and wonders about, for example, the options she has in selecting the context in which the communication is to occur and what influences each context will have on the eventual effectiveness of her message. What options does she have for expressing her message in terms, say, of formality–informality or friendly–businesslike, and what differences will these choices make in her effectiveness? See how her choices play out in the video "Summer Internship," and respond to the questions posed.

 **Watch** the **Video** "Summer Internship" at **MyCommunicationLab**

Can you draw/diagram a model of communication that contains source–receiver, messages, channel, noise, and context and illustrates the relationship among these elements? Can you define each of these elements?

PRINCIPLES OF INTERPERSONAL COMMUNICATION

Watch the **Video** "Going Up" at **MyCommunicationLab**

Another way to define interpersonal communication is to consider its major principles. These principles are significant in terms of explaining theory and also, as you'll see, have very practical applications.

Interpersonal Communication Is Purposeful

Interpersonal communication can be used to accomplish a variety of purposes. Understanding how interpersonal communication serves these varied purposes will help you more effectively achieve your own interpersonal goals.

VIEWPOINTS Interpersonal metaphors

How would you explain interpersonal communication or interpersonal relationships in terms of metaphors such as a seesaw, a ball game, a flower, ice skates, a microscope, a television sitcom, a work of art, a book, a rubber band, or a software program?

- *To learn.* Interpersonal communication enables you to learn, to better understand the world of objects, events, and people—whether you do this face to face or online. In fact, your beliefs, attitudes, and values are probably influenced more by interpersonal encounters than by formal education. Through interpersonal communication, you also learn about yourself—your strengths and your weaknesses.
- *To relate.* Interpersonal communication helps you relate to others and to form meaningful relationships whether it's face to face or online. Such relationships help to alleviate loneliness and depression, enable you to share and heighten your pleasures, and generally make you feel more positive about yourself.
- *To influence.* Very likely, you influence the attitudes and behaviors of others in your interpersonal encounters—to vote a particular way, to try a new diet, to see a movie, or to believe that something is true or false—the list is endless.
- *To help.* Therapists serve a helping function professionally by offering guidance through interpersonal interaction. But everyone interacts to help in everyday life: Online and offline, you console a friend who has broken off a love affair, counsel a student about courses to take, or offer advice to a colleague at work.
- *To play.* Tweeting your weekend activities, discussing sports or dates, posting a clever joke or photo on some social media site, and in general just passing the time are play functions. Far from frivolous, this extremely important purpose gives your activities a necessary balance and your mind a needed break from all the seriousness around you.

In research on the motivations/purposes for using social networking sites, it's the relationship purpose that dominates. One research study, for example, finds the following motivations/purposes, in order of frequency mentioned (Smith, 2011). As you'll see, the reasons are mostly to relate, but the other purposes are likely served in the process.

- Staying in touch with friends
- Staying in touch with family
- Connecting with friends with whom you've lost contact
- Connecting with those who share your interests
- Making new friends
- Reading comments by celebrities
- Finding romantic partners

Popular belief and recent research both agree that men and women use communication for different purposes. Generally, men seem to communicate more for information whereas women seem to communicate more for relationship purposes (Colley et al., 2004; Shaw & Grant, 2002). Gender differences also occur in computer communication. For example, women ICQ users chat more for relationship reasons while men chat more to play and to relax (Leung, 2001).

Interpersonal Communication Is a Package of Signals

Communication behaviors, whether they involve verbal messages, gestures, or some combination thereof, usually occur in "packages" (Pittenger, Hockett, & Danehy, 1960). Usually, verbal and nonverbal behaviors reinforce or support each other. All parts of a message system normally work together to communicate a particular meaning. You don't express fear with words while the rest of your body is relaxed. You don't express anger through your posture while your face smiles. Your entire body works together—verbally and nonverbally—to express your thoughts and feelings.

You probably pay little attention to its "packaged" nature. It goes unnoticed. But when there's an incongruity—when the chilly handshake belies the verbal greeting, when the nervous posture belies the focused stare, when the constant preening belies the expressions of being comfortable and at ease—you take notice. Invariably you begin to question the credibility, the sincerity, and the honesty of the individual.

Often, contradictory messages are sent over a period of time. Note, for example, that in the following interaction the employee is being given two directives: (1) Use initiative, and (2) don't use initiative. Regardless of what he or she does, rejection will follow.

Employer: You've got to learn to take more initiative. You never seem to take charge, to take control.
Employee: (Takes the initiative, makes decisions.)
Employer: You've got to learn to follow the chain of command and not do things just because you want to.
Employee: (Goes back to old ways, not taking any initiative.)
Employer: Well, I told you. We expect more initiative from you.

Contradictory messages may be the result of the desire to communicate two different emotions or feelings. For example, you may like a person and want to communicate a positive feeling, but you may also feel resentment toward this person and want to communicate a negative feeling as well. The result is that you communicate both feelings; for example, you say that you're happy to see the person, but your facial expression and body posture communicate your negative feelings (Beier, 1974). In this example, and in many similar cases, the socially acceptable message is usually communicated verbally, whereas the less socially acceptable message is communicated nonverbally.

Interpersonal Communication Involves Content *and* Relationship Messages

Interpersonal messages combine content and relationship dimensions. **Content messages** focus on the real world, to something external to both speaker and listener. **Relationship messages,** on the other hand, focus on the relationship/connection between the individuals. For example, a supervisor may say to a trainee, "See me after the meeting." This simple message has a content message that tells the trainee to see the supervisor after the meeting. It also contains a relationship message that says something about the connection between the supervisor and the trainee. Even the use of the simple command shows there is a status difference that allows the supervisor to command the trainee. You can appreciate this most clearly if you visualize this command being made by the trainee to the supervisor. It appears awkward and out of place because it violates the normal relationship between supervisor and trainee.

Deborah Tannen, in her book *You're Wearing That?* (2006), gives lots of examples of content and relationship communication and the problems that can result from different interpretations. For example, the mother who says, "Are you going to quarter those tomatoes?" thinks she is communicating solely a content message. To the daughter, however, the message is largely relational and is in fact a criticism of the way she intends to cut the tomatoes. Questions, especially, may appear to be objective and focused on content but often are perceived as attacks, as in the title of Tannen's book. For example, here are some questions that you may have been asked—or that you yourself may have asked. Try identifying the potential relationship messages that the listener might receive in each case.

- You're *calling* me?
- *Did you say you're applying to* medical *school?*
- *You're in* love?
- *You paid $100 for* that?
- *And that's* all *you did?*

"It's not about the story. It's about Daddy taking time out of his busy day to read you a story."

P. C. Vey/The New Yorker Collection/www.cartoonbank.com

Many conflicts arise because people misunderstand relationship messages and cannot clarify them. Other problems arise when people fail to see the difference between content messages and relationship messages. Arguments over the content dimension of a message—such as what happened in a movie—are relatively easy to resolve. You may, for example, simply ask a third person what took place or see the movie again. Arguments on the relationship level, however, are much more difficult to resolve, in part because people seldom recognize that the argument is about relationship messages.

Interpersonal Communication Is a Process of Adjustment

The principle of **adjustment** states that interpersonal communication can take place only to the extent that the people talking share the same communication system. We can easily understand this when dealing with speakers of two different languages; much miscommunication is likely to occur. The principle, however, takes on particular relevance when you realize that no two people share identical communication systems. Parents and children, for example, not only have very different vocabularies but also, more importantly, have different meanings for some of the terms they have in common. (Consider, for example, the differences between parents' and children's understanding of such terms as *music, success,* and *family.*) Different cultures and social groups, even when they share a common language, also have different nonverbal communication systems. To the extent that these systems differ, communication will be hindered.

Part of the art of interpersonal communication is learning the other person's signals, how they're used, and what they mean. People in close relationships—either as intimate friends or as romantic partners—realize that learning the other person's signals takes a long time and, often, great patience. If you want to understand what another person means—by smiling, by saying "I love you," by arguing about trivial matters, by making self-deprecating comments—you have to learn that person's system of signals. Furthermore, you have to share your own system of signals with others so that they can better understand you. Although some people may know what you mean by your

INTERPERSONAL CHOICE POINT

Corrective Messaging

In the heat of an argument, you said you never wanted to see your partner's family again. Your partner reciprocated, saying the feeling was mutual. Now, weeks later, there remains great tension between you, especially when you find yourself with one or both families. What communication choices do you have for apologizing and putting this angry outburst behind you? What channel would you use?

SKILL BUILDING EXERCISE

Distinguishing Content and Relationship Messages

How would you communicate both the content and the relationship messages in the following situations?

1. After a date that you didn't enjoy and don't want to repeat ever again, you want to express your sincere thanks, but you don't want to be misinterpreted as communicating any indication that you would go on another date with this person.
2. You're ready to commit yourself to a long-term relationship but want your partner to sign a prenuptial agreement before moving any further in the relationship. You need to communicate both your desire to keep your money and to move the relationship to the next level.
3. You're interested in dating a friend on Facebook who also attends the college you do and with whom you've been chatting for a few weeks. But you don't know if the feeling is mutual. You want to ask for the date but to do so in a way that, if you're turned down, you won't be embarrassed.

Content and relationship messages serve different communication functions. Being able to distinguish between them is prerequisite to using and responding to them effectively.

silence or by your avoidance of eye contact, others may not. You cannot expect others to decode your behaviors accurately without help.

This principle is especially important in intercultural communication, largely because people from different cultures use different signals and sometimes the same signals to signify quite different things. In much of the United States, focused eye contact means honesty and openness. But in Japan and in many Hispanic cultures, that same behavior may signify arrogance or disrespect if engaged in by, say, a youngster with someone significantly older.

An interesting theory largely revolving around adjustment is **communication accommodation theory**. This theory holds that speakers will adjust to or accommodate to the speaking style of their listeners to gain social approval and greater communication efficiency (Giles, 2009; Giles, Mulac, Bradac, & Johnson, 1987). For example, when two people have a similar speech rate, they seem to be attracted to each other more than to those with dissimilar rates (Buller, LePoire, Aune, & Eloy, 1992). Another study even showed that people accommodate in their e-mail. For example, responses to messages that contain politeness cues were significantly more polite than responses to e-mails that did not contain such cues (Bunz & Campbell, 2004). So, for example, if you say "thank you" and "please," others are more likely to use politeness cues as well.

Blog Post

Principles of Communication

For an application of some of these principles to a letter to Dear Abby, see "It's About Communication, Abby" at tcbdevito.blogspot.com. How would you have answered this writer's letter?

Interpersonal Communication Involves Power

Power is a major component of interpersonal communication. You cannot communicate without making some implicit comment on your power or lack of it. When in an interactional situation, therefore, recognize that on the basis of your verbal and nonverbal messages, people will assess your power and will interact accordingly.

No interpersonal relationship exists without a power dimension. Look at your own relationships and those of your friends and relatives. In each relationship, one person has more power than the other. In interpersonal relationships among most Americans, the more powerful person is often the one who is more attractive or the one who has more money. In other cultures the factors that contribute to power may be different and may include a person's family background, age, education, or wisdom.

Although all relationships involve power, they differ in the types of power that the people use and to which they respond. Before reading about the different types of power, take the following self-test.

Research has identified six types of power: legitimate, referent, reward, coercive, expert, and information or persuasion (French & Raven, 1968; Raven, Centers, & Rodrigues, 1975). As you listen to the messages of others (and your own) and as you observe the relationships of others (and your own), consider the role of power, how it's expressed, and how it's responded to. The more sensitive you become to the expression of power—in messages and in relationships—the more effective your interpersonal messages are likely to be.

- You hold **legitimate power** (self-test statement 1) when others believe you have a right—by virtue of your position—to influence or control their behaviors. For example, as an employer, judge, manager, or police officer, you'd have legitimate power by virtue of these roles. Relate your persuasive arguments and appeals to your own role and credibility.
- You have **referent power** (statement 2) when others wish to be like you. Referent power holders are often attractive, have considerable prestige, and are well liked and well respected. For example, you might have referent power over a younger brother because he wants to be like you. Demonstrate those qualities admired by those you wish to influence.
- You have **reward power** (statement 3) when you control the rewards that others want. Rewards may be material (money, promotion, jewelry) or social (love, friendship, respect). For example, teachers have reward power over students because they control grades, letters of recommendation, and social approval. Make rewards contingent on compliance, and follow through by rewarding those who comply with your requests.

INTERPERSONAL CHOICE POINT

Unwanted Talk

Your supervisor at work continually talks about sex. You fear your lack of reaction has been interpreted as a sign of approval. You need to change that but at the same time not alienate the person who can fire you. What are some of things you might do to stop this unwanted talk?

TEST YOURSELF

How Powerful Are You?

For each statement, indicate how appropriate it is to you. Use a ten-point scale with 1 = not true of me at all and 10 = very true of me. Use 5 if you don't know or aren't sure.

____ 1. My position is such that I often have to tell others what to do. For example, a mother's position demands that she tell her children what to do, a manager's position demands that he or she tell employees what to do, and so on.

____ 2. People wish to be like me or identified with me. For example, high school football players may admire the former professional football player who is now their coach and want to be like him.

____ 3. People see me as having the ability to give them what they want. For example, employers have the ability to give their employees increased pay, longer vacations, or improved working conditions.

____ 4. People see me as having the ability to administer punishment or to withhold things they want. For example, employers have the ability to reduce voluntary overtime, shorten vacation time, or fail to improve working conditions.

____ 5. Other people realize that I have expertise in certain areas of knowledge. For example, a doctor has expertise in medicine and so others turn to the doctor to tell them what to do.

____ 6. Other people realize that I possess the communication ability to present an argument logically and persuasively.

How Did You Do? These statements refer to the six major types of power, as described in the text. Low scores (1s, 2s, and 3s) indicate your belief that you possess little of these particular types of power, and high scores (8s, 9s, and 10s) indicate your belief that you possess a great deal of these particular types of power.

What Will You Do? How satisfied are you with your level of power? If you're not satisfied, what might you do about it? A good starting place, of course, is to learn the skills of interpersonal communication discussed in this text.

- You have **coercive power** (statement 4) when you have the ability to administer punishments to or remove rewards from others if they do not do as you wish. For example, teachers may give poor grades or withhold recommendations. Make clear the negative consequences that are likely to follow noncompliance.
- You have **expert power** (statement 5) when others see you as having expertise or knowledge. Your expert power increases when you're seen as unbiased with nothing personally to gain from exerting this power. For example, judges have expert power in legal matters, and doctors have expert power in medical matters. Cultivate your own expertise, and connect your persuasive appeals to this expertise.
- You have **information or persuasion power** (statement 6) when others see you as having the ability to communicate logically and persuasively. For example, researchers and scientists may be given information power because of their being perceived as informed and critical thinkers. Increase your communication competence; this book's major function, of course, is to explain ways for you to accomplish this.

Interpersonal Communication Is Ambiguous

All messages are ambiguous to some degree. **Ambiguity** is a condition in which a message can be interpreted as having more than one meaning. Sometimes ambiguity results when we use words that can be interpreted differently. Informal time terms offer good examples; different people may interpret terms such as *soon, right away, in a minute, early,* and *late* very differently. The terms themselves are ambiguous.

Some degree of ambiguity exists in all interpersonal communication. When you express an idea, you never communicate your meaning exactly and totally; rather, you communicate your meaning with some reasonable accuracy—enough to give the other person a reasonably clear idea of what you mean. Sometimes, of course, you're less accurate than you anticipated and your listener "gets the wrong idea" or "gets offended" when you only meant to be humorous or "misunderstands your emotional meaning." Because of this inevitable uncertainty, you may qualify what you're saying, give an example, or ask, "Do you know what I mean?" These clarifying tactics help the other person understand your meaning and reduce uncertainty (to some degree).

Similarly, all relationships contain uncertainty. Consider a close interpersonal relationship of your own, and ask yourself the following questions. Answer each question according to a six-point scale on which 1 means "completely or almost completely uncertain" and 6 means "completely or almost completely certain." How certain are you about these questions?

1. Do you know what you can and cannot say to each other? Are there certain topics that will cause problems?
2. Do you know how your partner feels about you, and does your partner know how you feel about him or her?
3. Do you know how you and your partner would characterize and describe the relationship? Would it be similar? Different? If different, in what ways?
4. How does your partner see the future of the relationship? Does your partner know how you feel about the relationship's future?

Very likely you were not able to respond with "6" for all four questions. And it's equally likely that your relationship partner would be unable to respond to every question with a 6. These questions, paraphrased from a relationship uncertainty scale (Knobloch & Solomon, 1999)—and similar others—illustrate that you probably experience some degree of uncertainty about the norms that govern your relationship communication (question 1), the degree to which the two of you see the relationship in similar ways (question 2), the definition of the relationship (question 3), and/or the relationship's future (question 4).

The skills of interpersonal communication presented throughout this text can give you tools for appropriately reducing ambiguity and making your meanings as unambiguous as possible.

INTERPERSONAL CHOICE POINT

How to Disambiguate

You've gone out with someone for several months and want to reduce ambiguity about the future of the relationship and discover your partner's level of commitment. But you don't want to scare your partner. What are some things you can say or do to find answers to your very legitimate questions?

Interpersonal Communication Is Punctuated

Interpersonal interactions are continuous transactions. There's no clear-cut beginning or ending. As a participant in or an observer of the communication act, you engage in punctuation: You divide up this continuous, circular process into causes and effects, or **stimuli** and **responses**. That is, you segment this continuous stream of communication into smaller pieces. You label some of these pieces causes, or stimuli, and others effects, or responses.

Consider an example. A married couple is in a restaurant. The husband is flirting with another woman, and the wife is talking to her sister on her cell phone. Both are scowling at each other and are obviously in a deep nonverbal argument. Recalling the situation later, the husband might observe that the wife talked on the phone, so he innocently flirted with the other woman. The only reason for his behavior (he says) was his anger over her talking on the phone when they were supposed to be having dinner together. Notice that he sees his behavior as a response to her behavior. In recalling the same incident, the wife might say that she phoned her sister when he started flirting. The more he flirted, the longer she talked. She had no intention of calling anyone until he started flirting. To her, his behavior was the stimulus and hers was the response; he caused her behavior. Thus, the husband sees the sequence as going from phoning to flirting, and the wife sees it as going from flirting to phoning. This example is depicted visually in Figure 1.5 and is supported by research showing that, among marrieds at least, the individuals regularly see their partner's behavior as the cause of conflict (Schutz, 1999).

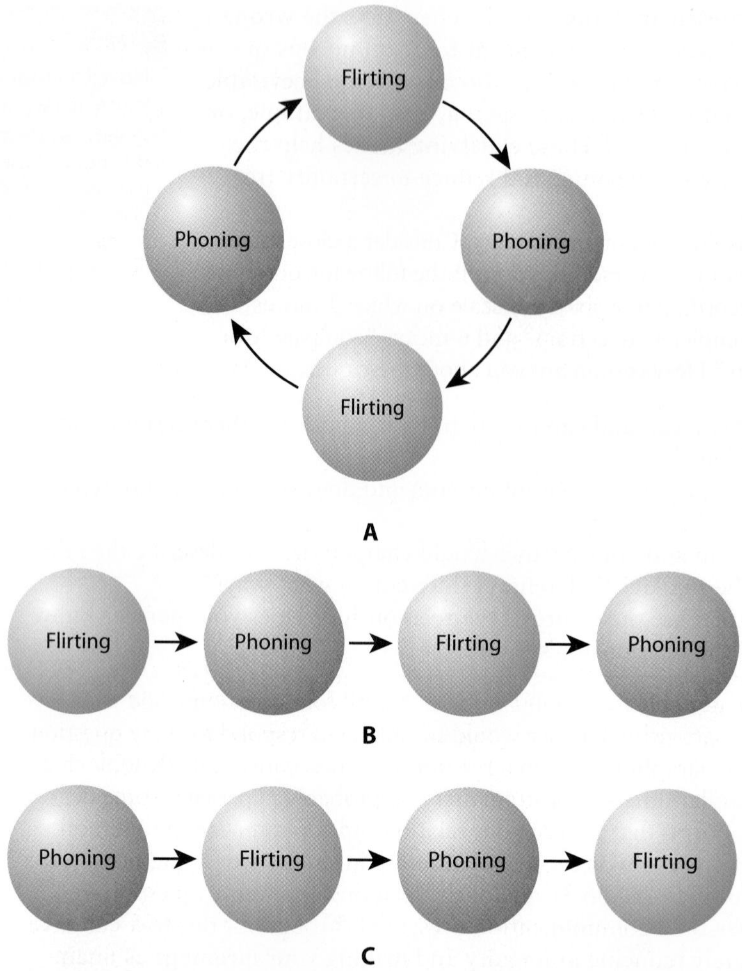

FIGURE 1.5

Punctuation and the Sequence of Events

Try using this three-part figure, discussed in the text, to explain what might go on in the following situation: One person complains about another person's nagging, and the nagging person complains about the other person's avoidance and silence.

This tendency to divide up the various communication transactions in sequences of stimuli and responses is referred to as **punctuation of communication** (Watzlawick, Beavin, & Jackson, 1967). People punctuate the continuous sequences of events into stimuli and responses for ease of understanding and remembering. And, as both the preceding examples illustrate, people punctuate communication in ways that allow them to look good and that are consistent with their own self-image.

Interpersonal Communication Is Inevitable, Irreversible, and Unrepeatable

Three characteristics often considered together are interpersonal communication's *inevitability, irreversibility,* and *unrepeatability*.

COMMUNICATION IS INEVITABLE Often communication is intentional, purposeful, and consciously motivated. Sometimes, however, you are communicating even though you may not think you are or may not even want to. Take, for example, the student sitting in the back of the room with an "expressionless" face, perhaps staring out the window. The student may think that she or he is not communicating with the teacher or with the other students. On closer inspection, however, you can see that the student *is* communicating something—perhaps lack of interest or simply anxiety about a private problem. In any event, the student is communicating whether she or he wishes to or not—demonstrating the principle of **inevitability**. Similarly, the color and type of your cell phone, the wallpaper in your room, and the type and power of your computer or cell phone communicate messages about you. You cannot *not* communicate. In the same way, you cannot *not* influence the person with whom you interact (Watzlawick, 1978). Persuasion, like communication, is also inevitable. The issue, then, is not whether you will or will not persuade or influence another; rather, it's how you'll exert your influence.

> **INTERPERSONAL CHOICE POINT**
>
> **The Irreversibility of Interpersonal Communication**
>
> You refer to your best friend's current romantic partner with the name of the ex-partner. From both their expressions, you can tell your friend never mentioned the ex. What can you say to get your friend out of the trouble you just created? To whom (primarily) would you address your explanation?

Communication Is Irreversible Notice that only some processes can be reversed. For example, you can turn water into ice and then reverse the process by turning the ice back into water. Other processes, however, are irreversible. You can, for example, turn grapes into wine, but you cannot reverse the process and turn wine into grapes. Interpersonal communication is an irreversible process. Although you may try to qualify, deny, or somehow reduce the effects of your message, you cannot withdraw the message you have conveyed. Similarly, once you press the send key, your e-mail is in cyberspace and impossible to reverse. Because of **irreversibility**, be careful not to say things you may wish to withdraw later.

In online communication, the messages are written and may be saved, stored, and printed. Both face-to-face and online messages may be kept confidential or revealed publicly. But computer messages can be made public more easily and spread more quickly than face-to-face messages. Interestingly enough, only 55 percent of online teens say they do not post content that might reflect negatively on them in the future (Lenhart et al., 2011). And, increasingly, employers and even some colleges are asking that candidates open their social networking accounts during the interview (Raby, 2012).

Because electronic communication often is permanent, you may wish to be cautious when you're e-mailing, posting your profile, or posting a message. Specifically:

- E-messages are virtually impossible to destroy. Often e-messages that you think you deleted will remain on servers and workstations and may be retrieved by a clever hacker or simply copied and distributed.
- E-messages can easily be made public. Your words, photos, and videos on your blog or on a social networking site can be sent to anyone.
- E-messages are not privileged communication and can easily be accessed by others and be used against you. And you'll not be able to deny saying something; it will be there in black and white.

Remember, too, that even when you restrict your information to one group or "circle of friends," you can never be sure that a person you intended to receive the message won't pass it on to someone you'd prefer to exclude from a particular post or photo.

> **INTERPERSONAL CHOICE POINT**
>
> **Getting Out of a Tight Spot**
>
> You write a gossipy e-mail about Ellen (revealing things that you promised to keep secret) to your mutual friend Ella but inadvertently send it to Ellen herself. What are some of the things you can say that might help you get out of this awkward situation?

Communication Is Unrepeatable The reason why communication is unrepeatable is simple: Everyone and everything are constantly changing. As a result, you never can recapture the exact same situation, frame of mind, or relationship dynamics that defined a previous interpersonal act. For example, you never can repeat meeting someone for the first time, comforting a grieving friend, or resolving a specific conflict.

You can, of course, try again; you can say, "I'm sorry I came off so pushy, can we try again?" Notice, however, that even when you say this, you have not erased the initial (and perhaps negative) impression. Instead, you try to counteract this impression by going through the motions again. In doing so, you hope to create a more positive impact that will lessen the original negative effect.

Can you explain and give examples of each of the principles governing interpersonal communication (it is purposeful, occurs in packages of signals, contains content and relationship messages, is a process of adjustment, involves power, is often ambiguous, is punctuated, and is inevitable, irreversible, and unrepeatable)?

INTERPERSONAL COMPETENCE

Explore the **Concept** "Perceived Communication Competence Questionnaire" at **MyCommunicationLab**

Your ability to communicate effectively is your **interpersonal competence** (Spitzberg & Cupach, 1989; Wilson & Sabee, 2003). A major goal of this text (and of your course) is to expand and enlarge your competence so you'll have a greater arsenal of communication options at your disposal. The greater your interpersonal competence, the more options you'll have for communicating with friends, lovers, and family; with colleagues on the job; and in just about any situation in which you'll communicate with another person. The greater your competence, the greater your own power to accomplish successfully what you want to accomplish—to ask for a raise or a date; establish temporary work relationships, long-term friendships, or romantic relationships; communicate empathy and support; or gain compliance or resist the compliance tactics of others.

In short, interpersonal competence includes knowing how interpersonal communication works and how to best achieve your purposes by adjusting your messages according to the context of the interaction, the person with whom you're interacting, and a host of other factors discussed throughout this text. Let's spell out more clearly the traits of a competent interpersonal communicator.

VIEWPOINTS Interpersonal competence

What characters in television sitcoms or dramas do you think demonstrate superior interpersonal competence? What characters demonstrate obvious interpersonal incompetence?

The Competent Interpersonal Communicator Thinks Critically and Mindfully

Without critical thinking, there can be no competent exchange of ideas. Critical thinking is logical thinking; it's thinking that is well reasoned, unbiased, and clear. It involves thinking intelligently, carefully, and with as much clarity as possible. It's the opposite of what you'd call sloppy, illogical, or careless thinking. And, not surprisingly, according to one study of corporate executives, critical thinking is one of the stepping stones to effective management (Miller, 1997).

A special kind of critical thinking is mindfulness. **Mindfulness** is a state of awareness in which you're conscious of your reasons for thinking or behaving. In its opposite, **mindlessness**, you lack conscious awareness of what or how you're thinking (Langer, 1989). To apply interpersonal skills effectively in conversation, you need to be mindful of the unique communication situation you're in, of your available communication options, and of the reasons why one option is likely to be better than the others (Burgoon, Berger, & Waldron, 2000; Elmes & Gemmill, 1990).

To increase mindfulness, try the following suggestions (Langer, 1989).

- *Create and re-create categories.* Group things in different ways; remember that people are constantly changing, so the categories into which you may group them also should change. Learn to see objects, events, and people as belonging to a wide variety of categories. Try to see, for example, your prospective romantic partner in a variety of roles—child, parent, employee, neighbor, friend, financial contributor, and so on.
- *Be open to new information and points of view,* even when these contradict your most firmly held beliefs. New information forces you to reconsider what might be outmoded ways of thinking and can help you challenge long-held but now inappropriate beliefs and attitudes.
- *Beware of relying too heavily on first impressions* (Chanowitz & Langer, 1981; Langer, 1989). Treat first impressions as tentative, as hypotheses that need further investigation. Be prepared to revise, reject, or accept these initial impressions.
- *Think before you act.* Especially in delicate situations such as anger or commitment messages, it's wise to pause and think over the situation mindfully (DeVito, 2003). In this way, you'll stand a better chance of acting and reacting appropriately.

INTERPERSONAL CHOICE POINT

Questionable Posts

Your friend has been posting some rather extreme socio-political statements that you think might turn out to be detrimental when searching for a graduate school or job. You've always been honest with each other but careful because you're both very sensitive to criticism. What are some ways you can bring up this topic without seeming critical?

The Competent Interpersonal Communicator Is Skillful

This text explains the theory and research in interpersonal communication in order to provide you with a solid understanding of how interpersonal communication works. With that understanding as a firm foundation, you'll be better able to develop and master the very practical skills of interpersonal communication, including those of empathy, power and influence, listening, politeness, using verbal and nonverbal messages, managing interpersonal conflict, and establishing and maintaining satisfying interpersonal relationships.

In learning the skills of interpersonal communication (or any set of skills), you'll probably at first sense an awkwardness and self-consciousness; the new behaviors may not seem to fit comfortably. As you develop more understanding and use the skills more, this awkwardness will gradually fade, and the new behaviors will begin to feel comfortable and natural. You'll facilitate your progress toward mastery if you follow a logical system of steps. Here's one possible system, called STEP (Skill, Theory, Example, Practice):

1. Get a clear understanding of what the *skill* is.
2. Understand the *theory;* if you understand the reasons for the suggestions offered, it will help make the skill more logical and easier to remember.
3. Develop *examples,* especially your own; this will help to make the material covered here a more integral part of communication behavior.
4. *Practice* with the Skill Building Exercises included in this text as well as with those on the website (www.MyCommunicationLab.com). Practice alone at first, then with supportive friends, and then in general day-to-day interactions.

Blog Post

Social Media

See "Social Media Warnings" and "Social Networking and Getting a Job" at tcbdevito.blogspot.com for some added insights into the dangers of posting inappropriate photos and messages on your social media site. Do you think this concern is warranted? Overblown?

SKILL BUILDING EXERCISE

Assessing Your Social Network Profile

Examine your own social network profile (or that of a friend) in terms of the principles of interpersonal communication discussed in this chapter:

1. What purposes does your profile serve? In what ways might it serve the five purposes of interpersonal communication identified here (to learn, relate, influence, play, and help)?
2. In what way is your profile page a package of signals? In what ways do the varied words and pictures combine to communicate meaning?
3. Can you identify and distinguish between content from relational messages?
4. In what ways, if any, have you adjusted your profile as a response to the ways in which others have fashioned their profiles?
5. In what ways does your profile exhibit interpersonal power? In what ways, if any, have you incorporated into your profile the six types of power discussed in this chapter (legitimate, referent, reward, coercive, expert, or information)?
6. What messages on your profile are ambiguous? Bumper stickers and photos should provide a useful starting point.
7. In what ways (if any) can you identify the process of punctuation?
8. What are the implications of inevitability, irreversibility, and unrepeatability for publishing a profile on and communicating via social network sites?

Heightened awareness of how messages help create meanings should increase your ability to make more reasoned and reasonable choices in your interpersonal interactions.

The Competent Interpersonal Communicator Is Culturally Aware and Sensitive

The term **culture** refers to the lifestyle of a group of people. A group's culture consists of its values, beliefs, artifacts, ways of behaving, and ways of communicating. Culture includes all that members of a social group have produced and developed—their language, ways of thinking, art, laws, and religion. Culture is transmitted from one generation to another not through genes but through communication and learning, especially through the teachings of parents, peer groups, schools, religious institutions, and government agencies. Because most cultures teach women and men different attitudes and ways of communicating, many of the gender differences we observe may be considered cultural. So, while not minimizing the biological differences between men and women, most people agree that gender differences are, in part, cultural.

Competence is sometimes culture specific; communications that prove effective in one culture will not necessarily prove effective in another. For example, giving a birthday gift to a close friend would be appreciated by members of many cultures and in some cases would be expected. But Jehovah's Witnesses frown on this practice because they don't celebrate birthdays (Dresser, 1999, 2005). Because of the vast range of cultural differences that affect interpersonal communication, every chapter discusses the role of culture, and Chapter 2 focuses exclusively on culture and intercultural communication.

Explore the **Exercise** "Ethics in Interpersonal Communication" at **MyCommunicationLab**

The Competent Interpersonal Communicator Is Ethical

Interpersonal communication also involves questions of **ethics**, the study of good and bad, of right and wrong, of moral and immoral. Ethics is concerned with actions, with behaviors; it's concerned with distinguishing between behaviors that are moral (ethical, good, and right) and those that are immoral (unethical, bad, and wrong). Not surprisingly, there's an ethical dimension to any interpersonal communication act (Bok, 1978; Neher & Sandin, 2007). In thinking about ethics, it's useful to distinguish between an objective and a subjective view of ethics.

If you take an **objective view** of ethics, you'd argue that the rightness or wrongness of an act is absolute and exists apart from the values or beliefs of any individual or culture. With this view, you'd hold that there are standards that apply to all people in all situations at all times. If lying, false advertising, using illegally obtained evidence, or revealing secrets you've promised to keep were considered unethical, then they would be unethical regardless of circumstances or of cultural values and beliefs. In an objective view, the end can never justify the means; an unethical act is never justified regardless of how good or beneficial its results (or ends) might be.

If you take a **subjective view**, you'd claim that the morality of an act depends on a specific culture's values and beliefs as well as on the particular circumstances. Thus, from a subjective position, you would claim that the end might justify the means—a good result can justify the use of unethical means to achieve that result. For example, you'd argue that lying is wrong to win votes or to sell cigarettes but that lying can be ethical if the end result is positive (such as trying to make someone who is unattractive feel better by telling them they look great or telling a critically ill person that they'll feel better soon).

Blog Post

Ethics

For a self-test, along with one interpretation of popular ethical guidelines, see "ABCD: Ethics" at tcbdevito.blogspot.com. Add your own comments.

Each field of study defines what is and what is not ethical to its concerns. Here are just a few to highlight some communication-oriented codes. In this connection, try looking up the code of ethics for the profession you're in or planning on entering.

- The National Communication Association Ethical Credo
- Blogger's Ethics
- Online Journalim
- Radio-Television News Directors Association and Foundation Code of Ethics and Professional Conduct

In addition to this introductory discussion, ethical dimensions of interpersonal communication are presented in each of the remaining chapters in "Ethical Messages" boxes. Here, as a kind of preview, are just a few of the ethical issues raised in these boxes. As you read these questions, think about your own ethical beliefs and how these beliefs influence the way you'd answer the questions.

- What are your ethical obligations as a listener? See Ethics box, Chapter 4.
- When it is unethical to remain silent? See Ethics box, Chapter 6.
- When is gossiping ethical, and when is it unethical? See Ethics box, Chapter 8.
- At what point in a relationship do you have an obligation to reveal intimate details of your life? See Ethics box, Chapter 9.
- Are there ethical and unethical ways to engage in conflict and conflict resolution? See Ethics box, Chapter 11.

Can you define and illustrate the four interpersonal competencies (mindful and critical thinking, an arsenal of interpersonal skills, an awareness of cultural differences and sensitivity to them, and an ethical foundation)?

MESSAGES IN THE MEDIA: WRAP UP

The plots of many sitcoms often revolve around problems in interpersonal communication. Watching such shows with a view to the principles of effective and ineffective interpersonal communication will provide a wide variety of specific examples.

SUMMARY OF CONCEPTS AND SKILLS

Listen to the **Audio Chapter Summary** at **MyCommunicationLab**

This chapter explored the reasons for studying interpersonal communication, its nature, its essential elements, several principles of interpersonal communication, and interpersonal competence.

Why Study Interpersonal Communication

1. It's an essential and inevitable part of human experience as well as having numerous personal and professional benefits.

The Nature of Interpersonal Communication

2. Interpersonal communication refers to a type of communication that occurs between interdependent individuals, is inherently relational, exists on a continuum, involves both verbal and nonverbal messages, exists in varied forms, and is best viewed as a transactional process involving choices.

The Elements of Interpersonal Communication

3. Essential to an understanding of interpersonal communication are the following elements: source–receiver, encoding–decoding, messages (including metamessages, feedback, and feedforward), channel, noise (physical, physiological, psychological, and semantic), and context (physical, social–psychological, temporal, and cultural).

Principles of Interpersonal Communication

4. Interpersonal communication is:
   - purposeful; through interpersonal communication we learn, relate, influence, play, and help.
   - a package of signals that usually reinforce but also may contradict one another.
   - a combination of content and relationship messages; we communicate about objects and events in the world but also about relationships between sources and receivers.
   - a process of adjustment in which each of us accommodates to the specialized communication system of the other.
   - integrally connected with power.
   - ambiguous to some extent.
   - punctuated (divided up into stimuli and responses) by observers.
   - inevitable (communication will occur whether we want it to or not), irreversible (once something is received, it remains communicated and cannot be erased from a listener's memory), and unrepeatable (no communication act can ever be repeated exactly).

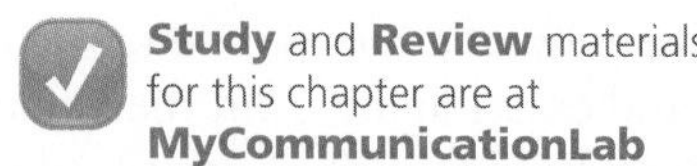

Study and **Review** materials for this chapter are at **MyCommunicationLab**

Interpersonal Competence

5. Interpersonal competence is best viewed as consisting of both a knowledge of and skill in interpersonal communication, an understanding and control of power strategies, effective listening, critical thinking and mindfulness, cultural understanding, politeness, and ethics.

In addition to the above concepts, this chapter also covered several interpersonal skills. As you read over the list, place a check in front of those you feel you'd like to work on:

____ 1. *Feedback.* Listen to both verbal and nonverbal feedback—from yourself and from others—and use these cues to help you adjust your messages.

____ 2. *Feedforward.* Use feedforward when you feel your listener needs background or when you want to ease into a particular topic, such as bad news.

____ 3. *Channel.* Assess your channel options (for example, face-to-face conversation versus e-mail or voicemail message) before communicating important messages.

____ 4. *Noise management.* Reduce physical, physiological, psychological, and semantic noise as best you can; use repetition and restatement and, when in doubt, ask if you're clear.

____ 5. *Mindfulness.* Create and re-create categories, be open to new information and points of view, avoid relying too heavily on first impressions, and think before you act.

____ 6. *Purposes.* Adjust your interpersonal communication strategies on the basis of your specific purpose.

____ 7. *Packaging.* Make your verbal and nonverbal messages consistent; inconsistencies often create uncertainty and misunderstanding.

____ 8. *Content and relationship.* Listen to both the content and the relationship aspects of messages, distinguish between them, and respond to both.

____ 9. *Context adjustment.* Adjust your messages to the physical, cultural, social–psychological, and temporal context.

____10. *Communication options.* Assess your communication options before communicating, in light of inevitability, irreversibility, and unrepeatability.

VOCABULARY QUIZZ: The Language of Interpersonal Communication

Match the terms of interpersonal communication with their definitions. Record the number of the definition next to the appropriate term.

____ interpersonal communication (3)
____ interpersonal competence (22)
____ feedback (10)
____ ambiguity (18)
____ cultural context (13)
____ feedforward (11)
____ relationship messages (15)
____ source–receiver (9)
____ encoding (9)
____ communication as a transactional process (7)

1. Messages sent back to the source in response to the source's messages.
2. Each person in the interpersonal communication act.
3. Information about messages that are yet to be sent.
4. Presence of more than one potential meaning.
5. The rules and norms, beliefs and attitudes of the people communicating.
6. Communication as an ongoing process in which each part depends on each other part.
7. Communication that takes place between persons who have a relationship.
8. Messages referring to the connection between the two people communicating.
9. The understanding of and ability to use the skills of interpersonal communication.
10. The process of sending messages; for example, in speaking or writing.

These ten terms and additional terms used in this chapter can be found in the glossary.

MyCommunicationLab

Visit MyCommunicationLab for a wealth of additional information on interpersonal communication. Flashcards, videos, skill building exercises, sample test questions, and additional exercises, examples, and discussions will help you continue your study of the fundamentals of interpersonal communication, its theory, and its skills.

CHAPTER

2

Culture and Interpersonal Communication

MESSAGES IN THE MEDIA

International news shows are becoming more and more popular, in part because we live in a global environment where events thousands of miles away in countries we've only read about exert powerful influences on us all. Understanding the role of culture in interpersonal communication—the subject of this chapter—is essential.

OBJECTIVES *After reading this chapter, you should be able to:*

1. Explain the role of culture in interpersonal communication; define *enculturation*, *ethnic identity*, and *acculturation*.
2. Define and illustrate four cultural principles for communicating efficiently and three principles for maintaining relationships.
3. Explain and give examples of the seven major ways in which cultures differ from one another.
4. Paraphrase the eight principles of intercultural communication, and apply these in intercultural interactions.

Listen to the **Chapter Audio** at **MyCommunicationLab**

Central to all forms of interpersonal communication is culture. The more you understand about culture, the more effective you'll be in a wide variety of interpersonal interactions. Here we explore the relationship between culture and interpersonal communication, the major principles of culture, the major differences among cultures, and the forms and skills of intercultural communication.

CULTURE

Explore the **Exercise** "Cultural Beliefs" at **MyCommunicationLab**

Culture (introduced briefly in Chapter 1) consists of (1) the relatively specialized lifestyle of a group of people (2) that is passed on from one generation to the next through communication, not through genes.

Included in a social group's "culture" is everything that members of that group have produced and developed—their values, beliefs, artifacts, and language; their ways of behaving and ways of thinking; and their art, laws, and religion.

Culture is passed on from one generation to the next through communication, not through genes. Culture is not synonymous with race or nationality. The term *culture* does not refer to color of skin or shape of eyes, as these are passed on through genes, not communication. But, because members of a particular race or country are often taught similar beliefs, attitudes, and values, it's possible to speak of "Hispanic culture" or "African American culture." It's important to realize, however, that within any large group—especially one based on race or nationality—there will be enormous differences. The Kansas farmer and the Wall Street executive may both be, say, German American, but they may differ widely in their attitudes, beliefs, and lifestyles. In some ways, the Kansas farmer may be closer in attitudes and values to a Chinese farmer than to the New York financier.

In ordinary conversation, *sex* and *gender* are often used synonymously. In academic discussions of culture, they're more often distinguished. **Sex** refers to the biological distinction between male and female; sex is determined by genes, by biology. **Gender**, on the other hand, refers to the cultural roles of "masculine" and "feminine" (Helgeson, 2009; Stewart, Cooper, & Stewart, 2003). Gender (masculinity and femininity) is what boys and girls learn from their culture; it's the attitudes, beliefs, values, and ways of communicating and relating to one another that boys and girls learn as they grow up.

Because of this, gender may be considered a cultural variable. Thus, you act like a man or a woman in part because your culture has taught you about how men and women should act. This does not, of course, deny that biological differences also play a role in the differences between male and female behavior. In fact, research continues to uncover biological roots of male/female differences we once thought were entirely learned (Wrench, McCroskey, & Richmond, 2008).

Table 2.1 provides a way of looking at the nature of culture through metaphors and will make some of the important concepts memorable.

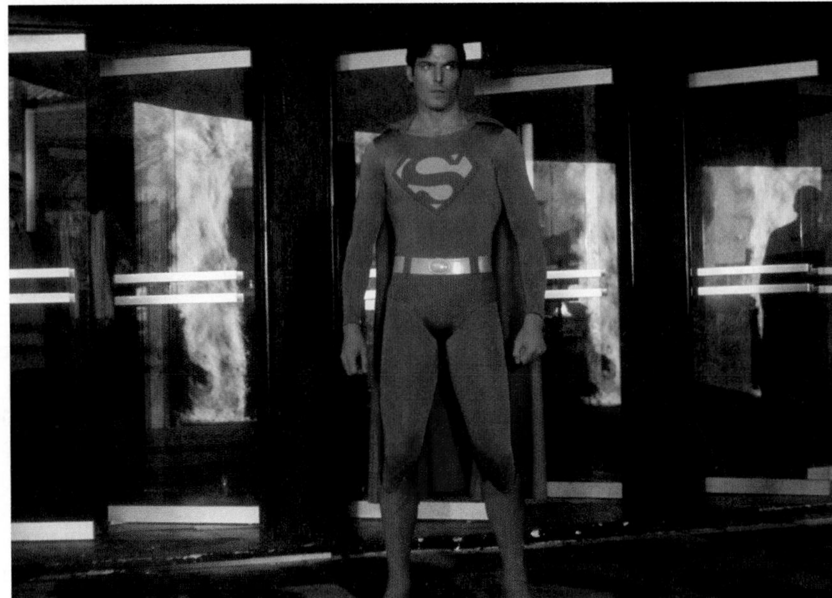

VIEWPOINTS Gender stereotypes

The stereotype of the male generally defines him as logical, decisive, aggressive, insensitive, unemotional, non-nurturing, mechanically talented, and impatient. The stereotype of the female generally defines her as illogical, variable, nurturing, emotional, sensitive, mechanically untalented, and impatient (Ciccarelli & White, 2012). Do your acquaintances maintain any of these stereotypes? What are some of the implications of thinking through these stereotypes?

Learning Culture

Culture is transmitted from one generation to another through **enculturation**, the process by which you learn the culture into which you're

TABLE 2.1

SEVEN METAPHORS OF CULTURE

Here are seven metaphors of culture; taken together they provide other ways of looking at the nature of culture. These insights are taken from a variety of sources including Hall (1976), Hofstede, Hofstede, and Minkov (2010), and the websites of Culture at Work and Culturally Teaching: Education across Cultures.

Metaphor	Metaphor's Claim/Assumption
Salad/jelly beans	Like items in a salad or bag of jelly beans, cultures are individual; yet they work together with other cultures to produce an even better combination.
Iceberg	Like the iceberg, only a small part of culture is visible; most of culture and its influences are hidden from easy inspection.
Tree	Like the tree, you only see the trunk, branches, and leaves, but the root system, which gives the tree its structure and function, is hidden from view.
Melting pot	Cultures blend into one amalgam and lose their individuality, but the blend is better than any one of the ingredients.
Software	Culture dictates what we do and don't do much as does a software program. Out of awareness, people are programmed, to some extent, to think and behave by their culture.
Organism	Culture, like an organism, uses the environment (other cultures) to grow but maintains boundaries so its uniqueness is not destroyed.
Mosaic	Like a beautiful mosaic is made up of pieces of different shapes, sizes, and colors, so is culture; the whole, the combination, is more beautiful than any individual piece.

born (your native culture). Parents, peer groups, schools, religious institutions, and government agencies are your main teachers of culture.

Explore the **Exercise** "Cultural Identities" at **MyCommunicationLab**

Through enculturation, you develop an **ethnic identity,** a commitment to the beliefs and philosophy of your culture that, not surprisingly, can act as a protective shield against discrimination (Ting-Toomy, 1981; Chung & Ting-Toomey, 1999; Lee, 2005). Ethnic identity refers to the degree to which you identify with your cultural group and see yourself as a member of your culture. As you can imagine, you acquire your ethnic identity from family and friends who observe ethnic holidays, patronize ethnic parades, and eat ethnic foods; from your schooling where you learn about your own culture and ethnic background; and from your own media and Internet exposure. If you begin looking at your culture's practices as the only right ones or look upon the practices of other cultures as inferior, ethnic identity can turn into ethnocentrism (see pp. 43–44).

A different process of learning culture is **acculturation,** the process by which you learn the rules and norms of a culture different from your native culture. In acculturation, your original or native culture is modified through direct contact with or exposure to a new and different culture. For example, when immigrants settle in the United States (the host culture), their own culture becomes influenced by the host culture. Gradually, the values, ways of behaving, and beliefs of the host culture become more and more a part of the immigrants' culture. At the same time, of course, the host culture changes, too, as it interacts with the immigrants' cultures. Generally, however, the culture of the immigrant changes more. The reasons for this are that the host country's members far outnumber the immigrant group and that the media are largely dominated by and reflect the values and customs of the host cultures (Kim, 1988).

New citizens' acceptance of the new culture depends on many factors (Kim, 1988). Immigrants who come from cultures similar to the host culture will become acculturated more easily. Similarly, those who are younger and better educated become acculturated more quickly than do older and less educated people. Personality factors also play a part. Persons who are risk takers and open-minded, for example, have greater acculturation potential. Also, persons who are familiar with the host culture before immigration—through interpersonal contact or through media exposure—will be acculturated more readily.

The Importance of Culture

Culture is important for a variety of reasons. Here are a few:

- *Demographic changes.* Whereas at one time the United States was a country largely populated by Europeans, it's now greatly influenced by the enormous number of new citizens from Latin and South America, Africa, and Asia. With these changes have come different customs and the need to understand and adapt to new ways of looking at communication.
- *Sensitivity to cultural differences.* As a people, we've become increasingly sensitive to cultural differences. U.S. society has moved from an *assimilationist perspective* (the idea that people should leave their native culture behind and adapt to their new culture) to a view that values *cultural diversity* (people should retain their native cultural ways). At the same time, the ability to interact effectively with members of other cultures often translates into financial gain and increased employment opportunities and advancement prospects.
- *Economic interdependence.* Today most countries are economically dependent on one another. Our economic lives depend on our ability to communicate effectively across cultures. Similarly, our political well-being depends in great part on that of other cultures. Political unrest or financial problems in any part of the world—Africa, Europe, or the Middle East, to take a few examples—affect our own security. Intercultural communication and understanding now seem more crucial than ever.
- *Communication technology.* Technology has made intercultural interaction easy, practical, and inevitable. It's common to have social network friends from different cultures, and these relationships require a new way of looking at communication and culture.
- *Culture-specific nature of interpersonal communication.* Still another reason culture is so important is that interpersonal competence is culture specific. As we'll see throughout this chapter, what proves effective in one culture may prove ineffective (even offensive) in another.

INTERPERSONAL CHOICE POINT

Violating Cultural Norms

You're invited to a holiday party by people you recently met at school. Having lots of money yourself and not knowing much about anyone else, you buy a really expensive present. As the gifts are being opened, you notice that everyone gave very inexpensive items—a photograph, a book, a scented candle. Your gift is next. What are some of the things you might say before your gift is opened to lessen the effect of your choice, which is sure to seem very strange to everyone else?

The Aim of a Cultural Perspective

As illustrated throughout this text, culture influences interpersonal communications of all types (Moon, 1996). It influences what you say to yourself and how you talk with friends, lovers, and family in everyday conversation. Adopting a cultural perspective will help you understand how interpersonal communication works and to develop successful interpersonal skills.

And, of course, you need cultural understanding to communicate effectively in a wide variety of intercultural situations. Success in interpersonal communication—on your job and in your social life—will depend on your ability to communicate effectively with persons who are culturally different from yourself.

Blog Post

Intercultural Communication Taboos

See "Intercultural Communication Taboos" at tcbdevito.blogspot.com for additional examples of the problems you can get into when cultural expectations are violated. Have you violated any cultural taboos lately?

SKILL BUILDING EXERCISE

Describing Cultural Attitudes

One of the best ways to appreciate the influence of culture on communication is to consider the attitudes people have about central aspects of culture. In a group of five or six people—try for as culturally diverse a group as possible—discuss how you think most of the students at your school feel (not how you feel) about each of the following. Use a five-point scale on which 5 = most students strongly agree; 4 = most students agree; 3 = most students are relatively neutral; 2 = most students disagree; 1 = most students strongly disagree. Also, note any gender, affectional orientation, and racial differences.

____ 1. Too many feminists are too sensitive about sexism.
____ 2. Courses on "women's studies" should be required in our schools.
____ 3. Gay rights means gay men and lesbians demand special privileges.
____ 4. Homosexuals have made many contributions to their societies.
____ 5. Racism isn't going to end overnight, so minorities need to be patient.
____ 6. White people benefit from racism whether they want to or not.

Attitudes strongly influence communication. Understanding your cultural attitudes is prerequisite to effective intercultural communication.

Source: These statements were adapted from the Human Relations Attitude Inventory (Koppelman, 2005). The authors note that this inventory is based on an inventory developed by Flavio Vega.

This emphasis on culture does not imply that you should accept all cultural practices or that all cultural practices are equal (Hatfield & Rapson, 1996). For example, cockfighting, foxhunting, and bullfighting are parts of the culture of some Latin American countries, England, and Spain, respectively, but you need not find these activities acceptable or equal to a cultural practice in which animals are treated kindly. Further, a cultural emphasis does not imply that you have to accept or follow even the practices of your own culture. For example, even if the majority in your culture holds sexist or homophobic attitudes, you need not agree with or adopt these attitudes yourself. Often, personality factors (such as your degree of assertiveness, extroversion, or optimism) will prove more influential than culture (Hatfield & Rapson, 1996). Of course, going against your culture's traditions and values is often very difficult. But it's important to realize that culture influences; it does not determine.

As demonstrated throughout this text, cultural differences exist across the interpersonal communication spectrum—from the way you use eye contact to the way you develop or dissolve a relationship (Chang & Holt, 1996). But these differences should not blind you to the great number of similarities existing among even the most widely separated cultures. Further, remember that differences are usually matters of degree. For example, most cultures value politeness, love, and honesty, but not all value these to the same degree. Also, the advances in media and technology and the widespread use of social

VIEWPOINTS Cultural evolution and cultural relativism

Cultural evolution (often called social Darwinism) holds that much as the human species evolved from earlier life forms to *Homo sapiens*, cultures also evolve. Under this view, some cultures may be considered advanced and others primitive. Most scholars reject this view, however, because the judgments that distinguish one culture from another have no basis in science and are instead based on individual values and preferences. **Cultural relativism,** on the other hand, holds that all cultures are different but that no culture is either superior or inferior to any other (Berry, Poortinga, Segall, & Dasen, 1992; Mosteller, 2008). What are some of the implications of these two views for intercultural communication?

media are influencing cultures and cultural change and are perhaps homogenizing different cultures to some degree, lessening differences and increasing similarities.

Can you explain the role and importance of culture in interpersonal communication (the culture-specific nature of interpersonal communication, an increased sensitivity to cultural differences, the economic and political interdependence of all people, the advances in communication technology, and the demographic changes that are so much a part of contemporary society)?
Can you define *enculturation, ethnic identity,* and *acculturation*?

INTERPERSONAL CHOICE POINT

Conflicting Cultural Beliefs

You're talking with new work colleagues, and one of the cultural practices you find unethical is discussed with approval; your colleagues argue that each culture has a right to its own practices and beliefs. Given your own beliefs about this issue and about cultural diversity and cultural sensitivity, what are some of the things you can say to be honest with yourself and yet not jeopardize your new position?

CULTURAL PRINCIPLES

As you learn about your culture's beliefs, values, and other aspects, you also learn the culture's principles (often referred to as "maxims") for communicating. Some of these cultural principles focus on enhancing communication efficiency (for example, how to make messages more easily understood) and some on maintaining interpersonal relationships (for example, how to get along with other people).

Explore the **Exercise** "Sources of Your Cultural Beliefs" at **MyCommunicationLab**

Principles for Communication Efficiency

When you communicate interpersonally, you probably follow the general principle of cooperation; there's a mutually agreed-upon assumption that you'll both try to understand each other (Grice, 1975). You cooperate largely by adhering to four maxims—rules that speakers and listeners in the United States and in many other cultures follow in conversation. As you'll see, following these maxims ensures efficient interpersonal communication.

The **quantity principle** requires that you be only as informative as necessary to communicate your intended meaning. Thus, you include information that makes the meaning clear but omit what does not. The maxim of quantity requires that you give neither too little nor too much information. Spam is the perfect example of messages that violate this principle; spam messages are unwanted noise and intrude on your own communication.

The **quality principle** states that you should say what you know or believe to be true and not say what you know to be false. When you're communicating, you assume that the other person's information is true—at least as far as he or she knows. For example when a friend tells you what happened on a trip, you assume that it's true.

The **relation principle** asks that you talk about what is relevant to the conversation. Speakers who digress widely and frequently interject irrelevant comments violate the maxim of relation.

The **manner principle** requires that you be clear, avoid ambiguities, be relatively brief, and organize your thoughts into a meaningful sequence. Thus, you use terms that the listener will understand and omit or clarify terms that you suspect the listener will not understand. When you talk to a young child, for example, you normally use familiar words and short sentences. You can also see this principle operating in computer-mediated communication's reliance on acronyms (for example, *BTW* for *by the way, IMHO* for *in my humble opinion,* and *TTYL* for *talk to you later*). This is an extremely efficient method of communicating (when sender and receiver both know the meanings), much like macros and autocorrect features in word processors.

Principles for Maintaining Relationships

Some communication principles help to maintain relationships rather than foster efficiency.

The **peaceful relations principle,** observed among the Japanese, requires that you say only what preserves peaceful relationships with others (Midooka, 1990). Under this principle, you wouldn't contradict another person or point out errors in what the other person said. This maxim of peaceful relationships is much more important in public than in private conversations, in which the maxim may be and often is violated.

The **self-denigration principle,** observed in the conversations of Chinese speakers, may require that you avoid taking credit for some accomplishment—saying, for example, "My colleagues really did most of the work." Or you might be expected to make less of some ability or talent you have—to say, for example, "I still have much to learn" (Gu, 1990). Putting yourself down helps to elevate the person to whom you're speaking.

The **politeness principle** is probably universal across all cultures (Brown & Levinson, 1987). Cultures differ, however, in how they define politeness and in how important politeness is in comparison with, say, openness or honesty. For example, not interrupting, saying "please" and "thank you," maintaining appropriate eye contact, and asking permission to do something are all examples of politeness messages, but their importance differs from one culture to another.

Cultures also differ in their rules for expressing politeness or impoliteness. Some cultures, for example, may require you to give extended praise when meeting, say, an important scientist or educator; other cultures expect you to assume a more equal position regardless of the stature of the other person.

There also are large gender differences (as well as similarities) in the expression of politeness (Holmes, 1995). Generally, studies from several different cultures show that women use more polite forms than men (Brown, 1980; Holmes, 1995; Wetzel, 1988). Both in informal conversation and in conflict situations, women tend to seek areas of agreement more than do men. There are also similarities. For example, both men and women in the United States and New Zealand seem to pay compliments in similar ways (Holmes, 1986, 1995; Manes & Wolfson, 1981), and both men and women use politeness strategies when communicating bad news in an organization (Lee, 1993).

INTERPERSONAL CHOICE POINT

Putting Your Foot in Your Mouth

At work, you tell an ageist joke, only to discover later that it has been resented and clearly violated the organizational norms for polite and unbiased talk. What are some of the things you can say to make this situation a little less awkward and less potentially damaging to your relationships with coworkers?

Can you describe and illustrate the cultural principles for more effective communication (quantity, quality, relation, and manner) and for establishing and maintaining relationships (peaceful relations, self-denigration, and politeness)?

VIEWPOINTS Cultural sensitivity and differences

Intercultural communication is especially important in political discussions between members of widely differing cultures. Take a look at one of the online news pages, especially the "world" section. How many news items can you identify that would profit from an understanding of intercultural communication? In what specific ways might intercultural communication competence be of value?

CULTURAL DIFFERENCES

For effective interpersonal communication to take place in a global world, goodwill and good intensions are helpful—but they are not enough. If you're going to be effective, you need to know how cultures differ and how these differences influence communication. Research supports several major cultural distinctions that are crucial for more effective interpersonal communication: (1) individualist or collectivist orientation, (2) emphasis on context (whether high or low), (3) power structure, (4) masculinity–femininity, (5) tolerance for ambiguity, (6) long- and short-term orientation, and (7) indulgence and restraint. Each of these dimensions of difference has significant impact on all forms of communication (Gudykunst, 1994; Hall & Hall, 1987; Hofstede et al., Hofstede, & Minkov, 2010). Following the major researchers in this area, these differences are discussed in terms of countries, even though in many cases different nations have very similar cultures (and so we often

TEST YOURSELF

What's Your Cultural Orientation?

For each of the items below, select either *a* or *b*. In some cases, you may feel that neither *a* nor *b* describes yourself accurately; in these cases, simply select the one that is closer to your feeling. As you'll see when you read the next section, these are not *either/or* preferences, but *more-or-less* preferences.

1. Success, to my way of thinking, is better measured by
   a. the extent to which I surpass others.
   b. my contribution to the group effort.
2. My heroes are generally
   a. people who stand out from the crowd.
   b. team players.
3. If I were a manager, I would likely
   a. reprimand a worker in public if the occasion warranted.
   b. always reprimand in private regardless of the situation.
4. In communicating, it's generally more important to be
   a. polite rather than accurate or direct.
   b. accurate and direct rather than polite.
5. As a student (and if I feel well informed), I feel
   a. comfortable challenging a professor.
   b. uncomfortable challenging a professor.
6. In choosing a life partner or even close friends, I feel more comfortable
   a. with just about anyone, not necessarily one from my own culture and class.
   b. with those from my own culture and class.
7. In a conflict situation, I'd be more likely to
   a. confront conflicts directly and seek to win.
   b. confront conflicts with the aim of compromise.
8. If I were a manager of an organization, I would stress
   a. competition and aggressiveness.
   b. worker satisfaction.
9. As a student, I'm more comfortable with assignments in which
   a. there is freedom for interpretation.
   b. there are clearly defined instructions.
10. Generally, when approaching an undertaking with which I've had no experience, I feel
    a. comfortable.
    b. uncomfortable.
11. Generally,
    a. I save money for the future.
    b. I spend what I have.
12. My general belief about child-rearing is that
    a. children should be cared for by their mothers.
    b. children can be cared for by others.
13. For the most part,
    a. I believe I'm in control of my own life.
    b. I believe my life is largely determined by forces out of my control.
14. In general,
    a. I have leisure time to do what I find fun.
    b. I have little leisure time.

How Did You Do?

- Items 1–2 refer to the **individualist–collectivist orientation;** *a* responses indicate an individualist orientation, and *b* responses indicate a collectivist orientation.
- Items 3–4 refer to the **high- and low-context** characteristics; *a* responses indicate a high-context focus, and *b* responses indicate a low-context focus.
- Items 5–6 refer to the **power distance** dimension; *a* responses indicate greater comfort with a low power distance, and *b* responses indicate comfort with a high power distance.
- Items 7–8 refer to the **masculine–feminine** dimension; *a* responses indicate a masculine orientation; *b* responses, a feminine orientation.
- Items 9–10 refer to the **tolerance for ambiguity** or uncertainty; *a* responses indicate high tolerance, and *b* responses indicate a low tolerance.
- Items 11–12 refer to the **long- or short-term orientation**; *a* responses indicate long-term orientation, and *b* responses indicate short-term orientation.
- Items 13–14 refer to **indulgent and restraint orientation**; *a* responses indicate indulgent, and *b* responses indicate restraint cultures.

What Will You Do? Understanding your preferences in a wide variety of situations as culturally influenced (at least in part) is a first step to controlling them and to changing them should you wish to do so. This understanding also helps you modify your behavior as appropriate for greater effectiveness in certain situations. The remaining discussion in this section further explains these orientations and their implications.

speak of *Hispanic culture,* which would include a variety of countries). In other cases, the same country includes varied cultures (for example, Hong Kong, although a part of China, is considered separately because it has a somewhat different culture) (Hofstede et al., 2010).

Before reading about these dimensions, take the accompanying self-test. It will help you think about your own cultural orientations and will personalize the text discussion and make it more meaningful.

Watch the **Video** "That's So Rude" at **MyCommunicationLab**

Individualist and Collectivist Cultures

In an **individualist culture** (the United States, Australia, United Kingdom, Netherlands, Canada, New Zealand, Italy, Belgium, Denmark, and Sweden), you're responsible for yourself and perhaps your immediate family; in a **collectivist culture** (Guatemala, Ecuador, Panama, Venezuela, Colombia, Indonesia, Pakistan, China, Costa Rica, and Peru), you're responsible for the entire group. The distinction between individualist and collectivist cultures revolves around the extent to which the individual's goals or the group's goals are given greater importance. Individualist and collectivist tendencies are not mutually exclusive; this is not an all-or-none orientation but rather one of emphasis. Thus, you may, for example, compete with other members of your basketball team for the most baskets or to get the most valuable player award. In a game, however, you will act in a way that will benefit the group. In actual practice, both individualist and collectivist tendencies will help you and your team each achieve your goals. Even so, at times these tendencies may conflict; for example, do you shoot for the basket and try to raise your own individual score, or do you pass the ball to another player who is better positioned to score the basket and thus benefit your team?

In an individualist culture, success is measured by the extent to which you surpass other members of your group; you will take pride in standing out from the crowd, and your heroes—in the media, for example—are likely to be those who are unique and who stand apart. In a collectivist culture, success is measured by your contribution to the achievements of the group as a whole; you will take pride in your similarity to other members of your group. Your heroes are more likely to be team players who do not stand out from the rest of the group's members. In individualist cultures, competition is promoted; in collectivist cultures, cooperation is promoted.

Another frequent difference and source of misunderstanding between individualist and collectivist cultures is relative importance of maintaining a positive public self-image, or what is frequently called **face-saving** (Hall & Hall, 1987). People in collectivist cultures place a great deal of emphasis on face-saving. For example, they are more likely to avoid argument for fear of causing others to lose face; people in individualist cultures are more likely to use argument to win a point. Similarly, in collectivist cultures, negative comments by a manager to an employee would be made only in private so that the person can save face. Individualistic cultures may not make this public–private distinction.

VIEWPOINTS Men, women, and culture

It's been argued that in the United States women are more likely to view themselves as interdependents, having a more collectivist orientation, whereas men are more likely to view themselves as independents, having a more individualist orientation (Cross & Madson, 1997). Does your experience support this? What implications do you see for the workplace?

High- and Low-Context Cultures

High-context cultures place a great deal of emphasis on the information that is in the context or in the person. For example, in high-context cultures, information that was communicated in previous interactions or through shared experiences—because it's part of the context—is not explicitly stated in verbal messages. **Low-context cultures** place more emphasis on the information that is explicitly stated in verbal messages or, in formal transactions, in written (contract) form.

High-context cultures are also collectivist cultures. These cultures (Japanese, Arabic, Latin American, Thai, Korean, Apache, and Mexican are examples) place great emphasis on personal relationships and oral agreements (Victor, 1992). Low-context cultures, on the other hand, are individualistic cultures. These cultures (German, Swedish, Norwegian, and American are examples) place less emphasis on personal relationships; they tend to emphasize explicit explanations and, for example, written contracts in business transactions.

INTERPERSONAL CHOICE POINT

Giving Directions in High- and Low-Context Situations

To further appreciate the distinction between high and low context, consider giving directions to some specific place on campus to someone who knows the campus and who you can assume knows the local landmarks (which would resemble a high-context situation) and to a newcomer to your campus who you cannot assume is familiar with campus landmarks (which would resemble a low-context situation). How would you give directions in the two different cases?

Members of high-context cultures spend lots of time getting to know one another before engaging in any important transactions. Because of this prior personal knowledge, a great deal of information is already shared and therefore does not have to be explicitly stated. High-context cultures, for example, rely more on nonverbal cues in reducing uncertainty (Sanders, Wiseman, & Matz, 1991). Members of low-context cultures spend less time getting to know each other and therefore do not have that shared knowledge. As a result, everything has to be stated explicitly. When this simple difference is not taken into account, misunderstandings can easily result. For example, the directness and explicitness characteristic of the low-context culture may be perceived as insulting, insensitive, or unnecessary by members of a high-context culture. Conversely, to members of a low-context culture, someone from a high-context culture may appear vague, underhanded, even dishonest in his or her reluctance to be explicit or to engage in communication that a low-context culture would consider open and direct.

Members of high-context cultures are reluctant to say no for fear of offending and causing a person to lose face. So, for example, it's necessary to understand when a Japanese executive's yes means yes and when it means no. The difference is not in the words but in the way they are used. It's easy to see how a low-context individual may interpret this reluctance to be direct—to say no when you mean no—as a weakness or as an unwillingness to confront reality.

Masculine and Feminine Cultures

When denoting cultural orientations, the terms *masculine* and *feminine*, used by Geert Hofstede and his associates to describe this cultural difference, should be taken not as perpetuating stereotypes but as reflecting some of the commonly held assumptions of a sizable number of people throughout the world. Some intercultural theorists note that equivalent terms would be cultures based on "achievement" and "nurturance," but, because research is conducted under the terms "masculine" and "feminine" and because these are the terms you would use to search the electronic databases, we use these terms here (Hofstede et al., 2010; Lustig & Koester, 2010).

In a highly **masculine culture,** men are valued for their aggressiveness, material success, and strength. Women, on the other hand, are valued for their modesty, focus on the quality of life, and tenderness. The ten countries with the highest masculinity scores are (beginning with the highest) Japan, Austria, Venezuela, Italy, Switzerland, Mexico, Ireland, Jamaica, Great Britain, and Germany. Of the 53 countries ranked, the United States ranks 15th most masculine (Hofstede et al., 2010). In

INTERPERSONAL CHOICE POINT

Feminine and Masculine Cultures

You come from a highly feminine culture and are working with colleagues who epitomize the highly masculine culture. Assertiveness (even aggressiveness) is rewarded and paid attention to while your cooperativeness leads you to be ignored. You want to explain this cultural difference to your colleagues and at the same time ensure that your contributions will be listened to and evaluated fairly instead of being ignored. What are some of the things you might say to achieve your goal? Through what channel would you send this message? To whom would you send it (to everyone, to one or two)?

"Because my genetic programming prevents me from stopping to ask directions—that's why!"

Donald Reilly/The New Yorker Collection/www.cartoonbank.com

masculine societies, there is a very clear distinction between men's and women's gender roles and expectations. Further, masculine cultures emphasize success and so socialize their members to be assertive, ambitious, and competitive. For example, members of masculine cultures are more likely to confront conflicts directly and to fight out any differences competitively; they're more likely to emphasize win–lose conflict strategies.

A highly **feminine culture,** on the other hand, values modesty, concern for relationships and the quality of life, and tenderness in both men and women. Here gender distinctions are much more fluid than in masculine cultures. The ten countries with the highest femininity scores are (beginning with the highest) Sweden, Norway, Netherlands, Denmark, Costa Rica, Yugoslavia, Finland, Chile, Portugal, and Thailand. Feminine cultures emphasize the quality of life and so socialize their members to be modest and to highlight close interpersonal relationships. Feminine cultures, for example, are more likely to use compromise and negotiation in resolving conflicts; they're more likely to seek win–win solutions.

Like countries, organizations can be viewed as masculine or feminine. Masculine organizations emphasize competitiveness and aggressiveness. They stress the bottom line and reward their workers on the basis of their contribution to the organization. Feminine organizations are less competitive and less aggressive. They emphasize worker satisfaction and reward their workers on the basis of need; those who have large families, for example, may get better raises than single people, even if they haven't contributed as much to the organization.

High- and Low-Power-Distance Cultures

In some cultures, power is concentrated in the hands of a few, and there's a great difference between the power held by these people and the power of the ordinary citizen. These are called **high-power-distance cultures;** examples are Mexico, Brazil, India, and the Philippines (Hofstede et al., 2010). In **low-power-distance cultures,** power is more evenly distributed throughout the citizenry; examples include Denmark, New Zealand, Sweden, and to a lesser extent the United States.

These differences influence communication in numerous ways. For example, in high-power-distance cultures, there's a great power differential between students and teachers; students are expected to be modest, polite, and totally respectful. In contrast, in low-power-distance cultures (and you can see this clearly in U.S. college classrooms), students are expected to demonstrate their knowledge and command of the subject matter, participate in discussions with the teacher, and even challenge the teacher—something many members of high-power-distance cultures wouldn't even think of doing.

Friendship and dating relationships also are influenced by power distances between groups (Andersen, 1991). In India, for example, such relationships are expected to take place within your cultural class. In Sweden, a person is expected to select friends and romantic partners not on the basis of class or culture but on the basis of personality, appearance, and the like.

In low-power-distance cultures, you're expected to confront a friend, partner, or supervisor assertively; there is in these cultures a general feeling of equality that is consistent with assertive behavior (Borden, 1991). An assistant who feels he or she is being treated unfairly is expected to bring the problem to the attention of the manager, for example. In high-power-distance cultures, however, direct confrontation and assertiveness may be viewed negatively, especially if directed at a superior.

Even in democracies in which everyone is equal under the law (or should be), there are still great power distances between those in authority—the employers, the police, the politicians—and ordinary citizens as there are between those who are rich and those who are poor, as we're seeing now in the Occupy movements throughout the United States.

High- and Low-Ambiguity-Tolerant Cultures

In some cultures, people do little to avoid uncertainty and have little anxiety about not knowing what will happen next. In some other cultures, however, uncertainty is strongly avoided, and there is much anxiety about uncertainty.

Members of **high-ambiguity-tolerant cultures** don't feel threatened by unknown situations; uncertainty is a normal part of life, and people accept it as it comes. Examples of such low-anxiety cultures include Singapore, Jamaica, Denmark, Sweden, Hong Kong, Ireland, Great Britain, Malaysia, India, Philippines, and the United States.

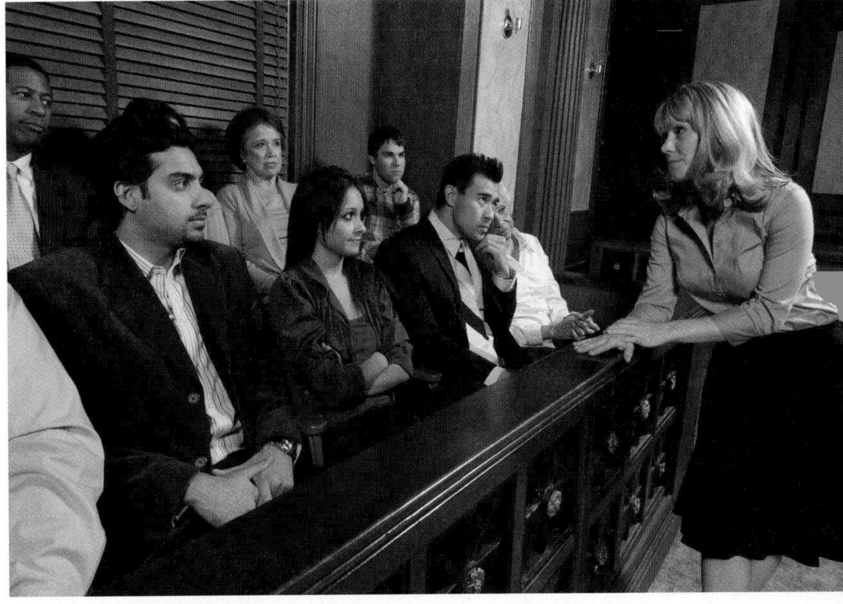

VIEWPOINTS Cultural defense

Assume you're a judge and the following case is presented to you: A Chinese immigrant killed his wife in New York because he suspected her of cheating. A "cultural defense" was offered, essentially claiming that infidelity so shames a man that he is uncontrollable in his anger. Would this cultural defense have influenced your judgment? In the actual case (reported in *Time,* December 2, 1993), influenced by an anthropologist's testimony that infidelity is so serious in Chinese culture that it pushed the defendant to commit the crime, the judge sentenced the defendant to five years' probation. How do you feel about "cultural defenses" in general? Are there some cultural defenses you'd accept and others you would not?

Because high-ambiguity-tolerant cultures are comfortable with ambiguity and uncertainty, they minimize the importance of rules governing communication and relationships (Hofstede et al., 2010; Lustig & Koester, 2010). People in these cultures readily tolerate individuals who don't follow the same rules as the cultural majority, and they may even encourage different approaches and perspectives.

Students in high-ambiguity-tolerant cultures appreciate freedom in education and prefer vague assignments without specific timetables. These students want to be rewarded for creativity and readily accept an instructor's lack of knowledge.

Members of **low-ambiguity-tolerant cultures** do much to avoid uncertainty and have a great deal of anxiety about not knowing what will happen next; they see uncertainty as threatening and as something that must be counteracted. Examples of such low-ambiguity-tolerant cultures include Greece, Portugal, Guatemala, Uruguay, Belgium, El Salvador, Japan, Yugoslavia, Peru, France, Chile, Spain, and Costa Rica (Hofstede et al., 2010).

Low-ambiguity-tolerant cultures create very clear-cut rules for communication that must not be broken. For example, students in these uncertainty-avoidant cultures prefer highly structured learning experiences with little ambiguity; they prefer specific objectives, detailed instructions, and definite timetables. An assignment to write a term paper on "anything" would be cause for alarm; it wouldn't be clear or specific enough. These students expect to be judged on the basis of producing the right answers and expect the instructor to have all the answers all the time (Hofstede et al., 2010).

Long- and Short-Term Orientation Cultures

Some cultures teach a **long-term orientation,** an orientation that promotes the importance of future rewards, and so, for example, members of these cultures are more apt to save for the future and to prepare for the future academically (Hofstede et al., 2010). The most long-term-oriented countries are South Korea, Taiwan, Japan, China,

Ukraine, Germany, Estonia, Belgium, Lithuania, and Russia. The United States ranks 69th out of 93 countries, making it less long-term than most countries. In these cultures, marriage is a practical arrangement rather than one based on sexual or emotional arousal and living with extended family (for example, in-laws) is common and considered quite normal. These cultures believe that mothers should be home with their children, that humility is a virtue for both men and women, and that old age should be a happy time of life.

Cultures fostering a **short-term orientation** (Puerto Rico, Ghana, Egypt, Trinidad, Nigeria, Dominican Republic, Colombia, Iran, Morocco, and Zimbabwe are the top ten) look more to the past and the present. Instead of saving for the future, members of this culture spend their resources for the present and, not surprisingly, want quick results from their efforts. These cultures believe and teach that marriage is a moral arrangement, living with in-laws causes problems, children do not have to be cared for by their mothers (others can do that), humility is a virtue only for women (not men), and old age is an unpleasant time of life.

These cultures also differ in their view of the workplace. Organizations in long-term-oriented cultures look to profits in the future. Managers or owners and workers in such cultures share the same values and work together to achieve a common good. Organizations in short-term-oriented cultures, on the other hand, look to more immediate rewards. Managers and workers are very different in their thinking and in their attitudes about work.

Even in educational outlook there are significant differences. Students in long-term cultures will attribute their success or failure in school to their own efforts while students in short-term cultures will attribute their success or failure to luck or chance.

Another perspective on this difference is offered by a study that asked Asian (long-term cultures) and American (short-term culture) executives to rank those values they considered most important in the workplace. The top six responses are presented in Table 2.2 and show a dramatic difference between the two cultural groups.

Indulgence and Restraint Cultures

Cultures also differ in their emphasis on indulgence or restraint (Hofstede et al., 2010). Cultures high in **indulgence** are those that emphasize the gratification of desires; they focus on having fun and enjoying life. Venezuela, Mexico, Puerto Rico, El Salvador, Nigeria, Colombia, Trinidad, Sweden, New Zealand, and Ghana are the top ten in indulgence; the United States ranks 15th out of 93 countries, making it considerably

TABLE 2.2

VALUES OF THE WORKPLACE

This table presents the six highest-ranked values (beginning with the highest-ranked value) by Asian and American executives (Hofstede et al., 2010). Notice that "hard work" makes both lists but in very different positions.

Values Selected by Asian (Long-Term Orientation) Executives	Values Selected by American (Short-Term Orientation) Executives
Hard work	Freedom of expression
Respect for learning	Personal freedom
Honesty	Self-reliance
Openness to new ideas	Individual rights
Accountability	Hard work
Self-discipline	Personal achievement

more indulgent than most countries. These cultures have more people who are happy, which depends on two major factors:

- *Life control.* This is the feeling that you may do as you please (at least to a significant degree), that you have freedom of choice to do or not do what you want.
- *Leisure.* This is the feeling that you have leisure time to do what you find fun.

Cultures high in **restraint** (Pakistan, Egypt, Latvia, Ukraine, Albania, Belarus, Lithuania, Bulgaria, Estonia, and Iraq are the top ten), on the other hand, are those that foster the curbing of such gratification and its regulation by social norms. Restraint cultures have more people who are unhappy: people who see themselves as lacking control of their own lives and with little or no leisure time to engage in fun activities. In contrast to indulgent cultures, members of cultures high in restraint are more cynical, pessimistic, and less likely to remember positive emotions. They have less satisfying family lives, rigid gender roles, and an unequal distribution of household tasks.

As you might expect, indulgent cultures do not place great value on thrift; instead the value is on spending to gratify one's needs. Restrained cultures place a great value on thrift. Also predictable is the finding that indulgent cultures place great importance on friendship and having lots of friends whereas restrained cultures place less importance on friendships. Although there are no studies offering evidence, it's likely that the Facebook pages of indulgent culture members will have a lot more friends than will those of members of restrained cultures. And not so predictable perhaps is the finding that death rates from cardiovascular diseases are significantly higher in restrained than in indulgent cultures and significantly more indulgent culture members describe their health as "very good" (Hofstede et al., 2010).

INTERPERSONAL CHOICE POINT

Culture Versus Culture

Your friend is pressed for time and asks you to do the statistical analyses for a term project. Your first impulse is to say yes because in your culture it would be extremely impolite to refuse to do a favor for someone you've known for so long. Yet you're aware that providing this kind of help is considered unethical at colleges in the United States. You want to help your friend but avoid doing anything that would be considered deceitful and might result in punishment. How might you respond to your friend's request while abiding by the standards of your college and, at the same time, not insulting your friend or contradicting your own cultural beliefs?

Can you explain and give examples of the seven major cultural distinctions and the ways in which these differences affect communication (individualist or collectivist orientation, emphasis on context [whether high or low], power structure, masculinity–femininity, tolerance for ambiguity, long- and short-term orientation, and indulgence and restraint)?

IMPROVING INTERCULTURAL COMMUNICATION

Intercultural communication is communication between persons who have different cultural beliefs, values, or ways of behaving. The model in Figure 2.1 illustrates this concept. The larger circles represent the cultures of the individual communicators. The inner circles identify the communicators (the sources–receivers). In this model, each communicator is a member of a different culture. In some instances, the cultural differences are relatively slight—say, between persons from Toronto and New York. In other instances, the cultural differences are great—say, between persons from Borneo and Germany or between persons from rural Nigeria and industrialized England.

Explore the **Concept** "Culture" at **MyCommunicationLab**

Explore the **Exercise** "Confronting Intercultural Obstacles" at **MyCommunicationLab**

All messages originate from a specific and unique cultural context, and that context influences their content and form. You communicate as you do largely as a result of your culture. Culture (along with the processes of enculturation and acculturation) influences every aspect of your communication experience. And, of course, you receive messages through the filters imposed by a unique culture. Cultural filters, like filters on a camera, color the messages you receive. They influence what you receive and how you receive it. For example, some cultures rely heavily on television or newspapers for their news and trust them implicitly. Others rely on face-to-face interpersonal interactions, distrusting any of the mass communication systems. Some look to religious leaders as guides to behavior; others generally ignore them.

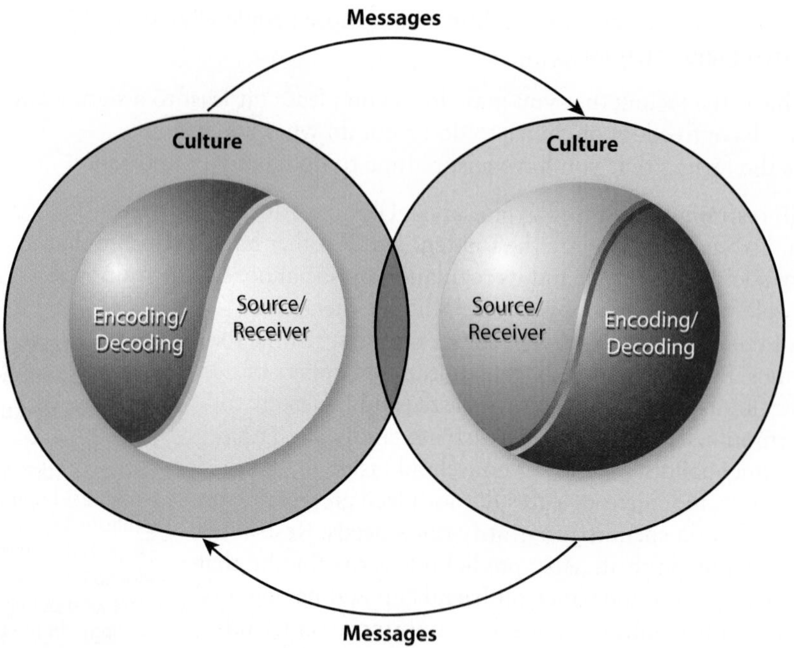

FIGURE 2.1
A Model of Intercultural Communication
This model of intercultural communication illustrates that culture is a part of every communication act. More specifically, it illustrates that the messages you send and the messages you receive will be influenced by your cultural beliefs, values, and attitudes. Note also that the circles overlap to some degree, illustrating that no matter how different the cultures of the two individuals are, there will always be some commonalities, some similarities, along with differences.

Murphy's law ("If anything can go wrong, it will") is especially applicable to intercultural communication. Intercultural communications is, of course, subject to all the same barriers and problems as are the other forms of communication discussed throughout this text. In this section, however, we'll consider some suggestions designed to counteract the barriers that are unique to intercultural communications (Barna, 1997; Ruben, 1985; Spitzberg, 1991).

Above all, intercultural communication depends on the cultural sensitivity of both individuals. **Cultural sensitivity** is an attitude and way of behaving in which you're aware of and acknowledge cultural differences. Cultural sensitivity is crucial on a global scale, as in efforts toward world peace and economic growth; it's also essential for effective interpersonal communication and for general success in life (Franklin & Mizell, 1995). Without cultural sensitivity, there can be no effective interpersonal communication between people who are different in gender or race or nationality or affectional orientation. So be mindful of the cultural differences between yourself and the other person. For example, the close physical distance that is normal in Arab cultures may prove too familiar or too intrusive in much of the United States and northern Europe. The empathy that most Americans welcome may be uncomfortable for most Koreans (Yun, 1976).

The following guidelines can help you achieve cultural sensitivity: (1) Prepare yourself, (2) reduce your ethnocentrism, (3) confront your stereotypes, (4) be mindful, (5) reduce uncertainty, (6) recognize differences, (7) adjust your communication, and (8) recognize culture shock—its inevitability and its symptoms. We'll take a look at each guideline in turn.

Prepare Yourself

There's no better preparation for intercultural communication than learning about the other culture. Fortunately, there are numerous sources to draw on. View a video or film that presents a realistic view of the culture. Read what members of the culture as well as "outsiders" write about the culture. Scan magazines and websites from the culture. Talk with members of the culture. Chat on international IRC channels. Read materials addressed to people who need to communicate with those from other cultures. The easiest way to do this is to search the online bookstores (for example, Barnes and Noble and Amazon) for such keywords as *culture, international,* and *foreign travel.*

Another part of this preparation is to recognize and face fears that may stand in the way of effective intercultural communication (Gudykunst, 1994; Stephan & Stephan, 1985). For example, you may fear for your self-esteem. You may be anxious about your ability to control the intercultural situation, or you may worry about your own level of discomfort. You may fear saying something that will be considered politically incorrect or culturally insensitive and thereby losing face.

VIEWPOINTS Cultural imperialism

The theory of cultural imperialism argues that certain developed countries, such as those of North America and Western Europe, dominate the cultures of countries importing their products, especially their Internet and television. What do you think of the influence that television and social media have on native cultures throughout the world? How do you evaluate this trend?

Some fears, of course, are reasonable. In many cases, however, fears are groundless. Either way, you need to assess your concerns logically and weigh their consequences carefully. Then you'll be able to make informed choices about your communications.

Reduce Your Ethnocentrism

Ethnocentrism is the tendency to see others and their behaviors through your own cultural filters, often as distortions of your own behaviors. It's the tendency to evaluate the values, beliefs, and behaviors of your own culture as superior—as more positive, logical, and natural than those of other cultures. For example, highly ethnocentric individuals would think that other cultures should be more like theirs, that people from other cultures often don't know what's good for them, that the lifestyles of people in other countries are not as good as theirs, and that people from other cultures are not as smart or trustworthy as people from their own culture (Neuliep & McCroskey, 1997). To achieve effective interpersonal communication, you need to see yourself and others as different but as neither inferior nor superior. You need to become aware of the potential blinders that ethnocentrism might impose—admittedly, not a very easily accomplished task.

Ethnocentrism exists on a continuum. People are not either ethnocentric or non-ethnocentric; rather, most people are somewhere between the extremes (see Table 2.3). We're all ethnocentric to at least some degree. The most important thing to see here is that your degree of ethnocentrism will influence your interpersonal (intercultural) communications, as both sender and receiver.

INTERPERSONAL CHOICE POINT

Dating an Ethnocentric

You've been dating this wonderful person for the past few months but increasingly are discovering that your "ideal" partner is extremely ethnocentric and sees little value in other religions, other races, and other nationalities. You want to educate your possible life partner but don't want to come off as a "teacher." What are some of the things you might say to at least initiate the topic?

Confront Your Stereotypes

Originally, the word *stereotype* was a printing term that referred to a plate that printed the same image over and over. A sociological or psychological **stereotype** is a fixed impression of a group of people. Everyone has attitudinal stereotypes—of national groups,

TABLE 2.3

The Ethnocentrism Continuum

Drawing from several researchers (Lukens, 1978; Gudykunst & Kim, 1992; Gudykunst, 1994), this table summarizes some interconnections between ethnocentrism and communication. The table identifies five levels of ethnocentrism; the general terms under "Communication Distances" characterize the major communication attitudes that dominate the various levels. Under "Communications" are some ways people might behave given their particular degree of ethnocentrism. How would you rate yourself on this scale?

Degree of Ethnocentrism	Communication Distances	Communications
Low	Equality	Treats others as equals; evaluates other ways of doing things as equal to own ways
	Sensitivity	Wants to decrease distance between self and others
	Indifference	Lacks concern for others but is not hostile
	Avoidance	Avoids and limits interpersonal interactions with others; prefers to be with own kind
High	Disparagement	Engages in hostile behavior; belittles others; views own culture as superior to other cultures

religious groups, or racial groups, or perhaps of criminals, prostitutes, teachers, or plumbers. Consider, for example, if you have any stereotypes of, say, bodybuilders, the opposite sex, a racial group different from your own, members of a religion very different from your own, hard drug users, or college professors. It is very likely that you have stereotypes of several, or perhaps all, of these groups. Although we often think of stereotypes as negative ("They're lazy, dirty, and only interested in getting high"), they may also be positive ("They're smart, hardworking, and extremely loyal").

If you have these fixed impressions, you may, on meeting a member of a particular group, see that person primarily as a member of that group. Initially this may provide you with some helpful orientation. However, it creates problems when you apply to the person all the characteristics you assign to members of that group without examining the

Tom Cheney/The New Yorker Collection/www.cartoonbank.com

unique individual. If you meet a politician, for example, you may have a host of characteristics for politicians that you can readily apply to this person. To complicate matters further, you may see in this person's behavior the manifestation of various characteristics that you would not see if you did not know that this person was a politician. Because there are few visual and auditory cues in online communication, it's not surprising to find that people form impressions of their online communication partner with a heavy reliance on stereotypes (Jacobson, 1999).

Stereotyping can lead to two major barriers. First, the tendency to group a person into a class and to respond to that person primarily as a member of that class can lead you to perceive that a person possesses those qualities (usually negative) that you believe characterize the group to which he or she belongs. If that happens, you will fail to appreciate the multifaceted nature of all people and all groups. For example, consider your stereotype of a high-frequency computer user. Very likely your image of such a person is quite different from the research findings, which show that such users are as often female as male and are as sociable, popular, and self-assured as their peers who are not into heavy computer use (Schott & Selwyn, 2000). And second, because stereotyping also can lead you to ignore the unique characteristics of an individual, you may fail to benefit from the special contributions each person can bring to an encounter.

Blog Post

Stereotyping in Cartoons, Etc.

For a brief rant on stereotyping of men, see "Stereotyping in Cartoons, Etc." at tcbdevito.blogspot.com. Can you add any examples from your own experience where stereotyping was involved?

Be Mindful

Being mindful rather than mindless is especially helpful in intercultural communication (Hajek & Giles, 2003). When you're in a mindless state, you behave in accordance with assumptions that would not normally pass intellectual scrutiny. For example, you know that cancer is not contagious, and yet many people will avoid touching cancer patients. You know that people who cannot see do not have hearing problems, and yet many people use a louder voice when talking to persons without sight. When the discrepancies between available evidence and behaviors are pointed out and your mindful state is awakened, you quickly realize that these behaviors are not logical.

When you deal with people from other cultures, you're often in a mindless state and therefore may function illogically in many ways. When your mindful state is awakened, you may then shift to a more critical-thinking mode—and recognize, for example, that other people and other cultural systems are different but not inferior or superior.

ETHICAL MESSAGES

Culture and Ethics

Throughout history, there have been cultural practices that today would be judged unethical. Sacrificing virgins to the gods, burning people who held different religious beliefs, and sending children to fight religious wars are obvious examples. But even today there are practices woven deep into the fabric of different cultures that you might find unethical. As you read these few examples of cultural practices with special relevance to interpersonal communication, consider what U.S. cultural practices people in other cultures might judge as unethical.

- Only men can initiate divorce, and only men are permitted to drive.
- Female genital mutilation, whereby part or all of a young girl's genitals are surgically altered so that she can never experience sexual intercourse without extreme pain, a practice designed to keep her a virgin until marriage.
- Women should not report spousal abuse because it will reflect negatively on the family.
- Sexual behavior between members of the same sex is punishable by imprisonment and even death.

Ethical Choice Point

Your neighbor is being abused by her husband—emotionally and physically. Although you've talked about this with her, she refuses to report her husband. It's not in her culture, she says; it will reflect badly on both families. What is your ethical obligation in this case?

Blog Post

Intercultural Communication: Gaining Weight?

For a similar example of cultural differences, see "Intercultural Communication Gaining Weight?" at tcbdevito.blogspot.com. Have you ever witnessed or been a part of such cultural misunderstandings?

Thus, these suggestions for increasing intercultural communication effectiveness may appear logical (even obvious) to your mindful state, even though they are probably often ignored in your mindless state.

Reduce Uncertainty

All communication interactions involve uncertainty and ambiguity. Not surprisingly, the uncertainty and ambiguity are greater when there are wide cultural differences (Berger & Bradac, 1982; Gudykunst, 1989, 1993). Because of this, in intercultural communication, it takes more time and effort to reduce uncertainty and thus to communicate meaningfully. Reducing your uncertainty about another person is worth the effort, however; it not only will make your communication more effective but also will increase your liking for the person (Douglas, 1994).

Techniques such as active listening (Chapter 5) and perception checking (Chapter 4) help you check on the accuracy of your perceptions and allow you to revise and amend any incorrect perceptions. Also, being specific reduces ambiguity and the chances of misunderstandings; misunderstanding is a lot more likely if you talk about "neglect" (a highly abstract concept) than if you refer to "forgetting my last birthday" (a specific event).

Recognize Differences

To communicate interculturally you need to recognize the differences between yourself and people who are culturally different, the differences within the culturally different group, and the numerous differences in meaning that arise from cultural differences.

Differences Between Yourself and Culturally Different People A common barrier to intercultural communication is the assumption that similarities exist but that differences do not. For example, though you may easily accept different hairstyles, clothing, and foods, you may assume that, in basic values and beliefs, everyone is really alike. But that's not necessarily true. When you assume similarities and ignore differences, you'll fail to notice important distinctions. As a result, you'll risk communicating to others that your ways are the right ways and that their ways are not important to you. Consider: An American invites a Filipino coworker to dinner. The Filipino politely refuses. The American is hurt, feels that the Filipino does not want to be friendly, and does not repeat the invitation. The Filipino is hurt and concludes that the invitation was not extended sincerely. Here, it seems, both the American and the Filipino assume that their customs for inviting people to dinner are the same—when, in fact, they aren't. A Filipino expects to be invited several times before accepting a dinner invitation. In the Philippines, an invitation given only once is viewed as insincere.

Differences Within the Culturally Different Group Within every cultural group, there are wide and important differences. Just as all Americans are not alike, neither are all Indonesians, Greeks, Mexicans, and so on. When you ignore these differences—when you assume that all persons covered by the same label (in this case, a national or racial label) are the same—you're guilty of stereotyping. A good example of this is the use of the term "African American." The term stresses the unity of Africa and those who are of African descent and is analogous to "Asian American" or "European American." At the same time, if the term is used in the same sense as "German American" or "Japanese American," it ignores the great diversity within the African continent. More analogous terms would be "Nigerian American" or "Ethiopian American."

Differences in Meaning Meanings exist not in words but in people (Chapter 5). Consider, for example, the different meanings of the word *woman* to an American and a Muslim, of *religion* to a born-again Christian and an atheist, or of *lunch* to a Chinese rice farmer and a Madison Avenue advertising executive. Even though different groups may use the same word, its meanings will vary greatly depending on the listeners' cultural definitions.

Similarly, nonverbal messages have different meanings in different cultures. For example, a left-handed American who eats with the left hand may be seen by a Muslim as obscene. Muslims do not use the left hand for eating or for shaking hands but solely to clean themselves after excretory functions. So using the left hand to eat or to shake hands is considered extremely impolite, even insulting and obscene.

VIDEO CHOICE POINT

Meet the Family

Charles will be meeting Mei Li's extended family for the first time, and both he and Mei Li are a bit nervous. They consider how the differences in their cultures may affect their relationship and their communication choices. "Meet the Family" explores the options you have for communicating in a cultural setting that is different from the one you grew up in. Illustrated here are choices that are both effective and ineffective communication among friends, romantic partners, and families. Watch to see how Charles and Mei Li's relationship is affected by their communication choices in the video "Meet the Family." Respond to the questions posed.

 **Watch** the **Video** "Meet the Family" at **MyCommunicationLab**

Adjust Your Communication

Intercultural communication (in fact, all interpersonal communication) takes place only to the extent that you and the person you're trying to communicate with share the same system of symbols. This principle takes on particular relevance when you realize that even within a given culture, no two persons share identical symbol systems. Parents and children, for example, not only have different vocabularies but also, even more important, associate different meanings with some of the terms they both use. People in close relationships—either as intimate friends or as romantic partners—realize that learning the other person's signals takes a long time and, often, great patience. If you want to understand what another person means—by smiling, by saying "I love you," by arguing about trivial matters, by self-deprecating comments—you have to learn the person's system of signals.

Adjusting your communication is especially important in intercultural situations, largely because people from different cultures use different signals—or sometimes use the same signals to signify quite different things. For example, focused eye contact means honesty and openness in much of the United States. But in Japan and in many Hispanic cultures, that same behavior may signify arrogance or disrespect, particularly if engaged in by a youngster with someone significantly older.

As you adjust your messages, recognize that each culture has its own rules and customs for communication (Barna, 1997; Ruben, 1985; Spitzberg, 1991). These rules identify what is appropriate and what is inappropriate. Thus, for example, in U.S. culture, you would call a person you wished to date three or four days in advance. In certain Asian cultures, you might call the person's parents weeks or even months in advance. In U.S. culture, you say, as a general friendly gesture and not as a specific invitation, "Come over and pay us a visit sometime." To members of other cultures, this comment is sufficient to prompt the listeners to actually visit at their convenience. Table 2.4 presents a good example of a set of cultural rules—guidelines for communicating with people with disabilities, an extremely large and important culture that many people don't understand.

INTERPERSONAL CHOICE POINT

Misusing Linguistic Privilege

You enter a group of racially similar people who are using terms normally considered offensive to refer to themselves. Trying to be one of the group, you too use such terms—but are met with extremely negative nonverbal feedback. What are some things you might say to lessen this negative reaction and to let the group know that you don't normally use such racial terms? What would you be sure not to say?

TABLE 2.4

Interpersonal Communication Tips Between People with and without Disabilities

Here we look at communication between those with general disabilities—for example, people in wheelchairs or with, say, cerebral palsy—and those who have no such disability.

If you're the person without a general disability:

Generally	Specifically
Use person-first language where the person, rather than the disability, is emphasized.	Avoid terms that define the person as disabled. Avoid such expressions as "the disabled man" or "the handicapped child." Instead, using "person-first" language, say "person with a disability."
Respect assistive devices such as wheelchairs, canes, walkers, or crutches.	Don't move these out of your way or lean on them; they're for the convenience of the person with the disability.
Shake hands with the person with the disability if you shake hands with others in a group.	Don't avoid shaking hands because the individual's hand has lost some normal function, for example.
Avoid talking about the person with a disability in the third person.	Direct your comments directly to the individual. Even if the person has an interpreter, direct your comments to the person with the disability, not the interpreter.
Don't assume that people who have a disability are intellectually impaired.	Slurred speech—such as may occur with people who have cerebral palsy or cleft palate—should not be taken as indicating a low-level intellect. Be careful not to talk down to such individuals as many people do.
When you're not sure of how to act, ask.	For example, if you're not sure if you should offer walking assistance, say, "Would you like me to help you into the dining room?" And accept the person's response; if he or she says no, then that means no.
Maintain similar eye level.	If the person is in a wheelchair, for example, it might be helpful for you to sit down or kneel down to get onto the same eye level.

If you're the person with a general disability:

Generally	Specifically
Communicate your feelings.	For example, if you want someone to speak in a louder voice, ask. If you want to relax and have someone push your wheelchair, say so.
Be patient and understanding.	Many people mean well but may simply not know how to act or what to say. Put them at ease as best you can.
Demonstrate your own comfort.	If you detect discomfort in the other person, you might talk about your disability to show your own comfort—and that you understand that others may not know how you feel. But you're under no obligation to educate the public, so don't feel this is something you have to do.

Sources: These suggestions are based on a wide variety of sources, including the websites of the United States Department of Justice, the World Health Organization, and the National Center for Access Unlimited.

SKILL BUILDING EXERCISE

Applying Cultural Awareness

Here are a few cases of obvious intercultural differences and difficulties. Assume you're a mediator and have been called in to help resolve or improve these difficult situations. How would you try to mediate these situations?

1. A couple is in an interracial, inter-religious relationship. The family of one partner ignores their "couplehood." For example, they are never invited to dinner as a couple or included in any family affairs. Neither the couple nor the family are very happy about the situation.
2. The parents of two teenagers hold and readily verbalize stereotypes about other religious, racial, and ethnic groups. As a result, the teenagers don't bring home friends. The parents are annoyed that they never get to meet their children's friends. It's extremely uncomfortable whenever there's a chance meeting.
3. A worker in a large office recently underwent a religious conversion and now persists in trying to get everyone else to undergo this same conversion. The workers are fed up and want it stopped. The worker, however, feels it's a duty, an obligation, to convert others.

Confronting intercultural differences is extremely difficult, especially because most people will deny they are doing anything inappropriate. Approach these situations carefully, relying heavily on the skills of interpersonal communication identified throughout this text.

Recognize Culture Shock

Culture shock is the psychological reaction you experience when you encounter a culture very different from your own (Furnham & Bochner, 1986). Culture shock is normal; most people experience it when entering a new and different culture. Going away to college, moving in together, or joining the military, for example, can also result in culture shock. Nevertheless, it can be unpleasant and frustrating. Entering a new culture often engenders feelings of alienation, conspicuousness, and difference from everyone else. When you lack knowledge of the rules and customs of the new society, you cannot communicate effectively. You're apt to blunder frequently and seriously. In your culture shock, you may not know basic things: how to ask someone for a favor or pay someone a compliment; how to extend or accept an invitation; how early or how late to arrive for an appointment or how long to stay; how to distinguish seriousness from playfulness and politeness from indifference; how to dress for an informal, formal, or business function; and how to order a meal in a restaurant or how to summon a waiter.

Culture shock occurs in four general stages, which apply to a wide variety of encounters with the new and the different (Oberg, 1960).

- *Stage one: The honeymoon.* At first you experience fascination, even enchantment, with the new culture and its people. Among people who are culturally different, the early (and superficial) relationships of this stage are characterized by cordiality and friendship.
- *Stage two: The crisis.* In the crisis stage, the differences between your own culture and the new one create problems. This is the stage at which you experience the actual shock of the new culture. For example, in a study of students from more than 100 countries who were studying in 11 foreign countries, 25 percent of the students experienced depression (Klineberg & Hull, 1979).
- *Stage three: The recovery.* During the recovery period, you gain the skills necessary to function effectively in the new culture. You learn the language and ways of the society. Your feelings of inadequacy subside.
- *Stage four: The adjustment.* At the final stage, you adjust to and come to enjoy the new culture and the new experiences. You may still experience periodic difficulties and strains, but, on a whole, the experience is pleasant.

People also may experience a kind of reverse culture shock when they return to their original culture after living in a foreign culture (Jandt, 2009). Consider, for example, Peace Corps volunteers who work in economically deprived rural areas around the world. On returning to Las Vegas or Beverly Hills, they too may experience culture shock. Sailors who serve long periods aboard ships and then return to, for example, isolated farming communities may also experience culture shock. In these cases, however, the recovery period is shorter and the sense of inadequacy and frustration is less.

Explore the **Exercise** "Random Pairs" at **MyCommunicationLab**

The suggestions outlined in the preceding subsections will go a long way in helping you communicate more effectively in all situations and especially in intercultural interactions. These suggestions are, however, most effective when they are combined with the essential skills of all interpersonal communication (listed on the inside covers and discussed throughout this text).

Can you paraphrase the eight principles of intercultural communication and apply the suggestions for increasing intercultural effectiveness (prepare yourself, reduce ethnocentrism, confront your stereotypes, increase mindfulness, reduce uncertainty, recognize differences, adjust your communication, and recognize and deal effectively with culture shock)?

MESSAGES IN THE MEDIA: WRAP UP

International news shows will help you increase your cultural awareness, which will most likely increase your own ability to communicate with those from other cultures.

SUMMARY OF CONCEPTS AND SKILLS

Listen to the **Audio Chapter Summary** at **MyCommunicationLab**

Study and **Review** materials for this chapter are at **MyCommunicationLab**

This chapter explored culture and intercultural communication, the ways in which cultures differ, and ways to improve intercultural communication.

Culture

1. Culture consists of the relatively specialized lifestyle of a group of people that is passed on from one generation to the next through communication rather than through genes.
2. Because of demographic changes, an increased sensitivity to cultural differences, economic and political interdependence of nations, advances in communication technology, and the culture-specific nature of interpersonal communication, culture is an essential ingredient in interpersonal communication.
3. Each generation transmits its culture to the next generation through the process of enculturation and helps to develop a member's ethnic identity.
4. Through acculturation, one culture is modified through direct contact with or exposure to another culture.

Cultural Principles

5. Cultural principles include principles for communication efficiency (grouped under the general quality of cooperation) and for maintaining interpersonal relationships such as those for maintaining peaceful relationships and politeness.

Cultural Differences

6. Cultures differ in the degree to which they teach an individualist orientation (the individual is the most important consideration) or a collectivist orientation (the group is the most important consideration).
7. Cultures differ in the way information is communicated. In high-context cultures, much information is in the context or in the person's nonverbals; in low-context cultures, most of the information is explicitly stated in the message.
8. Cultures differ in the degree to which gender roles are distinct or overlap. Highly "masculine" cultures view men as assertive, oriented to material success, and strong, and they view women as modest, focused on the quality of life, and tender. Highly feminine cultures encourage both men and women to be modest, oriented to maintaining the quality of life, and tender, and they socialize people to emphasize close relationships.
9. Cultures differ in their power structures; in high-power-distance cultures, there is much difference in power between rulers and the ruled, whereas in low-power-distance cultures, power is more evenly distributed.
10. Cultures differ in the degree to which they tolerate ambiguity and uncertainty. High-ambiguity-tolerant cultures are comfortable with uncertainty, whereas low-ambiguity-tolerant cultures are not.
11. Cultures different in their being long-term oriented (a focus that promotes future rewards) or short-term oriented (a focus hat stresses more immediate rewards.
12. Cultures differ in their degree of indulgence (emphasizing the gratification of desires) or restraint (emphasizing moderation).

Improving Intercultural Communication

13. Intercultural communication encompasses a broad range of interactions. This range includes communication between cultures, between races, between genders, between socioeconomic and ethnic groups, between age groups, between religions, and between nations.
14. Many tactics can help make intercultural communication more effective. For example, prepare yourself by learning about the culture, reduce ethnocentrism, confront your stereotypes, communicate mindfully, reduce uncertainty, recognize differences, adjust your communication on the basis of cultural differences, and recognize culture shock.

In addition, this chapter considered some important skills. Check those you wish to work on.

____1. *Cultural influences.* Communicate with an understanding that culture influences communication in all its forms.

____2. *Individualist and collectivist cultures.* Adjust your messages and your listening with an awareness of differences in individualist and collectivist cultures.

____3. *High- and low-context cultures.* Adjust your messages and your listening in light of the differences between high- and low-context cultures.

____4. *Masculine and feminine cultures.* Adjust your messages and your listening to differences in masculinity and femininity.

____5. *High- and low-power-distance cultures.* Adjust your messages on the basis of the power structure that is written into the culture.

____6. *High and low tolerance for ambiguity.* Adjust your messages on the basis of the degree of the ambiguity tolerance of the other people.

____7. *Ethnocentric thinking.* Recognize your own ethnocentric thinking and how it influences your verbal and nonverbal messages.

____8. *Intercultural communication.* Become mindful of (1) the differences between yourself and the culturally different, (2) the differences within the cultural group, (3) the differences in meanings, and (4) the differences in cultural customs.

____9. *Appreciating cultural differences.* Look at cultural differences not as deviations or deficiencies but as the differences they are. Recognizing differences, however, does not necessarily mean accepting them.

VOCABULARY QUIZ: The Language of Intercultural Communication

Match the terms of intercultural communication with their definitions. Record the number of the definition next to the appropriate term.

____ high-context culture (37)
____ acculturation (30)
____ intercultural communication (41)
____ low-context culture (37)
____ ethnocentrism (43)
____ culture (29)
____ low-power-distance cultures (38)
____ enculturation (29)
____ individualist cultures (36)
____ collectivist cultures (36)

1. A culture in which most information is explicitly encoded in the verbal message.
2. The values, beliefs, artifacts, and ways of communicating of a group of people.

3. The process by which culture is transmitted from one generation to another.
4. Communication that takes place between persons of different cultures or persons who have different cultural beliefs, values, or ways of behaving.
5. The process through which a person's culture is modified through contact with another culture.
6. The tendency to evaluate other cultures negatively and our own culture positively.
7. Cultures in which power is relatively evenly distributed.
8. Cultures that emphasize competition and individual success and in which your responsibility is largely to yourself.
9. A culture in which much information is in the context or the person and is not made explicit in the verbal message.
10. Cultures that emphasize the member's responsibility to the group.

These ten terms and additional terms used in this chapter can be found in the glossary.

MyCommunicationLab

Visit MyCommunicationLab for additional information on culture. Flashcards, videos, skill building exercises, sample test questions, and additional exercises, examples, and discussions will help you continue your study the role of culture in interpersonal communication and the skills of intercultural communication.

CHAPTER

3

Perception of Self and Others

MESSAGES IN THE MEDIA

In *Perception* you see a professor help the FBI solve a variety of cases because he understands human behavior and because he can perceive things that others cannot. With the exception of Dr. Pierce, all of us are limited in what we know of ourselves and others and in what we can perceive. Fortunately, we can increase our ability to understand ourselves and others, thereby increasing our accuracy in interpersonal perception and communication.

OBJECTIVES *After reading this chapter, you should be able to:*

1. Define *self-concept, self-awareness,* and *self-esteem,* and apply the suggestions for increasing self-awareness and self-esteem.
2. Explain the five stages of perception.
3. Define the six factors that influence interpersonal perception, and apply the suggestions for increasing accuracy in your own interpersonal perception.
4. Explain and give examples of the strategies of impression management, and use these when appropriate and ethical.

This chapter discusses two interrelated topics—the self and perception. After explaining the nature of the self (self-concept, self-awareness, and self-esteem) and the nature of perception, we look at the ways in which you form impressions of others and how you manage the impressions that you give to others.

THE SELF IN INTERPERSONAL COMMUNICATION

Let's begin this discussion by focusing on several fundamental aspects of the self: self-concept (the way you see yourself), self-awareness (your insight into and knowledge about yourself), and self-esteem (the value you place on yourself). In these discussions, you'll see how these dimensions influence and are influenced by the way you communicate.

Self-Concept

Watch the **Video** "Sarah's Blog" at **MyCommunicationLab**

You no doubt have an image of who you are; this is your **self-concept**. It consists of your feelings and thoughts about your strengths and weaknesses, your abilities and limitations, and your aspirations and worldview (Black, 1999). Your self-concept develops from at least four sources: (1) the image of you that others have and that they reveal to you, (2) the comparisons you make between yourself and others, (3) the teachings of your culture, and (4) the way you interpret and evaluate your own thoughts and behaviors (see Figure 3.1).

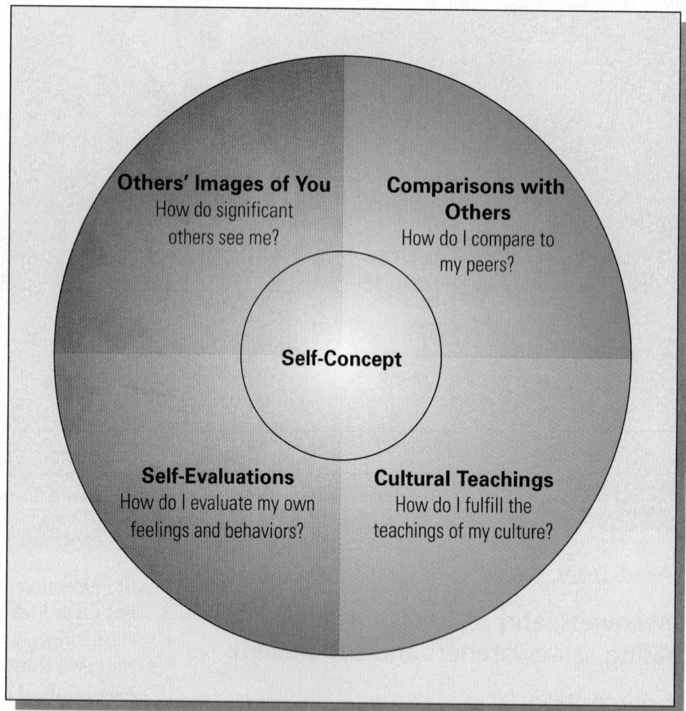

FIGURE 3.1

The Sources of Self-Concept

This diagram depicts the four sources of self-concept, the four contributors to how you see yourself: others' images of you; social comparisons; cultural teachings; and your own observations, interpretations, and evaluations. As you read about self-concept, consider the influence of each factor throughout your life. Which factor influenced you most as a preteen? Which influences you the most now? Which will influence you the most 25 or 30 years from now?

Others' Images of You According to Charles Horton Cooley's (1922) concept of the looking-glass self, when you want to discover, say, how friendly or how assertive you are, you would look at the image of yourself that others reveal to you through the way they treat you and react to you (Hensley, 1996). You'd look especially to those who are most significant in your life. As a child, you'd look to your parents and then to your teachers. As an adult, you might look to your friends, romantic partners, and colleagues at work. If these important others think highly of you, you'll see this positive image of yourself reflected in their behaviors; if they think little of you, you'll see a more negative image.

Comparisons with Others Another way you develop your self-concept is by comparing yourself with others. When you want to gain insight into who you are and how effective or competent you are, you probably look to your peers. For example, after an examination, you probably want to know how you performed relative to the other students in your class. If you play on a baseball team, it's important to know your batting average in comparison with others on the team. You gain an additional perspective when you see your score in comparison with the scores of your peers. And, if you want to feel good about yourself, you might compare yourself to those you know are less effective than you (it's called *downward social comparison*), though there are values in comparing yourself to those you think are better than you (*upward social comparison*). If you want a more accurate and objective assessment, you'd compare yourself with your peers, with others who are similar to you.

Social networking sites and social media generally have provided us with the tools (all very easy to use) to compare ourselves to others to perhaps estimate our individual worth or perhaps make us feel superior. Here are just a half-dozen ways social media enables you to find out how you stand.

- *Search engine reports.* Type in your name on Google, Bing, or Yahoo, for example, and you'll see the number of websites on which your name (and similarly named others) appears. Type in a colleague's name, and you get his or her score, which, you're hoping, is lower than yours.
- *Network spread.* Your number of friends on Facebook or your contacts on LinkedIn or Plaxo is in some ways a measure of your potential influence. Look at a friend's profile, and you have your comparison. Not surprisingly, there are websites that will surf the net to help you contact more social network friends.

"But otherwise I'll bet they lead very dull lives."

www.cartoonbank.com

- *Online influence.* Network sites such as Klout and PeerIndex provide you with a score (from 0–100) of your online influence. Your Klout score, for example, is a combination of your "true reach"—the number of people you influence, "amplification"—the degree to which you influence them, and "network"—the influence of your network. Postrank Analytics, on the other hand, provides you with a measure of engagement—the degree to which people interact with, pay attention to, read, or comment on what you write.
- *Twitter activities.* The number of times you tweet might be one point of comparison but, more important, is the number of times you are tweeted about or your tweets are repeated (retweets). Twitalyzer will provide you with a three-part score: an impact score, a Klout score, and a Peer Index score and will also enable you to search the "twitter elite" for the world as well as for any specific area (you can search by ZIP code). Assuming your Twitter score is what you'd like it to be, a single click will enable you to post this score on your own Twitter page.
- *Blog presence.* Your blog presence is readily available from your "stats" tab where you can see how many people visited your blog since inception or over the past year, month, week, or day. And you'll also see a map of the world indicating where people who are visiting your blog come from.
- *References to written works.* Google Scholar, for example, will enable you to see how many other writers have cited your works (and how many cited the works of the person you're comparing against) and the works in which you were cited. And, of course, Amazon and other online book dealers provide rankings of your books along with a star system based on reviewers' comments.

Explore the **Exercise** "How Open Are You Culturally" at **MyCommunicationLab**

CULTURAL TEACHINGS Through your parents, teachers, and the media, your culture instills in you a variety of beliefs, values, and attitudes—about success (how you define it and how you should achieve it); about your religion, race, or nationality; and about the ethical principles you should follow in business and in your personal life. These teachings provide benchmarks against which you can measure yourself. Your success in, for example, achieving what your culture defines as success will contribute to a positive self-concept. A perceived failure to achieve what your culture promotes (for example, not being in a permanent relationship by the time you're 30) may contribute to a negative self-concept.

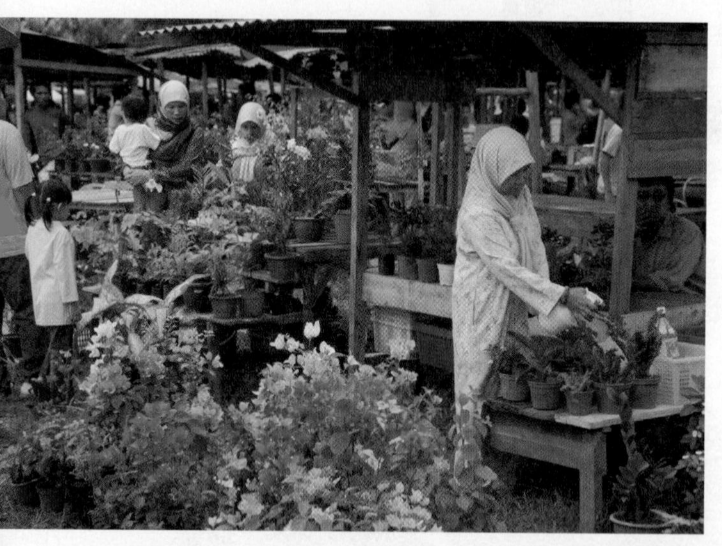

VIEWPOINTS Cultural Background

Your cultural background will significantly influence your responses to this simple "Who Am I?" test. In one study, for example, participants from Malaysia (a collectivist culture) and from Australia and Great Britain (individualist cultures) completed this test. Malaysians produced significantly more group self-descriptions and fewer idiocentric self-descriptions than did the Australian or British respondents (Bochner, 1994). If you completed the "Who Am I?" test, can you identify responses that were influenced by your cultural orientation, particularly your collectivist-individualist orientation? Did other cultural factors influence your statements?

SELF-EVALUATIONS Much in the way others form images of you based on what you do, you also react to your own behavior; you interpret and evaluate it. These interpretations and evaluations help to form your self-concept. For example, let us say you believe that lying is wrong. If you lie, you will evaluate this behavior in terms of your internalized beliefs about lying. You'll thus react negatively to your own behavior. You may, for example, experience guilt if your behavior contradicts your beliefs. In contrast, let's say you tutored another student and helped him or her pass a course. You would probably evaluate this behavior positively; you would feel good about this behavior and, as a result, about yourself.

Self-Awareness

Your **self-awareness** represents the extent to which you know yourself. Understanding how your self-concept develops is one way to increase your self-awareness: The more you understand about why you view yourself as you do, the more you will understand who you are. Additional insight is gained by looking at self-awareness through the Johari model of the self, or your four selves (Luft, 1984).

YOUR FOUR SELVES Self-awareness is neatly explained by the model of the four selves, the Johari window. This model, presented in Figure 3.2, has four basic areas, or quadrants, each of which represents a somewhat different self. The Johari model emphasizes that the several aspects of the self are not separate pieces but are interactive parts of a whole. Each part is dependent on each other part. Like that of interpersonal communication, this model of the self is transactional.

Each person's Johari window will be different, and each individual's window will vary from one time to another and from one interpersonal situation to another. By way of example, Figure 3.3 illustrates two possible configurations.

- *The open self* represents all the information, behaviors, attitudes, feelings, desires, motivations, and ideas that you and others know. The type of information included here might range from your name, skin color, and sex to your age, political and religious affiliations, and financial situation. Your open self will vary in size, depending on the situation you're in and the person with whom you're interacting.
- *The blind self* represents all the things about yourself that others know but of which you're ignorant. These may vary from the relatively insignificant habit of saying "You know," rubbing your nose when you get angry, or having a distinct body odor to things as significant as defense mechanisms, conflict strategies, or repressed experiences.
- *The hidden self* contains all that you know of yourself that you keep secret. In any interaction, this area includes everything you don't want to reveal, whether it's relevant or irrelevant to the conversation. At the extremes, the overdisclosers tell all—their relationship difficulties, their financial status, and just about everything else—while the underdisclosers tell nothing; they'll talk about you but not about themselves.
- *The unknown self* represents truths about yourself that neither you nor others know. Sometimes this unknown self is revealed through

Explore the **Exercise** "Disclosing Your Hidden Self" at **MyCommunicationLab**

INTERPERSONAL CHOICE POINT

Encouraging Self-Awareness

You have a friend who seems totally lacking in self-awareness—the blind self seems enormous. Assuming that this person wants to increase self-awareness, what are some of your options for helping your friend increase self-awareness without appearing to intrude too much into private matters?

FIGURE 3.2

The Johari Window

Visualize this model as representing your self. The entire model is of constant size, but each section can vary, from vary small to very large. As one section becomes smaller, one or more of the others grows larger. Similarly, as one section grows, one or more of the others must get smaller. For example, if you reveal a secret and thereby enlarge your open self, this shrinks your hidden self. Further, this disclosure may in turn lead to a decrease in the size of your blind self (if your disclosure influences other people to reveal what they know about you but that you have not known). How would you draw your Johari window to show yourself when interacting with your parents? With your friends? With your college instructors? The name Johari, by the way, comes from the first names of the two people who developed the model, Joseph Luft and Harry Ingham.

Source: Luft, J. (1984). Group processes: An introduction to group dynamics 60. Reprinted by permission of Mayfield Publishing Company, Mountain View, CA.

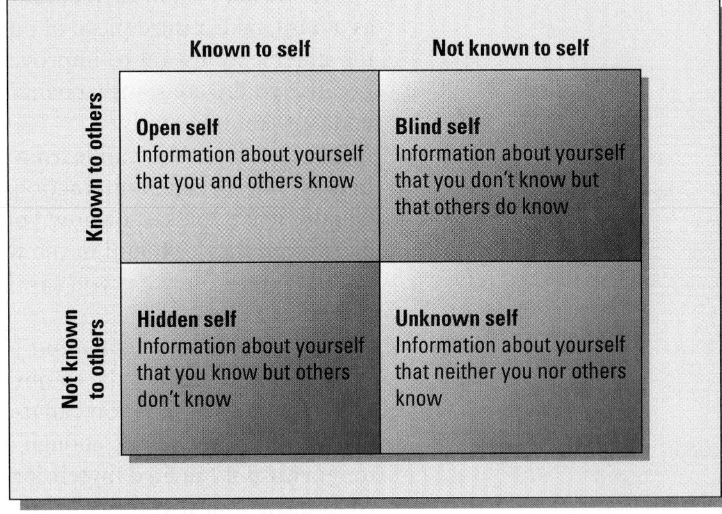

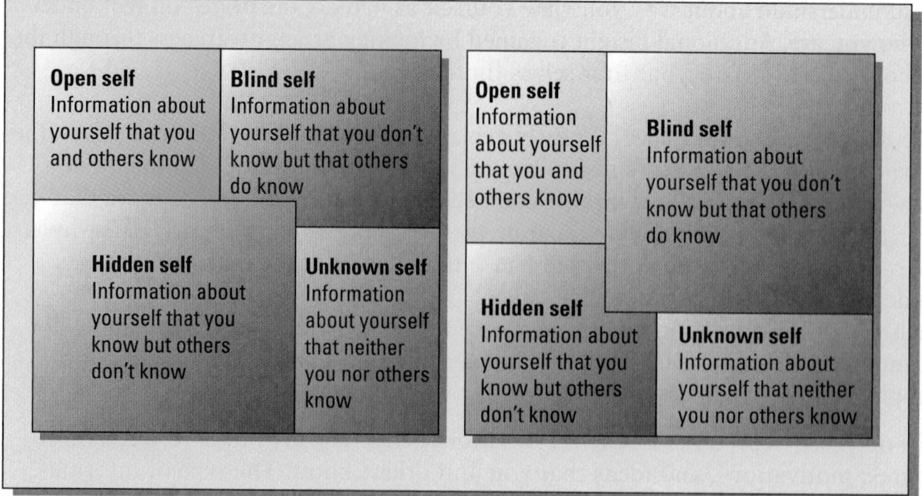

FIGURE 3.3
Johari Windows of Varied Structures
Notice that, as one self grows, one or more of the other selves shrink. Assume that each of these models depicts the self-awareness and self-disclosure of different people. How would you describe the type of interpersonal communication (especially self-disclosure) that characterizes each of these four people?

hypnosis, projective tests, or dreams. Mostly, however, it's revealed by the fact that you're constantly learning things about yourself that you didn't know before—for example, that you become defensive when someone asks you a question or voices disagreement or that you compliment others in the hope of being complimented back.

Growing in Self-Awareness Here are five ways you can increase your self-awareness:

- *Ask yourself about yourself.* One way to ask yourself about yourself is to take an informal "Who am I?" test (Bugental & Zelen, 1950; Grace & Cramer, 2003). Title a piece of paper "Who Am I?" and write 10, 15, or 20 times "I am.... " Then complete each of the sentences. Try not to give only positive or socially acceptable responses; just respond with what comes to mind first. Take another piece of paper and divide it into two columns; label one column "Strengths" and the other column "Weaknesses." Fill in each column as quickly as possible. Using these first two tests as a base, take a third piece of paper, title it "Self-Improvement Goals," and complete the statement "I want to improve my ... " as many times as you can in five minutes. Because you're constantly changing, these self-perceptions and goals also change, so update them frequently.
- *Listen to others.* You can learn a lot about yourself by seeing yourself as others do. In most interpersonal interactions, people comment on you in some way—on what you do, what you say, or how you look. Sometimes these comments are explicit; most often they're found in the way others look at you, in what they talk about, or in their interest in what you say. Pay close attention to this verbal and nonverbal information.
- *Actively seek information about yourself.* Actively seek out information to reduce your blind self. You need not be so obvious as to say, "Tell me about myself" or "What do you think of me?" But you can use everyday situations to gain self-information: "Do you think I was assertive enough when asking for the raise?" Or "Would I be thought too forward if I invited myself for dinner?" Do not, of course, seek this information constantly; your friends would quickly find others with whom to interact.

- *See your different selves.* Each person with whom you have an interpersonal relationship views you differently; to each you're a somewhat different person. Yet you are really all of these selves, and your self-concept will be influenced by each of these views as they are reflected back to you in everyday interpersonal interactions. For starters, visualize how you're seen by your mother, your father, your teachers, your best friend, the stranger you sat next to on the bus, your employer, your neighbor's child. The experience will give you new and valuable perspectives on yourself.
- *Increase your open self.* When you reveal yourself to others and increase your open self, you also reveal yourself to yourself. At the very least, you bring into clearer focus what you may have buried within. As you discuss yourself, you may see connections that you had previously missed, and with the aid of feedback from others, you may gain still more insight. Also, by increasing the open self, you increase the likelihood that a meaningful and intimate dialogue will develop that will enable you to get to know yourself better. This important process, called self-disclosure, is considered in Chapter 8, along with its advantages and disadvantages.

Self-Esteem

Self-esteem is a measure of how valuable you think you are. If you have high self-esteem, you think highly of yourself; if you have low self-esteem, you view yourself negatively. Before reading further about this topic, consider your own self-esteem by taking the accompanying self-test, "How's Your Self-Esteem?"

The basic idea behind self-esteem is that when you feel good about yourself—about who you are and what you're capable of doing—you will perform better. When you think like a success, you're more likely to act like a success. Conversely, when you think you're a failure, you're more likely to act like a failure. When you reach for the phone to ask the most popular student in the school for a date and you visualize yourself successful and effective, you're more likely to give a good impression. If, on the other hand, you think you're going to forget what you want to say or say something totally stupid, you're less likely to be successful.

INTERPERSONAL CHOICE POINT

Understanding Rejection

You've asked several different people at school for a date, but so far all you've received have been rejections. Something's wrong; you're not that bad. What are some of the things you can do to gain insight into the possible reasons for these rejections? From whom might you seek suggestions?

TEST YOURSELF

How's Your Self-Esteem?

Respond to each of the following statements with T (for true) if the statement describes you at least a significant part of the time and F (for false) if the statement describes you rarely or never.

____ 1. Generally, I feel I have to be successful in all things.

____ 2. A number of my acquaintances are often critical or negative of what I do and how I think.

____ 3. I often tackle projects that I know are impossible to complete to my satisfaction.

____ 4. When I focus on the past, I more often focus on my failures than on my successes and on my negative rather than my positive qualities.

____ 5. I make little effort to improve my personal and social skills.

How Did You Do? "True" responses to the questions generally are seen as getting in the way of building positive self-esteem. "False" responses indicate that you think much like a self-esteem coach would want you to think.

What Will You Do? The following discussion elaborates on these five issues and illustrates why each of them creates problems for the development of healthy self-esteem. You might also want to visit the National Association for Self-Esteem's website. There you'll find a variety of materials for examining and for bolstering self-esteem.

VIEWPOINTS Self-esteem

Despite its intuitive value, self-esteem has its critics (Epstein, 2005). Some researchers argue that high self-esteem is not necessarily desirable: It does nothing to improve academic performance, does not predict success, and may even lead to antisocial (even aggressive) behavior. Interestingly enough, a large number of criminals and delinquents are found to have high self-esteem. And conversely, many people who have low self-esteem have become quite successful in all fields (Owens, Stryker, & Goodman, 2002). How do you feel about the benefits or liabilities of self-esteem?

Interestingly enough, your self-esteem seems to influence the method of communication you choose. For example, if you have low self-esteem, you're likely to prefer e-mail, whereas if you have high self-esteem, you're more likely to prefer face-to-face interaction, at least in situations involving some degree of interpersonal risk (Joinson, 2001).

Here are five suggestions for increasing self-esteem that parallel the questions in the self-test.

Attack Self-Destructive Beliefs Challenge those beliefs you have about yourself that are unproductive or that make it more difficult for you to achieve your goals (Einhorn, 2006). Here, for example, are some beliefs that are likely to prove self-destructive (Butler, 1981):

- The belief that *you have to be perfect*; this causes you to try to perform at unrealistically high levels at work, school, and home; anything short of perfection is unacceptable.
- The belief that *you have to be strong* tells you that weakness and any of the more vulnerable emotions like sadness, compassion, or loneliness are wrong.
- The belief that *you have to please others* and that your worthiness depends on what others think of you.
- The belief that *you have to hurry up*; this compels you to do things quickly, to try to do more than can be reasonably expected in any given amount of time.
- The belief that *you have to take on more responsibilities* than any one person can be expected to handle.

Watch the **Video** "I'm Not Hungry" at **MyCommunicationLab**

Explore the **Exercise** "How Can You Attack Self-Defeating Drivers?" at **MyCommunicationLab**

These beliefs set unrealistically high standards and therefore almost always end in failure. As a result, you may develop a negative self-image, seeing yourself as someone who constantly fails. So, replace these self-destructive beliefs with more productive ones, such as "I succeed in many things, but I don't have to succeed in everything" and "It would be nice to be loved by everyone, but it isn't necessary to my happiness." See Table 3.1 for a summary and comparison of these destructive beliefs and constructive counterparts.

TABLE 3.1

Destructive and Constructive Beliefs

Destructive Beliefs	Constructive Beliefs
I need to **be perfect.**	I'm not perfect, no one is; and I don't need to be perfect, but I'm not bad.
I need to **be strong.**	It's nice to be strong sometimes but also nice to be able to show weakness.
I need **to please** everyone.	It would be nice if I pleased everyone, but that's really impossible; besides, there's no need to please everyone.
I need **to hurry;** I can't waste time.	I can stop and pause and not always be in a hurry.
I need to **do more.**	There is a limit on what one person can do; I do what I can do and don't do the rest.

Beware the Impostor Phenomenon The **impostor phenomenon** refers to the tendency to disregard outward signs of success and to consider yourself an "impostor," a fake, a fraud, one who doesn't really deserve to be considered successful (Clance, 1985; Harvey & Katz, 1985). Even though others may believe you are a success, you "know" that they are wrong. As you might expect, this tendency is more likely in new situations—a new job, say. One of the dangers of this belief is that it may prevent you from seeking advancement in your profession, believing you won't be up to the task. Becoming aware that such beliefs are not uncommon and that they are not necessarily permanent should help relieve some of these misperceptions. Another useful aid is to develop a relationship with an honest and knowledgeable mentor who will not only teach you the ropes but will let you know that you are successful.

"I've decided to leave my family to devote more time to myself."

Lee Lorenz/The New Yorker Collection/www.cartoonbank.com

Seek Out Nourishing People Psychologist Carl Rogers (1970) drew a distinction between noxious and nourishing people. Noxious people criticize and find fault with just about everything. Nourishing people, on the other hand, are positive and optimistic. Most important, they reward us, they stroke us, and they make us feel good about ourselves. To enhance your self-esteem, seek out these people. At the same time, avoid noxious people, those who make you feel negatively about yourself. At the same time, seek to become more nourishing yourself so that you each build up the other's self-esteem.

Identification with people similar to yourself also seems to increase self-esteem. For example, deaf people who identified with the larger deaf community had greater self-esteem than those who didn't so identify (Jambor & Elliott, 2005). Similarly, identification with your cultural group seems also helpful in developing positive self-esteem (McDonald et al., 2005).

Work on Projects That Will Result in Success Some people want to fail (or so it seems). Often, they select projects that will result in failure simply because these projects are impossible to complete. Avoid this trap and select projects that will result in success. Each success will help build self-esteem. Each success will make the next success a little easier. If a project does fail, recognize that this does not mean that you're a failure. Everyone fails somewhere along the line. Failure is something that happens to you; it's not something you've created, and it's not something inside you. Further, your failing once does not mean that you will fail the next time. So learn to put failure in perspective.

Remind Yourself of Your Successes Some people have a tendency to focus on and to exaggerate their failures, their missed opportunities, and their social mistakes. However, those witnessing these failures give them much less importance (Savitsky, Epley, & Gilovich, 2001). If your objective is to correct what you did wrong or to identify the skills that you need to correct these failures, then focusing on failures can have some positive value. However, if you just focus on failure without any plans for correction, then you're probably just making life more difficult for yourself and limiting your self-esteem. To counteract the tendency to recall failures, remind yourself of your successes. Recall these successes both intellectually and emotionally. Realize why they were successes, and relive the emotional experience when you sank the winning basketball, aced that test, or helped your friend overcome personal problems. And while you're at it, recall your positive qualities.

SECURE AFFIRMATION An affirmation is simply a statement asserting that something is true. In discussions of self-concept and self-awareness, affirmation is used to refer to positive statements about yourself, statements asserting that something good or positive is true of you. It's frequently recommended that you remind yourself of your successes with affirmations—that you focus on your good deeds; on your positive qualities, strengths, and virtues; and on your productive and meaningful relationships with friends, loved ones, and relatives (Aronson, Cohen, & Nail, 1998; Aronson, Wilson, & Akert, 2013). One useful way to look at self-affirmation is in terms of "I am," "I can," and "I will" statements (Van Praagh, 2010)

- *"I am" statements* focus on your self-image and how you see yourself and might include "I am a worthy person," "I am responsible," "I am capable of loving," and "I am a good team player."
- *"I can" statements* focus on your abilities and might include "I can accept my past but also let it go," "I can learn to be a more responsive partner," "I can assert myself when appropriate," and "I can control my anger."
- *"I will" statements* focus on useful and appropriate goals you want to achieve and might include "I will get over my guilty feelings," "I will study more effectively," "I will act more supportively," and "I will not take on more responsibility than I can handle."

The idea behind the advice in self-esteem is that the way you talk to yourself will influence what you think of yourself. If you affirm yourself—if you tell yourself that you're a friendly person, that you can be a leader, that you will succeed on the next test—you will soon come to feel more positively about yourself. Some research, however, argues that such affirmations—although extremely popular in self-help books—may not be very helpful. These critics contend that, if you have low self-esteem, you're not going to believe your self-affirmations simply because you don't have a high opinion of yourself to begin with (Paul, 2001). They propose that the alternative to self-affirmation is to secure affirmation from others. You'd do this largely by becoming more interpersonally competent. The more competent you become, the more positive affirmations you'll receive from others, and it is this affirmation from others that, these researchers argue, is more helpful than self-talk in raising self-esteem.

INTERPERSONAL CHOICE POINT

Lowering Self-Esteem

Your brother has entered a relationship with someone who constantly puts him down; this has lowered his self-esteem to the point where he has no self-confidence. If this continues, you fear your brother may again experience severe bouts of depression. What options do you have for dealing with this problem? What, if anything, would you do?

Can you define *self-concept, self-awareness,* and *self-esteem* and apply the suggestions for increasing your own self-awareness and self-esteem?

PERCEPTION IN INTERPERSONAL COMMUNICATION

Perception is the process by which you become aware of objects, events, and especially people through your senses: sight, smell, taste, touch, and hearing. Perception is an active, not a passive, process. Your perceptions result from what exists in the outside world and from your own experiences, desires, needs and wants, loves and hatreds. Among the reasons perception is so important in interpersonal communication is that it influences your communication choices. The messages you send and listen to will depend on how you see the world, on how you size up specific situations, on what you think of yourself and of the people with whom you interact.

Interpersonal perception is a continuous series of processes that blend into one another and can take place in a split second. For convenience of discussion, we can separate interpersonal perception into five stages: (1) You sense, you pick up some kind of stimulation; (2) you organize the stimuli in some way; (3) you interpret and evaluate what you perceive; (4) you store it in memory; and (5) you retrieve it when needed.

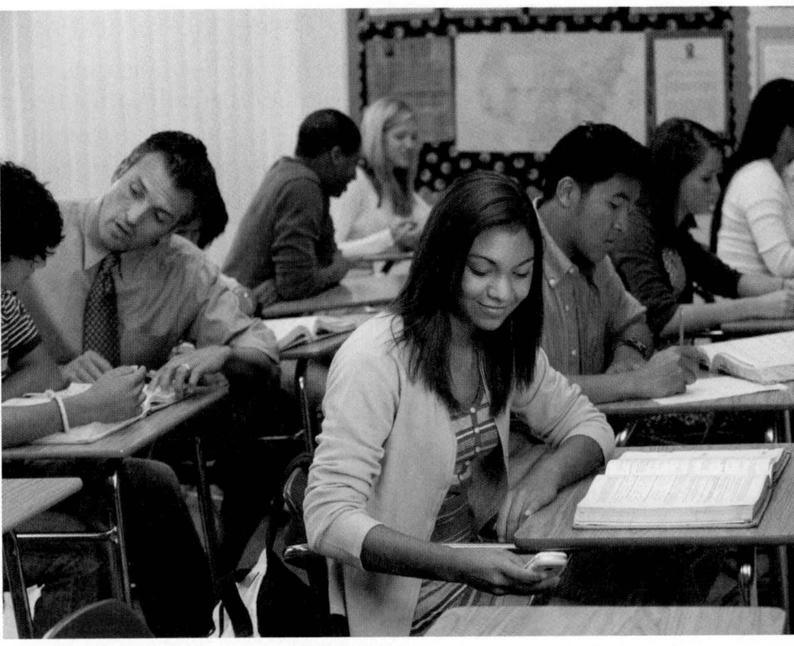

VIEWPOINTS Selective perception

Consider your own selective perception, particularly as it occurs in the classroom or in the workplace. In what ways is your selective perception useful? In what ways might it prove disadvantageous?

Stage One: Stimulation

At this first stage, your sense organs are stimulated—you hear a new CD, see a friend, smell someone's perfume, taste an orange, receive an instant message, or feel another's sweaty palm. Naturally, you don't perceive everything; rather, you engage in **selective perception**, a general term that includes selective attention and selective exposure:

- In **selective attention**, you attend to those things that you anticipate will fulfill your needs or will prove enjoyable. For example, when daydreaming in class, you don't hear what the instructor is saying until your name is called. Your selective attention mechanism then focuses your senses on your name.
- Through **selective exposure**, you expose yourself to messages that will confirm your existing beliefs, contribute to your objectives, or prove satisfying in some way. For example, after you buy a car, you're more apt to listen to advertisements for the car you just bought because these messages tell you that you made the right decision. At the same time, you'd likely avoid advertisements for the cars that you considered but eventually rejected because these messages would tell you that you made the wrong decision.

Stage Two: Organization

At the second stage, you organize the information your senses pick up. One of the major ways you organize information is by rules. One frequently used rule of perception is that of **proximity**, or physical closeness: Things that are physically close to each other are perceived as a unit. Thus, using this rule, you would perceive people who are often together or messages spoken one immediately after the other as units, as belonging together.

Another rule is **similarity**: Things that are physically similar (they look alike) are perceived to belong together and to form a unit. This principle of similarity would lead you to see people who dress alike as belonging together. Similarly, you might assume that people who work at the same jobs, who are of the same religion, who live in the same building, or who talk with the same accent belong together.

The rule of **contrast** is the opposite of similarity: When items (people or messages, for example) are very different from each other, you conclude that they don't belong together; they're too different from each other to be part of the same unit. If you're the only one who shows up at an informal gathering in a tuxedo, you'd be seen as not belonging to the group because you contrast too much with other members.

Blog Post

Perceptual Organization

For ways of organizing perceptions by schemata and scripts, see "Perceptual Organization" at tcbdevito.blogspot.com. How useful are these concepts to understanding your own perceptions?

Watch the **Video** "Art Appreciation" at **MyCommunicationLab**

Stage Three: Interpretation–Evaluation

The interpretation–evaluation step (a combined term because the two processes cannot be separated) is greatly influenced by your experiences, needs, wants, values, beliefs about the way things are or should be, expectations, physical and emotional state, and so on. Your interpretation–evaluation will be influenced by your gender; for example, women have been found to view others more positively than men (Winquist, Mohr, & Kenny, 1998).

Judgments about members of other cultures are often ethnocentric; because of your stereotypes, you can easily (but inappropriately) apply these to members of other cultures. And so it's easy to infer that when members of other cultures do things that conform to your ways of doing things, they're right, and when they do things that contradict your ways, they're wrong—a classic example of ethnocentric thinking. This tendency can easily contribute to intercultural misunderstandings.

Stage Four: Memory

Your perceptions and their interpretations–evaluations are put into memory; they're stored so that you may ultimately retrieve them at some later time. So, for example, you have in memory your stereotype for college athletes and the fact that Ben Williams is a football player. Ben Williams is then stored in memory with "cognitive tags" that tell you that he's strong, ambitious, academically weak, and egocentric. Despite the fact that you've not witnessed Ben's strength or ambitions and have no idea of his academic record or his psychological profile, you still may store your memory of Ben along with the qualities that make up your stereotype for college athletes.

Stage Five: Recall

At some later date, you may want to recall or access the information you have stored in memory. Let's say you want to retrieve your information about Ben because he's the topic of discussion among you and a few friends. As we'll see in our discussion of listening in the next chapter, memory isn't reproductive; you don't simply reproduce what you've heard or seen. Rather, you reconstruct what you've heard or seen into a whole that is meaningful to you. It's this reconstruction that you store in memory. When you want to retrieve this information, you may recall it with a variety of inaccuracies:

- *Stereotypes.* You're likely to recall information that is consistent with your stereotype; in fact, you may not even be recalling the specific information (say, about Ben) but may actually just be recalling your stereotype (which contains information about college athletes and, because of this, also about Ben).
- *Inconsistencies.* You're apt to fail to recall information that is inconsistent with your stereotype; you have no place to put that information, so you easily lose it or forget it.
- *Contradictions.* You're more likely to recall information that *drastically* contradicts your stereotype, because it forces you to think (and perhaps rethink) about your stereotype and its accuracy; it may even force you to revise your stereotype for college athletes in general.

INTERPERSONAL CHOICE POINT

Responding to Stereotypes

What are some of your communication options for dealing with people who persist in talking (and thinking) in stereotypes, assuming you want to educate them rather than alienate them?

Can you explain the five stages of perception (stimulation, organization, interpretation-evaluation, memory, and recall) and use the suggestions for increasing your own perceptual accuracy at each of the stages?

IMPRESSION FORMATION

Impression formation (sometimes referred to as person perception) refers to the processes you go through in forming an impression of another person, whether it's a person you meet face to face or a person whose profile you're reading on Facebook. Here you would make use of a variety of perception processes, each of which has pitfalls and potential dangers. Before reading about these processes that you use in perceiving other people, examine your own perception strategies by taking the accompanying self-test, "How Accurate Are You at People Perception?"

Impression Formation Processes

The ways in which you perceive another person and ultimately come to some kind of evaluation or interpretation of this person are influenced by a variety of processes. Here we consider some of the more significant: the self-fulfilling prophecy, personality theory, primacy recency, consistency, and attribution.

SELF-FULFILLING PROPHECY A **self-fulfilling prophecy** is a prediction that comes true because you act on it as if it were true. Self-fulfilling prophecies occur in such widely different situations as parent–child relationships, educational settings, and business (Merton, 1957; Madon, Guyll, & Spoth, 2004; Rosenthal, 2002; Tierney & Farmer, 2004). There are four basic steps in the self-fulfilling prophecy:

1. You make a prediction or formulate a belief about a person or a situation. For example, you predict that Pat is friendly in interpersonal encounters.
2. You act toward that person or situation as if that prediction or belief were true. For example, you act as if Pat were a friendly person.
3. Because you act as if the belief were true, it becomes true. For example, because of the way you act toward Pat, Pat becomes comfortable and friendly.

TEST YOURSELF

How Accurate Are You at People Perception?

Respond to each of the following statements with T if the statement is usually or generally true (accurate in describing your behavior) or with F if the statement is usually or generally false (inaccurate in describing your behavior).

____ 1. I make predictions about people's behaviors that generally prove to be true.

____ 2. When I know some things about another person, I can pretty easily fill in what I don't know.

____ 3. Generally my expectations are borne out by what I actually see; that is, my later perceptions usually match my initial expectations.

____ 4. I base most of my impressions of people on the first few minutes of our meeting.

____ 5. I generally find that people I like possess positive characteristics and people I don't like possess negative characteristics.

____ 6. I generally attribute people's attitudes and behaviors to their most obvious physical or psychological characteristic.

How Did You Do? This brief perception test was designed to raise questions to be considered in this chapter, not to provide you with a specific perception score. All statements refer to perceptual processes that many people use but that often get us into trouble, leading us to form inaccurate impressions. The questions refer to several processes to be discussed below: self-fulfilling prophecy (Statement 1), personality theory (2), perceptual accentuation (3), primacy–recency (4), and consistency (5). Statement 6 refers to overattribution, one of the problems we encounter as we try to identify the motives for other people's and even our own behaviors.

What Will You Do? As you read this section, think about these processes and consider how you might use them more accurately and not allow them to get in the way of accurate and reasonable people perception. At the same time, recognize that situations vary widely and that strategies for clearer perception will prove useful most of the time but not all of the time. In fact, you may want to identify situations in which you shouldn't follow the suggestions that this text will offer.

4. You observe your effect on the person or the resulting situation, and what you see strengthens your beliefs. For example, you observe Pat's friendliness, and this reinforces your belief that Pat is, in fact, friendly.

The self-fulfilling prophecy also can be seen when you make predictions about yourself and fulfill them. For example, suppose you enter a group situation convinced that the other members will dislike you. Almost invariably you'll be proved right; the other members will appear to you to dislike you. What you may be doing is acting in a way that encourages the group to respond to you negatively. In this way, you fulfill your prophecies about yourself.

Self-fulfilling prophecies can short-circuit critical thinking and influence others' behavior (or your own) so that it conforms to your prophecies. As a result, you may see what you predicted rather than what is really there (for example, you may perceive yourself as a failure because you have predicted it rather than because of any actual failures).

Personality Theory Each person has a personality theory (often unconscious or implicit) that tells you which characteristics of an individual go with which other characteristics. Consider, for example, the following brief statements. Note the word in parentheses that you think best completes each sentence.

- Carlo is energetic, eager, and (intelligent, stupid).
- Kim is bold, defiant, and (extroverted, introverted).
- Joe is bright, lively, and (thin, heavy).
- Eve is attractive, intelligent, and (likable, unlikable).
- Susan is cheerful, positive, and (outgoing, shy).
- Angel is handsome, tall, and (friendly, unfriendly).

What makes some of these choices seem right and others wrong is your implicit personality theory, the system of rules that tells you which characteristics go with which other characteristics. Your theory may, for example, have told you that a person who is energetic and eager is also intelligent, not stupid—although there is no logical reason why a stupid person could not be energetic and eager.

If you believe a person has some positive qualities, you're likely to infer that she or he also possesses other positive qualities (known as the **halo effect**). There is also a **reverse halo** (or "horns") effect: If you know a person possesses several negative qualities, you're more likely to infer that the person also has other negative qualities. The halo effect will lead you to perceive attractive people as more generous, sensitive, trustworthy, and interesting than those who are less attractive. And the reverse halo effect will lead you to perceive those who are unattractive as mean, dishonest, antisocial, and sneaky (Katz, 2003).

When forming impressions of others, consider if you're making judgments on the basis of your theory of personality, perceiving qualities in an individual that your theory tells you should be present but aren't, or seeing qualities that are not there (Plaks, Grant, & Dweck, 2005).

Perceptual Accentuation When poor and rich children were shown pictures of coins and later asked to estimate their size, the poor children's size estimates were much greater than the rich children's. Similarly, hungry people need fewer visual cues to perceive food objects and food terms than do people who are not hungry. This process, called **perceptual accentuation**, leads you to see what you expect or want to see. You see people you like as better looking and smarter than those you don't like. You magnify or accentuate what will satisfy your needs and desires: The thirsty person sees a mirage of water, the sexually deprived person sees a mirage of sexual satisfaction.

Perceptual accentuation can lead you to perceive what you need or want to perceive rather than what is really there and to fail to perceive what you don't want to perceive. For example, you may not perceive signs of impending relationship problems because you're only seeing what you want to see. Another interesting distortion created by perceptual accentuation is that you may perceive certain behaviors as indicative that someone likes you simply because you want to be liked. For example, you view general politeness and friendly behavior used as a persuasive strategy (say, by a salesperson) as an indication that the person genuinely likes you.

PRIMACY–RECENCY Assume for a moment that you're enrolled in a course in which half the classes are extremely dull and half extremely exciting. At the end of the semester, you evaluate the course and the instructor. Would your evaluation be more favorable if the dull classes occurred in the first half of the semester and the exciting classes in the second? Or would it be more favorable if the order were reversed? If what comes first exerts the most influence, you have a **primacy effect**. If what comes last (or most recently) exerts the most influence, you have a **recency effect**.

In the classic study on the effects of primacy–recency in interpersonal perception, college students perceived a person who was described as "intelligent, industrious, impulsive, critical, stubborn, and envious" more positively than a person described as "envious, stubborn, critical, impulsive, industrious, and intelligent" (Asch, 1946). Notice that the descriptions are identical; only the order was changed. Clearly, there's a tendency to use early information to get a general idea about a person and to use later information to make this impression more specific.

The tendency to give greater weight to early information and to interpret later information in light of early impressions can lead you to formulate a total picture of an individual on the basis of initial impressions that may not be typical or accurate. For example, if you form a picture of a potential date solely on the basis of an introductory video, you may have a tendency to filter future information about this person through this picture/image/impression. So, if your initial impression was that the individual was supportive, friendly, and warm, you may interpret future behaviors of this person as confirming your initial assessment. If you judge a job applicant as generally nervous when he or she may simply be showing normal nervousness at being interviewed for a much-needed job, you will have misperceived this individual. Similarly, this tendency can lead you to discount or distort subsequent perceptions so as not to disrupt your initial impression. For example, you may fail to see signs of deceit in someone you like because of your early impressions that this person is a good and honest individual.

> **INTERPERSONAL CHOICE POINT**
>
> **Reversing a First Impression**
>
> You made a really bad first impression in your interpersonal communication class. You meant to be funny but came off as just sarcastic. What are some of the things you might say (immediately as well as later) to lessen the impact of this first impression?

CONSISTENCY The tendency to maintain balance among perceptions or attitudes is called **consistency** (McBroom & Reed, 1992). You expect certain things to go together and other things not to go together. On a purely intuitive basis, for example, respond to the following sentences by noting your expected response:

1. I expect a person I like to (like, dislike) me.
2. I expect a person I dislike to (like, dislike) me.
3. I expect my friend to (like, dislike) my friend.
4. I expect my friend to (like, dislike) my enemy.
5. I expect my enemy to (like, dislike) my friend.
6. I expect my enemy to (like, dislike) my enemy.

According to most consistency theories, your expectations would be as follows: You would expect a person you liked to like you (1) and a person you disliked to dislike you (2). You would expect a friend to like a friend (3) and to dislike an enemy (4). You would expect your enemy to dislike your friend (5) and to like your other enemy (6). All these expectations are intuitively satisfying.

Further, you would expect someone you liked to possess characteristics you like or admire and would expect your enemies not to possess characteristics you like or admire. Conversely, you would expect people you liked to lack unpleasant characteristics and those you disliked to possess unpleasant characteristics.

Uncritically assuming that an individual is consistent can lead you to ignore or distort perceptions that are inconsistent with your picture of the whole person. For example, you may misinterpret Karla's unhappiness because your image of Karla is "happy, controlled, and contented."

Watch the **Video** "Tonya" at **MyCommunicationLab**

Explore the **Exercise** "How Do You Make Attributions?" at **MyCommunicationLab**

ATTRIBUTION OF CONTROL **Attribution** is the process by which you try to explain the motivation for a person's behavior. Perhaps the major way you do this is to ask yourself if the person was in control of his or her behavior. For example, suppose you invite your friend Desmond to dinner for 7 p.m. and he arrives at 9. Consider how you would respond to each of these reasons:

- Reason 1: I just couldn't tear myself away from the beach. I really wanted to get a great tan.
- Reason 2: I was driving here when I saw some young kids mugging an old couple. I broke it up and took the couple home. They were so frightened that I had to stay with them until their children arrived. Their phone was out of order, so I had no way of calling to tell you I'd be late.
- Reason 3: I got in a car accident and was taken to the hospital.

Depending on the reason, you would probably attribute very different motives to Desmond's behavior. With reasons 1 and 2, you'd conclude that Desmond was in control of his behavior; with reason 3, that he was not. Further, you would probably respond negatively to reason 1 (Desmond was selfish and inconsiderate) and positively to reason 2 (Desmond was a good Samaritan). Because Desmond was not in control of his behavior in reason 3, you would probably not attribute either positive or negative motivation to his behavior. Instead, you would probably feel sorry that he got into an accident.

In perceiving and especially in evaluating other people's behavior, you frequently ask if they were in control of the behavior. Generally, research shows that if you feel a person was in control of negative behaviors, you'll come to dislike him or her. If you believe the person was not in control of negative behaviors, you'll come to feel sorry for and not blame the person.

In your attribution of controllability—or in attributing motives on the basis of any other reasons (for example, hearsay or observations of the person's behavior)—beware of several potential errors: (1) the self-serving bias, (2) overattribution, and (3) the fundamental attribution error.

- You commit the **self-serving bias** when you take credit for the positive and deny responsibility for the negative. For example, you're more likely to attribute your positive outcomes (say, you get an A on an exam) to internal and controllable factors—to your personality, intelligence, or hard work. And you're more likely to attribute your negative outcomes (say, you get a D) to external and uncontrollable factors—to the exam's being exceptionally difficult or to your roommate's party the night before (Bernstein, Stephan, & Davis, 1979; Duval & Silva, 2002).
- **Overattribution** is the tendency to single out one or two obvious characteristics of a person and attribute everything that person does to this one or these two characteristics. For example, if a person is blind or was born into great wealth, there's often a tendency to attribute everything that person does to such factors. And so you might say, "Alex overeats because he's blind" or "Lillian is irresponsible because she never had to work for her money." To prevent overattribution, recognize that most behaviors and personality characteristics result from lots of factors. You almost always make a mistake when you select one factor and attribute everything to it.
- The **fundamental attribution error** occurs when you overvalue the contribution of internal factors (for example, a person's personality) and undervalue the influence of external factors (for example, the context or situation the person is in). The fundamental attribution error leads you to conclude that people do what they do because that's the kind of people they are, not because of the situation they're in. When Pat is late for an appointment, you're more likely to conclude that Pat is inconsiderate or irresponsible than to attribute the lateness to a bus breakdown or a traffic accident.

INTERPERSONAL CHOICE POINT

Overattribution

Your work colleagues attribute your behavior, attitudes, values, and just about everything you do to your racial origins—a clear case of overattribution. What are some of the things you can say to explain the illogic of this thinking without alienating people you're going to have to work with for a considerable time?

Increasing Accuracy in Impression Formation

Successful interpersonal communication depends largely on the accuracy of the impressions you form of others. We've already identified the potential barriers that can arise with each of the perceptual processes, for example, the self-serving bias or overattribution. In addition to avoiding these barriers, here are some ways to increase your accuracy in impression formation.

Blog Post

Perceiving Nonverbal Cues

For an interesting application of perception research and theory, see "Perceiving Nonverbal Cues" at tcbdevito.blogspot.com. In what other fields would a knowledge of nonverbal behavior prove useful?

ANALYZE YOUR IMPRESSIONS Subject your perceptions to logical analysis and to critical thinking. Here are three suggestions:

- *Recognize your own role in perception.* Your emotional and physiological state will influence the meaning you give to your perceptions. A movie may seem hysterically funny when you're in a good mood but just plain stupid when you're in a bad mood. Understand your own biases; for example, do you tend to perceive only the positive in people you like and only the negative in people you don't like?
- *Avoid early conclusions.* On the basis of your observations of behaviors, formulate hypotheses to test against additional information and evidence; avoid drawing conclusions that you then look to confirm. Look for a variety of cues pointing in the same direction. The more cues point to the same conclusion, the more likely your conclusion will be correct. Be especially alert to contradictory cues that seem to refute your initial hypotheses. At the same time, seek validation from others. Do others see things in the same way you do? If not, ask yourself if your perceptions may be distorted in some way.
- *Beware the just world hypothesis.* Many people believe that the world is just: Good things happen to good people, and bad things happen to bad people (Aronson et al., Wilson, & Akert, 2013; Hunt, 2000). Put differently, you get what you deserve! Even when you mindfully dismiss this assumption, you may use it mindlessly when perceiving and evaluating other people. Consider a particularly vivid example: If a woman is raped in certain cultures (for example, in Bangladesh, Iran, or Yemen), she is considered by many in that culture (certainly not all) to have disgraced her family and to be deserving of severe punishment—in many cases, even death. And although you may claim that this is unfair (and it surely is), much research shows that even in the United States, many people do blame the victim for being raped, especially if the victim is male (Adams-Price, Dalton, & Sumrall, 2004; Andersen, 2004). The belief that the world is just creates perceptual distortions by leading you to overemphasize the influence of internal factors (this happened because this person is good or bad) and to deemphasize the influence of situational factors (the external circumstances) in your attempts to explain the behaviors of other people or even your own behaviors.

Explore the **Exercise** "Louder Than Words" at **MyCommunicationLab**

REDUCE YOUR UNCERTAINTY In every interpersonal situation, there is some degree of uncertainty. A variety of strategies can help reduce uncertainty (Berger & Bradac, 1982; Brashers, 2007; Gudykunst, 1994).

- Observing another person while he or she is engaged in an active task, preferably interacting with others in an informal social situation, will often reveal a great deal about the person, as people are less apt to monitor their behaviors and more likely to reveal their true selves in informal situations. When you log on to an Internet chat group and lurk, reading

VIEWPOINTS Impression formation

What one suggestion for increasing accuracy in impression formation do you wish others would follow more often when they make judgments about you?

INTERPERSONAL CHOICE POINT

Relationship Uncertainty

You've been dating someone casually over the past six months and want to take the relationship to the next level. But you first want to find out if your partner feels the same way. What are some of the things you can do to reduce this relationship uncertainty?

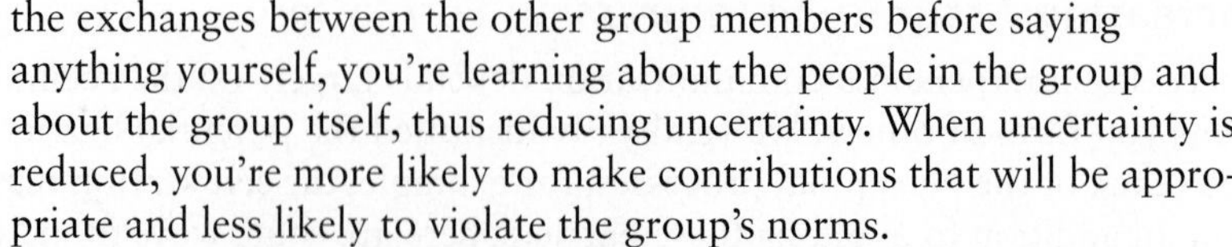

the exchanges between the other group members before saying anything yourself, you're learning about the people in the group and about the group itself, thus reducing uncertainty. When uncertainty is reduced, you're more likely to make contributions that will be appropriate and less likely to violate the group's norms.

- You can sometimes manipulate situations so as to observe the person in more specific and revealing contexts. Employment interviews, theatrical auditions, and student teaching are good examples of situations arranged to get an accurate view of the person in action.

- Learn about a person through asking others. You might inquire of a colleague if a third person finds you interesting and might like to have dinner with you.
- Interact with the individual. For example, you can ask questions: "Do you enjoy sports?" "What did you think of that computer science course?" "What would you do if you got fired?"

Explore the **Exercise** "How Might You Perceive Other's Perceptions" at **MyCommunicationLab**

CHECK YOUR PERCEPTIONS **Perception checking** is another way to help you further reduce your uncertainty and to make your perceptions more accurate. The goal of perception checking is to further explore the thoughts and feelings of the other person, not to prove that your initial perception is correct. In its most basic form, perception checking consists of two steps:

- Describe what you see or hear or, better, what you *think* is happening. Try to do this as descriptively (not evaluatively) as you can. Sometimes you may wish to offer several possibilities: *You've called me from work a lot this week. You seem concerned that everything is all right at home* or *You've not wanted to talk with me all week. You say that my work is fine, but you don't seem to want to give me the same responsibilities that other editorial assistants have.*
- Seek confirmation: Ask the other person if your description is accurate. Don't try to read the thoughts and feelings of another person just from observing his or her behaviors. Regardless of how many behaviors you observe and how carefully you examine them, you can only guess what is going on in someone's mind. So be careful that your request for confirmation does not sound as though you already know the answer. Avoid phrasing your questions defensively, as in, "You really don't want to go out, do you? I knew you didn't when you turned on that lousy television." Instead, ask for confirmation in as supportive a way as possible: *Would you rather watch TV?* or *Are you worried about me or the kids?* or *Are you displeased with my work? Is there anything I can do to improve my job performance?*

INCREASE YOUR CULTURAL SENSITIVITY Becoming aware of and being sensitive to cultural differences will help increase your accuracy in perception. For example, Russian or Chinese artists such as ballet dancers will often applaud their audience by clapping. Americans seeing this may easily interpret this as egotistical. Similarly, a German man will enter a restaurant before the woman in order to see if the place is respectable enough for the woman to enter. This simple custom can easily be interpreted as rude when viewed by people from cultures in which it's considered courteous for the woman to enter first (Axtell, 1994, 2007).

Cultural awareness will help you exercise caution in decoding the nonverbal behaviors of others, especially important perhaps in deciphering facial expressions. For example, it's easier to interpret the facial expressions of members of your own culture than those of members of other cultures (Weathers, Frank, & Spell, 2002). This "in-group advantage" will assist your perceptional accuracy for members of your own culture but will often hinder your accuracy for members of other cultures, especially if you assume that all people express themselves similarly (Elfenbein & Ambady, 2002).

The suggestions for improving intercultural communication offered in Chapter 2 (pp. 41–50) are applicable to increasing your cultural sensitivity in perception. For

SKILL BUILDING EXERCISE

Explaining Your Perceptions

Complete the following table by providing a description of how you perceive the incident and how you'd go about seeking confirmation. If you have several possible explanations for the incident, describe each of these in the second column. In the third column, indicate the choices you have for seeking clarification of your initial impressions—what are your choices for asking for clarification?

Incident	Your Perceptions and Possible Interpretations or Meanings	Choices for Seeking Clarification
You've extended an invitation to a classmate to be a Facebook friend but have heard nothing back.		
Your manager at work seems to spend a lot of time with your peers but very little time with you. You're concerned about the impression you're making.		
The person you've been dating for the past several months has stopped calling for a date. The messages have become fewer and less personal.		

example, educate yourself, reduce uncertainty, recognize differences (between yourself and people from other cultures, among members of other cultures, and between your meanings and the meanings that people from other cultures might have), confront your stereotypes, and adjust your communication.

Can you define the factors that influence interpersonal perception (self-fulfilling prophecy, personality theory, perceptual accentuation, primacy–recency, consistency, and the attribution of control)? Can you apply the skills for increasing your accuracy in impression formation?

IMPRESSION MANAGEMENT: GOALS AND STRATEGIES

Explore the **Exercise** "Perceiving My Selves" at **MyCommunicationLab**

Impression management (some writers use the term "self-presentation" or "identity management") refers to the processes you go through to create the impression you want the other person to have of you.

Impression management is largely the result of the messages you communicate. In the same way that you form impressions of others largely on the basis of how they communicate (verbally and nonverbally), you also communicate an impression of yourself through what you say (your verbal messages) and how you act and dress as well as how you decorate your office or apartment (your nonverbal messages). Communication messages, however, are not the only means for impression formation and management. For example, you also communicate your self-image and judge others by the people with whom they associate, the number of friends they have on their social media site; their Twitter score; their financial status; or their race or gender. Or you might rely on what others have said or posted about the person and form impressions that are consistent with these comments.

Part of the art of interpersonal communication is to be able to manage the impressions you give to others. Mastering the art of impression management will enable you to present yourself as you want others to see you, at least to some extent.

The strategies you use to achieve this desired impression will naturally depend on your specific goal. Here are seven major interpersonal communication goals and their corresponding strategies.

To Be Liked: Affinity-Seeking and Politeness Strategies

If you want to be liked—say you're new at school or on the job and you want to be well liked, included in the activities of other students or work associates, and thought of highly by these other people—you'd likely use affinity-seeking strategies and politeness strategies.

VIDEO CHOICE POINT

Mike Tries to Get a Date

Mike would like to ask Chloe, a classmate from his biology class, out on a date so that he can get to know her better. Mike is not always successful when asking girls for a date, so he's a bit apprehensive. Mike is an average guy who is pleasant and reasonably good-looking, but he often gets rejected and isn't sure why. "Mike Tries to Get a Date" looks at how Mike's own self-expectations and impression management skills affect the outcome of this interaction. See how various strategies for how to approach Chloe work out for Mike in the video "Mike Tries to Get a Date." Respond to the questions posed.

 **Watch** the **Video** "Mike Tries to Get a Date" at **MyCommunicationLab**

Affinity-Seeking Strategies As you can see from examining the list of affinity-seeking strategies that follows, their use is likely to increase your chances of being liked (Bell & Daly, 1984). Such strategies are especially important in initial interactions, and their use has even been found to increase student motivation when used by teachers (Martin & Rubin, 1994; Myers & Zhong, 2004; Wrench, McCroskey, & Richmond, 2008).

- Be of help to Other (the other person).
- Present yourself as comfortable and relaxed when with Other.
- Follow the cultural rules for polite, cooperative conversation with Other.
- Appear active, enthusiastic, and dynamic.
- Stimulate and encourage Other to talk about himself or herself; reinforce disclosures and contributions of Other.
- Include Other in your social activities and groupings.
- Listen to Other attentively and actively.
- Communicate interest in Other.
- Appear optimistic and positive rather than pessimistic and negative.
- Show respect for Other, and help Other to feel positively about himself or herself.
- Communicate warmth and empathy to Other.
- Demonstrate that you share significant attitudes and values with Other.
- Communicate supportiveness in Other's interpersonal interactions.

Although this research was conducted before much of social media, you can easily see how the same strategies could be used in online communication. For example, you can post photos to show that you're active and enthusiastic; you can follow the rules for polite interaction by giving "likes" and "+1s" to others; and you can communicate interest in the other person by inviting him or her to hang out or join a group, by commenting on a post, or by retweeting. Not surprisingly, plain old flattery goes a long way toward making you liked. Flattery has been found to increase your chances for success in a job interview, increase the tip a customer is likely to leave, and even increase the credibility you're likely to be seen as having (Sieter, 2007; Varma, Toh, & Pichler, 2006; Vonk, 2002).

There is also, however, a negative effect that can result from the use of affinity-seeking strategies—as there is for all of these impression-management strategies. Using affinity-seeking strategies too often or in ways that appear insincere may lead people to see you as trying to ingratiate yourself for your own advantage and not really meaning "to be nice."

INTERPERSONAL CHOICE POINT

Face to Face

You've been communicating with Pat over the Internet for the past seven months, and you finally have decided to meet for coffee. You really want Pat to like you. What are some impression-management strategies you might use to get Pat to like you? What messages would you be sure not to communicate?

POLITENESS STRATEGIES We can view politeness strategies, which are often used to make ourselves appear likeable, in terms of negative and positive types (Brown & Levinson, 1987; Goffman, 1967; Goldsmith, 2007; Holmes 1995). Both of these types of politeness are responsive to two needs that we each have:

- **positive face**—the desire to be viewed positively by others, to be thought of favorably
- **negative face**—the desire to be autonomous, to have the right to do as we wish

Politeness in interpersonal communication, then, refers to behavior that allows others to maintain both positive and negative face and impoliteness refers to behaviors that attack either positive face (for example, you criticize someone) or negative face (for example, you make demands on someone).

To help another person maintain *positive face,* you speak respectfully to and about the person, you give the person your full attention, and you say "excuse me" when appropriate. In short, you treat the person as you would want to be treated. In this way, you allow the person to maintain positive face through what is called *positive politeness.* You *attack* the person's positive face when you speak disrespectfully about the person, ignore the person or the person's comments, and fail to use the appropriate expressions of politeness such as *thank you* and *please.*

Blog Post

Politeness Functions

For a discussion of the functions of politeness, see "The Communication Functions of Politeness" at tcbdevito.blogspot.com. What function do you think is most important? Are there other functions that should be added here?

ETHICAL MESSAGES

The Ethics of Impression Management

Impression management strategies may also be used unethically and for less-than-noble purposes. As you read these several examples, ask yourself at what point impression management strategies become unethical:

- People who use affinity-seeking strategies to get you to like them so that they can extract favors from you.
- People who present themselves as credible (as being competent, moral, and charismatic) when in fact they are not.
- People who use self-handicapping strategies to get you to see their behavior from a perspective that benefits them rather than you.
- People who use self-deprecating strategies to get someone to do what they should be doing.
- People who use self-monitoring strategies to present a more polished image than one that might come out without this self-monitoring.
- People who use influence strategies to deceive and for self-gain.
- People who use image-confirming strategies to exaggerate their positive and minimize their negative qualities.

Ethical Choice Point

You're ready to join one (perhaps several) of the online dating services. You need to write your profile and are wondering if everyone (or nearly everyone) exaggerates, shouldn't you also? Specifically, you're considering saying that you earn a very good salary (actually, it's not so great, but you're hoping for a promotion), are twenty pounds lighter (actually, you intend to lose weight), and own a condo (actually, that's a goal once you get the promotion and save a down payment). If you don't exaggerate, you reason, you'll disadvantage yourself and not meet the people you want to meet. Also, you figure that people expect you to exaggerate and assume that you're probably a lot less ideal than your profile would indicate. Would this be ethical?

INTERPERSONAL CHOICE POINT

Like and Unlike

Social media sites generally emphasize positiveness and so there is a "like" on Facebook and a "+1" on Google+ but there is no "unlike" and no "-1", though there is a "thumbs up" and a "thumbs down" on StumbleUpon and there is a "+1" and a "-1" on Reddit. What are some other things you might do to signal online positiveness? How might you signal negative reactions?

To help another person maintain *negative face,* you respect the person's right to be autonomous and so you request rather than demand that he or she do something; you say, "Would you mind opening a window?" rather than "Open that window, damn it!" You might also give the person an "out" when making a request, allowing the person to reject your request if that is what the person wants. And so you say, "If this is a bad time, please tell me, but I'm really strapped and could use a loan of $100" rather than "Loan me $100" or "You have to lend me $100." If you want a recommendation, you might say, "Would it be possible for you to write me a recommendation for graduate school?" rather than "You have to write me a recommendation for graduate school." In this way, you enable the person to maintain negative face through what is called *negative politeness.*

Explore the **Exercise** "Perspective Taking" at **MyCommunicationLab**

Of course, we do this almost automatically, and asking for a favor without any consideration for the person's negative face needs would seem totally insensitive. In most situations, however, this type of attack on negative face often appears in more subtle forms. For example, your mother saying "Are you going to wear that?"—to use Deborah Tannen's (2006) example—attacks negative face by criticizing or challenging your autonomy. This comment also attacks positive face by questioning your ability to dress properly.

As with all the strategies discussed here, politeness too may have negative consequences. Overpoliteness, for example, is likely to be seen as phony and is likely to be resented. Overpoliteness will also be resented if it's seen as a persuasive strategy.

Blog Post

Politeness

For politeness as it relates to customer-server relationships, see "Drugstore Politeness" at tcbdevito.blogspot.com. How do you view politeness between customer and server?

To Be Believed: Credibility Strategies

If you were a politician and wanted people to vote for you, at least part of your strategy would involve attempts to establish your **credibility** (which consists of your competence, your character, and your charisma). For example, to establish your competence, you might mention your great educational background or the courses you took that qualify you as an expert. Or you can post a photo with a Harvard diploma on the wall. To establish that you're of good character, you might mention how fair and honest you are, the causes you support, or your concern for those less fortunate. And to establish your charisma—your take-charge, positive personality—you might demonstrate enthusiasm in your face-to-face interactions as well as in your posts and in your photos, be emphatic, or focus on the positive while minimizing the negative.

Of course, if you stress your competence, character, and charisma too much, you risk being seen as someone who is afraid of being seen as lacking these very qualities that you seem too eager to present to others. Generally, people who are truly competent need to say little directly about their own competence; their knowledgeable, insightful, and appropriate messages will reveal their competence.

To Excuse Failure: Self-Handicapping Strategies

If you were about to tackle a difficult task and were concerned that you might fail, you might use what are called **self-handicapping strategies.** In the more extreme form of this strategy, you actually set up barriers or obstacles to make the task impossible, so when you fail, you won't be blamed or thought ineffective—after all, you can tell yourself, the task was impossible. Let's say you aren't prepared for your history exam and you feel you're going to fail. With this self-handicapping strategy, you might go out and party the night before so that when you do poorly on the exam, you can blame it on the all-night party rather than on your intelligence or knowledge. In the less extreme form, you manufacture excuses for failure and have them ready if you do fail. "The exam was unfair" is one such popular excuse, but you might blame a long period without a date on your being too intelligent or too shy or too poor or blame a poorly cooked dinner on your defective stove.

On the negative side, using self-handicapping strategies too often may lead people to see you as incompetent or foolish—after all, partying the night before an exam for which you are already unprepared doesn't make a whole lot of sense and can easily reflect on your overall competence.

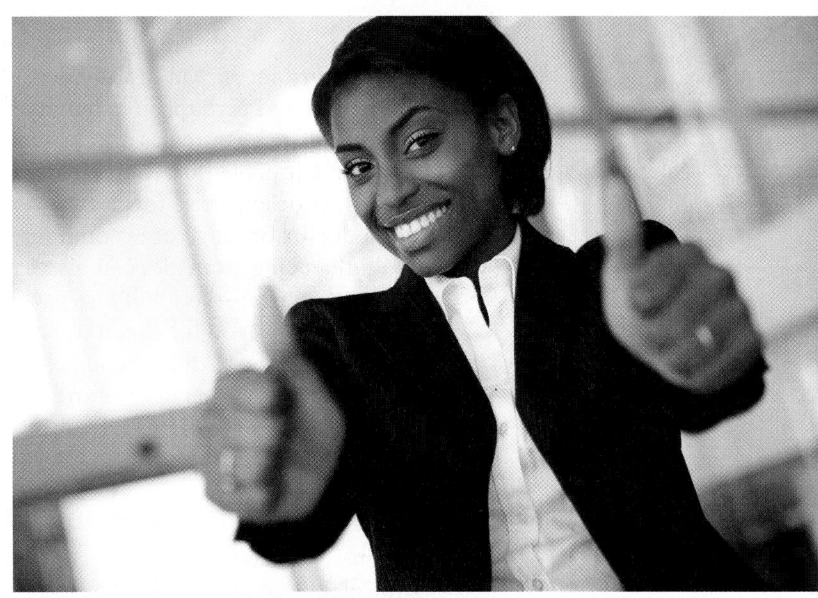

VIEWPOINTS Impression management
Take a good look at yourself, and consider the strategies of impression management you used (or were used by others) during the past week. Did they work?

To Secure Help: Self-Deprecating Strategies

If you want to be taken care of and protected or simply want someone to come to your aid, you might use **self-deprecating strategies**. Confessions of incompetence and inability often bring assistance from others. And so you might say, "I just can't fix that drain and it drives me crazy; I just don't know anything about plumbing" with the hope that the other person will offer help.

But be careful: Your self-deprecating strategies may convince people that you are in fact just as incompetent as you say you are. Or people may see you as someone who doesn't want to do anything yourself and so feigns incompetence to get others to do it for you. This is not likely to get you help in the long run.

To Hide Faults: Self-Monitoring Strategies

Much impression management is devoted not merely to presenting a positive image but to suppressing the negative, or **self-monitoring strategies**. Here you carefully monitor (self-censor) what you say or do. You avoid your normal slang so as to make your colleagues think more highly of you; you avoid chewing gum so you don't look juvenile or unprofessional; you avoid posting the photos from the last party. While you readily disclose favorable parts of your experience, you actively hide the unfavorable parts.

However, if you self-monitor too often or too obviously, you risk being seen as someone unwilling to reveal himself or herself and perhaps not trusting of the others to feel comfortable disclosing your weaknesses as well as your strengths. In more extreme cases, you may be seen as dishonest, as hiding your true self, or as trying to fool other people.

SKILL BUILDING EXERCISE

Applying Impression Management Strategies

Here are a few interpersonal situations in which you might want to use impression-management strategies. Identify at least two impression-management strategies you could use to achieve your goals in each of these situations.

1. You're interviewing for a job; you want to be seen as credible and as a good team player.
2. Your term paper is not up to par; you don't want your instructor to think this is the level at which you normally function.
3. You want to ask a former instructor to be a friend on a social network site.
4. You've just started at a new school and you want to be careful not to make a fool of yourself—as you had at your previous school.
5. You're a police officer assigned to a neighborhood patrol; you want to be seen as firm but approachable.

Everyone uses impression-management strategies; using them effectively and ethically is not always easy but almost always an available choice.

To Be Followed: Influencing Strategies

In many instances, you'll want to get people to see you as a leader, as one to be followed in thought and perhaps in behavior. Here you can use a variety of **influencing strategies.** One set of such strategies are those normally grouped under power and identified in Chapter 1 (pp. 00–00). And so, for example, you'd stress your knowledge (information power), your expertise (expert power), your right to lead by virtue of your position as, say, a doctor or judge or accountant (legitimate power).

Influencing strategies can also easily backfire. If your influence attempts fail—for whatever reason—you will lose general influence. That is, if you try to influence someone but it fails, you'll be seen to have less power now than before you tried this failed influence attempt. And, of course, if you're seen as someone who is influencing others for self-gain, your persuasive attempts are likely to be rejected and perhaps seen as self-serving and resented.

To Confirm Self-Image: Image-Confirming Strategies

At times, you communicate to confirm your self-image, and so you'll use **image-confirming strategies.** If you see yourself as the life of the party, you'll tell jokes, post photos in which you are in fact the life of the party, and try to amuse people. At the same time that you confirm your own self-image, you also let others know that this is who you are, this is how you want to be seen. And, while you reveal aspects of yourself that confirm your desired image, you actively suppress revealing aspects of yourself that would disconfirm this image. Unfavorable wall postings, for example, are quickly removed.

If you use image-confirming strategies too frequently, you risk being seen as "too perfect to be for real." If you try to project this all-positive image, it's likely to turn people off—people want to see their friends and associates as having some faults, some imperfections. Also, image-confirming strategies invariably involve your talking about yourself, and with that comes the risk of being seen as self-absorbed.

A knowledge of these impression-management strategies and the ways in which they are effective and ineffective will give you a greater number of choices for achieving such widely diverse goals as being liked, being believed, excusing failure, securing help, hiding faults, being followed, and confirming your self-image.

Can you explain and give examples of the strategies of impression management for being liked, being believed, excusing failure, securing help, hiding faults, influencing others, and confirming your image? Can you apply the skills for effective (and ethical) impression management?

MESSAGES IN THE MEDIA: WRAP UP

Crime shows provide numerous and excellent examples where one person perceives something that others do not and, in effect, solves the crime. Identifying the clues and cues used in such shows can help you see the principles of perception in action and increase your own perceptual accuracy.

SUMMARY OF CONCEPTS AND SKILLS

Listen to the **Audio Chapter Summary** at **MyCommunicationLab**

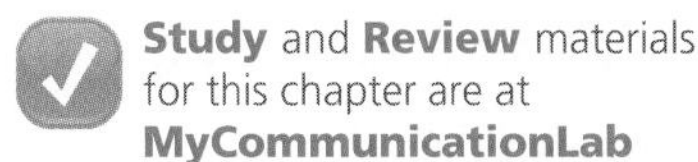
Study and **Review** materials for this chapter are at **MyCommunicationLab**

This chapter looked at the self and perception in interpersonal communication.

The Self in Interpersonal Communication

1. Self-concept is the image you have of who you are. Sources of self-concept include others' images of you, social comparisons, cultural teachings, and your own interpretations and evaluations.
2. Self-awareness is your knowledge of yourself, the extent to which you know who you are. A useful way of looking at self-awareness is with the Johari window, which consists of four parts. The open self holds information known to self and others; the blind self holds information known only to others; the hidden self holds information known only to self; and the unknown self holds information known to neither self nor others.
3. Self-esteem is the value you place on yourself, your perceived self-worth.

Perception in Interpersonal Communication

4. Perception is the process by which you become aware of objects and events in the external world.
5. Perception occurs in five stages: (1) stimulation, (2) organization, (3) interpretation–evaluation, (4) memory, and (5) recall.

Impression Formation

6. Six important processes influence the way you form impressions: self-fulfilling prophecies may influence the behaviors of others; personality theory allows you to conclude that certain characteristics go with certain other characteristics; primacy–recency may influence you to give extra importance to what occurs first (a primacy effect) or to what occurs last (a recency effect); the tendency to seek and expect consistency may influence you to see what is consistent and not to see what is inconsistent; and attributions of control, the process through which you try to understand the behaviors of others, are made in part on the basis of your judgment of controllability.

Impression Management: Goals and Strategies

7. Among the goals and strategies of impression management are to be liked (affinity-seeking and politeness strategies); to be believed (credibility strategies that establish your competence, character, and charisma); to excuse failure (self-handicapping strategies); to secure help (self-deprecating strategies); to hide faults (self-monitoring strategies); to be followed (influencing strategies); and to confirm one's self-image (image-confirming strategies).
8. Each of these impression-management strategies can backfire and give others negative impressions. And each of these strategies may be used to reveal your true self or to present a false self and deceive others in the process.

This chapter also considered some useful skills. As you review these skills, check those you wish to work on.

____ 1. *Self-awareness.* To increase self-awareness, ask yourself about yourself, listen to others, actively seek information about yourself, see your different selves, and increase your open self.

____ 2. *Self-esteem.* To increase self-esteem, try attacking your self-destructive beliefs, seeking affirmation, seeking out nourishing people, and working on projects that will result in success. Most importantly, develop interpersonal competence.

____ 3. *Selective perception.* Recognize the influence that your own selective attention and selective exposure have on your perceptual accuracy.

____ 4. *Impression formation.* In forming impressions, take into consideration the possible influence of your own self-fulfilling prophecies, personality theories, tendencies to favor primacy or recency, expectations of consistency, and the attribution errors (self-serving bias, overattribution, and the fundamental attribution error) and adjust your perceptions accordingly.

____ 5. *Perceptual accuracy.* In increasing your accuracy in impression formation: Analyze your impressions (recognize your role in perception, avoid early conclusions, and beware of the just world assumptions), reduce uncertainty, check your perceptions, and become culturally sensitive by recognizing the differences between you and others and also the differences among people from other cultures.

____ 6. *Impression management.* Use the strategies of impression management ethically and with a clear understanding of their potential to backfire.

VOCABULARY QUIZ: The Language of the Self and Perception

Match the terms listed here with their definitions. Record the number of the definition next to the appropriate term.

____ open self (57)
____ self-esteem (59)
____ the hidden self (57)
____ self-monitoring strategies (75)
____ affinity-seeking strategies (72)
____ perception checking (70)
____ just world hypothesis (69)
____ the fundamental attribution error (68)
____ halo effect (66)
____ impression management (71)

1. Overvaluing internal factors and undervaluing external factors in impression formation.
2. Techniques designed to hide certain information from others.
3. The belief that good things happen to good people≈and bad things to bad people.
4. A process of gaining confirmation for your impressions.
5. The value you place on yourself.
6. That part of you that you and others know about yourself.
7. Seeing good things in people we have already evaluated positively.
8. Techniques to make you appear more likeable
9. The processes by which one controls his or her desired impression.
10. That part of yourself that you normally do not reveal to others.

These ten terms and additional terms used in this chapter can be found in the glossary.

Study and **Review** the **Flashcards** at **MyCommunicationLab**

MyCommunicationLab

Visit MyCommunicationLab for a wealth of additional information on the self and perception. Flashcards, videos, skill building exercises, sample test questions, and additional exercises, examples, and discussions will help you continue your study of the role of the self and perception in interpersonal communication and the skills of impression formation and management.

CHAPTER

4

Listening in Interpersonal Communication

MESSAGES IN THE MEDIA

Television talk shows will generally demonstrate the principles of effective listening, and when they do, they're enjoyable to watch. When ineffective listening is used—and everyone speaks at the same time, for example—the shows become boring. The same is true outside the television studio. This chapter discusses listening and the principles for making your own listening more effective and more productive.

OBJECTIVES *After reading this chapter, you should be able to:*

1. Define *listening* and its five stages, and use the suggestions to increase your own listening accuracy at each stage.
2. Describe the four major barriers to effective listening, and apply the suggestions for effectiveness in your own listening.
3. Identify the five styles of listening, and select and use the appropriate style for the specific situation.
4. Explain the major cultural and gender differences found in listening, and assess their influence on interpersonal communication/listening.

In light of Facebook, Twitter, wikis, blogs, and other social media, we need to expand the traditional definition of listening as the receiving and processing of auditory signals. If posting messages on social media sites is part of interpersonal communication (which it surely is), then reading and responding to these messages must also be part of communication and most logically a part of listening. **Listening**, then, may be defined as *the process of receiving, understanding, remembering, evaluating, and responding to verbal and/or nonverbal messages.*

Regardless of what you do, listening will prove a crucial communication component and will serve both task functions (or work-related activities) and relationship functions (establishing and maintaining relationships). Whether a temporary intern or a high-level executive, you need to listen if you're going to function effectively in today's workplace. If you're not convinced of this, take a look at the many websites that talk about the skills needed for success in today's workplace (the websites of Career.com, Buzzle, and the Department of Labor are especially revealing).

Listening also is crucial to developing and maintaining relationships of all kinds. You expect a friend or a romantic partner to listen to you, and you're expected to listen to them in turn. Listening also plays a significant role in the management of interpersonal conflict; listening effectively to the other person, even during a heated argument, will go a long way toward helping you manage the conflict and preventing it from escalating into a major blowup.

Here we look at the stages of the listening process, the major barriers to listening effectiveness, the varied styles of listening for different situations, and some cultural and gender differences in listening.

THE STAGES OF LISTENING

Listening is a five-stage process of (1) receiving, (2) understanding, (3) remembering, (4) evaluating, and (5) responding to verbal and/or nonverbal messages, as represented in Figure 4.1. As you'll see from the following discussion, listening involves a collection

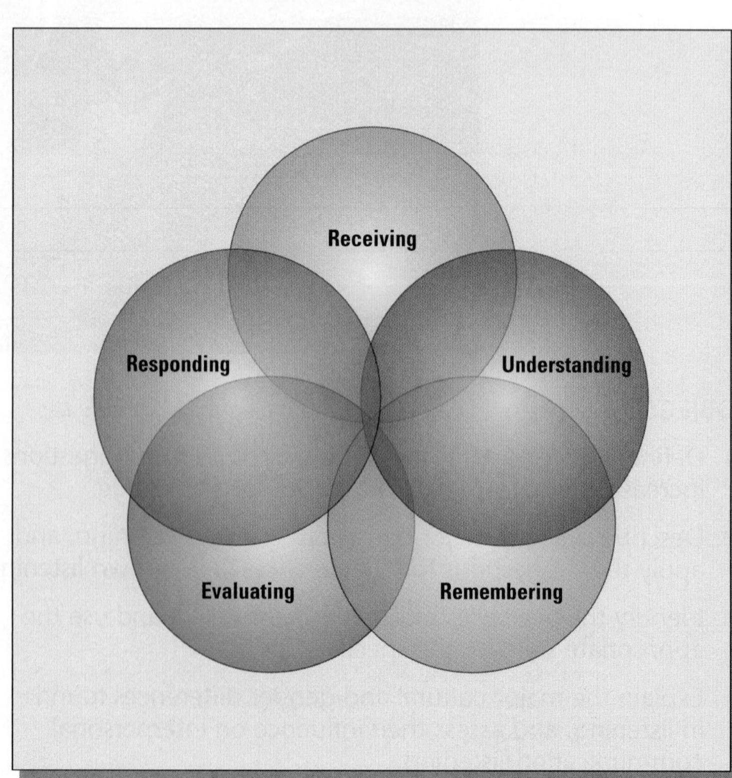

FIGURE 4.1
The Five Stages of Listening
Both this model and the suggestions for listening improvement throughout this chapter draw on theories and models that listening researchers have developed (for example, Barker & Gaut, 2002; Brownell, 2010; Nichols & Stevens, 1957; Nichols, 1995; Steil, Barker, & Watson, 1983).

of skills that work together at each of these five stages. Listening can go wrong at any stage; by the same token, you can enhance your listening ability by strengthening the skills needed for each step of the process.

All five stages overlap. When you listen, you're performing all five processes at essentially the same time. For example, when listening in conversation, you're not only processing what you hear for understanding, but you're also putting it into memory storage, critically evaluating what was said, and responding (nonverbally and perhaps with verbal messages as well).

VIEWPOINTS Hedging

Research shows that hedging reflects negatively on both male and female speakers when it indicates a lack of certainty or conviction resulting from some inadequacy on the speaker's part (Pearson, West, & Turner, 1995). The hedging will be more positively received, however, if listeners feel it reflects the speaker's belief that tentative statements are the only kinds a person can reasonably make. What are some of the implications of this for effective workplace communication?

Receiving

Listening begins, but does not end, with receiving messages the speaker sends. In listening, you receive both the verbal and the nonverbal messages—not only the words but also the gestures, facial expressions, variations in volume and rate, accompanying photos, and lots more.

The following suggestions should help you receive messages more effectively:

- *focus attention* on the speaker's verbal and nonverbal messages, on both what is said and what is not said, rather than on how you'll respond.
- *maintain your role* as listener, and avoid interrupting the speaker until he or she is finished.
- *avoid assuming you understand* what the speaker is going to say before he or she actually says it.

In this brief discussion of receiving (and in this entire chapter on listening), the unstated assumption is that both individuals can receive auditory signals without difficulty. For the many people who have hearing impairments, however, listening presents a variety of problems. Table 4.1 (page 82) provides tips for communication between people with and without hearing loss.

Blog Post

Disclaimers

For a brief discussion of disclaimers—statements that ask others to listen without prejudice—see "Disclaimers" at tcbdevito.blogspot.com. In what ways do you use disclaimers?

Understanding

Understanding occurs when you learn what the speaker means or when the meaning you get is essentially the same as what the speaker sent. Understanding includes both the thoughts that are expressed and the emotional tone that accompanies them, for example, the urgency or the joy or the sorrow expressed in the message.

Right now, a large part of your listening will take place in the classroom—listening to the instructor and to other students, essentially for understanding. (See Table 4.2, page 83.)

In understanding, try to:

- *see the speaker's messages from the speaker's point of view.* Avoid judging the message until you've fully understood it—as the speaker intended it.
- *rephrase/paraphrase* the speaker's ideas in your own words.
- *ask questions* to clarify or to secure additional details or examples if necessary.

TABLE 4.1

Interpersonal Communication Tips Between People with and without Hearing Difficulties

People with hearing loss differ greatly in their hearing ability: Some are totally deaf and can hear nothing, others have some hearing loss and can hear some sounds, and still others have impaired hearing but can hear most speech. Although people with profound hearing loss can speak, their speech may appear labored and may be less clear than the speech of those with unimpaired hearing. Here are some suggestions for more effective communication between people who hear well and those who have hearing problems.

If you have unimpaired hearing:

Generally	Specifically
Set up a comfortable context.	Reduce the distance between yourself and the person with a hearing impairment. Reduce background noise. Make sure the lighting is adequate.
Avoid interference.	Make sure the visual cues from your speech are clearly observable; face the person squarely and avoid smoking, chewing gum, or holding your hand over your mouth.
Speak at an adequate volume.	But avoid shouting, which can distort your speech and may insult the person. Be careful to avoid reducing volume at the ends of your sentences.
Phrase ideas in different ways.	Because some words are easier to lip-read than others, it often helps if you can rephrase your ideas in different words.
Avoid overlapping speech.	In group situations, only one person should speak at a time. Similarly, direct your comments to the person with hearing loss himself or herself; don't talk to the person through a third party.
Ask for additional information.	Ask the person if there is anything you can do to make it easier for him or her to understand you.
Don't avoid common terms.	Use terms like *hear, listen, music,* or *deaf* when they're relevant to the conversation. Trying to avoid these common terms will make your speech sound artificial.
Use nonverbal cues.	Nonverbals can help communicate your meaning; gestures indicating size or location and facial expressions indicating feelings are often helpful.

If you have impaired hearing:

Generally	Specifically
Do your best to eliminate background noise.	Reduce the distance between yourself and the person with a hearing impairment. Reduce background noise. Make sure the lighting is adequate.
Move closer to the speaker if this helps you hear better.	Alert the speaker that this closer distance will help you hear better.
Ask for adjustments.	If you feel the speaker can make adjustments, ask the speaker to repeat a message, to speak more slowly, or to increase volume.
Position yourself for best reception.	If you hear better in one ear than another, position yourself accordingly and, if necessary, clue the speaker in to this fact.
Ask for additional cues.	If necessary, ask the speaker to write down certain information, such as phone numbers or website addresses. Carrying a pad and pencil will prove helpful for this and in the event that you wish to write something down for others.

Sources: These suggestions were drawn from a variety of sources including the websites of the Rochester Institute of Technology, the National Technical Institute for the Deaf, and the United States Department of Labor.

TABLE 4.2

LISTENING IN THE CLASSROOM

In addition to following the general guidelines for listening noted throughout this chapter, here are a few additional suggestions for making your listening for understanding in the classroom more effective.

General Suggestions	Specifically
Prepare yourself to listen.	Sit up front where you can see your instructor and any visual aids clearly and comfortably. Remember that you listen with your eyes as well as your ears.
Avoid distractions.	Avoid mental daydreaming, and put away physical distractions like your laptop, smartphone, or newspaper.
Pay special attention to the introduction.	Listen for orienting remarks and for key words and phrases such as "major reasons," "three main causes," and "first." These cues will help you outline the lecture.
Take notes in outline form.	Listen for headings, and then use these as major topics in your outline. When the instructor says, "There are four kinds of noise," you have your heading and can record a numbered list of four kinds of noise.
Assume relevance.	A piece of information may eventually prove irrelevant (unfortunately), but if you listen with the assumption of irrelevancy, you'll never hear anything relevant.
Listen for understanding.	Avoid taking issue with what is said until you understand fully and then, of course, take issue if you wish. But, generally, don't waste listening time rehearsing your responses; you risk missing additional explanation or qualification.

Remembering

Effective listening depends on **remembering**. For example, when Susan says she is planning to buy a new car, the effective listener remembers this and at a later meeting asks about the car. When Joe says his mother is ill, the effective listener remembers this and inquires about her health later in the week.

In some small group and public speaking situations, you can augment your memory by taking notes or by taping the messages. And in many work situations, taking notes is common and may even be expected. In most interpersonal communication situations, however, note taking is inappropriate—although you often do write down a telephone number, an appointment, or directions.

Perhaps the most important point to understand about memory is that what you remember is not what was said but what you remember was said. Memory for speech is not reproductive; you don't simply reproduce in your memory what the speaker said. Rather, memory is reconstructive; you actually reconstruct the messages you hear into a system that makes sense to you.

If you want to remember what someone says or the names of various people, this information needs to pass from your **short-term memory** (the memory you use, say, to remember a phone number just long enough to write it down) into long-term memory. Short-term memory is very limited in capacity—you can hold only a small amount of information there. **Long-term memory** is unlimited. To facilitate the passage of information from short- to long-term memory, here are FOUR suggestions:

- *Focus* your attention on the central ideas. Even in the most casual conversation, there are central ideas. Fix these in your mind. Avoid focusing on minor details that often lead to detours in listening and in conversation.

- *Organize* what you hear; summarize the message in a more easily retained form. Chunk the message into categories; for example, if you want to remember 15 or 20 items to buy in the supermarket, you'll remember more if you group them into chunks—say, produce, canned goods, and meats.
- *Unite* the new with the old; relate new information to what you already know. Avoid treating new information as totally apart from all else you know. There's probably some relationship, and if you identify it, you're more likely to remember the new material.
- *Repeat* names and key concepts to yourself or, if appropriate, aloud. By repeating the names or key concepts, you rehearse them and, as a result, learn and remember them. If you're introduced to Alice, you'll stand a better chance of remembering her name if you say, "Hi, Alice" than if you say just "Hi."

Evaluating

Evaluating consists of judging messages in some way. At times you may try to evaluate the speaker's underlying intent, often without conscious awareness. For example, Elaine tells you that she is up for a promotion and is really excited about it. You may then try to judge her intention. Does she want you to use your influence with the company president? Is she preoccupied with her accomplishment and thus telling everyone about it? Is she looking for a pat on the back? Generally, if you know the person well, you'll be able to identify the intention and therefore be able to respond appropriately.

In evaluating:

- *resist evaluation* until you fully understand the speaker's point of view.
- *assume that the speaker is a person of goodwill.* Give the speaker the benefit of any doubt by asking for clarification on issues that you feel you must object to.
- *distinguish facts from opinions* and personal interpretations as well as identify any biases, self-interests, or prejudices that may lead the speaker to slant unfairly what is presented.

Blog Post

E-mail Responding

Take a look at "E-mail Responding" at tcbdevito.blogspot.com for a list of reasons people may not respond to an email—even though you expect one.

Responding

Responding occurs in two forms: (1) responses you make while the speaker is talking and (2) responses you make after the speaker has stopped talking. Responses made while the speaker is talking should be supportive and should acknowledge that you're listening. These responses are **backchanneling cues:** messages (words and gestures) that let the speaker know you're paying attention, as when you nod in agreement or say, "I see" or "Uh-huh."

Responses after the speaker has stopped talking are generally more elaborate and might include empathy ("I know how you must feel"); requests for clarification ("Do you mean this new health plan will replace the old plan, or will it only be a supplement?"); challenges ("I think your evidence is weak"); and/or agreement ("You're absolutely right, and I'll support your proposal when it comes up for a vote"). You can improve this responding phase of listening if you:

- *express support* and understanding for the speaker throughout the conversation.
- *use varied cues that say "I'm listening"* (for example, nodding, using appropriate facial expressions, or saying "I see").
- *own your own responses;* that is, state your thoughts and feelings as your own, using "I-messages"—for example, saying, "I don't agree" rather than "No one will agree with that."
- *avoid the common problem-causing listening responses* such as being static or overly expressive, giving feedback that is monotonous and not responsive to the messages, avoiding eye contact, or appearing preoccupied with, say, a cell phone.

Table 4.3 provides a comparison of effective and ineffective listening at each of these five stages.

INTERPERSONAL CHOICE POINT

Giving Anti-listening Cues

One of your friends is a storyteller; instead of talking about the world and about people, he tells endless stories—about things that happened a long time ago that he finds funny (though no one else does). You just can't deal with this any longer. What are some options you have for ending this kind of "conversation"?

TABLE 4.3

INEFFECTIVE AND EFFECTIVE LISTENING

Listening Stage	Ineffective Listening	Effective Listening
At the **receiving** stage, you note not only what is said (verbally and nonverbally) but also what is omitted.	Attention wanders, distractions are attended to	1. **Focus your attention** on the speaker's verbal and nonverbal messages. 2. **Avoid distractions** in the environment. 3. **Maintain your role as listener** and avoid interrupting.
Understanding is the stage at which you learn what the speaker means, the stage at which you grasp both the thoughts and the emotions expressed.	Assume you understand what the speaker is going to say; interpret the speaker's message from your own point of view; make no attempt to seek clarification	1. **Avoid assuming you understand** what the speaker is going to say before he or she actually says it. 2. **See the speaker's messages from the speaker's point of view.** 3. **Ask questions** for clarification. 4. **Rephrase (paraphrase)** the speaker's ideas in your own words.
Effective listening depends on **remembering**.	Fail to distinguish between central and peripheral ideas	1. **Focus** your attention on the central ideas. 2. **Organize** what you hear. 3. **Unite** the new with the old. 4. **Rehearse;** repeat names and key concepts to yourself or, if appropriate, aloud.
Evaluating consists of judging the messages in some way.	Evaluate immediately; group facts and opinions together; fail to notice biases; influenced by fallacious reasoning	1. **Resist evaluation** until you fully understand the speaker's point of view. 2. **Distinguish facts from opinions** and personal interpretations by the speaker. 3. **Identify any biases,** self-interests, or prejudices in the speaker. 4. **Recognize some of the popular but fallacious forms of "reasoning"** speakers may employ, such as **name-calling, testimonial, and bandwagon.**
Responding occurs in two phases: responses you make while the speaker is talking and responses you make after the speaker has stopped talking.	Fail to give the speaker appropriate feedback	1. **Support the speaker.** 2. **Own your responses.** 3. **Resist "responding to another's feelings" with "solving the person's problems."** 4. **Focus on the other person.** 5. **Avoid being a thought-completing listener.**

Can you define *listening* and its five stages (receiving, understanding, remembering, evaluating, and responding)? Can you apply the skills for more effective listening recommended for each of these stages?

Watch the **Video** "Fast Food" at **MyCommunicationLab**

Explore the **Exercise** "Reducing Barriers to Listening" at **MyCommunicationLab**

LISTENING BARRIERS

In addition to practicing the various skills for each stage of listening, consider some of the common general barriers to listening. Here are just four such barriers and some suggestions for dealing with them as both listener and speaker, as both speaker and listener are responsible for effective listening.

Blog Post

Teacher Bias

Do you notice bias in your instructors? See "Teacher Bias?" at tcbdevito.blogspot.com. How might this type of research help instructors and students alike?

Distractions: Physical and Mental

Physical barriers might include, for example, hearing impairment, a noisy environment, or loud music. Multitasking (say, watching TV, texting, and listening to someone) with the aim of being supportive simply doesn't work. As both listener and speaker, try to remove whatever physical barriers can be removed; for those that you can't remove, adjust your listening and speaking to lessen the effects as much as possible. As a listener, focus on the speaker; you can attend to the room and the other people later.

Mental distractions are in many ways similar to physical distractions; they get in the way of focused listening. These barriers are often seen when you're thinking about your upcoming Saturday night date or becoming too emotional to think (and listen) clearly. In listening, recognize that you can think about your date later. In speaking, make what you say compelling and relevant to the listener.

Biases and Prejudices

In biased and prejudiced listening, you hear what the speaker is saying through stereotypes. This type of listening occurs when you listen differently to a person because of his or her race, affectional orientation, age, or gender when these characteristics are irrelevant to the message.

Such listening can occur in a wide variety of situations. For example, when you dismiss a valid argument or attribute validity to an invalid argument because the speaker is of a particular race, affectional orientation, age, or gender, you're listening with prejudice.

However, there are many instances in which these characteristics are pertinent to your evaluation of the message. For example, the sex of a speaker talking about pregnancy, fathering a child, birth control, or surrogate motherhood probably is, most would agree, relevant to the message. So, in these cases it is not sexist listening to take the gender of the speaker into consideration. It is, however, sexist listening to assume that only one gender can be an authority on a particular topic or that one gender's opinions are without value. The same is true when listening through the filter of a person's race, affectional orientation, or age.

INTERPERSONAL CHOICE POINT

Ageist Language

At the organization where you work, ageist language is rampant in small groups but totally absent in formal meetings. You want to point out this hypocrisy but don't want to make enemies or have people think you're going to cause legal problems for them. What options do you have for accomplishing what you want but without incurring negative reactions?

Lack of Appropriate Focus

Focusing on what a person is saying is obviously necessary for effective listening. And yet there are many influences that can lead you astray. For example, listeners often get lost because they focus on irrelevancies, say, on an especially vivid example that conjures up old memories. Try not to get detoured from the main idea; don't get hung up on unimportant details. Try to repeat the idea to yourself and see the details in relation to this main concept. As a speaker, try to avoid language or examples that may divert attention away from your main idea.

At times people will listen only for information that has an obvious relevance to them. But this type of listening only prevents you from expanding your horizons. And it's quite possible that information that you originally thought irrelevant will eventually prove helpful.

"All these years, and you haven't listened to a damn thing I've said, have you?"

Charles Barsotti/The New Yorker Collection/www.cartoonbank.com

ETHICAL MESSAGES

Ethical Listening

As a listener, you have at least two ethical obligations (generally):

First, you generally owe the other person an honest hearing, without prejudgment, putting aside prejudices and preconceptions as best you can. At the same time, you owe the person your best effort at understanding emotionally as well as intellectually what he or she means. This does not mean, however, that there are not situations when you don't owe the speaker a fair hearing.

Second, you generally owe the other person honest responses. Just as you should be honest with the listener when speaking, you should be honest with the speaker when listening. This means giving open and honest feedback and also reflecting honestly on the questions that the speaker raises. Again, this does not mean that there are not situations in which you would not owe the speaker an honest response.

These obligations, as you might have guessed, will vary with the interpersonal relationship between yourself and the other person. If this "other person" is a life partner, then your obligations are considerable. If this "other person" is a stranger, your obligations are less. Generally, as the intimacy of a relationship increases, so do your obligations to serve as a supportive and honest listener.

Ethical Choice Point

Your partner of ten years has decided to come clean about a sordid past, essentially the ten years before you met. You really don't want to hear this (it just depresses you), but your partner insists on self-disclosing. What is your ethical obligation to both your partner and to yourself?

Avoid interpreting everything in terms of what it means to you; see other perspectives. As a speaker, be sure to make what you say relevant to your specific listener.

Another misplaced focus is often on the responses a listener is going to make while the speaker is still speaking. Anticipating how you're going to respond or what you're going to say (and even interrupting the speaker) just prevents you from hearing the message in full. Instead, make a mental note of something and then get back to listening. As a speaker, when you feel someone is preparing to argue with you, ask the person to hear you out—*I know you disagree with this, but let me finish and we'll get back to that.*

Premature Judgment

Perhaps the most obvious form of premature judgment is assuming you know what the speaker is going to say—and so there's no need to really listen. Let the speaker say what he or she is going to say before you decide that you already know it. As a speaker, of course, it's often wise to assume that listeners will do exactly this, so it may be helpful to make clear that what you're saying will be unexpected.

A common listener reaction is to draw conclusions or judgments on incomplete evidence. Sometimes listeners will stop listening after hearing, for example, an argument they disagree with or some sexist or culturally insensitive remark. Instead, this is a situation that calls for especially concentrated listening so that you don't rush to judgment. Instead, wait for the evidence or argument; avoid making judgments before you gather all the information. Listen first, judge second. As a speaker, be aware of this tendency, and when you feel this is happening, ask for a suspension of judgment. A simple *Hear me out* is often sufficient to prevent a listener's too early judgment.

VIEWPOINTS Listening barriers

The four barriers discussed here are certainly not the only ones that get in the way of effective listening. What other types of barriers can you identify? Put differently, in what types of interpersonal situations do you have difficulty listening?

SKILL BUILDING EXERCISE

Explaining the Barriers to Listening

Taking into consideration your own attitudes, beliefs, values, and opinions, what obstacles to listening would you identify for each of the following interpersonal situations?

1. Colleagues at work are discussing how they can persuade management to restrict the company gym to men only.
2. Students in your computer science class are talking about planting a virus in the college computer as a way of protesting recent decisions by the administration.
3. A campus religious group is conferring about its plan to prevent same-sex couples from attending the college prom.
4. A group of faculty and students is discussing a campaign to prevent the military from recruiting on campus.

No one can listen apart from his or her own attitudes, beliefs, values, and opinions; these always get in the way of accurate listening. Your objective should be to minimize these effects.

VIDEO CHOICE POINT

A Bad Day at Work

Sue's partner Harry is visibly upset, but she doesn't know why. Sue considers the elements of the listening process and the various barriers that can interfere with effective listening as she contemplates her communication choices. This video looks at how Sue's listening choices will affect the outcome of this interaction and potentially help Harry better cope with his issues. See how Sue's choices play out in the video "A Bad Day at Work," and respond to the questions posed.

 **Watch** the **Video** "A Bad Day at Work" at **MyCommunicationLab**

Can you describe the four major barriers to effective listening (physical and mental distractions, biases and prejudices, lack of appropriate focus, and premature judgment)? Can you apply the suggestions for effectiveness in your own listening?

Explore the **Concept** "Listening" at **MyCommunicationLab**

STYLES OF LISTENING EFFECTIVELY

Listening is situational (Brownell, 2010). As we've seen, the way you listen should depend on the situation you are in. You don't listen to a State of the Union address in the same way that you listen to Jay Leno's monologue or to a proposal for a date. At the least, you need to adjust your listening on the basis of (1) your purposes (are you listening to learn? to give comfort?) and (2) your knowledge of and relationship to the other person (does this person exaggerate or lie? or need support or perhaps a reality check?). The following discussion will provide specific suggestions for how to adjust your listening style and how you can avoid the pitfalls and barriers to ineffective listening. We'll look at five dimensions of listening: the empathic–objective, nonjudgmental–critical, surface–deep, polite–impolite, and active–inactive dimensions. Before doing so, take the following self-test.

Explore the **Exercise** "Listening with Empathy" at **MyCommunicationLab**

Empathic and Objective Listening

If you're going to understand what a person means and what a person is feeling, you need to listen with some degree of **empathy** (Rogers, 1970; Rogers & Farson, 1981). To **empathize** with others is to feel with them, to see the world as they see it, to feel what they feel.

TEST YOURSELF

How Do You Listen?

Respond to each statement using the following scale: **1** = always, **2** = frequently, **3** = sometimes, **4** = seldom, and **5** = never.

____ 1. I listen actively, communicate acceptance of the speaker, and prompt the speaker to further explore his or her thoughts.

____ 2. I listen to what the speaker is saying and feeling; I try to feel what the speaker feels.

____ 3. I listen without judging the speaker.

____ 4. I listen to the literal meanings that a speaker communicates; I don't look too deeply into hidden meanings.

____ 5. I listen without active involvement; I generally remain silent and take in what the other person is saying.

____ 6. I listen objectively; I focus on the logic of the ideas rather than on the emotional meaning of the message.

____ 7. I listen politely even to messages that contradict my attitudes and beliefs.

____ 8. I'll interrupt a speaker when I have something really relevant to say.

____ 9. I listen critically, evaluating the speaker and what the speaker is saying.

____10. I look for the hidden meanings, the meanings that are revealed by subtle verbal or nonverbal cues.

How Did You Do? These statements focus on the ways of listening discussed in this chapter. All of these ways are appropriate at some times but not at other times. It depends. So the only responses that are really inappropriate are "always" and "never." Effective listening is listening that is tailored to the specific communication situation.

What Will You Do? Consider how you might use these statements to begin to improve your listening effectiveness. A good way to do this is to review these statements and identify situations in which each statement would be appropriate and situations in which each statement would be inappropriate.

When you listen empathically as a neighbor tells of having her apartment burgled and all her prized possessions taken, you can share on some level the loss and emptiness she feels. Only when you achieve empathy can you fully understand another person's meaning. Empathic listening will also help you enhance your relationships (Barrett & Godfrey, 1988; Snyder, 1992).

Although for most communication situations, empathic listening is the preferred mode of responding, there are times when you need to go beyond it and measure the speaker's meanings and feelings against some objective reality. It's important to listen to Peter tell you how the entire world hates him and to understand how Peter feels and why he feels this way. But then you need to look a bit more objectively at the situation and perhaps see Peter's paranoia or self-hatred. Sometimes you have to put your empathic responses aside and listen with objectivity and detachment.

In adjusting your empathic and objective listening focus, keep the following recommendations in mind.

- *See from the speaker's point of view.* See the sequence of events as the speaker does, and try to figure out how this perspective can influence what the speaker says and does.

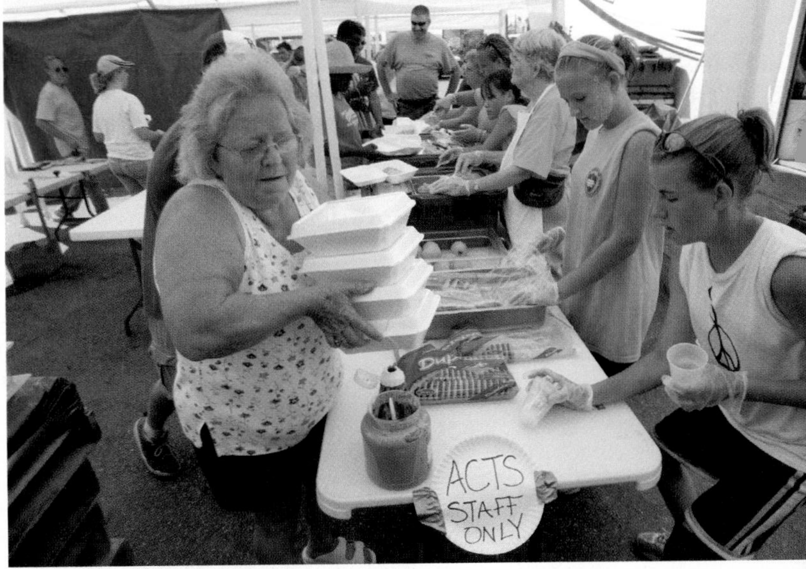

VIEWPOINTS Empathy

There is some evidence to show that empathy also has a negative side. For example, the more empathy you feel toward people who are similar to you racially and ethnically, the less empathy you feel toward those who are different. The same empathy that increases your understanding of your own group decreases your understanding of other groups. So although empathy may encourage understanding, it also can create dividing lines between your group and "them" (Angier, 1995). Have you ever witnessed these negative effects of empathy?

INTERPERSONAL CHOICE POINT

Listening Empathically

Your mother has been having a difficult time at work. She was recently passed up for a promotion and received one of the lowest merit raises given in the company. "I'm not sure what I did wrong," she tells you. "I do my work, mind my own business, don't take my sick days like everyone else. How could they give that promotion to Helen, who's only been with the company for two years? Maybe I should just quit." What can you do and say that will demonstrate empathic listening?

- *Engage in equal, two-way conversation.* To encourage openness and empathy, try to eliminate any physical or psychological barriers to equality. For example, step from behind the large desk separating you from your employees. Avoid interrupting the speaker—a sign that you think what you have to say is more important.
- *Seek to understand both thoughts and feelings.* Don't consider your listening task finished until you've understood what the speaker is feeling as well as what he or she is thinking.
- *Avoid "offensive listening"*—the tendency to listen to bits and pieces of information that will enable you to attack the speaker or find fault with something the speaker has said (Floyd, 1985).
- *Strive to be objective* when listening to friends or foes alike. Your attitudes may lead you to distort messages—to block out positive messages about a foe or negative messages about a friend. Guard against "expectancy hearing," in which you fail to hear what the speaker is really saying and instead hear what you expect.

Nonjudgmental and Critical Listening

Effective listening includes both *nonjudgmental* and *critical* responses. You need to listen *nonjudgmentally*—with an open mind and with a view toward understanding. But you also need to listen *critically*—with a view toward making some kind of evaluation or judgment. Clearly, it's important to listen first for understanding while suspending judgment. Only after you've fully understood the relevant messages should you evaluate or judge.

Supplement nonjudgmental listening with critical listening. When you listen critically, you think logically and dispassionately about, for example, the stories your friends tell you or the sales pitch of the car dealer. Listening with an open mind will help you understand the messages better; listening with a critical mind will help you analyze and evaluate the messages. In adjusting your nonjudgmental and critical listening, focus on the following guidelines:

Explore the **Exercise** "How Might You Listen to New Ideas?" at **MyCommunicationLab**

- *Keep an open mind.* Avoid prejudging. Delay your judgments until you fully understand both the content and the intention the speaker is communicating. Avoid either positive or negative evaluation until you have a reasonably complete understanding. Even when a friend tells you he or she did something you disapprove of, nonjudgmental listening requires that you withhold making value judgments (in your mind as well as in your responses) that can get in the way of your understanding your friend.
- *Avoid filtering out or oversimplifying complex messages.* Similarly, avoid filtering out undesirable messages. Clearly, you don't want to hear that something you believe is untrue, that people you care for are unkind, or that ideals you hold are self-destructive. Yet it's important that you reexamine your beliefs by listening to these messages.
- *Recognize your own biases.* These may interfere with accurate listening and cause you to distort message reception through a process of assimilation—the tendency to integrate and interpret what you hear or think you hear in keeping with your own biases, prejudices, and expectations. For example, are your ethnic, national, gender, or religious biases preventing you from appreciating a speaker's point of view?
- *Combat the tendency to sharpen*—to highlight, emphasize, and perhaps embellish one or two aspects of a message. Often the concepts that we tend to *sharpen* are incidental remarks that somehow stand out from the rest of the message. Be careful, therefore, about sharpening your blind date's "Thank you, I had a nice time" and assuming that the date was a big success—while ignoring the signs that it was just so-so, such as the lack of eye contact, the awkward silences, and the cell phone interruptions.

INTERPERSONAL CHOICE POINT

Relationship Listening

A young nephew tells you that he can't talk with his parents. No matter how hard he tries, they don't listen. "I tried to tell them that I can't play baseball and I don't want to play baseball," he confides. "But they ignore me and tell me that all I need is practice." What are some of the things you can say or do that will show your nephew that you're listening?

- *Avoid uncritical listening* when you need to make evaluations and judgments. Especially watch out for what are called "fallacies of language," language used to serve less than noble purposes, to convince or persuade you without giving you any reasons, and sometimes to fool you. Several of these are presented in Table 4.4.

INTERPERSONAL CHOICE POINT

Listening without Judging

A classmate says to you: I got a C on that paper. That's the worst grade I've ever received. I just can't believe that I got a C. This is my major. What am I going to do? What options do you have in this case for communicating without judging?

Surface and Depth Listening

In most messages, there's an obvious meaning that you can derive from a literal reading of the words and sentences. But in reality, most messages have more than one level of meaning. Sometimes the other level is the opposite of the literal meaning; at other times, it seems totally unrelated. Consider some frequently heard types of messages. Carol asks you how you like her new haircut. On one level, the meaning is clear: Do you like the haircut? But there's also another and perhaps more important level: Carol is asking you to say something positive about her appearance. In the same way, the parent who complains about working hard at the office or in the home may, on a deeper level, be asking for an expression of appreciation. The child who talks about the unfairness of the other children on the playground may be asking for comfort and love, for some expression of caring.

TABLE 4.4

LISTENING TO FALLACIES OF LANGUAGE

Here are four language fallacies that often get in the way of meaningful communication and need to be identified in critical listening. After reviewing these fallacies, take a look at some of the commercial websites for clothing, books, music, or any such product you're interested in and try to find examples of these fallacies.

Fallacy	Examples	Critical Notes
Weasel words are those whose meanings are slippery and difficult to pin down, for example, "help," "virtually," "as much as," "like" (as in "it will make you feel like new"), and "more economical."	A commercial claiming that medicine M works "better than Brand X" but doesn't specify how much better or in what respect Medicine M performs better. It's quite possible that it performs better in one respect but less effectively according to nine other measures.	Ask yourself, "Exactly what is being claimed?" For example, "What does 'may reduce cholesterol' mean? What exactly is being asserted?"
Euphemisms make the negative and unpleasant appear positive and appealing.	An executive calls the firing of 200 workers "downsizing" or "reallocation of resources."	Euphemisms can make the mundane seem extraordinary or lies seem like the truth. Don't let words get in the way of accurate firsthand perception.
Jargon is the specialized language of a professional class, which may be used to intimidate or impress people who aren't members of the profession.	For example, the language of the computer hacker, the psychologist, and the advertiser.	Don't be intimidated by jargon; ask questions when you don't understand.
Gobbledygook is overly complex language that overwhelms the listener instead of communicating meaning.	Extra-long sentences, complex grammatical constructions, and rare or unfamiliar words.	Some people just normally speak in complex language, but others use complexity to confuse and mislead. Ask for simplification when appropriate.

To appreciate these other meanings, you need to engage in *depth* listening. If you respond only to the *surface-level* communication (the literal meaning), you miss the opportunity to make meaningful contact with the other person's feelings and needs. If you say to the parent, "You're always complaining. I bet you really love working so hard," you fail to respond to the person's call for understanding and appreciation. In regulating your surface and depth listening, consider the following guidelines:

- *Focus on both verbal and nonverbal messages.* Recognize both consistent and inconsistent "packages" of messages, and use these as guides for drawing inferences about the speaker's meaning. Ask questions when in doubt. Listen also to what is omitted. Remember that speakers communicate by what they leave out as well as by what they include. When Harry says things will be okay now that his relationship is finally over but says it with downcast eyes, deep breathing, and clenched hands, consider the possibility that Harry is really hurting and that things are not okay.
- *Listen for both content and relational messages.* The student who constantly challenges the teacher is on one level communicating disagreement over content. However, on another level—the relationship level—the student may be voicing objections to the instructor's authority or authoritarianism. The instructor needs to listen and respond to both types of messages.
- *Make special note of statements that refer back to the speaker.* Remember that people inevitably talk about themselves. Whatever a person says is, in part, a function of who that person is. Attend carefully to those personal, self-referential messages. Realize that, when Sara tells you she fears the economy is not going well, she may be voicing her own financial worries but phrasing them in the abstract.
- *Don't, however, disregard the literal meaning of interpersonal messages* in trying to uncover the more hidden meanings. Balance your listening between surface and underlying meanings. Respond to the different levels of meaning in the messages of others as you would like others to respond to yours—sensitively but not obsessively, readily but not over ambitiously. When Tommy tells you he's not feeling well, don't ignore this literal meaning and assume that Tommy is just looking for attention.

Blog Post

Impolite Questions, What Are They?

As you've no doubt experienced, some questions are polite and some aren't. For a brief discussion of impolite questions, see "Impolite Questions, What Are They?" at tcbdevito .blogspot.com. Have you ever asked or been asked an impolite question?

Polite and Impolite Listening

Politeness is often thought of as the exclusive function of the speaker, as solely an encoding or sending function. But politeness (or impoliteness) may also be signaled through listening (Fukushima, 2000).

Of course, there are times when you would not want to listen politely (for example, if someone is being verbally abusive or condescending or using racist or sexist language). In these cases, you might want to show your disapproval by showing that you're not even listening. But most often you'll want to listen politely, and you'll want to express this politeness through your listening behavior. Here are a few suggestions for demonstrating that you are in fact listening politely. As you read these strategies, you'll notice that they are designed to be supportive of the speaker's positive and negative face needs:

- *Avoid interrupting the speaker.* Avoid trying to take over the speaker's turn. Avoid changing the topic. If you must say something in response to something the speaker said and can't wait until he or she finishes, then say it as briefly as possible and pass the speaker's turn back to the speaker.
- *Give supportive listening cues.* These might include nodding your head, giving minimal verbal responses such as "I see" or "yes, it's true," or moving closer to the speaker. Listen in a way that demonstrates that what the speaker is saying is important. In some cultures, polite listening cues must be cues of agreement (Japanese culture is often used as an example); in other cultures, polite listening cues are attentiveness and support rather than cues of agreement (much of United States culture is an example).

INTERPERSONAL CHOICE POINT

Responding Politely

You are working as a manager at a restaurant, and a regular customer complains about the server: "I don't like the way she treated me, and I'm not coming back here." What are some of the things you might say without losing the customer or your server (who is usually excellent)? Are there things you'd be sure not to say?

- *Show empathy with the speaker.* Demonstrate that you understand and feel the speaker's thoughts and feelings by giving responses that show this level of understanding—smiling or cringing or otherwise echoing the feelings of the speaker. If you echo the speaker's nonverbal expressions, your behavior is likely to be seen as empathic.
- *Maintain eye contact.* In much of the United States, this is perhaps the single most important rule. If you don't maintain eye contact when someone is talking to you, then you'll appear to be not listening and definitely not listening politely. This rule, however, does not hold true in all cultures. In some Latin and Asian cultures, polite listening would consist of looking down and avoiding direct eye contact when, for example, listening to a superior or much older person.
- *Give positive feedback.* Throughout the listening encounter and perhaps especially after the speaker's turn (when you continue the conversation as you respond to what the speaker has said), positive feedback will be seen as polite and negative feedback as impolite. If you must give negative feedback, then do so in a way that does not attack the person's negative face, for example, first mention areas of agreement or what you liked about what the person said and stress your good intentions. And, most important, do it in private. Public criticism is especially threatening and will surely be seen as a personal attack.

A somewhat different slant on politeness and listening can be seen in "forcing" people to listen when they don't want to. Generally, the polite advice is to be sensitive when the other person wants to leave and to stop asking the person to continue listening. And closely related to this is the "forced" listening that many cell phone users impose on others (or the forced waiting while someone reads and responds to texts), a topic addressed in Table 4.5 (page 94).

VIEWPOINTS Politeness in social media

Much of the thinking and research on listening and politeness has focused on them as face-to-face communication skills. How would you describe listening politeness on the phone or on social network sites? Are the same principles applicable, or do we need an entirely different set to describe social networking listening politeness?

Active and Inactive Listening

One of the most important communication skills you can learn is that of active listening (Gordon, 1975). Consider the following interaction. You're disappointed that you have to redo your entire budget report, and you say, "I can't believe I have to redo this entire report. I really worked hard on this project, and now I have to do it all over again." To this you get three different responses:

Watch the **Video** "Listening and Nonverbal Communication" at **MyCommunicationLab**

Explore the **Exercise** "Experience Active Listening" at **MyCommunicationLab**

Apollo: That's not so bad; most people find they have to redo their first reports. That's the norm here.

Athena: You should be pleased that all you have to do is a simple rewrite. Peggy and Michael both had to completely redo their entire projects.

Diana: You have to rewrite that report you've worked on for the past three weeks? You sound really angry and frustrated.

TABLE 4.5

Politeness and the Mobile Device

The ubiquity of the cell phone and texting has led to enormous increases in communication, but it has also created problems, many of which are problems of politeness. Because much use occurs in public spaces, people often are forced to listen to conversations that don't involve them or to lose your attention when you send or respond to a text message.

General Rule	Specifics	Adjustments
Avoid using cell phones where inappropriate.	Especially avoid calling in restaurants, hospitals, theaters, museums, commuter buses or trains, and the classroom.	If you must make or take a call when in these various situations, try to move to a less public area.
Avoid texting when in a group.	Unless the text message concerns everyone and will be shared, avoid making everyone wait until you're finished.	If the text is especially important, excuse yourself and apologize for the inconvenience.
Silence your cell.	Put your phone on vibrate mode, or let your voicemail answer and take a message when your call might interfere with others.	When you can't avoid taking a call, speak as quietly as possible and as briefly as possible.
Avoid unwanted photo taking.	Don't take pictures of people who aren't posing for you, and delete photos if the person you photographed requests it.	Of course, if there's an accident or a robbery, you may want to photograph the events.
Avoid extended talking when your reception is weak.	Talking on your cell on a crowded street will probably result in poor reception, which is annoying to the other person.	In an emergency, caution trumps politeness.
Consider the other person.	It's easy to assume that when you have nothing better to do, the person you're calling also has nothing better to do.	As with any phone call, it's wise to ask if this is a good time to call—a strategy that helps maintain the autonomy (negative face) of the person you're calling.

All three listeners are probably trying to make you feel better. But they go about it in very different ways and, we can be sure, with very different results. Apollo tries to lessen the significance of the rewrite. This type of well-intended response is extremely common but does little to promote meaningful communication and understanding. Athena tries to give the situation a positive spin. With these responses, however, both these listeners are also suggesting that you should not be feeling the way you do. They're also implying that your feelings are not legitimate and should be replaced with more logical feelings.

Diana's response, however, is different from the others. Diana uses active listening. **Active listening** owes its development to Thomas Gordon (1975), who made it a cornerstone of his P-E-T (Parent Effectiveness Training) technique; it is a process of sending back to the speaker what you as a listener think the speaker meant—both in content and in feelings. Active listening, then, is not merely repeating the speaker's exact words but rather putting together into some meaningful whole your understanding of the speaker's total message.

INTERPERSONAL CHOICE POINT

Listening Actively

Your life partner comes home from work and is visibly upset. Your partner clearly has a need to talk about what happened but simply says, "Work sucks!" You're determined to use active listening techniques. What are some of the things you can say?

Functions of Active Listening Active listening serves several important functions.

Perhaps most obvious is that active listening enables you to *check understanding*. It helps you as a listener check your understanding of what the speaker said and, more important, what he or she meant.

Reflecting back perceived meanings to the speaker gives the speaker an opportunity to offer clarification and correct any misunderstandings.

Second, through active listening you let the speaker know that you *acknowledge and accept his or her feelings*. In the sample responses given, the first two listeners challenged your feelings. Diana, the active listener, who reflected back to you what she thought you meant, accepted what you were feeling. In addition, she also explicitly identified your emotions; she commented that you sounded "angry and frustrated," allowing you an opportunity to correct her interpretation if necessary. Do be careful, however, to avoid sending what Gordon (1975) calls "solution messages." Solution messages tell the person how he or she *should* feel or what he or she *should* do. The four types of messages that send solutions and that you'll want to avoid in your active listening are (1) ordering messages—*Do this..., Don't touch that...*; (2) warning and threatening messages—*If you don't do this, you'll..., If you do this, you'll...*; (3) preaching and moralizing messages—*People should all..., We all have responsibilities*...and (4) advising messages—*Why don't you..., What I think you should do is...*

Third, active listening *stimulates the speaker to explore his or her feelings and thoughts*. For example, Diana's response encourages you to elaborate on your feelings. This opportunity to elaborate also helps you deal with your feelings by talking them through.

TECHNIQUES OF ACTIVE LISTENING Three simple techniques may help you succeed in active listening:

- *Paraphrase the speaker's meaning*. Stating in your own words what you think the speaker means and feels can help ensure understanding and also shows interest in the speaker. Paraphrasing gives the speaker a chance to extend what was originally said. Thus, when Diana echoes your thoughts, you're given the opportunity to elaborate on why rewriting the budget report is so daunting to you.

  But in paraphrasing, be objective; be especially careful not to lead the speaker in the direction you think he or she should go. Also, be careful that you don't overdo it; only a very small percentage of statements need paraphrasing. Paraphrase when you feel there's a chance for misunderstanding or when you want to express support for the other person and keep the conversation going.
- *Express understanding of the speaker's feelings*. In addition to paraphrasing the content, echo the feelings the speaker expressed or implied ("You must have felt horrible"). This expression of feelings will help you further check your perception of the speaker's feelings. This also will allow the speaker to see his or her feelings more objectively—especially helpful when they're feelings of anger, hurt, or depression—and to elaborate on these feelings.
- *Ask questions*. Asking questions strengthens your own understanding of the speaker's thoughts and feelings and elicits additional information ("How did you feel when you read your job appraisal report?"). Ask questions to provide just enough stimulation and support so the speaker will feel he or she can elaborate on these thoughts and feelings. These questions should further confirm your interest and concern for the speaker but not pry into unrelated areas or challenge the speaker in any way.

Blog Post

Listening Doctors

For a brief discussion of the importance of listening in health care, see "Listening Doctors" at tcbdevito.blogspot.com. In what other areas would you like to see people listening more effectively?

Explore the **Exercise** "Regulating Your Listening Perspective" at **MyCommunicationLab**

Consider this dialogue and note the active listening techniques used throughout:

Pat: That jerk demoted me. He told me I wasn't an effective manager. I can't believe he did that, after all I've done for this place.
Chris: I'm with you. You've been manager for three or four months now, haven't you?
Pat: A little over three months. I know it was probationary, but I thought I was doing a good job.
Chris: Can you get another chance?
Pat: Yes, he said I could try again in a few months. But I feel like a failure.

SKILL BUILDING EXERCISE

Identifying Examples of Listening Styles

Go to YouTube or any online video site and select interpersonal interactions from any of a variety of talk shows (for example, *The Jay Leno Show, Jerry Springer, The View, Charlie Rose*) and identify one or two of the following:

1. An example of empathic or objective listening. How does the person communicate this?
2. An example of nonjudgmental or critical listening. What does the person say or do that indicates he or she is listening in this way?
3. An example of surface or deep listening. What verbal and nonverbal behaviors enable you to distinguish between the two styles of listening?
4. An example of polite or impolite listening. What cues are used to communicate this?
5. An example of active or inactive listening. What does the person say that indicates he or she is listening actively or inactively?

Being able to identify the varied styles of listening is a first step in controlling and adjusting our own style of listening for greatest effectiveness.

Chris: I know what you mean. It sucks. What else did he say?
Pat: He said I had trouble getting the paperwork done on time.
Chris: You've been late filing the reports?
Pat: A few times.
Chris: Is there a way to delegate the paperwork?
Pat: No, but I think I know now what needs to be done.
Chris: You sound as though you're ready to give that manager's position another try.
Pat: Yes, I think I am, and I'm going to let him know that I intend to apply in the next few months.

Even in this brief interaction, Pat has moved from unproductive anger and feelings of failure to a determination to correct an unpleasant situation. Note, too, that Chris didn't offer solutions but "simply" listened actively.

As stressed throughout this discussion, listening is situational; the type of listening that is appropriate varies with the situation. You can visualize a listening situation as one in which you have to make choices among at least the five styles of effective listening just discussed. Each listening situation should call for a somewhat different configuration of listening responses; the art of effective listening is largely one of making appropriate choices along these five dimensions.

Can you explain the five styles of listening (empathic and objective, nonjudgmental and critical, surface and deep, polite and impolite, and active and inactive listening)? Can you regulate your listening along these dimensions as appropriate for the situation you're in?

LISTENING, CULTURE, AND GENDER

Listening is difficult in part because of the inevitable differences in communication systems between speakers and listeners. Because each person has had a unique set of experiences, each person's communication and meaning system is going to be different from each other person's. When speaker and listener come from different cultures or are of different genders, the differences and their effects are naturally so much greater. Let's look first at culture.

Culture and Listening

"Anything you say with an accent may be used against you."

Paul Noth/The New Yorker Collection/www.cartoonbank.com

The culture in which you were raised will influence your listening in a variety of ways. Here we look at some of these: language and speech, direct and indirect styles, nonverbal differences, and feedback.

Even when speaker and listener speak the same language, they speak it with different meanings and different accents. No two speakers speak exactly the same language. Every speaker speaks an *idiolect*: a unique variation of the language. Speakers of the same language will, at the very least, have different meanings for the same terms because they have had different experiences.

Speakers and listeners who have different native languages and who may have learned English as a second language will have even greater differences in meaning. Translations are never precise and never fully capture the meaning in the other language. If you learned your meaning for *house* in a culture in which everyone lived in their own house with lots of land around it, then communicating with someone whose meaning was learned in a neighborhood of high-rise tenements is going to be difficult. Although each of you will hear the word *house,* the meanings you'll develop will be drastically different. In adjusting your listening—especially when in an intercultural setting—understand that the speaker's meanings may be very different from yours even though you're speaking the same language.

Explore the **Exercise** "Listening to Other's Perspectives" at **MyCommunicationLab**

Watch the **Video** "American Spoken Here" at **MyCommunicationLab**

Some cultures—those of Western Europe and the United States, for example—favor **direct speech** in communication; they advise you to "say what you mean and mean what you say." Many Asian cultures, on the other hand, favor **indirect speech**; they emphasize politeness and maintaining a positive public image rather than literal truth. Listen carefully to persons with different styles of directness. Consider the possibility that the meanings the speaker wishes to communicate with, say, indirectness, may be very different from the meanings you would communicate with indirectness.

Another area of difference is that of accents. In many classrooms throughout the United States, there will be a wide range of accents. Those whose native language is a tonal one such as Chinese (in which differences in pitch signal important meaning differences) may speak English with variations in pitch that may be puzzling to others. Those whose native language is Japanese may have trouble distinguishing *l* from *r*, because Japanese does not include this distinction. The native language acts as a filter and influences the accent given to the second language.

Accents are often stereotyped. A British accent may seem "upper class" whereas a southern European accent—Spanish, Italian, or Greek, for example—may seem "lower class." These accent stereotypes reflect nationality stereotypes and are invariably illogical.

Speakers from different cultures also have different *display rules*: cultural rules that govern which nonverbal behaviors are appropriate and which are inappropriate in a public setting. As you listen to other people, you also "listen" to their nonverbals. If these are drastically different from what you expect on the basis of the verbal message, you may

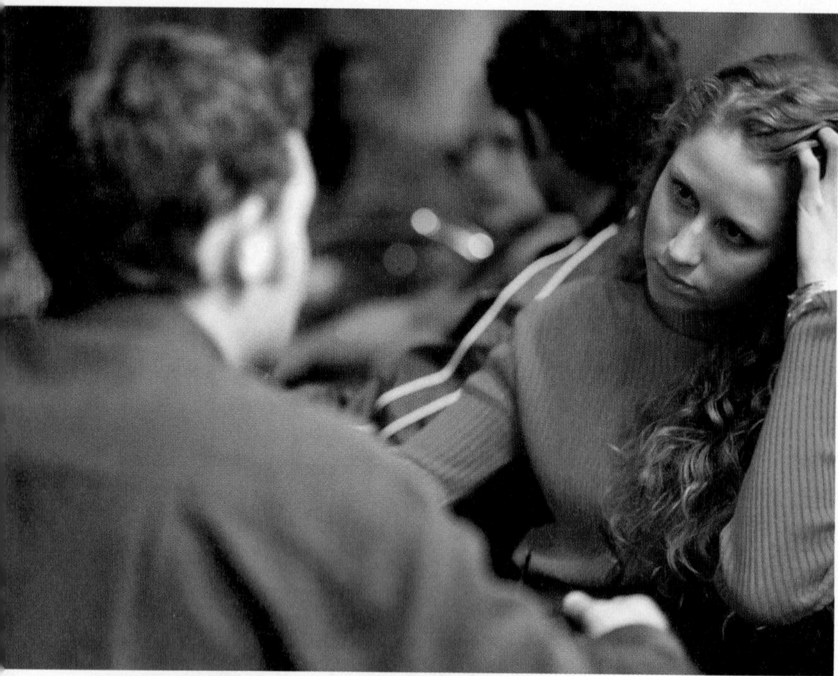

VIEWPOINTS Gender differences

A popular belief is that men listen in the way they do to prove themselves superior and that women listen as they do to ingratiate themselves. Although there is no evidence to show that these images are valid, they persist in the assumptions that people make. What do you believe accounts for the differences in the way men and women listen?

perceive a kind of noise or interference or even contradictory messages. Also, of course, different cultures may give very different meaning to a particular nonverbal gesture than you do, creating another potential listening obstacle.

Variations in directness are often especially clear when people give feedback. Members of some cultures tend to give direct and honest feedback. Speakers from these cultures—the United States is a good example—expect feedback to be an honest reflection of what their listeners are feeling. In other cultures—Japan and Korea are good examples—it's more important to be positive than to be truthful; listeners may respond with positive feedback (say, in commenting on a business colleague's proposal) even though they don't feel positive. Listen to feedback, as you would all messages, with a full recognition that various cultures view feedback very differently.

Gender and Listening

Men and women learn different styles of listening, just as they learn different styles for using verbal and nonverbal messages. Not surprisingly, these different styles can create difficulties in opposite-sex interpersonal communication.

INTERPERSONAL CHOICE POINT

Support, Not Solutions

You need to make some major decisions in your life, and you need to bounce these off someone, just to clarify these in your own mind. Your romantic partner almost always tries to solve your problems rather than just be a supportive listener. What can you say in preface (in feed forward) to get your partner to listen supportively and not try to solve your problem? What would you be sure not to say?

Rapport and Report Talk According to Deborah Tannen (1990) in her best-selling *You Just Don't Understand: Women and Men in Conversation*, women seek to build rapport and establish closer relationships and use listening to achieve these ends. Men, on the other hand, will play up their expertise, emphasize it, and use it in dominating the interaction. They will talk about things; they report. Women play down their expertise and are more interested in talking about feelings and relationships and in communicating supportiveness (rapport talk). Tannen argues that the goal of a man in conversation is to be given respect, so he seeks to show his knowledge and expertise. A woman's goal, on the other hand, is to be liked, so she expresses agreement.

Listening Cues Men and women display different types of listening cues and consequently show that they're listening in different ways. In conversation, a woman is more apt to give lots of listening cues—interjecting "Yeah" or "Uh-huh," nodding in agreement, and smiling. A man is more likely to listen quietly, without giving lots of listening cues as feedback. Women also make more eye contact when listening than do men, who are more apt to look around and often away from the speaker (Brownell, 2006). As a result of these differences, women seem to be more engaged in listening than do men.

Explore the **Exercise** "Typical Man, Typical Woman" at **MyCommunicationLab**

Amount and Purposes of Listening Tannen argues that men listen less to women than women listen to men. The reason, says Tannen, is that listening places the person in an inferior position, whereas speaking places the person in a superior position. Men may seem to assume a more argumentative posture while listening, as if getting ready to disagree. They also may appear to ask questions that are more argumentative or that seek to puncture holes in your position as a way to play up their own expertise. Women, on

MESSAGES IN THE MEDIA: WRAP UP

Television talk shows provide lots of examples of effective and ineffective listening. When you watch such shows, focus some attention to the listening patterns the panelists use. You'll learn a great deal about listening.

the other hand, are more likely to ask supportive questions and perhaps offer evaluations that are more positive than those of men. Men and women act this way to both men and women; their customary ways of talking don't seem to change depending on whether the listener is male or female.

Gender differences are changing drastically and quickly; it's best to take generalizations about gender as starting points for investigation and not as airtight conclusions (Gamble & Gamble, 2003). Further, as you no doubt observed, the gender differences—although significant—are far outnumbered by the similarities. It's important to be mindful of both similarities and differences.

Can you explain the major cultural and gender differences in listening and assess their influence on your own interpersonal interactions?

SUMMARY OF CONCEPTS AND SKILLS

Listen to the **Audio Chapter Summary** at **MyCommunicationLab**

This chapter defined listening and some of its benefits; identified the five stages of listening; explained some of the barriers to listening, the styles of effective listening, and how best to adjust your listening to achieve maximum effectiveness; and looked at the wide cultural and gender differences in listening.

1. Listening has both task and relationship benefits and serves the same purposes as communication: to learn, to relate, to influence, to play, and to help.

The Stages of Listening

2. Listening may be viewed as a five-step process: receiving, understanding, remembering, evaluating, and responding. Listening difficulties and obstacles exist at each of these stages.

Listening Barriers

3. Among the obstacles to effective listening are physical and mental distractions, biases and prejudices, lack of appropriate focus, and premature judgment.

Study and **Review** materials for this chapter are at **MyCommunicationLab**

Styles of Listening Effectively

4. Effective listening depends on finding appropriate balances among empathic and objective, nonjudgmental and critical, surface and depth, polite and impolite, and active and inactive listening.
5. Both listener and speaker share in the responsibility for effective listening.

Listening, Culture, and Gender

6. Members of different cultures vary on a number of communication dimensions that influence listening: speech and language, nonverbal behavioral differences, and approaches to feedback.
7. Men and women appear to listen differently; generally, women give more specific listening cues to show they're listening than do men.

This chapter also covered a wide variety of listening skills. Check those that you wish to work on.

___ 1. *Receiving.* Focus attention on both the verbal and the nonverbal messages; both communicate essential parts of the total meaning.

___ 2. *Understanding.* Relate new information to what you already know, ask questions, and paraphrase what you think the speaker said to make sure you understand.

___ 3. *Remembering.* Identify the central ideas of a message, summarize the message in an easier-to-retain form, and repeat ideas (aloud or to yourself) to help you remember.

___ 4. *Evaluating.* Try first to understand fully what the speaker means, then look to identify any biases or self-interests that might lead the speaker to give an unfair presentation.

___ 5. *Responding.* Express support for the speaker by using I-messages instead of you-messages.

___ 6. *Empathic and objective listening.* Punctuate the interaction from the speaker's point of view, engage in dialogue, and seek to understand the speaker's thoughts and feelings.

___ 7. *Nonjudgmental and critical listening.* Keep an open mind, avoid filtering out difficult messages, and recognize your own biases. When listening to make judgments, listen extra carefully, ask questions when in doubt, and check your perceptions before criticizing.

___ 8. *Surface and depth listening.* Focus on both verbal and nonverbal messages, on both content and relationship messages, and on statements that refer back to the speaker. At the same time, do not avoid the surface or literal meaning.

___ 9. *Active and inactive listening.* Be an active listener: Paraphrase the speaker's meaning, express understanding of the speaker's feelings, and ask questions when necessary.

___10. *Cultural differences in listening.* Be especially flexible when listening in a multicultural setting, realizing that people from other cultures give different listening cues and may operate with different rules for listening.

___11. *Gender differences in listening.* Understand that women give more cues that they're listening and appear more supportive in their listening than men.

VOCABULARY QUIZ: The Language of Listening

Match these terms about listening with their definitions. Record the number of the definition next to the appropriate term.

___ listening (80)
___ offensive listening (90)
___ receiving (81)
___ empathic listening (88)
___ supportive listening (92)
___ backchanneling cues (84)
___ active listening (93)
___ memory (83)
___ paraphrase (95)
___ evaluating (84)

1. A reconstructive (not a reproductive) process.
2. A process of sending back to the speaker what the listener thinks the speaker means.
3. Hearing.
4. A stage in the listening process in which you make judgments about a message.
5. A restatement of something said in your own words.
6. Listening for ideas to attack.
7. A process of receiving, understanding, remembering, evaluating, and responding to messages.
8. Listening in which you place yourself in the position of the speaker so that you feel as the speaker feels.
9. Responses listeners send back to the speaker as a kind of feedback.
10. Listening without judgment or evaluation; listening for understanding.

The above terms and additional key terms from this chapter can be found in the glossary.

MyCommunicationLab

Visit MyCommunicationLab for additional information on listening. Flash cards, videos, skill building exercises, sample test questions, and additional examples and discussions will help you continue your study of the role of listening in interpersonal communication and the skills of effective listening.

CHAPTER

5

Verbal Messages

MESSAGES IN THE MEDIA

Cartoon shows are interesting in part because the characters are all given very distinctive verbal communication styles, making them all easily identifiable. In much the same way, we each have a distinctive verbal style that, as this chapter will demonstrate, can be improved and made more effective.

OBJECTIVES *After reading this chapter, you should be able to:*

1. Paraphrase the eight principles of verbal messages.
2. Distinguish between disconfirmation and confirmation, and use appropriate cultural identifiers, without sexism, heterosexism, racism, and ageism.
3. Explain the ways in which language can distort thinking and apply the suggestions for greater guidelines for communicating more logically.

Listen to the **Audio Chapter** at **MyCommunicationLab**

Explore the **Exercise** "Integrating Verbal and Nonverbal Messages" at **MyCommunicationLab**

As you communicate, you use two major signal systems—the verbal and the nonverbal. Verbal messages are those sent with words. The word *verbal* refers to words, not to orality; verbal messages consist of both oral and written words. Verbal messages would not include laughter; vocalized pauses you make when you speak such as *er*, *hmh*, and *uh-uh*; and responses you make to others that are oral but don't involve words such as *hah-hah*, *aha*, and *ugh*. These would be considered nonverbal—as are, of course, facial expressions, eye movements, gestures, and so on. This chapter focuses on verbal messages; the next focuses on nonverbal messages.

PRINCIPLES OF VERBAL MESSAGES

A useful way to study verbal messages is to examine the principles that govern the way verbal messages work. Here we look at eight such principles: (1) meanings are in people, (2) messages are both denotative and connotative and communicate objective meanings as well as attitudes and values, (3) messages can be onymous or anonymous, (4) messages vary in abstraction, (5) messages vary in politeness, (6) messages vary in immediacy, (7) messages can deceive, and (8) messages vary in assertiveness.

Message Meanings Are in People

If you wanted to know the meaning of the word *love*, you'd probably turn to a dictionary. There you'd find, according to Webster's, "the attraction, desire, or affection felt for a person who arouses delight or admiration or elicits tenderness, sympathetic interest, or benevolence." This is the denotative meaning. But where would you turn if you wanted to know what Pedro means when he says, "I'm in love"? Of course, you'd turn to Pedro to discover his meaning. It's in this sense that meanings are not in words but in people. Consequently, to uncover meaning, you need to look into people and not merely into words.

Also recognize that, as you change, you also change the meanings you created out of past messages. Thus, although the message sent may not change, the meanings you created from it yesterday and the meanings you create today may be quite different. Yesterday, when a special someone said, "I love you," you created certain meanings. But today, when you learn that the same "I love you" was said to three other people or when you fall in love with someone else, you drastically change the meanings you draw from those three words.

Meanings Are Denotative and Connotative

Explore the **Concept** "Verbal Communication" at **MyCommunicationLab**

Two general types of meaning are essential to identify: denotation and connotation. The term *denotation* refers to the meaning you'd find in a dictionary; it's the meaning that members of the culture assign to a word. Connotation is the emotional meaning that specific speakers/listeners give to a word. Take as an example the word *death*. To a doctor, this word might mean (denote) the time when the heart stops. This is an objective description of a particular event. On the other hand, to a mother who is informed of her son's death, the word means (connotes) much more. It recalls her son's youth, ambitions, family, illness, and so on. To her, *death* is a highly emotional, subjective, and personal word. These emotional, subjective, or personal associations make up the word's connotative meaning. The denotation of a word is its objective definition. The connotation of a word is its subjective or emotional meaning.

Semanticist S. I. Hayakawa (Hayakawa & Hayakawa, 1989) coined the terms "snarl words" and "purr words" to further clarify the distinction between denotative and connotative meanings. Snarl words are highly negative ("She's an idiot," "He's a pig," "They're a bunch of losers"). Sexist, racist, heterosexist, and ageist language, and hate speech generally, provide lots of other examples. Purr words are highly positive ("She's a real sweetheart," "He's a dream," "They're the greatest").

Snarl and purr words, although they may sometimes seem to have denotative meaning and to refer to the "real world," are actually connotative in meaning. These terms do not describe people or events in the real world but rather reflect the speaker's feelings about these people or events. Compare the term *migrants* (used to designate Mexicans coming into the United States to better their economic condition) with the term *settlers* (used to designate Europeans who came to the United States for the same reason) (Koppelman, 2005). Though both terms describe people engaged in essentially the same activity (and are essentially the same denotatively), one label is often negatively evaluated, and the other is more often positively valued (so that the terms differ widely in their connotations).

Blog Post

Names

Do women communicate different messages when they change their names to their husband's, when they hyphenate their birth name with their husband's, or when they retain their birth name? Check out "Names" at tcbdevito .blogspot.com. How do you feel about this topic? Do men and women view this similarly or differently?

Messages Can Be Onymous or Anonymous

Onymous messages are "signed"; that is, the author of the message is clearly identified, as it is in your textbooks, news-related editorials, and feature articles and, of course, when you communicate face to face and, usually, by phone or chat. In many cases, you have the opportunity to respond directly to the speaker/writer and voice your opinions, your agreement or disagreement, for example. **Anonymous messages** are those for which the author is not identified. For example, on faculty evaluation questionnaires and on RateMyProfessor.com, the ratings and the comments are published anonymously.

The Internet has made anonymity extremely easy, and there are currently a variety of websites that offer to send your e-mails to your boss, your ex-partner, your secret crush, your noisy neighbors, or your inadequate lawyer—all anonymously. Thus, your message gets sent but you are not identified with it. For good or ill, you don't have to deal with the consequences of your message.

One obvious advantage of anonymity is that it allows people to voice opinions that may be unpopular and may thus encourage greater honesty. In the case of RateMyProfessor.com, for example, anonymity ensures that the student writing negative comments about an instructor will not be penalized. An anonymous e-mail to a sexual partner informing him or her about your having an STD and suggesting testing and treatment might never get said in a face-to-face or phone conversation. The presumption is that anonymity encourages honesty and openness.

Anonymity also enables people to disclose their inner feelings, fears, hopes, and dreams with a depth of feeling that they may be otherwise reluctant to do. A variety of websites that enable you to maintain anonymity are available for these purposes. And in these cases, not only are you anonymous, but the people who read your messages are also anonymous, a situation that is likely to encourage a greater willingness to disclose and to make disclosures at a deeper level than otherwise.

An obvious disadvantage is that anonymity might encourage people to go to extremes—because there are no consequences to the message—to voice opinions that are outrageous. This in turn can easily spark conflict that is likely to prove largely unproductive. With anonymous messages, you can't evaluate the credibility of the source. Advice on depression, for example, may come from someone who knows nothing about depression and may make useless recommendations.

VIEWPOINTS Communication changes

When asked what they would like to change about the communication patterns of the opposite sex, men said they wanted women to be more direct, and women said they wanted men to stop interrupting and offering advice (Noble, 1994). What one change would you like to see in the communication system of the opposite sex? Of your own sex?

Explore the **Exercise** "Using the Abstraction Ladder as a Critical Thinking Tool" at **MyCommunicationLab**

Message Meanings Vary in Abstraction

Consider the following terms:

- entertainment
- film
- American film
- classic American films
- *Casablanca*

At the top is an **abstraction**, or general concept—*entertainment*. Note that *entertainment* includes all the other items on the list plus various other items—*television, novels, drama, comics,* and so on. *Film* is more specific and concrete. It includes all of the items below it as well as various other items such as *Indian film* or *Russian film*. It excludes, however, all entertainment that is not film. *American film* is again more specific than *film* and excludes all films that are not American. *Classic American film* further limits *American film* to those considered to be timeless. *Casablanca* specifies concretely the one item to which reference is made.

A verbal message that uses the most general term—in this case, entertainment—will conjure up many different images in listeners' minds. One person may focus on television, another on music, another on comic books, and still another on radio. To some listeners, the word *film* may bring to mind the early silent films; to others it may connote high-tech special effects; to still others it will recall Disney's animated cartoons. *Casablanca* guides listeners still further—in this case, to one film. So, as you get more specific—less abstract—you more effectively guide the images that come to your listeners' minds.

Effective verbal messages include words that range widely in abstractness. At times, a general term may suit your needs best; at other times, a more specific term may serve better. The widely accepted recommendation for effective communication is to use abstractions sparingly and to express your meanings explicitly with words that are low in abstraction.

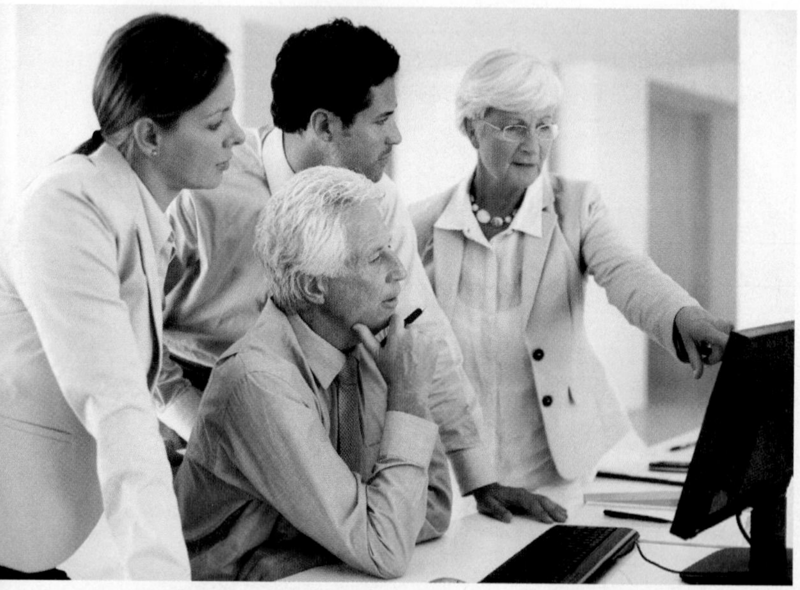

VIEWPOINTS Indirectness

Research finds that women are more indirect in giving orders whereas men are more likely to be indirect when they express weakness, reveal a problem, or admit an error. Three sets of reasons have been advanced to explain these differences (Holmes, 1995): gender differences are due to (1) *innate biological differences;* (2) *socialization,* in the way they are raised; and (3) *social power* differences and inequalities. To what do you attribute observed gender differences?

Message Meanings Vary in Politeness

It will come as no surprise that messages vary greatly in politeness. Polite messages reflect positively on the other person (for example, compliments or pats on the back) and respect the other person's right to be independent and autonomous (for example, asking permission or acknowledging the person's right to refuse). Impolite messages attack our needs to be seen positively (for example, criticism or negative facial expressions) and to be autonomous (making demands or forcing another to do something). A special case of politeness concerns the ever popular social networking sites (see Table 5.1).

Politeness and Directness Directness is usually less polite and may infringe on a person's need to maintain negative face—*Write me a recommendation; lend me $100.* Indirectness—*Do you think you could write a recommendation for me? Would it be possible to lend me $100?*—is often more polite because it allows the person to maintain autonomy and provides an acceptable way for the person to refuse your request (thus helping to maintain the person's negative face needs).

TABLE 5.1

Social Networking Politeness

The social networking sites such as Facebook, MySpace, and Google+ have developed their own rules of politeness. Here are just five rules.

Rules of Politeness	The Rule in Operation
Engage in networking feedforward before requesting friendship.	Sending a message complimenting the person's latest post provides some background and eases the way for a friendship request.
Avoid negativity.	Avoid writing negative or embarrassing messages or posting unflattering photos that may generate conflict.
Keep networking information confidential.	It's considered inappropriate and impolite to relay information on Facebook, for example, to those who are not themselves friends.
Be gentle in refusals.	Refuse any request for friendship gently or, if you wish, ignore it. If you're refused, don't ask for reasons; it's considered impolite.
Avoid making potentially embarrassing requests.	Avoid asking to be friends with someone who you suspect may have reasons for not wanting to admit you. For example, your work associate may not want you to see her or his profile.

Explore the **Exercise** "How Can You Vary Directness for Greatest Effectiveness" at **MyCommunicationLab**

Indirect messages allow you to express a desire without insulting or offending anyone; they allow you to observe the rules of polite interaction. So instead of saying, "I'm bored with this group," you say, "It's getting late and I have to get up early tomorrow," or you look at your watch and pretend to be surprised by the time. Instead of saying, "This food tastes like cardboard," you say, "I just started my diet." In each instance you're stating a preference but are saying it indirectly so as to avoid offending someone.

The differences between direct and indirect messages may easily create misunderstandings. For example, a person who uses an indirect style of speech may be doing so to be polite and may have been taught this

INTERPERSONAL CHOICE POINT

Rejecting Directly

A colleague at work continues to ask you for a date, but you're just not interested. You've used every polite excuse in the book and now feel you have to be more direct and more honest. What are some choices you have for expressing your feelings that would help you achieve your goal and yet not alienate or insult your colleague?

VIDEO CHOICE POINT

We Have Work to Do

Zach, an employee at a small office, is trying to cope with a coworker. Katie is just a little too friendly, constantly chatting and Zach is becoming increasingly annoyed with Katie's over-friendliness, but does not want to alienate her. However, his work is beginning to suffer and Zach doesn't want either of them to lose their jobs and would like to remain on good speaking terms with Katie. Zach has two objectives: getting his work done and maintaining a cordial relationship with Katie. He tries a couple of strategies with varying levels of success. See how his choices play out in the video "We Have Work to Do" and respond to the questions posed.

 **Watch** the **Video** "We Have Work to Do" at **MyCommunicationLab**

Blog Post

Gender Differences

For a brief discussion of some gender differences, see "Gender Differences" at tcbdevito.blogspot.com. What gender differences do you observe?

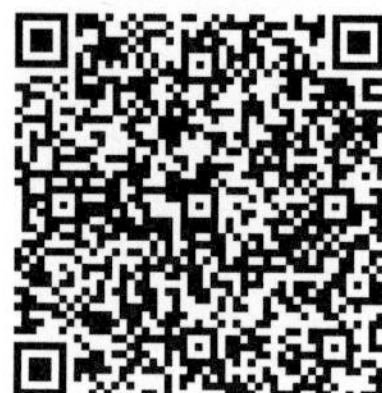

style by his or her culture. If you assume, instead, that the person is using indirectness to be manipulative because your culture regards it so, then miscommunication is inevitable.

POLITENESS AND GENDER There are considerable gender differences in politeness (Dindia & Canary, 2006; Holmes, 1995; Kapoor, Hughes, Baldwin, & Blue, 2003; Tannen, 1994b). Among the research findings are, for example, that women are more polite and more indirect in giving orders than are men; they are more likely to say, for example, "it would be great if these letters could go out today" than "Have these letters out by 3." Generally, men speak indirectly when expressing meanings that violate the masculine stereotype (for example, messages of weakness, doubt, or incompetence). Women's greater politeness is also seen in the finding that women express empathy, sympathy, and supportiveness more than men. Women also apologize more than men, and women make more apologies to other women whereas men make more apologies to women.

Messages Vary in Immediacy

Immediacy is the creation of closeness, a sense of togetherness, of oneness, between speaker and listener. When you communicate immediacy you convey a sense of interest and attention, a liking for and an attraction to the other person. You communicate immediacy with both verbal and nonverbal messages.

And, not surprisingly, people like people who communicate immediacy. You increase your interpersonal attractiveness, the degree to which others like you and respond positively toward you, when you use immediacy behaviors. In addition, there is considerable evidence to show that immediacy behaviors are also effective in workplace communication, especially between supervisors and subordinates (Richmond, McCroskey, & Hickson, 2012). For example, when a supervisor uses immediacy behaviors, he or she is seen by subordinates as interested and concerned; subordinates are therefore likely to communicate more freely and honestly about issues that can benefit the supervisor and the organization. Also, workers with supervisors who communicate immediacy behaviors have higher job satisfaction and motivation.

Not all cultures or all people respond in the same way to immediacy messages. For example, in the United States, immediacy behaviors are generally seen as friendly and appropriate. In other cultures, however, the same immediacy behaviors may be viewed as overly familiar—as presuming that a relationship is close when only acquaintanceship exists (Axtell, 1994). Similarly, recognize that some people may take your immediacy behaviors as indicating a desire for increased intimacy in the relationship. So although you may be trying merely to signal a friendly closeness, the other person may perceive a romantic invitation.

Here are a few suggestions for communicating immediacy (Mottet & Richmond, 1998; Richmond, McCroskey, & Hickson, 2012):

- Self-disclose; reveal something significant about yourself.
- Refer to the other person's good qualities of, say, dependability, intelligence, or character—"you're always so reliable."
- Talk about commonalities, things you and the other person have done together or share.
- Demonstrate your responsiveness by giving feedback cues that indicate you want to listen more and that you're interested—"And what else happened?"
- Maintain appropriate eye contact, smile, and express your interest in the other person.
- Focus on the other person's remarks. Make the speaker know that you heard and understood what was said, and give the speaker appropriate verbal and nonverbal feedback.

Explore the **Concept** "'Must Lie' Situations" at **MyCommunicationLab**

Messages Can Deceive

Although we operate on the assumption that people tell the truth, it should come as no surprise to learn that some people do lie. Lying also begets more lying; when one person lies, the likelihood of the other person lying increases (Tyler, Feldman, & Reichert,

2006). **Lying** refers to the act of (1) sending messages (2) with the intention of giving another person information you believe to be false.

Large cultural differences exist in the way lying is defined and in the way lying is treated. For example, as children get older, Chinese and Taiwanese (but not Canadians) see lying about the good deeds that they do as positive (as you'd expect for cultures that emphasize modesty), and taking credit for these same good deeds is seen negatively (Lee et al., 2002). Some cultures consider lying to be more important than others—in one study, for example, European Americans viewed lies less negatively than did Ecuadorians. Both, however, felt that lying to an out-group member was more acceptable than lying to an in-group member (Mealy, Stephan, & Urrutia, 2007).

TYPES OF LIES Lies vary greatly in type; each lie seems a bit different from every other lie. Here is one useful system that classifies lies into four types (McGinley, 2000).

Watch the **Video** "Please Don't Lie to Me" at **MyCommunicationLab**

- *Pro-social deception: To achieve some good* These are lies that are designed to benefit the person lied to or lied about, for example, praising a person's effort to give him or her more confidence.
- *Self-enhancement deception: To make yourself look good* Presenting yourself as younger or as having a better job in your social networking profile is a common example.
- *Selfish deception: To protect yourself* These lies protect you, for example, not answering the phone because you want to do something else.
- *Anti-social deception: To harm someone* These lies are designed to hurt another person, for example, spreading false rumors about someone or falsely accusing an opposing candidate of some wrongdoing.

THE BEHAVIOR OF LIARS One of the more interesting questions about lying is how liars act. Do they act differently from those telling the truth? And, if they do act differently, how can we tell when someone is lying? These questions are not easy to answer, and we are far from having complete answers to such questions. But we have learned a great deal.

ETHICAL MESSAGES

Lying

Not surprisingly, lies have ethical implications. Some lies (pro-social, self-enhancement, and selfish deception lies) are considered ethical (for example, publicly agreeing with someone you really disagree with to enable the person to save face, saying that someone will get well despite medical evidence to the contrary, or simply bragging about your accomplishments). Some lies are considered not only ethical but required (for example, lying to protect someone from harm or telling the proud parents that their child is beautiful). Other lies (largely those in the anti-social category) are considered unethical (for example, lying to defraud investors or to falsely accuse someone).

Ethical Choice Point

Of course, not all lies are easy to classify as ethical or unethical. For example, what would you do in each of these situations?

- *Would it be ethical for you to lie to get what you deserve but couldn't get any other way? For example, would it be ethical to lie to get a well-earned promotion or a raise?*
- *Would it be ethical for you to lie to your relationship partner to avoid a conflict and, perhaps, splitting up? Would it make a difference if the issue was a minor one (e.g., you were late for an appointment because you wanted to see the end of the football game) or a major one (e.g., continued infidelity)?*
- *Would it be ethical for you to lie to get yourself out of an unpleasant situation, for example, an unpleasant date, an extra office chore, or a boring conversation?*

INTERPERSONAL CHOICE POINT

Confronting a Lie

You ask about the previous night's whereabouts of your romantic partner of two years and are told something you know beyond any doubt to be false. You don't want to break up the relationship over this, but you do want the truth and an opportunity to resolve the problems that contributed to this situation. What are some of the things you might say to achieve your purposes? What are some types of things you'd definitely want to avoid saying?

For example, after an examination of 120 research studies, the following behaviors were found to most often accompany lying (DePaulo et al., 2003; Knapp, 2008):

- *Liars hold back.* They speak more slowly (perhaps to monitor what they're saying), take longer to respond to questions (again, perhaps monitoring their messages), and generally give less information and elaboration.
- *Liars make less sense.* Liars' messages contain more discrepancies, more inconsistencies.
- *Liars give a more negative impression.* Generally, liars are seen as less willing to be cooperative, smile less than truth-tellers, and are more defensive.
- *Liars are tense.* The tension may be revealed by their higher-pitched voices and their excessive body movements.

It is very difficult to detect when a person is lying and when a person is telling the truth. The hundreds of research studies conducted on this topic find that in most instances people judge lying accurately in less than 60 percent of the cases, only slightly better than chance (Knapp, 2008).

Lie detection is even more difficult (that is, less accurate) in long-standing romantic relationships—the very relationships in which the most significant lying occurs (Guerrero, Andersen, & Afifi, 2007). One important reason for this is the **truth bias:** we assume that the person is telling the truth. This truth bias is especially strong in long-term relationships where it's simply expected that each person tells the truth (Knapp, 2008).

Watch the **Video** "Hey Roomie" at **MyCommunicationLab**

Message Meanings Vary in Assertiveness

Assertive messages express your real thoughts—even if they involve disagreeing or arguing with others—but are nevertheless respectful of the other person. Consider your own message behavior. If you disagree with other people in a group, do you speak your mind? Do you allow others to take advantage of you because you're reluctant to say what you want? Do you feel uncomfortable when you have to state your opinion in a group? Questions such as these revolve around your degree of assertiveness. Increasing your level of assertiveness will enable you to deal with these experiences positively and productively. Before reading further about this type of communication, take the accompanying self-test, "How Assertive Are Your Messages?"

TEST YOURSELF

How Assertive Are Your Messages?

Indicate how true each of the following statements is about your own communication. Respond instinctively rather than in the way you feel you should respond. Use a scale in which **5** = always or almost always true; **4** = usually true; **3** = sometimes true, sometimes false; **2** = usually false; and **1** = always or almost always false.

____ 1. I would express my opinion in a group even if it contradicted the opinions of others.

____ 2. When asked to do something that I really don't want to do, I can say no without feeling guilty.

____ 3. I can express my opinion to my superiors on the job.

____ 4. I can start up a conversation with a stranger on a bus or at a business gathering without fear.

____ 5. I voice objection to people's behavior if I feel it infringes on my rights.

How Did You Do? All five items in this test identify characteristics of assertive communication. High scores (about 20 and above) would indicate a high level of assertiveness. Low scores (about 10 and below) would indicate a low level of assertiveness.

What Will You Do? The remaining discussion in this section clarifies the nature of assertive communication and offers guidelines for increasing your own assertiveness. These suggestions can help you not only to increase your assertiveness but also, when appropriate, to reduce your aggressive tendencies.

NONASSERTIVE, AGGRESSIVE, AND ASSERTIVE MESSAGES In addition to identifying some specific assertive behaviors (as in the assertiveness self-test), we can further understand the nature of assertive communication by distinguishing it from nonassertiveness and aggressiveness (Alberti, 1977).

Explore the **Exercise** "Analyzing Assertiveness" at **MyCommunicationLab**

Nonassertive Messages. The term *nonassertiveness* refers to a lack of assertiveness in certain types of (or even in all) communication situations. People who are nonassertive fail to stand up for their rights. They operate with a "you win, I lose" philosophy; they give others what they want without concern for themselves (Lloyd, 2001). Nonassertive people often ask permission from others to do what is their perfect right.

Aggressive Messages. Aggressiveness is the other extreme. Aggressive people operate with an "I win, you lose" philosophy; they care little for what the other person wants and focus only on their own needs. Aggressive communicators think little of the opinions, values, or beliefs of others and yet are extremely sensitive to others' criticisms of their own behavior. Consequently, they frequently get into arguments with others.

Assertive Messages. Assertive behavior—behavior that enables you to act in your own best interests without denying or infringing on the rights of others—is the generally desired alternative to nonassertiveness (which prevents you from expressing yourself) or aggressiveness (which creates resentment and conflict). Assertive people operate with an "I win, you win" philosophy; they assume that both people can gain something from an interpersonal interaction, even from a confrontation. People who are assertive in interpersonal communication display four major behavior patterns (Norton & Warnick, 1976):

- They express their feelings frankly and openly to people in general as well as to those in whom they may have a romantic interest.
- They volunteer opinions and beliefs, deal directly with interpersonal communication situations that may be stressful, and question others without fear.
- They stand up and argue for their rights, even if this may entail a certain degree of disagreement or conflict with relatives or close friends.
- They make up their own minds on the basis of evidence and argument instead of just accepting what others say.

Research shows that people who are assertive generally answer yes to these questions. Assertive people are more open, less anxious, more contentious, and less likely to be intimidated or easily persuaded than nonassertive people. People who are low in assertiveness generally answer no to the questions above. Such unassertive people are less open, more anxious, less contentious, and more likely to be intimidated and easily persuaded.

GUIDELINES FOR INCREASING ASSERTIVENESS Most people are nonassertive in certain situations. If you're one of these people and if you wish to modify your behavior in some situations, there are steps you can take to increase your assertiveness. (If you're nonassertive always and everywhere and are unhappy about this, then you may need to work with a therapist to change your behavior.)

Analyze Assertive Messages. The first step in increasing your assertiveness skills is to understand the nature of these communications. Observe and analyze the messages of others. Learn to distinguish the differences among assertive, aggressive, and nonassertive messages. Focus on what makes one behavior assertive and another behavior nonassertive or aggressive.

After you've gained some skills in observing the behaviors of others, turn your analysis to yourself. Analyze situations in which you're normally assertive and situations in which you're more likely to act nonassertively or aggressively. What circumstances characterize these situations? What do the situations in which you're normally assertive have in common? How do you speak? How do you communicate nonverbally?

Rehearse Assertive Messages. To rehearse assertiveness, select a situation in which you're normally nonassertive. Build a ladder (or hierarchy) whose first step is a relatively nonthreatening message and whose second step would be a bit more risky but still safe and so on, until the final step, the desired communication. For example, let us say that you have difficulty voicing your opinion to your supervisor at work. The desired behavior, then, is to tell your supervisor your opinions. A ladder or hierarchy of situations leading up to this desired behavior might begin with visualizing yourself talking with your boss. Visualize this scenario until you can do it without any anxiety or discomfort. Once you have mastered this visualization, visualize a step closer to your goal: say, walking into your boss's office. Again, do this until your visualization creates no discomfort. Continue with these successive visualizations until you can visualize yourself telling your boss your opinion. As with the other visualizations, practice this until you can do it while totally relaxed. This is the mental rehearsal.

You might add a vocal dimension to this by actually acting out (with voice and gesture) telling your boss your opinion. Again, do this until you experience no difficulty or discomfort. Next, try doing this in front of a trusted and supportive friend or group of friends. Ideally this interaction will provide you with useful feedback. After this rehearsal, you're probably ready for the next step: putting assertiveness into action.

INTERPERSONAL CHOICE POINT

Acting Assertively

The person you've been dating for the past few months is wonderful, and you're looking forward to continuing this relationship. The only problem is that your partner uses language more vulgar than you can stand. You've expressed your displeasure about this, but nothing has changed. You need to be more assertive. What options do you have for communicating more assertively?

Communicate Assertively. Communicating assertively is naturally the most difficult step but obviously the most important. Here's a generally effective pattern to follow:

1. Describe the problem; don't evaluate or judge it. "We're all working on this advertising project together. You're missing half our meetings, and you still haven't produced your first report."
2. State how this problem affects you. Be sure to use I-messages and to avoid messages that accuse or blame the other person. "My job depends on the success of this project, and I don't think it's fair that I have to do extra work to make up for what you're not doing."
3. Propose solutions that are workable and that allow the person to save face. "If you can get your report to the group by Tuesday, we'll still be able to meet our deadline. And I could give you a call an hour before the meetings to remind you."
4. Confirm understanding. "Is it clear that we just can't produce this project if you're not going to pull your own weight? Will you have the report to us by Tuesday?"
5. Reflect on your own assertiveness. Think about what you did. How did you express yourself verbally and nonverbally? What would you do differently next time?

Be cautious, however. It's easy to visualize a situation in which, for example, people are talking behind you in a movie and, with your newfound enthusiasm for assertiveness, you tell them to be quiet. It's also easy to see yourself getting smashed

VIEWPOINTS Concept importance

A widely held assumption in anthropology, linguistics, and communication is that the importance of a concept to a culture can be measured by the number of words the language has for talking about the concept. So, for example, in English, there are lots of words for money, transportation, and communication—all crucial to the English-speaking world. With this principle in mind, consider these findings (Thorne, Kramarae, & Henley, 1983): In a search of English-language terms indicating sexual promiscuity, there were 220 terms referring to a sexually promiscuous woman but only 22 terms for a sexually promiscuous man. What does this finding suggest about our culture's attitudes and beliefs about promiscuity in men and women? In what ways is this changing?

SKILL BUILDING EXERCISE

Evaluating Assertiveness

For any one of the following situations, discuss in a group or write individually (a) an aggressive, (b) a nonassertive, and (c) an assertive response. Then, in one sentence of 15 words or less, explain why your assertiveness message will prove more effective than the aggressive or nonassertive message.

1. You've just redecorated your apartment, expending considerable time and money in making it exactly as you want it. A good friend of yours brings you a house gift—the ugliest poster you've ever seen—and insists that you hang it over your fireplace, the focal point of your living room.
2. Your friend borrows $150 and promises to pay you back tomorrow. But tomorrow passes, as do 20 subsequent tomorrows, and there is still no sign of the money. You know that your friend has not forgotten about the debt, and you also know that your friend has more than enough money to pay you back.
3. Your next-door neighbor repeatedly asks you to take care of her four-year-old while she runs some errand or another. You don't mind helping out in an emergency, but this occurs almost every day. You feel you're being taken advantage of and simply do not want to do this anymore.

Assertiveness is the most direct and honest response in situations such as these. Usually it's also the most effective.

in the teeth as a result. In applying the principles of assertive communication, be careful that you do not go beyond what you can handle effectively.

Can you explain in your own words the eight principles of verbal messages (meanings are in people; meanings are denotative and connotative; meanings vary in abstraction, politeness, and immediacy; messages can deceive; and messages vary in assertiveness)? Can you apply the skills that are a part of these principles in your own verbal message sending and receiving?

CONFIRMATION AND DISCONFIRMATION

Explore the **Exercise** "Confirming, Rejecting, and Disconfirming" at **MyCommunicationLab**

The terms *confirmation* and *disconfirmation* refer to the extent to which you acknowledge another person. **Disconfirmation** is a communication pattern in which you ignore someone's presence as well as that person's communications. You say, in effect, that this person and what this person has to say are not worth serious attention or effort, that this person and this person's contributions are so unimportant or insignificant that there is no reason to concern yourself with them.

Note that disconfirmation is not the same as **rejection**. In rejection, you acknowledge but disagree with the person; you indicate your unwillingness to accept something the other person says or does. In disconfirming someone, however, you deny that person's significance; you claim that what this person says or does simply does not count.

Confirmation is the opposite communication pattern. In **confirmation**, you not only acknowledge the presence of the other person but also indicate your acceptance of this person, of this person's self-definition, and of your relationship as defined or viewed by this other person.

Consider this situation. You've been living with someone for the past six months, and you arrive home late one night. Your partner, let's say Pat, is angry and complains about your being so late. Which of the following is most likely to be your response?

- Stop screaming. I'm not interested in what you're babbling about. I'll do what I want, when I want. I'm going to bed.
- What are you so angry about? Didn't you get in three hours late last Thursday when you went to that office party? So knock it off.

INTERPERSONAL CHOICE POINT

Discouraging Disconfirmation

For the past several months, you've noticed how disconfirming your neighbors are toward their preteen children; it seems the children can never do anything to the parents' satisfaction. What are some of the things you might say (if you do decide to get involved) to make your neighbors more aware of their communication patterns and the possible negative effects these might have? Through what channel would you send these messages?

- You have a right to be angry. I should have called to tell you I was going to be late, but I got involved in an argument at work, and I couldn't leave until it was resolved.

In the first response, you dismiss Pat's anger and even indicate dismissal of Pat as a person. In the second response, you reject the validity of Pat's reasons for being angry but do not dismiss either Pat's feelings of anger or Pat as a person. In the third response, you acknowledge Pat's anger and the reasons for it. In addition, you provide some kind of explanation and, in doing so, show that both Pat's feelings and Pat as a person are important and that Pat has the right to know what happened. The first response is an example of disconfirmation, the second of rejection, and the third of confirmation. You can communicate both confirmation and disconfirmation in a wide variety of ways; Table 5.2 shows just a few.

You can gain insight into a wide variety of offensive language practices by viewing them as types of disconfirmation—as language that alienates and separates. One such practice is "ableism," or discrimination against people with disabilities. This particular practice is handled throughout this text in a series of tables offering tips for communication between people with and without a variety of disabilities. These tables address communication:

- between people with and without visual impairment (Chapter 1).
- between people with and without disabilities (Chapter 2).
- between people with and without hearing impairment (Chapter 4).
- between people with and without speech and language disorders (Chapter 8).

TABLE 5.2

Confirmation and Disconfirmation

This table identifies some specific confirming and disconfirming messages. As you review this table, try to imagine a specific illustration for each of the ways of communicating disconfirmation and confirmation (Galvin, Bylund, & Brommel, 2012; Pearson, 1993).

Disconfirmation	Confirmation
Ignores the presence or contributions of the other person; expresses indifference to what the other person says.	**Acknowledges** the presence and the contributions of the other person by either supporting or taking issue with what he or she says.
Makes no nonverbal contact; avoids direct eye contact; avoids touching and general nonverbal closeness.	**Makes nonverbal contact** by maintaining direct eye contact and otherwise demonstrating acknowledgment of the other.
Monologues; engages in communication in which one person speaks and one person listens; there is no real interaction.	**Dialogues;** engages in communication in which both persons are speakers and listeners; both are involved.
Jumps to interpretation or evaluation rather than working at understanding what the other person means.	**Demonstrates understanding** of what the other says or, when in doubt, asks questions.
Discourages, interrupts, or otherwise makes it difficult for the other person to express himself or herself.	**Encourages** the other person to express his or her thoughts and feelings by showing interest and asking questions.
Avoids responding or responds tangentially but shifting the focus of the message in another direction.	**Responds directly** and exclusively to what the other person says.

Blog Post

Because I Said So

For an application of this concept of confirmation, see "Because I Said So" at tcbdevito.blogspot.com. How do you see confirmation denied?

Here we'll consider four additional disconfirming practices—racism, heterosexism, ageism, and sexism. We'll then look at preferred "cultural identifiers," or confirming language practices, that are recommended for use with many groups.

VIEWPOINTS Negative terms

Many people feel that it's permissible for members of a particular culture to refer to themselves in terms that if said by outsiders would be considered racist, sexist, or heterosexist. Some researchers suggest a possible problem with this—the idea that these terms may actually reinforce negative stereotypes that the larger society has already assigned to the group (Guerin, 2003). Others would argue that, by using such labels, groups weaken the terms' negative impact. Do you refer to yourself using terms that would be considered offensive or politically incorrect if said by "outsiders"? What effects, if any, do you think such self-talk has?

Racism

Racism—like all the "isms" discussed in this section—exists on both an individual and an institutional level, as pointed out by educational researchers Kent Koppelman and R. Lee Goodhart (2005) and others. *Individual* racism consists of negative attitudes and beliefs that people hold about specific races or ethnic groups. The assumption that certain groups are intellectually inferior to others or are incapable of certain achievements are clear examples of individual racism. Prejudices against American Indians, African Americans, Hispanics, Arabs, and others have existed throughout history and are still a part of many people's lives today.

Institutionalized racism is seen in organizational behaviors such as de facto school segregation, corporations' reluctance to hire members of minority groups, and banks' unwillingness to extend mortgages and business loans to members of some groups or residents of some neighborhoods. Racial profiling, in which people become crime suspects solely because of their apparent race, is another form of institutionalized racism.

Racist language is used by members of one culture to disparage members of other cultures, their customs, or their accomplishments. Racist language emphasizes differences rather than similarities and separates rather than unites members of different cultures.

SKILL BUILDING EXERCISE

Distinguishing among Confirming, Rejecting, and Disconfirming Responses

For each of the following scenarios, (1) write a confirming, a rejecting, and a disconfirming response, and (2) indicate what effects each type of response is likely to generate.

1. Enrique receives this semester's grades in the mail; they're a lot better than previous semesters' grades but are still not great. After opening the letter, Enrique says, "I really tried hard to get my grades up this semester." Enrique's parents respond:
   a. with disconfirmation
   b. with rejection
   c. with confirmation
2. Pat, who has been out of work for the past several weeks, says: "I feel like such a failure; I just can't seem to find a job. I've been pounding the pavement for the past five weeks and still nothing." Pat's friend responds:
   a. with disconfirmation
   b. with rejection
   c. with confirmation
3. Judy's colleague at work comes to her, overjoyed, and tells her that she has just been promoted to vice president of marketing, skipping three steps in the hierarchy and tripling her salary. Judy responds:
   a. with disconfirmation
   b. with rejection
   c. with confirmation

Although each type of response serves a different purpose, confirming responses seem most likely to promote communication satisfaction.

INTERPERSONAL CHOICE POINT

Insults

Your colleague frequently tells jokes that insult various nationalities. With the idea that meanings are in people, not in words, what are some of your options for responding to these "jokes"? What would you say?

Generally, the dominant group uses racist language to establish and maintain power over other groups.

According to Andrea Rich (1974), "any language that, through a conscious or unconscious attempt by the user, places a particular racial or ethnic group in an inferior position is racist." Racist language expresses racist attitudes. It also, however, contributes to the development of racist attitudes in those who use or hear the language. Even when racism is subtle, unintentional, or even unconscious, its effects are systematically damaging (Dovidio, Gaertner, Kawakami, & Hodson, 2002).

Examine your own language racism and avoid:

- using derogatory terms for members of a particular race or group of people.
- interacting with members of other races through stereotypes perpetuated by the media.
- including reference to race when it's irrelevant, as in referring to "an African American surgeon" or "an Asian athlete."
- attributing economic or social problems to the race of individuals rather than to institutionalized racism or to general economic problems that affect everyone.

Heterosexism

Heterosexism also exists on both an individual and an institutional level. On an individual level, the term **heterosexism** refers to attitudes, behaviors, and language that disparage gay men and lesbians and in the belief that all sexual behavior that is not heterosexual is unnatural and deserving of criticism and condemnation. Beliefs such as these are at the heart of antigay violence and "gay bashing." Individual heterosexism also includes such beliefs as the ideas that homosexuals are more likely to commit crimes (there's actually no difference) and to molest children than are heterosexuals (actually, heterosexual married men are overwhelmingly the child molesters) (Abel & Harlow, 2001; Koppelman, 2005). It also includes the belief that homosexuals cannot maintain stable relationships or effectively raise children, beliefs that contradict research evidence (Fitzpatrick, Jandt, Myrick, & Edgar, 1994; Johnson & O'Connor, 2002).

Institutional heterosexism is easy to identify. For example, the ban on gay marriage in many states and the fact that at this time only a few states allow gay marriage are good examples of institutional heterosexism. Other examples include the Catholic Church's ban on homosexual priests, the U.S. military's former "don't ask, don't tell" policy, and the many laws prohibiting adoption of children by gay people. In some cultures, homosexual relations are illegal (for example, in Pakistan, Yemen, and Iran, with sentences that can range from years in prison to death). And, interestingly enough, in some cultures homosexual relationships are illegal for men but legal for women (for example, in Palau, Cook Islands, Tonga, and Guyana).

Heterosexist language includes derogatory terms used for lesbians and gay men. For example, surveys in the military showed that 80 percent of those surveyed had heard "offensive speech, derogatory names, jokes or remarks" about gay people and that 85 percent believed that such derogatory speech was "tolerated" (*New York Times*, March 25, 2000, p. A12). You also see heterosexism in more subtle forms of language usage; for example, when you qualify a professional—as in "gay athlete" or "lesbian doctor"—you, in effect, say that athletes and doctors are not normally gay or lesbian.

Still another instance of heterosexism is the presumption of heterosexuality. Usually, people assume the person they're talking to or about is heterosexual. And usually they're correct because most people are heterosexual. At the same time, however, this presumption denies the lesbian or gay identity a certain legitimacy. The practice is very similar to the presumptions of whiteness and maleness that we have made significant inroads in eliminating.

Explore the **Exercise** "Identifying the Barriers to Communication" at **MyCommunicationLab**

Here are a few additional suggestions for avoiding heterosexist (or what some call homophobic) language:

- Avoid offensive nonverbal mannerisms that parody stereotypes when talking about gay men and lesbians. Avoid the "startled eye blink" with which some people react to gay couples (Mahaffey, Bryan, & Hutchison, 2005).
- Avoid "complimenting" gay men and lesbians by saying that they "don't look it." To gay men and lesbians, this is not a compliment. Similarly, expressing disappointment that a person is gay—often intended to be complimentary, as in comments such as "What a waste!"—is not really flattering.
- Avoid making the assumption that every gay or lesbian knows what every other gay or lesbian is thinking. It's very similar, as one comic put it, to asking an African American, "What do you think Jesse Jackson meant by that last speech?"
- Avoid overattribution, the tendency to attribute just about everything a person does, says, and believes to the fact that the person is gay or lesbian. This tendency helps to activate and perpetuate stereotypes.
- Remember that relationship milestones are important to all people. Ignoring anniversaries or birthdays of, say, a relative's partner is likely to cause hurt and resentment.

> **INTERPERSONAL CHOICE POINT**
>
> **Homophobia**
>
> You're bringing your college roommate home for the holidays; he's an outspoken gay activist, whereas your family is extremely homophobic, though you suspect it's largely because of a lack of knowledge. What are some of the things you can say to help prepare your family and your roommate for their holiday get-together? What channels might you use? What would you say?

Ageism

Ageism is discrimination based on age and also comes in individual and institutionalized forms. On an individual level, ageism is seen in the general disrespect many have for older people. More specifically, it's seen in negative stereotypes that many people have about those who are older.

Although used mainly to refer to prejudice against older people, the word *ageism* can also refer to prejudice against other age groups. For example, if you describe all teenagers as selfish and undependable, you're discriminating against a group purely because of their age and thus are ageist in your statements. In some cultures—some Asian and some African cultures, for example—the old are revered and respected. Younger people seek them out for advice on economic, ethical, and relationship issues.

Institutional ageism is seen in mandatory retirement laws and in age restrictions in certain occupations, such as those of pilot or air traffic controller (which impose age cutoffs rather than basing requirements on demonstrated competence). In some countries, people in their 70s are not able to rent cars. In less obvious forms, institutional ageism is seen in the media's portrayal of old people as incompetent, complaining, and—perhaps most clearly evidenced in television and films—without romantic feelings. Rarely, for example, do TV shows or films show older people working productively, being cooperative and pleasant, and engaging in romantic and sexual relationships.

Popular language is replete with ageist phrases; as with racist and heterosexist language, we can all provide plenty of examples. Similarly, qualifying a description of someone in terms of his or her age—especially when it's irrelevant to the discussion—demonstrates ageism. You also communicate ageism when you speak to older people in overly simple words or explain things that don't need explaining. Also, it's a mistake to speak to an older person at an overly high volume; this suggests that all older people have hearing difficulties, and it tends to draw attention to the fact that you are talking down to the older person.

One useful way to avoid ageism is to recognize and avoid the illogical stereotypes that ageist language is based on, for example:

- Avoid talking down to a person because he or she is older. Older people are not mentally slow; most people remain mentally alert well into old age.
- Refrain from refreshing an older person's memory each time you see the person. Older people can and do remember things.

> **INTERPERSONAL CHOICE POINT**
>
> **Ageism**
>
> One of your instructors is extremely sensitive in talking about women, different races, and different affectional orientations but consistently speaks of old people using stereotypical and insulting language. What are some of the things you can say (you're in your early 20s and your instructor is at least 65) to voice your objection to this type of talk?

- Avoid implying that relationships are no longer important. Older people continue to be interested in relationships.
- Speak at a normal volume, and maintain a normal physical distance. Being older does not necessarily mean being hard of hearing or being unable to see; most older people hear and see quite well, sometimes with hearing aids or glasses.
- Engage older people in conversation as you would wish to be engaged. Older people are interested in the world around them.

Sexism

Explore the Concept "Sexist Language" at **MyCommunicationLab**

Sexism refers to the prejudicial attitudes and beliefs about men or women based on rigid beliefs about gender roles. Individual sexism may take the form of beliefs such as the ideas that women should be caretakers, should be sensitive at all times, and should acquiesce to men's decisions concerning political or financial matters. It also includes beliefs such as the notions that men are insensitive, are interested only in sex, and are incapable of communicating feelings.

Institutional sexism, on the other hand, consists of customs and practices that discriminate against people because of their gender. Two very clear examples are the widespread practice of paying women less than men for the same job and the discrimination against women in the upper levels of management. Another clear example of institutionalized sexism is the practice of automatically or near-automatically granting child custody to the mother rather than the father in divorce cases.

Blog Post

Gender Gap

For an article on sexual equality in different countries, see "Gender Gap" at tcbdevito.blogspot.com. Do you see "gender gaps"? Where are they most prevalent?

Of particular interest here is **sexist language**: language that puts down someone because of his or her gender (usually, language derogatory toward women). The National Council of Teachers of English has proposed guidelines for nonsexist (gender-free, gender-neutral, or sex-fair) language. These guidelines concern the use of the generic word *man*, the use of generic *he* and *his*, and sex role stereotyping (Penfield, 1987).

- Avoid using the word *man* generically. The word *man* refers most clearly to an adult male. To use the term to refer to both men and women emphasizes maleness at the expense of femaleness. Gender-neutral terms can easily be substituted. Instead of *mankind*, you can say *humanity*, *people*, or *human beings*. Instead of the *common man*, you can say *the average person* or *ordinary people*. Similarly, the use of terms such as *policeman* or *fireman* and other terms that presume maleness as the norm—and femaleness as a deviation from this norm—are clear and common examples of sexist language.
- Avoid using the words *he* and *his* as generic. There seems no legitimate reason why the feminine pronoun cannot alternate with the masculine pronoun to refer to hypothetical individuals, or why terms such as *he and she* or *her and him* cannot be used instead of just *he* or *him*. Alternatively, you can restructure your sentences to eliminate any reference to gender. For example, the NCTE Guidelines (Penfield, 1987) suggest that instead of saying, "The average student is worried about his grades," you say, "The average student is worried about grades." Instead of saying, "Ask that each student hand in his work as soon as he is finished," say, "Ask students to hand in their work as soon as they're finished."
- Avoid sex role stereotyping. The words you use often reflect a sex role bias—the assumption that certain roles or professions belong to men and others belong to women. When you make the hypothetical elementary school teacher female and the college professor male, or when you refer to doctors as male and nurses as female, you're sex role stereotyping. This is also true when you include the sex of a professional, as in referring to a "female doctor" or a "male nurse."

INTERPERSONAL CHOICE POINT

Cultural Identifiers

You're at an international students open house, and all students are asked to talk about the cultural identifiers they prefer to have used in reference to themselves as well as the cultural identifiers they do not like. How might you explain the cultural identifiers you like and don't like?

Cultural Identifiers

Perhaps the best way to develop nonracist, nonheterosexist, nonageist, and nonsexist language is to examine the preferred **cultural identifiers** to use in talking to and about members of different groups. Keep in mind, however, that preferred terms frequently change over time and that there is a difference of opinion, so keep in touch with the most current preferences and be aware of the preference of the group to which you're referring. The preferences and many of the specific examples identified here are drawn largely from the findings of the Task Force on Bias-Free Language of the Association of American University Presses (Faigley, 2009; Schwartz, 1995).

"It doesn't have a damn thing to do with political correctness, pal. I'm a sausage, and that guy's a wienie."

Charles Barsotti/The New Yorker Collection/www.cartoonbank.com

RACE AND NATIONALITY Some research finds that the term African American is preferred over black in referring to Americans of African descent (Hecht, Jackson, & Ribeau, 2003). Other research, however, concludes that "a majority of blacks in America today do not have a preference" (Newport, 2007). *Black* is often used with *white*, as well as in a variety of other contexts (for example, Department of Black and Puerto Rican Studies, the *Journal of Black Studies*, and Black History Month). The American Psychological Association recommends that both terms be capitalized, but the *Chicago Manual of Style* recommends using lowercase. The terms *Negro* and *colored*, although used in the names of some organizations (for example, the United Negro College Fund and the National Association for the Advancement of Colored People), are not appropriately used outside these contexts.

White is generally used to refer to those whose roots are in European cultures and usually does not include Hispanics. Analogous to African American (which itself is based on a long tradition of terms such as Irish American and Italian American) is the phrase *European American*. Few European Americans, however, call themselves that; most prefer their national origins emphasized, as in, for example, German American or Greek American. *People of color*—a more literary-sounding term appropriate perhaps to public speaking but awkward in most conversations—is preferred to *nonwhite*, which implies that whiteness is the norm and nonwhiteness is a deviation from that norm. The same is true of the term *non-Christian*: It implies that people who have other beliefs deviate from the norm.

Generally, the term *Hispanic* refers to anyone who identifies himself or herself as belonging to a Spanish-speaking culture. *Latina* (female) and *Latino* (male) refer to persons whose roots are in one of the Latin American countries, such as Haiti, the Dominican Republic, Nicaragua, or Guatemala. *Hispanic American* refers to U.S. residents whose ancestry is in a Spanish culture; the term includes Mexican, Caribbean, and Central and South Americans. In emphasizing a Spanish heritage, however, the term is really inaccurate because it leaves out the large numbers of people in the Caribbean and in South America whose origins are African, Native American, French, or Portuguese. *Chicana* (female) and *Chicano* (male) refer to persons with roots in Mexico, although they often connote a nationalist attitude (Jandt, 2009) and is considered offensive by many Mexican Americans. *Mexican American* is generally preferred.

Inuk (plural, *Inuit*), also spelled with two n's (*Innuk* and *Innuit*), is preferred to *Eskimo* (a term the U.S. Census Bureau uses), which was applied to the indigenous peoples of Alaska and Canada by Europeans and literally means "raw meat eaters."

The word *Indian* technically refers only to someone from India, not to the indigenous peoples of North America. *American Indian* or *Native American* is preferred, even though many Native Americans do refer to themselves as *Indian people*. The word *squaw*, used to refer to a Native American woman and still used in the names of some places in the United States and in some textbooks, is clearly a term to be avoided; its usage is almost always negative and insulting (Koppelman, 2005).

In Canada, indigenous people are called *first people* or *first nations*. The term *native American* (with a lowercase n) is most often used to refer to persons born in the United

States. Although technically the term could refer to anyone born in North or South America, people outside the United States generally prefer more specific designations such as *Argentinean*, *Cuban*, or *Canadian*. The term *native* describes an indigenous inhabitant; it is not used to indicate someone having a less developed culture.

Muslim (rather than the older *Moslem*) is the preferred form to refer to a person who adheres to the religious teachings of Islam. *Quran* (rather than *Koran*) is the preferred term for the scriptures of Islam. *Jewish people* is often preferred to *Jews*, and *Jewess* (a Jewish female) is considered derogatory.

When history was being written from a European perspective, Europe was taken as the focal point, and the rest of the world was defined in terms of its location relative to that continent. Thus, Asia became the East or the Orient, and *Asians* became *Orientals*—a term that is today considered "Eurocentric." People from Asia are *Asians*, just as people from Africa are *Africans* and people from Europe are *Europeans*.

AFFECTIONAL ORIENTATION Generally, *gay* is the preferred term to refer to a man who has an affectional preference for other men, and *lesbian* is the preferred term for a woman who has an affectional preference for other women (Lever, 1995). (Lesbian means "homosexual woman," so the term *lesbian woman* is redundant.) *Homosexual* refers to both gay men and lesbians but more often to a sexual orientation to members of one's own sex and is often considered derogatory when used instead of *gay*. Gay and lesbian refer to a lifestyle and not just to sexual orientation. Gay as a noun, although widely used, may prove offensive in some contexts, as in "We have two gays on the team." Because most scientific thinking holds that sexuality is not a matter of choice, the terms *sexual orientation* and *affectional orientation* are preferred to sexual preference or sexual status (which is also vague).

In the case of same-sex marriages—there are two husbands or two wives. In a male–male marriage, each person is referred to as husband, and in the case of female–female marriage, each person is referred to as wife. Some same-sex couples—especially those who are not married—prefer the term "partner" or "lover."

AGE AND SEX *Older person* is preferred to *elder, elderly, senior*, or *senior citizen* (which technically refers to someone older than 65). Usually, however, terms designating age are unnecessary. There are times, of course, when you'll need to refer to a person's age group, but most of the time it isn't necessary—in much the same way that racial or affectional orientation terms are usually irrelevant.

Generally, the term *girl* should be used only to refer to very young females and is equivalent to *boy*. Neither term should be used for people older than 17 or 18. *Girl* is never used to refer to a grown woman, nor is *boy* used to refer to people in blue-collar positions, as it once was. *Lady* is negatively evaluated by many because it connotes the stereotype of the prim and proper woman. *Woman* or *young woman* is preferred. Although there are regional variations, the term *ma'am*, originally an honorific used to show respect, is probably best avoided because today it's often used as a verbal tag to comment (indirectly) on the woman's age or marital status (Angier, 2010).

Transgendered people (people who identify themselves as members of the sex opposite to the one they were assigned at birth and who may be gay or straight, male or female) are addressed according to their self-identified sex. Thus, if the person identifies herself as a woman, then the feminine name and pronouns are used—regardless of the person's biological sex. If the person identifies himself as a man, then the masculine name and pronouns are used.

Transvestites (people who prefer at times to dress in the clothing of the sex other than the one they were assigned at birth and who may be gay or straight, male or female) are addressed on the basis of their clothing. If the person is dressed as a woman—regardless of the birth-assigned sex—she is referred to and addressed with feminine

INTERPERSONAL CHOICE POINT

Cultural Insensitivity

You inadvertently say something that you thought would be funny, but it turns out that you offended a friend with some culturally insensitive remark. What might you say to make it clear that you don't normally talk this way?

pronouns and feminine name. If the person is dressed as a man—regardless of the birth-assigned sex—he is referred to and addressed with masculine pronouns and masculine name.

Can you distinguish between confirmation and disconfirmation? Can you use appropriate cultural identifiers, without language that might be considered racist, heterosexist, ageist, and sexist?

GUIDELINES FOR USING VERBAL MESSAGES EFFECTIVELY

The principles governing the verbal messages system suggest a wide variety of suggestions for using language more effectively. Here are some additional guidelines for making your own verbal messages more effective and a more accurate reflection of the world in which we live. Here we consider six such guidelines: (1) extensionalize: avoid intensional orientation, (2) recognize complexity: avoid allness, (3) distinguish between facts and inferences: avoid fact–inference confusion, (4) discriminate among: avoid indiscrimination, (5) talk about the middle: avoid polarization, and (6) update messages: avoid static evaluation.

Watch the **Video** "Interpersonal Communication" at **MyCommunicationLab**

Extensionalize: Avoid Intensional Orientation

The term **intensional orientation** (the "s" is intentional) refers to the tendency to view people, objects, and events in terms of how they're talked about or labeled rather than in terms of how they actually exist. *Extensional orientation* is the opposite: the tendency to look first at the actual people, objects, and events and then at the labels. It's the tendency to be guided by what you see happening rather than by the way something or someone is talked about or labeled.

Intensional orientation occurs when you act as if the words and labels were more important than the things they represent—as if the map were more important than the territory. In its extreme form, intensional orientation is seen in the person who is afraid of dogs and who begins to sweat when shown a picture of a dog or when hearing people talk about dogs. Here the person is responding to a label as if it were the actual thing. In its more common form, intensional orientation occurs when you see people through your schemata instead of on the basis of their specific behaviors. For example, it occurs when you think of a professor as an unworldly egghead before getting to know the specific professor.

The corrective to intensional orientation is to focus first on the object, person, or event and then on the way in which the object, person, or event is talked about. Labels are certainly helpful guides, but don't allow them to obscure what they're meant to symbolize.

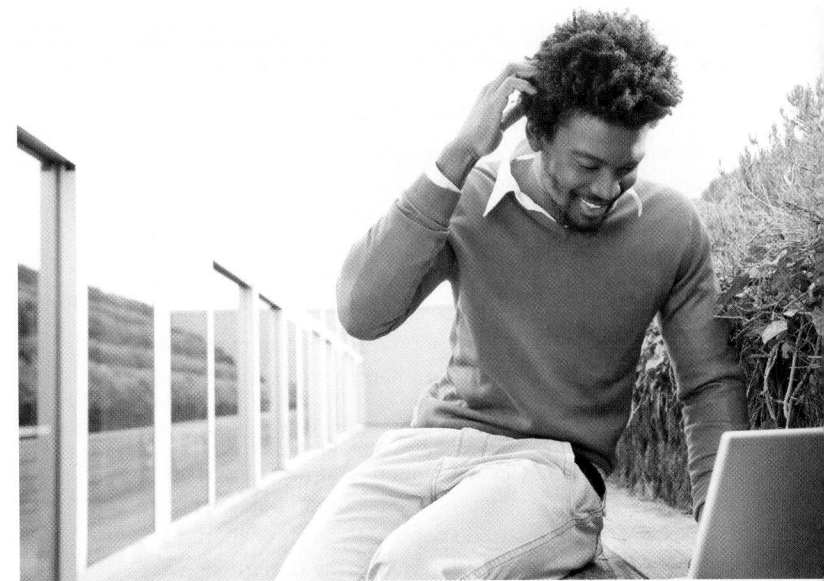

VIEWPOINTS Labels
One of the problems with the tendency to respond to labels is that these labels set up a kind of template through which you then see the thing or person. Having been told someone is deceitful, for example, you may then interpret future behaviors of this person through this *deceitful* label. What are some of the implications of this for writing your profile on social networking sites such as Facebook and LinkedIn? On dating sites such as Match.com and eHarmony?

Recognize Complexity: Avoid Allness

The world is infinitely complex, and because of this, you can never say all there is to say about anything—at least not logically. When you assume you do, you're committing the fallacy of **allness**, which is particularly relevant when you are dealing with people. You may think you know all there is to know about certain individuals or about why they did what they did, yet clearly you don't know all. You can never know all the reasons you yourself do something, so there is no way you can know all the reasons your parents, friends, or enemies did something.

You may, for example, go on a first date with someone who, at least during the first hour or so, turns out to be less interesting than you would have liked. Because of this initial impression, you may infer that this person is dull, always and everywhere. Yet it could be that this person is simply ill at ease or shy during first meetings. The problem here is that you run the risk of judging a person on the basis of a very short acquaintanceship. Further, if you then define this person as dull, you're likely to treat the person as dull and fulfill your own prophecy.

A useful extensional device that can help you avoid allness is to end each statement, sometimes verbally but always mentally, with an "etc." (**et cetera**)—a reminder that there is more to learn, know, and say; that every statement is inevitably incomplete. To be sure, some people overuse the et cetera. They use it as a substitute for being specific, which defeats its purpose. Instead, it should be used to mentally remind yourself that there is more to know and more to say.

Explore the **Concept** "Perception" at **MyCommunicationLab**

Distinguish Between Facts and Inferences: Avoid Fact–Inference Confusion

Before reading this section, test your ability to distinguish facts from inferences by taking the accompanying self-test, "Can You Distinguish Facts from Inferences?"

Language enables you to form statements of facts and inferences without making any linguistic distinction between the two. For example, you can make statements about things that you observe, and you can make statements about things that you have not observed. In form or structure, these statements are similar; they cannot be distinguished from each

TEST YOURSELF

Can You Distinguish Facts from Inferences?

Carefully read the following report and the observations based on it. Indicate whether you think, on the basis of the information presented in the report, that the observations are true, false, or doubtful. Write *T* if the observation is definitely true, *F* if the observation is definitely false, and *?* if the observation may be either true or false. Judge the observations in order. Do not reread the observations after you have indicated your judgment, and do not change any of your answers.

A well-liked college teacher had just completed making up the final examinations and had turned off the lights in the office. Just then a tall, broad figure with dark glasses appeared and demanded the examination. The professor opened the drawer. Everything in the drawer was picked up, and the individual ran down the corridor. The dean was notified immediately.

____ 1. The thief was tall and broad and wore dark glasses.
____ 2. The professor turned off the lights.
____ 3. A tall figure demanded the examination.
____ 4. The examination was picked up by someone.
____ 5. The examination was picked up by the professor.
____ 6. A tall, broad figure appeared after the professor turned off the lights in the office.
____ 7. The man who opened the drawer was the professor.
____ 8. The professor ran down the corridor.
____ 9. The drawer was never actually opened.
____10. Three persons are referred to in this report.

How Did You Do? After you answer all 10 questions, form small groups of five or six and discuss the answers. Look at each statement from each member's point of view. For each statement, ask yourself, "How can you be absolutely certain that the statement is true or false?" You should find that only one statement can be clearly identified as true and only one as false; eight should be marked *?*.

What Will You Do? Try to formulate specific guidelines that will help you distinguish facts from inferences.

other by any grammatical analysis. For example, you can say, "She is wearing a blue jacket" as well as "She is harboring an illogical hatred." In the first sentence, you can observe the jacket and the blue color; the sentence constitutes a factual statement. But how do you observe "illogical hatred"? Obviously, this is an inferential statement, a statement that you make not solely on what you observe but on what you observe plus your own conclusions.

Distinguishing between these two types of statements does not imply that one type is better than the other. Both types of statements are useful; both are important. The problem arises when you treat an inferential statement as if it were fact. Phrase your inferential statements as tentative. Recognize that such statements may be wrong. Leave open the possibility of other alternatives.

"Are you the angry young artist or the angry young bloodsucking dealer?"

Michael Crawford/The New Yorker Collection/www.cartoonbank.com

Discriminate Among: Avoid Indiscrimination

Nature seems to abhor sameness at least as much as vacuums, for nowhere in the universe can you find identical entities. Everything is unique. Language, however, provides common nouns, such as *teacher*, *student*, *friend*, *war*, *politician*, and the like, that may lead you to focus on similarities. Such nouns can lead you to group together all teachers, all students, and all friends and perhaps divert attention from the uniqueness of each individual, object, and event.

The misevaluation known as **indiscrimination**—a form of stereotyping (see Chapter 2)—occurs when you focus on classes of individuals, objects, or events and fail to see that each is unique and needs to be looked at individually. Indiscrimination can be seen in such statements as *He's just like the rest of them: lazy, stupid, a real slob*; or *I really don't want another ethnic on the board of directors. One is enough for me*; or *Read a romance novel? I read one when I was 16. That was enough to convince me.*

A useful antidote to indiscrimination is the extensional device called the **index**, a spoken or mental subscript that identifies each individual in a group as an individual even though all members of the group may be covered by the same label. For example, when you think and talk of an individual politician as just a "politician," you may fail to see the uniqueness in this politician and the differences between this particular politician and other politicians. However, when you think with the index—when you think not of politician but of politician_1 or politician_2 or politician_3—you're less likely to fall into the trap of indiscrimination and more likely to focus on the differences among politicians. The more you discriminate among individuals covered by the same label, the less likely you are to discriminate against any group.

Talk About the Middle: Avoid Polarization

Polarization, often referred to as the fallacy of "either/or," is the tendency to look at the world and to describe it in terms of extremes—good or bad, positive or negative, healthy or sick, brilliant or stupid, rich or poor, and so on. Polarized statements come in many forms, for example: *After listening to the evidence, I'm still not clear who the good guys are and who the bad guys are*; or *Well, are you for us or against us?* or *College had better get me a good job. Otherwise, this has been a big waste of time.*

Most people exist somewhere between the extremes of good and bad, healthy and sick, brilliant and stupid, rich and poor. Yet there seems to be a strong tendency to view only the extremes and to categorize people, objects, and events in terms of these polar opposites.

You can easily demonstrate this tendency by filling in the opposites for each of the following words:

Blog Post

General Semantics

These guidelines are derived from the work of General Semanticists. For a look at this area of study concerned with the relationships among language, thought, and behavior, see "General Semantics" at tcbdevito.blogspot.com. Which of these principles/guidelines do you see violated most often?

								Opposite
tall:	______:	______:	______:	______:	______:	______:	______:	________
heavy:	______:	______:	______:	______:	______:	______:	______:	________
strong:	______:	______:	______:	______:	______:	______:	______:	________
happy:	______:	______:	______:	______:	______:	______:	______:	________
legal:	______:	______:	______:	______:	______:	______:	______:	________

Filling in the opposites should have been relatively easy and quick. The words should also have been fairly short. Further, if different people supplied the opposites, there would be a high degree of agreement among them. Now try to fill in the middle positions with words meaning, for example, "midway between tall and short," "midway between heavy and light," and so on. Do this before reading any further.

These midway responses (compared with the opposites) were probably more difficult to think of and took you more time. The responses should also have been long words or phrases of several words. Further, different people would probably agree less on these midway responses than on the opposites.

This exercise illustrates the ease with which you can think and talk in opposites and the difficulty you have in thinking and talking about the middle. But recognize that the vast majority of cases exist between extremes. Don't allow the ready availability of extreme terms to obscure the reality of what lies in between (Read, 2004).

Update Messages: Avoid Static Evaluation

Language changes very slowly, especially when compared with the rapid pace at which people and things change. When you retain an evaluation of a person, despite the inevitable changes in the person, you're engaging in **static evaluation**.

While you would probably agree that everything is in a constant state of flux, the relevant question is whether you act as if you know this. Do you act in accordance with the notion of change, instead of just accepting it intellectually? Do you treat your little sister as if she were 10 years old, or do you treat her like the 20-year-old woman she has become? Your evaluations of yourself and others need to keep pace with the rapidly changing real world. Otherwise, you'll be left with attitudes and beliefs—static evaluations—about a world that no longer exists.

To guard against static evaluation, use a device called the **date**: Mentally date your statements and especially your evaluations. Remember that Gerry Smith$_{2010}$ is not Gerry Smith$_{2014}$; academic abilities$_{2010}$ are not academic abilities$_{2014}$. T. S. Eliot, in *The Cocktail Party*, said that "what we know of other people is only our memory of the moments during which we knew them. And they have changed since then... at every meeting we are meeting a stranger."

These six guidelines will not solve all problems in verbal communication, but they will help you to more accurately align your language with the real world, the world of words and not words, infinite complexity, facts and inferences, sameness and difference, extremes and middle ground, and constant change.

Can you explain the nature of intensional orientation, infinite complexity, the distinction between facts and inferences, indiscrimination, polarization, and static evaluation? Can you use verbal messages that avoid such misevaluations? Can you identify these misevaluations in the messages of others?

MESSAGES IN THE MEDIA: WRAP-UP

In watching such shows, try identifying what makes a verbal communication style effective and pleasant and what makes it ineffective and unpleasant.

SUMMARY OF CONCEPTS AND SKILLS

Listen to the **Audio Chapter Summary** at **MyCommunicationLab**

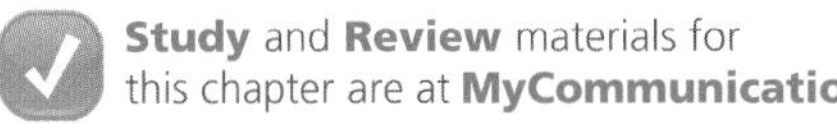

Study and **Review** materials for this chapter are at **MyCommunicationLab**

This chapter looked at verbal messages: the nature of language and the ways in which language works; the concept of disconfirmation and how it relates to racism, heterosexism, ageism, and sexist language; and the ways in which you can use language more effectively.

Principles of Verbal Messages

1. Message meanings are in people, not in things.
2. Verbal messages are both denotative (objective and generally easily agreed upon) and connotative (subjective and generally highly individual in meaning).
3. Verbal messages can be onymous or anonymous.
4. Verbal messages vary in abstraction; they can vary from extremely general to extremely specific.
5. Verbal messages vary in politeness, which can be viewed as strategies that enable a person to maintain a positive public image and autonomy.
6. Verbal messages can deceive, sometimes for acceptable reasons and sometimes for unethical and unacceptable reasons.
7. Messages vary in assertiveness and need to be clearly distinguished from nonassertive and aggressive messages.

Confirmation and Disconfirmation

8. Disconfirmation is the process of ignoring the presence and the communications of others. Confirmation means accepting, supporting, and acknowledging the importance of the other person.
9. Racist, heterosexist, ageist, and sexist messages unfairly put down and negatively evaluate groups and are seen in both individual and institutionalized forms.

Guidelines for Using Verbal Messages Effectively

10. Using verbal messages effectively involves eliminating conceptual distortions and substituting more accurate assumptions about language, the most important of which are:
    - intensional orientation, giving primary attention to the way something is talked about instead of to the actual thing.
    - allness, assuming that all can be known or said about something.
    - fact–inference confusion, treating inferences with the same certainty as facts.
    - indiscrimination, failing to see differences.
    - polarization, assuming that the extremes define the world,
    - static evaluation, assuming non-change.

In addition, this chapter discussed a variety of verbal messages skills. Check those you wish to work on:

____ 1. *Meanings.* Look for meanings in people, not just in words.

____ 2. *Connotative meanings.* Clarify your connotative meanings if you have any concern that your listeners might misunderstand you; as a listener, ask questions if you have doubts about the speaker's connotations.

____ 3. *Abstractions.* Use both abstract and concrete language when describing or explaining.

____ 4. *Politeness.* Be careful of messages that will be perceived as impolite, messages that attack a person's positive or negative face.

____ 5. *Deception.* Be alert to messages that seek to deceive but careful in reading signs of deception where there may be no deception involved.

____ 6. *Confirmation.* When you wish to be confirming, acknowledge (verbally and/or nonverbally) others in your group and their contributions.

____ 7. *Disconfirming language.* Avoid racist, heterosexist, ageist, and sexist language, which is disconfirming and insulting and invariably creates communication barriers.

____ 8. *Cultural identifiers.* Use cultural identifiers that are sensitive to the desires of others; when appropriate, make clear the cultural identifiers you prefer.

____ 9. *Intensional orientation.* Avoid intensional orientation. Look to people and things first and to labels second.

____ 10. *Allness.* Avoid allness statements; they invariably misstate the reality and will often offend the other person.

____ 11. *Facts and inferences.* Distinguish facts (verifiably true past events) from inferences (guesses or hypotheses), and act on inferences with tentativeness.

____ 12. *Indiscrimination.* Treat each situation and each person as unique (when possible) even when they're covered by the same label. Index key concepts.

____ 13. *Polarization.* Avoid thinking and talking in extremes by using middle terms and qualifiers. But remember that too many qualifiers may make you appear unsure of yourself.

____ 14. *Dating statements.* Date your statements to avoid thinking of the world as static and unchanging. Reflect the inevitability of change in your messages.

VOCABULARY QUIZ: The Language of Verbal Messages

Match these terms about language with their definitions. Record the number of the definition next to the appropriate term.

____ polarization (121)
____ intensional orientation (119)
____ connotative meaning (102)
____ fact–inference confusion (120)
____ confirmation (111)
____ static evaluation (122)
____ indiscrimination (121)
____ ageism (115)
____ level of abstraction (104)
____ ableism (112)

1. Treating inferences as if they were facts.
2. The denial of change in language and in thinking.
3. The emotional, subjective aspect of meaning.
4. A communication pattern of acknowledgement and acceptance.
5. Discrimination against people with disabilities.
6. The degree of generality or specificity of a term.
7. Discrimination based on age.
8. The failure to see the differences among people or things covered by the same label.
9. A focus on the way things are talked about rather than on the way they exist.
10. A focus on extremes to the neglect of the middle.

The above terms and additional key terms from this chapter can be found in the glossary.

Study and **Review** the **Flashcards** at **MyCommunicationLab**

MyCommunicationLab

Visit MyCommunicationLab for more information on verbal messages. Flashcards, videos, skill building exercises, sample test questions, and additional exercises, examples, and discussions will help you continue your study of verbal messages in interpersonal communication and the skills of using verbal messages effectively.

CHAPTER

6

Nonverbal Messages

MESSAGES IN THE MEDIA

In *The Mentalist,* police consultant Patrick Jane solves crimes largely through noticing some nonverbal items that escape the attention of everyone else. Although other members of the team inspect the same crime scene, Jane notices what others do not. The same is true in interpersonal communication. Often the meaning of a message will turn on some small nonverbal cue that will be perceived by the effective communicator and ignored by those less effective. Understanding these nonverbal behaviors and the meanings they communicate are the topics of this chapter.

OBJECTIVES *After reading this chapter, you should be able to:*

1. Explain the six principles that identify the ways in which nonverbal communication functions.
2. Define the ten channels of nonverbal messages, and give examples of messages in each channel.
3. Apply the encoding and decoding suggestions in your own nonverbal interactions.

Listen to the **Audio Chapter** at **MyCommunicationLab**

A good way to begin the study of **nonverbal communication** (communication without words) is to consider your own beliefs about nonverbal communication. Which of the following statements do you believe are true?

____ **1.** Nonverbal communication conveys more meaning than verbal communication.
____ **2.** Understanding nonverbal communication will enable you to tell what people are thinking, "to read a person like a book."
____ **3.** Studying nonverbal communication will enable you to detect lying.
____ **4.** Unlike verbal communication, the meanings of nonverbal signals are universal throughout the world.
____ **5.** When verbal and nonverbal messages contradict each other, it's wise to believe the nonverbal.

Actually, all of these statements are popular myths about nonverbal communication. Briefly, (1) in some instances, nonverbal messages may communicate more meaning than verbal messages, but, in most cases, it depends on the situation. You won't get very far discussing science and mathematics nonverbally, for example. (2) This is an impossible task; you may get ideas about what someone is thinking, but you really can't be certain on the basis of nonverbal behaviors alone. (3) Lie detection is a far more difficult process than any chapter or even series of courses could accomplish. (4) Although some nonverbal behaviors may be universal in meaning, many signals communicate very different meanings in different cultures. (5) People can be deceptive verbally as well as nonverbally; it's best to look at the entire group of signals before making a judgment, but even then it won't be an easy or sure thing.

Studying nonverbal communication and developing your nonverbal competence can yield two principal benefits (Burgoon, Guerrero, & Floyd, 2010; Burgoon & Hoobler, 2002). First, the greater your ability to encode and decode nonverbal signals, the higher your popularity and psychosocial well-being are likely to be. Not surprisingly, encoding and decoding abilities are highly correlated; if you're good at expressing yourself nonverbally, then you're likely to also be good at reading the nonverbal cues of others. This relationship is likely part of a more general relationship: people who are high in interpersonal skills are perceived to be high on such positive qualities as expressiveness, self-esteem, outgoingness, social comfort, sociability, and gregariousness. Interpersonal skills really do matter.

Second, the greater your nonverbal skills, the more successful you're likely to be in a wide variety of interpersonal situations, including close relationships, workplace relationships, teacher–student relationships, intercultural communication, courtroom communication, politics, and health care (Knapp, 2008; Richmond, McCroskey, & Hickson, 2008; Riggio & Feldman, 2005).

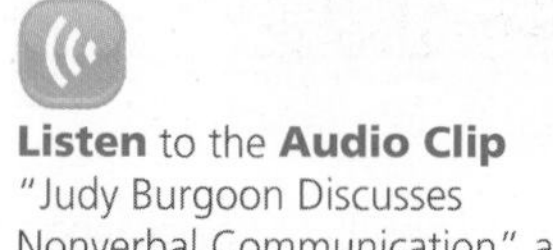
Listen to the **Audio Clip** "Judy Burgoon Discusses Nonverbal Communication" at **MyCommunicationLab**

PRINCIPLES OF NONVERBAL COMMUNICATION

In this section, we look at several principles of nonverbal communication, which, as you'll see, also identify the varied functions that nonverbal messages serve (Afifi, 2007; Burgoon & Bacue, 2003; Burgoon et al., 2010). These principles, as you'll see, are applicable in personal and in workplace situations.

Nonverbal Messages Interact with Verbal Messages

Verbal and nonverbal messages interact with each other in six major ways: to accent, to complement, to contradict, to control, to repeat, and to substitute for each other.

- *Accent.* Nonverbal communication is often used to accent or emphasize some part of the verbal message. You might, for example, raise your voice to underscore a particular word or phrase or look longingly into someone's eyes when saying "I love you."
- *Complement.* Nonverbal communication may be used to complement, to add nuances of meaning not communicated by your verbal message. Thus, you might smile when

telling a story (to suggest that you find it humorous) or frown and shake your head when recounting someone's deceit (to suggest your disapproval).

- *Contradict.* You may deliberately contradict your verbal messages with nonverbal movements; for example, by crossing your fingers or winking to indicate that you're lying.
- *Control.* Nonverbal movements may be used to control, or to indicate your desire to control, the flow of verbal messages, as when you purse your lips, lean forward, or make hand movements to indicate that you want to speak.
- *Repeat.* You can repeat or restate the verbal message nonverbally. You can, for example, follow your verbal "Is that all right?" with raised eyebrows and a questioning look, or you can motion with your head or hand to repeat your verbal "Let's go."
- *Substitute.* You may also use nonverbal communication to substitute for verbal messages. You can, for example, signal "OK" with a hand gesture. You can nod your head to indicate yes or shake your head to indicate no.

When you communicate electronically, of course, your message is communicated by means of typed letters without facial expressions or gestures that normally accompany face-to-face communication and without the changes in rate and volume that are a part of normal telephone communication. To compensate for this lack of nonverbal behavior, you post and refer to photos and videos that convey some of your message's meaning. This lack of nonverbal behavior was the reason the emoticon was created (see Table 6.1). Sometimes called a "smiley" after the ever-present :), the emoticon is a typed symbol that communicates through a keyboard the nuances of the message normally conveyed by nonverbal expression. The absence of the nonverbal channel through which you can clarify your message—for example, smiling or winking to communicate sarcasm or humor—make such typed symbols extremely helpful. As you'll also see from the table, emoticons are specific to a given culture.

Blog Post

Tweets

Even the emotional tone of tweets seems to vary with the time of day. See "Tweets" at tcbdevito.blogspot.com. If you tweet, do you notice differences in the emotional tone?

Nonverbal Messages Help Manage Impressions

It is largely through the nonverbal communications of others that you form impressions of them. Based on a person's body size, skin color, and dress (which you may see face to face or online in photos and videos), as well as on the way the person smiles, maintains

Watch the **Video** "Louder Than Words" at **MyCommunicationLab**

TABLE 6.1

Some Popular Emoticons

These are some of the emoticons used in computer communication. The first six are widely used in the United States; the last three are popular in Japan and illustrate how culture influences such symbols. Because Japanese culture considers it impolite for women to show their teeth when smiling, the emoticon for a woman's smile shows a dot signifying a closed mouth. Depending on your computer, these typed symbols often auto-correct (as in the first two examples) into the graphic smileys. Additional emoticons, acronyms, and abbreviations—in varied cultures—are plentiful on the Internet.

Emoticon	Meaning	Emoticon	Meaning
:-) ☺	Smile: I'm kidding	{*****}	Hugs and kisses
:-(☹	Frown: I'm feeling down	^ . ^	Woman's smile
;-)	Wink	^ _ ^	Man's smile
*	Kiss	^0^	Happy
{ }	Hug		

"Well, just look at you—that's why I'm king."

Charles Barsotti/The New Yorker Collection/www.cartoonbank.com

eye contact, and expresses himself or herself facially, you form impressions—you judge who the person is and what the person is like.

And, at the same time that you form impressions of others, you are also managing the impressions they form of you. As explained in the discussion of impression management in Chapter 3 (pp. 71–76), you use different strategies to achieve different impressions. And of course many of these strategies involve nonverbal messages. For example:

- *To be liked,* you might smile, pat another on the back, and shake hands warmly. See Table 6.2 for some additional ways in which nonverbal communication may make you seem more attractive and more likeable.
- *To be believed,* you might use focused eye contact, a firm stance, and open gestures.
- *To excuse failure,* you might look sad, cover your face with your hands, and shake your head.
- *To secure help* by indicating helplessness, you might use open hand gestures, a puzzled look, and inept movements.
- *To hide faults,* you might avoid self-adaptors.
- *To be followed,* you might dress the part of a leader or display your diploma or awards where others can see them.
- *To confirm self-image and to communicate it to others,* you might dress in certain ways or decorate your apartment with things that reflect your personality.

Nonverbal Messages Help Form Relationships

Much of your relationship life is lived nonverbally. You communicate affection, support, and love, in part at least, nonverbally (Floyd & Mikkelson, 2005). At the same time, you also communicate displeasure, anger, and animosity through nonverbal signals.

You also use nonverbal signals to communicate the nature of your relationship to another person; and you and that person communicate nonverbally with each other. These **tie signs** are signals that communicate your relationship status; they indicate the ways in which your relationship is tied together (Goffman, 1967; Knapp & Hall, 2007). Tie signs are also used to confirm the level of the relationship; for example, you might hold hands to see if this is responded to positively. And of course tie signs are often used to let others know that the two of you are tied together.

Tie signs vary in intimacy and may extend from the relatively informal handshake through more intimate forms such as hand holding and arm linking to very intimate contact such as full mouth kissing (Andersen, 2004).

Nonverbal Messages Structure Conversation

When you're in conversation, you give and receive cues—signals that you're ready to speak, to listen, to comment on what the speaker just said. These cues regulate and structure the interaction. These **turn-taking cues** may be verbal (as when you say, "What do

TABLE 6.2

TEN NONVERBAL WAYS TO INCREASE YOUR ATTRACTIVENESS

Here are ten nonverbal messages that help communicate your attractiveness and ten that will likely create the opposite effect (Andersen, 2004; Riggio & Feldman, 2005).

Do	But Don't
Gesture to show liveliness and animation in ways that are appropriate to the situation and to the message.	Gesture for the sake of gesturing or gesture in ways that may prove offensive to members of other cultures.
Nod and lean forward to signal that you're listening and are interested.	Go on automatic pilot, nodding without any coordination with what is being said or lean forward so much that you intrude on the other's space.
Smile and otherwise show your interest, attention, and positiveness facially.	Overdo it; inappropriate smiling is likely to be perceived negatively.
Make eye contact in moderation.	Stare, ogle, glare, or otherwise make the person feel that he or she is under scrutiny.
Touch in moderation when appropriate.	Touch excessively or too intimately. When in doubt, avoid touching another.
Use vocal variation in rate, rhythm, pitch, and volume to communicate your animation and involvement in what you're saying.	Fall into the pattern where, for example, your voice goes up and down, up and down, up and down without any relationship to what you're saying.
Use silence to listen the same amount of time as you speak. Show that you're listening with appropriate facial reactions, posture, and backchanneling cues, for example.	Listen motionlessly or in ways that suggest you're only listening half-heartedly.
Stand reasonably close to show a connectedness.	Exceed the other person's comfort zone.
Present a pleasant smell and be careful to camouflage the onion, garlic, or smoke that you're so used to, you can't smell it.	Overdo the cologne or perfume or wear your body sweat as a sign of a heavy workout.
Dress appropriately to the situation.	Wear clothing that proves uncomfortable or that calls attention to itself and hence away from your message.

you think?" and thereby give the speaking turn over to the listener). Most often, however, they're nonverbal; a nod of the head in the direction of someone else, for example, signals that you're ready to give up your speaking turn and want this other person to say something. You also show that you're listening and that you want the conversation to continue (or that you're not listening and want the conversation to end) largely through nonverbal signals of posture and eye contact (or the lack thereof).

Nonverbal Messages Can Influence and Deceive

You can influence others not only through what you say but also through your nonverbal signals. A focused glance that says you're committed; gestures that further explain

Blog Post

Deception Detection

For additional reasons why identifying lying is so difficult, see "Deception Detection" at tcbdevito .blogspot.com. Based on your own deception detection experiences, do you agree/disagree with what is said here?

Explore the **Exercise** "Communicating Emotions Nonverbally" at **MyCommunicationLab**

what you're saying; and appropriate dress that says, "I'll easily fit in with this organization" are just a few examples of ways in which you can exert nonverbal influence.

And with the ability to influence, of course, comes the ability to deceive—to mislead another person into thinking something is true when it's false or that something is false when it's true. One common example of nonverbal deception is using your eyes and facial expressions to communicate a liking for other people when you're really interested only in gaining their support in some endeavor. Not surprisingly, you also use nonverbal signals to detect deception in others. For example, you may suspect a person of lying if he or she avoids eye contact, fidgets, and conveys inconsistent verbal and nonverbal messages.

Nonverbal Messages Are Crucial for Expressing Emotions

Nonverbal signals communicate a great part of your emotional experience. For example, you reveal your level of happiness or sadness or confusion largely through facial expressions. You also reveal your feelings by posture (for example, whether tense or relaxed), gestures, eye movements, and even the dilation of your pupils. You can also use nonverbal messages to communicate unpleasant messages that you might feel uncomfortable putting into words (Infante, Rancer, & Avtgis, 2010). For example, you might avoid eye contact and maintain large distances between yourself and someone with whom you didn't want to interact or with whom you wanted to decrease the intensity of your relationship.

At the same time, you also use nonverbal messages to hide your emotions. You might, for example, smile even though you feel sad so as not to dampen the party spirit. Or you might laugh at someone's joke even though you think it silly.

Can you explain the basic principles of nonverbal communication (that nonverbal messages work together with verbal messages, help form impressions, define relationships, structure conversation, can influence and deceive, and are crucial to emotional expression)? Can you identify instances in which your own nonverbal messages illustrate each of these principles?

THE CHANNELS OF NONVERBAL MESSAGES

Nonverbal communication messages may use a variety of channels. Here we'll survey eleven channels: body gestures, body appearance, face, eye, space, artifactual, touch, paralanguage, silence, time, and smell.

Explore the **Concept** "Nonverbal Communication" at **MyCommunicationLab**

Body Gestures

An especially useful classification in **kinesics**, or the study of communication through body movement, identifies five types: emblems, illustrators, affect displays, regulators, and adaptors (Ekman & Friesen, 1969).

Emblems are body gestures that directly translate into words or phrases—for example, the OK sign, the thumbs-up for "good job," and the V for victory. You use these consciously and purposely to communicate the same meaning as the words. But emblems are culture specific, so be careful when using your culture's emblems in other cultures (Axtell, 2007). For example, in the United States, to say "hello" you wave with your whole hand moving from side to side, but in a large part of Europe, that same signal means "no." In Greece, such a gesture would be considered insulting to the person to whom you're waving.

Illustrators enhance (literally "illustrate") the verbal messages they accompany. Most often you illustrate with your hands, but you can also illustrate with head and general body movements. For example, when referring to something on the left, you might gesture toward the left or nod in that direction. You also use illustrators to communicate the shape or size of objects you're talking about.

Affect displays include movements of the face (smiling or frowning, for example), as well as of the hands and general body (body tension or relaxation, for example), that communicate emotional meaning. You use affect displays to accompany and reinforce your verbal messages but also as substitutes for words; for example, you might smile while saying how happy you are to see your friend, or you might simply smile. Affect displays are often unconscious; frequently, example, you smile or frown without awareness. At other times, however, you may smile with awareness, consciously trying to convey pleasure or friendliness.

Regulators are behaviors that monitor, control, coordinate, or maintain the speaking of another individual. When you nod your head, for example, you tell the speaker to keep on speaking; when you lean forward and open your mouth, you tell the speaker that you would like to say something.

Adaptors are gestures that satisfy some personal need. **Self-adaptors** are self-touching movements; for example, rubbing your nose, scratching to relieve an itch, or moving your hair out of your eyes. **Alter-adaptors** are movements directed at the person with whom you're speaking, such as removing lint from a person's jacket, straightening a person's tie, or folding your arms in front of you to keep others a comfortable distance from you. **Object-adaptors** are gestures focused on objects; for example, doodling on or shredding a Styrofoam coffee cup.

Body Appearance

Your general body appearance also communicates. Height, for example, has been shown to be significant in a wide variety of situations. Tall presidential candidates have a much better record of winning elections than do their shorter opponents. Tall people seem to be paid more and are favored by personnel interviewers over shorter job applicants (Guerrero & Hecht, 2008; Jackson & Ervin, 1992; Keyes, 1980; Knapp & Hall, 1996). Taller people also have higher self-esteem and greater career success than do shorter people (Judge & Cable, 2004).

Your body also reveals your race (through skin color and tone) and may even give clues as to your specific nationality. Your weight in proportion to your height will also communicate messages to others, as will the length, color, and style of your hair.

Your general attractiveness, which includes both visual appeal and pleasantness of personality, is also a part of body communication. Attractive people have the advantage in just about every activity you can name. They get better grades in school, are more valued as friends and lovers, and are preferred as coworkers (Burgoon et al., 2010). Not surprisingly, positive facial expressions contribute to the perception of attractiveness for both men and women (Koscriski, 2007).

Facial Messages

Throughout your interpersonal interactions, your face communicates many things, especially your emotions. Facial movements alone seem to communicate messages about pleasantness, agreement, and sympathy; the rest of the body doesn't provide any additional information in those realms. But you'll need both facial and bodily cues to express the intensity with which an emotion is felt (Graham & Argyle, 1975; Graham, Bitti, & Argyle, 1975).

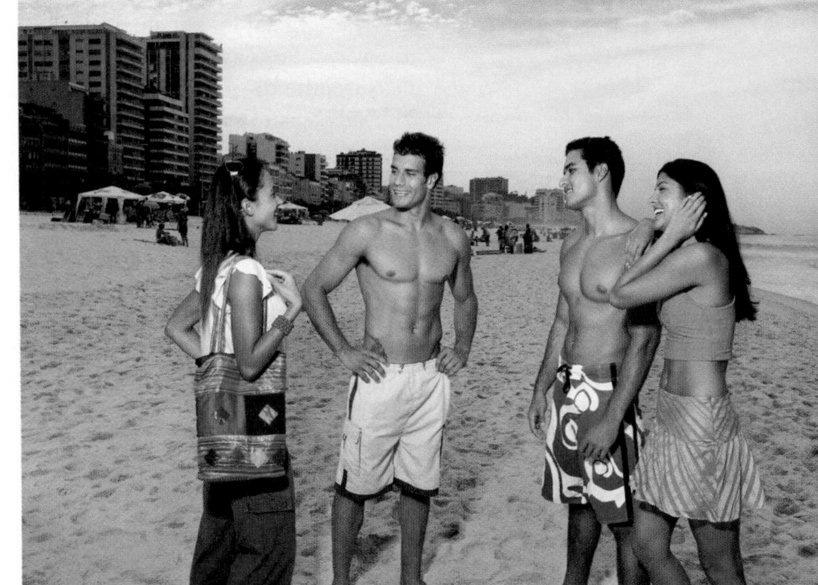

VIEWPOINTS Body appearance

On a ten-point scale, with 1 indicating "not at all important" and 10 indicating "extremely important," how important is body appearance to your own romantic interest in another person? Do the men and women you know conform to the stereotypes that say males are more concerned with the physical and females more concerned with personality?

Try to express surprise using only facial movements. Do this in front of a mirror, and try to describe in as much detail as possible the specific movements of the face that make up a look of surprise. If you signal surprise like most people, you probably use raised and curved eyebrows, long horizontal forehead wrinkles, wide-open eyes, a dropped-open mouth, and lips parted with no tension. Even if there were differences from one person to another—and clearly there would be—you probably could recognize the movements listed here as indicative of surprise.

As you've probably experienced, you may interpret the same facial expression differently depending on the context in which it occurs. For example, in a classic study, when researchers showed participants a smiling face looking at a glum face, the participants judged the smiling face to be vicious and taunting. But when presented with the same smiling face looking at a frowning face, they saw it as peaceful and friendly (Cline, 1956).

Not surprisingly, people who smile are judged to be more likable and more approachable than people who don't smile or people who pretend to smile (Gladstone & Parker, 2002; Kluger, 2005).

> **INTERPERSONAL CHOICE POINT**
>
> **Smiling to Bad Effect**
>
> Sally smiles almost all the time. Even when she criticizes or reprimands a subordinate, she ends with a smile, and this dilutes the strength of her message. As Sally's supervisor, you need her to realize what she's doing and to change her nonverbals. What are some of the things you can say to Sally that will not offend her but at the same time get her to change her habit of smiling?

FACIAL MANAGEMENT As you learn your culture's nonverbal system of communication, you also learn certain facial management techniques that enable you to communicate your feelings in order to achieve the effect you want—for example, to hide certain emotions and to emphasize others. Consider your own use of such facial management techniques; which of the following facial management techniques do you use or see used by others (Richmond et al., 2012)?

- *To intensify,* for example, to exaggerate surprise when friends throw you a party to make your friends feel better
- *To deintensify,* for example, to cover up your own joy in the presence of a friend who didn't receive such good news
- *To neutralize,* for example, to cover up your sadness to keep from depressing others
- *To mask,* for example, to express happiness to cover up your disappointment at not receiving the gift you expected

These facial management techniques help you display emotions in socially acceptable ways. For example, when someone gets bad news in which you may secretly take pleasure, the display rule dictates that you frown and otherwise nonverbally signal your displeasure. If you place first in a race and your best friend barely finishes, the display rule requires that you minimize your expression of pleasure in winning and avoid any signs of gloating. If you violate these display rules, you'll be judged as insensitive. So, although these techniques may be deceptive, they're also expected—and, in fact, required—by the rules of polite interaction.

FACIAL FEEDBACK The **facial feedback hypothesis** holds that your facial expressions influence physiological arousal. In one study, for example, participants held a pen in their teeth to simulate a sad expression and then rated a series of photographs. Results showed that mimicking sad expressions actually increased the degree of sadness the participants reported feeling when viewing the photographs (Larsen, Kasimatis, & Frey, 1992). Generally, research finds that facial expressions can produce or heighten feelings of sadness, fear, disgust, and anger. But this effect does not occur with all emotions; smiling, for example, doesn't seem to make us feel happier (Burgoon et al., 2010). Further, it has not been demonstrated that facial expressions can eliminate one feeling and replace it with another. So if you're feeling sad, smiling will not eliminate the sadness and replace it with gladness. A reasonable conclusion seems to be that your facial expressions can influence some feelings but not all (Burgoon et al., 2010; Cappella, 1993).

CULTURE AND FACIAL EXPRESSION The wide variations in facial communication that you observe in different cultures seem to reflect which reactions are publicly permissible,

"Damn it, when things were going well there was nothing but eye contact."

Charles Barsotti/The New Yorker Collection/www.cartoonbank.com

rather than a difference in the way emotions are facially expressed. For example, Japanese and American students watched a film of a surgical operation (Ekman, 1985a). The students were videotaped both while being interviewed about the film and alone while watching the film. When alone, all students showed very similar reactions. In the interview, however, the American students displayed facial expressions indicating displeasure, whereas the Japanese students did not show any great emotion.

Similarly, cultural differences exist in decoding the meaning of a facial expression. In one study, for example, American and Japanese students judged the meaning of a smiling and a neutral facial expression. The Americans rated the smiling face as more attractive, more intelligent, and more sociable than the neutral face. The Japanese, however, rated the smiling face as more sociable but not as more attractive—and they rated the neutral face as more intelligent (Matsumoto & Kudoh, 1993).

Eye Messages

Research on communication via the eyes (a study known technically as **oculesics**) shows that the duration, direction, and quality of eye movements communicate different messages. For example, in every culture there are strict, though unstated, rules for the proper duration for eye contact. In our culture, the average length of gaze is 2.95 seconds. The average length of mutual gaze (two persons gazing at each other) is 1.18 seconds (Argyle, 1988; Argyle & Ingham, 1972). When eye contact falls short of this amount, you may think the person is uninterested, shy, or preoccupied. When the appropriate amount of time is exceeded, you may perceive the person as showing unusually high interest. Along with this discussion of eye messages, take a look at Table 6.3 (page 134); it identifies some suggestions for communicating between people with and people without visual impairment.

Explore the **Exercise** "Eye Contact" at **MyCommunicationLab**

Blog Post

The Eye Roll

Another type of eye movement is the eye roll. Take a look at "The Eye Roll" at tcbdevito.blogspot.com. Do you use the eye roll? What messages would you be most likely to communicate with the eye roll?

EYE CONTACT With eye contact, you send a variety of messages. One such message is a request for feedback. In talking with someone, we look at her or him intently, as if to say, "Well, what do you think?" As you might expect, listeners gaze at speakers more than speakers gaze at listeners.

Another function of eye contact is to inform the other person that the channel of communication is open and that he or she should now speak. You see this regularly in conversation, when one person asks a question or finishes a thought and then looks to you for a response.

Eye contact may also send messages about the nature of the relationship. For example, if you engage in prolonged eye contact coupled with a smile, you'll signal a positive relationship. If you stare or glare at the person while frowning, you'll signal a negative

TABLE 6.3

INTERPERSONAL COMMUNICATION TIPS BETWEEN PEOPLE WITH AND PEOPLE WITHOUT VISUAL IMPAIRMENTS

People vary greatly in their visual abilities; some are totally blind, some are partially sighted, and some have unimpaired vision. Ninety percent of people who are "legally blind" have some vision. All people, however, have the same need for communication and information. Here are some tips for making communication better between those who have visual impairments and those without such difficulties.

Generally	Specifically
If you're the person without visual impairment and are talking with a visually impaired person:	
Identify yourself.	Don't assume the visually impaired person will recognize your voice.
Face your listener; you'll be easier to hear.	Don't shout. Most people who are visually impaired are not hearing impaired. Speak at your normal volume.
Encode into speech all the meanings you wish to communicate.	Remember that your gestures, eye movements, and facial expressions cannot be seen by the visually impaired.
Use audible turn-taking cues.	When you pass the role of speaker to a person who is visually impaired, don't rely on nonverbal cues; instead, say something like "Do you agree with that, Joe?"
Use normal vocabulary and discuss topics that you would discuss with sighted people.	Don't avoid terms like "see" or "look" or even "blind." Don't avoid discussing a television show or the way your new car looks; these are normal topics for all people.
If you are a person with visual impairment and are talking with a person without visual impairment:	
Help the sighted person meet your special communication needs.	If you want your surroundings described, ask. If you want the person to read the road signs, ask.
Be patient with the sighted person.	Many people are nervous talking with people who are visually impaired for fear of offending. Put them at ease in a way that also makes you more comfortable.
Demonstrate your comfort.	When appropriate, let the other person know that you're comfortable with the interaction, verbally or nonverbally.

Sources: These suggestions were drawn from a variety of sources, including the websites of the Cincinnati Association for the Blind and Visually Impaired, the Association for the Blind of WA, the National Federation of the Blind, and the American Foundation for the Blind, all accessed May 9, 2012.

Blog Post

Eye Contact

For a brief note on something you may have encountered in a restaurant or similar place, take a look at "Eye Contact" at tcbdevito.blogspot.com. What's been your experience in situations like this?

relationship. If you roll your eyes, you'll signal disappointment or disgust or disagreement. Research indicates that it's one of the most hurtful of nonverbal aggressive behaviors (Rancer, Lin, Durbin, & Faulkner, 2010)

EYE AVOIDANCE The eyes are "great intruders," observed sociologist Erving Goffman (1967). When you avoid eye contact or avert your glance, you help others to maintain their privacy. You may do this when you see a couple arguing in public: You turn your eyes away (though your eyes may be wide open) as if to say, "I don't mean to intrude; I respect your privacy," a behavior called **civil inattention**.

Eye avoidance can also signal lack of interest—in a person, a conversation, or some visual stimulus. At times you may hide your eyes to block off unpleasant stimuli (a particularly gory or violent scene in a movie, for example) or close your eyes to block out visual stimuli and thus heighten other senses. For example, you may listen to music with your eyes closed. Lovers often close their eyes while kissing, and many prefer to make love in a dark or dimly lit room.

Culture, Gender, and Eye Messages Not surprisingly, eye messages vary with both culture and gender. Americans, for example, consider direct eye contact an expression of honesty and forthrightness, but the Japanese often view this as a lack of respect. A Japanese person will glance at the other person's face rarely, and then only for very short periods (Axtell, 1990). Interpreting another's eye contact messages with your own cultural rules is a risky undertaking; eye movements that you may interpret as insulting may have been intended to show respect.

Women make eye contact more and maintain it longer (both in speaking and in listening) than men. This holds true whether women are interacting with other women or with men. This difference in eye behavior may result from women's greater tendency to display their emotions (Wood, 1994). When women interact with other women, they display affiliative and supportive eye contact, whereas when men interact with other men, they avert their gaze (Gamble & Gamble, 2003).

VIEWPOINTS Gaze

Listeners gaze at speakers more than speakers gaze at listeners (Knapp & Hall, 2006). The percentage of interaction time spent gazing while listening, for example, ranges from 62 percent to 75 percent; the percentage of time spent gazing while talking, however, ranges from 38 percent to 41 percent. When these percentages are reversed—when a speaker gazes at the listener for longer than "normal" periods or when a listener gazes at the speaker for shorter than "normal" periods—the conversational interaction becomes awkward. Try this out with a friend and see what happens. Even with mutual awareness, you'll notice the discomfort caused by this seemingly minor communication change

Spatial Messages

Proxemics is the study of the ways in which people use space to communicate varied meanings (Hall, 1959, 1963, 1966). We can examine this broad area by looking at the messages communicated by proxemic distances and territory.

Proxemic Distances Not surprisingly, the major proxemic distances correspond closely to the major types of relationships: intimate, personal, social, and public (see Table 6.4, page 136).

In **intimate distance**, ranging from actual touching to 18 inches, the presence of the other individual is unmistakable. Each person experiences the sound, smell, and feel of the other's breath. You use intimate distance for lovemaking, comforting, and protecting. This distance is so short that most people do not consider it proper in public.

Personal distance refers to the protective "bubble" that defines your personal space, ranging from 18 inches to 4 feet. This imaginary bubble keeps you protected and untouched by others. You can still hold or grasp another person at this distance but only by extending your arms; this allows you to take certain individuals such as loved ones into your protective bubble. At the outer limit of personal distance, you can touch another person only if both of you extend your arms. At this distance you conduct much of your interpersonal interactions—for example, talking with friends and family.

At **social distance**, ranging from 4 to 12 feet, you lose the visual detail you have at personal distance. You conduct impersonal business and interact at a social gathering at this social distance. The more distance you maintain in your interactions, the more formal they appear. In offices of high officials, the desks are positioned so the official is assured at least this distance from clients.

Public distance, from 12 to 25 feet or more, protects you. At this distance, you could take defensive action if threatened. On a public bus or train, for example, you might try to keep at least this distance from a drunken passenger. Although at this distance you lose fine details of the face and eyes, you're still close enough to see what is happening.

INTERPERSONAL CHOICE POINT

Inappropriate Spacing

Like in an episode of *Seinfeld*, your friend is a "close talker" and stands much too close to others when talking and makes others feel uncomfortable. What (if anything) can you say or do to help your friend use space to communicate more effectively?

Watch the **Video** "Personal Space" at **MyCommunicationLab**

TABLE 6.4

RELATIONSHIPS AND PROXEMIC DISTANCES

These four distances can be further divided into close and far phases; the far phase of one level (say, personal) blends into the close phase of the next level (social). Do your relationships also blend into one another? Or are, say, your personal relationships totally separated from your social relationships?

Relationship	Distance
Intimate Relationship	Intimate Distance 0 ——— 18 inches close phase — far phase
Personal Relationship	Personal Distance 1½ ——— 4 feet close phase — far phase
Social Relationship	Social Distance 4 ——— 12 feet close phase — far phase
Public Relationship	Public Distance 12 ——— 25+ feet close phase — far phase

The specific distances that you maintain between yourself and other individuals depend on a wide variety of factors (Burgoon et al., 2010). Among the most significant factors are gender (women in same-sex dyads sit and stand closer to each other than do men and people approach women more closely than they approach men); age (people maintain closer distances with similarly aged others than they do with those much older or much younger); and personality (introverts and highly anxious people maintain greater distances than do extroverts). You'll also tend to maintain shorter distances with people you're familiar with than with strangers and with people you like than with those you don't like.

TERRITORIALITY Another type of communication having to do with space is territoriality, a possessive reaction to an area or to particular objects. You interact basically in three types of territories (Altman, 1975):

- **Primary territories** are areas that you might call your own; these areas are your exclusive preserve. Primary territories might include your room, your desk, or your office.
- **Secondary territories** are areas that don't belong to you but which you have occupied and with which you're associated. They might include your usual table in the cafeteria, your regular seat in the classroom, or your neighborhood turf.
- **Public territories** are areas that are open to all people; they may be owned by some person or organization, but they are used by everyone. They are places such as movie theaters, restaurants, and shopping malls.

When you're in your primary territory, you have an interpersonal advantage, often called the home field advantage. In their own home or office, people take on a kind of leadership role: They initiate conversations, fill in silences, assume relaxed and comfortable postures, and maintain their positions with greater conviction. In your own territory, you're dominant, and, therefore you stand a better chance of getting your raise approved, your point accepted, or a contract resolved in your favor if you're in your own territory (your office, your home) rather than in someone else's (Marsh, 1988).

Like animals, humans mark both their primary and secondary territories to signal ownership. Humans use three types of markers: central markers, boundary markers, and earmarkers (Goffman, 1971). **Central markers** are items you place in a territory to reserve it for you—for example, a drink at the bar, books on your desk, or a sweater over a library chair.

Boundary markers serve to divide your territory from that of others. In the supermarket checkout line, the bar placed between your groceries and those of the person behind you is a boundary marker, as are fences, armrests that separate your chair from those on either side, and the contours of the molded plastic seats on a bus.

Earmarkers—a term taken from the practice of branding animals on their ears—are identifying marks that indicate your possession of a territory or object. Trademarks, nameplates, and initials on a shirt or attaché case are all examples of earmarkers.

Markers are also important in giving you a feeling of belonging. For example, one study found that students who marked their college dorm rooms by displaying personal items stayed in school longer than did those who didn't personalize their spaces (Marsh, 1988).

> **INTERPERSONAL CHOICE POINT**
>
> **Inviting and Discouraging Conversation**
> Sometimes you want to encourage people to come into your office and chat, and at other times you want to be left alone. What are some of the things you might do nonverbally to achieve each goal?

Artifactual Messages

Artifactual messages are messages conveyed through objects or arrangements made by human hands. The colors you prefer, the clothing or jewelry you wear, the way you decorate your space, and even bodily scents communicate a wide variety of meanings.

COLOR There is some evidence that colors affect us physiologically. For example, respiratory movements increase with red light and decrease with blue light. Similarly, eye blinks increase in frequency when eyes are exposed to red light and decrease when exposed to blue. This seems consistent with our intuitive feelings that blue is more soothing and red more arousing. When a school changed the color of its walls from orange and white to blue,

Explore the **Exercise** "The Meaning with Color" at **MyCommunicationLab**

> **SKILL BUILDING EXERCISE**
>
> ### Choosing the Right Seat
>
> The graphic here represents a meeting table with 12 chairs, one of which is already occupied by the boss. Below are listed five messages you might want to communicate. For each of these messages, indicate (a) where you would sit to communicate the desired message, (b) any other possible messages that your choice of seat would likely communicate, and (c) the messages that your choice of seat would make it easier for you to communicate.
>
> 1. You want to ingratiate yourself with your boss.
> 2. You aren't prepared and want to be ignored.
> 3. You want to challenge your boss on a certain policy that will come up for a vote.
> 4. You want to help your boss on a certain policy that will come up for a vote.
> 5. You want to be accepted as a new (but important) member of the company.

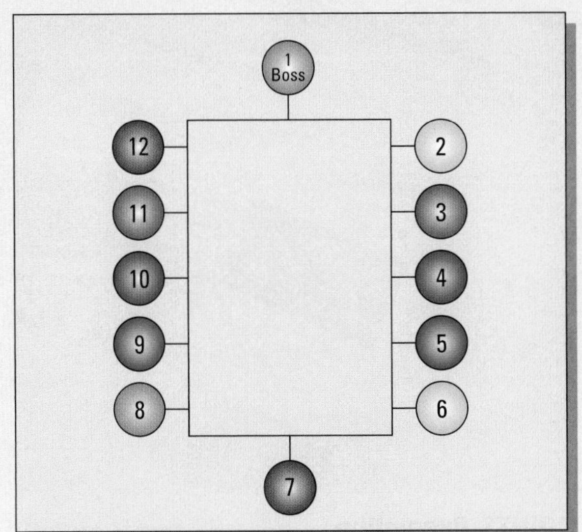

Nonverbal choices (such as the seat you select or the clothes you wear) have an impact on communication and on your image as a communicator.

Blog Post

Artifactual Communication: Color

Take a look at "Artifactual Communication: Color" (and, while on the blog, also look at "The Nonverbal Message of RED"). What do you think?

the blood pressure of the students decreased and their academic performance increased (Malandro, Barker, & Barker, 1989).

Color communication also influences perceptions and behaviors (Kanner, 1989). People's acceptance of a product, for example, can be largely determined by its packaging, especially its color. In one study, participants described the very same coffee taken from a yellow can as weak, from a dark brown can as too strong, from a red can as rich, and from a blue can as mild. Even your acceptance of a person may depend on the colors the person wears. Consider, for example, the comments of one color expert (Kanner, 1989): "If you have to pick the wardrobe for your defense lawyer heading into court and choose anything but blue, you deserve to lose the case ..." Black is so powerful it could work against the lawyer with the jury. Brown lacks sufficient authority. Green would probably elicit a negative response.

Colors vary greatly in their meanings from one culture to another. To illustrate this cultural variation, here are just some of the many meanings that popular colors communicate in a variety of different cultures (Dresser, 1999, 2005; Dreyfuss, 1971; Hoft, 1995; Singh & Pereira, 2005). As you read this section, you may want to consider your own meanings for these colors and where your meanings came from.

- *Red.* In China, red signifies prosperity and rebirth and is used for festive and joyous occasions; in France and the United Kingdom, it indicates masculinity; in many African countries, blasphemy or death; and in Japan, anger and danger.
- *Green.* In the United States, green signifies capitalism, go ahead, and envy; in Ireland, patriotism; among some Native Americans, femininity; to the Egyptians, fertility and strength; and to the Japanese, youth and energy.
- *Black.* In Thailand, black signifies old age; in parts of Malaysia, courage; and in much of Europe, death.
- *White.* In Thailand, white signifies purity; in many Muslim and Hindu cultures, purity and peace; and in Japan and other Asian countries, death and mourning.
- *Blue.* In Iran, blue signifies something negative; in Ghana, joy; among the Cherokee, it signifies defeat; for the Egyptians, virtue and truth; and for the Greeks, national pride.
- *Yellow.* In China, yellow signifies wealth and authority; in the United States, caution and cowardice; in Egypt, happiness and prosperity; and in many countries throughout the world, femininity.
- *Purple.* In Latin America, purple signifies death; in Europe, royalty; in Egypt, virtue and faith; in Japan, grace and nobility; in China, barbarism; and in the United States, nobility and bravery.

VIEWPOINTS Pygmalion

The "Pygmalion gift" is a gift that is designed to change the recipient into what the donor wants that person to become. For example, the parent who gives a child books or science equipment may be asking the child to be a scholar or a scientist. Examine the virtual gifts on social networking sites. Are any of these Pygmalion gifts? Have you given or received Pygmalion virtual gifts?

Clothing and Body Adornment People make inferences about who you are, at least in part, from the way you dress. Whether accurate or not, these inferences will affect what people think of you and how they react to you. Your socioeconomic class, your seriousness, your attitudes (for example, whether you're conservative or liberal), your concern for convention, your sense of style, and perhaps even your creativity will all be judged in part by the way you dress (Burgoon et al., 2010; Knapp & Hall, 1996; Molloy, 1977). In the business world, your clothing may communicate your position within the hierarchy and your willingness and desire to conform to the clothing norms of the organization. It may also communicate your professionalism, which seems to be the reason why some organizations favor dress codes (Smith, 2003). On the other hand, many of the technology companies like Google, Yahoo, and Apple encourage a more informal, casual style of dress.

In the college classroom, research indicates, college students tend to perceive an instructor dressed informally as friendly, fair, enthusiastic, and flexible and the same instructor dressed formally as prepared, knowledgeable, and organized (Malandro et al., 1989).

Body adornment also communicates about who you are—from a concern about being up to date, to a desire to shock, to perhaps a lack of interest in appearances. Your jewelry, too, sends messages about you. Some jewelry is a form of **cultural display**, indicating a particular cultural or religious affiliation. Wedding and engagement rings are obvious examples that communicate specific messages. College rings and political buttons likewise convey messages. If you wear a Rolex watch or large precious stones, others are likely to infer that you're rich. Men who wear earrings will be judged differently from men who don't. What judgments people make will depend, of course, on whom the receiver is, on the communication context, and on all the other factors identified throughout this text.

Blog Post

The Divorce Ring

For another function of rings, see "The Divorce Ring" at tcbdevito.blogspot.com. If you were divorced, would you wear a divorce ring?

Body piercings have become increasingly popular, especially among the young. Nose and nipple rings and tongue and belly-button jewelry send a variety of messages. Although people wearing such jewelry may wish to communicate different meanings, those interpreting the messages of body piercings seem to infer that the wearers are communicating an unwillingness to conform to social norms and a willingness to take greater risks than those without such piercings (Forbes, 2001). Further, health care providers sometimes see tattoos and piercings as signs of such undesirable traits as impulsiveness, unpredictability, and a tendency toward being reckless or violent (Rapsa & Cusack, 1990; Smith, 2003).

Tattoos—whether temporary or permanent—likewise communicate a variety of messages, often the name of a loved one or some symbol of allegiance or affiliation.

Although body piercings and tattoos are becoming more accepted generally, business experts continue to note the negative effects in terms of getting a job and suggest hiding them during job interviews (Ingegneri, 2008; Varenik, 2010).

Space Decoration The way you decorate your private spaces speaks about you. The office with a mahogany desk and bookcases and oriental rugs communicates your importance and status within the organization, just as a metal desk and bare floor indicate a worker much further down in the hierarchy.

Similarly, people will make inferences about you based on the way you decorate your home. The expensiveness of the furnishings may communicate your status and wealth; their coordination may express your sense of style. The books and magazines reflect your interests, and the arrangement of chairs around a television set may reveal how important watching television is to you. In fact, there is probably little in your home that would not send messages from which others would draw inferences about you.

In a similar way, the absence of certain items will communicate something about you. Consider

VIEWPOINTS Defense tactic

A popular defense tactic in sex crimes against women, gay men, and lesbians is to blame the victim by referring to the way the victim was dressed and implying that the victim, by wearing certain clothing, provoked the attack. What do you think of this tactic? Is it likely to be effective? Is it ethical?

INTERPERSONAL CHOICE POINT

Smelling

Your colleague in the next cubicle wears extremely strong cologne that you find horrendous. You can't continue smelling this horrible scent any longer. What choices do you have to correct this situation but not alienate your colleague?

what messages you would get from a home where no television, phone, or books could be seen.

SMELL Smell communication, or **olfactory communication**, is extremely important in a wide variety of situations and is now big business. There is some evidence (though clearly not very conclusive evidence) that the smell of lemon contributes to a perception of health; the smells of lavender and eucalyptus seem to increase alertness; and the smell of rose oil seems to reduce blood pressure. The smell of chocolate seems to reduce theta brain waves and thus produce a sense of relaxation and a reduced level of attention (Martin, 1998). Findings such as these have contributed to the growth of aromatherapy and to a new profession of aromatherapists. Because humans possess so many scent glands, it has been argued that it only remains for us to discover how we use scent to communicate a wide variety of messages (Furlow, 1996, p. 41). Two particularly important messages scent communicates are those of attraction and identification.

Blog Post

Nonverbal Communication: Scent

Take a look at "Nonverbal Communication: Scent" at tcbdevito.blogspot.com for a brief discussion of the connection between scent and memory. Have you ever experienced this?

- *Attraction messages.* People use perfumes, colognes, aftershave lotions, powders, and the like in an effort to enhance attractiveness. You also use scents to make yourself feel better. When you smell pleasant, you feel better about yourself; when you smell unpleasant, you feel less good about yourself—and probably shower and perhaps put on some cologne.
- *Identification messages.* Smell is often used to create an image or an identity for a product (Spence, 2008). Advertisers and manufacturers spend millions of dollars each year creating scents for cleaning products and toothpastes, for example, which have nothing to do with products' cleaning power; instead, they function solely to create an image for the products. There is also evidence that we can identify specific significant others by smell. For example, young children were able to identify the T-shirts of their brothers and sisters solely by smell (Porter & Moore, 1981).

Touch Messages

Touch communication, or **tactile communication**, is perhaps the most primitive form of communication (Montagu, 1971). Touch develops before the other senses; even in the womb, the child is stimulated by touch. Soon after birth, the child is fondled, caressed, patted, and stroked. In turn, the child explores its world through touch and quickly learns to communicate a variety of meanings through touch. The nature of touch communication also varies with relationship stages. In the early stages of a relationship, you touch little; in intermediate stages (involvement and intimacy), you touch a great deal; and at stable or deteriorating stages, you again touch little (Guerrero & Andersen, 1991).

THE MEANINGS OF TOUCH Researchers in the field of **haptics**—the study of touch—have identified the major meanings of touch (Jones & Yarbrough, 1985):

- *Positive feelings.* Touch may communicate such positive feelings as support, appreciation, inclusion, sexual interest or intent, or affection.
- *Playfulness.* Touch often communicates the desire to play, sometimes affectionately, sometimes aggressively.
- *Control.* Touch may control or direct the behaviors, attitudes, or feelings of the other person. To get attention, for example, you may touch a person as if to say, "Look at me" or "Look over here."
- *Ritual.* Touching may also serve a ritual function, for example, shaking hands to say hello or putting your arm around another's shoulder when saying farewell.
- *Task-related.* Touching often occurs while you're performing some function, such as removing a speck of dust from another person's face or helping someone out of a car.

Different cultures view these types of touching differently. For example, some task-related touching, viewed as acceptable in much of the United States, would be viewed negatively in some cultures. Among Koreans, for example, it's considered disrespectful for a storekeeper to touch a customer in, say, handing back change; it's considered too intimate a gesture. But members of other cultures, expecting some touching, may consider the Koreans' behavior cold and insulting.

INTERPERSONAL CHOICE POINT

Touching

Your supervisor touches just about everyone. You don't like it and want it to stop—at least as far as you're concerned. What are some ways you can nonverbally show your aversion to this unwanted touching?

TOUCH AVOIDANCE Much as we touch and are touched, we also avoid touch from certain people and in certain circumstances. Researchers in nonverbal communication have found some interesting relationships between **touch avoidance** and other significant communication variables (Andersen & Leibowitz, 1978; Hall, 1996). Among research findings, for example, is the fact that touch avoidance is positively related to communication apprehension; those who fear oral communication also score high on touch avoidance. Touch avoidance is also high with those who self-disclose little. Both touch and self-disclosure are intimate forms of communication; thus, people who are reluctant to get close to another person by self-disclosing also seem reluctant to get close by touching.

Older people have higher touch-avoidance scores for opposite-sex persons than do younger people. As we get older, we're touched less by members of the opposite sex, and this decreased frequency may lead us to avoid touching.

Males score higher on same-sex touch avoidance than do females, a finding that confirms popular stereotypes. Men avoid touching other men, but women may and do touch other women. On the other hand, women have higher touch-avoidance scores for opposite-sex touching than do men.

CULTURE AND TOUCH Cultures vary greatly in their touching behavior. For example, Muslim children are socialized not to touch members of the opposite sex, a practice that can easily be interpreted as unfriendly by American children who are used to touching each other (Dresser, 2005).

One study on touch surveyed college students in Japan and in the United States (Barnlund, 1975) and found that students from the United States reported being touched twice as much as did the Japanese students. In Japan, there is a strong taboo against strangers touching, and the Japanese are therefore especially careful to maintain sufficient distance.

Some cultures—including many in southern Europe and the Middle East—are considered *contact cultures*, and others—such as those of northern Europe and Japan—are *noncontact cultures*. Members of contact cultures maintain close distances, touch one another in conversation, face each other more directly, and maintain longer and more focused eye contact. Members of noncontact cultures maintain greater distances in their interactions, touch each other rarely (if at all), avoid facing each other directly, and maintain much less direct eye contact.

As you can imagine, touching may also get you into trouble in another way. For example, touching that is too positive (or too intimate) too early in a relationship may send the wrong signals. Similarly, playing too rough or holding someone's arm to control their movements may be resented. Using ritualistic touching incorrectly or in ways that may be culturally insensitive may likewise get you into difficulty.

Paralanguage Messages

The term **paralanguage** refers to the vocal but nonverbal dimensions of speech. It refers to how you say something, not what you say. A traditional exercise students use to increase their ability to express different emotions, feelings, and attitudes is to repeat a sentence while accenting or stressing different words. One popular sentence is "Is this the face that launched a thousand ships?" Examine your own sensitivity to paralanguage

Explore the **Exercise** "Praising and Criticizing" at **MyCommunicationLab**

variations by seeing if you get different meanings for each of the following questions based on where the emphasis or **stress** is.

- *Is* this the face that launched a thousand ships?
- Is *this* the face that launched a thousand ships?
- Is this *the face* that launched a thousand ships?
- Is this the face that *launched* a thousand ships?
- Is this the face that launched *a thousand ships*?

In addition to stress and **pitch** (highness or lowness), paralanguage includes such voice qualities or vocal characteristics as **rate** (speed), **volume** (loudness), and **rhythm** as well as the vocalizations you make in crying, whispering, moaning, belching, yawning, and yelling (Argyle, 1988; Trager, 1958, 1961). A variation in any of these features communicates. When you speak quickly, for example, you communicate something different from when you speak slowly. Even though the words may be the same, if the speed (or volume, rhythm, or pitch) differs, the meanings people receive also will differ.

Judgments About People We often use paralanguage cues as a basis for judgments about people—for example, evaluations of their emotional state or even their personality. A listener can accurately judge the emotional state of a speaker from vocal expression alone, if both speaker and listener speak the same language. Paralanguage cues are not so accurate when used to communicate emotions to those who speak a different language (Albas, McCluskey, & Albas, 1976). Some emotions, of course, are easier to identify than others; it's easy to distinguish between hate and sympathy but more difficult to distinguish between fear and anxiety. And, of course, listeners vary in their ability to decode, and speakers in their ability to encode, emotions (Scherer, 1986).

Less reliable are judgments made about personality. Some people, for example, may conclude that those who speak softly feel inferior, believing that no one wants to listen to them, or that people who speak loudly have over-inflated egos. Such conclusions may be mistaken, however. There are lots of reasons why people might speak softly or loudly.

INTERPERSONAL CHOICE POINT

Criticizing with Kindness

A close friend is going to an important job interview dressed totally inappropriately and asks, "How do I look?" What are some of the things you can say that will boost your friend's confidence but at the same time get your friend to dress differently?

Judgments About Communication Effectiveness The rate or speed at which people speak is the aspect of paralanguage that has received the most attention (MacLachlan, 1979; Swanbrow, 2011). Rates of speech are of interest to the advertiser, the politician, and, in fact, anyone who tries to convey information or influence others. They are especially important when time is limited or expensive.

In one-way communication (when one person is doing all or most of the speaking and the other person is doing all or most of the listening), those who talk fast (about 50 percent faster than normal) are more persuasive. People agree more with a fast speaker than with a slow speaker and find the fast speaker more intelligent and objective. Generally, research finds that a 50 percent faster-than-normal speech rate lowers comprehension by only about 5 percent (Jones, Berry, & Stevens, 2007; MacLachlan, 1979). When the rate is doubled, the comprehension level drops only 10 percent. These 5 percent and 10 percent losses are more than offset by the increased speed; thus, the faster rates are much more efficient in communicating information. If speeds are more than twice the rate of normal speech, however, comprehension begins to fall dramatically.

Rate seems also to influence persuasion. For example, interviewers who called to ask people to participate in a survey were more successful when they spoke moderately fast, at a rate of about 3.5 words per second. Interviewers who spoke overly fast or very slowly were much less successful in gaining compliance (Swanbrow, 2011).

Not all cultures view speech rate in the same way. In one study, for example, Korean male speakers who spoke rapidly were given unfavorable credibility ratings, as opposed to the results obtained by Americans who spoke rapidly. Researchers have suggested that in individualistic societies, a rapid-rate speaker is seen as more competent than a slow-rate speaker, whereas in collectivist cultures, a speaker who uses a slower rate is judged more competent (Lee & Boster, 1992).

Silence Messages

Like words and gestures, **silence**, too, communicates important meanings and serves important functions (Jaworski, 1993; Johannesen, 1974). For example, silence allows the speaker time to think, time to formulate and organize his or her verbal communications. Before messages of intense conflict, as well as before those confessing undying love, there is often silence. Again, silence seems to prepare the receiver for the importance of these messages.

Some people use silence as a weapon to hurt others. We often speak of giving someone "the silent treatment." After a conflict, for example, one or both individuals may remain silent as a kind of punishment. Silence used to hurt others may also take the form of refusal to acknowledge the presence of another person, as in disconfirmation (see Chapter 5); here silence is a dramatic demonstration of the total indifference one person feels toward the other.

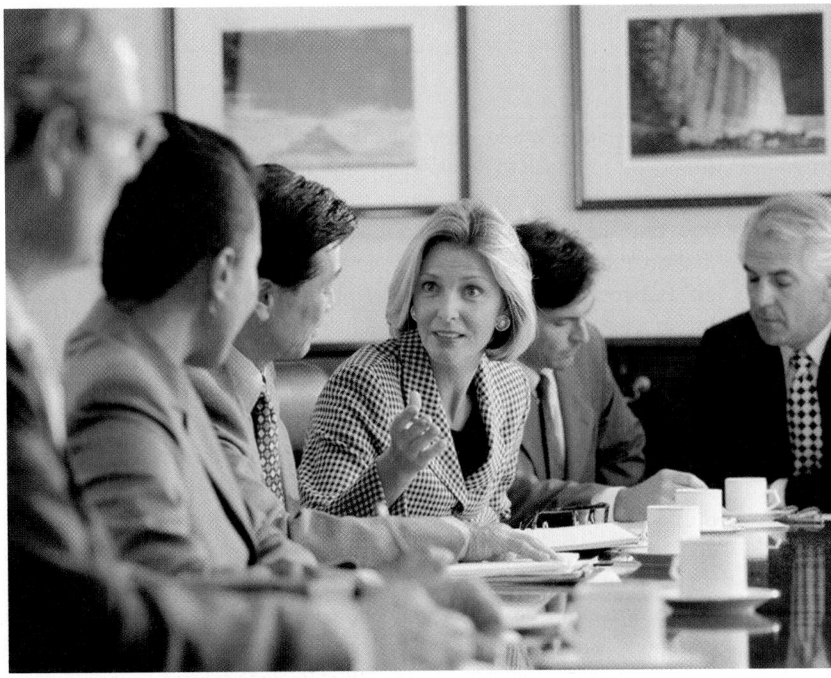

VIEWPOINTS Spiral of silence

The spiral of silence theory holds that you're more likely to voice agreement than disagreement, which creates the belief that there's even more agreement than there really is (because people who disagree aren't voicing their disagreement) (Noelle-Neumann, 1991). If you were talking with a group of new work colleagues, would you be more likely to voice opinions that agreed with the majority? Would you hesitate to voice opinions that differed greatly from what the others were expressing? Under what conditions are you likely to voice disagreement?

Sometimes silence is used as a response to personal anxiety, shyness, or threats. You may feel anxious or shy among new people and prefer to remain silent. By remaining silent, you preclude the chance of rejection. Only when you break your silence and make an attempt to communicate with another person do you risk rejection.

Silence may be used to prevent communication of certain messages. In conflict situations, silence is sometimes used to prevent certain topics from surfacing and to prevent one or both parties from saying things they may later regret. In such situations, silence often allows us time to cool off before expressing hatred, severe criticism, or personal attacks—which, as we know, are irreversible.

Like the eyes, face, or hands, silence can also be used to communicate emotional responses (Ehrenhaus, 1988). Sometimes silence communicates a determination to be uncooperative or defiant; by refusing to engage in verbal communication, you defy the authority or the legitimacy of the other person's position. Silence is often used to communicate annoyance, particularly when accompanied by a pouting expression, arms crossed in front of the chest, and nostrils flared. Silence may express affection or love, especially when coupled with long and longing gazes into each other's eyes.

Silence also may be used strategically, to achieve specific effects. You may, for example, strategically position a pause before what you feel is an important comment to make your idea stand out. Interestingly enough, interviewers who paused about every 20 seconds were more successful in gaining compliance than were those who spoke without a pause (Swanbrow, 2011). A prolonged silence after someone voices disagreement may give the appearance of control and superiority. It's a way of saying, "I can respond in my own time."

Silence is also seen in computer-mediated communication. For example, when a close friend posts a message that asks for support or

INTERPERSONAL CHOICE POINT

Remaining Silent

Your college roommate has developed a small business selling term papers and uses your jointly owned computer to store them. You've remained silent about this for some time, but you've become increasingly uncomfortable about the situation and want to distance yourself from what you feel is unethical. How might you break your silence to distance yourself or, better, sever yourself entirely from this entire operation without creating too much trouble in the small dorm room you'll have to continue sharing for the next year?

ETHICAL MESSAGES

Silence

In the U.S. legal system, you have the right to remain silent and to refuse to reveal information about yourself that could be used against you or that might incriminate you. But you don't have the right to refuse to reveal information about, for example, the criminal activities of others that you may have witnessed. Rightly or wrongly (and this in itself is an ethical issue), psychiatrists, clergy, and lawyers are often exempt from this general rule. Similarly, a wife can't be forced to testify against her husband or a husband against his wife.

In interpersonal situations, however, there are no such written rules, so it's not always clear if or when silence is ethical. For example, most people (but not all) would agree that you have the right to withhold information that has no bearing on the matter at hand. Thus, your previous relationship history, affectional orientation, or religion is usually irrelevant to your ability to function as a doctor or police officer and may thus be kept private in most job-related situations. On the other hand, these issues may be relevant when, for example, you're about to enter a more intimate phase of a relationship—then there may be an obligation to reveal information about yourself that could have been kept hidden at earlier relationship stages.

As you consider the ethical dimensions of silence, ask yourself what types of information you can ethically withhold from, say, your relationship partner or family or best friend. What types of information would it be unethical to withhold?

Ethical Choice Point

After 30 years together, Pat has fallen out of love with Chris and in love with TJ. But TJ isn't interested, and so Pat has decided to stay in the relationship with Chris and say nothing about this change. Would you see this as ethical if you were Pat? If you were Chris?

help and you remain silent, you're communicating a message—perhaps you simply didn't know what to say or you weren't interested or you didn't have online access (an excuse that is becoming increasingly difficult to advance convincingly). Or when someone sends you a lengthy email and you fail to respond to its main theme (indicating you haven't really read the email), you're communicating some message.

Not all cultures view silence in the same way (Vainiomaki, 2004). In the United States, for example, silence is often interpreted negatively. At a business meeting or even in informal social groups, a silent person may be seen as not listening, as having nothing interesting to add, or as not understanding the issues. Other cultures, however, view silence more positively. In many situations in Japan, for example, silence is a response that is considered more appropriate than speech (Haga, 1988).

Time Messages

The study of **temporal communication**, known technically as **chronemics**, concerns the use of time—how you organize it, react to it, and communicate messages through it (Bruneau, 1985, 1990, 2009/2010). Time is important in both face-to-face and computer-mediated communication. The time you take to poke someone back on Facebook or the time you take to respond to an e-mail request for a favor or the delay in returning a phone call will all communicate varied messages. Often, as you have probably already discovered, the meanings that the sender intends to communicate are not the same as the meanings the receiver constructs.

Blog Post

Interpersonal Time

In this connection take a look at "Interpersonal Time" at tcbdevito.blogspot.com for a consideration of the varied ways time is used in interpersonal interactions.

Before reading further about time, take a look at your own time orientation by taking the accompanying self-test.

The time orientation you develop, or **psychological time**, depends to a great extent on your socioeconomic class and your personal experiences (Gonzalez & Zimbardo, 1985). For example, parents with unskilled and semiskilled occupations are likely to teach their children a present-orientated fatalism and a belief that enjoying yourself is more important than planning for the future. Parents who are teachers, managers, or other professionals tend to teach their children the importance of planning and preparing for the future, along with other strategies for success. In the United States, not surprisingly, future income is positively related to future orientation; the more future oriented you are, the greater your income is likely to be.

TEST YOURSELF

What's Your Time?

Instructions: For each statement, indicate whether the statement is true (T) or false (F) of your general attitude and behavior.

____ 1. I work hard today basically because of tomorrow's expected rewards.
____ 2. I enjoy life as it comes.
____ 3. I enjoy planning for tomorrow and the future generally.
____ 4. I avoid looking too far ahead.
____ 5. I'm willing to endure difficulties if there's a payoff/reward at the end.
____ 6. I frequently put off work to enjoy the moment.
____ 7. I prepare "to do" lists fairly regularly.
____ 8. I am late with assignments at least 25 percent of the time.
____ 9. I get very disappointed with myself when I'm late with assignments.
____10. I look for immediate payoffs/rewards.

How Did You Do? These questions were designed to raise the issue of present and future time orientation, whether you focus more on the present or more on the future. Future-oriented individuals would respond with T to odd-numbered statements (1, 3, 5, 7, and 9) and F to even-numbered questions (2, 4, 6, 8, and 10). Present-oriented individuals would respond in reverse: F for odd-numbered statements and T for even-numbered statements.

What Will You Do? As you read more about time and nonverbal communication generally, consider how these time orientations work for or against you. For example, will your time orientation help you achieve your social and professional goals? If not, what might you do about changing these attitudes and behaviors?

Different time perspectives also account for much intercultural misunderstanding, as different cultures often teach their members drastically different time orientations. For example, people from some Latin cultures would rather be late for an appointment than end a conversation abruptly or before it has come to a natural end. So the Latin cultures may see an individual's lateness as a result of politeness. But others may see the lateness as impolite to the person with whom the individual had the appointment (Hall & Hall, 1987).

Similarly, the future-oriented person who works for tomorrow's goals will frequently see the present-oriented person as lazy and poorly motivated for enjoying today and not planning for tomorrow. In turn, the present-oriented person may see those with strong future orientations as obsessed with amassing wealth or rising in status.

Not surprisingly, culture influences our approaches to time in a variety of ways. Here we look at three types of cultural time: formal and informal time, monochronism and polychronism, and the social clock.

FORMAL AND INFORMAL TIME In the United States and in most of the world, **formal time** is divided into seconds, minutes, hours, days, weeks, months, and years. Some cultures, however, may use seasons or phases of the moon to delineate their most important time periods. In the United States, if your college is on the semester system, your courses are divided into 50- or 75-minute periods that meet two or three times a week for 14-week periods. Eight semesters of 15 or 16 periods per week equal a college education. As these examples illustrate, formal time units are arbitrary. The culture establishes them for convenience.

In contrast, the term **informal time** refers to people's understanding of general time terms—for example, expressions such as "forever," "immediately," "soon," "right away," and "as soon as possible." Communication about informal time creates the most problems because the terms have different meanings for different people. And this is especially true when these terms are used interculturally. For example, what does "late" mean when applied to a commuter train? Apparently, it depends on your culture. In the New York area, "late" means six minutes, and in Britain, it means five minutes. But in Japan, it means one minute. And recently, the most deadly train crash in Japan in decades—which killed 90 people—was attributed to speeding resulting from the Japanese concern (or obsession) with being on time (Onishi, 2005).

Other attitudes toward time also vary from one culture to another. In one study, for example, the accuracy of clocks was measured in six countries—Japan, Indonesia, Italy, England, Taiwan, and the United States. Japan had the most accurate and Indonesia had the least accurate clocks. The researchers also measured the speed at which people in these six cultures walked, and results showed that the Japanese walked the fastest, the Indonesians the slowest (LeVine & Bartlett, 1984).

MONOCHRONISM AND POLYCHRONISM Another important distinction is that between **monochronic** and **polychronic time orientations** (Hall, 1959, 1976; Hall & Hall, 1987). Monochronic people or cultures—such as those of the United States, Germany, Scandinavia, and Switzerland—schedule one thing at a time. In these cultures, time is compartmentalized, and there is a time for everything. Polychronic people or cultures—such as those of Latin America, Mediterranean peoples, and Arab peoples—on the other hand, schedule multiple things at the same time. Members of these cultures feel comfortable eating, conducting business with several different people, and taking care of family matters all at the same time.

No culture is entirely monochronic or polychronic; rather, these are general tendencies that are found across a large part of the culture. Some cultures combine both time orientations; Japanese and parts of American culture are examples where both orientations are found.

THE SOCIAL CLOCK Another interesting aspect of cultural time is your **social clock** (Neugarten, 1979). Your culture, as well as your more specific society, maintains a schedule for the right time to do a variety of important things—for example, the right time to start dating, to finish college, to buy your own home, or to have a child. And you no doubt learned about this "clock" as you were growing up. You may tend to evaluate your own social and professional development on the basis of this social clock. If you're on time relative to the rest of your peers—for example, if you all started dating at around the same age or you're all finishing college at around the same age—then you will feel well adjusted, competent, and a part of the group. If you're late, you will probably experience feelings of dissatisfaction. Research in recent decades, however, shows that this social clock is becoming more flexible; people are becoming more willing to tolerate deviations from the established, socially acceptable timetable for accomplishing many of life's transitional events (Peterson, 1996).

Can you define and give examples of messages in each of the basic channels through which you send and receive nonverbal signals (gestures, body appearance, face, eyes, space and territory, artifacts, touch, paralanguage, silence, and time)?

NONVERBAL COMMUNICATION COMPETENCE

Throughout the discussion of nonverbal communication, you've probably deduced a number of suggestions for improving your own nonverbal communication. Here we bring together some suggestions for both receiving and sending nonverbal messages.

Perhaps the most general skill that applies to both receiving and sending is to become mindful of nonverbal messages—those of others as well as your own. Observe those whose nonverbal behavior you find particularly effective and those you find ineffective and try to identify exactly what makes one effective and one ineffective. Consider this chapter a brief introduction to a lifelong study.

In addition to mindfulness, general suggestions can be offered for encoding (or sending) nonverbal messages and for decoding (or interpreting) nonverbal messages.

SKILL BUILDING EXERCISE

Identifying Connections Between Verbal and Nonverbal Messages

To demonstrate that the way you say something influences the meanings you communicate, try reading each of the sentences below aloud—first to communicate a positive meaning and then to communicate a negative meaning. As you communicate these meanings, try to identify the nonverbal differences between the ways you express positive meanings and the ways you express negative meanings. Look specifically at (a) how you read the statements in terms of rate, pauses, and volume and (b) how your facial and eye expressions differ.

1. Oh, yeah, I have the relationship of a lifetime.
2. I can't wait to receive my test results.
3. Did you see her Facebook profile and the new photos?
4. I had some fantastic date last night.
5. Did you see him pitch that great game last night?

You cannot speak a sentence without using nonverbal signals, and these signals influence the meaning you send to the receiver.

Encoding Skills

In using nonverbal messages to express your meanings, consider these suggestions:

Watch the **Video** "Go for It" at **MyCommunicationLab**

1. Consider your choices for your nonverbal communication just as you do for your verbal messages. Identify and think mindfully about the choices you have available for communicating what you want to communicate.
2. Keep your nonverbal messages consistent with your verbal messages; avoid sending verbal messages that say one thing and nonverbal messages that say something else—at least not when you want to be believed.
3. Monitor your own nonverbal messages with the same care that you monitor your verbal messages. If it's not appropriate to say "this meal is terrible," then it's not appropriate to have a negative expression when you're asked if you want seconds.
4. Avoid extremes and monotony. Too little nonverbal communication or too much are likely to be responded to negatively. Similarly, always giving the same nonverbal message—say, continually smiling and nodding your head when listening to a friend's long story—is likely to be seen as insincere.
5. Take the situation into consideration. Effective nonverbal communication is situational; to be effective, adapt your nonverbal messages to the specific situation. Nonverbal behavior appropriate to one situation may be totally inappropriate in another.
6. Maintain eye contact with the speaker—whether at a meeting, in the hallway, or on an elevator; it communicates politeness and says that you are giving the person the consideration of your full attention. Eye contact that is too focused and too prolonged is likely to be seen as invasive and impolite.
7. Avoid using certain adaptors in public—for example, combing your hair, picking your teeth, or putting your pinky in your ear; these will be seen as impolite. And, not surprisingly, the greater the formality of the situation, the greater the perception of impoliteness is likely to be. So, for example, combing your hair while sitting with two or three friends would probably not be considered impolite (or perhaps only mildly so), but in a classroom or at a company meeting, it would be considered inappropriate.
8. Avoid strong cologne or perfume. While you may enjoy the scent, those around you may find it unpleasant and intrusive. Much like others do not want to hear your cell messages, they probably don't want to have their sense of smell invaded, either.
9. Be careful with touching; it may or may not be considered appropriate or polite depending on the relationship you have with the other person and on the context in which you find yourselves. The best advice to give here is to avoid touching unless it's part of the culture of the group or organization.

VIDEO CHOICE POINT

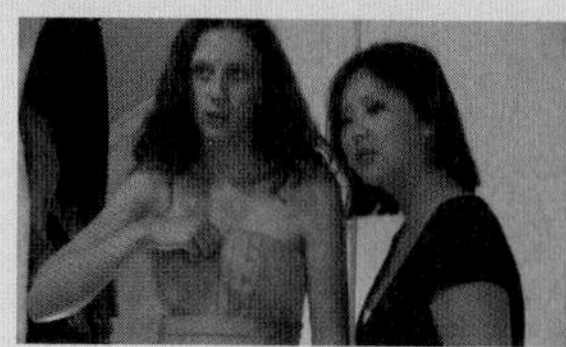

Bridesmaid

Vicki is getting married in a few months, and she has asked her best friend Marisol to be in the wedding party. Vicki is clearly tense about her wedding, and Marisol doesn't want to make things worse, but Marisol can't afford the designer dress that Vicki has selected for the wedding party. She also feels that the dress is unflattering on her. Marisol is from Brazil and this is the first American wedding she has been asked to participate in. She doesn't know what expectations Vicki has of her. Marisol needs to find out the expectations of being a bridesmaid, but does not want to further upset her already tense friend as she finds out. She considers the topics covered in this chapter as she contemplates her communication choices. See how her choices play out in the video "Bridesmaid" and respond to the questions posed.

 **Watch** the **Video** "Bridesmaid" at **MyCommunicationLab**

Decoding Skills

When you make judgments or draw conclusions about another person on the basis of her or his nonverbal messages, consider these suggestions:

INTERPERSONAL CHOICE POINT

Demonstrating Credibility

At work, people don't attribute any credibility to you, though you're probably as competent as anyone else. You need to increase the nonverbal credibility cues you give off. What nonverbal cues can you use to communicate your competence and ability? How might you begin to integrate these into your everyday interactions?

1. Be tentative. Resist the temptation to draw conclusions from nonverbal behaviors. Instead, develop hypotheses (educated guesses) about what is going on, and test the validity of your hypotheses on the basis of other evidence.
2. When making judgments, mindfully seek alternative judgments. Your first judgment may be in error, and one good way to test it is to consider alternative judgments. When your romantic partner creates a greater-than-normal distance between you, it may signal an annoyance with you, but it can also signal that your partner needs some space to think something out.
3. Notice that messages come from lots of different channels and that reasonably accurate judgments can only be made when multiple channels are taken into consideration. Although textbooks (like this one) must present the areas of nonverbal communication separately, the various elements all work together in actual communication situations.
4. Even after you've explored the different channels, consider the possibility that you are incorrect. This is especially true when you make a judgment that another person is lying based on, say, eye avoidance or long pauses. These nonverbal signals may mean lots of things (as well as the possibility of lying).
5. Interpret your judgments and conclusions against a cultural context. Consider, for example, if you interpret another's nonverbal behavior through its meaning in your own culture. So, for example, if you interpret someone's "overly close" talking distance as intrusive or pushy because that's your culture's interpretation, you may miss the possibility that this distance is simply standard in the other person's culture or it's a way of signaling closeness and friendliness.
6. Consider the multitude of factors that can influence the way a person behaves nonverbally; for example, a person's physical condition, personality, or particular situation may all influence a person's nonverbal communication. A sour stomach may be more influential in unpleasant expressions than any interpersonal factor. A low grade in an exam may make your normally pleasant roommate scowl and grumble.

Without knowing these factors, it's difficult to make an accurate judgment.

Can you use the suggestions to more effectively decode the nonverbal messages of others? Can you use the suggestions to more effectively encode your own nonverbal messages?

MESSAGES IN THE MEDIA: WRAP-UP

Almost all television crime shows but especially shows like *The Mentalist, Psych,* and *Castle* use subtle nonverbal cues as the keys to solving crimes. Watching such shows with a view to noticing the nonverbal cues they use to solve the crime is a great way to sensitize yourself to these same cues as they occur in your everyday interpersonal interactions.

SUMMARY OF CONCEPTS AND SKILLS

Listen to the **Audio Chapter Summary** at **MyCommunicationLab**

This chapter explored nonverbal communication—communication without words—and considered such areas as body language, body appearance, facial messages, eye messages, spatial and territorial communication, artifactual communication, touch communication, paralanguage, silence, time, and smell communication.

Principles of Nonverbal Communication

1. Nonverbal messages often interact with verbal messages to accent, complement, contradict, regulate, repeat, or substitute.
2. Nonverbal messages help manage impressions. We present ourselves nonverbally to give people the desired impression.
3. Nonverbal messages help form relationships.
4. Nonverbal messages structure conversation.
5. Nonverbal messages can influence and deceive.
6. Nonverbal messages are crucial for expressing emotions.

The Channels of Nonverbal Messages

7. Body gestures are classified into five categories: emblems (which rather directly translate words or phrases); illustrators (which accompany and literally "illustrate" verbal messages); affect displays (which communicate emotional meaning); regulators (which coordinate, monitor, maintain, or control the speaking of another individual); and adaptors (which usually are unconscious and serve some kind of need, as in scratching an itch).
8. Body appearance (for example, height and general attractiveness) communicates a variety of messages.
9. Facial movements may communicate a variety of emotions. The most frequently studied are happiness, surprise, fear, anger, sadness, and disgust/contempt. Facial management techniques enable you to control your facial expression of emotions.

Study and **Review** materials for this chapter are at **MyCommunicationLab**

The facial feedback hypothesis claims that facial display of an emotion can lead to physiological and psychological changes.

10. Eye movements may seek feedback, invite others to speak, signal the nature of a relationship, or compensate for physical distance.
11. The study of proxemics investigates the communicative functions of space and spatial relationships. Four major proxemic distances are: (1) intimate distance, ranging from actual touching to 18 inches; (2) personal distance, ranging from 18 inches to 4 feet; (3) social distance, ranging from 4 to 12 feet; and (4) public distance, ranging from 12 to 25 or more feet. Your treatment of space is influenced by such factors as status, culture, context, subject matter, sex, age, and positive or negative evaluation of the other person. Territoriality involves people's possessive reactions to particular spaces or objects.
12. Artifactual communication consists of messages conveyed by objects or arrangements created by humans, for example, by the use of color, clothing, body adornment, space decoration, or scent/smell.
13. Touch communication, or haptics, may communicate a variety of meanings, the most important being positive affect, playfulness, control, ritual, and task-relatedness. Touch avoidance is the desire to avoid touching and being touched by others.
14. Paralanguage has to do with the vocal but nonverbal dimension of speech. It includes rate, pitch, volume, resonance, and vocal quality as well as pauses and hesitations. Based on paralanguage, we make judgments about people, sense conversational turns, and assess believability.
15. Silence communicates a variety of meanings, from anger (as in the "silent treatment") to deep emotional responses.
16. Time communication, or chronemics, consists of messages communicated by our treatment of time.

17. Cultural variations in nonverbal communication are great. Different cultures, for example, assign different meanings to gestures, facial expressions, and colors; have different spatial rules; and treat time very differently.

Nonverbal Communication Competence

18. Encoding skills (maintaining eye contact, avoiding intrusive touching) will enable you to communicate more effective with nonverbal messages.
19. Decoding skills (being conscious of the several nonverbal channels sending messages simultaneously, interpreting messages in a cultural context) will enable you to more effectively understand the meanings being communicated with nonverbal signals.

This chapter also covered some significant nonverbal communication skills. Check those you wish to work on.

____ 1. *Body movements.* Use body and hand gestures to reinforce your communication purposes.

____ 2. *Facial messages.* Use facial expressions to communicate involvement. In listening, look to the emotional expressions of others as cues to their meaning.

____ 3. *Eye movements.* Use eye movements to seek feedback, exchange conversational turns, signal the nature of your relationship, or compensate for increased physical distance.

____ 4. *Spatial and proxemic conversational distances.* Maintain distances that are comfortable and that are appropriate to the situation and to your relationship with the other person.

____ 5. *Giving space.* Give others the space they need. Look to the other person for any signs of spatial discomfort.

____ 6. *Artifactual communication.* Use artifacts (for example, color, clothing, body adornment, space decoration) to communicate desired messages.

____ 7. *Touch and touch avoidance.* Respect the touch-avoidance tendencies of others; pay special attention to cultural and gender differences in touch preferences.

____ 8. *Paralanguage.* Vary paralinguistic features to communicate nuances of meaning and to add interest and color to your messages.

____ 9. *Silence.* Examine silence for meanings just as you would eye movements or body gestures.

____10. *Time cues.* Interpret time cues from the perspective of the person with whom you're interacting. Be especially sensitive to the person's leave-taking cues—remarks such as "It's getting late" or glances at the clock.

____11. *Smell.* Avoid strong smell that might offend.

____12. *Nonverbal communication and culture.* Interpret the nonverbal cues of others from the perspective of the other person's cultural meanings (insofar as you can).

VOCABULARY QUIZ: The Language of Nonverbal Communication

Match the terms of nonverbal communication with their definitions. Record the number of the definition next to the appropriate term.

____ emblems (130)
____ affect displays (131)
____ proxemics (135)
____ territoriality (136)
____ haptics (140)
____ paralanguage (141)
____ chronemics (144)
____ artifactual communication (137)
____ social clock (146)
____ psychological time (144)

1. Movements of the facial area that convey emotional meaning.
2. The study of how time communicates.
3. The time that a culture establishes for achieving certain milestones.
4. Nonverbal behaviors that directly translate words or phrases.
5. Communication by touch.
6. Your orientation to the past, present, or future.
7. The meanings communicated by clothing, jewelry, or buttons.
8. The study of how space communicates.
9. A possessive or ownership reaction to space or to particular objects.
10. The vocal but nonverbal aspects of speech—for example, rate and volume.

These ten terms and additional terms used in this chapter can be found in the glossary.

Study and **Review** the **Flashcards** at **MyCommunicationLab**

MyCommunicationLab

Visit MyCommunicationLab for more on nonverbal messages. Flashcards, videos, skill building exercises, sample test questions, and additional exercises, examples, and discussions will help you continue your study of the role of nonverbal messages in interpersonal communication and the skills of nonverbal communication.

CHAPTER

7

Emotional Messages

MESSAGES IN THE MEDIA

Soap operas and telenovelas both attempt to tell stories that viewers can identify with but that are generally more extreme. To achieve this often over-the-top intensity these stories rely heavily on emotional expression, the subject of this chapter where we consider the nature of emotions, the major obstacles, and how we can become more effective in both expressing your own feelings and in responding to the feelings of others.

OBJECTIVES *After reading this chapter, you should be able to:*

1. Explain the nine principles of emotions and emotional messages.
2. Describe the three obstacles to communicating emotions, and combat these in your own emotional communication.
3. Communicate your own emotions effectively.
4. Respond appropriately to the emotions of others.

Listen to the **Audio Chapter** at **MyCommunicationLab**

VIEWPOINTS Strong emotions

Some societies permit and even expect men (but not women) to show strong emotions such as anger. What has your culture taught you about the expression of anger and particularly about gender differences in the expression of anger?

Among our most difficult interpersonal communication situations are those that involve strong **emotions**. This chapter addresses this crucial topic, offers insight into the nature of emotions and emotional expression, and explores some of the obstacles to communicating emotions. With this understanding as a base, suggestions for communicating emotions and for responding to the emotions of others are offered.

PRINCIPLES OF EMOTIONS AND EMOTIONAL MESSAGES

Communicating emotions is both difficult and important. It's difficult because your thinking often gets confused when you're intensely emotional. It's also difficult because you probably weren't taught how to communicate emotions—and you probably have few effective models to imitate. Communicating emotions is also important. Feelings constitute a great part of your meanings. If you leave your feelings out or if you communicate them inadequately, you will fail to communicate a great part of your meaning. Consider what your communications would be like if you left out your feelings when talking about failing a recent test, winning the lottery, becoming a parent, getting engaged, driving a car for the first time, becoming a citizen, or being promoted to supervisor. Emotional expression is so much a part of communication that, even in the cryptic e-mail message style, emoticons are becoming more popular.

So important is **emotional communication** that it is at the heart of what is now called "emotional intelligence" or "social intelligence" (Goleman, 1995a, b), and the inability to engage in emotional communication—as sender and as receiver—is part of the learning disability known as *dyssemia*, a condition in which individuals are unable to appropriately read the nonverbal messages of others or to communicate their own meanings nonverbally (Duke & Nowicki, 2005). Persons suffering from dyssemia, for example, fail to return smiles, look uninterested, and use facial expressions that are inappropriate to the situation and the interaction. As you can imagine, people who are poor senders and receivers of emotional messages will likely have problems in developing and maintaining relationships. When interacting with such people, you're likely to feel uncomfortable because of their inappropriate emotional communication (Goleman, 1995a, b).

Let's look first at several general principles of emotions and emotional expression; these will establish a foundation for our consideration of the skills of emotional communication.

Blog Post

Emotional Checker

It's interesting to note that programs are available for checking the emotional tone of your e-mail, highlighting problematic terms, and suggesting alternative expressions, another indication of the importance the workplace puts on emotions and their expression. See "Emotional Checker" at tcbdevito.blogspot.com. What do you think of this?

Emotions May Be Primary or Blended

How would you feel in each of the following situations?

- You won the lottery.
- You got the job you applied for.
- Your best friend just died.
- Your parents tell you they're getting divorced.

You would obviously feel very differently in each of these situations. In fact, each feeling is unique and unrepeatable. Yet amid all these differences, there are some similarities. For example, most people would claim that the feelings in the first two examples are more similar to each other than they are to the last two. Similarly, the last two are more similar to each other than they are to the first two.

To capture the similarities among emotions, many researchers have tried to identify basic or **primary emotions**. Robert Plutchik (1980; Havlena, Holbrook, & Lehmann, 1989) developed a most helpful model. In this model, there are eight basic emotions (Figure 7.1): joy, acceptance, fear, surprise, sadness, disgust, anger, and anticipation. Emotions that are

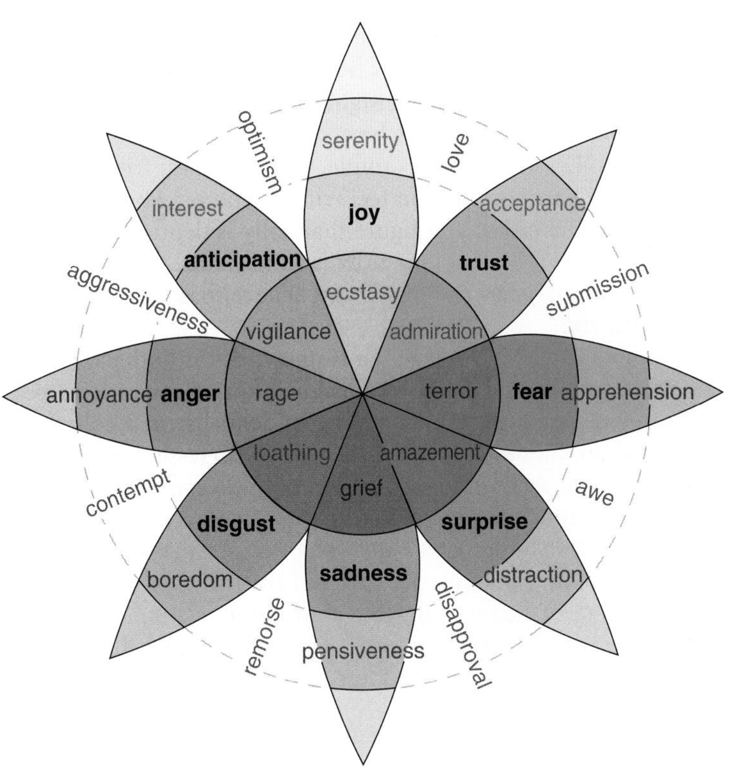

FIGURE 7.1
A Model of the Emotions
Do you agree with the basic assumptions of this model?
Reprinted with permission from Annette deFerrari Design.

close to each other on this wheel are also close to each other in meaning. For example, joy and anticipation are more closely related than are joy and sadness or acceptance and disgust. Emotions that are opposite each other on the wheel are also opposite each other in their meaning. For example, joy is the opposite of sadness; anger is the opposite of fear.

In this model, there are also **blended emotions**. These are emotions that are combinations of the primary emotions. These are noted outside the emotion wheel. For example, according to this model, love is a blend of joy and acceptance. Remorse is a blend of disgust and sadness.

Emotions Are Influenced by Body, Mind, and Culture

Emotion involves at least three parts: bodily reactions (such as blushing when you're embarrassed), mental evaluations and interpretations (as in calculating the odds of drawing an inside straight at poker), and cultural rules and beliefs (such as the pride parents feel when their child graduates from college).

Bodily reactions are the most obvious aspect of our emotional experience because we can observe them easily. Such reactions span a wide range. They include the blush of embarrassment, the sweating palms that accompany nervousness, and the playing with your hair or touching your face that goes with discomfort. When you judge people's emotions, you probably look to these nonverbal behaviors. You conclude that Ramon is happy to see you because of his smile and his open body posture. You conclude that Lisa is nervous from her damp hands, vocal hesitations, and awkward movements.

INTERPERSONAL CHOICE POINT

Dealing with Sadness and Joy

The parents of your neighbor who has lived next door to you for the past 10 years were recently killed in a car accident. Now your neighbor, who has had many difficult financial times, will inherit a large estate. You meet in the hallway of your apartment house. What are some of the things you can say to your neighbor at this time? What would you say?

The mental or cognitive part of emotional experience involves the evaluations and interpretations you make on the basis of your behaviors. For example, psychotherapist Albert Ellis (1988; Ellis & Harper, 1975), whose insights are used throughout this chapter, claims that your evaluations of what happens have a greater influence on your feelings than what actually happens. Let us say, for example, that your best friend, Sally, ignores you in the college cafeteria. The emotions you feel will depend on what you think this behavior means. You may feel pity if you figure that Sally is depressed because her father died. You may feel anger if you believe that Sally is simply rude and insensitive and snubbed you on purpose. Or you may feel sadness if you believe that Sally is no longer interested in being friends with you.

The culture you were raised in and live in gives you a framework for both expressing feelings and interpreting the emotions of others. A colleague of mine gave a lecture in Beijing, China, to a group of Chinese college students. The students listened politely but made no comments and asked no questions after her lecture. At first my colleague concluded that the students were bored and uninterested. Later, she learned that Chinese students show respect by being quiet and seemingly passive. They think that asking questions would imply that she was not clear in her lecture. In other words, the culture—whether American or Chinese—influenced the interpretation of the students' feelings. In a recent study, Japanese students, when asked to judge the emotion in a computer icon, looked to the eyes to determine the emotion. Students from the United States, however, focused on the mouth (Masuda et al., 2008; Yuki, Maddux, & Masuda, 2007).

Emotional Arousal Is a Multi-Step Process

If you were to describe the events leading up to emotional arousal, you would probably describe three stages: (1) An event occurs. (2) You experience an emotion such as surprise, joy, or anger. (3) You respond physiologically; your heart beats faster, your face flushes, and so on. The process would go like this:

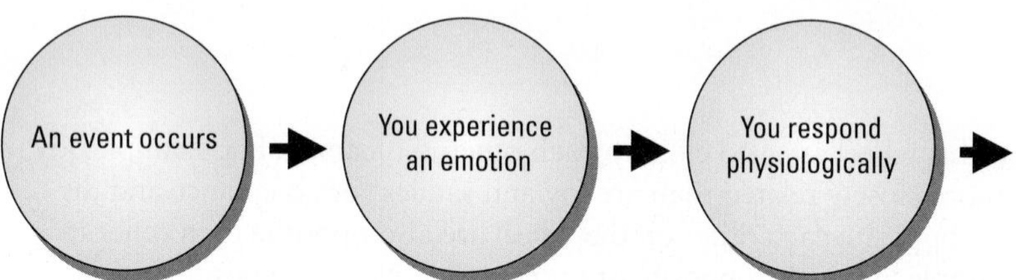

An early theory of emotion was offered by psychologist William James and physiologist Carl Lange (James, 1884). Their theory places the physiological arousal before the experience of the emotion. The sequence of events according to the **James–Lange theory** is: (1) An event occurs. (2) You respond physiologically. And (3) you experience an emotion; for example, you feel joy or sadness. This process would look like this:

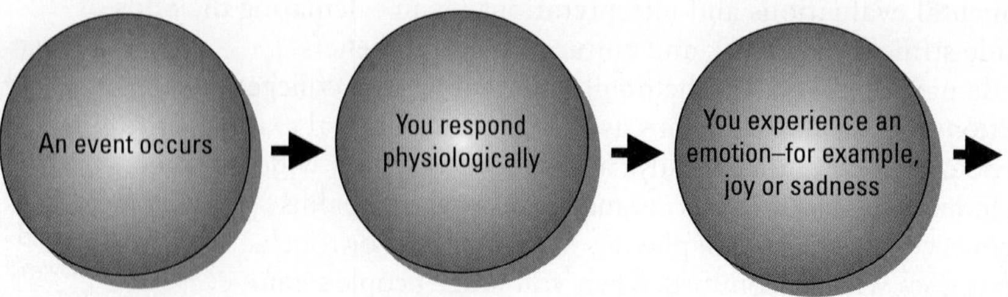

According to a third explanation, the **cognitive labeling theory**, you interpret the physiological arousal and, on the basis of this, experience the emotions of joy, sadness, or whatever (Reisenzein, 1983; Schachter, 1971;). The sequence goes like this: (1) An event occurs. (2) You respond physiologically. (3) You interpret this arousal—that is, you decide what emotion you're experiencing. And (4) you experience the emotion. Your interpretation of your arousal will depend on the situation you're in. For example, if you experience an increased pulse rate after someone you've been admiring smiles at you, you may interpret this as joy. If three suspicious-looking strangers approach you on a dark street, however, you may interpret that same increased heartbeat as fear. It's only after you make the interpretation that you experience the emotion; for example, the joy or the fear. This process looks like this:

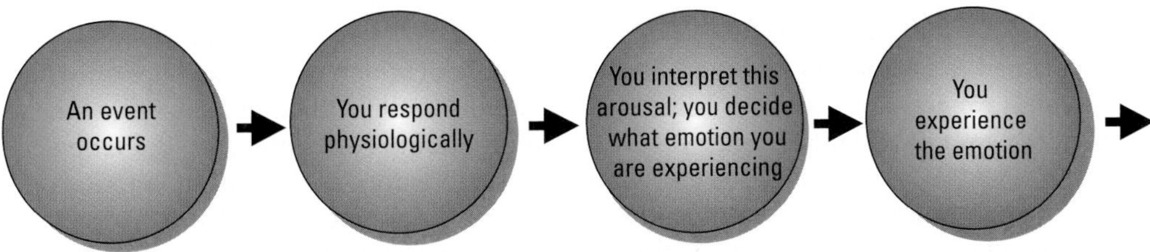

As you continue reading this chapter, consider these three alternative explanations. Though none of them explains the process fully, they each offer interesting insights that help explain the nature of emotional communication.

Emotions May Be Adaptive and Maladaptive

Emotions are often adaptive and help you adjust to the situation. For example, if you feel anxious about not doing well on an exam, it might lead you to study harder. If you fear losing your partner, you might act more supportively and lovingly. If you become suspicious of someone following you down a dark street, it might motivate you to take safety precautions. All of these situations are examples of emotions aiding you in accomplishing useful goals.

At other times, emotions may be maladaptive and may get in the way of your accomplishing your goals. For example, you may be so anxious about a test that you just stop thinking and do more poorly than you would have if you walked in totally cold. Or you might fear losing your partner and, as a result, become suspicious and accusatory, making your relationship even less likely to survive.

Another way in which emotions may create problems is in what some theorists have cleverly called catastrophizing (or awfulizing)—taking a problem, even a minor one, and making it into a catastrophe: "If I don't do well on this test, I'll never get into law school" or "If this relationship doesn't work, I'm doomed." As you tell yourself (and convince yourself) of these impending catastrophes, your emotional responses can easily get out of hand (Bach & Wyden, 1968; Willson & Branch, 2006).

Emotions Are Communicated Verbally and Nonverbally

Although emotions are especially salient in conflict situations and in relationship development and dissolution, they are actually a part of all messages. Emotions are always present—sometimes to a very strong extent, though sometimes only mildly. Therefore, they must be recognized as a part of the communication experience. This is not to say that emotions should always be talked about or that all emotions you feel should be expressed. Emotional feeling and emotional communication are two different things. In some instances, you may want to say exactly what you feel, to reveal your emotions without any censorship. At other times, however, you may want to avoid revealing your

INTERPERSONAL CHOICE POINT

Spending Time

Your grandmother is dying and calls to ask you to spend some time with her. She says that she knows she is dying, that she wants you to know how much she has always loved you, and that her only regret in dying is not being able to see you anymore. You want her to feel comforted, yet it's so emotional for you. What are some of the things you might say?

INTERPERSONAL CHOICE POINT

Responding to Betrayal

A colleague at work has made a post on his Facebook wall containing information about you that you confided in him and in him alone. You're steaming as you pass a group of colleagues commenting on your current relationship problems. What are some choices you have for reacting to this? What would you do first?

emotions. For example, you might not want to reveal your frustration over a customer's indecision, or you might not want to share with your children your worries about finding a job.

Theorists do not agree over whether you can choose the emotions you feel. Some argue that you can; others argue that you cannot. You are, however, in control of the ways in which you express your emotions. Whether or not you choose to express your emotions will depend on your own attitudes about emotional expression. You may wish to explore these by taking the self-test below.

Emotional Expression Is Governed by Display Rules

As explained in Chapter 6, different **display rules** govern which emotions are permissible and which are not permissible to communicate. For example, although men and women experience emotions similarly, they display them differently (Cherulnik, 1979; Oatley & Duncan, 1994; Wade & Tavris, 1998). Women talk more about feelings and emotions and use communication for emotional expression more than men (Barbato & Perse, 1992). Perhaps because of this, they also express themselves facially more than men. Even junior and senior high schoolers show this gender difference.

Women are also more likely to express socially acceptable emotions than are men (Brody, 1985). Women smile significantly more than men. In fact, women smile even when smiling is not appropriate—for example, when reprimanding a subordinate. Men, on the other hand, are more likely than women to express anger and aggression (DePaulo, 1992; Fischer, 1993; Wade & Tavris, 1998). Similarly, women are more effective at communicating happiness, and men are more effective at communicating anger (Coats & Feldman, 1996). Women also cry more than men (Metts & Planalp, 2002).

TEST YOURSELF

How Do You Feel About Communicating Feelings?

Respond to each of the following statements with T if you feel the statement is a generally true description of your attitudes about expressing emotions or with F if you feel the statement is a generally false description of your attitudes.

____ 1. Expressing feelings is healthy; it reduces stress and prevents wasting energy on concealment.
____ 2. Expressing feelings can lead to interpersonal relationship problems.
____ 3. Expressing feelings can help others understand you.
____ 4. Emotional expression is often an effective means of persuading others to do as you wish.
____ 5. Expressing emotions may lead others to perceive you negatively.
____ 6. Emotional expression can lead to greater and not less stress; expressing anger, for example, may actually increase your feelings of anger.

How Did You Do? These statements are arguments that are often made for and against expressing emotions. Statements 1, 3, and 4 are arguments made in favor of expressing emotions; 2, 5, and 6 are arguments made against expressing emotions. You can look at your responses as revealing (in part) your attitude favoring or opposing the expression of feelings. "True" responses to statements 1, 3, and 4 and "False" responses to statements 2, 5, and 6 would indicate a favorable attitude to expressing feelings. "False" responses to statements 1, 3, and 4, and "True" responses to statements 2, 5, and 6 indicate a negative attitude.

What Will You Do? There is evidence suggesting that expressing emotions can lead to all six outcomes—the positives and the negatives—so general suggestions for increasing your willingness to express your emotions are not offered. These potential consequences underscore the importance of critically assessing your options for emotional expression. Especially, be flexible, remembering that what will work in one situation may not work in another.

SKILL BUILDING EXERCISE

Analyzing Cultural and Gender Emotional Display Rules

Examine each of the following situations, and identify the cultural and gender display rules that would most likely influence your emotional expression (or lack of it).

1. You're watching a movie with a group of friends, and you're emotionally moved by the film and feel like crying.
2. You've just been severely criticized by your supervisor in front of six workers you supervise. You're so stunned that the supervisor walks away before you can say anything. You're now alone with your six subordinates, and you want to scream.
3. One of your close friends accuses you of stealing money, which you did not do. This person has told several mutual friends who seem to believe the story. You're angry, and you want this rumor stopped.
4. You just found out that your romantic partner of the past five years is being unfaithful with a mutual friend. You feel hurt, angry, resentful, jealous, and like a real fool. You want to stop this affair, but you also want to retain your romantic relationship and hopefully bring it back to the way it used to be.

All people are influenced in their emotional expression by the display rules they learned from their culture. Becoming mindful of emotional display rules will increase your understanding of the emotional expression of others and will inform your own choices for emotional expression.

Emotions Can Be Used Strategically

Although you may at first think of emotional expression as honest reflections of what a person is feeling, emotions can be and often are used strategically. In **strategic emotionality**, emotions (for example, crying, ranting, screaming, and threatening to commit self-harm) are used for one's personal ends. Such emotions can take a variety of forms and serve a variety of purposes. But the basic idea behind strategic emotionality is to control the situation or the other person. For example, in a conflict situation, emotions are often used to win. If someone cries enough and loud enough, the other person may just give in. It works for the baby who wants to be picked up, and it often works for the adult and enables the person to win the fight. This strategy is more likely to be used by members of individualist cultures, which emphasize the winning of a conflict rather than compromise or negotiation (which would be more likely in collectivist cultures).

Not surprisingly, this strategy, which is essentially one of manipulation, often creates resentment and perhaps a desire to retaliate—neither of which is good for a relationship. Another negative outcome of this strategy is that the other person can never be sure how accurately your emotions reflect your true feelings, and this is likely to create communication problems whenever emotions are involved. The effect of this lack of transparency—of not knowing if your partner is trying to manipulate you or expressing strong and honest feelings—is likely to be greatest in intimate relationships where these expressions are likely to have long term effects.

VIEWPOINTS Sex differences

Which of these theories seems the most reasonable based on your own observations of sex differences in communication (Guerrero, Jones, & Boburka, 2006)?

- **Biological theory:** Differences in brains and chemistry account for the differences in the ability to express and detect emotions in others.
- **Evolutionary theory:** Emotional expression was basic to survival; those who were good at it lived and passed on their genes to others.
- **Socialization theory:** Men and women are taught differently about emotions and have been socialized into expressing emotions as they do.

Emotions Are Contagious

Emotional messages are often contagious (Cappella & Schreiber, 2006). If you've ever watched an infant and mother interacting, you can readily see how quickly the infant mimics the emotional expressions of the mother. If the mother smiles, the infant smiles; if the mother frowns, the infant frowns. As children get older, they begin to pick up more subtle expressions of emotions. For example, children quickly identify and often mimic a parent's anxiety or fear. Even among college roommates, the depression of one roommate can spread to the other over a period of just three weeks (Joiner, 1994). In short, emotions pass easily from one person to another; women are especially prone to **emotional contagion** (Cappella & Schreiber, 2006; Doherty, Orimoto, Singelis, Hatfield, & Hebb, 1995). In conversation and in small groups, the strong emotions of one person can easily prove contagious to others present; this can be productive when the emotions are productive or unproductive when the emotions are unproductive.

One view of this process goes like this:

1. You perceive the emotional expression of others.
2. You mimic this emotional expression, perhaps unconsciously.
3. The feedback you get from your expressions recalls (consciously or unconsciously) the feelings you had when you last expressed yourself in this way, and this recall creates the feelings.

Blog Post

Loneliness Is Contagious

Even loneliness seems to be contagious. See "Loneliness Is Contagious" at tcbdevito.blogspot.com. Does your experience support this view?

Another view of this process would hold that the process is under more conscious control. That is, you look at others who are expressing emotions to see how you should be feeling—you take nonverbal cues from those you observe—and then feel the feeling you feel you should be feeling.

You see more intentional emotional contagion in many attempts at persuasion. One popular appeal, which organizations use frequently in fund-raising for children's orphanages, is to the emotion of pity. By showing you images of hungry and destitute children, these fund-raisers hope to get you to experience so much pity that you'll help finance their efforts. Similarly, people who beg for money often emphasize their difficulties in an effort to evoke pity and donations.

Emotional contagion also seems the goal of certain organizational display rules (Ashkanasy & Humphrey, 2011). For example, it may be required (at least expected) that the sales force cheer enthusiastically as each new product is unveiled. This cheering is extremely useful and is likely to make the sales representatives more enthusiastic about and more emotionally committed to the product than if they didn't engage in this cheering.

Emotions Have Consequences

Like all communications, emotions and emotional expression have consequences and affect your relationships in important ways. By revealing your emotions, you may create close bounds with others. At the same time, you may also scare people with too much and too intimate of disclosure.

Revealing your emotions communicates important information about who you are and how you feel about those you're communicating with. If you talk about your loneliness, you're revealing important information about yourself and also expressing a confidence in the person with whom you're talking. When you support a cause on Facebook and ask your friends to join you, you're revealing what's important to you. Do realize, of course, that in revealing strongly felt emotions, you may be exposing vulnerabilities or weaknesses that conceivably could be used against you.

INTERPERSONAL CHOICE POINT

Emotional Frankness

Joe is extremely honest and open; he regularly says everything he feels without self-censorship. Not surprisingly, he often offends people. Joe is entering a new work environment and worries that his frankness may not be the best way to win friends and influence people. What are some things Joe can do to better understand this problem? What can he do to correct it?

Emotions and emotional expression also affect your work life, and, in fact, organizations are devoting energy to dealing with worker emotion, trying to turn the negative into the positive. See Table 7.1.

With these principles of emotions and emotional expression as a foundation, we can now look at some of the obstacles to effective emotional expression.

Can you explain the nine principles of emotions and emotional expression (primary and blended, the influences, the multi-step nature, the adaptive and maladaptive nature, verbal and nonverbal display, display rules, strategic uses, contagion, and consequences)?

TABLE 7.1

NEGATIVE EMOTIONS AND WORK

Here are the five most frequently experienced negative emotions on the job (Fisher, 1997). Assuming these emotions are unproductive, what recommendations would you offer a colleague who experiences each of these negative emotions? After making your recommendations, take a look at Mindtools.com (Managing Your Emotions at Work).

Negative Emotions	Recommendations
Frustration over feeling stuck in a rut	______________
Worry and anxiety over job security	______________
Anger over the actions or decisions of others	______________
Dislike of others you work with and for	______________
Disappointment over your position, accomplishments, and prospects	______________

OBSTACLES TO COMMUNICATING EMOTIONS

The expression of feelings is a part of most meaningful relationships. Yet it's often very difficult. Three major obstacles stand in the way of effective emotional communication: (1) society's rules and customs, (2) fear, and (3) inadequate interpersonal skills. Let's look more closely at each of these barriers.

Social and Cultural Customs

If you grew up in the United States, you probably learned the display rule that we should not express emotions. This is especially true for men and has been aptly called "the cowboy syndrome," after a pattern of behavior seen in the old Westerns (Balswick & Peck, 1971). The cowboy syndrome describes the closed and unexpressive male. This

ETHICAL MESSAGES

Motivational Appeals

Appeals to motives are commonplace. For example, if you want a friend to take a vacation with you, you're likely to appeal to such motives as the friend's desire for fun and excitement and perhaps to your friend's hopes of finding true love. If you look at the advertisements for cruises and vacation packages, you'll see appeals to very similar motives. Fear appeals are also common: Persons who want to censor the Internet may appeal to your fear of children accessing pornographic materials; those who want to restrict media portrayals of violence may appeal to your fear of increased violence in your community. Advertisers appeal to your vanity and your desire for increased sexual attractiveness in trying to sell you cosmetics, expensive clothing, and cars.

On a more interpersonal level, one partner may use fear to intimidate the other and to get one's own way. Or one may appeal to your desire to be popular when the real motive is sex. There can be no doubt that such motivational appeals are effective. But are they ethical?

Ethical Choice Point

Would it be ethical to use fear appeals to deter/prevent your 16-year-old nephew from engaging in sexual relationships? From smoking? From associating with people of other races?

"I've been thinking—it might be good for Andrew if he could see you cry once in a while."

Robert Weber/The New Yorker Collection/www.cartoonbank.com

man is strong but silent. He never feels any of the softer emotions (such as compassion, love, or contentment). He would never, ever cry, experience fear, or feel sorry for himself. Unfortunately, many men grow up trying to live up to this unrealistic image. It's a syndrome that prevents open and honest expression. Boys are taught early in life not to cry and not to be "babies" if hurt.

Nor are women exempt from the difficulties of emotional expression. At one time, our society permitted and encouraged women to express emotions openly. The tide now is turning, especially for women in executive and managerial positions. Today, the executive woman is being forced into the same cowboy syndrome. She is not allowed to cry or to show any of the once acceptable "soft" emotions. She is especially denied these feelings while she is on the job.

For both men and women, the best advice is to express your emotions selectively. Carefully weigh the arguments for and against expressing your emotions. Consider the situation, the people you're with, the emotions themselves, and all the elements that make up the communication act. And, most important, consider your choices for communicating emotions—not only what you'll say but also how you'll say it. And realize that one choice is *not* to express your emotions.

Fear

A variety of types of fear stand in the way of emotional expression. Emotional expression exposes a part of you that makes you vulnerable to attack. For example, if you express your love for another person, you risk being rejected. When you expose a weakness, you can more easily be hurt by the uncaring and the insensitive. Of course, you may also fear hurting someone else by, say, voicing your feelings about past loves. Or you may be angry and want to say something but fear that you might hurt the person and then feel guilty yourself.

In addition, you may not reveal your emotions for fear of causing a conflict. Expressing your dislike for your new romantic partner's friends, for example, may create difficulties for the two of you, and you may not be willing to risk the argument and its aftermath. Because of fears such as these, you may deny to others and perhaps even to yourself that you have certain feelings. In fact, this kind of denial is the way many people were taught to deal with emotions.

As you can appreciate, fear can also be adaptive and may lead you to not say things you may be sorry for later. It may lead you to consider more carefully whether you should express yourself and how you might do it. When it debilitates us and contradicts what logic and reason might tell us, then the fear becomes maladaptive.

Inadequate Interpersonal Skills

Perhaps the most important obstacle to effective emotional communication is lack of interpersonal skills. Many people simply don't know how to express their feelings. Some people, for example, can express anger only through violence or avoidance. Others can deal with anger only by blaming and accusing others. And many people cannot express love. They literally cannot say, "I love you."

Expressing negative feelings is doubly difficult. Many of us suppress or fail to communicate negative feelings for fear of offending the other person or making matters worse. But failing to express negative feelings will probably not help the relationship, especially if these feelings are concealed frequently and over a long time.

Watch the **Video** "Sam's Surprise" at **MyCommunicationLab**

Both communicating your emotions and responding appropriately to the emotional expressions of others are as important as they are difficult (Burleson, 2003).

VIDEO CHOICE POINT

Communicating Change

Tobin, the manager of a small firm, has called a team leader meeting. There are going to be some unpopular changes in the work teams, and each leader will be responsible for giving the news to their respective teams. Tobin has to describe how upcoming changes will affect workers and how this should be communicated by team leaders. Tobin realizes that his expressed emotional state will directly affect the message he delivers and how it is received. "Communicating Change" looks at how tone and word choice affect how information is received. In the video, you can see how Tobin's emotional state affects the choices he makes about how to deliver the message. Respond to the questions posed.

 **Watch** the **Video** "Communicating Change" at **MyCommunicationLab**

Can you describe the three obstacles to emotional communication (societal and cultural customs, fear, and inadequate communication skills)? Can you avoid these obstacles in your own intercultural communication?

SKILLS FOR COMMUNICATING EMOTIONS

Much as emotions are a part of your psychological life, emotional expression is a part of your interpersonal life; it is not something you could avoid even if you wanted to. In specific cases, you may decide to hide your emotions and not express them, but in other cases, you'll want to express your emotions, and this calls for what we might call **emotional competence**, the skills for expressing and responding to the emotions of others. We can group these under three major headings: emotional understanding, emotional expression, and emotional responding (see Table 7.2).

TABLE 7.2

EMOTIONAL HAPPINESS

A somewhat different view of emotional competence would be emotional happiness; after all, if you're emotionally competent, it should contribute to your individual happiness. Here are a few "dos" (but with qualifications) for achieving emotional satisfaction, contentment, and happiness.

Do	But
Think positively.	Don't be a Pollyanna; don't gloss over problems.
Associate with positive people.	Don't avoid others because they have different ideas or backgrounds; you'll miss out on a lot.
Do what you enjoy.	Don't forget your responsibilities or ignore obligations.
Talk about your feelings.	Don't substitute talk for action or talk too much.
Imagine yourself positively.	Don't become egotistical; after all, we all have faults, and these need to be addressed if we're to improve.
Think logically; keep emotions in perspective.	Don't ignore the crucial role that emotions and emotional expression often play in interpersonal communication.

INTERPERSONAL CHOICE POINT

The Crying Child

A young child about 6 or 7 years old is crying because the other children won't play with her. What are some things you can say to make the child feel better (but without trying to solve the child's problems by asking the other children to play with her)?

Emotional Understanding

Your first task is to develop self-awareness: recognizing what your feelings are, understanding why you feel as you do, and understanding the potential effects of your feelings (Stein & Book, 2011). Here you ask yourself a few pertinent questions.

- *"What am I feeling, and what made me feel this way?"* That is, understand your emotions. Think about your emotions as objectively as possible. Identify, in terms as specific as possible, the antecedent conditions that may be influencing your feelings. Try to answer the question "Why am I feeling this way?" or "What happened to lead me to feel as I do?"
- *"What exactly do I want to communicate?"* Consider also whether your emotional expression will be a truthful expression of your feelings. When emotional expressions are faked—when, for example, you smile though feeling angry or say "I forgive you" when you don't—you may actually be creating emotional and physical stress (Grandey, 2000). Remember, too, the irreversibility of communication; once you communicate something, you cannot take it back.
- *"What are my communication choices?"* Evaluate your communication options in terms of both effectiveness (what will work best and help you achieve your goal) and ethics (what is right or morally justified).

Watch the **Video** "Emotional Intelligence" at **MyCommunicationLab**

Explore the **Exercise** "Expressing Negative Feelings" at **MyCommunicationLab**

Emotional Expression

Your second step is interpersonal. Here are a few suggestions for this type of special communication. A special box on expressing anger complements this discussion. (See pages 166–168).

- *Be specific.* Consider, for example, the frequently heard "I feel bad." Does it mean "I feel guilty" (because I lied to my best friend)? "I feel lonely" (because I haven't had a date in the past two months)? "I feel depressed" (because I failed that last exam)? Specificity helps. Describe also the intensity with which you feel the emotion: "I feel so angry I'm thinking of quitting the job." "I feel so hurt I want to cry." Also describe any mixed feelings you might have. Very often feelings are a mixture of several emotions, sometimes even of conflicting emotions. Learn the vocabulary to describe your emotions and feelings in specific and concrete terms.

  Table 7.3 provides a list of terms for describing your emotions verbally. It's based on the eight primary emotions identified by Plutchik (refer to Figure 7.1,

SKILL BUILDING EXERCISE

Communicating Emotions Effectively

The following statements are all ineffective expressions of feelings. For each statement, (1) identify why the statement is ineffective (for example, what problem or distortion the statement creates) and (2) rephrase it into a more effective statement.

1. You hurt me when you ignore me. Don't ever do that again.
2. I'll never forgive that louse. The hatred and resentment will never leave me.
3. Look. I really can't bear to hear about your problems of deciding whom to date tomorrow and whom to date the next day and the next. Give me a break. It's boring. Boring.
4. You did that just to upset me. You enjoy seeing me get upset, don't you?
5. Don't talk to me in that tone of voice. Don't you dare insult me with that attitude of yours.

Learning to express emotions effectively will help you think about emotions more logically.

page 153). Notice that the terms included for each basic emotion provide you with lots of choices for expressing the intensity level you're feeling. For example, if you're extremely fearful, *terror* or *dread* might be appropriate, but if your fear is mild, perhaps *apprehension* or *concern* might be an appropriate term. In addition, the table provides a list of antonyms, providing additional choices for emotional expression.

- *Describe the reasons you're feeling as you are.* "I'm feeling guilty because I was unfaithful." "I feel lonely; I haven't had a date for the past two months." "I'm really depressed from failing that last exam." If your feelings were influenced by something the person you're talking to did or said, describe this also. For example, "I felt so angry when you said you wouldn't help me." "I felt hurt when you didn't invite me to the party."
- *Address mixed feelings.* If you have mixed feelings—and you really want the other person to understand you—then address these mixed or conflicting feelings. "I want so much to stay with Pat and yet I fear I'm losing my identity." Or "I feel anger and hatred, but at the same time, I feel guilty for what I did."
- *Anchor your emotions in the present.* Coupled with specific description and the identification of the reasons for your feelings, such statements might look like this: "I feel like a failure right now; I've erased this computer file three times today." "I felt foolish when I couldn't think of that formula." "I feel stupid when you point out my grammatical errors."
- *Own your feelings; take personal responsibility for your feelings.* Consider the following statements: "You make me angry." "You make me feel like a loser." "You

Blog Post

Alexithymia

Take a look at a discussion of the lack of vocabulary needed to describe feelings, "alexithymia," at tcbdevito.blogspot.com. Do you see the lack of a vocabulary a problem among people you know?

TABLE 7.3

VERBAL EXPRESSIONS OF EMOTION

Basic Emotion	Synonyms	Antonyms
Joy	happiness, bliss, cheer, contentment, delight, ecstasy, enchantment, enjoyment, felicity, rapture, gratification, pleasure, satisfaction, well-being	sadness, sorrow, unhappiness, woe, depression, gloom, misery, pain
Trust	confidence, belief, hope, assurance, faith, reliance, certainty, credence, certitude, conviction	distrust, disbelief, mistrust, uncertainty
Fear	anxiety, apprehension, awe, concern, consternation, dread, fright, misgiving, phobia, trepidation, worry, qualm, terror	courage, fearlessness, heroism, unconcern
Surprise	amazement, astonishment, awe, eye-opener, incredulity, jolt, revelation, shock, unexpectedness, wonder, startle, catch off-guard, unforeseen	expectation, assurance, confidence, fear, intention, likelihood, possibility, prediction, surmise
Sadness	dejected, depressed, dismal, distressed, grief, loneliness, melancholy, misery, sorrowful, unhappiness	happiness, gladness, joy, cheer
Disgust	abhorrence, aversion, loathing, repugnance, repulsion, revulsion, sickness, nausea, offensiveness	admiration, desire, esteem, fondness, liking, loving, reverence, respect
Anger	acrimony, annoyance, bitterness, displeasure, exasperation, fury, ire, irritation, outrage, rage, resentment, tantrum, umbrage, wrath, hostility	calmness, contentment, enjoyment, peace, joy, pleasantness
Anticipation	contemplation, prospect, expectancy, hope, foresight, expectation, foreboding, forecast, forethought	unreadiness, doubt, uncertainty

INTERPERSONAL CHOICE POINT

Responding Emotionally (or Not)

Your supervisor seems to constantly belittle your experience, which you thought was your strong point. Often your supervisor will say that your experiences were "in school" or "with only a few people" or some such negative phrase. You think your experience has more than prepared you for this job, and you want to make sure your supervisor knows this. What are your options for communicating this feeling? What would you say?

make me feel stupid." "You make me feel like I don't belong here." In each of these statements, the speaker blames the other person for the way he or she is feeling. Of course, you know, on more sober reflection, that no one can make you feel anything. Others may do things or say things to you, but it is you who interpret them. That is, you develop feelings as a result of the interaction between what these people say, for example, and your own interpretations. **Owning feelings** means taking responsibility for them—acknowledging that your feelings are your feelings. The best way to own your statements is to use **I-messages** rather than the kinds of you-messages given above. With this acknowledgment of responsibility, the above statements would look like these: "I get angry when you come home late without calling." "I begin to think of myself as a loser when you criticize me in front of my friends." "I feel so stupid when you use medical terms that I don't understand." "When you ignore me in public, I feel like I don't belong here." These rephrased statements identify and describe your feelings about those behaviors; they don't attack the other person or demand that he or she change certain behaviors and consequently don't encourage defensiveness. With I-message statements, it's easier for the other person to acknowledge behaviors and to offer to change them.

For good or ill, some social network sites (and the same is true with blogs) make it very easy to *not* own your own messages by enabling you to send comments anonymously.

"So, would anyone in the group care to respond to what Clifford has just shared with us?"

Tom Cheney/The New Yorker Collection/www.cartoonbank.com

- *Ask for what you want.* Depending on the emotions you're feeling, you may want the listener to assume a certain role or just listen or offer advice. Let the listener know what you want. Use I-messages to describe what, if anything, you want the listener to do: "I'm feeling sorry for myself right now; just give me some space. I'll give you a call in a few days." Or, more directly: "I'd prefer to be alone right now." Or "I need advice." Or "I just need someone to listen to me."
- *Respect emotional boundaries.* Each person has a different level of tolerance for communication about emotions or communication that's emotional. Be especially alert to nonverbal cues that signal that boundaries are near to being broken. And it's often useful to simply ask, "Would you rather change the subject?" At the same time, realize that you also have a certain tolerance for revealing your own feelings as well as for listening to and responding to the emotions of others.

INTERPERSONAL CHOICE POINT

Giving Emotional Advice

Your best friend tells you that he suspects his girlfriend is seeing someone else. He's extremely upset; he tells you that he wants to confront her with his suspicions but is afraid of what he'll hear. What options does your friend have for dealing with his suspicions (short of a lie detector test on *Maury*)? What would you advise him to say (or not say)?

Table 7.4 provides a comparison and summary of effective and ineffective emotional expression.

Can you communicate your own emotions effectively?

TABLE 7.4

INEFFECTIVE AND EFFECTIVE EMOTIONAL EXPRESSION

Effective Emotional Expression	Ineffective Emotional Expression
Specific; talks about emotions with specific terms and with specific examples and behavioral references	**General;** talks about emotions and feelings in general terms and without specifics
Mindful; identifies the reasons for the feelings; seeks to understand the causes of emotions.	**Mindless;** mindlessly accepts emotions without asking about their causes.
Present focused; concentrates on present feelings.	**Past focused;** concentrates on past feelings (perhaps as a way to avoid focusing on present feelings)
Uses I-messsages; demonstrates ownership of feelings and their expressions; *I feel angry, I'm hurt, I don't feel loved.*	**Uses You-messages;** attributes feelings to others—*You made me angry, you hurt me, you don't love me.*
Polite; talks about emotions (even anger) without anger and with respect for the other person and the relationship.	**Impolite;** lashes out in anger without regard for the feelings of the other person.

SKILLS FOR RESPONDING TO EMOTIONS

Expressing your feelings is only half of the process of emotional communication; the other half is listening and responding to the feelings of others. Here are a few guidelines for making an often difficult process a little easier. A special box on responding to the grief stricken complements this discussion (see page 168).

- *Look at nonverbal cues to understand the individual's feelings.* For example, overly long pauses, frequent hesitations, eye contact avoidance, or excessive fidgeting may be a sign of discomfort that it might be wise to talk about. Similarly, look for inconsistent messages, as when someone says that "everything is okay" while expressing facial sadness; these are often clues to mixed feelings. But be sure to use any verbal or nonverbal cues as hypotheses, never as conclusions. Check your perceptions before acting on them. Treat inferences as inferences and not as facts.
- *Look for cues as to what the person wants you to do.* Sometimes, all the person wants is for someone to listen. Don't equate (as the stereotypical male supposedly does) "responding to another's feelings" with "solving the other person's problems." Instead, provide a supportive atmosphere that encourages the person to express his or her feelings.
- *Use active listening techniques.* These will encourage the person to talk should he or she wish to. Paraphrase the speaker. Express understanding of the speaker's feelings. Ask questions as appropriate.

Explore the **Exercise** "Emotional Advice" at **MyCommunicationLab**

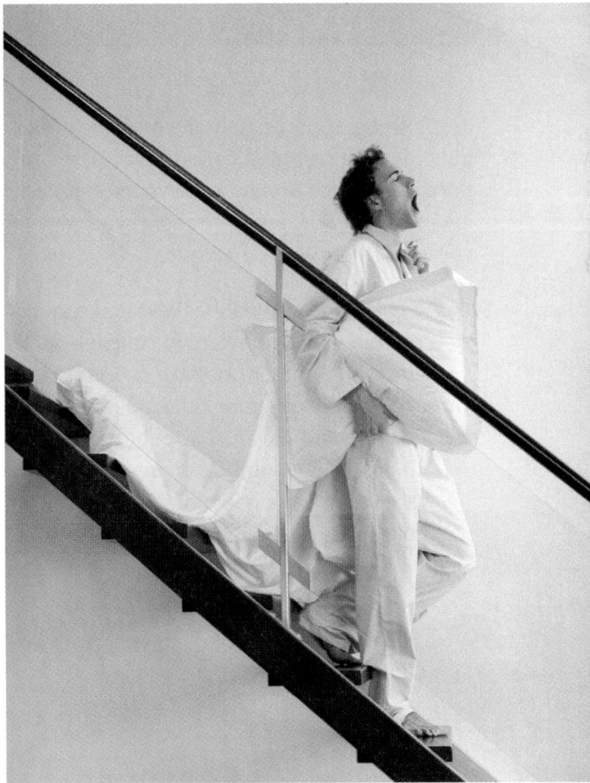

VIEWPOINTS Decoding emotions

Research finds that sleep deprivation hinders your ability to accurately recognize the emotions expressed facially by others (Gordon, 2010). What other factors (about yourself, the context, your relationship to the other person, and so on) might influence your ability to accurately detect the emotions of others?

INTERPERSONAL CHOICE POINT

The Break-In

Fellow students have just had their dorm room broken into, their computers stolen, and their furnishings trashed. They come to you to tell you what happened. Your room was not touched. What might you say? What should you be sure you don't say?

- *Empathize.* See the situation from the point of view of the speaker. Don't evaluate the other person's feelings. For example, comments such as "Don't cry; it wasn't worth it" or "You'll get promoted next year" can easily be interpreted to mean "Your feelings are wrong or inappropriate."
- *Focus on the other person.* Interjecting your own similar past situations is often useful for showing your understanding, but it may create problems if it refocuses the conversation away from the other person. Show interest by encouraging the person to explore his or her feelings. Use simple encouragers like "I see" or "I understand." Or ask questions to let the speaker know that you're listening and that you're interested.
- *Remember the irreversibility of communication.* Whether expressing emotion or responding to the emotions of others, it's useful to recall the irreversibility of communication. You won't be able to take back an insensitive or disconfirming response. Responses to another's emotional expressions are likely to have considerable impact, so be especially mindful to avoid inappropriate responding.

Can you use the suggestions offered here to respond appropriately to the emotions of others?

SKILL BUILDING EXERCISE

Responding to Emotions

Responding appropriately to emotions is one of the most difficult of all communication tasks. Here are some situations to practice on. Visualize yourself in each of the following situations, and respond as you think an effective communicator would respond.

1. A colleague at work has revealed some of the things you did while you were in college—many of which you would rather not have others on the job know about. You told your colleague these things in confidence, and now just about everyone on the job knows. You're angry and are considering the advantages (and the disadvantages) of confronting your colleague.
2. A close friend comes to your apartment in deep depression and tells you that her (or visualize a male) spouse of 22 years has fallen in love with another person and wants a divorce. Your friend is at a total loss as to what to do and comes to you for comfort and guidance.
3. Neighbors who have lived next door to you for the past 10 years and who have had many difficult financial times have just won the lottery worth several million dollars. You meet in the hallway of your apartment house; they're glowing.

Communicating emotions is difficult, but often there is no alternative.

HANDLING ANGER: A SPECIAL CASE ILLUSTRATION

As a kind of summary of the guidelines for expressing your emotions, this section looks at anger. **Anger** is one of the eight basic emotions identified in Plutchik's model (Figure 7.1). It's also an emotion that can create considerable problems if not managed properly. Anger varies from mild annoyance to intense rage; increases in pulse rate and blood pressure usually accompany these feelings.

Anger is not necessarily always bad. In fact, anger may help you protect yourself, energizing you to fight or flee. Often, however, anger does prove destructive—as when, for example, you allow it to obscure reality or to become an obsession.

Anger doesn't just happen; you make it happen by your interpretation of events. Yet life events can contribute mightily. There are the road repairs that force you to detour so you wind up late for an important appointment. There are the moths that attack your favorite sweater. There's the water leak that ruins your carpet. People, too, can contribute to your anger: the driver who tailgates, the clerk who overcharges you, the supervisor who ignores your contributions to the company. But it is you who interpret these events and people in ways that stimulate you to generate anger.

Writing more than a hundred years ago, Charles Darwin observed in his *The Expression of the Emotions in Man and Animals* (1872) that "The free expression by outside signs of an emotion intensifies it . . . the repression, as far as this is possible, of all outside signs softens our emotions. He who gives way to violent gestures will increase his rage." Popular psychology ignored Darwin's implied admonition in the 1960s and '70s, when the suggested prescription for dealing with anger was to "let it all hang out" and "tell it like it is." Express your anger, many people advised, or risk its being bottled up and eventually exploding. This idea is called the **ventilation hypothesis**—the notion that expressing emotions allows you to ventilate your negative feelings and that this will have a beneficial effect on your physical health, your mental well-being, and even your interpersonal relationships (Kennedy-Moore & Watson, 1999; Spett, 2004).

Later thinking has returned to Darwin, however, and suggests that venting anger may not be the best strategy (Tavris, 1989). Expressing anger doesn't get rid of it but makes it grow: Angry expression increases anger, which promotes more angry expression, which increases anger, and on and on. Some support for this idea that expressing emotions makes them stronger comes from a study that compared (a) participants who felt emotions such as happiness and anger with (b) participants who both felt and expressed these emotions. The results of the study indicated that people who felt and expressed the emotions became emotionally aroused faster than did those who only felt the emotion (Hess, Kappas, McHugo, & Lanzetta, 1992). And of course this spiral of anger can make conflicts all the more serious and all the more difficult to manage.

A better strategy seems to be to reduce the anger. With this principle in mind, here are some suggestions for managing and communicating anger.

Anger Management: SCREAM Before You Scream

Perhaps the most popular recommendation for dealing with anger is to count to 10. The purpose is to give you a cooling-off period, and the advice is not bad. A somewhat more difficult but probably far more effective strategy, however, would be to use that cooling-off period not merely for counting but for mindfully analyzing and ultimately managing your anger. The **anger management** procedure offered here is similar to those available in popular books on anger management but is couched in a communication framework. It's called SCREAM, an acronym for the major components of the communication process that you need to consider:

1. *Self.* How important is this matter to you? Is it worth the high blood pressure and the general aggravation? Are you interpreting the "insult" as the other person intended, or could you be misperceiving the situation or the intent? Are you confusing factual with inferential knowledge? Are you sure that what you think happened really happened?
2. *Context.* Is this the appropriate time and place to express your anger? Do you have to express your anger right now? Do you have to express it right here? Might a better time and place be arranged?
3. *Receiver.* Is this person the one to whom you wish to express your anger? For example, do you want to express your anger to your life partner if you're really angry with your supervisor for not recommending your promotion?
4. *Effect (immediate).* What effect do you want to achieve? Do you want to express your anger to help you get the promotion? To hurt the other person? To release pent-up emotions? To stand up for your rights? Each purpose would obviously require a different communication strategy. Consider, too, the likely effect of your anger display. For example, will the other person also become angry? And if so, is it possible that the entire situation will snowball and get out of hand?
5. *Aftermath (long-range).* What are the likely long-term repercussions of this expression of anger? What will be the effects on your relationship? Your continued employment?

HANDLING ANGER: A SPECIAL CASE ILLUSTRATION (continued)

6. *Messages.* Suppose that after this rather thorough analysis, you do decide to express your anger. What messages would be appropriate? How can you best communicate your feelings to achieve your desired results? This question brings us to the subject of anger communication.

Anger Communication

Anger communication is not angry communication. In fact, it might be argued that the communication of anger ought to be especially calm and dispassionate. Here, then, are a few suggestions for communicating your anger in a nonangry way.

- *Get ready to communicate calmly and logically.* First, relax. Try to breathe deeply; think pleasant thoughts; perhaps tell yourself to "take it easy," "think rationally," and "calm down." Try to get rid of any unrealistic ideas you may have that might contribute to your anger. For example, ask yourself if this person's revealing something about your past to a third party is really all that serious or was really intended to hurt you.
- *Examine your communication choices.* In most situations, you'll have a range of choices. There are lots of different ways to express yourself, so don't jump to the first possibility that comes to mind. Assess your options for the form of the communication—should you communicate face to face? By e-mail? By telephone? Similarly, assess your options for the timing of your communication, for the specific words and gestures you might use, for the physical setting, and so on.
- *Consider the advantages of delaying the expression of anger.* For example, consider writing the e-mail but sending it to yourself, at least until the next morning. Then the options of revising it or not sending it at all will still be open to you.
- *Remember that different cultures have different display rules* —norms for what is and what is not appropriate to display. Assess the culture you're in as well as the cultures of the other people involved, especially these cultures' display rules for communicating anger.
- *Apply the relevant skills of interpersonal communication.* For example, be specific, use I-messages, avoid allness, avoid polarized terms, and in general communicate with all the competence you can muster.
- *Recall the irreversibility of communication.* Once you say something, you'll not be able to erase or delete it from the mind of the other person.

These suggestions are not going to solve the problems of road rage, gang warfare, or domestic violence. Yet they may help—a bit—in reducing some of the negative consequences of anger and perhaps even some of the anger itself.

COMMUNICATING WITH THE GRIEF STRICKEN: A SPECIAL CASE ILLUSTRATION

Communicating with people who are experiencing grief, a common but difficult type of communication interaction, requires special care (Zunin & Zunin, 1991). Consideration of this topic also will offer a useful recap of some of the principles of responding to the emotions of others.

A person may experience grief because of illness or death, the loss of a job or highly valued relationship (such as a friendship or romantic breakup), the loss of certain physical or mental abilities, the loss of material possessions (a house fire or stock losses), or the loss of some ability (for example, the loss of the ability to have children or to play the piano). Each situation seems to call for a somewhat different set of dos and don'ts.

A Problem

Before considering specific suggestions for responding to a person experiencing grief, read the following expression of sympathy, what we might call "the problem."

I just heard that Harry died—I mean—passed away. Excuse me. I'm so sorry. We all are. I know exactly how you feel. But, you know, it's for the best. I mean the man was suffering. I remember seeing him last month; he could hardly stand up, he was so weak. And he looked so sad, so lonely, so depressed. He must have been in constant pain. It's better this way; believe me. He's at peace now. And you'll get over it. You'll see. Time heals all wounds. It was the same way with me, and you know how close we were. I mean, we were devoted to each other. Everyone said we were the closest pair they ever saw. And I got over it. So, how about we'll go to dinner tonight? We'll take about old times. Come on. Come on. Don't be a spoilsport. I really need to get out. I've been in the house all week, and you know what a drag that can be. So, do it for me; come to dinner. I won't take no for an answer; I'll pick you up at 7.

COMMUNICATING WITH THE GRIEF STRICKEN: A SPECIAL CASE ILLUSTRATION (continued)

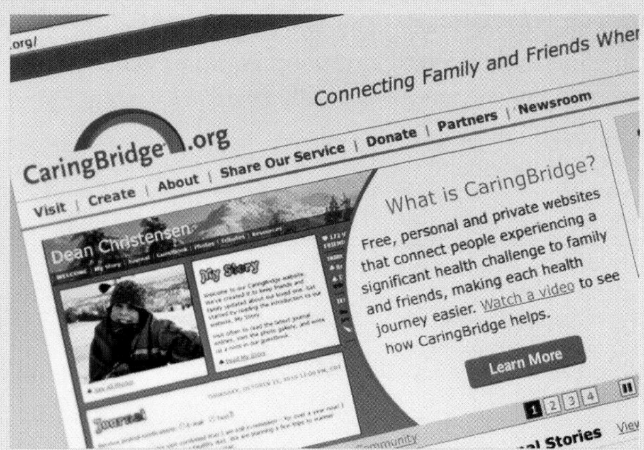

VIEWPOINTS Expressing grief
Social media websites such as CaringBridge enable people to express their caring/support/love for someone experiencing grief by writing in a guestbook that all people who are signed up can read. What general purposes do such websites serve?

Obviously, this is not the way to talk to the grief stricken. In fact, this paragraph was written to illustrate several popular mistakes. After you read the suggestions below, you may wish to return to this "expression of sympathy," reanalyze it, and rework it into an effective expression of sympathy.

A Solution

Here are some suggestions for communicating more effectively with the grief stricken, offering at least some solutions to the above problems.

- *Confirm the other person and the person's emotions.* A simple "You must be worried about finding another position" or "You must be feeling very alone right now" confirms the person's feelings. This type of expressive support lessens feelings of grief (Reed, 1993).
- *Give the person permission to grieve.* Let the person know that it's acceptable and okay with you if he or she grieves in the ways that feel most comfortable—for example, crying or talking about old times. Don't try to change the subject or interject too often. As long as the person is talking and seems to be feeling better for it, be supportive.
- *Avoid trying to focus on the bright side.* Avoid expressions such as "You're lucky you have some vision left" or "It's better this way; Pat was suffering so much." These expressions may easily be seen as telling people that their feelings should be redirected, that they should be feeling something different.
- *Encourage the person to express feelings and talk about the loss.* Most people will welcome this opportunity. On the other hand, don't try to force people to talk about experiences or feelings they may not be willing to share.
- *Be especially sensitive to leave-taking cues.* Behaviors such as fidgeting or looking at a clock and statements such as "It's getting late" or "We can discuss this later" are hints that the other person is ready to end the conversation. Don't overstay your welcome.
- *Let the person know you care and are available.* Saying you're sorry is a simple but effective way to let the person know you care. Express your empathy; let the grief-stricken person know that you can feel (to some extent) what he or she is going through. But don't assume that your feelings, however empathic you are, are the same in depth or in kind. At the same time, let the person know that you are available—"If you ever want to talk, I'm here" or "If there's anything I can do, please let me know."

Even when you follow the principles and do everything according to the book, you may find that your comments are not appreciated or are not at all effective in helping the person feel any better. Use these cues to help you readjust your messages.

MESSAGES IN THE MEDIA WRAP-UP

Watching a soap or telenovela with a view to identifying effective and ineffective emotional expression is a good way to sensitize yourself to more effective ways of expressing your emotions and responding to the emotions of others.

SUMMARY OF CONCEPTS AND SKILLS

Listen to the **Audio Chapter Summary** at **MyCommunicationLab**

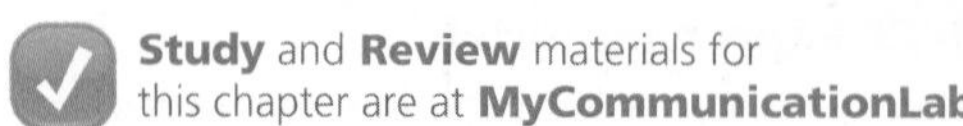

Study and **Review** materials for this chapter are at **MyCommunicationLab**

This chapter explored the nature and principles of emotions in interpersonal communication, the obstacles to meaningful emotional communication, and some guidelines that will help you communicate your feelings and respond to the feelings of others more effectively.

Principles of Emotions and Emotional Messages

1. Emotions consist of a physical part (our physiological reactions), a cognitive part (our interpretations of our feelings), and a cultural part (our cultural traditions' influence on our emotional evaluations and expressions).
2. Emotions may be primary or blends. The primary emotions, according to Robert Plutchik, are joy, acceptance, fear, surprise, sadness, disgust, anger, and anticipation. Other emotions, such as love, awe, contempt, and aggressiveness, are blends of primary emotions.
3. There are different views as to how emotions are aroused. One proposed sequence is this: An event occurs, you respond physiologically, you interpret this arousal, and you experience emotion based on your interpretation.
4. Emotions are communicated verbally and nonverbally, and the way in which you express emotions is largely a matter of choice.
5. Cultural and gender display rules identify what emotions may be expressed, where, how, and by whom.
6. Emotions are often contagious.

Obstacles to Communicating Emotions

7. Among the obstacles to emotional expression are societal rules and customs, the fear of appearing weak or powerless, and not knowing how to express emotions.

Skills for Communicating Emotions

8. Develop self-awareness: recognize what your feelings are, understand why you feel as you do, and understand the potential effects of your feelings.
9. Practice the skills for effective verbal and nonverbal expression, for example, be specific and own your own messages.

Skills for Responding to Emotions

10. Learn what the other person is feeling by understanding the verbal and nonverbal cues.

This chapter also covered a wide variety of skills for more effective emotional communication. Check those you wish to work on.

____ 1. *Understanding feelings.* Understand your feelings. Understand what you are feeling and what made you feel this way.

____ 2. *Communication goals.* Formulate a communication goal. What exactly do you want to accomplish when expressing emotions?

____ 3. *Consider choices.* Identify your communication choices and evaluate them, and only then make your decision as to what to say.

____ 4. *Communicating feelings.* Describe your feelings as accurately as possible, identify the reasons for your feelings, anchor your feelings and their expression to the present time, own your own feelings, and handle your anger as appropriate.

____ 5. *Emotional cues.* Look for cues to understand the person's feelings.

____ 6. *Emotional wants.* Look for cues as to what the person wants you to do, and try to be responsive to these wants.

____ 7. *Active listening.* Use active listening techniques.

____ 8. *Empathize.* See the situation from the other person's perspective.

____ 9. *Other-focus.* Focus on the other person; avoid changing the focus to oneself.

____10. *Irreversibility.* Remember the irreversibility of communication; once something is said, it cannot be unsaid.

VOCABULARY QUIZ: The Language of Emotions

Match the following terms in emotional communication with their definitions. Record the number of the definition next to the appropriate term.

____ blended emotions (153)
____ display rules (156)
____ strategic emotionality (157)
____ emotional communication (152)
____ ventilation hypothesis (166)
____ emotional contagion (158)
____ primary emotions (152)
____ anger (166)
____ emotion (152)
____ anger management (167)

1. using emotions to achieve some personal end
2. the idea that expressing emotions allows you to express your negative feelings and this will have beneficial effects
3. combinations of the basic emotions
4. the process by which the strong emotions of one person can easily be transferred to others present
5. acrimony, annoyance, bitterness, displeasure, exasperation, fury, ire, irritation, outrage, rage, resentment, tantrum, umbrage, wrath, hostility
6. norms for what is and what is not appropriate to express
7. the most basic of emotions, often thought to consist of joy, acceptance, fear, surprise, sadness, disgust, anger, and anticipation
8. the process by which you handle anger
9. the expression of feelings—for example, feelings of guilt, happiness, or sorrow
10. feeling; a mental stage of agitation or excitement, for example

These ten terms and additional terms used in this chapter can be found in the glossary.

MyCommunicationLab

Visit MyCommunicationLab for a wealth of additional information on interpersonal communication. Flashcards, videos, skill building exercises, sample test questions, and additional exercises, examples, and discussions will help you continue your study of the fundamentals of interpersonal communication, its theory, and its skills.

CHAPTER

8

Conversation Messages

MESSAGES IN THE MEDIA

In *Blue Bloods* you see amazingly effective conversation around the dinner table. Although not likely to be representative of most family meals, we can learn a great deal from seeing how conversations are managed and made more effective—the subject of this chapter.

OBJECTIVES *After reading this chapter, you should be able to:*

1. Explain the stages of conversation, its dialogic nature, and the roles of turn-taking and politeness.
2. Define *self-disclosure,* disclose with recognition of its rewards and its dangers, and use the suggestions to respond to the disclosures of others and to resist the pressure to self-disclose.
3. Communicate effectively in making small talk, introductions, and apologies and in giving compliments and advice.

 **Listen** to the **Audio Chapter** at **MyCommunicationLab**

Conversation can be defined as "relatively informal social interaction in which the roles of speaker and hearer are exchanged in a non-automatic fashion under the collaborative management of all parties" (McLaughlin, 1984). Examining conversation provides an excellent opportunity to look at verbal and nonverbal messages as they're used in day-to-day communications and thus serves as a useful culmination for this second part of the text. In this chapter, we look at three aspects of conversation: (1) principles of conversation, (2) conversational disclosure where you reveal yourself to others, and (3) some special types of conversations, grouped under the heading "Everyday Conversations." The general purpose of this discussion is to increase your understanding of the conversation process and also to enable you to engage in conversations with greater comfort, effectiveness, and satisfaction.

PRINCIPLES OF CONVERSATION

Although conversation is an everyday process and one we seldom think about, it is, like most forms of communication, governed by several principles.

Explore the **Concept** "Talkaholic Scale" at **MyCommunicationLab**

The Principle of Process: Conversation Is a Developmental Process

Conversation is best viewed as a process rather than as an act. It's convenient to divide up this process into chunks or stages and to view each stage as requiring a choice as to what you'll say and how you'll say it. Here we divide the sequence into five steps: opening, feedforward, business, feedback, and closing. These stages and the way people follow them will vary depending on the personalities of the communicators, their culture, the context in which the conversation occurs, the purpose of the conversation, and the entire host of factors considered throughout this text.

- *Opening.* The first step is to open the conversation, usually with some kind of greeting: "Hi. How are you?" "Hello, this is Joe." The greeting is a good example of phatic communion. It's a message that establishes a connection between two people and opens up the channels for more meaningful interaction. Openings, of course, may be nonverbal as well as verbal. A smile, kiss, or handshake may be as clear an opening as "Hello." Greetings are so common that they often go unnoticed. But when they're omitted—as when the doctor begins the conversation by saying, "What's wrong?"—you may feel uncomfortable and thrown off guard.
- *Feedforward.* At the second step, you (usually) provide some kind of **feedforward**, which gives the other person a general idea of the conversation's focus: "I've got to tell you about Jack," "Did you hear what happened in class yesterday?," or "We need to talk about our vacation plans." Feedforward also may identify the tone of the conversation ("I'm really depressed and need to talk with you") or the time required ("This will just take a minute") (Frentz, 1976; Reardon, 1987). Conversational awkwardness often occurs when feedforwards are used inappropriately, for example, using overly long feedforwards or omitting feedforward before a truly shocking message.
- *Business.* The third step is the "business," the substance or focus of the conversation. The term *business* is used to emphasize that most conversations are goal directed. That is, you converse to fulfill one or several of the general purposes of interpersonal communication: to learn, relate, influence, play, or help (see Chapter 1). The term is also sufficiently general to incorporate all kinds of interactions. In general, the business is conducted through an exchange of speaker and listener roles. Brief, rather than long, speaking turns characterize most satisfying conversations. In the business stage, you talk about Jack, what happened in class, or your vacation plans. This is obviously the longest part of the conversation and the reason for the opening and the feedforward.

Blog Post

ABCD: Phatic Communion

For a more extended discussion of phatic communication (also and originally called phatic communion), see "ABCD: Phatic Communion" at tcbdevito.blogspot.com. In what ways do you use phatic communication/ communion?

INTERPERSONAL CHOICE POINT

Prefacing to Extremes

A friend whom you talk to on the phone fairly regularly seems to take phatic communication to a new level—the preface is so long that it makes you want to get off the phone, and frequently you make excuses to do just that. What are some things you might do to change this communication pattern?

VIEWPOINTS Gender differences
One of the stereotypes about gender differences in communication that is widely reported in the popular writings on gender is that women talk more than men. However, a recent study of 396 college students finds that women and men talk about the same number of words per day, about 16,000 (Mehl, Vazire, Ramirez-Esparza, Slatcher, & Pennebaker, 2007). Do your own experiences support the stereotype, or do they support these research findings?

- *Feedback.* The fourth step is **feedback,** the reverse of the second step. Here you (usually) reflect back on the conversation to signal that, as far as you're concerned, the business is completed: "So you want to send Jack a get-well card," "Wasn't that the craziest class you ever heard of?," or "I'll call for reservations, and you'll shop for what we need."
- *Closing.* The fifth and last step, the opposite of the first step, is the closing, the goodbye, which often reveals how satisfied the participants were with the conversation: "I hope you'll call soon" or "Don't call us, we'll call you." The closing also may be used to schedule future conversations: "Give me a call tomorrow night" or "Let's meet for lunch at 12."

  When closings are indefinite or vague, conversation often becomes awkward; you're not quite sure if you should say goodbye or if you should wait for something else to be said.

The Principle of Dialogue: Conversation Is Dialogic

Often the term *dialogue* is used as a synonym for *conversation.* But it's more than simple conversation; it's conversation in which there is genuine two-way interaction (Buber, 1958; McNamee & Gergen,

SKILL BUILDING EXERCISE

Opening and Closing a Conversation

Effectively opening and closing conversations often can be challenging. Consider, first, a few situations in which you might want to open a conversation. For each situation, develop a possible opening message in which you seek to accomplish one or more of the following: (a) telling others that you're accessible and open to communication, (b) showing that you're friendly, or (c) showing that you like the other person.

1. You're one of the first guests to arrive at a friend's party and are now there with several other people to whom you've only just been introduced. Your friend, the host, is busy with other matters.
2. You're in the college cafeteria eating alone. You see another student who is also eating alone and whom you recognize from your English literature class. But you're not sure if this person has noticed you in class.

Here are two situations in which you might want to bring a conversation to a close. For each situation, develop a possible closing message in which you seek to accomplish one or more of the following: (a) end the conversation without much more talk, (b) leave the other person with a favorable impression of you, or (c) keep the channels of communication open for future interaction.

1. You and a friend have been talking on the phone for the past hour, but not much new is being said. You have a great deal of work to do and want to wrap it up. Your friend just doesn't seem to hear your subtle cues.
2. You're at a party and are anxious to meet a person with whom you've exchanged eye contact for the past ten minutes. The problem is that another person is demanding all your attention. You don't want to insult this person, but you need to end the conversation in order to make contact with this other person.

Opening and closing conversations are often difficult; your handling of these steps is going to help create an impression that's likely to be long lasting and highly resistant to change.

"Conversation? I thought we were just meeting for coffee."

Michael Maslin/The New Yorker Collection/www.cartoonbank.com

1999; Yau-fair Ho, Chan, Peng, & Ng, 2001). It's useful to distinguish the *ideal* dialogic (two-way) communicator from the opposite, the totally monologic (one-way) communicator.

In **dialogue**, each person is both speaker and listener, sender and receiver. It's a type of conversation in which there is deep concern for the other person and for the relationship between the two. The objective of dialogue is mutual understanding, supportiveness, and empathy. There is respect for the other person, not because of what this person can do or give but simply because this person is a human being and therefore deserves to be treated honestly and sincerely.

Monologue is the opposite side; it's communication in which one person speaks and the other listens—there's no real interaction between participants. The monologic communicator is focused only on his or her own goals and has no real concern for the listener's feelings or attitudes; this speaker is interested in the other person only insofar as that person can serve his or her purposes.

To increase dialogue and decrease monologic tendencies, try the following:

- *Demonstrate respect for the other person.* Allow that person the right to make his or her own choices without coercion, without the threat of punishment, and without fear or social pressure. A dialogic communicator believes that other people can make decisions that are right for them and implicitly or explicitly lets them know that whatever choices they make, they will still be respected as people.
- *Avoid negative criticism* ("I didn't like that explanation") and negative judgments ("You're not a very good listener, are you?"). Instead, practice using positive criticism ("I like those first two explanations best; they were really well reasoned").
- *Keep the channels of communication open* by displaying a willingness to listen. Give cues (nonverbal nods, brief verbal expressions of agreement, paraphrasing) that tell the speaker you're listening.
- *Acknowledge the presence and importance of the other person.* Ask for suggestions, opinions, and clarification. This will ensure that you understand what the

other person is saying from that person's point of view and will also signal a real interest in the person.

- *Avoid manipulating the conversation* to get the person to say something positive about you or to force the other person to think, believe, or behave in any particular way.

Watch the **Video** "Talk, Talk, Talk" at **MyCommunicationLab**

Explore the **Exercise** "Responding Effectively in Conversation" at **MyCommunicationLab**

The Principle of Turn Taking: Conversation Is a Process of Turn Taking

The defining feature of conversation is **turn-taking** (introduced briefly in Chapter 6), where the speaker and listener exchange roles throughout the interaction. You accomplish this through a wide variety of verbal and nonverbal cues that signal conversational turns—the changing or maintaining of the speaker or listener role during the conversation. In hearing people, turn taking is regulated by both audio and visual signals. Among blind speakers, the turn taking is governed in larger part by audio signals and often touch. Among deaf speakers, turn-taking signals are largely visual and also may involve touch (Coates & Sutton-Spence, 2001). Combining the insights of a variety of communication researchers (Burgoon et al., 2010; Duncan, 1972; Pearson & Spitzberg, 1990), let's look more closely at conversational turns in terms of cues that speakers use and cues that listeners use.

SPEAKER CUES As a speaker, you regulate conversation through two major types of cues: turn-maintaining and turn-yielding. **Turn-maintaining cues** help you maintain the speaker's role. You can do this with a variety of cues, for example, by continuing a gesture to show that you have not completed the thought, avoiding eye contact with the listener so there's no indication that you're passing on the speaking turn, or sustaining your intonation pattern to indicate that you intend to say more (Burgoon et al., 2010; Duncan, 1972). In most cases, speakers are expected to maintain relatively brief speaking turns and to turn over the speaking role willingly to the listener, when so signaled by the listener.

With **turn-yielding cues**, you tell the listener that you're finished and wish to exchange the role of speaker for that of listener. For example, at the end of a statement, you might add some paralinguistic cue such as "eh?" that asks one of the listeners to assume the role of speaker. You can also indicate that you've finished speaking by dropping your intonation, by prolonged silence, by making direct eye contact with a listener, by asking some general question, or by nodding in the direction of a particular listener.

Blog Post

Conversational Coolers and Warmers

For a somewhat different take on achieving conversational effectiveness and satisfaction, see "Conversational Coolers and Warmers" at tcbdevito.blogspot.com. What is the single most annoying conversational habit you can think of? What is the single most pleasant conversational habit?

LISTENER CUES As a listener, you can regulate the conversation by using a variety of cues. **Turn-requesting cues** let the speaker know that you'd like to take a turn as speaker. Sometimes you can do this by simply saying, "I'd like to say something," but often you do it more subtly through some vocalized "er" or "um" that tells the mindful speaker that you'd now like to speak. This request to speak is also often made with facial and mouth gestures. You can, for example, indicate a desire to speak by opening your eyes and mouth widely as if to say something, by beginning to gesture with your hand, or by leaning forward.

You can also indicate your reluctance to assume the role of speaker by using **turn-denying cues**. For example, intoning a slurred "I don't know" or a brief grunt signals you have nothing to say. Other ways to refuse a turn are to avoid eye contact with the speaker who wishes you to take on the role of speaker or to engage in some behavior that is incompatible with speaking—for example, coughing or blowing your nose.

BACKCHANNELING CUES **Backchanneling cues** are used to communicate various types of information back to the speaker *without* your assuming the role of speaker and are generally supportive and confirming and show that you're listening and are involved in the interaction (Kennedy & Camden, 1988). You can communicate a variety of messages with these backchanneling cues; here are four of the most important messages (Burgoon et al., 2010; Pearson & Spitzberg, 1990).

- *To indicate agreement or disagreement.* Smiles, nods of approval, brief comments such as "Right" and "Of course," or a vocalization like "uh-huh" signal agreement. Frowning, shaking your head, or making comments such as "No" or "Never" signal disagreement.

- *To indicate degree of involvement.* An attentive posture, forward leaning, and focused eye contact tell the speaker that you're involved in the conversation. An inattentive posture, backward leaning, and avoidance of eye contact communicate a lack of involvement.
- *To pace the speaker.* You ask the speaker to slow down by raising your hand near your ear and leaning forward or to speed up by repeatedly nodding your head. Or you may cue the speaker verbally by asking the speaker to slow down or to speed up.
- *To ask for clarification.* Puzzled facial expressions, perhaps coupled with a forward lean, or direct interjection of "Who?," "When?," or "Where?" signal your need for clarification.

INTERRUPTIONS In contrast to backchanneling cues, **interruptions** are attempts to take over the role of the speaker. These are not supportive and are often disconfirming. Interruptions are often interpreted as attempts to change the topic to a subject that the interrupter knows more about or to emphasize the person's authority. Interruptions are often seen as attempts to assert power and to maintain control. Not surprisingly, research finds that superiors (bosses and supervisors) and those in positions of authority (police officers and interviewers) interrupt those in inferior positions more than the other way around (Ashcraft, 1998; Carroll, 1994). In fact, it would probably strike you as strange to see a worker repeatedly interrupting a supervisor.

Another and even more often studied aspect of interruption is that of gender difference. The popular belief is that men interrupt more than women. This belief, research finds, is basically accurate. Men interrupt both women and other men more than women do. For example, one analysis of 43 published studies showed that men interrupted significantly more than women (Anderson, 1998). In addition, the more male-like the person's gender identity—regardless of the person's biological sex—the more likely it is that the person will interrupt (Drass, 1986). Fathers, one research study shows, interrupt their children more than mothers do (Greif, 1980). These gender differences, however, are small. More important than gender in determining who interrupts is the specific type of situation; some contexts (for example, task-oriented situations) may call for more interruptions, whereas others (such as relationship discussions) may call for more backchanneling cues (Anderson, 1998).

The various turn-taking cues and how they correspond to the conversational wants of speaker and listener are summarized in Figure 8.1.

INTERPERSONAL CHOICE POINT

Interrupting

You're supervising a group of six people who are working to revise your college's website. But one member of the group interrupts so much that other members have simply stopped contributing. It's become a one-person group, and you can't have this. Ask yourself: What are some of the things that you might say to correct this situation without coming across as the bossy supervisor?

The Principle of Politeness: Conversation Is (Usually) Polite

Not surprisingly, conversation is expected (at least in many cases) to follow the principle of politeness. Six maxims of politeness have been identified by linguist Geoffrey Leech (Leech, 1983) and seem to encompass a great deal of what we commonly think of as conversational politeness. Before reading about these maxims, take the following self-test to help you personalize the material that follows.

The *maxim of tact* (statement 1 in the self-test) helps to maintain the other's autonomy (what we referred to earlier as negative face, p. 00). Tact in your conversation would mean that you do not impose on others or challenge their right to do as they wish. For example, if you wanted to ask someone a favor, using the maxim of tact, you might say something like, "I know you're very busy but..." or "I don't mean to impose, but..." Not using the maxim of tact, you might say something like, "You have to lend me your car this weekend" or "I'm going to use your ATM card."

The *maxim of generosity* (statement 2) helps to confirm the other person's importance, for example, the importance of the person's time, insight, or talent. Using the maxim of generosity, you might say, "I'll walk the dog; I see you're busy," and violating the maxim, you might say, "I'm really busy, why don't you walk the dog; you're not doing anything important."

Blog Post

Politeness in the Workplace: Self-Test

For a similar self-test but oriented to the workplace, see "Politeness in the Workplace: Self-Test" at tcbdevito.blogspot.com. What other politeness behaviors would you identify?

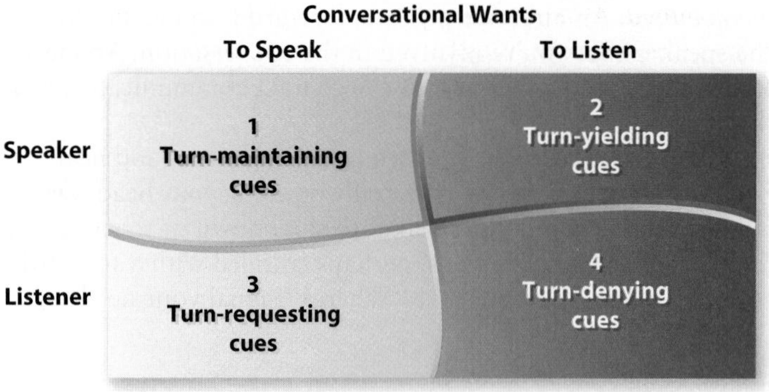

	Conversational Wants	
	To Speak	To Listen
Speaker	1 Turn-maintaining cues	2 Turn-yielding cues
Listener	3 Turn-requesting cues	4 Turn-denying cues

FIGURE 8.1
Turn Taking and Conversational Wants
Each quadrant represents a different type of turn-taking:

- Quadrant 1 represents the speaker who wishes to speak (or to continue speaking) and uses turn-**maintaining** cues.
- Quadrant 2 represents the speaker who wishes to listen and uses turn-**yielding** cues.
- Quadrant 3 represents the listener who wishes to speak and uses turn-**requesting** cues.
- Quadrant 4 represents the listener who wishes to listen (or to continue listening) and uses turn-**denying** cues.

Backchanneling cues would also appear in quadrant 4, as they are cues that listeners use while they continue to listen. Interruptions would appear in quadrant 3, though they're not so much cues that request a turn as takeovers of the speaker's position.

How responsive would you say you are to the turn-taking cues of others? How responsive would you say others are of your turn-taking cues?

The *maxim of approbation* (statement 3) refers to praising someone or complimenting the person in some way (for example, "I was really moved by your poem") and minimizing any expression of criticism or disapproval (for example, "For a first effort, that poem wasn't half bad").

TEST YOURSELF

How Polite Are You?

Try estimating your own level of politeness. For each of the statements below, indicate how closely it describes your typical communication behavior. Avoid giving responses that you feel might be considered "socially acceptable"; instead, give responses that accurately represent your typical communication behavior. Use a ten-point scale with 10 being "very accurate description of my typical conversation" and 1 being "very inaccurate description of my typical conversation."

____ 1. I tend not to ask others to do something or to otherwise impose on others.
____ 2. I tend to put others first, before myself.
____ 3. I maximize the expression of approval of others and minimize any disapproval.
____ 4. I seldom praise myself but often praise others.
____ 5. I maximize the expression of agreement and minimize disagreement.
____ 6. I maximize my sympathy for another and minimize any feelings of antipathy.

How Did You Do? All six statements would characterize politeness, so high numbers, say 8–10, would indicate politeness whereas low numbers, say 1–4, would indicate impoliteness.

What Will You Do? As you read this material, personalize it with examples from your own interpersonal interactions, and try to identify specific examples and situations in which increased politeness might have been more effective.

The *maxim of modesty* (statement 4) minimizes any praise or compliments *you* might receive. At the same time, you might praise and compliment the other person. For example, using this maxim you might say something like, "Well, thank you, but I couldn't have done this without your input; that was the crucial element." Violating this maxim, you might say, "Yes, thank you, it was one of my best efforts, I have to admit."

The *maxim of agreement* (statement 5) refers to your seeking out areas of agreement and expressing them ("That color you selected was just right; it makes the room exciting") and at the same time avoiding and not expressing (or at least minimizing) disagreements ("It's an interesting choice, very different"). In violation of this maxim, you might say "That color—how can you stand it?"

The *maxim of sympathy* (statement 6) refers to the expression of understanding, sympathy, empathy, supportiveness, and the like for the other person. Using this maxim, you might say "I understand your feelings; I'm so sorry." If you violated this maxim, you might say, "You're making a fuss over nothing" or "You get upset over the least little thing; what is it this time?"

An awareness of these several principles will likely lead to more effective and more satisfying conversations. Table 8.1 provides a different perspective on conversational effectiveness and satisfaction.

Blog Post

Annoying Conversation

One of the things that make conversations unsatisfying is those annoying phrases. For a brief list of these, see "Annoying Conversation" at tcbdevito.blogspot.com. What do you feel are the most annoying phrases?

TABLE 8.1

UNSATISFYING CONVERSATIONAL PARTNERS AND HOW NOT TO BECOME ONE OF THEM

As you read this table, consider your own conversations. Have you met any of these people? Have you ever been one of these people?

Unsatisfying Conversational Partners	How Not to Become One of Them
The **Detour Taker** begins to talk about a topic and then goes off pursuing a totally different subject.	Follow a logical pattern in conversation, and avoid frequent and long detours.
The **Monologist** gives speeches rather than engaging in dialogue.	Dialogue; give the other person a chance to speak and keep your own "lectures" short.
The **Complainer** has many complaints and rarely tires of listing each of them.	Be positive; emphasize what's good before what's bad.
The **Moralist** evaluates and judges everyone and everything.	Avoid evaluation and judgment; see the world through the eyes of the other person.
The **Inactive Responder** gives no reaction regardless of what you say.	Respond overtly with verbal and nonverbal messages; let the other person see and hear that you're listening.
The **Story Teller** tells stories, too often substituting them for two-way conversation.	Talk about yourself in moderation; be other-oriented.
The **Egotist** talks only about topics that are self-related.	Be other-oriented; focus on the other person; listen as much as you speak.
The **Thought Completer** "knows" exactly what you're going to say and so says it for you.	Don't interrupt; assume that the speaker wants to finish her or his own thoughts.
The **Self-Discloser** discloses more than you need or want to hear.	Disclose selectively, in ways appropriate to your relationship with the listener.
The **Advisor** regularly and consistently gives advice, whether you want it or not.	Don't assume that the expression of a problem is a request for a solution.

Can you explain the stages of conversation, its dialogic nature, and the roles of turn-taking and politeness? Can you effectively converse in conversation that is dialogic (rather than monologic), operates with appropriate turn-taking, and is generally polite?

CONVERSATIONAL DISCLOSURE: REVEALING YOURSELF

One of the most important forms of interpersonal communication that you can engage in is talking about yourself, or self-disclosure. **Self-disclosure** refers to communicating information about yourself (usually information that you normally keep hidden) to another person. It may involve information about (1) your values, beliefs, and desires ("I believe in reincarnation"); (2) your behavior ("I shoplifted but was never caught"); or (3) your self-qualities or characteristics ("I'm dyslexic"). Overt and carefully planned statements about yourself as well as slips of the tongue would be classified as self-disclosing communications.

Similarly, you could self-disclose nonverbally by, for example, wearing gang colors, a wedding ring, or a shirt with slogans that reveal your political or social concerns, such as "Pro-choice" or "Go green."

Self-disclosure occurs in all forms of communication, not just interpersonal. It frequently occurs in small group settings, in public speeches, and on television talk shows such as *Maury, Jerry Springer, The View*, or even Leno and Letterman. Self-disclosure can occur in face-to-face settings as well as through television and the Internet. On social network sites, for example, a great deal of self-disclosure goes on (verbally and in photos, bumper stickers, and just about any addition you make to your profile), as it does when people reveal themselves in personal e-mails, newsgroups, and blog posts.

You probably self-disclose for a variety of reasons. Perhaps you feel the need for catharsis—a need to get rid of guilty feelings or to confess some wrongdoing. You might also disclose to help the listener—to show the listener, for example, how you dealt with an addiction or succeeded in getting a promotion. And you may self-disclose to encourage relationship growth, to maintain or repair a relationship, or even as a strategy for ending a relationship.

Although self-disclosure may occur as a single message—for example, you tell a stranger on a train that you're thinking about getting a divorce—it's best viewed as a developing process in which information is exchanged between people in a relationship over the period of their relationship (Spencer, Spencer, 1993; Spencer, 1994). If we view it as a developing process, we can then appreciate how self-disclosure changes as the relationship changes; for example, as a relationship progresses from initial contact through involvement to intimacy, the self-disclosures increase. If the relationship deteriorates and perhaps dissolves, the disclosures will decrease.

Self-disclosure involves at least one other individual; it cannot be an intrapersonal communication act. To qualify as self-disclosure, the information must be received and understood by another individual.

VIEWPOINTS Disinhibition
Some researchers have pointed to a "disinhibition effect" that occurs in online communication. We seem less inhibited in communicating in e-mail or in chat groups, for example, than we do face to face. Among the reasons for this seems to be the fact that in online communication there is a certain degree of anonymity and invisibility (Suler, 2004). Does your relative anonymity in online communication lead you to self-disclose differently than you do in face-to-face interactions?

Influences on Self-Disclosure

Many factors influence whether you disclose, what you disclose, and to whom you disclose. Among the most important factors are who you are, your culture, your gender, who your listeners are, and what your topic is.

- *Who You Are.* Highly sociable and extroverted people self-disclose more than those who are less sociable and more introverted. People who are apprehensive about talking in general also self-disclose less than do those who are more comfortable in communicating. Competent people and those with high self-esteem engage in self-disclosure more than less competent people and those with low self-esteem (Dolgin, Meyer, & Schwartz, 1991; McCroskey & Wheeless, 1976).

- *Your Culture.* Different cultures view self-disclosure differently. People in the United States, for example, disclose more than do those in Great Britain, Germany, Japan, or Puerto Rico (Gudykunst, 1983). Americans also reported greater self-disclosure when communicating with other Americans than when communicating interculturally (Allen, Long, O'Mara, & Judd, 2003). In Japan, it's considered undesirable for colleagues to reveal personal information, whereas in much of the United States, it's expected (Barnlund, 1989; Hall & Hall, 1987).
- *Your Gender.* Generally, research finds great self-disclosure between women, a moderate amount in opposite-sex dyads, and the least between men (Aries, 2006; Dindia & Allen, 1992). Women disclose more than men about their previous romantic relationships, their feelings about their closest same-sex friends, their greatest fears, and what they don't like about their partners (Sprecher, 1987; Stewart, Cooper, & Stewart, 2003). A notable exception occurs in initial encounters, where men disclose more intimately than women (Derlega, Winstead, Wong, & Hunter, 1985).
- *Your Listeners.* Because you disclose on the basis of the support you receive, you disclose to people you like (Collins & Miller, 1994; Derlega, Winstead, Greene, Serovich, & Elwood, 2004) and to people you trust and love (Sprecher & Hendrick, 2004; Wheeless & Grotz, 1977). Not surprisingly, you're more likely to disclose to people who are close to you in age (Parker & Parrott, 1995). You also come to like those to whom you disclose (Berg & Archer, 1983).
- *Your Topic.* You're more likely to disclose about some topics than others. You're more likely to self-disclose information about your job or hobbies than about your sex life or financial situation (Jourard, Jourard, 1968; Jourard, 1971). You're also more likely to disclose favorable than unfavorable information. Generally, the more personal and negative the topic, the less likely you are to self-disclose.

Rewards and Dangers of Self-Disclosure

Research shows that self-disclosure has both significant rewards and dangers. In making choices about whether to disclose, consider both.

INTERPERSONAL CHOICE POINT

Breaking Up

You're engaged to Pat, but over the past few months, you've fallen in love with someone else. You now have to break your engagement and disclose your new relationship. What are some options for this disclosure? What channel would be most appropriate? What kind of feedforward would you use?

Rewards of Self-Disclosure Self-disclosure may help increase self-knowledge, communication and relationship effectiveness, and physiological well-being.

- *Self-knowledge.* Self-disclosure helps you gain greater self-knowledge, a new perspective on yourself, a deeper understanding of your own behavior. Through self-disclosure you may bring to consciousness a great deal that you might otherwise keep from conscious analysis. Also, the interaction that follows your disclosures is likely to increase your self-awareness.
- *Communication and relationship effectiveness.* Self-disclosure is an essential condition for communication and relationship effectiveness, largely because you understand the messages of another person largely to the extent that you understand the person. Self-disclosure helps you achieve a closer relationship with the person to whom you self-disclose and increases relationship satisfaction (Meeks, Hendrick, & Hendrick, 1998; Schmidt & Cornelius, 1987; Sprecher, 1987). Research also finds that persons who engage in in-depth self-disclosure seem to experience less psychological abuse (Shirley, Powers, & Sawyer, 2007).
- *Physiological health.* Self-disclosure seems to have a positive effect on health. People who self-disclose are less vulnerable to illnesses (Pennebacker, 1991). Not surprisingly, health benefits also result from disclosing in e-mails (Sheese, Brown, & Graziano, 2004).

Watch the **Video** "Friends" at **MyCommunicationLab**

Dangers of Self-Disclosure: Risks Ahead There are also, however, personal, relational, and professional risks to self-disclosure.

- *Personal Risks.* If you self-disclose aspects of your life that vary greatly from the values of those to whom you disclose, you may incur personal risks, perhaps rejection

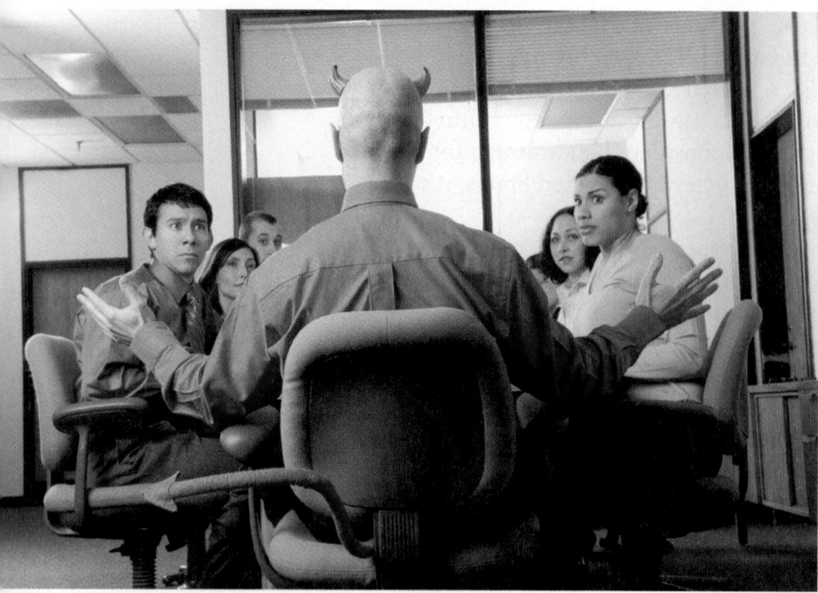

VIEWPOINTS Remaining mysterious

The more you reveal about yourself to others, the more areas of your life you expose to possible attack. Especially in the competitive context of work (or even romance), the more that others know about you, the more they'll be able to use against you. This simple fact has prompted power watcher Michael Korda (Korda, 1975, p. 302) to advise that you "never reveal all of yourself to other people." This advice is not to suggest that you be secretive; rather, Korda is advocating "remaining slightly mysterious, as if [you] were always capable of doing something surprising and unexpected." What's your view on this issue?

from even your closest friends and family members. Men and women who disclose that they have cheated on their relationship partner, have stolen, or are suffering from prolonged depression, for example, may find their friends and family no longer wanting to be quite as close as before.

- *Relational Risks.* Even in close and long-lasting relationships, self-disclosure can pose relational risks (Bochner, 1984). Total self-disclosure may prove threatening to a relationship by causing a decrease in mutual attraction, trust, or any of the bonds holding the individuals together. Self-disclosures concerning infidelity, romantic fantasies, past indiscretions or crimes, lies, or hidden weaknesses and fears could easily have such negative effects.
- *Professional Risks.* Revealing political views or attitudes toward different religious or racial groups may open you to professional risks and create problems on the job, as may disclosing any health problems (Fesko, 2001). Teachers who disclose former or current drug use or cohabitation with students may find themselves denied tenure, teaching at undesirable hours, and eventually falling victim to "budget cuts."

In making your choice between disclosing and not disclosing, keep in mind—in addition to the advantages and dangers already noted—the irreversible nature of communication. Regardless of how many times you may try to qualify something or take it back, once you have disclosed, you cannot undisclose it. You cannot erase the conclusions and inferences listeners have made on the basis of your disclosures.

Explore the **Concept** "Interpersonal" at **MyCommunicationLab**

Guidelines for Self-Disclosure

Because self-disclosure is so important and so delicate a matter, guidelines are offered here for (1) deciding whether and how to self-disclose, (2) responding to the disclosures of others, and (3) resisting pressures to self-disclosure.

GUIDELINES FOR MAKING SELF-DISCLOSURES The following guidelines will help you raise the right questions before you make a choice that must ultimately be your own.

INTERPERSONAL CHOICE POINT

To Disclose or Not

You discover that your close friend's romantic partner of the past two years is being unfaithful. You feel you have an obligation to tell your friend and decide to do so (though you still have doubts that this is the right thing to do). What are some of the choices you have for communicating this information to your friend? What choice seems the most logical for this specific situation? After you formulate your response, take a look at Zhang & Merolla, 2006.

- *Disclose out of appropriate motivation.* Self-disclosure should be motivated by a concern for the relationship, for the others involved, and for oneself. Avoid disclosing to hurt the listener (for example, children telling parents that they hindered their emotional development may be disclosing out of a desire to hurt and punish rather than a desire to improve the relationship).
- *Disclose in the appropriate context.* Before making any significant self-disclosure, ask whether this is the right time and place. Could a better time and place be arranged? Ask, too, whether this self-disclosure is appropriate to the relationship. Generally, the more intimate the disclosures, the closer the relationship should be.
- *Disclose gradually.* During your disclosures, give the other person a chance to reciprocate with his or her own disclosures. If reciprocal

disclosures are not made, reassess your own self-disclosures. It may be a signal that, for this person at this time and in this context, your disclosures are not welcome or appropriate.

- *Disclose without imposing burdens on yourself or others.* Carefully weigh the potential problems that you may incur as a result of your disclosure. Can you afford to lose your job if you disclose your arrest record? Are you willing to risk relational difficulties if you disclose your infidelities?

Blog Post

Self-Disclosure

Take a look at "Self-Disclosure" at tcbdevito.blogspot.com. What do you see as the advantages and the disadvantages of this form of disclosure?

Guidelines for Facilitating and Responding to Self-Disclosures When someone discloses to you, it's usually a sign of trust and affection. In serving this most important receiver function, keep the following guidelines in mind. These guidelines will also help you facilitate the disclosures of another person.

- *Practice the skills of effective and active listening.* The skills of effective listening are especially important when you are listening to self-disclosures: Listen actively, listen for different levels of meaning, listen with empathy, and listen with an open mind. Express an understanding of the speaker's feelings to allow the speaker the opportunity to see them more objectively and through the eyes of another. Ask questions to ensure your own understanding and to signal your interest and attention.
- *Support and reinforce the discloser.* Express support for the person during and after the disclosures. Concentrate on understanding and empathizing with (rather than evaluating) the discloser. Make your supportiveness clear to the discloser through your verbal and nonverbal responses: Maintain eye contact, lean toward the speaker, ask relevant questions, and echo the speaker's thoughts and feelings.
- *Be willing to reciprocate.* When you make relevant and appropriate disclosures of your own in response to the other person's disclosures, you're demonstrating your understanding of the other's meanings and at the same time showing a willingness to communicate on this meaningful level.
- *Keep the disclosures confidential.* When people disclose to you, it's because they want you to know their feelings and thoughts. If you reveal these disclosures to others, negative outcomes are inevitable, and your relationship is almost sure to suffer for it.

INTERPERSONAL CHOICE POINT

Disclosure Encouragement

Your teen-aged nephew seems on edge, and you think he needs to talk about what's on his mind. You want to encourage greater disclosure but don't want to seem pushy or nosy. How might you begin a conversation that encourages your nephew to self-disclose?

Guidelines for Resisting Self-Disclosure You may, on occasion, find yourself in a position where a friend, colleague, or romantic partner pressures you to self-disclose. In such situations, you may wish to weigh the pros and cons of self-disclosure and then

SKILL BUILDING EXERCISE

Disclosing Your Hidden Self

This experience is an extremely powerful one for exploring some of the dimensions of self-disclosure and is based on a suggestion by Gerard Egan (Egan, 1970). The procedure is simple: Each person in the class writes on an index card a statement of information that is currently in his or her hidden self (that is, currently undisclosed to all or most of the others in this class). No names should be used here; the statements are dealt with anonymously. The cards should be collected and read aloud to the entire group. No comments should be made as the cards are read; no indications of evaluation should be made. The comments are to be dealt with in a totally supportive atmosphere.

After the cards are read, consider some or all of the following issues:

- What topics did the statements deal with? Are they generally the topics about which you too keep information hidden?
- Why do you suppose this type of information is kept in the hidden self? What advantages might there be in keeping it hidden? What disadvantages?
- How would you react to people who disclosed such statements to you? For example, what difference, if any, would these types of disclosures make in your closest interpersonal relationships?

Understanding the topics others are willing and are not willing to disclose (and their reasons) will likely give you insight into your own disclosure patterns.

INTERPERSONAL CHOICE POINT

Refusing to Self-Disclose

You've dated this person three or four times, and each time you're pressured to self-disclose your past experiences and personal information you're just not ready to talk about, at least not at this early stage of the relationship. What are some of the things you can say or do to resist this pressure to self-disclose? What might you say to discourage further requests that you reveal yourself?

make your decision as to whether and what you'll disclose. If your decision is not to disclose and you're still being pressured, then you need to say something. Here are a few suggestions.

- *Don't be pushed.* Although there may be certain legal or ethical reasons for disclosing, generally, if you don't want to disclose, you don't have to. Don't be pushed into disclosing because others are doing it or because you're asked to.
- *Be indirect and move to another topic.* Avoid the question, and change the subject. This is a polite way of saying, "I'm not talking about it," and it may be the preferred choice in certain situations. Most often people will get the hint and understand your refusal to disclose.
- *Delay a decision.* If you don't want to say "No" directly but still don't want to disclose, delay the decision, saying something like, "That's pretty personal; let me think about that before I make a fool of myself" or "This isn't really a good time (or place) to talk about this."
- *Be assertive in your refusal to disclose.* Say, very directly, "I'd rather not talk about that now" or "Now is not the time for this type of discussion." More specific guidelines for communicating assertiveness are offered in Chapter 5 (pp. 109–111).

Blog Post

Outing

For a brief discussion of the dangers of revealing normally hidden information about others, see "Outing" at tcbdevito.blogspot.com. Have you ever been "outed"? Ever "outed" others? What were the consequences?

Can you define *self-disclosure*? Can you apply the guidelines for making, facilitating, and resisting self-disclosure?

EVERYDAY CONVERSATIONS

Here we discuss a variety of everyday conversation situations: making small talk, introducing other people or ourselves, apologizing, complimenting, and giving advice. When reading about and thinking about of conversation, keep in mind that not everyone speaks with the fluency and ease that many textbooks often assume. Speech and language disorders, for example, can seriously disrupt the conversation process when some elementary guidelines aren't followed. Table 8.2 offers suggestions for making such conversations run more smoothly.

Small Talk

Small talk is pervasive; all of us engage in small talk. Sometimes, we use small talk as a preface to big talk. For example, before a conference with your boss or even an employment interview, you're likely to engage in some preliminary small talk. *How are you doing? I'm pleased this weather has finally cleared up. That's a great-looking jacket.* The purpose with much of this face-to-face small talk is to ease into the major topic or the big talk. On Facebook and Twitter, however, small talk may actually be an end in itself—simply a way of letting your "friends" know that you went to the movies last night and not necessarily to get into an extended discussion of the movie.

Sometimes, small talk is a politeness strategy and a bit more extensive way of saying hello as you pass someone in the hallway or a neighbor you meet at the post office. And so you might say, "Good seeing you, Jack. You're ready for the big meeting?" or "See you in geology at 1."

Sometimes your relationship with another person revolves totally around small talk, perhaps with your barber or hair dresser, a colleague at work, your next-door neighbor, or a student you sit next to in class. In these relationships, neither person makes an effort to deepen the relationship, and it remains on a small-talk level.

TABLE 8.2

Interpersonal Communication Tips Between People with and without Speech and Language Disorders

Speech and language disorders vary widely—from fluency problems such as stuttering, to indistinct articulation, to difficulty in finding the right word (aphasia). Following a few simple guidelines can facilitate communication between people with and without speech and language disorders.

If you're the person without a speech or language disorder:

Generally	Specifically
Avoid finishing another's sentences.	Finishing the person's sentences may communicate the idea that you're impatient and don't want to spend the extra time necessary to interact effectively.
Avoid giving directions to the person with a speech disorder.	Saying "slow down" or "relax" will often seem insulting and will make further communication more difficult.
Maintain eye contact.	Show interest and at the same time avoid showing any signs of impatience or embarrassment.
Ask for clarification as needed.	If you don't understand what the person said, ask him or her to repeat it. Don't pretend that you understand when you don't.
Don't treat people who have language problems like children.	A person with aphasia, say, who has difficulty with names or nouns generally, is in no way childlike. Similarly, a person who stutters is not a slow thinker; in fact, stutterers differ from non-stutterers only in their oral fluency.

If you're the person with a speech or language disorder:

Generally	Specifically
Let the other person know what your special needs are.	If you stutter, you might tell others that you have difficulty with certain sounds and so they need to be patient.
Demonstrate your own comfort.	Show that you have a positive attitude toward the interpersonal situation. If you appear comfortable and positive, others will also.
Be patient	For example, have patience with those who try to finish your sentences; They're likely just trying to be helpful.

Sources: These suggestions were drawn from a variety of sources including the websites of the National Stuttering Association, the National Aphasia Association, the United States Department of Labor, and the American Speech and Hearing Association, all accessed May 9, 2012.

Before reading about the guidelines for effective small talk, take the accompanying self-test to start thinking about how you engage in small talk.

Although "small," this talk still requires the application of the interpersonal communication skills for "big" talk. Keep especially in mind, as already noted, that the best topics are noncontroversial and that most small talk is relatively brief. Here are a few additional guidelines for more effective small talk.

- *Be positive.* No one likes a negative doomsayer.
- *Talk about noncontroversial topics.* If there are wide differences of opinion on a topic, it's probably not appropriate for small talk.
- *Be sensitive to leave-taking cues.* Small talk is necessarily brief, but at times one person may want it to be a preliminary to the big talk and another person may see it as the sum of the interaction.

INTERPERSONAL CHOICE POINT

Making Small Talk

You're on an elevator with three other people from your office building. The elevator gets stuck without any indication of when power will go back on. What are some of your options for initiating small talk? What would your first sentence be?

TEST YOURSELF

How Do You Small Talk?

Examine your small talk communication by responding to the following questions.

____ 1. On an elevator with three or four strangers, I'd be most likely to
   a. seek to avoid interacting.
   b. respond to another but not initiate interaction.
   c. be the first to talk.

____ 2. When I'm talking with someone and I meet a friend who doesn't know the person I'm with, I'd be most apt to
   a. avoid introducing them.
   b. wait until they introduce each other.
   c. introduce them to each other.

____ 3. At a party with people I've never met before, I'd be most likely to
   a. wait for someone to talk to me.
   b. nonverbally indicate that I'm receptive to someone interacting with me.
   c. initiate interaction with others nonverbally and verbally

____ 4. When confronted with someone who doesn't want to end the conversation, I'd be most apt to
   a. just stick it out and listen.
   b. tune out the person and hope time goes by quickly.
   c. end it firmly myself.

____ 5. When the other person monologues, I'd be most apt to
   a. listen politely.
   b. try to change the focus.
   c. exit as quickly as possible.

How Did You Do? The *a* responses are unassertive, the *b* responses are indirect (not totally unassertive but not assertive, either), and the *c* responses are direct and assertive. Very likely, if you answered with 4 or 5 *c* responses, you're comfortable and satisfied with your small talk experiences. Lots of *a* responses would indicate some level of dissatisfaction and discomfort with the experience of small talk. If you had lots of *b* responses, you probably experience both satisfaction and dissatisfaction with small talk.

What Will You Do? If your small talk experiences are not satisfying to you, read on. The entire body of interpersonal skills will prove relevant here as will a number of suggestions unique to small talk.

- *Talk in short sequences;* dialogue, don't monologue.
- *Stress similarities* rather than differences; this is a good way to ensure that this small talk is noncontroversial.
- *Answer questions with enough elaboration* to give the other person information that can then be used to interact with you. Let's say someone sees a book you're carrying and says, "I see you're taking interpersonal communication." If you say simply "yes," you've not given the other person anything to talk with you about. Instead, if you say, "Yes, it's a great course; I think I'm going to major in communication," then you have given the other person information that can be addressed. Of course, if you do not want to interact, then a simple one-word response will help you achieve your goal.

VIDEO CHOICE POINT

First Day of Class

Tim would like to initiate a conversation with his classmate Emad, but feels awkward. Tim considers some of the principles of conversation that you will read about in this chapter as he makes both effective and ineffective communication choices. See how his choices play out in the video "First Day of Class" and respond to the questions posed.

 **Watch** the **Video** "First Day of Class" at **MyCommunicationLab**

ETHICAL MESSAGES

The Ethics of Gossip

Gossip is social talk that involves making evaluations about persons who are not present during the conversation; it generally occurs when two people talk about a third party (Eder & Enke, 1991; Wert & Salovey, 2004). As you obviously know, a large part of our conversation at work and in social situations, whether face to face or online, is spent gossiping (Carey, 2005; Lachnit, 2001; Waddington, 2004). In fact, one study estimates that approximately two-thirds of people's conversation time is devoted to social topics and that most of these topics can be considered gossip (Dunbar, 2004). And, not surprisingly, gossip occupies a large part of online communication (Morgan, 2008).

Gossip serves a number of purposes. For example, gossip bonds people together and solidifies their relationship; it creates a sense of camaraderie (Greengard, 2001; Hafen, 2004). At the same time, of course, it helps to create an in-group (those doing the gossiping) and an out-group (those being gossiped about). Gossip also teaches people what behaviors are acceptable (the positive gossip) and which are unacceptable (from the negative gossip) (Baumeister, Zhang, & Vohs, 2004; Hafen, 2004).

As you might expect, gossiping often has ethical implications, and in many instances, gossip would be considered unethical. Some such instances generally identified as unethical are the following (Bok, 1983). As you read these, consider whether there are other types of gossip that you might consider unethical.

- when gossip is used to unfairly hurt another person, for example, spreading gossip about an office romance or an instructor's past indiscretions.
- when you know that what you're saying is not true, for example, lying to make another person look bad.
- when no one has the right to such personal information, for example, revealing the income of neighbors to others or revealing another student's poor grades to other students.
- when you've promised secrecy, for example, revealing something that you promised not to repeat to others.

Ethical Choice Point

You're supervising a new group of interns, and you're wondering if you should tell them about the general supervisor, who has made romantic overtures to several past interns. Would this just be unethical gossip, or would it be ethical and well within your mission to warn them?

Introducing People

One of the interpersonal communication situations that often create difficulties is the introduction of one person to another person. Let's say you're with Jack and bump into Jill who stops to talk. Because they don't know each other, it's your job to introduce them. Generally, it's best to do this simply but with enough detail to provide a context for further interaction. It might go something like this: "Jill Williams, this is Jack Smith, who works with me at ABC as marketing manager. I went to college with Jill and, if I'm not mistaken, she has just returned from Hawaii."

With this introduction, Jack and Jill can say something to each other based on the information provided in this brief (32-word) introduction. They can talk about working at ABC, what it's like being a marketing manager, what Jill majored in, what Hawaii is like, what Jill did in Hawaii, and on and on. If you simply said: "Jack this is Jill; Jill, Jack," there would be virtually nothing for Jack and Jill to talk about.

Some introductions need special handling, as the following examples show:

- *Forgetting the person's name.* If you forget the person's name, the best thing to do here is to admit it and say something like: "I don't know why I keep thinking your name is Joe; I know it's not. I'm blocking." You're not the only one who forgets names, and few people take great offense when this happens.
- *Reluctance to self-disclose.* If you don't want to reveal what your relationship with the person you're with is, don't. Simply say, "This is Jack." You don't have to identify what your relationship to Jack is if you don't want to. And, hopefully, the other person won't ask. Of course, if you want to reveal your relationship, then do so. This is Jack, my lover, boyfriend, life partner, parole officer, or whatever term you want to use to define your relationship.

- *Be culturally sensitive.* In using names, it's best to be consistent with the norms operating in your specific culture. So, if just first names are exchanged in the introduction, use just first names. If the norm is to use first and last names, follow that pattern. Also, be consistent with the two people you introduce. Use just the first name for both or first name plus last name for both.
- *Rank differences.* If the two people are of obviously different ranks, then the person of lower rank is introduced to the person of higher rank. Thus, you'd introduce the child to the adult, the junior executive to the senior executive, the student to the professor. Another commonly practiced rule is to introduce the man to the woman: *Marie, this is Stephen.* Or *Marie, I'd like to introduce Stephen to you.*

In the United States, the handshake is the most essential gesture of introduction (see Table 8.3). In Muslim cultures, people hug same-sex people but not the opposite sex. In Latin America, South America, and the Mediterranean, people are more likely to hug (and perhaps kiss on the cheek) than are Northern Europeans, Asians, and many from the United States. Asians are more reluctant to extend their hands and more often bow, with lower bows required when people of lower status meet someone of higher status, for example, an intern meeting a company executive or a private meeting a general.

INTERPERSONAL CHOICE POINT

Introducing Yourself

You're in class early with a few students; no one knows anyone. What are some of the ways you can introduce yourself and engage in some small talk? What would you say?

Apologies

Watch the **Video** "I Didn't Do It" at **MyCommunicationLab**

Despite your best efforts, there are times when you'll say or do the wrong thing and an apology may be necessary. An **apology** is an expression of regret or sorrow for having done what you did or for what happened; it's a statement that you're sorry. And so, the most basic of all apologies is simply: *I'm sorry.* In popular usage, the apology includes some admission of wrongdoing on the part of the person making the apology. Sometimes the wrongdoing is acknowledged explicitly (I'm sorry I lied) and sometimes only by implication (I'm sorry you're so upset). In many cases, the apology also includes a request for forgiveness (*Please forgive my lateness*) and some assurance that this won't happen again (*Please forgive my lateness; it won't happen again*).

TABLE 8.3

SIX STEPS TO AN EFFECTIVE HANDSHAKE

Dos	Don'ts
Make eye contact at the beginning and maintain it throughout the handshake.	Look away from the person or down at the floor or at your shaking hand.
Smile and otherwise signal positiveness.	Appear static or negative.
Extend your entire right hand.	Extend just your fingers or your left hand.
Grasp the other person's hand firmly but without so much pressure that it would be uncomfortable.	Grasp the other person's fingers as if you really don't want to shake hands but you're making a gesture to be polite.
Pump three times; a handshake in the United States lasts about three to four seconds. In other cultures, it might be shorter or, more often, longer.	Give the person a "dead fish." Be careful that the other person's pumping doesn't lead you to withdraw your own pumping. Pump much more than three times.
Release grasp while still maintaining eye contact.	Hold grasp for an overly long time or release too early.

"What flower says you're sorry without admitting wrongdoing?"

Mike Twohy/The New Yorker Collection/www.cartoonbank.com

An effective apology must be crafted for the specific situation. Effective apologies to a longtime lover, to a parent, or to a new supervisor are likely to be very different because the individuals are different and your relationships are different. And so the first rule of an effective apology is to take into consideration the uniqueness of the situation—the people, the context, the cultural rules, the relationship, the specific wrongdoing—for which you might want to apologize. Each situation will call for a somewhat different message of apology. Nevertheless, we can offer some general recommendations.

- *Admit wrongdoing* (if indeed wrongdoing occurred). Accept responsibility. Own your own actions; don't try to pass them off as the work of someone else. Instead of *Smith drives so slow, it's a wonder I'm only 30 minutes late*, say *I should have taken traffic into consideration.*
- *Be apologetic.* Say (and mean) the words *I'm sorry*. Don't justify your behavior by mentioning that everyone does it, for example, *Everyone leaves work early on Friday.* Don't justify your behavior by saying that the other person has done something equally wrong: *So I play poker; you play the lottery.*
- *Be specific.* State, in specific rather than general terms, what you've done. Instead of *I'm sorry for what I did*, say *I'm sorry for flirting at the party.*
- *Empathize.* Express understanding of how the other person feels and acknowledge the legitimacy of these feelings, for example, *You have every right to be angry; I should have called.* Express your regret that this has created a problem for the other person:

VIEWPOINTS Apologies
What kinds of apologies do you hear most often from your peers? Can you identify what makes some apologies acceptable and others unacceptable?

I'm sorry I made you miss your appointment. Don't minimize the problem that this may have caused. Avoid such comments as *So the figures arrived a little late. What's the big deal?*

- *Give assurance* that this will not happen again. Say, quite simply, *It won't happen again* or, better and more specifically, *I won't be late again.* And, whenever possible, offer to correct the problem: *I'm sorry I didn't clean up the mess I made; I'll do it now.*
- *Avoid excuses.* Be careful of including excuses with your apology, for example, *I'm sorry the figures are late, but I had so much other work to do.* An excuse often takes back the apology and says, in effect, I'm really not sorry because there was good reason for what I did, but I'm saying "I'm sorry" to cover all my bases and to make this uncomfortable situation go away.
- *Choose the appropriate channel.* Don't take the easy way out and apologize through e-mail (unless the wrongdoing was committed in e-mail or if e-mail is your only or main form of communication). Generally, it's more effective to use a more personal mode of communication—face-to-face or phone, for example. It's harder, but it's more effective.

> **INTERPERSONAL CHOICE POINT**
>
> **Apologizing**
>
> You borrowed a friend's car and got into an accident—and, to make matters worse, it was totally your fault. What are some of the things you might say that would help you explain the situation, alleviate any anxiety your friend will have over the accident, and pave the way for a request to borrow the car again next week for the most important date of your life? What would be your first sentence?

Complimenting

A **compliment** is a message of praise, flattery, or congratulations. It's the opposite of criticism, insult, or complaint. It can be expressed in face-to-face interaction or on social media sites when, for example, you retweet someone's post or indicate "like" or "+1" or when you comment on a blog post. The compliment functions like a kind of interpersonal glue; it's a way of relating to another person with positiveness and immediacy. It's also a conversation starter, "I like your watch; may I ask where you got it?" In online communication—when you poke, tag, +1, or retweet, for example—it's a reminder that you're thinking of someone (and being complimentary). Another purpose the compliment serves is to encourage the other person to compliment you—even if not immediately (which often seems inappropriate).

A *backhanded compliment* is really not a compliment at all; it's usually an insult masquerading as a compliment. For example, you might give a backhanded compliment if you say "That beautiful red sweater takes away from your pale complexion; it makes you look less washed out" (it compliments the color of the sweater but criticizes the person's complexion) or "Looks like you've finally lost a few pounds, am I right?" (it compliments a slimmer appearance but points out the person's being overweight).

Yet compliments are sometimes difficult to express and even more difficult to respond to without discomfort or embarrassment. Fortunately, there are easy-to-follow guidelines.

Giving a Compliment Here are a few suggestions for giving compliments.

- *Be real and honest.* Say what you mean, and omit giving compliments you don't believe in. They'll likely sound insincere and won't serve any useful purpose.
- *Compliment in moderation.* A compliment that is too extreme (say, for example, "that's the best decorated apartment I've ever seen in my life") may be viewed as dishonest. Similarly, don't compliment at every possible occasion; if you do, your compliments will seem too easy to win and not really meaningful.
- *Be totally complimentary.* Avoid qualifying your compliments. If you hear yourself giving a compliment and then adding a "but" or a "however," be careful; you're likely going to qualify your compliment. Unfortunately, in such situations, many people will remember the qualification rather than the compliment, and the entire compliment + qualification will appear as a criticism.
- *Be specific.* Direct your compliment at something specific rather than something general. Instead of saying something general, such as *I like your design*, you might say something more specific, such as *I like your design; the colors and fonts are perfect.*

- *Be personal in your own feelings.* For example, say *Your song really moved me; it made me recall so many good times.* At the same time, avoid any compliment that can be misinterpreted as overly sexual.

RECEIVING A COMPLIMENT In receiving a compliment, people generally take either one of two options: denial or acceptance.

Many people deny the compliment ("It's nice of you to say, but I know I was terrible"), minimize it ("It isn't like I wrote the great American novel; it was just an article that no one will read"), change the subject ("So, where should we go for dinner?"), or say nothing. Each of these responses creates problems. When you deny the legitimacy of the compliment, you're saying that the person isn't being sincere or doesn't know what he or she is talking about. When you minimize it, you say, in effect, that the person doesn't understand what you've done or what he or she is complimenting. When you change the subject or say nothing, again, you're saying, in effect, that the compliment isn't having any effect; you're ignoring it because it isn't meaningful.

Accepting the compliment seems the much better alternative. An acceptance might consist simply of (1) a smile with eye contact—avoid looking at the floor; (2) a simple "thank you," and, if appropriate, (3) a personal reflection where you explain (very briefly) the meaning of the compliment and why it's important to you (for example, "I really appreciate your comments; I worked really hard on that design, and it's great to hear it was effective"). Depending on your relationship with the person, you might use his or her name; people like to hear their names spoken and doubly so when it's associated with a compliment.

Advice Giving

Advice is the process of giving another person a suggestion for thinking or behaving, usually to change his or her thinking or ways of behaving. The popularity of the "Dear Abby" type of columns in print and in online newspapers and magazines and the many websites that offer advice on just about everything attests to our concern with asking for and getting advice.

In many ways, you can look at advice giving as a suggestion to solve a problem. So, for example, you might advise friends to change their ways of looking at broken love affairs or their financial situations or their career paths. Or you might advise someone to do something, to behave in a certain way, for example, to start dating again or to invest in certain stocks or to go back to school and take certain courses.

Notice that you can give advice in at least two ways. One way is to give specific advice, and another is to give **meta-advice**, or advice about advice. Thus, you can give advice to a person that addresses the problem or issue directly—buy that condo, take this course, or vacation in Hawaii. But you can also give advice about advice. For example, you might suggest that the individual explore additional options and choices. So, when confronted with a request for advice, this meta-advice would focus on helping the person explore the available options. For example, if a friend asks what he or she should do about never having a date, you might give meta-advice and help your friend explore the available options and the advantages and disadvantages (the rewards and the

VIEWPOINTS Giving advice

Men are frequently accused of offering advice even when it isn't solicited (Tannen, 1994a, 1994b). When a problem or question is expressed, the stereotype goes, men will try to solve the problem while women will be more likely to express empathy for the speaker. Do you find this true from your own interactions?

costs) of each. Another type of meta-advice is to suggest the individual seek expert advice. If confronted with a request for advice concerning some technical issue in which you have no competence, the best advice is often meta-advice, in this case, to seek advice from someone who is an expert in the field. When a friend asks what to do about a persistent cough, the best advice seems to be the meta-advice to "talk to your doctor." Still another form of meta-advice is to suggest that the decision be delayed (assuming that it doesn't have to be made immediately). So, for example, if your advice-seeking friend has two weeks to decide on whether to take a job with XYZ Company, meta-advice would suggest that the decision be delayed while the company is researched more thoroughly.

Blog Post

Advice Giving

Take a look at the comments on "Advice Giving" at tcbdevito.blogspot.com. What advice would you have given?

GIVING ADVICE In addition to giving meta-advice, there is also the option of giving specific advice. Here are a few suggestions:

- *Listen.* This is the first rule for advice giving. Listen to the person's thoughts and feelings. Listen to what the person wants—the person may actually want support and active listening and not advice. Or the person may simply want to vent in the presence of a friend.
- *Empathize.* Try to feel what the other person is feeling. Perhaps you might recall similar situations you were in or similar emotions you experienced. Think about the importance of the issue to the person, and, in general, try to put yourself into the position, the circumstance, or the context of the person asking your advice.
- *Be tentative.* If you give advice, give it with the qualifications it requires. The advice seeker has a right to know how sure (or unsure) you are of the advice or what evidence (or lack of evidence) you have that the advice will work.
- *Ensure understanding.* Often people seeking advice are emotionally upset and may not remember everything in the conversation. So seek feedback after giving advice, for example, "Does that make sense?" "Is my suggestion workable?"
- *Keep the interaction confidential.* Often advice seeking is directed at very personal matters, so it's best to keep such conversations confidential, even if you're not asked to do so.
- *Avoid should statements.* People seeking advice still have to make their own decisions rather than being told what they should or should not do. So it's better to say, for example, "You *might* do X" or "You *could* do Y" rather than "You *should* do Z." Don't demand—or even imply—that the person has to follow your advice. This attacks the person's negative face, the person's need for autonomy.

INTERPERSONAL CHOICE POINT

Unwanted Advice

One of your close friends has the annoying habit of trying to give you advice, which you don't want and only depresses you. What are some of your options for dealing with this problem? What are some of the things you might say to your friend?

RESPONDING TO ADVICE Responding appropriately to advice is an often difficult process. Here are just a few suggestions for making receiving advice more effective.

- *Accept the advice.* If you asked for the advice, then accept what the person says. You don't have to follow the advice; you just have to listen to it and process it.
- *Avoid negative responses.* And even if you didn't ask for advice (and don't like it), resist the temptation to retaliate or criticize the advice giver. Instead of responding with "Well, your hair doesn't look that great either," consider if the advice has any merit.
- *Interact with the advice.* Talk about it with the advice giver. A process of asking and answering questions is likely to produce added insight into the problem.
- *Express appreciation.* Express your appreciation for the advice. It's often difficult to give advice, so it's only fair that the advice giver receive some words of appreciation.

In each of these everyday conversations, you have choices in terms of what you say and in terms of how you respond. Consider these choices mindfully, taking into consideration the variety of influencing factors discussed throughout this text and their potential advantages and disadvantages. Once you lay out your choices in this way, you'll be more likely to select effective ones.

Can you communicate effectively in small talk? In making introductions? In apologizing? In giving compliments? In advice giving?

MESSAGES IN THE MEDIA: WRAP-UP

Watching a show such as *Blue Bloods* (or almost any drama) will provide lots of specific examples of effective and ineffective conversational patterns that you might want to compare with your own conversation behavior.

SUMMARY OF CONCEPTS AND SKILLS

Listen to the **Audio Chapter Summary** at **MyCommunicationLab**

Study and **Review** materials for this chapter are at **MyCommunicationLab**

This chapter reviewed the principles of conversation, conversational disclosure, and some everyday conversation situations.

Principles of Conversation

1. Conversation can be viewed as a developmental process, consisting of a series of stages: opening, feedforward, business, feedback, and closing.
2. Conversation is best viewed as dialogic.
3. Conversation is a process of turn taking.
4. Conversation is, usually at least, a polite interaction.

Conversational Disclosure: Revealing Yourself

5. Self-disclosure is revealing information about yourself to others, information that is normally hidden, and is influenced by a variety of factors: who you are, your culture, your gender, your listeners, and your topic and channel.
6. Among the rewards of self-disclosure are self-knowledge, ability to cope, communication effectiveness, meaningfulness of relationships, and physiological health. Among the dangers are personal risks, relational risks, professional risks, and the fact that communication is irreversible; once something is said, you can't take it back.

Everyday Conversations

7. Small talk is pervasive and noncontroversial and often serves as a polite way of introducing one's self or a topic.
8. Introducing one person to another or yourself to others will vary with the culture.
9. Apologies are expressions of regret or sorrow for having done what you did or for what happened.
10. A compliment is a message of praise, flattery, or congratulations and often enables you to interact with positiveness and immediacy.
11. Advice—telling another person what he or she should do—can be specific or general (meta-advice).

In addition, this chapter covered a variety of conversational skills. Check those you wish to work on.

____ 1. *Dialogue.* Engage in conversation as dialogue rather than as monologue.

____ 2. *Turn-taking cues.* Be responsive to turn-taking cues that you give and that others give.

____ 3. *Politeness.* Follow the maxims of politeness: tact, generosity, approbation, modesty, agreement, and sympathy.

____ 4. *Self-disclosing.* In self-disclosing consider your motivation, the appropriateness of the disclosure to the person and context, the disclosures of others (the dyadic effect), and the possible burdens that the self-disclosure might impose on yourself or on others.

____ 5. *Responding to disclosures.* In responding to the disclosures of others, listen effectively, support and reinforce the discloser, keep disclosures confidential, and don't use disclosures as weapons.

____ 6. *Resisting self-disclosure.* When you wish to resist self-disclosing, don't be pushed, try indirectness or delaying the disclosures, or be assertive in your determination not to disclose.

____ 7. *Small talk.* Engage in small talk in a variety of situations with comfort and ease by keeping the conversation noncontroversial.

____ 8. *Introductions.* Introduce people to each other and yourself to others in any interaction that looks like it will last more than a few minutes.

____ 9. *Apologies.* Formulate effective apologies, and use them appropriately (and ethically) in interpersonal interactions.

____ 10. *Complimenting.* Extend and receive a compliment graciously, honestly, and without avoidance.

____ 11. *Advising.* Give advice carefully and mindfully, considering the advantages of meta-advice (when you're not an expert).

VOCABULARY QUIZ: The Language of Conversation

Match the following conversation-related terms with their definitions. Record the number of the definition next to the appropriate term.

____ backchanneling cues (176)
____ turn-taking cues (176)
____ apology (188)
____ meta-advice (191)
____ backhanded compliment (190)
____ interruption (177)
____ self-disclosure (180)
____ dialogic communication (174)
____ maxim of approbation (178)
____ phatic communication (173)

1. Communication that opens the channels for further communication
2. Attempts to take over the speaker's role
3. Revealing information about yourself (usually information that you normally keep hidden) to another person.
4. An insult masquerading as praise
5. Verbal or nonverbal cues used to communicate various types of information back to the speaker *without* your assuming the role of speaker
6. A principle of politeness advocating praising others and minimizing criticism.
7. Conversational cues that indicate you want to change your role as speaker or listener
8. An expression of regret or sorrow for having done what you did or for what happened
9. Communication in which there is a genuine two-way interaction
10. Advice about advice

These ten terms and additional terms used in this chapter can be found in the glossary.

MyCommunicationLab

Visit MyCommunicationLab for a wealth of additional information on interpersonal communication. Flashcards, videos, skill building exercises, sample test questions, and additional exercises, examples, and discussions will help you continue your study of the fundamentals of interpersonal communication, its theory, and its skills.

CHAPTER

9

Interpersonal Relationships

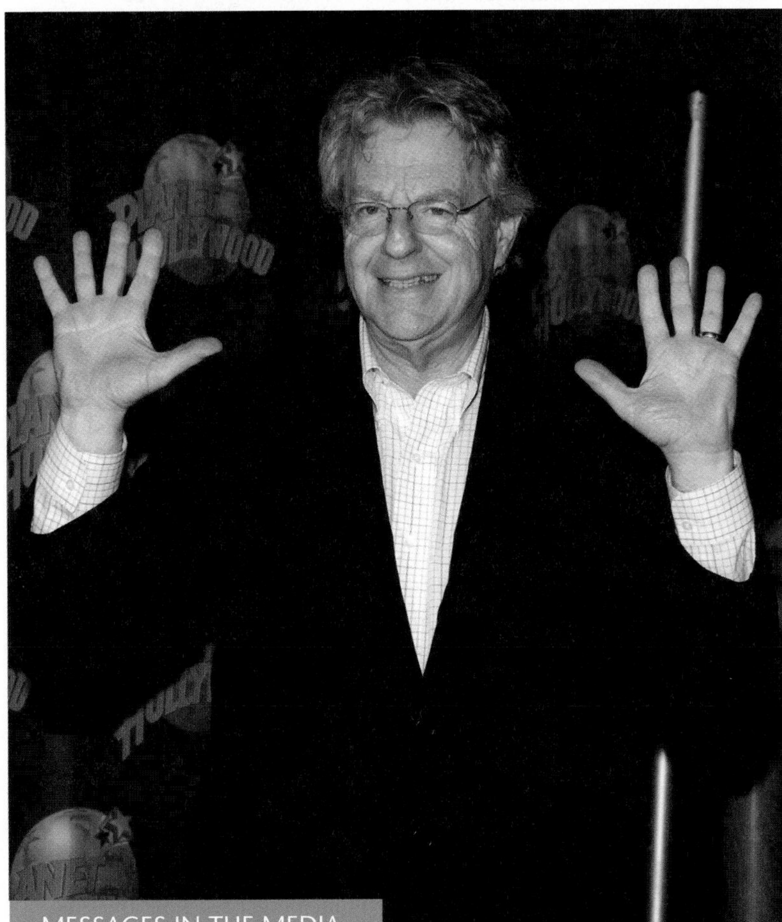

MESSAGES IN THE MEDIA

On *The Jerry Springer Show* and similar shows like *Maury* and *The Steve Wilkos Show,* you see all sorts of relationship problems, often ineffectively dealt with by the guests. This chapter introduces interpersonal relationships, explains what they are, how and why they develop and perhaps deteriorate, and some of the inappropriate types of relationships.

OBJECTIVES *After reading this chapter, you should be able to:*

1. Describe the advantages and disadvantages of interpersonal relationships and assess your own relationships in light of these.
2. Explain the relationship stages of contact, involvement intimacy, deterioration, repair, and dissolution and give examples of the types of messages that occur at each.
3. Define *jealousy, bullying,* and *relationship violence* and use the suggestions for managing such relationship dark sides.

Listen to the **Audio Chapter** at **MyCommunicationLab**

Interpersonal relationships are among the most important assets you have, and your ability to form meaningful and satisfying relationships rests largely on your interpersonal communication competencies. Here we consider the advantages and disadvantages of interpersonal relationships, the stages relationships go through, and some examples of the "dark side" of relationships.

ADVANTAGES AND DISADVANTAGES OF INTERPERSONAL RELATIONSHIPS

All relationships have advantages and disadvantages, and it is helpful to consider what these may be.

A good way to begin the study of interpersonal relationships is to examine your own relationships (past, present, or those you look forward to) by asking yourself what your relationships do for you. What are the advantages and the disadvantages? Focus on your own relationships in general (friendship, romantic, family, and work), on one particular relationship (say, your life partner or your child or your best friend), or on one type of relationship (say, friendships), and respond to the following statements by indicating the extent to which your relationship(s) serve each of these functions. Visualize a 10-point scale on which 1 indicates that your relationship(s) never serves this function, 10 indicates that your relationship(s) always serves this function, and the numbers in between indicate levels between these extremes. You may wish to do this twice—once for your face-to-face relationships and once for your online relationships.

____ 1. My relationships help to lessen my loneliness.
____ 2. My relationships help me gain in self-knowledge and in self-esteem.
____ 3. My relationships help enhance my physical and emotional health.
____ 4. My relationships maximize my pleasures and minimize my pains.
____ 5. My relationships help me to secure stimulation (intellectual, physical, and emotional).

Let's elaborate just a bit on each of these commonly accepted advantages of interpersonal communication.

VIEWPOINTS Online relationship advantages

Among the advantages of online relationships is that they reduce the importance of physical characteristics and instead emphasize such factors as rapport, similarity, and self-disclosure and in the process promote relationships that are based on emotional intimacy rather than physical attraction (Cooper & Sportolari, 1997). What do you see as the main advantages of online relationships?

1. One of the major benefits of relationships is that they help to lessen loneliness (Rokach, 1998; Rokach & Brock, 1995). They make you feel that someone cares, that someone likes you (the popularity of the "like" button on Facebook and +1 on Google+ attests to the importance of this benefit), that someone will protect you, that someone ultimately will love you.
2. Through contact with others you learn about yourself and see yourself from different perspectives and in different roles, as a child or parent, as a coworker, as a manager, as a best friend. This function is significantly strengthened by the availability of so many international relationship sites that can expose you to widely varied ways of viewing yourself and relationships. Healthy interpersonal relationships also help enhance self-esteem and self-worth. Simply having a friend or romantic partner (at least most of the time) makes you feel desirable and worthy.
3. Research consistently shows that interpersonal relationships contribute significantly to physical and emotional health (Goleman, 1995; Pennebacker, 1991; Rosen, 1998; Rosengren, 1993) and to personal happiness (Berscheid & Reis, 1998). Without

close interpersonal relationships you're more likely to become depressed—and this depression, in turn, contributes significantly to physical illness. Relationship isolation, in fact, contributes as much to mortality as high blood pressure, high cholesterol, obesity, smoking, or lack of physical exercise (Goleman, 1995).

4. The most general function served by interpersonal relationships, and the function that encompasses all the others, is that of maximizing pleasure and minimizing pain. Your good friends, for example, will make you feel even better about your good fortune and less hurt when you're confronted with hardships.
5. As plants are heliotropic and orient themselves to light, humans are stimulotropic and orient themselves to sources of stimulation (Davis, 1973). Human contact is one of the best ways to secure this stimulation—intellectual, physical, and emotional. Even an imagined relationship seems better than none.

Now respond to these sentences as you did to the above.

____ 6. My relationships put uncomfortable pressure on me to expose my vulnerabilities.
____ 7. My relationships increase my obligations.
____ 8. My relationships prevent me from developing other relationships.
____ 9. My relationships scare me because they may be difficult to dissolve.
____ 10. My relationships hurt me.

These statements express what most people would consider disadvantages of interpersonal relationships.

6. Close relationships put pressure on you to reveal yourself and to expose your vulnerabilities. While this is generally worthwhile in the context of a supporting and caring relationship, it may backfire if the relationship deteriorates and these weaknesses are used against you.
7. Close relationships increase your obligations to other people, sometimes to a great extent. Your time is no longer entirely your own. And although you enter relationships to spend more time with these special people, you also incur time (and perhaps financial) obligations with which you may not be happy.
8. Close relationships can lead you to abandon other relationships. Sometimes the other relationship involves someone you like but your partner can't stand. More often, however, it's simply a matter of time and energy; relationships take a lot of both, and you have less to give to these other and less intimate relationships.
9. The closer your relationships, the more emotionally difficult they are to dissolve, a feeling which may be uncomfortable for some people. If a relationship is deteriorating, you may feel distress or depression. In some cultures, for example, religious pressures may prevent married couples from separating. And if lots of money is involved, dissolving a relationship can often mean giving up the fortune you've spent your life accumulating.
10. And, of course, your partner may break your heart. Your partner may leave you—against all your pleading and promises. Your hurt will be in proportion to how much you care and need your partner. If you care a great deal, you're likely to experience great hurt; if you care less, the hurt will be less—it's one of life's little ironies.

To complement this discussion of the disadvantages of interpersonal relationships, we'll look also at what has come to be called the "dark side" of interpersonal relationships later in this chapter.

VIEWPOINTS Parasocial relationships

Parasocial relationships are relationships that audience members perceive themselves to have with media personalities (Giles, 2001; Giles & Maltby, 2004; Rubin & McHugh, 1987). At times, viewers develop these relationships with real media personalities—Wendy Williams, Anderson Cooper, or Ellen DeGeneres, for example—and at other times, the relationship is with a fictional character—an investigator on *CSI*, a scientist on *Bones*, or a doctor on a soap opera. Interestingly enough, Google+ seems to encourage this by suggesting that you "follow public posts from interesting and famous people." You'll even get updates and photos from them—not unlike "real" relationships. What's your view of parasocial relationships? Are there advantages to these relationships? Disadvantages? What's your experience with parasocial relationships?

Can you describe the major advantages and disadvantages of interpersonal relationships? Can you assess and evaluate your own relationships in terms of its advantages and disadvantages?

Explore the **Concept** "Relationships" at **MyCommunicationLab**

Blog Post

Facial Attraction

For a seldom-discussed view on attraction, see "Facial Attraction" at tcbdevito.blogspot.com. Does this all seem logical?

RELATIONSHIP STAGES

The quality that makes a relationship interpersonal is interdependency: The actions of one person affect the other; one person's actions have consequences for the other person. The actions of a stranger—such as working overtime or flirting with a coworker—will have no impact on you; you and the proverbial stranger are independent, and your actions have no effect on each other. If, however, you were in an interpersonal relationship and your partner worked overtime or flirted with a coworker, these actions would affect you and the relationship in some way.

The six-stage model shown in Figure 9.1 describes the significant stages you may go through as you try to achieve your relationship goals. We'll explain the arrows after describing the stages. As a general description of relationship development (and sometimes dissolution), the stages seem standard: They apply to all relationships, whether friendship or love, whether face to face or online. The six stages are contact, involvement,

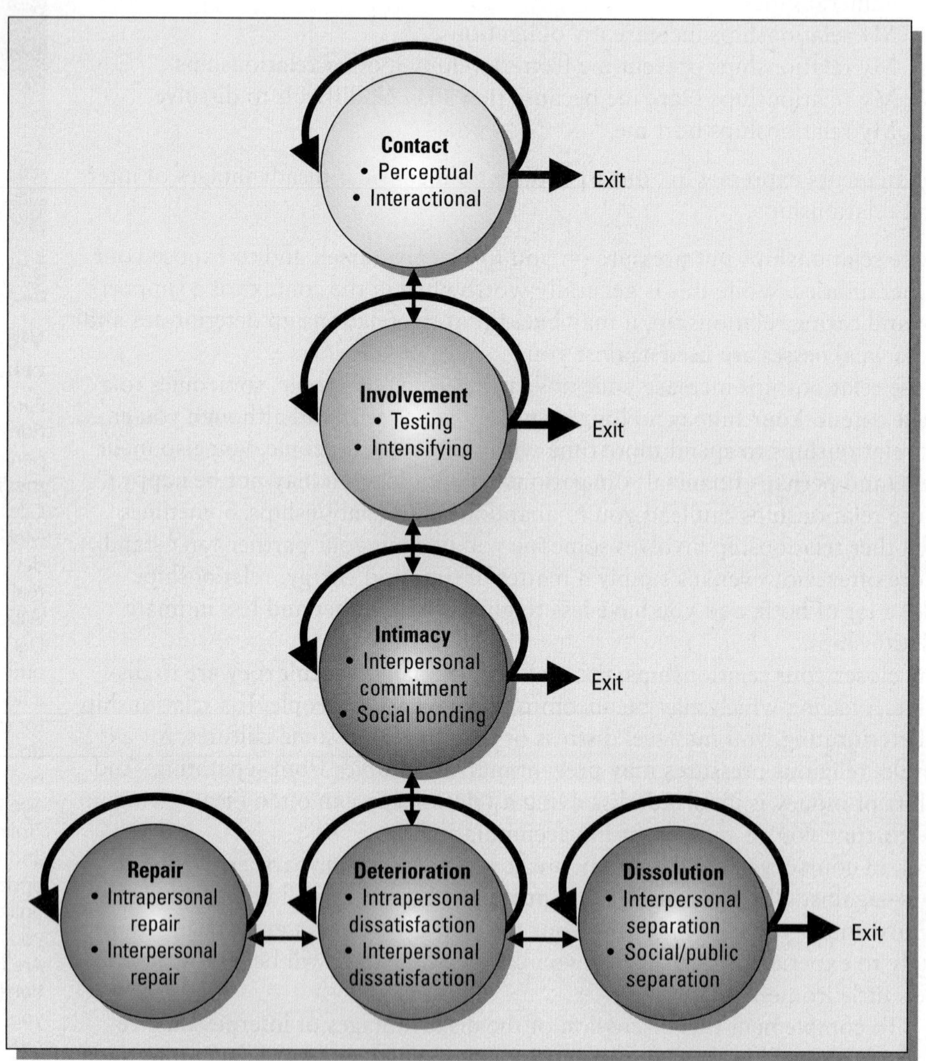

FIGURE 9.1

The Six Stages of Relationships

Because relationships differ so widely, it's best to think of any relationship model as a tool for talking about relationships rather than as a specific map that indicates how you move from one relationship stage to another. The six-stage model is certainly not the only way you can look at relationships. If you want to see an additional model of relationships, go to MyCommunicationLab.

Explore the **Exercise** "Analyzing Stage Talk" at **MyCommunicationLab**

intimacy, deterioration, repair, and dissolution. Each stage can be divided into an initial and a final phase.

Social network sites seem to recognize this stage nature of relationships by enabling you to treat your online "friends" differently. For example, the circles on Google+ and the "friends lists" on Facebook enable you to group people on the basis of the information that you want them to be able to access. This makes it very easy to distinguish acquaintances from intimate friends, for example, as well as family from friends from workplace colleagues.

"I can't wait to see what you're like online."

Paul Noth/The New Yorker Collection/www.cartoonbank.com

Contact

At the **contact** stage, there is first perceptual contact—you see what the person looks like, you hear what the person sounds like, you may even smell the person. Or you might browse a group of photos and profiles from an online dating site. From this contact, you get a physical picture: gender, approximate age, height, and so on.

After this perception, there is usually interactional contact. Here the interaction is superficial and impersonal. This is the stage of "Hello, my name is Joe"—the stage at which you exchange basic information that needs to come before any more intense involvement. This interactional contact also may be nonverbal, as in, for example, exchanging smiles, concentrating your focus on one person, or decreasing the physical distance between the two of you. With online relationships, each of you will have read the other's profile and so will know quite a lot about each other before you even begin to talk.

This is the stage at which you initiate interaction ("Hello, I'm Pat") and engage in invitational communication ("May I join you?" "Will you be friends with me?"). The invitational messages in online communication may involve moving to a face-to-face meeting or to phoning each other. According to some researchers, it's at this contact stage—within the first four minutes of initial interaction—that you decide whether you want to pursue the relationship (Zunin & Zunin, 1972).

Physical appearance is especially important in the initial development of attraction because it's the characteristic most readily available to sensory inspection. Yet through both verbal and nonverbal behaviors, qualities such as friendliness, warmth, openness, and dynamism also are revealed at the contact stage. With online relations, people may profile themselves as warm or open or dynamic, and as a result, you may actually see the person's messages confirming this labeling.

The contact stage is also the stage at which you start flirting—messages that signal your romantic interest. Table 9.1 elaborates on the dos and don'ts of flirting.

Involvement

At the **involvement** stage, a sense of mutuality, of being connected, develops. Your ability to empathize with each other increases. During this stage, you experiment and try to learn more about the other person. At the early phase of involvement, a kind of preliminary testing goes on. You want to see if your initial judgment—perhaps at the contact stage, perhaps from reading the person's profile—proves reasonable. So you may ask questions: "Where do you work?" "What are you majoring in?"

Blog Post

Body Language

For some tips on nonverbal behaviors to avoid during dating and courtship, see "Body Language" at tcbdevito.blogspot.com. What additional suggestions would you add?

TABLE 9.1

How to Flirt and Not to Flirt

Here are a few nonverbal and verbal ways people flirt and some cautions to observe. The most general caution, which applies to all the suggestions, is to recognize that different cultures view flirting very differently and to observe the prevailing cultural norms.

Flirtatious Messages	Cautions
Maintain an open posture; face the person; lean forward; tilt your head to one side (to get a clearer view of the person you're interested in).	Don't move so close that you make it uncomfortable for the other person.
Maintain eye contact for a somewhat longer than normal time; raise your eyebrows to signal interest; wink.	Be careful that your direct eye contact doesn't come off as leering or too invasive; avoid excessive blinking.
Smile and otherwise displace positive emotions with your facial expressions.	Avoid overdoing this; laughing too loud at lame jokes is probably going to appear phony.
Touch the person's hand.	Be careful that the touching is appropriate and not perceived as intrusive.
Mirror the other's behaviors.	Don't overdo it. It will appear as if you're mimicking.
Introduce yourself.	Avoid overly long or overly cute introductions.
Ask a question (most commonly, "Is this seat taken?").	Avoid sarcasm or joking; these are likely to be misunderstood.
Compliment ("great jacket").	Avoid any compliment that might appear too intimate.
Be polite; respect the individual's positive and negative face needs.	But don't be overly polite. It will appear phony.

Here you're committed to getting to know the person even better, and so you might follow the person on Twitter or read the postings, photos, and causes, for example, on Facebook. And at this stage, you continue your involvement by intensifying your interaction; the texting becomes more frequent, the Facebook postings become more complimentary and more frequent, and the photos exchanged become increasingly more personal and revealing.

Here, you not only try to get to know the other person better, but you also begin to reveal yourself. It's at this stage that you begin to share your feelings and your emotions. If this is to be a romantic relationship, you might date. If it's to be a friendship, you might share in activities related to mutual interests—go to the movies or to some sports event together.

INTERPERSONAL CHOICE POINT

Coming Clean

You're getting ready to meet someone you've only communicated with over the Internet, and you're going to have to admit that you lied about your age and a few other things. What are the things about which you'd have to come clean with most immediately? What are your options for expressing this? What seems the best option?

Intimacy

At the **intimacy** stage, you feel you can be honest and open when talking about yourself; you can express thoughts and feelings that you don't reveal in other relationships (Mackey, Diemer, & O'Brien, 2000). Because intimacy is essentially an emotional/communication connection, it can occur in face-to-face and in online relationships equally. At the intimacy stage, you commit yourself still further to the other person, establishing

ETHICAL MESSAGES

Your Obligation to Reveal Yourself

If you're in a close relationship, your influence on your partner is considerable, so you may have an obligation to reveal certain things about yourself. Conversely, you may feel that the other person—because he or she is so close to you—has an ethical obligation to reveal certain information to you.

Ethical Choice Point

Consider: At what point in a relationship—if any—do you feel you would have an ethical obligation to reveal each of the 10 items of information listed here? Visualize a relationship as existing on a continuum from initial contact at 1 to extreme intimacy at 10, and use the numbers from 1 to 10 to indicate at what point you would feel your romantic partner or close friend has a right to know each type of information about you. If you feel you would never have the obligation to reveal this information, use 0. As you respond to these items, ask yourself, what gives one person the right to know personal information about another person? What principle of ethics requires another person to disclose this information in a relationship?

At what point do you have an ethical obligation to reveal:	Romantic Partner	Friend
Age	______	______
History of family genetic disorders	______	______
HIV status	______	______
Past sexual experiences	______	______
Marital history	______	______
Annual salary and net financial worth	______	______
Affectional orientation	______	______
Attitudes toward other races and nationalities	______	______
Religious beliefs	______	______
Past criminal activity or incarceration	______	______

a kind of relationship in which this individual becomes your best or closest friend, lover, or companion. Your communication becomes more personalized, more synchronized, and easier (Gudykunst, Nishida, & Chua, 1987). Usually the intimacy stage divides itself quite neatly into two phases: an interpersonal commitment phase, in which you commit yourselves to each other in a kind of private way, and a social bonding phase, in which the commitment is made public—perhaps to family and friends, perhaps to the public at large through formal marriage. Here the two of you become a unit, a pair.

To some people, relational intimacy seems extremely risky. To others, it involves only low risk. Consider your own view of relationship risk by responding to the following questions.

- Is it dangerous to get really close to people?
- Are you afraid to get really close to someone because you might get hurt?

VIDEO CHOICE POINT

Taking the Next Step

Tim and Marisol have been dating for several weeks and things between them have been going well. Tim now realizes that he wants the relationship to be permanent and exclusive, and he wants to express his feelings to Marisol. He isn't sure how to bring this issue up in conversation because he's never felt this strongly about someone before. He considers the topics covered in this chapter as he contemplates his communication choices. See how his choices play out in the video "Taking the Next Step" and respond to the questions posed.

 **Watch** the **Video** "Taking the Next Step" at **MyCommunicationLab**

SKILL BUILDING EXERCISE

Talking Cherishing

Cherishing behaviors are those small gestures you enjoy receiving from your partner (a smile, a wink, a phone call, an e-mail saying "I'm thinking of you," a kiss). They are (1) specific and positive—nothing overly general or negative; (2) focused on the present and future rather than related to issues about which the partners have argued in the past; (3) capable of being performed daily; and (4) easily executed—nothing you really have to go out of your way to accomplish. Cherishing behaviors are an especially effective way to affirm another person and to increase "favor exchange," a concept that comes from the work of William Lederer (1984).

Prepare a list of 10 cherishing behaviors that you would like to receive from your real or imagined relationship partner. After each partner prepares a list, exchange lists and, ideally, perform the desired cherishing behaviors. At first, these behaviors may seem self-conscious and awkward. In time, however, they'll become a normal part of your interaction, which is exactly what you want.

Lists of cherishing behaviors—yours or your partner's—will also give you insight into your relationship needs and the kind of communicating partner you want.

- Do you find it difficult to trust other people?
- Do you believe that the most important thing to consider in a relationship is whether you might get hurt?

People who answer *yes* to these and similar questions see intimacy as involving considerable risk (Pilkington & Richardson, 1988). Such people have fewer close friends, are less likely to have romantic relationships, have less trust in others, have lower levels of dating assertiveness, have lower self-esteem, are more possessive and jealous, and are generally less sociable and extroverted than those who see intimacy as involving little risk (Pilkington & Woods, 1999). The nature of risk in online relationships is similar to that in face-to-face relationships; for example, in both kinds of relationships you risk losing face and damaging your self-esteem. So there's likely to be considerable similarity in any given individual's attitudes toward risk in both types of relationships.

Explore the **Exercise** "Learning to Hear Stage Talk" at **MyCommunicationLab**

Deterioration

Although many relationships remain at the intimacy stage, some enter the stage of **deterioration**—the stage that sees the weakening of bonds between the parties and that represents the downside of the relationship progression. Relationships deteriorate for many reasons. When the reasons for coming together are no longer present or change drastically, relationships may deteriorate. Thus, for example, when your relationship no longer lessens your loneliness or when it fails to increase your self-esteem or to maximize pleasures, it may be in the process of deteriorating. Other reasons for deterioration are third-party relationships, sexual dissatisfaction, dissatisfaction with work, or financial difficulties.

The first phase of deterioration is usually intrapersonal dissatisfaction. You begin to feel that this relationship may not be as important as you had previously thought. You may experience personal dissatisfaction with everyday interactions and begin to view the future together negatively. If this dissatisfaction continues or grows, you may pass to the second phase, interpersonal deterioration, in which you discuss these dissatisfactions with your partner.

During the process of deterioration, communication patterns change drastically. These patterns are in part a response to the deterioration; you communicate as you do because of the way you feel your relationship is deteriorating. However, the way you communicate (or fail to communicate) also influences the fate of your relationship. During the deterioration

INTERPERSONAL CHOICE POINT

Virtual Infidelity

You discover that your partner of the past 15 years is being unfaithful with someone online (and in another country). You understand that generally such infidelity is seen as a consequence of a failure in communication (Young, Griffin-Shelley, Cooper, O'Mara, & Buchanan, 2000). You want to discover the extent of this online relationship and your partner's intentions concerning this affair. What choices do you have for opening up this topic for honest conversation without making your partner defensive and hence uncommunicative?

stage, you may, for example, increase withdrawal, communicate less, respond to Facebook pokes and requests for "likes" less often, text infrequently, and have fewer face-to-face meetings. In communication, each person reduces his or her level of self-disclosure.

Repair

Explore the **Exercise** "Giving Repair Advice" at **MyCommunicationLab**

The first phase of **repair** is intrapersonal repair, in which you analyze what went wrong and consider ways of solving your relational difficulties. At this phase, you may consider changing your behaviors or perhaps changing your expectations of your partner. You may also weigh the rewards of your relationship as it is now against the rewards you could anticipate if your relationship ended.

If you decide that you want to repair your relationship, you may discuss this with your partner at the interpersonal repair level. Here you may talk about the problems in the relationship, the corrections you would want to see, and perhaps what you would be willing to do and what you would want the other person to do. This is the stage of negotiating new agreements, new behaviors. You and your partner may try to solve your problems yourselves, or you may seek the advice of friends or family or perhaps seek advice from the numerous anonymous websites.

You can look at the strategies for repairing a relationship in terms of the following six suggestions, which conveniently spell out the word REPAIR, a useful reminder that repair is not a one-step but a multistep process: Recognize the problem, Engage in productive conflict resolution, Pose possible solutions, Affirm each other, Integrate solutions into normal behavior, and Risk (see Figure 9.2).

INTERPERSONAL CHOICE POINT

Strengthening Similarities

You're dating a person you really like, but you are both so different—in values, politics, religion, and just about everything else. But you enjoy each other more than you do anyone else. What are some of the things you can do to encourage greater similarity while not losing the excitement created by the differences?

- *Recognize the problem.* What is wrong with your present relationship? What specific changes will make it better?
- *Engage in productive conflict resolution.* Conflict is an inevitable part of relationship life, but if it's approached through productive strategies, it may be resolved and the relationship may actually emerge stronger and healthier.
- *Pose possible solutions.* Ideally, each person will ask, "What can we do to resolve the difficulty that will allow both of us to get what we want?"
- *Affirm each other.* Social media sites make this especially easy by providing you with cards, virtual gifts, and the like to help you express your desire to repair the relationship.
- *Integrate solutions into your life.* In other words, make the solutions a part of your normal behavior.
- *Risk.* Risk giving favors without any certainty of reciprocity. Risk rejection by making the first move to make up or say you're sorry. Be willing to change, to adapt.

"When a relationship needs maintenance, it would be great if you could just call a super."

Victoria Roberts/The New Yorker Collection/www.cartoonbank.com

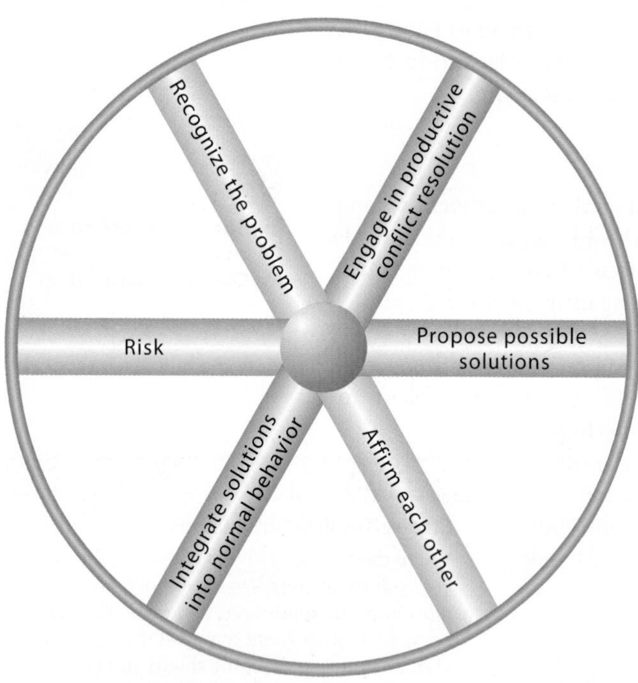

FIGURE 9.2
The Relationship Repair Wheel
The wheel seems an apt metaphor for the repair process; the specific repair strategies—the spokes—all work together in constant process. The wheel is difficult to get moving, but once in motion it becomes easier to turn. Also, it's easier to start when two people are pushing, but it is not impossible for one to move it in the right direction. What metaphor do you find helpful in thinking about relationship repair?

Dissolution

The **dissolution** stage, in both friendship and romance, is the cutting of the bonds that tie you together. Not surprisingly, there are both advantages and disadvantages of relationship dissolution. Often the relationship deserves to be dissolved; it was no longer productive or satisfying. When a "friend" reveals your confidential disclosures on Facebook or otherwise betrays your confidence and this becomes a pattern, it may be time to move from the level of friendship to that of seldom-seen acquaintanceship. Not surprisingly, social networking sites have provided you with easy means for "defriending" and "uncircling." Even in families, certain members or relationships within the family may become toxic and the relationship may be deserving of dissolution. Partners, parents, or children often become enablers, helping a family member to engage in destructive behavior—for example, helping to hide the alcoholism from friends and relatives and thus helping the partner to continue drinking more comfortably and without social criticism. Gay and lesbian children who are rejected by their families after coming out may be better off away from homophobic (and guilt-instilling) parents, siblings, and assorted relatives.

The decision to stay in a relationship that does not fulfill your needs or is destructive or to end the relationship is not an easy one to make because so many factors come into play. Religious beliefs, the attitudes of family members and close friends, and the economic implications of staying together versus separating are just a few of the more obvious factors that would logically influence such decisions.

In most cases, relationship dissolution creates difficulties, most often for both parties. Here are some suggestions for dealing with this often difficult period:

- *Break the loneliness–depression cycle.* Avoid sad passivity, a state in which you feel sorry for yourself, sit alone, and perhaps cry. Instead, engage in active solitude (exercise, write, study, play computer games) and seek distraction (do things to put loneliness out of your mind; for example, take a long drive or shop).
- *Take time out.* Take some time for yourself. Renew your relationship with yourself. Get to know yourself as a unique individual, standing alone now but fully capable of entering a meaningful relationship in the future.
- *Bolster self-esteem.* Positive and successful experiences are most helpful in building self-esteem. As in dealing with loneliness, helping others is one of the best ways to raise your own self-esteem.
- *Seek the support of others.* Avail yourself of your friends and family for support; it's an effective antidote to the discomfort and unhappiness that occur when a relationship ends.
- *Avoid repeating negative patterns.* Ask yourself, at the start of a new relationship, if you're entering a relationship modeled on the previous one. If the answer is yes, be especially careful that you do not repeat the problems. At the same time, avoid becoming a prophet of doom. Do not see in every new relationship vestiges of the old.

INTERPERSONAL CHOICE POINT

Ending the Relationship

You want to break up your eight-month romantic relationship and still remain friends. What are the possible contexts in which you might do this? What types of things can you say that might help you accomplish your dual goal?

Movement among the Stages: Explaining the Arrows

Relationships are not static; we move from one stage to another largely as a result of our interpersonal interactions. It is some of these movements that the arrows in Figure 9.1 depict. Let's look at some relationship processes that revolve around movement.

VIEWPOINTS Gender differences in breaking up

Popular myth would have us believe that most heterosexual love affairs break up as a result of the man's outside affair. But the research does not support this (Blumstein & Schwartz, 1983; Janus & Janus, 1993). When surveyed as to the reason for breaking up, only 15 percent of the men indicated that it was their interest in another partner, whereas 32 percent of the women noted this as a cause of the breakup. These findings are surely dated. What do you think we'd find if the same survey were done today? More important, why do you think differences exist at all?

STAGE MOVEMENT The six-stage model illustrates the kinds of movement that take place in interpersonal relationships. In the model, you'll note three types of arrows:

- *The exit arrows* show that each stage offers the opportunity to exit the relationship. After saying "Hello" you can say "Goodbye" and exit. And, of course, you can end even the most intimate of relationships.
- *The vertical arrows* between the stages represent the fact that you can move to another stage: either to a stage that is more intense (say, from involvement to intimacy) or to a stage that is less intense (say, from intimacy to deterioration).
- *The self-reflexive arrows*—the arrows that return to the beginning of the same level or stage—signify that any relationship may become stabilized at any point. You may, for example, continue to maintain a relationship at the intimate level without its deteriorating or going back to the less intense stage of involvement. Or you may remain at the "Hello, how are you?" stage—the contact stage—without getting any further involved.

As you can imagine, movement from one stage to another depends largely on your communication skills—for example, your abilities to initiate a relationship, to present yourself as likable, to express affection, to self-disclose appropriately, and, when necessary, to dissolve the relationship with the least possible amount of acrimony (Dindia & Timmerman, 2003).

INTERPERSONAL CHOICE POINT

Moving Through Relationship Stages

Your current romantic partner seems to be moving too fast for your liking. You want to take things a lot slower, yet you don't want to turn this person off; this may be The One. What might you say (and where might you say it) to get your partner to proceed more slowly?

TURNING POINTS Movement through the various stages takes place both gradually and in leaps. Sometimes the arrow/movement proceeds slowly from one stage to another, sometimes by leaps and jumps. Most often, you progress from one stage to another gradually. You don't jump from contact to involvement to intimacy; rather, you progress gradually, a few degrees at a time. In addition to this gradual movement, however, there are leaps called **relationship turning points** (Baxter & Bullis, 1986). These are significant relationship events that have important consequences for the individuals and the relationship and may turn its direction or trajectory. For example, a relationship that is progressing slowly might experience a rapid rise after the first date, the first kiss, the first sexual encounter, or the first meeting with the partner's child.

And, not surprisingly, turning points vary with culture. In some cultures, the first sexual experience is a major turning point; in others, it's a minor progression in the normal dating process. What constitutes a turning point will also vary with your relationship stage. For example, an expensive and intimate gift may be a turning point at the involvement or the repair stage, an ordinary event if you're at the intimate stage where such gifts are exchanged regularly, and an inappropriate gift if given too early in the relationship.

Blog Post

From Dating to Mating

For an interesting article on moving from involvement to intimacy, see "From Dating to Mating" at tcbdevito.blogspot.com. Any further suggestions?

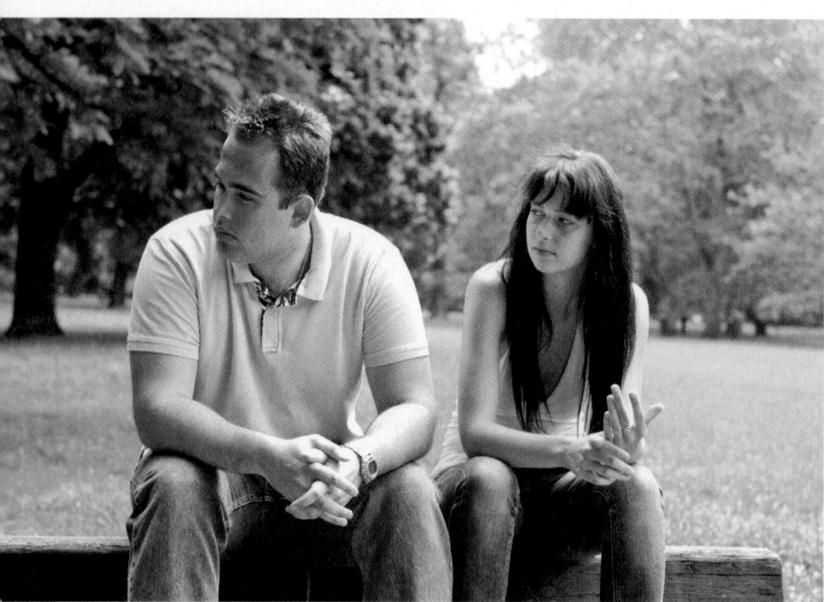

VIEWPOINTS Negative turning points
Turning points are often positive, as the examples in the text indicate, but they can also be negative. For example, the first realization that a partner has been unfaithful, lied about past history, or revealed a debilitating condition would likely be significant turning points for many romantic relationships. What have been your experiences with negative relationship turning points?

THE RELATIONSHIP LICENSE Movement of a somewhat different type can be appreciated by looking at what might be called the **relationship license**—the license or permission to break some relationship rule as a result of your relationship stage. As the relationship develops, so does the relationship license; as you become closer and approach the intimacy stage, you have greater permission to say and do things that you didn't have at the contact or involvement stage. The license becomes broader as the relationship develops and becomes more restrictive as the relationship deteriorates. For example, long-term friends or romantic couples (say, at the intimacy stage) may taste each other's food in a restaurant or may fix each other's clothing or pat each other on the rear. These are violations of rules that normally hold for non-intimates, casual acquaintances, or people in the initial stages of a relationship. In relationships that are deteriorating, the licenses become more limited or may be entirely withdrawn.

In some relationships, the license is reciprocal; each person's license is the same. In other relationships, it's nonreciprocal; one person has greater license than the other. For example, perhaps one person has license to come home at any time but the other is expected to stay on schedule. Or one person has license to spend the couple's money without explanation but the other has no such right. Or one perhaps has the right to be unfaithful but the other doesn't. For example, in some cultures, men are expected to have intimate relationships with many women, whereas women are expected to have relationships only with a legally approved partner. In this case, a nonreciprocal license is built into the culture's rules.

INTERPERSONAL CHOICE POINT

Meeting the Parents
You're dating someone from a very different culture and have been invited to meet the parents and have a traditional ethnic dinner. What are some of the things you might do to make this potentially difficult situation go smoothly?

Part of the art of relationship communication—as you move through the various stages—is to negotiate the licenses that you want without giving up the privacy you want to retain. This negotiation is almost never made explicit; most often it is accomplished nonverbally and in small increments. The license to touch intimately, for example, is likely to be arrived at through a series of touches that increase gradually, beginning with touching that is highly impersonal.

RELATIONSHIP COMMITMENT. An important factor influencing the movement in any relationship is the degree of **relationship commitment** that you and your relationship partner have toward each other and toward the relationship. Not surprisingly, commitment is especially strong when individuals are satisfied with their relationship and grows weaker as individuals become less satisfied (Hirofumi, 2003). Three types of commitment are often distinguished and can be identified from your answers to the following questions (Johnson, 1973, 1982, 1991; Knapp & Taylor, 1994; Knapp & Vangelisti, 2009; Kurdek, 1995):

- Do I have a **desire** to stay in this relationship? Do I have a desire to keep this relationship going?

INTERPERSONAL CHOICE POINT

Refusing a Gift Positively
A coworker with whom you're becoming friendly gives you a very intimate gift, much too intimate for the relationship as you see it. What are some things you might say to refuse the gift but not close off the possibility of dating?

- Do I have a moral **obligation** to stay in this relationship?
- Do I have to stay in this relationship? Is it a **necessity** for me to stay in this relationship?

All relationships are held together, in part, by commitment based on desire, obligation, or necessity or on some combination of these factors. And the strength of the relationship, including its resistance to possible deterioration, is related to your degree of commitment. When a relationship shows signs of deterioration and yet there's a strong commitment to preserving it, you may well surmount the obstacles and reverse the process. For example, couples with high relationship commitment will avoid arguing about minor grievances and also will demonstrate greater supportiveness toward each other than will those with lower commitment (Roloff & Solomon, 2002). Similarly, those who have great commitment are likely to experience greater jealousy in a variety of situations (Rydell, McConnell, & Bringle, 2004). When commitment is weak and the individuals doubt that there are good reasons for staying together, the relationship deteriorates faster and more intensely.

Relationship Politeness Not surprisingly, your level of politeness will vary with your relationship stage. Figure 9.3 depicts a proposed relationship between the levels of politeness and the relationship stages discussed earlier. Politeness, according to this model, is greatest during the contact and involvement stages—you want to put your best foot forward if the relationship is to be established and perhaps moved forward.

During the intimacy stage, you're likely to relax your politeness, at least the rules of politeness that would operate in social settings. As noted earlier, as the relationship becomes more interpersonal, the rules that guide the relationship are not so much the rules of society as they are the rules established by the individuals themselves. With intimates, you know each other so well that you feel you can dispense with the "please" and "excuse me" or with prefacing requests with, for example, "Can I please ask you a favor?" or "Would you mind helping me here?"

Relaxing politeness in intimacy, however, is not necessarily a good thing; in fact, politeness during the intimacy stage helps to maintain the relationship and ensure relationship satisfaction. Relaxing politeness too much may be interpreted as a decrease in

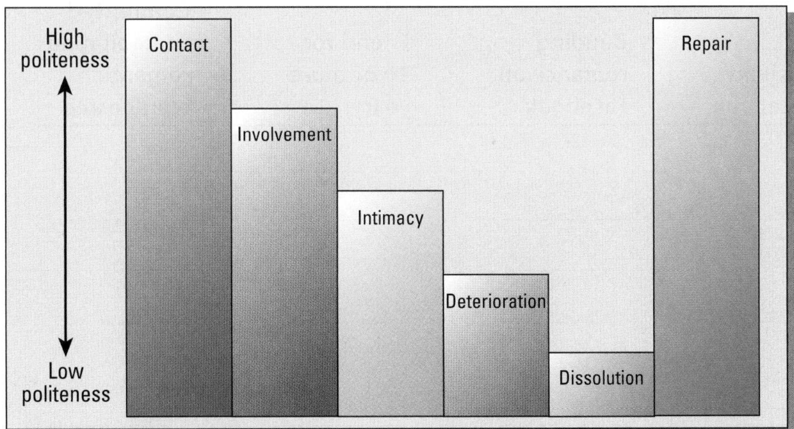

FIGURE 9.3
Politeness and Relationship Stages
Although politeness will not vary in the same way in all relationships, the general pattern depicted here is likely to be representative of many relationships. As you review this figure, analyze your own history of relationship politeness. Did it follow the pattern predicted here? If not, how did it differ?

caring and respect for the other person, which will increase dissatisfaction and perhaps move the relationship away from intimacy.

During the deterioration and dissolution stages, you're not likely to be concerned with politeness. You may even go out of your way to be impolite as an expression of your dislike or even hostility. In some cases, of course, the dissolution of a relationship is an amicable one where politeness would be relatively high with perhaps the idea of remaining friends but at a less intimate level than previously.

If you wish to repair the relationship, then you're likely to be extremely polite, perhaps on the same level as during the contact and involvement stages. Your politeness in starting and growing the relationship is likely to be echoed in your attempts to restart (or repair) your relationship.

Can you explain the stages of interpersonal relationships (contact, involvement, intimacy, deterioration, repair, and dissolution) and the major movements (stage movement, turning points, relationship license, relationship commitment, and relationship politeness)? Can you give examples of the types of messages that occur at each stage?

SKILL BUILDING EXERCISE

Assessing the End of a Relationship

This exercise is designed to stimulate you to examine the factors that might lead you to dissolve an interpersonal relationship. Here are listed a number of factors that might lead someone to end such a relationship. For each factor, identify the likelihood that you would dissolve relationships of various types, using a 10-point scale with 10 = would definitely dissolve the relationship, 1 = would definitely not dissolve the relationship, and the numbers 2–9 representing intermediate levels. Use 5 for "don't know what I'd do" or "not sure." What factor would lead you to dissolve one or more of your present relationships?

Often the same relationship factors can create mild dissatisfaction or result in the total dissolution of the relationship.

Factor	New friend on Facebook	Budding romance on Facebook	Friend for 10 or more years	Committed co-habitating romantic relationship
1. Person lies frequently about insignificant and significant issues	______	______	______	______
2. Person lacks ambition and doesn't want to do anything of significance	______	______	______	______
3. Person is not supportive and rarely compliments or confirms you	______	______	______	______
4. Person is unwilling to reveal anything significant about past behavior or present feelings	______	______	______	______
5. Person embarrasses you because of bad manners, poor grammar, inappropriate posts and photos	______	______	______	______

THE DARK SIDE OF INTERPERSONAL RELATIONSHIPS

Although relationships serve a variety of vital functions and provide enormous advantages, as already noted, not all relationships are equally satisfying and productive. Consequently, it's necessary to explore this "dark" side. Here we consider three such dark sides: jealousy, bullying, and violence in close relationships.

Relationship Jealousy

Watch the **Video** "Getting Even" at **MyCommunicationLab**

Jealousy is similar to envy in that in both cases, we experience a negative emotion about our relationship and we often use the terms interchangeably. But they are actually very different. Envy is an emotional feeling that we experience when we desire what someone else has or has more of than we do. And so we might feel envious of a friend who has lots of friends or romantic partners or money when we have significantly less. When we feel **envy**, we may feel that we are inferior to or of lesser importance than someone else. **Jealousy**, on the other hand, is a feeling (most researchers would view it as a type or form of anger) we have when we feel our relationship is in danger due to some rival. Jealousy is a reaction to relationship threat: If you feel that someone is moving in on your relationship partner, you may experience jealousy—especially if you feel that this interloper is succeeding. Usually, the rival is a potential romantic partner, but it could also be a close friend or a job that occupies all our partner's time and thoughts. When we feel jealousy, we may feel angry and anxious.

THE PARTS OF JEALOUSY Jealousy has at least three components (Erber & Erber, 2011): a cognitive, an emotional, and a behavioral.

- *Cognitive jealousy.* Cognitive jealousy would involve your suspicious thinking, worrying, and imagining the different scenarios in which your partner may be interested in another person.
- *Emotional jealousy.* Emotional jealousy would involve the feelings you have when you see your partner, say, laughing or talking intimately with or kissing a rival. It includes "emotional infidelity"—feelings of love and arousal.
- *Behavioral jealousy.* Behavioral jealousy refers to what you actually do in response to the jealous feelings and emotions, for example, reading your partner's e-mail, looking on Facebook for incriminating photos, or going through the back seat of the car with the proverbial fine-tooth comb.

Blog Post

Cyberflirting, Etc.

For cyberflirting, see "Cyberflirting, Etc." at tcbdevito.blogspot.com. How do you see cyberflirting? What cyberflirting techniques do you find most interesting?

Sometimes we feel jealousy because of some suspicion that a rival is looking to steal our relationship partner. In this case, we may do a variety of things to guard our relationship and our relationship partner, a process called **mate guarding** (Buss, 1988; Erber & Erber, 2011). One popular strategy is concealment. We don't introduce our partner to any potential rival and avoid interaction with any potential rivals. Another strategy is vigilance; we constantly look out for occasions when we might lose our partner to a rival. The least suspicious glance becomes a major problem. Still another strategy is to monopolize the partner, to always be together, and to avoid leaving the partner without anything to do for too long a time. Of course, we also would experience jealousy if our rival actually succeeded.

Much research has reported that heterosexual men and women experience jealousy for different reasons, which are rooted in our evolutionary development (Buller, 2005; Buss, 2000; Buunk & Dijkstra, 2004). Basically, research finds that men experience jealousy from their partner being *physically* intimate with another man whereas women experience jealousy from their partner being *emotionally* intimate with another woman. The evolutionary reason given is that men provided food and shelter for the family and would resent his partner's physical intimacy with another because he would then be providing food and shelter for another man's child. Women, because they depended on men for food and shelter, became especially jealous when their partner was emotionally intimate with another because this might mean he might leave her and she'd thus lose the food and shelter protection.

INTERPERSONAL CHOICE POINT

Jealousy

Your partner is excessively jealous—at least from your point of view. You can't meet other people or even communicate with them online without your partner questioning your fidelity. What might you do to reduce (or ideally stop) this jealousy without destroying the relationship?

Not all research supports this finding and not all theory supports this evolutionary explanation (Harris, 2003). For example, among Chinese men, only 25 percent reported physical infidelity was the more distressing while 75 percent reported emotional infidelity to be more distressing.

Another commonly assumed gender difference is that jealous men are more prone to respond with violence. This assumption, however, does not seem to be the case; men and women apparently are equally likely to respond with violence (Harris, 2003).

DEALING WITH JEALOUSY So what do you do when you experience jealousy (short of violence)? Communication researchers find several popular but generally negative interactive responses (Dindia & Timmerman, 2003; Guerrero, Andersen, Jorgensen, Spitzberg, & Eloy, 1995). You may:

- nonverbally express your displeasure; for example, cry or express hurt.
- threaten to become violent or actually engage in violence.
- be verbally aggressive; for example, be sarcastic or accusatory.
- withdraw affection or be silent, sometimes denying that anything is wrong.

On the more positive side are responses known as "integrative communication": messages that attempt to work things out with your partner, such as self-disclosing your feelings, being honest, practicing effective conflict management, listening actively, and, in short, all the skills we talk about in this text.

Bullying

Bullying, whether in a close relationship, the workplace, or the playground, consists of abusive acts repeatedly committed by one person (or a group) against another. Bullying is behavior that has become a pattern; it's repeated frequently rather than being an isolated instance. On the playground, bullying often involves physical abuse; in the workplace, bullying is generally verbal.

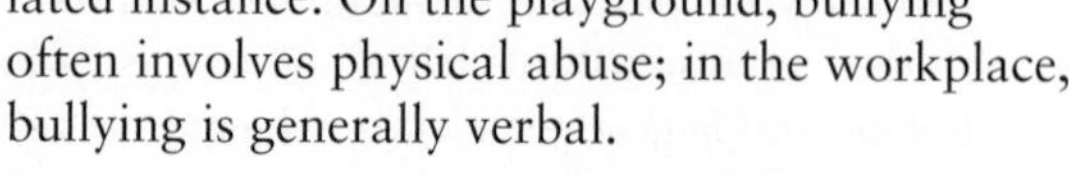

VIEWPOINTS Bullying

Sometimes, bullying is a part of the organization's culture, where, for example, first-year interns in a law office are treated unfairly and often abused by their superiors (demonstrated on a variety of lawyer TV shows such as *The Good Wife*). Sometimes it's perpetrated by a group who perhaps bully the newcomers or those who do less creative jobs. What's the status of bullying in organizations with which you're familiar?

TYPES OF BULLYING Here are some of the types of bullying found in the workplace:

- gossiping about someone, making others the butt of jokes
- treating others as inferior, for example, frequently interrupting them or otherwise not giving their ideas due attention
- excluding members from social functions
- verbal insults, name calling
- negative facial expressions, sneering, avoiding eye contact
- excessive blaming
- being supervised (watched, monitored) more closely than others
- being unnecessarily criticized, often with shouting and in public

The problem with bullying from the employer's point of view is that it reduces productivity and hurts the bottom line. If one or even a few workers are bullied, they're probably not going to be as productive as they would be if they weren't bullied. It also is likely to lead to workers leaving the company—after the company has trained them but before they have become productive team members—with the added cost of hiring and training new people (and perhaps attendant lawsuits).

A special type of bullying is cyberbullying, which can take place through any electronic communication system—Facebook, Twitter, e-mail, instant messages, blog posts—and can take the form of sending threatening messages or images, posting negative comments, revealing secrets, or lying about another person. In one 2009 survey of 13- to 18-year-olds, 15 percent said they had been cyberbullied, and in another study of 12- to 17-year-olds, one-third said they were threatened or embarrassed by things said about them online. In another study, 88 percent of social media–using teenagers said they witnessed other people being mean or cruel on the sites and 15 percent say they were the targets of such meanness (Lenhart et al., 2011).

Among the reasons why cyberbullying is so important is that it can occur at any time; the messages, photos, and videos can be distributed quickly and widely; and the bully can hide behind false names. Websites, in fact, will do this for you and send messages anonymously. In this way, the person receives a bullying message but without any name attached. Cyberbullying attacks—because they occur electronically—are often more cruel than those made in face-to-face attacks (Hinduja & Patchin, 2008).

According to a Washington State Department of Labor & Industries report, victims of bullying may suffer significant mental and physical problems including high stress, financial problems, reduced self-esteem, and sleep and digestion disturbances. From the point of view of the worker being bullied, it obviously creates an uncomfortable atmosphere, perhaps a desire to avoid going into work, perhaps a preoccupation with the bullying rather than the job. And this is likely to spill over into the person's private life; after all, it would be strange if bullying at work did not create problems with other aspects of life. And although the bullies probably derive some personal satisfaction from wielding power over someone else, they too are likely to fail to be as productive as they might be and may well be personally troubled. From an ethical point of view, bullying destroys a person's right to personal dignity and a workplace free from intimidation and is therefore unethical. And yet bullying is not illegal in the United States, unless it involves harassment based on a person's gender or race, for example.

Dealing with Bullying Among the actions recommended for combating bullying are these:

1. Workers and organizations need to be clear about their opposition to bullying and that it doesn't profit anyone and will not be tolerated. Accusations of bullying will be investigated promptly and fairly.
2. If possible and there is no danger (physical or institutional), sometimes confronting the bully assertively (not aggressively) will be enough—*I don't like it when you make fun of the way I dress and I want you to stop—it's not funny and it just makes me feel bad.*
3. Taking action when you or someone else is bullied. This suggestion is not always easy to implement, especially if the bullying is part of the corporate culture or is carried out by your boss. But well-kept records of such incidents will often convince even the most reluctant.

INTERPERSONAL CHOICE POINT

Bullying

Your colleagues at your new job have been bullying a junior colleague ever since you arrived at the job a few months ago. What are some of your choices for helping your colleague without doing anything that will make you the next victim?

Violence

Perhaps the most obvious dark side is seen in the varied forms of relationship violence. Before reading about this important but often neglected topic, take the following self-test.

TEST YOURSELF

Is Violence a Part of Your Relationship?

Based on your present relationship or one you know, respond to the following questions with *yes* or *no*.

Do either of you:

____ 1. get angry to the point of making the other person fearful?
____ 2. engage in behavior that could be considered humiliating to the other person?
____ 3. verbally abuse the other?
____ 4. threaten the other with violence?
____ 5. engage in slapping, hitting, or pushing the other?
____ 6. throw things in anger?
____ 7. make accusations of sexual infidelity?
____ 8. force the other to have sex?
____ 9. use abusive sexual terms in reference to the other?

How Did You Do? These nine items are all signs of a violent relationship (it only takes one to make a relationship violent). Items 1–3 are examples of verbal or emotional abuse, 4–6 of physical abuse, and 7–9 of sexual abuse—all of which are explained more fully in the text.

What Will You Do? If any of these questions describes your relationship, you may wish to seek professional help (which is likely available on your campus). Additional suggestions are offered in the text and are readily available online.

Source: These questions were drawn from a variety of websites, including those from SUNY at Buffalo Counseling Services; The American College of Obstetricians and Gynecologists, Women's Heath Care Physicians; and the University of Texas at Austin, Counseling and Mental Health Center.

TYPES OF RELATIONSHIP VIOLENCE Three types of **relationship violence** may be distinguished: verbal or emotional abuse, physical abuse, and sexual abuse (Rice, 2007).

- *Verbal or emotional abuse* may include humiliating you; engaging in economic abuse such as controlling the finances or preventing you from working; and/or isolating, criticizing, or stalking you. Not surprisingly, some research shows that people who use verbal or emotional abuse are more likely than others to escalate to physical abuse (Rancer & Avtgis, 2006).
- *Physical abuse* includes threats of violence as well as pushing, hitting, slapping, kicking, choking, throwing things at you, and breaking things.
- *Sexual abuse* involves touching that is unwanted, accusations of sexual infidelity without reason, forced sex, and references to you in abusive sexual terms. Table 9.2 offers a brief comparison and summary of violent and nonviolent relationships.

A great deal of research has centered on trying to identify the warning signs of relationship violence. For example, the State University of New York at Buffalo compiled the following list to help you start thinking about your own relationship or those that you know of. It may be a warning sign if your partner:

- belittles, insults, or ignores you.
- controls pieces of your life; for example, the way you dress or who you can be friends with.
- gets jealous without reason.
- can't handle sexual frustration without anger.
- is so angry or threatening that you've changed your life so as not to provoke additional anger.

As you might expect, there are a variety of consequences to relationship violence: physical injuries, psychological injuries, and economic "injuries."

Perhaps the image that comes most quickly to mind with the issue of relationship violence is that of physical violence, and that element

INTERPERSONAL CHOICE POINT

Verbal Abuse

On your way to work, you witness a father verbally abusing his 3-year-old child. You worry that he might psychologically harm the child, and your first impulse is to speak up and tell this man that verbal abuse can have lasting effects on the child and often leads to physical abuse. At the same time, you don't want to interfere with his right to speak to his child, and you certainly don't want to make him angrier. What are some things you might say or do in this difficult situation?

TABLE 9.2

VIOLENT AND NONVIOLENT RELATIONSHIPS

Here are some characteristics that distinguish a nonviolent from a violent relationship, drawn largely from the University of Texas website on relationship violence.

Violent Relationships	Nonviolent Relationships
Emotional abuse	Fairness; you look for resolutions to conflict that will be fair to both of you.
Control and isolation	Communication that makes the partner feel safe and comfortable expressing himself or herself.
Intimidation	Mutual respect, mutual affirmation, and valuing of each other's opinions.
Economic abuse	The partners make financial decisions together.
Threats	Accountability—each person accepts responsibility for his or her own behavior.
Power over the other	Fair distribution of responsibilities.
Sexual abuse	Trust and respect for what each person wants and doesn't want.

is certainly a big part of overall relationship violence. Physical injuries may range from scratches and bruises to broken bones, knife wounds, and central nervous system damage. Such injuries can range from minor to life-ending.

Even when physical injuries are relatively minor, however, psychological injuries may be major and may include, for example, depression, anxiety, fear of intimacy, and, of course, low self-esteem. In fact, relationship violence often attacks self-esteem to the point where the victims come to believe that the violence against them was and is justified.

In addition to the obvious physical and psychological injuries, consider the economic impact. It's been estimated that in the United States relationship violence costs approximately $6.2 billion for physical assaults and almost $500 million for rape. Interpersonal violence also results in lost days of work. The Centers for Disease Control and Prevention estimates that in this country interpersonal violence costs the equivalent of 32,000 full-time jobs in lost work each year. Additional economic costs are incurred when interpersonal violence prevents women from maintaining jobs or continuing their education.

DEALING WITH RELATIONSHIP VIOLENCE Whether you're a victim or a perpetrator of relationship violence, it is important to seek professional help (and, of course, the help of friends and family where appropriate). In addition, here are several further suggestions.

If your partner has been violent:

- Realize that you're not alone. There are other people who suffer similarly, and there is a mechanism in place to help you.
- Realize you're not at fault. You did not deserve to be the victim of violence.
- Plan for your safety. Violence, if it occurred once, is likely to occur again, and part of your thinking needs to be devoted to your own safety.
- Know your resources—the phone numbers you need to contact help, the locations of money and a spare set of keys.

If you are the violent partner:

- Realize that you too are not alone and that help and support are available.
- Know that you can change. It won't necessarily be easy or quick, but you can change.
- Own your own behaviors; take responsibility. This is an essential step if any change is to occur.

Relationship violence is not an inevitable part of interpersonal relationships; in fact, it occurs in a minority of relationships. Yet it's important to know that there is the potential for violence in all relationships, as there is the potential for friendship, love, support, and all the positive things we look for in relationships. Knowing the difference between productive and destructive relationships seems the best way to make sure that your own relationships are as you want them to be.

Can you define *jealousy, bullying,* and *relationship violence?* Can you use the suggestions offered here to help you effectively deal with such relationships in your own personal or workplace life?

MESSAGES IN THE MEDIA: WRAP-UP

It's instructive to watch such shows with a view to identifying what went wrong in the relationship. And, Jerry Springer's summary and relationship advice at the end of the show is always logical and well-reasoned.

SUMMARY OF CONCEPTS AND SKILLS

Listen to the **Audio Chapter Summary** at **MyCommunicationLab**

Study and **Review** materials for this chapter are at **MyCommunicationLab**

This chapter explored the nature of interpersonal relationships, including the stages relationships go through, the movements in relationships, the dark side of interpersonal relationships, relationship types and theories, and the role of culture and technology in relationships.

Advantages and Disadvantages of Interpersonal Relationships

1. Interpersonal relationships have both advantages and disadvantages. Among the advantages are that they stimulate you, help you learn about yourself, and generally enhance your self-esteem. Among the disadvantages are that they force you to expose your vulnerabilities, make great demands on your time, and often cause you to abandon other relationships.

Relationship Stages

2. Interpersonal relationships may be viewed as occurring in stages. Recognize at least these: contact, involvement, intimacy, deterioration, repair, and dissolution.
3. In contact, there is first perceptual contact and then interaction.
4. Involvement includes a testing phase (will this be a suitable relationship?) and an intensifying of the interaction; often a sense of mutuality, of connectedness, begins.
5. In intimacy, there is an interpersonal commitment and perhaps a social bonding, in which the commitment is made public.
6. Some relationships deteriorate, proceeding through a period of intrapersonal dissatisfaction to interpersonal deterioration.

7. Along the process, repair may be initiated. Intrapersonal repair generally comes first (should I change my behavior?); it may be followed by interpersonal repair, in which you and your partner discuss your problems and seek remedies.
8. If repair fails, the relationship may dissolve, moving first to interpersonal separation and later, perhaps, to public or social separation.
9. Relationships are fluid, and movement from one stage to another is characteristic of most relationships.

The Dark Side of Interpersonal Relationships

10. Jealousy is a feeling that a relationship is in danger due to some rival and may be cognitive, emotional, and/or behavioral.
11. Bullying consists of abusive acts repeatedly committed by one person or group against another and is especially prevalent n the workplace.
12. Relationship violence may be verbal, physical, and/or sexual.

This chapter also considered a variety of skills. As you review these skills, check those you wish to work on.

____ 1. *Advantages and disadvantages of relationships.* In evaluating, entering, or dissolving relationships, consider both the advantages and the disadvantages.

____ 2. *Relationship messages.* Formulate messages that are appropriate to the stage of the relationship. Also, listen to messages from relationship partners that may reveal differences in perceptions about your relationship stage.

____ 3. *Relationship repair.* Recognize the problem, engage in productive conflict resolution, pose possible solutions, affirm each other, integrate solutions into normal behavior, and take risks as appropriate.

____ 4. *Managing relationship dissolution.* Break the loneliness–depression cycle, take time out, bolster self-esteem, seek support from others, and avoid repeating negative patterns.

____ 5. *Jealousy.* Recognize the generally unproductive nature of jealousy.

____ 6. *Bullying.* Become aware of the tactics of bullies and ways to combat them.

____ 7. *Violence in relationships.* Become sensitive to the development of violence in a relationship and learn the ways to deal with this problem, should it arise.

VOCABULARY QUIZ: The Language of Interpersonal Relationships

Match the terms dealing with interpersonal relationships with their definitions. Record the number of the definition next to the appropriate term.

____ turning points (205)
____ politeness (207)
____ repair (203)
____ verbal abuse (212)
____ jealousy (209)
____ involvement (199)
____ intimacy (200)
____ contact (199)
____ dissolution (204)
____ desire, obligation, and necessity (207)

1. Humiliation, criticizing, isolating
2. Testing and intensifying a relationship
3. Types of commitment
4. Perceptual and interactional
5. Commitment and social bonding
6. Separation, the breaking of relationship bonds
7. Significant relationship events
8. Highest in contact and lowest in dissolution
9. Attempts to improve a relationship
10. Reaction to relationship threat

These ten terms and additional terms used in this chapter can be found in the glossary.

Study and **Review** the **Flashcards** at **MyCommunicationLab**

MyCommunicationLab

Visit MyCommunicationLab for a wealth of additional information on interpersonal communication. Flashcards, videos, skill building exercises, sample test questions, and additional exercises, examples, and discussions will help you continue your study of the fundamentals of interpersonal communication, its theory, and its skills.

CHAPTER

10

Interpersonal Relationship Types and Theories

MESSAGES IN THE MEDIA

In *Modern Family* (and lots of other shows like *Mad Men*) you see a wide variety of relationships—the subject of this chapter. In *Modern Family*, as in life, some relationships are effective and some are ineffective.

OBJECTIVES *After reading this chapter, you should be able to:*

1. Define the types and stages of friendship and explain the roles of culture, gender, and technology in friendships.
2. Describe the six types of love and explain the role of culture, gender, and technology on love.
3. Define *family* and the types of couples and families and explain the roles of culture, gender, and technology in family.
4. Explain the nature of work relationships.
5. Define *online-only relationships* and communicate more effectively in these relationships.
6. Summarize the theories of attraction, social exchange, equity, dialectics, and rules and apply their insights to your own interpersonal relationships.

Listen to the **Audio Chapter** at **MyCommunicationLab**

This chapter looks at two broad topics, relationship types and relationship theories (explanations of how and why our relationships work or don't work). Together these two topics will provide you with different perspectives on relationships and considerable insights to help you manage your own relationships more effectively.

In these first sections, we look at some of the major types of relationships: friendship, love, family, and work relationships. In the next section, we'll look at relationship theories, at explanations of what leads us to form, maintain, and sometimes dissolve interpersonal relationships.

VIEWPOINTS Friendship choices

Before reading any further, examine your own friendship choices. On what basis do you choose to call someone "friend"? On what basis do you choose to extend your friendship to another? In what ways do the reasons for these choices differ in face-to-face interactions versus social networking interactions?

FRIENDSHIP RELATIONSHIPS

Friendship is an interpersonal relationship between two people that is mutually productive and characterized by mutual positive regard. Friendship is an *interpersonal* relationship; communication interactions must have taken place between the people. Further, the interpersonal relationship involves a "personalistic focus" (Wright, 1978, 1984). That is, friends react to each other as complete persons—as unique, genuine, and irreplaceable individuals. In online friendships, people often have friends numbering in the hundreds. In a 2011 survey, Facebook users had an average of 229 friends (Hampton, Goulet, Rainie, & Purcell, 2011). Because these numbers are so large, this personalistic focus may easily be lost. Yet it remains a goal even when the numbers are extremely large. Facebook's "friends" lists and Google+'s circles enable you to group your friends based on degree of closeness—or any other grouping you find useful. Interestingly enough, research finds that Facebook users have more people with whom they can share important matters than non-users.

Friendships must be *mutually productive*; by definition, they cannot be destructive to either person. Once destructiveness enters into a relationship, it no longer qualifies as friendship. For example, a relationship in which one person intimidates, controls, or ridicules the other can hardly be called a friendship. Love relationships, marriage relationships, parent–child relationships, and just about any other possible relationship can be either destructive or productive. But friendship must enhance the potential of each person and can only be productive.

Friendships are characterized by *mutual positive regard*. Liking people is essential if we are to call them friends. Three major characteristics of friendship—trust, emotional support, and sharing of interests—testify to this positive regard (Blieszner & Adams, 1992). And, of course, the "like" and +1 icons on social media sites make the expression of this positive regard extremely easy.

The closer friends are, the more interdependent they become; that is, when friends are especially close, the actions of one will affect more significantly the other than they would if the friends were just casual acquaintances. Similarly, the friends of one will become the friends of others—more easily on social media sites but also in face-to-face friendships. Close friends are less influenced by the societal rules that govern more casual relationships; close friends are likely to make up their own rules for interacting with each other; they decide what they will talk about and when, what they can say to each other without offending and what they can't, when and for what reasons one friend can call the other, and so on.

Types of Friendships

Not all friendships are the same. But how do they differ? One way of answering this question is by distinguishing among the three major types of friendship: reciprocity, receptivity, and association (Reisman, 1979, 1981).

- *Reciprocity.* The friendship of reciprocity is characterized by loyalty, self-sacrifice, mutual affection, and generosity. A friendship of reciprocity is based on equality:

Watch the **Video** "Juggling Act" at **MyCommunicationLab**

SKILL BUILDING EXERCISE

Identifying Friendship Functions in Social Media

Friendships, as you know, serve a variety of functions or needs. The following five functions were identified in a pre-social media communication environment and are based largely on face-to-face friendships (Wright, 1978, 1984; Reiner & Blanton, 1997). However, these functions are also served by social media friendships. Indicate the specific means used (and specific examples) in social media communication to serve each of these five needs/functions:

Identifying the functions that friendships serve will help you communicate in such relationships as friend and as befriended.

Function	Generally	In Social Media
Utility	Friends can do useful things for you, for example, helping you get a better job or introducing you to a possible romantic partner.	
Affirmation	Friends can affirm your personal value and help you to appreciate your qualities.	
Ego Support	Friends can be supportive, encouraging, and complimentary, helping you develop a healthy ego.	
Stimulation	Friends can introduce you to new ideas and new ways of seeing the world.	
Security	Friends come to your aid when you need them, supportively and nonjudgmentally.	

Each individual shares equally in giving and receiving the benefits and rewards of the relationship.

- *Receptivity.* In the friendship of receptivity, in contrast, there is an imbalance in giving and receiving; one person is the primary giver and one the primary receiver. This imbalance, however, is a positive one because each person gains something from the relationship. The different needs of both the person who receives and the person who gives are satisfied. This is the friendship that may develop between a teacher and a student or between a doctor and a patient.
- *Association.* The friendship of association is a transitory one. It might be described as a friendly relationship rather than a true friendship. Associative friendships are the kind we often have with classmates, neighbors, or coworkers. There is no great loyalty, no great trust, no great giving or receiving. The association is cordial but not intense. Most of the friendships on social network sites would fall into this category, though the friendships of reciprocity and receptivity would also be represented.

INTERPERSONAL CHOICE POINT

Friend Request

You get a request to be friends with someone you really don't want to have in your network. Assuming you don't want to create animosity, what are some of your options in this case?

Friendship, Culture, Gender, and Technology

Your friendships and the way you look at friendships will be influenced by your culture, gender, and the technology around us.

CULTURE In the United States, you can be friends with someone yet never really be expected to go much out of your way for the other person. Many Middle Easterners, Asians, and Latin Americans would consider going significantly out of their way an absolutely essential ingredient in friendship; if you're not willing to sacrifice for your friend, then this person is not really your friend (Dresser, 2005).

Generally friendships are closer in collectivist cultures than in individualist cultures (see Chapter 2). In their emphasis on the group and on cooperating, collectivist cultures foster the development of close friendship bonds. Members of collectivist cultures are expected to help others in the group, certainly a good start for a friendship. Members of individualist cultures, on the other hand, are expected to look out for "number one," themselves. Consequently, they're more likely to compete and to try to do better than each other—conditions that don't support, generally at least, the development of friendships.

Blog Post

Friendship, Gay and Straight

For a brief discussion of gay–straight friendships and their problems and advantages, see "Friendship, Gay and Straight" at tcbdevito .blogspot.com. How do you see such friendships?

GENDER Gender also influences your friendships—who becomes your friend and the way you look at friendships. Women engage in significantly more affectional behaviors with their friends than do males; this difference may account for the greater difficulty men experience in beginning and maintaining close friendships (Hays, 1989). Women engage in more casual communication; they also share greater intimacy and more confidences with their friends than do men. Communication, in all its forms and functions, seems a much more important dimension of women's friendships.

Men's friendships are often built around shared activities—attending a ball game, playing cards, working on a project at the office. Women's friendships, on the other hand, are built more around a sharing of feelings, support, and "personalism." Similarity in status, in willingness to protect a friend in uncomfortable situations, in academic major, and even in proficiency in playing the game Password were significantly related to the relationship closeness of male–male friends but not of female–female or female–male friends (Griffin & Sparks, 1990). Perhaps similarity is a criterion for male friendships but not for female or mixed-sex friendships.

TECHNOLOGY Whereas not so many years ago, friends met at school, at work, or in their neighborhood, today online friendships in some form are a major part of our relationship life. Social networking sites such as Facebook, Google+, and LinkedIn, for example, make it increasingly easy and interesting to both meet new friends and to keep in touch with old friends. Establishing and maintaining friendships, in fact, are the major reasons for online communication (instant messaging and texting, social network sites, and e-mail) among college students and among teens (Lenhart, Madden, Macgill, & Smith, 2007).

What is especially striking when you look at online friendships is that the number of "friends" on Facebook, for example, is often in the hundreds and even the thousands. Clearly, this is a very different definition of *friend* and probably results from what researchers call network convergence, the process that occurs when people in a relationship begin to share their network of friends with each other (Parks, 1995; Parks & Floyd, 1996). So, if you're friends with Pat, Pat's friends become your friends and your friends

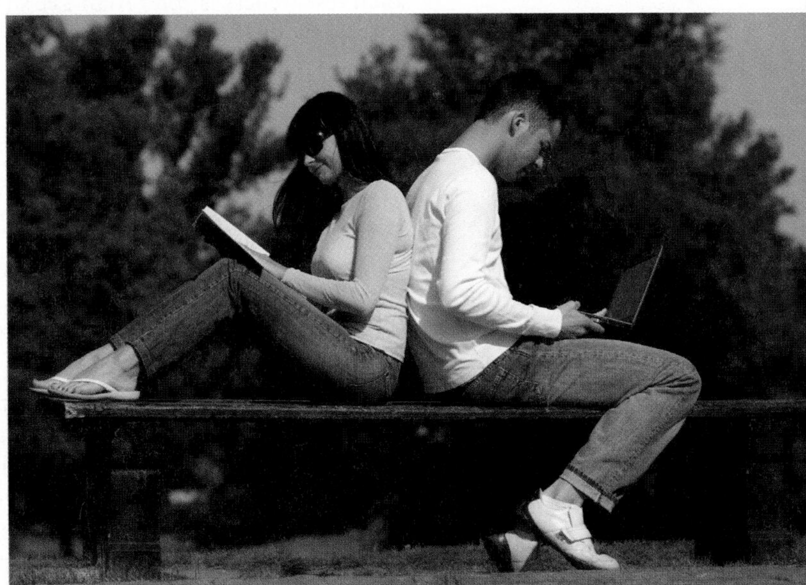

VIEWPOINTS Social information processing

Social information processing (SIP) theory claims that whether you're communicating face to face or online, you can communicate the same degree of personal involvement and develop similar close relationships (Walther, 2011). Communicators are clever people; they will make whatever adjustments are needed to communicate what they want and to develop the relationships they want. In short, communication and the relationships can be as personal online as face to face. In what ways do you adjust your online communication to make it resemble face-to-face communication? What do you think of this theory?

INTERPERSONAL CHOICE POINT

Getting Back in Touch

You've been out of touch with some friends for over a year, and as many web watchers recommend, they seem to have pruned you from their list of friends. What are some of your choices for getting back in touch with (and in the good graces of) these friends?

become Pat's. To some people, the number of friends seems to be taken as a measure of the person's importance; the more friends you have, the more important you must be.

Online friendships are now important and are becoming more so in providing a sense of belonging that may once have been thought possible only through face-to-face interactions. And with more choices available, you can easily discover those people with whom you want to develop a face-to-face friendship.

Can you define the types and stages of friendship and explain the roles of culture, gender, and technology in friendships?

LOVE RELATIONSHIPS

Of all the qualities of interpersonal relationships, none seems as important as love. **Love** is a feeling characterized by closeness and caring and by intimacy, passion, and commitment. It's also an interpersonal relationship developed, maintained, and sometimes destroyed through communication—and at the same time a relationship that can be greatly enhanced with communication skills (Dindia & Timmerman, 2003).

Explore the **Exercise** "Mate Preferences" at **MyCommunicationLab**

Types of Love

Although there are many theories about love, a model that has long interested interpersonal researchers is John Alan Lee's (1976) proposal that not one but six types of love exist. View the following descriptions of the six types as broad characterizations that are generally but not always true.

- *Eros: Beauty and sexuality.* Like Narcissus, who fell in love with the beauty of his own image, the erotic lover focuses on beauty and physical attractiveness, sometimes to the exclusion of qualities some might consider more important and more lasting. Also like Narcissus, the erotic lover has an idealized image of beauty that is unattainable in reality. Consequently, the erotic lover often feels unfulfilled.
- *Ludus: Entertainment and excitement.* Ludus love is experienced as a game, as fun; love is not to be taken too seriously. Passions never rise to the point where they get out of control. A ludic lover is self-controlled, always aware of the need to manage love rather than allowing it to be in control. Not surprisingly, the ludic lover retains a partner only as long as the partner remains interesting and amusing.
- *Storge: Peace and slowness.* Storgic lovers set out not to find a lover but to establish a companionable relationship with someone they know and with whom they can share interests and activities. Storgic love is a gradual process of unfolding thoughts and feelings; the changes seem to come so slowly and so gradually that it's often difficult to define exactly where the relationship is at any point in time.
- *Pragma: Practicality and tradition.* The pragma lover is practical and seeks a relationship that will work. Pragma lovers want compatibility and a relationship in which their important needs and desires will be satisfied. The pragma lover views love as a useful relationship, a relationship that makes the rest of life easier, so the pragma lover asks such questions of a potential mate as "Will this person earn a good living?" or "Will my family get along with this person?"

INTERPERSONAL CHOICE POINT

Virtual Infidelity

You discover that your partner of the past 15 years is being unfaithful with someone online. You want to discover your partner's intentions in regard to this affair. What choices do you have for opening up this topic for honest conversation without making your partner defensive and hence uncommunicative?

VIDEO CHOICE POINT

Asking for a Date

Alice and Judy have become acquainted in several contexts and have enjoyed each other's company, but they have not confided to each other about their affectional orientation. Alice, a lesbian, decides to ask Judy for a date and self-disclose in the process. "Asking for a Date" looks at various relationship types and needs and the roles communication choices play in friendship and love relationships. See how Alice's choices play out in the video "Asking for a Date" and respond to the questions posed.

 **Watch** the **Video** "Asking for a Date" at **MyCommunicationLab**

- *Mania: Elation and depression.* Mania is characterized by extreme highs and extreme lows. The manic lover loves intensely and at the same time worries intensely about the loss of the love. Manic love is obsessive; the manic lover has to possess the beloved completely. In return, the manic lover wishes to be possessed, to be loved intensely. The manic lover's self-image seems capable of being improved only by being loved.
- *Agape: Compassion and selflessness.* Agape (ah-guh-pay) is a compassionate, egoless, self-giving love. The agapic lover loves even people with whom he or she has no close ties. Agape is a spiritual love, offered without concern for personal reward or gain. This lover loves without expecting that the love will be reciprocated.

Explore the **Exercise** "How Can You Talk Cherishing?" at **MyCommunicationLab**

Love, Culture, Gender, and Technology

Like friendship, love is heavily influenced by culture, gender, and technology.

CULTURE Although most of the research on the six love styles has been done in the United States, some research has been conducted in other cultures (Bierhoff & Klein, 1991). Here is just a sampling of the research findings—just enough to illustrate that culture is an important factor in love.

In their love style, Asians have been found to be more friendship oriented than are Europeans (Dion & Dion, 1993b). Members of individualist cultures (for example, Europeans) are likely to place greater emphasis on romantic love and on individual fulfillment. Members of collectivist cultures are likely to spread their love over a large network of relatives (Dion & Dion, 1993a). When compared with their Chinese counterparts, American men scored higher on ludic and agapic love and lower on erotic and pragma love. American men also are less likely to view emotional satisfaction as crucial to relationship maintenance (Sprecher & Toro-Morn, 2002).

In the United States, both men and women can initiate relationships, and both can dissolve them. Both men and women are expected to derive satisfaction from their interpersonal relationships, and when that satisfaction isn't present, either person may seek to exit the relationship. In Iran, on the other hand, only the man has the right to dissolve a marriage without giving reasons.

Further, your culture will influence the difficulty that you go through when relationships do break up. For example, married persons whose religion forbids divorce and remarriage will experience religious disapproval and condemnation as well as the same economic and social difficulties everyone else goes through. In the United States, child custody almost invariably goes to the woman, and this presents an added emotional burden for the man. In Iran, child custody goes to the man, which presents added emotional burdens for the woman. In India, women experience greater difficulty than men in divorce because of their economic

INTERPERSONAL CHOICE POINT

From Friendship to Love

You have a great friendship with a colleague at work, but recently these feelings of friendship are turning to feelings of love. How can you move this friendship to love or at least discover if the other person would be receptive to this change?

dependence on men, the cultural beliefs about women, and the patriarchal order of the family (Amato, 1994). And it was only as recently as 2002 that the first wife in Jordan was granted a divorce. Prior to this, only men had been granted divorces.

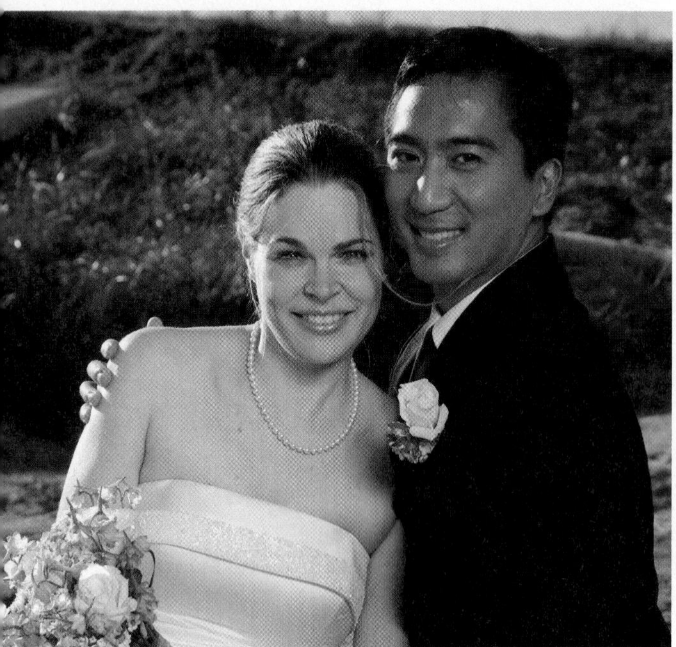

VIEWPOINTS Gender differences

Men and women from different cultures were asked the following question: "If a man (woman) had all the other qualities you desired, would you marry this person if you were not in love with him (her)?" Results varied from one culture to another (Levine, Sato, Hashimoto, & Verma, 1994). For example, 50 percent of the respondents from Pakistan said yes and 49 percent of those from India said yes. At the other extreme were those from Japan (only 2 percent said yes) and the United States (only 3.5 percent said yes). How would you answer this question? How is your answer influenced by your culture?

GENDER In the United States the differences between men and women in love are considered great. In poetry, novels, and the mass media, women and men are depicted as acting very differently when falling in love, being in love, and ending a love relationship.

Men and women differ in the types of love they prefer (Hendrick, Hendrick, Foote, & Slapion-Foote, 1984). For example, on one version of the love self-test presented earlier, men scored higher on erotic and ludic love, whereas women scored higher on manic, pragmatic, and storgic love. No difference was found for agapic love.

Some research finds that men place more emphasis on romance than women. For example, when college students were asked the question "If a man (woman) had all the other qualities you desired, would you marry this person if you were not in love with him (her)?" approximately two-thirds of the men responded *no*, which seems to indicate that a high percentage were concerned with love and romance. However, less than one-third of the women responded *no* (LeVine, Sato, Hashimoto, & Verma, 1994). Further, when men and women were surveyed concerning their view on love—whether it's basically realistic or basically romantic—it was found that married women had a more realistic (less romantic) conception of love than did married men (Knapp & Vangelisti, 2009). This difference seems to increase as the romantic relationship develops: Men become more romantic and women less romantic (Fengler, 1974; Sprecher & Metts, 1989).

TECHNOLOGY Unlike relationships established in face-to-face encounters, in which physical appearance tends to outweigh personality, online communication reveals your inner qualities first. Rapport and mutual self-disclosure become more important than physical attractiveness in promoting intimacy (Cooper & Sportolari, 1997). And contrary to some popular opinions, online relationships rely just as heavily on the ideals of trust, honesty, and commitment as do face-to-face relationships (Whitty & Gavin, 2001). Online romantic interaction is a natural boon to shut-ins and extremely shy people for whom face-to-face ways of meeting someone are often difficult. Computer talk is empowering for those with "physical disabilities or disfigurements," for whom face-to-face interactions are often superficial and often end with withdrawal (Bull & Rumsey, 1988; Lea & Spears, 1995). By eliminating the physical cues, computer talk equalizes the interaction and doesn't put the person who is disfigured, for example, at an immediate disadvantage in a society where physical attractiveness is so highly valued.

Online, people can present a false self with little chance of detection; minors may present themselves as adults, and adults may present themselves as children. Similarly, people can present themselves as poor when they're rich, as mature when they're immature, as serious and committed when they're just enjoying the online experience. Although people can also misrepresent themselves in face-to-face relationships, the fact that it's easier to do online probably accounts for greater frequency of misrepresentation in computer relationships (Cornwell & Lundgren, 2001).

INTERPERSONAL CHOICE POINT

Discovering Personal Information

You're becoming romantically involved with someone from school, but before this relationship goes any further, you want to know about this person's HIV status and adherence to safe sex practices. What are some of the things that you might say that will elicit truthful information but at the same time will not create a rift in the relationship?

Can you describe the six types of love (eros, ludus, storge, pragma, mania, and agape) and explain how love is influenced by culture, gender, and technology?

FAMILY RELATIONSHIPS

If you had to define the term *family*, you might say that a family consists of a husband, a wife, and one or more children. When pressed, you might add that some families also include other relatives—in-laws, brothers and sisters, grandparents, aunts and uncles, and so on. But other types of relationships are, to their own members, "families." One example is the family without children, a pattern that has been increasing. Also on the increase is the single parent family. Table 10.1 provides a few findings from the U.S. Census to further illustrate some of these changes.

Another example is people living together in an exclusive relationship who are not married. For the most part, these cohabitants live as if they were married. These relationships mirror traditional marriages, except that they lack the legal marriage union that is recognized by a religious body, the state, or both; also, only marrieds can profit from federal benefits and protections.

Another example is the gay or lesbian couple who live together as "domestic partners" in a "civil union" or in marriage in households that have all the characteristics of a family. Many of these couples have children from previous heterosexual unions, through artificial insemination, or by adoption. Although accurate statistics are difficult to secure, primary relationships among gays and lesbians seem more common than the popular media lead us to believe. And most relational experts agree that being in a committed relationship is the goal of most people, regardless of affectional orientation (Fitzpatrick & Caughlin, 2002; Kurdek, 2000, 2004; Patterson, 2000).

The communication principles that apply to the traditional nuclear family (the mother–father–child family) also apply to these other kinds of families. In the following discussion, the term *primary relationship* denotes the relationship between the two principal parties—the husband and wife, the lovers, the domestic partners, for example—and the term *family* denotes the broader constellation that includes children, relatives, and assorted significant others.

"If you don't have anything profound to say, don't say anything at all."

Robert Leighton/The New Yorker Collection/www.cartoonbank.com

Characteristics of Families

All primary relationships and families have several qualities that further characterize this relationship type: defined roles, recognition of responsibilities, shared history and future, and shared living space.

- *Defined roles.* Many heterosexual couples divide their roles rather traditionally, with the man as primary wage earner and maintenance person and the woman as primary cook, child rearer, and housekeeper. This is less true among more highly educated couples and those in

TABLE 10.1

The American Family

Here are several findings on the American family from the U.S. Census. For each finding, indicate what you think the reasons for these changes might be and the possible trends they may indicate. In one sentence of not more than 140 characters, summarize the changes you see happing in the American family.

- The percentage of one-person households increased from 25 percent in 1990 to 27 percent in 2010.
- The percentage of multigenerational households increased from 14 percent in 1990 to 16 percent in 2010.
- The percentage of births by unmarried women increased from 26 percent in 1990 to 41 percent in 2010.
- Fifty percent of women who marry did so at 24 in 1990; in 2010, 50 percent married at 26.
- In 2000 (the first year the Census Bureau allowed people to indicate more than one race), 1.6 percent indicated mixed race; in 2010, it was 2 percent.
- In 2005, 53 percent of men and 46 percent of women between the ages of 18 and 24 lived with their parents; in 2011, the percentage was 59 percent for men and 50 percent for women.
- In 2000, 57 percent of all adults were married; in 2010, 51 percent were married.
- In 2000, the average size of the family was 2.62; in 2010 it was 2.59.

Watch the **Video** "Please Don't Lie to Me" at **MyCommunicationLab**

the higher socioeconomic classes, where changes in traditional role assignments are seen first. However, among gay and lesbian couples, clear-cut, stereotypical male and female roles are not found (Cloud, 2008; Peplau, 1988).

- *Recognition of responsibilities.* Family members see themselves as having certain obligations and responsibilities to one another. For example, individuals have an obligation to help each other financially. There are also emotional responsibilities: to offer comfort when family members are distressed, to take pleasure in their pleasures, to feel their pain, to raise their spirits.
- *Shared history and future.* Primary relationship partners have a shared history and the prospect of a shared future. For a relationship to become primary, there must be some history, some significant past interaction. Despite researchers' prediction that 50 percent of couples now entering first marriages will divorce (the rate is higher for second marriages) and that 41 percent of all persons of marriageable age will experience divorce, most couples entering a relationship such as marriage view it—ideally, at least—as permanent.
- *Shared living space.* In general American culture, persons in primary interpersonal relationships usually share the same living space. In some other cultures, however, men and women don't share the same living space; the women may live with the children while the men live together in a communal arrangement (Harris, 1993). Even in the United States, the number of long-distance relationships is not insignificant. For example, the Center for the Study of Long Distance Relationships puts the number of married persons who do not share a living space at more than 3,500,000, which is 2.9 percent of all U.S. marrieds. Skype and Google+'s Hangout feature, to name just two, effectively enable users to bridge this long-distance gap by providing low-cost (in many cases, free) means for video-talking as well as, of course, sharing thoughts, photos, and videos.

INTERPERSONAL CHOICE POINT

Maintaining Long-Distance Relationships

You and your romantic partner are going to separate graduate schools—some 2,000 miles apart. You both want your relationship to continue and eventually to be together after completing graduate school. What are some communication options you have for maintaining long-distance relationships?

Couple Types

Based on responses from more than 1,000 couples to questions concerning their degree of sharing, their space needs, their conflicts, and the time they spend together, researchers have identified three basic types of primary relationships: traditionals, independents, and separates (Fitzpatrick, 1983, 1988, 1991; Noller & Fitzpatrick, 1993).

TRADITIONAL Traditional couples share a basic belief system and philosophy of life. They see themselves as a blending of two persons into a single couple rather than as two separate individuals. They're interdependent and believe that each individual's independence must be sacrificed for the good of the relationship. Traditionals believe in mutual sharing and do little separately. This couple holds to the traditional gender roles, and there are seldom any role conflicts. There are few power struggles and few conflicts in general because each person knows and adheres to a specified role within the relationship. In their communications, traditionals are highly responsive to each other. Traditionals lean toward each other, smile, talk a lot, interrupt each other, and finish each other's sentences.

INDEPENDENT COUPLES Independent couples stress their individuality. The relationship is important, but never more important than each person's individual identity. Although independents spend a great deal of time together, they don't ritualize it, for example, with schedules. Each individual spends time with outside friends. Independents see themselves as relatively androgynous—as individuals who combine the traditionally feminine and the traditionally masculine roles and qualities. The communication between independents is responsive. They engage in conflict openly and without fear. Their disclosures are quite extensive and include high-risk and negative disclosures that are typically absent among traditionals.

SEPARATE COUPLES Separate couples live together but view their relationship more as a matter of convenience than a result of their mutual love or closeness. They seem to have little desire to be together and, in fact, usually are together only at ritual functions, such as mealtime or holiday get-togethers. It's important to separates that each has his or her own physical as well as psychological space. Separates share little; each seems to prefer to go his or her own way. Separates hold relatively traditional values and beliefs about gender roles, and each person tries to follow the behaviors normally assigned to each role. What best characterizes this type, however, is that each person sees himself or herself as a separate individual and not as a part of a "we."

INTERPERSONAL CHOICE POINT

Couple Types

Your current relationship—which is a good one for the most part—is becoming too "separate" for your liking. You'd like it to be more "traditional." What are some of your options for changing your couple type? What would you do or say to begin this transformation?

Family Types

Families can be classified in any number of ways, for example, according to the number of people in the family, their affectional orientation, the presence or absence of children or of extended family members. In a communication-oriented typology families are looked at in terms of conformity and conversation (Arnold, 2008; Caughlin, Koerner, Schrodt, & Fitzpatrick, 2011; Galvin, Bylund, & Brommel, 2012; Koerner & Fitzpatrick, 1997, 2004).

Conformity-orientation refers to the degree to which family members express similar or dissimilar attitudes, values, and beliefs. So, we can speak of high-conformity families as those who express highly similar attitudes, beliefs, and values and try to avoid conflict and low-conformity families as those whose members express highly divergent attitudes, beliefs, and values and may frequently engage in conflict interactions. As you can appreciate, families high in conformity are likely to be harmonious with children who are expected to obey their parents, largely without question. Families low in conformity are likely to be less harmonious with children who are given greater freedom to say or do as they wish.

Watch the **Video** "Saga of Susan and Juan" at **MyCommunicationLab**

Conversation-orientation refers to the degree to which family members can speak their mind. A family high on conversation orientation encourages members to discuss a variety of issues and the voicing of members' opinions. A family low on conversation orientation discourages discussion and the voicing of opinions.

With these two dimensions in mind, we can identify four types of families:

- *Consensual families:* High in conversation and high in conformity. These families encourage open communication and agreement.
- *Protective families:* High in conformity and low in conversation. These families stress agreement and strive to avoid conflict but with little communication.
- *Pluralistic families:* Low in conformity and high in conversation. These family members are encouraged to express different attitudes and points of view and to engage in open communication while being supportive of each other.
- *Laissez-faire families:* Low in confirmation and low in conversation. These families avoid interaction and communication and encourage privacy and a "do what you want" attitude.

These family types are simply descriptions and are not meant to be evaluative; no assumption is made that one family type is better or more productive than another. What works for some people will not work for others.

Families, Culture, Gender, and Technology

As with friendship and love, families also vary from one culture to another, are viewed differently by men and women, and are influenced by technology.

Culture and Families U.S. researchers study—and textbook authors write about—how relationships dissolve and how to survive relationship breakups. It's assumed that you have the right to exit an undesirable relationship. But in some cultures, you cannot simply dissolve a relationship once it's formed or once there are children. In the practice of Roman Catholicism, once people are validly married, they're always married and cannot dissolve that relationship. More important in such cultures may be such issues as "How do you maintain a relationship that has problems?" "What can you do to survive in this unpleasant relationship?" or "How can you repair a troubled relationship?" (Moghaddam, Taylor, & Wright, 1993).

Further, your culture will influence the difficulty that you go through when relationships do break up. For example, married persons whose religion forbids divorce and remarriage will experience religious disapproval and condemnation as well as the same economic and social difficulties everyone else goes through. In the United States, child custody almost invariably goes to the woman, and this presents added emotional burdens for the man. In Iran, child custody goes to the man, which presents added emotional burdens for the woman.

Gender and Families In the United States, both men and women can initiate relationships, and both can dissolve them. Both men and women are expected to derive satisfaction from their interpersonal relationships, and when that satisfaction isn't present, either person may seek to exit the relationship. In Iran, on the other hand, only the man has the right to dissolve a marriage without giving reasons.

Gay and lesbian families are accepted in some cultures and condemned in others. In the United States, some states allow same sex couples to legally marry. In other states, "domestic partnerships" may be registered, and these grant gay men, lesbians, and (in some cases) unmarried heterosexuals rights that were formerly reserved only for married couples, such as health insurance benefits and the right to make decisions when one member is incapacitated. In Belgium, the Netherlands, Spain, South Africa, and Canada, same-sex couples can marry; in Norway, Sweden, and Denmark, same-sex relationship partners have the same rights as married partners. And, as mentioned in our discussion of heterosexism in Chapter 5, in many countries same-sex couples would be considered criminals and could face severe punishment—in some cultures, even death.

TECHNOLOGY AND FAMILIES You know from your own family interactions that technology has greatly changed communication among family members. Cell phones enable parents and children to keep in close touch in case of emergencies or just to chat. College students today stay in closer touch with their parents, in part because of the cell phone but also through e-mail, instant messaging, Facebook, and Twitter. And you can "hang out" (on Google+, for example) with family members and with one click change from text to audio and video interaction.

On the other hand, some people—in some cases parents, in most cases children—become so absorbed with their online community that they have little time for their biological family members. In some cases, as in South Korea, Internet use seems to be contributing further to the already significant generational conflict between children and parents (Rhee & Kim, 2004). Similarly, a study on young people (ages 10 to 17) in the United States found that for both girls and boys, those who formed close online relationships were more likely to have low levels of communication with their parents and to be more "highly troubled" than those who didn't form such close online relationships (Wolak, Mitchell, & Finkelhor, 2003).

Can you define *family* and the types of couples and families and explain the roles of culture, gender, and technology in family interactions?

Blog Post

Relationship and Work Esteem

For a brief discussion of how the media *might* influence self-esteem, see "Relationship and Work Esteem" at tcbdevito.blogspot.com. Have the media influenced your image of yourself?

WORKPLACE RELATIONSHIPS

The workplace is a context in which all forms of communication take place and, not surprisingly, all kinds of relationships may be seen. This context is especially influenced by culture—both by the wider culture and by the particular culture of a given workplace. Here we look at three kinds of work relationships (mentoring, networking, and romance) and then at the interpersonal communication skills particularly appropriate to the workplace and the role of politeness on the job.

Mentoring

In a mentoring relationship, an experienced individual (mentor) helps to train a less-experienced person who is sometimes referred to as a mentee or, more often, a protégé (Ragins & Kram, 2007). An accomplished teacher, for example, might mentor a newly arrived or novice teacher. The mentor shows the new person through the "ropes," teaches the strategies and techniques for success, and otherwise communicates his or her knowledge and experience to the newcomer.

Not surprisingly, mentoring is frequently conducted online. One great advantage of e-mentoring is the flexibility it allows for communication. E-mail messages, for example, can be sent and received at times that are convenient for the individuals involved (Stewart, 2006). Further, because the individuals may be separated geographically, it's possible to have mentor–protégé relationships with people in foreign countries and in widely differing cultures, relationships that would be impossible

VIEWPOINTS Being liked at work

Among the suggestions offered by organization theorists for being liked at work are: looking and dressing the part and being positive, culturally sensitive, respectful and friendly, polite, and interested. What other qualities would make you like a workplace colleague?

without online communication. Still another advantage is that persons with disabilities (mentor or protégé), who cannot easily travel, can still enjoy and profit from e-mentoring relationships (Burgstahler, 2007).

Mentoring usually involves a one-on-one relationship between an expert and a novice—a relationship that is supportive and trusting. There's a mutual and open sharing of information and thoughts about the job. The relationship enables the novice to try out new skills under the guidance of an expert, to ask questions, and to obtain the feedback so necessary in learning complex skills.

At the same time that a mentor helps a novice, the mentor benefits from clarifying his or her thoughts, from seeing the job from the perspective of a newcomer, and from considering and formulating answers to a variety of questions. Much the way a teacher learns from teaching and from his or her students, a mentor learns from mentoring and from his or her protégés.

Networking

Networking is more than a technique for securing a job. It is a broad process of enlisting the aid of other people to help you solve a problem or to offer insights that bear on your problem—for example, on how to publish your manuscript, where to go for low-cost auto insurance, how to find an apartment, or how to empty your cache (Heenehan, 1997). Here are a few principles for effective networking, which have special application to the workplace but which you'll find generally useful. Serious networking would include social media networking sites such as LinkedIn or Plaxo. They offer opportunities for networking simply not available offline.

Start your networking with people you already know. You'll probably discover that you know a great number of people with specialized knowledge who can be of assistance (Rector & Neiva, 1996). You can also network with people who know the people you know. Thus, you may contact a friend's friend to find out if the firm where he or she works is hiring. Or you may contact people with whom you have no connection. Perhaps you've read something the person wrote or heard the person's name raised in connection with an area in which you're interested and you want to get more information. With e-mail addresses so readily available, it's now quite common to e-mail individuals who have particular expertise and ask your questions. Newsgroups and chat rooms are other obvious networking avenues.

Try to establish relationships that are mutually beneficial. If you can provide others with helpful information, it's more likely that they'll provide helpful information for you. In this way, you establish a mutually satisfying and productive network.

Be proactive; initiate contacts rather than waiting for them to come to you. If you're also willing to help others, there's nothing wrong in asking these same people to help you. If you're respectful of your contacts' time and expertise, it's likely that they will respond favorably to your networking attempts. Following up your requests with thank-you notes—the polite thing to do—will help you establish networks that can be ongoing relationships.

INTERPERSONAL CHOICE POINT

Networking

You want to establish a small mail-order business selling framed prints; you plan to buy the frames and prints separately and inexpensively at yard sales, restore them, and sell them. What types of network connections might be appropriate in this situation? How would you go about the actual networking?

Blog Post

Communication on the Job

For additional suggestions for on-the-job communication, for example, getting a promotion, see "Communication on the Job" at tcbdevito.blogspot.com. Any other suggestions?

Romantic Relationships at Work

Unlike television depictions, in which workers are always best friends who would do anything for one another and in which the characters move in and out of office romances with little difficulty—at least with no difficulty that can't be resolved in 24 minutes—real-life office romance can be complicated.

Opinions vary widely concerning workplace romances. Some organizations, on the assumption that romantic relationships are basically detrimental to the success of the workplace, have explicit rules prohibiting romantic involvements. In some organizations, members can be fired for such relationships. In other organizations, the prohibitions are unwritten and informal but nevertheless clearly in opposition to office romances. Yet in some other organizations, the taboos against office romance are lessening, with a variety of business professionals supporting such relationships—or at least recognizing that such relationships are inevitable.

On the positive side, the work environment seems a perfect place to meet a potential romantic partner. After all, by virtue of the fact that you're working in the same office, probably you both are interested in the same field, have similar training and ambitions, and will spend considerable time together—all factors that foster the development of a successful interpersonal relationship. Also, given that Americans are marrying later in life, they are less likely to meet prospective partners in school, so work seems the logical alternative.

However, even when the relationship is good for the two individuals, it may not be good for others. Workplace romantic relationships may cause problems for management when, for example, a promotion is to be made or relocation decisions are necessary. Can you legitimately ask one lover to move to Boston and the other to move to San Francisco? Will it prove difficult for management to promote one lover who then becomes the supervisor of the other? When the romance goes bad or when it's one-sided, there are even more disadvantages. Other workers may feel they have to take sides, being supportive of one partner and critical of the other. This can easily cause friction throughout the organization.

Organizations generally advise workers not to romance their colleagues. Friendships, on the other hand, are encouraged by setting up sports teams, dinners, and lounge and exercise areas. In fact, research finds that office friendships increase employees' job satisfaction and commitment to the organization and decrease turnover (Morrison, 2004). And friendships often serve as the basis for mentoring and networking.

Blog Post

Romance in the Workplace

For another perspective on office romance, see "Romance in the Workplace" at tcbdevito.blogspot.com. What are your feelings about office romance?

INTERPERSONAL CHOICE POINT

Intern in Love

You're a young intern, but you're convinced that your supervisor is romantically interested in you, and the feeling is mutual. What are some of your choices in dealing with this?

Politeness at Work

Politeness at work is important from your initial interview at a college job fair through the face-to-face interview to your first day on the job, and, of course, to your progression up the organizational ladder. A search of Google for "politeness + business" recently yielded more than 1,000,000 sites. Politeness on the job follows the same general rules for effective interpersonal interaction stressed throughout this text. For example, be positive, be expressive, listen carefully, and so on. There are, however, certain rules for polite interaction that take on special importance in the workplace. To complicate matters just a bit, each organization—much like each culture—will have somewhat different rules for what is considered polite. Nevertheless, here are a few general suggestions for politeness on the job, which seem near universal.

Watch the Video "Power Moment" at **MyCommunicationLab**

- **Be respectful of a colleague's time.** Don't copy those who don't need to be copied, don't tag people just for the sake of tagging, be brief and organized, respond to requests as soon as possible, and, when not possible, alert the other person that, for example, "the figures will be sent as soon as they arrive, probably by the end of the day."
- **Be respectful of a person's territory.** Don't invade another's office or desk space; don't overstay your welcome. Treat another's work space as someone's private territory into which you must be invited.
- **Follow the rules for effective electronic communication.** Discover and follow the rules governing the use of e-mails, Internet game playing, cell phones, social networking, and instant messaging.
- **Discard your Facebook grammar.** Abbreviations, acronyms, and smileys—so common in social media—are best avoided here. These may be seen as not showing sufficient respect or seriousness of purpose.

SKILL BUILDING EXERCISE

Describing Television Relationships

Watch a television sitcom or drama that focuses on one of the four major kinds of relationships discussed in this chapter (friendship, love, family, and workplace relationships), and respond to the following questions:

1. How are the relationships defined? What specific verbal or nonverbal behaviors cue you into the kind of relationship existing between or among the characters?
2. What types of attraction exist between or among the characters?
3. How would you describe the relationship in terms of social exchange and equity theories?
4. Can you identify any example of relationship dialectics operating here?
5. What rules do the relationship partners follow? What rules do they violate?

Television is popular, in part, because it both reflects and exaggerates real life. Seeing the concepts of interpersonal relationships as they exist on television is a useful first step to seeing the concepts in operation in our own relationships.

- **Use the appropriate medium for sending messages.** Generally, the rule is to respond in kind—for example, if a question is texted to you, text back; if in e-mail, answer it in e-mail.
- **Avoid touching except in shaking hands.** Touching is often interpreted as a sexual overture, so it's best avoided on the job. Touching may also imply a familiarity that the other person may not welcome. Your best bet is to avoid initiating touching.
- **Treat everyone politely,** even the newest intern, as if that person will one day be your boss. Follow the organization's rules of politeness, for example, in answering phones, addressing management, dress, lateness, and desk materials.

Can you explain the nature of work relationships (mentoring, networking, and the issues involved in office romances and politeness)?

ONLINE-ONLY RELATIONSHIPS

In addition to the friendships, romantic, family, and workplace relationships—which will probably involve both face-to-face and online interactions—there are another group of what might be called "online-only" relationships. These are the relationships that exist between a tweeter and a follower, a blogger and a reader, a friend or contact on Facebook or LinkedIn, for example. The suggestions for more effective relationships are the same as the suggestions for more effective communication. In all of these relationships, it is dialogue (rather than monologue) that is emphasized. In fact, the defining characteristic of Web 2.0 is to move the online experience from monologue (for example, reading newspapers online) to dialogue, where commenting/reviewing/liking/+1ing) are essential parts of the communication experience.

Tweeting

Unlike other social network sites, people can follow you on Twitter whether you like it or not. Assuming that you want some kind of relationships between yourself and those who follow you, consider these suggestions.

- Leave room for retweets (if you want retweets). Keep your tweet to 120 characters.
- Avoid "fast following" tools. These will likely create problems for you.
- Tweet items of interest to yourself, but also keep in mind your readers.

- Treat criticism as the start of a dialogue rather than a personal attack.
- Tweet in moderation. Not everything that happens deserves a tweet.
- Tweet positively; avoid angry tweets.
- Create a complete profile, revealing what you want and keeping hidden what you don't want revealed.
- Limit promotional materials; Twitter is personal.
- Retweet if you wish to be retweeted.

Blogging

Although many people use blogs as a monologue, their great value is in creating dialogue. An effective blog post provides information with a personal slant for a specific audience that elicits discussion. Here are a few suggestions for making the blog a more effective interaction.

- Offer syndication. RSS feeds will greatly help in spreading the word.
- Be both informational and personal; blog posts are more personal in nature than are articles or websites, which are more purely informational.
- Be consistent in style and format. It will help brand your blog as unique—not unlike the way McDonald's presents consistent food; readers will know what to expect.
- Build your blog and your posts around a theme. Posts unrelated to the theme are generally perceived as noise and are likely to lose you readers.
- Reply to comments. Dialogue.
- Track statistics so you can get insight into the posts that are read often and those that aren't.
- Create attractive titles and relevant identifying labels. Make it as easy as possible for others to retrieve your materials.

Social/Workplace Networking

Perhaps the social media network that comes first to mind is Facebook, by far largest of the social networking sites. But Google+ and MySpace serve similar purposes as do numerous others. LinkedIn and Plaxo, on the other hand, serve mainly business purposes, for example, getting a job or promotion, finding likely candidates for a job, networking, or mentoring. Despite these differences, some similar suggestions govern effective relationships and communication in these types of sites.

- Do not post photos that will reflect on you negatively.
- Be positive about your current position. Complaining about your job online for all to see is likely to make management less positive toward you.
- Avoid revealing any negative work habits or discussing inappropriate workplace behavior.
- Use the friends list or the Google+ circles to distinguish the people you want to see certain information and those you wouldn't.
- Give your social network profile even more attention than you give to dressing up for a long-anticipated face-to-face date. After all, a lot more people are going to see your online profile than the way you dressed for a date.
- Keep your posts (at least on Facebook and Google+) personal and informational. Avoid promoting any commercial enterprise.
- Poke and tag in moderation. Learn first the norms of the group with which you're communicating.
- Avoid asking to be friends with anyone you think may have difficulty with your seeing their more personal side.

Can you define *online-only relationships?* Can you use the suggestions offered here to communicate more effectively on social network sites?

INTERPERSONAL CHOICE POINT

Friending

You want to ask your instructor/advisor to be your friend on Facebook, but you don't want to embarrass your instructor who may not want to bridge the professional teacher–student relationship. What are some of your options for dealing with this?

RELATIONSHIP THEORIES

Numerous theories attempt to explain the hows and whys of interpersonal relationships. Let's take a look at several of the most interesting approaches. As you'll see when you read the following discussions, each theory offers considerable insight into relationships, but none provides a complete explanation.

Attraction Theory

Attraction theory holds that people develop relationships on the basis of such factors as physical appearance and personality, proximity, similarity, socioeconomic and educational status, and the perception of reciprocity of liking. This theory tries to answer the question of what draws one person to another, what makes a person like another person. To explore your own theory of attraction, take the accompanying self-test.

PHYSICAL APPEARANCE AND PERSONALITY Not surprisingly, you probably prefer physically attractive to physically unattractive people, and you probably like people who possess a pleasant rather than an unpleasant personality. You're more likely to find those who are culturally similar as more attractive than those who are culturally different (Pornpitakpan, 2003). You're also more likely to help someone who is similar in race, attitude, and general appearance. Even the same first name is significant. For example, when an e-mail asking recipients to fill out surveys of their food habits identified the sender as someone with the same name as the recipient, there was a greater willingness to comply with the request (Gueguen, 2003).

PROXIMITY Generally, we find people who live or work close to us more attractive than those who are less physically close. Repeated interaction—if the initial interaction is

TEST YOURSELF

What Is Attractive to You?

For each of the following characteristics, indicate how important each one is to you in a potential (or actual) romantic/life partner. Use the following scale:
5 = very important; I wouldn't consider a long-term relationship with someone who didn't possess this characteristic
4 = important
3 = neither important nor unimportant
2 = unimportant
1 = very unimportant; I wouldn't even think about this characteristic.

____ 1. Facial appearance
____ 2. General body structure (weight, height, shape)
____ 3. Grooming and general cleanliness
____ 4. Appropriate financial resources
____ 5. Intelligence
____ 6. Similarity in religious beliefs
____ 7. Sense of humor
____ 8. Positive toward me
____ 9. Optimistic toward life in general
____10. Honest/ethical
____11. Ambitious
____12. Communicative
____13. Similarity in cultural backgrounds including race and nationality
____14. Available
____15. Sexual compatibility

How Did You Do? There are no correct or incorrect answers and people are likely to respond to such characteristics very differently. This self-test was designed to stimulate you to think in specific terms about the characteristics of another person that are important to you. Those given here are often mentioned in research and theory as being significant in evaluating a potential life partner.

What Will You Do? Consider the importance of these characteristics to your own relationship happiness and well-being. At the same time, consider the importance of these characteristics to your potential partner. Consider, too, other characteristics that you consider important. Another way to use this self-test is to review each of the characteristics and specify more concretely what each of them means to you. For example, how attractive must a person be for you to be attracted to him or her? What constitutes "appropriate financial resources"? How ambitious would you want your partner to be?

positive—will generally lead to increased attraction. Very similar to proximity's focus on frequency of interaction is the frequency of communication. Here the same relationship is found; the more people communicate with each other, the more attractive they find each other (Reis, Maniaci, Caprariello, Eastwick, & Finkel, 2011).

Similarity Although there are exceptions, you're probably attracted to your own mirror image—to people who are similar to you in nationality, race, ability, physical characteristics, intelligence, and so on. What's more, all cultures seem to be similar in being attracted to people of similar attitudes (Hatfield & Rapson, 1992). The alternative explanation—that "opposites attract"—has received much less research support; similarity clearly wins out over differences.

Socioeconomic and Educational Status Popular belief holds that among heterosexual men and women, men are more interested in a woman's physical attributes than in her socioeconomic status. And, indeed, research shows that women flirt on the Internet by stressing their physical attributes whereas men stress their socioeconomic status (Whitty, 2003). Men report greater likelihood of a romantic relationship with a woman lower in socioeconomic status than they are. Further, men find women with a higher educational level (which is often responsible for the higher socioeconomic status) less likable and less faithful and as a result see less likelihood of a romantic relationship with such women (Greitemeyer, 2007).

Reciprocity of Liking It will come as no surprise that research supports what you already know from your own experience: You tend to be attracted to people you think are attracted to you. You come to like those who you think like you. You initiate potential friendships and romantic relationships with people who you think like you, certainly not with those you think dislike you. Group members who are told that certain other members like them will later express greater liking for these members than for others. Public speakers are advised to compliment the audience and express liking for them largely on the theory that this liking will be reciprocated. There is even evidence to show that people like "likers"—people who like others generally—more than they like people who don't express such liking (Eastwick & Finkel, 2009).

INTERPERSONAL CHOICE POINT

Estimating Interest

You've become interested in a friend of a friend on Facebook, and you want to ask this person on a date, but first you'd like to estimate the person's interest in you. You don't want a rejection. What are some of the things you can do to estimate your prospective date's interest in you?

Social Exchange Theory

Social exchange theory tries to answer the question of why some relationships develop and last and others don't and is based on an economic model of profits and losses. You seek to develop the relationships (friendship and romantic) that will give you the greatest profit—relationships in which the rewards are greater than the costs. The preferred relationships, according to this theory, are those that are most profitable and thus give you the greatest rewards with the least costs (Chadwick-Jones, 1976; Gergen, Greenberg, & Willis, 1980; Thibaut & Kelley, 1959). The theory begins with the following equation:

Profits = Rewards − Costs

Rewards are anything that you want, that you enjoy, and that you'd be willing to incur costs to obtain. For example, to acquire the reward of financial gain, you might have to work rather than play; to acquire more followers on

Jack Ziegler/The New Yorker Collection/www.cartoonbank.com

ETHICAL MESSAGES

Relationship Ethics

A starting place for considering the ethics of interpersonal relationships—the ethical issues and guidelines that operate within a friendship, romantic, family, or workplace relationship—can be identified with the acronym ETHICS—empathy (Cheney & Tompkins, 1987), talk rather than force, honesty (Krebs, 1989), interaction management, confidentiality, and supportiveness (Johannesen, 2001). As you read these, consider what other qualities you feel should be a part of relationship ethics.

- Empathy: People in relationships have an ethical obligation to try to understand what other individuals are feeling as well as thinking from those individuals' points of view.
- Talk: Decisions in a relationship should be arrived at by talk rather than by force—by persuasion, not coercion.
- Honesty: Relationship communication should be honest and truthful.
- Interaction management: Relationship communication should be satisfying and comfortable and is the responsibility of both individuals.
- Confidentiality: People have a right to expect that what they say in confidence will not be revealed to others.
- Supportiveness: A supportive and cooperative climate should characterize the interpersonal interactions of people in relationships.

Ethical Choice Point

A neighbor, with whom you're generally friendly, repeatedly wants you to listen to everything she did during the day—a kind of "twitter" (but much longer) monologue. You just don't want to do this anymore. What is your ethical obligation in this case—to your neighbor as well as to yourself?

Twitter, you might have to put more effort into your tweets. Love, affection, status, money, gifts, security, social acceptance, companionship, friendship, and intimacy are just a few examples of rewards for which you would be willing to work (that is, incur costs). Costs are those things that you normally try to avoid—things you consider unpleasant or difficult. Working overtime, washing dishes and ironing clothes, viewing the 200 photographs your grandmother posted on Facebook, or watching a television show that your partner enjoys but you find boring might all be considered costs.

Equity Theory

Equity theory tries to answer the same question as social exchange theory (why some relationships develop while others don't) and uses the concepts of social exchange. But it goes a step further. Equity theory claims that you develop and maintain relationships in which your ratio of rewards to costs is approximately equal to your partner's (Messick & Cook, 1983; Walster, Walster, & Berscheid, 1978). In an equitable relationship, both partners should derive rewards that are proportional to their costs. For example, if you work harder for the relationship than your partner does, then equity demands that you should get greater rewards than your partner. If you both work equally hard for the relationship, then equity demands that each of you should get approximately equal rewards. Online friends likewise expect equity, for example, that each friend contributes to the conversation, to poke back, to contribute a similar amount of likes and +1s. In the workplace, you're expected to help others network in response to the networking help others gave you.

Much research finds that people in Western societies want equity and feel that relationships should be characterized by equity (Ueleke et al., 1983). As you can appreciate, however, this theory is decidedly a product of Western culture. For example, in Europe and the United States, each person is paid according to his or her contributions; the more you contribute to an organization—or to a relationship—the more rewards you should get out of it. In other cultures, especially collectivist cultures, a principle of equality or need might operate. According to the

INTERPERSONAL CHOICE POINT

Complaining

Your partner complains constantly; no matter what the situation, your partner has a complaint about it. It's becoming painful to listen to this, and you want to stop it. What are some of the things you might do to help lessen the complaining? Alternatively, what might you be doing to encourage the complaints, and therefore what might you stop doing?

principle of equality, each person would get equal rewards regardless of his or her individual contribution. According to the principle of need, each person would get rewards according to his or her need (Moghaddam et al., 1993).

Relationship Dialectics Theory

Watch the **Video** "Give Me a Break" at **MyCommunicationLab**

Relationship dialectics theory tries to answer the question of the conflicting motives that people in relationships often experience. The theory argues that people in a relationship experience dynamic tensions between at least three pairs of opposing motives or desires (Baxter, 2004; Baxter & Braithwaite, 2007; Baxter & Simon, 1993; Rawlins, 1989, 1992).

- *Closedness and openness.* This tension focuses on the desire to be in a closed, exclusive relationship and also the desire to be in a relationship that is open to different people. Not surprisingly, this tension manifests itself most during the early stages of relationship development. You like the exclusiveness of your pairing, and yet you want also to relate to a larger group.
- *Autonomy and connection.* This tension seems to occur more often as the relationship progresses and involves the desire to remain an autonomous, independent individual but also the desire to connect intimately to another person and to a relationship. You want to be close and connected with another person, but you also want to be independent (Sahlstein, 2004).
- *Novelty and predictability.* This tension centers on the competing desire for newness, different experiences, and adventure on the one hand and the desire for sameness, stability, and predictability on the other. You're comfortable with being able to predict what will happen, and yet you also want newness, difference, and novelty.

INTERPERSONAL CHOICE POINT

Presenting the Self

Consider the tensions between presenting yourself as a professional, motivated, reliable worker on social networking sites (for any employer who might look at your online profile) and presenting yourself as fun loving, friendly, and popular (to your peers, for example). In what specific ways might you accomplish both aims?

Each individual in a relationship may experience a somewhat different set of desires. For example, one person may want exclusivity above all, whereas that person's partner may want greater openness. There seem to be three main ways that you can deal with these tensions.

First, you can simply *accept the imbalance* as part of dating or as part of a committed relationship. You may even redefine it as a benefit and tell yourself something like: "I had been spending too much time at work. It's probably better that I come home earlier and don't work weekends"—accepting the closeness and giving up the autonomy.

Second, you can simply *exit the relationship*. For example, if the loss of autonomy is so great that you can't live with it, then you may choose to simply end the relationship and achieve your desired autonomy.

A third alternative is to *rebalance your life*. For example, if you find the primary relationship excessively predictable, you may seek to satisfy the need for novelty elsewhere, perhaps with a vacation to exotic places, perhaps with a different partner. You can also rebalance by negotiating with your partner, for example, taking separate vacations or each going out separately with old friends once or twice a week.

As you can appreciate, meeting your partner's needs—while also meeting your own needs—is one of the major relationship challenges you'll face. Knowing and empathizing with these tensions and discussing them seem a useful (even necessary) step for relationship maintenance and satisfaction.

Relationship Rules Theory

Explore the **Exercise** "Friendship Behaviors" at **MyCommunicationLab**

The general assumption of **relationship rules theory** is that relationships—friendship and love, in particular—are held together by adherence to certain rules. When those rules are broken, the relationship may deteriorate and even dissolve.

FRIENDSHIP RULES When friendship rules are followed, the friendship is strong and mutually satisfying. When these rules are broken, the friendship suffers and may die (Argyle,

1986; Argyle & Henderson, 1984). The rules for keeping a friendship include such behaviors as standing up for your friend in his or her absence, sharing information and feelings about successes, demonstrating emotional support for a friend, trusting and offering to help a friend in need, and trying to make a friend happy when you're together. As you can see from this list, these rules operate in face-to-face and in online relationships. On social media sites, for example, a friend is expected to stand up for a friend by supporting causes, liking, including the other in "hangouts," and +1ing. Similarly, a friend is expected to share information online and respond to the posts and comments of friends. On the other hand, a friendship is likely to be in trouble when one or both friends are intolerant of the other's friends, discuss confidences with third parties, fail to demonstrate positive support, nag, or fail to trust or confide in the other.

Romantic Rules Romantic rules vary considerably from one culture to another. For example, the different attitudes toward permissiveness and sexual relations with which Chinese and American college students view dating influence the romantic rules each group will establish and live by (Tang & Zuo, 2000). One research study identified eight major romantic rules that will provide a clear idea of the rules approach to romantic relationships (Baxter, 1986). When these rules are followed, the relationship stays together; when they are broken, the relationship is heading to deterioration:

- acknowledge each other's individual identities and lives beyond the relationship.
- express similar attitudes, beliefs, values, and interests.
- enhance each other's self-worth and self-esteem.
- be open, genuine, and authentic with each other.
- remain loyal and faithful to each other.
- have substantial shared time together.
- reap rewards commensurate with their investments relative to the other party.
- experience a mysterious and inexplicable "magic" in each other's presence.

VIEWPOINTS The family

If you looked at the family from an evolutionary–Darwinian point of view, one research watcher notes, you'd have to conclude that families are "inherently unstable" and that it's necessity, not choice, that keeps them together. If they had better opportunities elsewhere, many family members would leave immediately (Goleman, 1995b). What do you see as the greatest advantages of family? What do you see as the greatest disadvantages?

Family Rules Family rules concern three main interpersonal communication issues (Galvin, Bylund, & Brommel, 2012; Satir, 1983):

- What can you talk about? Can you talk about the family finances? Grandpa's drinking? Your sister's lifestyle?
- How can you talk about something? Can you joke about your brother's disability? Can you address directly questions of family history or family skeletons?
- To whom can you talk? Can you talk openly to extended family members such as cousins and aunts and uncles? Can you talk to close neighbors about family health issues?

All families teach rules for communication. Some of these are explicit, such as "Never contradict the family in front of outsiders" or "Never talk finances with outsiders." Other rules are unspoken; you deduce them as you learn the communication style of your family. For example, if financial issues are always discussed in secret and in hushed tones, then you rather logically infer that you shouldn't tell other more distant family members or neighbors about family finances.

Not surprisingly, the rules a family develops are greatly influenced by the culture. Although there are many similarities among families throughout the world, there are also differences (Georgas et al., 2001). For example, members of collectivist cultures are more likely to restrict family information from outsiders as a way of protecting the family than are members of individualist cultures. This tendency to protect the family can create serious problems in cases of wife abuse. Many women will not report spousal abuse due to this desire to protect the family image and not let others know that things aren't perfect at home (Dresser, 2005).

Workplace Rules Rules also govern your workplace relationships. These rules are usually a part of the corporate culture that an employee would learn from observing other employees (especially those who move up the hierarchy) as well as from official memos on dress, sexual harassment, and the like. Of course, each organization will have different rules, so it's important to see what rules are operating in any given situation. Among the rules that you might find are:

- work very hard.
- be cooperative in teams; the good of the company comes first.
- don't reveal company policies and plans to workers at competing firms.
- don't form romantic relationships with other workers.
- avoid even the hint of sexual harassment.
- be polite to other workers and especially to customers.

Though each relationship is unique, relationships for many people possess similar characteristics. It is these general patterns that these theories try to explain. Taken together, the theories actually illuminate a great deal about why you develop relationships, the way relationships work, the ways you seek to maintain relationships, and the reasons why some relationships are satisfying and others are not. With an understanding of these aspects of relationships, you'll be in a better position to regulate and manage your own friendship, romantic, and family relationships. Table 10.2 (page 238) compares movement toward and away from intimacy as seen by the various theories.

Blog Post

Politeness as an Interpersonal Relationship Theory

Another theory that might be mentioned here is politeness theory; take a look at "Politeness as an Interpersonal Relationship Theory" at tcbdevito.blogspot.com. What role does politeness play in your relationships?

Can you summarize the nature of the varied theories of interpersonal relationships (attraction, social exchange, equity, relationship dialectics, and rules)? Can you apply the insights from these theories to you own relationships—to better understand them and to improve them?

MESSAGES IN THE MEDIA: WRAP-UP

Television dramas and sitcoms are excellent laboratories for studying the varied types of relationships. Identifying why some work and why others don't is a useful exercise in learning the principles of effective interpersonal interaction.

TABLE 10.2

MOVEMENT AMONG THE STAGES AS PREDICTED BY RELATIONSHIP THEORIES

You move toward intimacy when:	Relationship Stages	You move away from intimacy when:
Attraction increases	Contact	Attraction decreases
Rewards increase, costs decrease, profits increase	Involvement	Rewards decrease, costs increase, profits decrease
Equity prevails; each derives rewards in proportion to the costs paid	Intimacy	Inequities exist and grow greater; one person is under-benefited and one person is over-benefited
Tensions are at acceptable limits	Deterioration	Tensions become too high and unacceptable
Rules are followed	Dissolution	Rules are broken, disregarded

SUMMARY OF CONCEPTS AND SKILLS

Listen to the **Audio Chapter Summary** at **MyCommunicationLab**

Study and **Review** materials for this chapter are at **MyCommunicationLab**

This chapter explored the types of relationships (friendship, love, family, and work relationships) and the theories that try to explain something about how they work.

Friendship Relationships

1. Friendship is an interpersonal relationship between two persons that is mutually productive and characterized by mutual positive regard.

Love Relationships

2. Love—a romantic relationship existing between two people—comes in a variety of forms. Eros, ludus, storge, pragma, mania, and agape are some of the commonly distinguished types of love.

Family Relationships

3. Family relationships are those existing between two or more people who have defined roles, recognize their responsibilities to each other, have a shared history and a prospect of a shared future, and interact according to a shared system of communication rules.

Workplace Relationships

4. Among the important workplace relationships are mentoring, networking, and office romances.
5. Culture and technology both influence relationships in various and important ways. Relationships in one culture are very different from relationships in another culture, and face-to-face relationships are different from online relationships. Amid these differences, there are also similarities.

Online-Only Relationships

6. Online-only relationships include those between tweeter and follower or blogger and reader. Each of these social media has its own rules for promoting more effective communication and relationships.

Relationship Theories

7. Attraction theory holds that you development relationships with those you find physically attractive, similar to you, and in close proximity.

8. Social exchange theory holds that you develop relationships in which you derive profits—that is, in which the rewards are greater than the costs.
9. Equity theory holds that you develop and maintain relationships you find equitable, in which your rewards are in proportion to your costs.
10. Relationship dialectics theory holds that you experience tensions in your relationship between, for example, being autonomous and being a part of a pair.
11. Rules theory holds that we develop and maintain relationships with those who follow important rules and that we dissolve relationships with those who break the rules.

This chapter also considered a variety of skills. As you review these skills, check those you wish to work on.

____ 1. *Friendships.* Establish friendships to help serve such needs as utility, ego support, stimulation, and security. At the same time, seek to serve your friends' similar needs.

____ 2. *Workplace competence.* Be supportive, self-disclose selectively, avoid bringing problems from home into the workplace, learn and follow the rules of the organization, and be positive.

____ 3. *Romantic workplace relationships.* Establish romantic relationships at work with a clear understanding of the potential problems.

____ 4. *Cultural and technology.* Both culture and technology exert influence on all types of relationships, encouraging some and discouraging others, making some easy and some difficult.

____ 5. *Relationship satisfaction.* Relationships are likely to be more satisfying when the rules of the relationships are followed, when there are profits for both people, and when there is fairness or equity.

VOCABULARY QUIZ: The Language of Interpersonal Relationships

Match the terms dealing with interpersonal relationships with their definitions. Record the number of the definition next to the appropriate term.

____ friendship (217)
____ agape (221)
____ equity theory (234)
____ network convergence (219)
____ social exchange theory (233)
____ family (236)
____ relationship dialectics theory (235)
____ networking (228)
____ reciprocity (217)
____ mentoring (227)

1. A relationship characterized by defined roles, recognition of mutual responsibilities, a shared history and future, shared living space, and rules for communicating
2. A theory of relationships based on costs and rewards
3. A type of friendship based on loyalty, self-sacrifice, and equality
4. A systematic process of enlisting the aid of others
5. The sharing of one another's friends
6. A theory that all relationships can be defined by a series of competing opposite motivations or desires
7. A relationship in which an experienced individual helps to train a less-experienced person
8. An interpersonal relationship that is mutually productive and characterized by mutual positive regard
9. A selfless, compassionate love
10. A theory of relationships postulating that people seek to get rewards commensurate with their costs

These ten terms and additional terms used in this chapter can be found in the glossary.

MyCommunicationLab

Visit MyCommunicationLab for a wealth of additional information on interpersonal communication. Flashcards, videos, skill building exercises, sample test questions, and additional exercises, examples, and discussions will help you continue your study of the fundamentals of interpersonal communication, its theory, and its skills.

CHAPTER

11

Interpersonal Conflict Management

MESSAGES IN THE MEDIA

In *Dancing with the Stars* each team is in a kind of conflict with the others—there is one goal and only one team can win. This is a zero-sum game—if one team wins, the others must lose. Interpersonal conflict, the kind we discuss here, is not a zero-sum game; both parties can win and, unfortunately, both can lose. The task of achieving win-win outcomes is the focus of this chapter.

Listen to the **Audio Chapter** at **MyCommunicationLab**

OBJECTIVES *After reading this chapter, you should be able to:*

1. Define *interpersonal conflict* and identify the popular myths about conflict.
2. Explain the six principles describing the nature of interpersonal conflict.
3. Define and illustrate the stages of conflict management and use these in resolving interpersonal conflicts.
4. Define and distinguish between the conflict management strategies of win–lose and win–win approaches, avoiding and fighting actively, defensiveness and supportiveness, face-attacking and face-enhancing, and verbal aggressiveness and argumentativeness and use these strategies constructively.

Among the most important of all your interpersonal interactions are those involving conflict. Interpersonal conflict creates uncertainty, anxiety, and problems for the relationship but also, as you'll soon see, opportunities for improving and strengthening the relationship. Understanding interpersonal conflict and mastering the skills of conflict management—the subject of this final chapter—will prove immensely effective in making your own relationship life more satisfying and more productive.

WHAT IS INTERPERSONAL CONFLICT?

Interpersonal conflict is a special type of conflict, so we need here to define what this type of conflict is and what it isn't.

A Definition of Interpersonal Conflict

You want to go to the movies with your partner. Your partner wants to stay home. Your insisting on going to the movies interferes with your partner's staying home, and your partner's determination to stay home interferes with your going to the movies. Your goals are incompatible; if your goal is achieved, your partner's goal is not. Conversely, if your partner's goal is achieved, your goal is not.

As this example illustrates, **interpersonal conflict** is disagreement between or among interdependent individuals (for example, friends, lovers, family members) who perceive their goals as incompatible (Cahn & Abigail, 2007; Folger, Poole, & Stutman, 2013; Hocker & Wilmot, 2007). More specifically, conflict occurs when people:

- *are interdependent* (they're connected in some significant way); what one person does has an effect on the other person.
- *are mutually aware of incompatible goals*; if one person's goal is achieved, then the other person's goal cannot be achieved. For example, if one person wants to buy a new car and the other person wants to pay down the mortgage, there is conflict. Note that this situation would not pose a conflict if the couple had unlimited resources, in which case, they could both buy the car and pay down the mortgage.
- *perceive each other as interfering* with the attainment of their own goals. For example, you may want to study but your roommate may want to party; the attainment of either goal would interfere with the attainment of the other goal.

One of the implications of this concept of interdependency is that the greater the interdependency (1) the greater the number of issues about which conflict can center and (2) the greater the impact of the conflict on the individuals and on the relationship. Looked at in this way, it's easy to appreciate how important understanding interpersonal conflict and the strategies of effective conflict management are to your relationship life. Figure 11.1 (p. 242) illustrates this relationship between interdependency and the breadth and depth of conflict issues.

VIEWPOINTS Conflict issues
What issues do television characters fight about? Are the issues fought over in situation comedies different from those in dramas?

Myths About Conflict

Many people have problems dealing with **conflict** because they hold false assumptions about what conflict is and what it means. Think about your own assumptions about interpersonal and small group conflict, which were probably

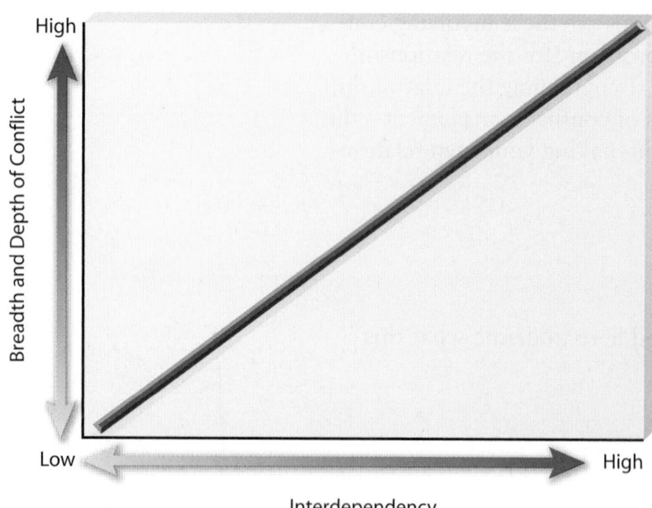

FIGURE 11.1
Conflict and Interdependency
This figure illustrates that as interdependency increases, so do the potential and the importance of conflict. How effectively does the relationship predicted in this figure depict your own interpersonal conflicts?

derived from the communications you witnessed in your family and in your social interactions. For example, do you think the following are true or false?

- Conflict is best avoided. Time will solve the problem; it will all blow over.
- If two people experience relationship conflict, it means their relationship is in trouble.
- Conflict damages an interpersonal relationship.
- Conflict is destructive because it reveals our negative selves—our pettiness, our need to be in control, our unreasonable expectations.
- In any conflict, there has to be a winner and a loser. Because goals are incompatible, someone has to win and someone has to lose.

These are myths and, as we'll see in this chapter, they can interfere with your ability to deal with conflict effectively. Some methods of approaching conflict can resolve difficulties and differences and can actually improve a relationship. Other reactions to conflict can hurt the relationship; they can destroy self-esteem, create bitterness, and foster suspicion. Conflict does not mean that someone has to lose and someone has to win. Both parties can win. Your task, therefore, is not to try to create relationships that will be free of conflict but rather to learn appropriate and productive ways of managing conflict so that neither person can be considered a loser.

Can you define *interpersonal conflict* and identify the popular myths about conflict?

PRINCIPLES OF INTERPERSONAL CONFLICT

Interpersonal conflict is a process that is complex and often difficult to understand. The following principles will help clarify how interpersonal conflict works: (1) Conflict is inevitable—you can't avoid it, (2) conflict can center on content and/or relationship issues, (3) interpersonal conflict can occur in all communication forms, (4) conflict can have positive as well as negative effects, (5) conflict is heavily influenced by gender and culture, and (6) the style of conflict you use will have significant effects on your relationship.

Blog Post
Relationships and Relationship Conflict
See "Relationships and Relationship Conflict" at tcbdevito.blogspot.com for a discussion of the relationship between health and effective conflict management. What other advantages do you see for effective conflict management?

Conflict Is Inevitable

Conflict is a part of every interpersonal relationship, between parents and children, brothers and sisters, friends, lovers, coworkers. One study found that people have approximately seven conflicts per week (Benoit & Benoit, 1990). A more recent poll claims that married couples have 182 conflicts each year (approximately 3.5 conflicts per week), each lasting on average 25 minutes, with another 30 minutes for sulking.

The very fact that people are different, have had different histories, and have different goals will invariably produce differences. If the individuals are interdependent, as shown above, these differences may well lead to conflicts, and, if so, they can focus on a wide variety of issues and be extremely personal. And, of course, some people have greater tolerance for disagreement and consequently are more apt to let things slide and not become emotionally upset or hostile than are those with little tolerance for disagreement (Teven, Richmond, & McCroskey, 1998; Wrench, McCroskey, & Richmond, 2008).

"This isn't really about the beagles, is it."

Paul Noth/The New Yorker Collection/www.cartoonbank.com

Conflict Can Center on Content and Relationship Issues

Using concepts developed in Chapter 1, we can distinguish between content conflict and relationship conflict. Content conflict centers on objects, events, and persons in the world that are usually, though not always, external to the parties involved in the conflict. Content conflicts have to do with the millions of issues that we argue and fight about every day—the merit of a particular movie, what to watch on television, the fairness of the last examination or job promotion, the way to spend our savings.

Relationship conflicts are equally numerous and include clashes between, for example, a younger brother who refuses to obey his older brother, two partners who each want an equal say in making vacation plans, or a mother and daughter who each want to have the final word concerning the daughter's lifestyle. Here the conflicts are concerned not so much with some external object as with the relationships between the individuals—with issues like who is in charge, how equal the members in a family relationship are, or who has the right to set down rules of behavior.

Explore the **Exercise** "Conflict" at **MyCommunicationLab**

Content and relationship dimensions are always easier to separate in a textbook than they are in real life, in which many conflicts contain elements of both. For example, you can probably imagine both content and relationship dimensions in each of the "content" issues mentioned earlier. Yet certain issues seem oriented more toward one dimension than the other. For example, differences on political and social issues are largely content focused, whereas intimacy and power issues are largely relational.

In the workplace, conflicts also center on both content and relationship issues. As you can appreciate, conflict is an especially important issue in the workplace because of its many potential negative effects such as personnel leaving the job (necessitating new recruitment and retraining), low morale, and lessening of the desire to perform at top efficiency. Workplace conflicts, according to one study, center on such issues as these, a clear mix of both content and relationship issues (Psychometrics, 2010):

- personality differences and resulting clashes, 86 percent
- ineffective leadership, 73 percent
- lack of openness, 67 percent
- physical and emotional stress, 64 percent
- differences in values and resulting clashes, 59 percent

INTERPERSONAL CHOICE POINT

Escalating to Relationship Conflict

Your own interpersonal conflicts often start out as content conflicts but quickly degenerate into relationship conflicts, and that's when things get ugly. You want to keep the argument and its eventual resolution focused on the content. What are some of the things you can say to prevent this move to relationship conflict?

Conflict Can Occur in All Communication Forms

In large part, the same conflicts you experience in face-to-face relationships can also arise in online communication. Yet there are a few conflict issues that seem to be unique to online communication, whether in e-mail, in social networking sites such as Facebook or MySpace, or in blog postings. For the most part, online conflict results when people violate the rules of politeness identified throughout this text. For example, sending commercial messages to those who didn't request them often creates conflict, or sending a message to an entire listserv when it's relevant to only one member may annoy members who expect to receive messages relevant to the entire group and not personal exchanges between two people. Sending someone unsolicited mail (spamming or spimming), repeatedly sending the same mail, or posting the same message in lots of newsgroups (especially when the message is irrelevant to the focus of one or more groups) will also create conflict. Putting out purposefully incorrect information or outrageous viewpoints to watch other people correct you or get emotionally upset by your message (trolling) can obviously lead to conflict, though some see it as fun. Other potential causes of online conflict are ill-timed cell phone calls, calling someone at work just to chat, or criticizing someone unfairly or posting an unflattering photo on social network sites.

Conflict Can Be Negative or Positive

Although interpersonal conflict is always stressful, it's important to recognize that it has both negative and positive aspects.

Negative Aspects of Interpersonal Conflict Conflict often leads to increased negative regard for the opponent. One reason for this is that many conflicts involve unfair fighting methods and are focused largely on hurting the other person. When one person hurts the other, increased negative feelings are inevitable; even the strongest relationship has limits.

At times, too, conflict may lead you to close yourself off from the other person. When you hide your true self from an intimate, you prevent meaningful communication from taking place. Because the need for intimacy is so strong, one or both parties may then seek intimacy elsewhere. This often leads to further conflict, mutual hurt, and resentment—qualities that add heavily to the costs carried by the relationship. Meanwhile, rewards may become difficult to exchange. In this situation, the costs increase and the rewards decrease, which often results in relationship deterioration and eventual dissolution.

Positive Aspects of Interpersonal Conflict The major value of interpersonal conflict is that it forces you to examine a problem and work toward a potential solution. If the participants use productive conflict strategies, the relationship may well emerge from the encounter stronger, healthier, and more satisfying than before. And you may emerge stronger, more confident, and better able to stand up for yourself (Bedford, 1996).

Through conflict and its resolution, we also can stop resentment from increasing and let our needs be known. For example, suppose I need lots of attention when I come home from work, but you need to review and get closure on the day's work. If we both can appreciate the legitimacy of these needs, then we can find solutions. Perhaps you can make your important phone call after my attention needs are met, or perhaps I can delay my need for attention until you get closure about work. Or perhaps I can learn to provide for your closure needs and in doing so get my attention needs met. We have a win–win solution; each of us gets our needs met.

Consider, too, that when you try to resolve conflict within an interpersonal relationship, you're saying in effect that the relationship is worth the effort; otherwise, you would walk away from such a conflict. Usually, confronting a conflict indicates commitment and a desire to preserve the relationship.

Conflict Is Influenced by Culture and Gender

As in other areas of interpersonal communication, it helps to view conflict in light of culture and gender. Both exert powerful influences on how people view and resolve conflicts.

Conflict and Culture Culture influences not only the issues that people fight about but also what people consider appropriate and inappropriate in terms of dealing with conflict. Researchers have found, for example, that cohabiting 18-year-olds are more likely to experience conflict with their parents about their living style if they live in the United States than if they live in Sweden, where cohabitation is much more accepted. Similarly, male infidelity is more likely to cause conflict between American spouses than in southern European couples. Students from the United States are more likely to engage in conflict with other U.S. students than with someone from another culture. Chinese students, on the other hand, are more likely to engage in conflict with non-Chinese students than with fellow Chinese (Leung, 1988).

The types of conflicts that arise depend on the cultural orientation of the individuals involved. For example, in collectivist cultures, such as those of Ecuador, Indonesia, and Korea, conflicts are more likely to center on violations of collective or group norms and values, for example, the failure to provide for family members or publicly disagreeing with a superior. Conversely, in individualist cultures, such as those of the United States, Canada, and Western Europe, conflicts are more likely to occur when people violate individual norms, for example, not defending a position in the face of disagreement (Ting-Toomey, 1985).

The cultural norms of organizations also influence the types of conflicts that occur and the ways people may deal with them. Some work environments, for example, would not tolerate employees' expressing disagreement with high-level management; others might welcome it. In individualist cultures, there is greater tolerance for conflict, even when it involves different levels of an organizational hierarchy. In collectivist cultures, there's less tolerance. And, not surprisingly, the culture influences how the conflict will be resolved. For example, managers in the United States (an individualist culture) deal with workplace conflict by seeking to integrate the demands of the different sides; managers in China (a collectivist culture) are more likely to call on higher management to make decisions—or not to resolve the conflict at all (Tinsley & Brett, 2001).

CONFLICT AND GENDER Not surprisingly, research finds significant gender differences in interpersonal conflict. For example, men are more apt to withdraw from a conflict situation than are women. It's been argued that this may be due to the fact that men become more psychologically and physiologically aroused during conflict (and retain this heightened level of arousal much longer) than do women, and so they may try to distance themselves and withdraw from the conflict to prevent further arousal (Goleman, 1995b; Gottman & Carrere, 1994). Another position would argue that men withdraw because the culture has taught men to avoid conflict, and still another would claim that withdrawal is an expression of power.

Women, on the other hand, want to get closer to the conflict; they want to talk about it and resolve it. Even adolescents reveal these differences. In research on boys and girls ages 11 to 17, boys withdrew more than girls (Heasley, Babbitt, & Burbach, 1995; Lindeman, Harakka, & Keltikangas-Jarvinen, 1997). Other research has found that women are more emotional and men are more logical when they argue. Women have been defined as conflict "feelers" and men as conflict "thinkers" (Sorenson, Hawkins, & Sorenson, 1995). Another difference is that women are more apt to reveal their negative feelings than are men (Canary, Cupach, & Messman, 1995; Schaap, Buunk, & Kerkstra, 1988).

It should be mentioned, however, that some research fails to support these stereotypical gender differences in conflict style—the differences that cartoons, situation comedies, and films portray so readily and so clearly. For example, several studies dealing with both college students and men and women in business found no significant differences in the ways men and women engage in conflict (Canary & Hause, 1993; Gottman & Levenson, 1999; Wilkins & Andersen, 1991).

Watch the **Video** "Time Troubles" at **MyCommunicationLab**

INTERPERSONAL CHOICE POINT

Preventing Conflicts in Social Media

In a variety of social media sites, you can disable comments on a post that might be causing conflict, prevent it from being shared, or remove your post entirely. In what ways might these abilities be applied to face-to-face conflict?

Conflict Styles Have Consequences

The way in which you engage in conflict has consequences for the resolution of the conflict and for the relationship between the conflicting parties. Here we consider five basic styles (Blake & Mouton, 1985). As you read through these styles, try to identify your own conflict style as well as the styles of those with whom you have close relationships.

Competing: I Win, You Lose The competitive conflict style involves great concern for your own needs and desires and little for those of others. As long as your needs are met, the conflict has been dealt with successfully (for you). In conflict motivated by competitiveness, you'd be likely to be verbally aggressive and to blame the other person.

This style represents an *I win, you lose* philosophy. As you can tell, this style might be appropriate in a courtroom or at a used-car lot, two settings where one person benefits from the other person's losses. But in interpersonal situations, this philosophy can easily lead to resentment on the part of the person who loses, which can easily cause additional conflicts. Further, the fact that you win and the other person loses probably means that the conflict hasn't really been resolved but only concluded (for now).

Avoiding: I Lose, You Lose Conflict avoiders are relatively unconcerned with their own or with their opponents' needs or desires. They avoid any real communication about the problem, change topics when the problem is brought up, and generally withdraw from the scene both psychologically and physically.

As you can appreciate, the avoiding style does little to resolve any conflicts and may be viewed as an *I lose, you lose* philosophy. Interpersonal problems rarely go away of their own accord; rather, if they exist, they need to be faced and dealt with effectively. Avoidance merely allows the conflict to fester and probably grow, only to resurface in another guise.

Accommodating: I Lose, You Win In accommodating, you sacrifice your own needs for the needs of the other person(s). Your major purpose is to maintain harmony and peace in the relationship or group. This style may help maintain peace and may satisfy the opposition, but it does little to meet your own needs, which are unlikely to go away.

Accommodation represents an *I lose, you win* philosophy. And although this conflict style may make your partner happy (at least on this occasion), it's not likely to prove a lasting resolution to an interpersonal conflict. You'll eventually sense unfairness and inequality and may easily come to resent your partner and perhaps even yourself.

Collaborating: I Win, You Win In collaborating, you address both your own and the other person's needs. This conflict style, often considered the ideal, takes time and a willingness to communicate—and especially to listen to the perspectives and needs of the other person.

Ideally, collaboration enables each person's needs to be met, an *I win, you win* situation. This is obviously the style that, in an ideal world, most people would choose for interpersonal conflict.

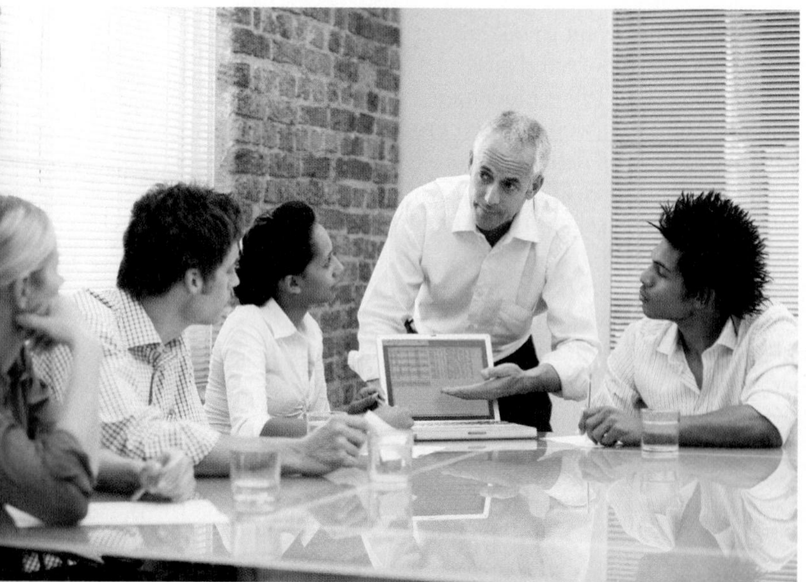

VIEWPOINTS Conflict changes

What changes would you like to see your workplace colleagues make in their own conflict management strategies? What might you do to more effectively regulate your own ways of dealing with conflict on the job?

Compromising: I Win and Lose, You Win and Lose The **compromising** style is in the middle: There's some concern for your own needs and some concern for the other's needs. Compromise is the kind of strategy you might refer to as "meeting each other halfway," "horse trading," or "give and take." This strategy is likely to result in maintaining peace, but there will be a residue of dissatisfaction over the inevitable losses that each side has to endure.

Compromise represents an *I win and lose, you win and lose* philosophy. There are lots of times when you can't both get exactly what you want. You can't both get a new car if the available funds allow for only one. And yet you might each get a better used car than the one you now have. So, each of you might win something, though not everything.

SKILL BUILDING EXERCISE

Generating Win–Win Solutions

To get into the habit of looking for win–win solutions, consider the following conflict situations. For each situation, generate as many win–win solutions as you can—solutions in which both persons win. After you complete your list, explain what you see as the major advantages of win–win solutions.

1. For their vacation, Pat wants to go to the shore and relax by the water; Chris wants to go hiking and camping in the mountains.
2. Pat wants to spend a weekend with Jesse to make sure their relationship is over. Chris doesn't want this.
3. Pat hangs around the house in underwear. Chris really hates this, and they argue about it almost daily.
4. Pat wants to pool their income whereas Chris wants to keep each person's income and savings separate.
5. Pat wants Chris to commit to their relationship and move in together. Chris wants to wait to make sure this is the right thing.

Win–win solutions exist for most conflict situations (though not necessarily all); with a little effort, win–win solutions can be identified for most interpersonal conflicts.

Can you explain the six principles of interpersonal conflict (that it's inevitable, can center on content and relationship issues, occurs in all communication forms, can be positive or negative, is heavily influenced by both culture and gender, and that conflict styles have consequences)?

CONFLICT MANAGEMENT STAGES

The model in Figure 11.2 (p. 248) provides guidance for dealing with conflicts effectively. This five-stage model is based on the problem-solving technique first introduced by John Dewey (1910) and still used by contemporary theorists. The assumption made here is that interpersonal conflict is essentially a problem that needs to be solved. This model should not be taken as suggesting that there is only one path to conflict resolution, however. It is a general way of envisioning the process that should help you better understand how conflict works and how you can work toward resolving the conflict.

Before getting to the five stages of conflict, consider a few "before the conflict" suggestions.

- *Try to fight in private.* You may not be willing to be totally honest when third parties are present; you may feel you have to save face and therefore must win the fight at all costs.
- *Make sure you're both relatively free* of other problems and ready to deal with the conflict at hand.
- *Fight about problems that can be solved.* Fighting about past behaviors or about family members or situations over which you have no control solves nothing; in fact, it's more likely to create additional difficulties.

INTERPERSONAL CHOICE POINT

Confronting a Problem

Your next-door neighbor never puts out the garbage in time for pickup. As a result, the garbage—often broken into by stray animals—remains until the next pickup. You're fed up with the rodents the garbage draws, the smell, and the horrible appearance. What are some of the things you can say to get your neighbor to be more responsive and yet not hate you in the process? What channel would you use?

Define the Conflict

At the first stage, you define the conflict. Here are several techniques to help you accomplish this essential task.

- *Define both content and relationship issues.* Define the obvious content issues (who should do the dishes, who should take the kids to school) as well as the underlying relationship issues (who's been avoiding household responsibilities, whose time is more valuable).

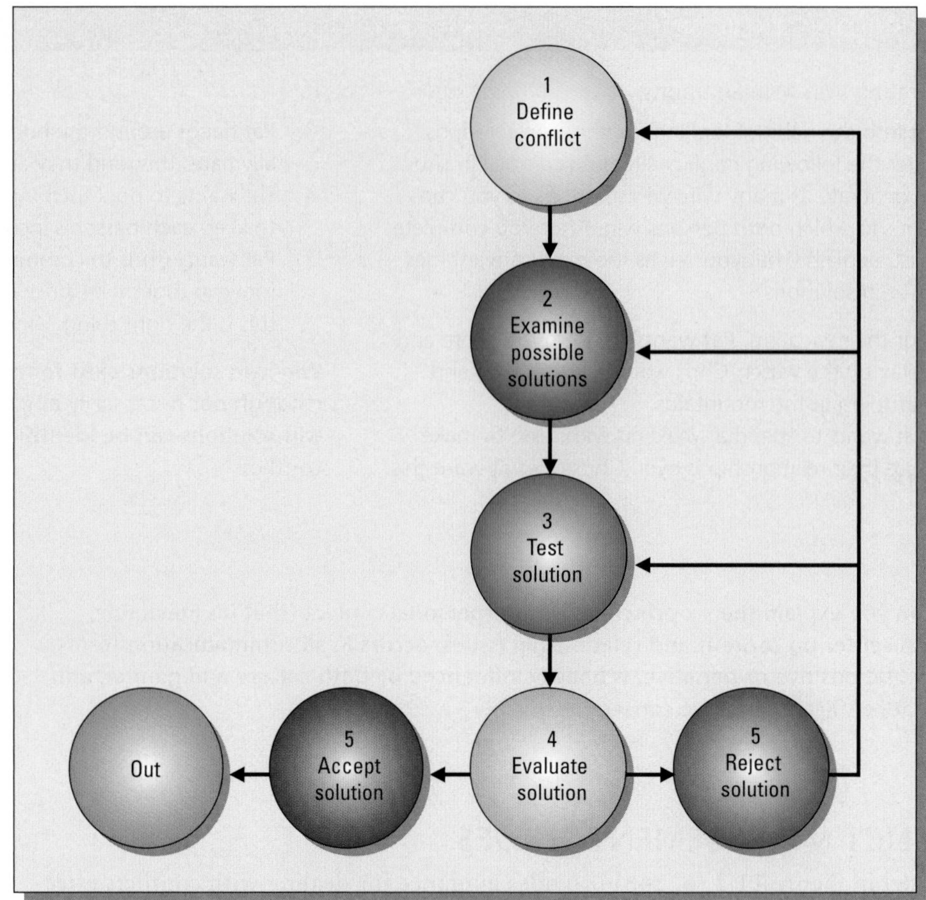

FIGURE 11.2
The Stages of Conflict Management
This model derives from John Dewey's stages of reflecting thinking and is a general pattern for understanding and resolving any type of problem.

- *Define the problem in specific terms.* It's one thing for a person to say "you don't seem to like me" and quite another to say "you don't include me in your hangouts, you don't respond to my posts." It's one thing for a husband to say that his wife is "cold and unfeeling" and quite another for him to say that she does not call him at the office, kiss him when he comes home, or hold his hand when they're at a party. Specific behaviors can be agreed on and dealt with, but the abstract "you don't seem to like me" or "cold and unfeeling" remains elusive.
- *Empathize.* Try to understand the nature of the conflict from the other person's point of view. Once you have empathically understood the other person's feelings, validate those feelings when appropriate. If your partner is hurt or angry and you believe such feelings are justified, say so: "You have a right to be angry; I shouldn't have said that."
- *Avoid mind reading.* Don't try to read the other person's mind. Ask questions to make sure you understand the problem as the other person is experiencing it.

Let's take an example and work with it through the remaining conflict stages. This conflict revolves around Raul's not wanting to socialize with Julia's friends. Julia thinks her friends are wonderful and exciting; Raul thinks they're unpleasant and boring.

INTERPERSONAL CHOICE POINT

Conflict Management

Your dorm mate is very popular and has an open-door policy. So, throughout the day and evening, friends drop by to chat, borrow a book, check their e-mail, and do a range of things—all of which prevents you from studying. You need to resolve this problem. What can you say to your roommate to begin to resolve this conflict?

Examine Possible Solutions

The second step in conflict is to look for possible ways of resolving the issue. Because most conflicts can probably be resolved in a variety of ways, it's useful at this stage to identify as many solutions as possible.

As noted in the discussion of conflict styles earlier, win–win solutions are the ideal, so look for these whenever possible. Most solutions, of course, will involve costs to one or both parties (after all, someone has to take the dog out), so it's unlikely that solutions to real interpersonal problems are going to involve only rewards for both persons. But you can try to seek solutions in which the costs and the rewards will be evenly shared.

In our example, let's say Raul and Julia identify these possible solutions:

1. Julia should not interact with her friends anymore.
2. Raul should interact with Julia's friends.
3. Julia should see her friends without Raul.

Clearly solutions 1 and 2 are win–lose solutions. In 1, Raul wins and Julia loses; in 2, Julia wins and Raul loses. These involve a competing or accommodating style in which one wins and one loses. Solution 3 (which may be collaborating or compromising), however, might be a possibility. Both might win, and neither must necessarily lose. The next step would be to test this possible solution.

Test a Solution

Once you have examined all possible solutions, select one and test it out. First test the solution mentally. How does it feel? Are you comfortable with the solution? Will Raul be comfortable about Julia's socializing with her friends without him? Will Julia be comfortable socializing with her friends without Raul? Will she feel guilty? Will she enjoy herself without Raul?

Then test the solution in actual practice. Give the idea a fair chance. Perhaps Julia might go out once without Raul to try it out. Did her friends think there was something wrong with her relationship with Raul? Did she feel guilty? Did she enjoy herself? Did Raul feel jealous?

Evaluate the Solution

In the evaluation stage, ask whether the tested solution helped resolve the conflict. Is the situation better now than it was before the solution was put into operation? Share your feelings and evaluations of the solution. Raul and Julia now need to share their perceptions of this possible solution. Would they be comfortable with this solution on a monthly basis? Is the solution worth the costs that each will pay? Are the costs and the rewards about evenly distributed? Might other solutions be more effective?

Critical thinking pioneer Edward deBono (1985) suggests that in evaluating problems or proposed solutions, you use six "thinking hats." With each hat, you look at the problem or the solution from a different perspective. Here's how looking at Julia and Raul's problem with the six hats might work:

- The **fact hat** focuses attention on the facts and figures that bear on the problem. For example, how can Raul learn more about the rewards that Julia gets from her friends? How can Julia find out why Raul doesn't like her friends?
- The **feeling hat** focuses attention on the emotional responses to the problem. How does Raul feel when Julia goes out with her friends? How does Julia feel when Raul refuses to meet them?
- The **negative argument hat** asks you to become the devil's advocate. How might this relationship deteriorate if Julia continues seeing her friends without Raul or if Raul resists interacting with Julia's friends?

INTERPERSONAL CHOICE POINT

Teaching Confrontation

You're a new teacher at an elementary school. The parents of a student who has been doing very poorly and has created all sorts of discipline problems complain that their daughter hates school and isn't learning anything. They want her transferred to another class with another teacher. What are some of the things you can say as feedforward that might help lessen their anger?

- The **positive benefits hat** asks you to look at the upside. What are the opportunities that Julia's seeing friends without Raul might yield? What benefits might Raul and Julia get from this new arrangement?
- The **creative new idea hat** focuses on new ways of looking at the problem. In what other ways can Raul and Julia look at this problem? What other possible solutions might they consider?
- The **control of thinking hat** helps you analyze what you're doing. It asks you to reflect on your own thinking. Have Raul and Julia adequately defined the problem? Are they focusing too much on insignificant issues? Have they given enough attention to possible negative effects?

Accept or Reject the Solution

If you accept a solution, you're ready to put this solution into more permanent operation. But if you decide, on the basis of your evaluation, that this is not the right solution for the conflict, then there are two major alternatives. First, you might test another solution. Perhaps you might now reexamine a runner-up idea or approach. Second, you might go back to the definition of the conflict. As the diagram in Figure 11.2 illustrates, you can reenter the conflict-resolution process at any of the first three stages.

Let us say that Raul is actually quite happy with the solution. He takes the opportunity of his evening alone to visit his brother. Next time Julia goes out with her friends, Raul intends to go to wrestling. And Julia feels pretty good about seeing her friends without Raul. She simply explains that occasionally she and Raul socialize separately and that both are comfortable with this.

After a conflict is resolved, it is not necessarily over. Consider a few "after the conflict" suggestions.

- *Learn from the conflict* and from the process you went through in trying to resolve it. For example, can you identify the fight strategies that aggravated the situation? Do you, or does your partner, need a cooling-off period? Can you tell when minor issues are going to escalate into major arguments?
- *Attack your negative feelings.* Often such feelings arise because unfair fight strategies were used (as we'll see in the next section)—for example, blame or verbal aggressiveness. Resolve to avoid such unfair tactics in the future, but at the same time, let go of guilt and blame. And be prepared to forgive each other.
- *Increase the exchange of rewards* and cherishing behaviors. These will show your positive feelings and demonstrate that you're over the conflict and want the relationship to survive.

Blog Post

Conflict Management

Take a look at "Conflict Management" at tcbdevito.blogspot.com for some additional suggestions. What management strategies do you find especially effective?

Can you define and illustrate the stages of conflict management (definition of the conflict, examination of possible solutions, testing a solution, evaluating a solution, and making a decision to accept or reject the solution)? Can you apply the insights of this model to your own interpersonal conflict management?

CONFLICT MANAGEMENT STRATEGIES

In managing conflict, you can choose from a variety of strategies, which we will consider here. Realize, however, that a variety of factors will influence the strategies you choose (Koerner & Fitzpatrick, 2002). Understanding these factors may help you select more effective strategies to manage conflict with success.

- The *goals* (short-term and long-term) you wish to achieve: If you merely want to enjoy the moment, you may want to simply "give in" and ignore the difficulty. On the other hand, if you want to build a long-term relationship, you may want to fully analyze the cause of the problem and to choose cooperative strategies.

- Your *emotional state:* When you're sorry, you're likely to use conciliatory strategies designed to make peace; when you're angry, you're more likely to use strategies that attack the other person.
- Your *assessment* of the situation: For example, your attitudes and beliefs about what is fair and equitable will influence your readiness to acknowledge the fairness in the other person's position. Your own assessment of who (if anyone) is the cause of the problem also will influence your conflict style.
- Your *personality and communication competence:* If you're shy and unassertive, you may want to avoid a conflict rather than fighting actively. If you're extroverted and have a strong desire to state your position, you may be more likely to fight actively and to argue forcefully.
- Your *family history:* If your parents argued about money or gave each other the silent treatment when conflict arose, you're likely to repeat these patterns yourself if you aren't mindful of your conflict strategies.

VIEWPOINTS **Social network conflicts**

How would you compare interpersonal conflicts in face-to-face encounters and on social media sites? Are the issues argued about the same? Are the attempts at resolving the conflict the same?

Before examining these various strategies, take the self-test "Conflict Management Strategies," and examine your own patterns of conflict management.

Win–Lose and Win–Win Strategies

As noted in the discussion of conflict styles, you can look at interpersonal conflict in terms of winning and losing. Obviously, solutions in which both parties win are the most

TEST YOURSELF

Conflict Management Strategies

The following statements refer to ways in which people engage in interpersonal conflict. Respond to each statement with *True* if this is a generally accurate description of your interpersonal conflict behavior and *False* if the statement is a generally inaccurate description of your behavior.

____ 1. I strive to seek solutions that will benefit both of us.
____ 2. I look for solutions that will give me what I want.
____ 3. I confront conflict situations as they arrive.
____ 4. I avoid conflict situations as best I can.
____ 5. My messages are basically descriptive of the events leading up to the conflict.
____ 6. My messages are often judgmental.
____ 7. I take into consideration the face needs of the other person.
____ 8. I advance the strongest arguments I can find even if these attack the other person.
____ 9. I center my arguments on issues rather than on personalities.
____10. I use messages that may attack a person's self-image if this will help me win the argument.

How Did You Do? This self-test was designed to sensitize you to some of the conflict strategies to be discussed in this section of the chapter. It is not intended to give you a specific score. Generally, however, you'd be following the general principles of effective interpersonal conflict management if you answered True to the odd-numbered statements (1, 3, 5, 7, and 9) and False to the even-numbered statements (2, 4, 6, 8, and 10).

What Will You Do? As you think about your responses and read the text discussion, ask yourself what you can do to improve your own conflict management skills. That's the overriding goal of this section.

desirable. Perhaps the most important reason is that win–win solutions lead to mutual satisfaction and prevent the kind of resentment that win–lose solutions often engender. Another reason is that looking for and developing win–win solutions makes the next conflict less unpleasant; conflict can more easily be viewed as "solving a problem" rather than as "fighting." Also, win–win solutions promote mutual face-saving; both parties can feel good about themselves. Finally, people are more likely to abide by the decisions reached in a win–win conflict than they are in win–lose or lose–lose situations. In sum, you can look for solutions in which you or your side wins and the other person or side loses (win–lose solutions). Or you can look for solutions in which you and the other person both win (win–win solutions). Too often, we fail to even consider the possibility of win–win solutions and what they might be.

Take an interpersonal example: Let's say that I want to spend our money on a new car (my old one is unreliable), and you want to spend it on a vacation (you're exhausted and feel the need for a rest). Ideally, through our conflict and its resolution, we learn what each really wants. We may then be able to figure out a way for each of us to get what we want. I might accept a good used car, and you might accept a less expensive vacation. Or we might buy a used car and take an inexpensive road trip. Each of these win–win solutions will satisfy both of us; each of us wins, in the sense that each of us gets what we wanted.

Instead of approaching conflict with a win–lose mentality, consider the advantages of win–win possibilities:

- Brainstorm potential win–win solutions.
- Focus on areas of agreement; see the other person's point of view.
- Be willing to give up something (but not everything) for the sake of the other person and the relationship.

Avoidance and Fighting Actively

Conflict **avoidance** may involve actual physical flight: You may leave the scene of the conflict (walk out of the apartment or go to another part of the office or shop), fall asleep, or blast the stereo to drown out all conversation. It also may take the form of emotional or intellectual avoidance, in which you may leave the conflict psychologically by not dealing with any of the arguments or problems raised.

Nonnegotiation is a special type of avoidance. Here you refuse to discuss the conflict or to listen to the other person's argument. At times, nonnegotiation takes the form of hammering away at your own point of view until the other person gives in—a technique called "steamrolling."

Another form of avoidance is **gunnysacking**. The term *gunnysack* refers to the kind of burlap bag that years ago held potatoes. As a conflict strategy, gunnysacking involves storing up grievances (as if in a gunnysack) and then unloading them on the other person—even when the grievances have nothing to do with the present conflict. As you can imagine, as a conflict strategy, gunnysacking is highly unproductive. The immediate occasion for unloading stored-up grievances may be relatively simple (or so it may seem at first); for example, you come home late one night without calling. Instead of arguing about this, the gunnysacker pours out a mass of unrelated past grievances. As you probably know from experience, however, gunnysacking often begets gunnysacking. Frequently, the trigger problem never gets addressed. Instead, resentment and hostility escalate. Instead of avoiding the issues:

- *Take an active role* in your interpersonal conflicts and involve yourself actively as both speaker and listener. Turn off the phone, television, or computer; face the other person. Devote your total attention to the other person.
- *Voice your feelings, and listen carefully* to the voicing of the other person's feelings. When appropriate, consider taking a moratorium, a time-out. Be careful to keep these

INTERPERSONAL CHOICE POINT

Avoiding Conflict

Your work team members all seem to have the same conflict style: avoidance. When differing alternatives are discussed or there is some kind of disagreement, they refuse to argue for one side or the other or even to participate in the discussion. What are some things you can say to stimulate spirited discussion and honest debate (which seem essential if your team is going to come up with appropriate solutions)?

feelings between the two of you; avoid writing on the person's wall, for example, and thus airing the conflict for your entire network to read.

- *Own your thoughts and feelings.* For example, when you disagree with your partner or find fault with her or his behavior, take responsibility for these feelings, saying, for example, "I disagree with..." or " I don't like it when you..." Avoid statements that deny your responsibility, for example, "Everybody thinks you're wrong about..." or "Chris thinks you shouldn't..."
- *Focus on the present,* on the here and now, rather than on an issue that occurred two months ago.
- *Express your support, empathy, and agreement:* "I can understand how you feel. I know I control the checkbook, and I realize that can create a feeling of inequality."

Defensiveness and Supportiveness

Although talk is preferred to force, not all talk is equally productive in conflict resolution. One of the best ways to look at destructive versus productive talk is to look at how the style of your communications can create unproductive **defensiveness** or a productive sense of **supportiveness**, an approach developed by Jack Gibb (1961) that is still used widely by communication and conflict theorists and interpersonal textbook writers. The type of talk that generally proves destructive and sets up defensive reactions in the listener is talk that is evaluative, controlling, strategic, indifferent or neutral, superior, and certain.

EVALUATION When you evaluate or judge another person or what that person has done, that person is likely to become resentful and defensive and is likely to respond with attempts to defend himself or herself and perhaps at the same time to become equally evaluative and judgmental. In contrast, when you describe what happened or what you want, it creates no such defensiveness and is generally seen as supportive. The distinction between **evaluation** and description can be seen in the differences between you-messages and I-messages.

Evaluative You-Messages	Descriptive I-Messages
You never reveal your feelings.	I'd like hearing how you feel about this.
You just don't plan ahead.	I need to know what our schedule for the next few days will be.
You never call me.	I'd enjoy hearing from you more often.

If you put yourself in the role of the listener hearing these statements, you probably can feel the resentment or defensiveness that the evaluative messages (you-messages) would create and the supportiveness from the descriptive messages (I-messages).

SKILL BUILDING EXERCISE

Rewriting You- to I-Messages

Recognizing a conflict starter—some incident that signals that this is the beginning of an interpersonal conflict—early can often diffuse a later and more extensive conflict. Here, for example, are accusatory comments using you-messages. Turn each of these into an I-message. What do you see as the major differences between you- and I-messages?

1. You're late again. You're always late. Your lateness is so inconsiderate!
2. All you do is sit home and watch cartoons; you never do anything useful.
3. Well, there goes another anniversary that you forgot.
4. You think I'm fat, don't you?
5. You never want to do what I want. We always have to do what you want.

Generally and perhaps especially in conflict situations, I-messages are less likely to aggravate conflict than are you-messages.

CONTROL When you try to control the behavior of the other person, when you order the other person to do this or that, or when you make decisions without mutual discussion and agreement, defensiveness is a likely response. Control messages deny the legitimacy of the person's contributions and in fact deny his or her importance. They say, in effect, "You don't count; your contributions are meaningless." When, on the other hand, you focus on the problem at hand—not on controlling the situation or getting your own way—defensiveness is much less likely. This problem orientation invites mutual participation and recognizes the significance of each person's contributions.

STRATEGY When you use **strategy** and try to get around other people or situations through manipulation—especially when you conceal your true purposes—others are likely to resent it and to respond defensively. But when you act openly and with spontaneity, you're more likely to create an atmosphere that is equal and honest.

NEUTRALITY When you demonstrate **neutrality**—in the sense of indifference or a lack of caring for the other person—it's likely to create defensiveness. Neutrality seems to show a lack of empathy or interest in the thoughts and feelings of the other person; it is especially damaging when intimates are in conflict. This kind of talk says, in effect, "You're not important or deserving of attention and caring." When, on the other hand, you demonstrate empathy, defensiveness is unlikely to occur. Although it can be especially difficult in conflict situations, try to show that you can understand what the other person is going through and that you accept these feelings.

SUPERIORITY When you present yourself as superior to the other person, you're in effect putting the other person in an inferior position, and this is likely to be resented. Such **superiority** messages say in effect that the other person is inadequate or somehow second-class. It's a violation of the implicit equality contract that people in a close relationship have—namely, the assumption that each person is equal. The other person may then begin to attack your superiority; the conflict can easily degenerate into a conflict over who's the boss, with personal attack being the mode of interaction.

CERTAINTY The person who appears to know it all is likely to be resented, so **certainty** often sets up a defensive climate. After all, there is little room for negotiation or mutual problem solving when one person already has the answer. An attitude of provisionalism—"Let's explore this issue together and try to find a solution"—is likely to be much more productive than closed-mindedness.

Instead of defensiveness, try supportiveness:

- **Talk descriptively** rather than evaluatively.
- **Focus on the problem** rather than on the person. Even when the problem is the person's behavior, focus on the behavior rather than the whole person.
- **Act and react honestly**, spontaneously.
- **Empathize** with the other person.
- **See equality**; act as an equal. Avoid pulling rank.
- **Be provisional**; suggest rather than order or demand.

INTERPERSONAL CHOICE POINT

Fighting with Trolls

Someone trolls your posts, and no matter what you say, this person takes issue with it, criticizes it, and says all sorts of negative things. What are some of the ways you might deal with trolling in general?

Face-Attacking and Face-Enhancing Strategies: Politeness in Conflict

In Chapter 3, we introduced the concept of face and politeness. As you might have guessed, this concept has special relevance to interpersonal conflict. Face-attacking conflict strategies are those that attack a person's positive face (for example, comments that criticize the person's contribution to a relationship or any of the person's abilities) or a person's negative face (for example, making demands on a person's time or resources or comments that attack the person's autonomy). Face-enhancing strategies are those that support and confirm a person's positive face (praise, a pat on the back, a sincere smile) or negative face (giving the person space and asking rather than demanding).

One popular but destructive face-attacking strategy is **beltlining** (Bach & Wyden, 1968). Much like fighters in a ring, each of us has a "beltline" (here, an emotional one). When you hit below this emotional beltline, you can inflict serious injury. When you hit above the belt, however, the person is able to absorb the blow. With most interpersonal relationships, especially those of long standing, you know where the beltline is. You know, for example, that to hit Kristen or Matt with the inability to have children is to hit below the belt. You know that to hit Jack or Jill with the failure to get a permanent job is to hit below the belt. This type of face-attacking strategy causes all persons involved added problems.

VIEWPOINTS The importance of face

Cultures vary widely in how important they consider face. How important is it to maintain face in a conflict situation in your culture and the cultures with which you're familiar?

Another such face-attacking strategy is **blame**. Instead of focusing on a solution to a problem, some members try to affix blame on the other person. Whether true or not, blaming is unproductive; it diverts attention away from the problem and from its potential solution, and it creates resentment that is likely to be responded to with additional resentment. The conflict then spirals into personal attacks, leaving the individuals and the relationship worse off than before the conflict was ever addressed.

Strategies that enhance a person's self-image and that acknowledge a person's autonomy will not only be polite, but they're likely to be more effective than strategies that attack a person's self-image and deny a person's autonomy. Even when you get what you want, it's wise to help the other person retain positive face because it makes it less likely that future conflicts will arise (Donohue & Kolt, 1992).

Instead of face-attacking, try face-enhancing strategies:

- Use messages that enhance a person's self-image.
- Use messages that acknowledge a person's autonomy.
- Compliment the other person even in the midst of a conflict.
- Make few demands, respect another's time, give the other person space especially in times of conflict.
- Keep blows to areas above the belt.
- Avoid blaming the other person.
- Express respect for the other's point of view even when it differs greatly from your own.

INTERPERSONAL CHOICE POINT

Dealing with Face Attacks

Sara and Margaret want to go to Canada and get married, but both sets of parents are adamantly opposed to same-sex marriage and want Sara and Margaret to stop seeing each other and enter therapy. What are some of the ways Sara and Margaret might begin to deal with this conflict situation?

Verbal Aggressiveness and Argumentativeness

An especially interesting perspective on conflict has emerged from work on verbal aggressiveness and argumentativeness, concepts developed by communication researchers that have quickly spread to other disciplines—such as psychology, education, and management, among others (Infante, Rancer, & Avtgis, 2010; Rancer & Avtgis, 2006). Understanding these two concepts will help you understand some of the reasons why things go wrong and some of the ways in which you can use conflict to improve rather than damage your relationships.

Explore the **Exercise** "Jim and Jack Joust" at **MyCommunicationLab**

VERBAL AGGRESSIVENESS **Verbal aggressiveness** is an unproductive conflict strategy in which a person tries to win an argument by inflicting psychological pain, by attacking the other person's self-concept (Infante & Wigley, 1986; Rancer & Avtgis, 2006). The

VIEWPOINTS Relationship violence

One of the most puzzling findings on violence is that many victims interpret it as a sign of love. For some reason, they see being beaten or verbally abused as a sign that their partner is fully in love with them. Also, many victims blame themselves for the violence instead of blaming their partners (Gelles & Cornell, 1985). Why do you think this is so? What part does force or violence play in conflicts in your own interpersonal relationships?

technique is a type of disconfirmation in that it seeks to discredit the individual's view of self. The verbally aggressive individual is likely to

- attack the character of the other person.
- insult the other person; post an unflattering photo.
- lose his or her temper during a dispute; write really negative comments on someone's wall for all to see.
- make fun of others.
- yell and scream.
- make the other person feel unreasonable or stupid or defensive.

Now, let's consider the alternative, argumentativeness.

ARGUMENTATIVENESS **Argumentativeness** refers to your willingness to argue for a point of view, your tendency to speak your mind on significant issues. It's the mode of dealing with disagreements that is the preferred alternative to verbal aggressiveness.

As you can appreciate, argumentativeness differs greatly from verbal aggressiveness (see Table 11.1). Argumentativeness is constructive; the outcomes are positive in a variety of communication situations (interpersonal, group, organizational, family, and intercultural). Verbal aggressiveness is destructive; the outcomes are negative.

INTERPERSONAL CHOICE POINT

Talking Aggressively

Your partner is becoming more and more verbally aggressive, and you're having trouble with this new communication pattern. Regardless of what the conflict is about, your self-concept is attacked. You've had enough; you want to stop this kind of attack and yet preserve the relationship. What are your options for communicating in this situation? What would you say?

Argumentativeness leads to relationship satisfaction, and even in organizations, it enhances relationships between subordinates and supervisors. Aggressiveness, on the other hand, leads to relationship dissatisfaction, and in an organization, it demoralizes workers on many levels of the hierarchy.

Argumentative individuals are generally seen as having greater credibility; they're seen as more trustworthy, committed, and dynamic than their aggressive counterparts. In addition, argumentativeness is likely to increase your power of persuasion and will also increase the likelihood that you'll be seen as a leader. Aggressiveness tactics, on the other hand, decrease your power and your likelihood of being seen as a leader.

VIDEO CHOICE POINT

Dorm Room Conflict

Tim needs to study, but there is just too much commotion going on in his dorm room for him to concentrate. Tim's dorm mate Luis is very popular and has an open-door policy. Day and night, friends drop by to chat, borrow books, check their e-mail, and socialize—all of which prevents Tim from studying. Normally, Tim puts up with the heavy traffic, but midterms are coming up and he needs to focus. As he tries to resolve this problem, he considers the topics covered in this chapter and his communication choices. See how his choices play out in the video "Dorm Room Conflict" and respond to the questions posed.

 **Watch** the **Video** "Dorm Room Conflict" at **MyCommunicationLab**

ETHICAL MESSAGES

Ethical Fighting

This chapter focuses on the dimension of effectiveness versus ineffectiveness in conflict strategies. But all communication strategies also have an ethical dimension, and it's important to look at the ethical implications of conflict resolution strategies. For example:

- Does conflict avoidance have an ethical dimension? For example, is it unethical for one relationship partner to refuse to discuss disagreements or to walk out of an argument?
- Can the use of physical force to influence another person ever be ethical? Can you identify a situation in which it would be appropriate for someone with greater physical strength to overpower another to compel the other to accept his or her point of view?
- Are face-attacking strategies inherently unethical, or might it be appropriate to use them in certain situations? Can you identify such situations?
- What are the ethical implications of verbal aggressiveness?
- Is it ethical to lie to help resolve an interpersonal conflict?

Ethical Choice Point

Jim spent the night gambling (and lost a lot of money) but knows that revealing this will cause conflict and hurt his partner. He'd be able to hide the loss without difficulty. Would it be ethical for Jim to say he had to work late to avoid the conflict and hurt?

TABLE 11.1

DIFFERENCES BETWEEN VERBAL AGGRESSIVENESS AND ARGUMENTATIVENESS

As discussed in the text, there are numerous differences between argumentativeness and verbal aggressiveness. Here is a brief summary (Infante & Rancer, 1996; Rancer & Atvgis, 2006).

Verbal Aggressiveness	Argumentativeness
Is destructive; the outcomes are negative in a variety of interpersonal communication situations	Is constructive; the outcomes are positive in a variety of interpersonal communication situations
Leads to relationship dissatisfaction, not surprising for a strategy that aims to attack another's self-concept	Leads to relationship satisfaction
May lead to relationship violence	May prevent relationship violence especially in domestic relationships
Damages organizational life and demoralizes workers on varied levels	Enhances organizational life; subordinates prefer supervisors who encourage argumentativeness
Prevents meaningful parent–child communication; makes corporal punishment more likely	Enhances parent–child communication and enables parents to gain greater compliance without corporal punishment
Decreases the user's credibility, in part because it's seen as a tactic to discredit the opponent rather than address the argument	Increases the user's credibility; argumentatives are seen as trustworthy, committed, and dynamic
Decreases the user's power of persuasion	Increases the user's power of persuasion; argumentatives are more likely to be seen as leaders

Explore the **Exercise** "Analyzing a Conflict Episode" at **MyCommunicationLab**

"Look, if we never went to bed angry we'd never sleep."

Pat Byrnes/The New Yorker Collection/www.cartoonbank.com

Blog Post

Interpersonal Communication and . . .

Take a look at "Interpersonal Communication and . . ." at tcbdevito.blogspot.com for a discussion of interpersonal conflict training. Would interpersonal conflict training be useful to people in the profession you're in or hope to enter?

Instead of verbal aggressiveness, consider the more effective argumentativeness:

- Treat disagreements as objectively as possible; avoid assuming that because someone takes issue with your position or your interpretation, they're attacking you as a person.
- Center your arguments on issues rather than personalities. Avoid attacking a person (rather than a person's arguments), even if this would give you a tactical advantage—it will probably backfire at some later time and make your relationship or group participation more difficult.
- Reaffirm the other person's sense of competence; compliment the other person as appropriate.
- Allow the other person to state her or his position fully before you respond; avoid interrupting.
- Stress equality, and stress the similarities that you have with the other person or persons; stress your areas of agreement before attacking the disagreements.
- Express interest in the other person's position, attitude, and point of view.
- Avoid getting overemotional; using an overly loud voice or interjecting vulgar expressions will prove offensive and eventually ineffective.
- Allow people to save face; never humiliate another person.

INTERPERSONAL CHOICE POINT

Choices for Conflict Competence

Take a good look at your own conflict behaviors. What are some of your options for improving the ways in which you engage in conflict and conflict resolution?

Can you define and distinguish between the basic conflict strategies (win–lose and win–win, avoidance and fighting actively, defensiveness and supportiveness, face-attacking and face-enhancing, and verbal aggressiveness and argumentativeness)? Can you apply the suggestions for effective conflict management strategies to you own interpersonal conflicts?

MESSAGES IN THE MEDIA: WRAP-UP

Television shows generally provide great examples of interpersonal conflict. Watching these with a view to identifying productive and unproductive conflict resolution strategies will help you master the appropriate strategies in your own interpersonal conflicts.

SUMMARY OF CONCEPTS AND SKILLS

Listen to the **Audio Chapter Summary** at **MyCommunicationLab**

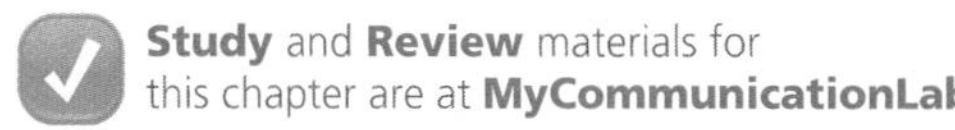

This chapter examined interpersonal conflict, including key principles of interpersonal conflict, the distinction between content and relationship conflict, and conflict's positive and negative effects; the chapter explained a model of conflict resolution and described a variety of unproductive conflict strategies and their more productive counterparts.

What Is Interpersonal Conflict?

1. Interpersonal conflict is disagreement between or among connected individuals. The positions in interpersonal conflicts are to some degree interrelated and incompatible.

Principles of Interpersonal Conflict

2. Interpersonal conflict is inevitable. If a relationship exists, conflict in some form will also exist.
3. Interpersonal conflict may focus on content and/or relationship issues.
4. Interpersonal conflict can occur in all forms of communication and through all channels.
5. Interpersonal conflict can be negative or positive; any conflict encounter may be destructive or constructive.
6. Interpersonal conflict is influenced by culture and gender.
7. Interpersonal conflict may be approached with different styles, each of which has different consequences.

Conflict Management Stages

8. Before the conflict, try to fight in private, be sure you're each ready to fight, know what you're fighting about, and avoid fighting about problems that cannot be solved.
9. A five-step model is often helpful in resolving conflict: Define the conflict, examine possible solutions, test a solution, evaluate the solution, and accept or reject the solution.
10. After the conflict, keep the conflict in perspective, challenge your negative feelings, and increase the exchange of rewards.

Conflict Management Strategies

11. Unproductive and productive conflict strategies include win–lose and win–win approaches, avoidance and fighting actively, defensiveness and supportiveness, face-attacking and face-enhancing strategies, and verbal aggressiveness and argumentativeness.
12. To cultivate argumentativeness, treat disagreements objectively and avoid attacking the other person; reaffirm the other's sense of competence; avoid interrupting; stress equality and similarities; express interest in the other's position; avoid presenting your arguments too emotionally; and allow the other to save face.

This chapter also focused on the major skills for managing interpersonal conflict. Check those you wish to work on.

____1. *Negatives and positives of conflict.* Approach conflict to minimize its negative aspects and to maximize the positive benefits of conflict and its resolution.

____2. *Conflict, culture, and gender.* Approach conflict with the understanding of the cultural and gender differences in attitudes toward what constitutes conflict and toward how it should be pursued.

____ 3. *Conflict styles.* Choose your conflict style carefully; each style has consequences. In relationship conflict, look for win–win solutions rather than solutions in which one person wins and the other loses.

____ 4. *Content and relationship conflicts.* Analyze conflict messages in terms of content and relationship dimensions, and respond to each accordingly.

____ 5. *Problem-solving conflicts.* Deal with interpersonal conflicts systematically as problems to be solved: Define the problem, examine possible solutions, test a solution, evaluate the solution, and accept or reject the solution.

____ 6. *Active interpersonal conflict.* Engage in interpersonal conflict actively; be appropriately revealing, and listen to your partner.

____ 7. *Supportive conflict.* Engage in conflict using a supportive approach, so as not to create defensiveness; avoid messages that evaluate or control, that are strategic or neutral, or that express superiority or certainty.

____ 8. *Face-saving strategies.* Use strategies that allow your opponents to save face; avoid beltlining, or hitting opponents with attacks that they will have difficulty absorbing and will resent.

____ 9. *Open expression in conflict.* Try to express your feelings openly rather than resorting to silence or avoidance.

____ 10. *Present-focus conflict.* Focus your conflict resolution messages on the present; avoid gunnysacking, or dredging up old grievances and unloading these on the other person.

____ 11. *Argumentativeness.* Avoid aggressiveness (attacking the other person's self-concept); instead, focus logically on the issues, emphasize finding solutions, and work to ensure that what is said will result in positive self-feelings for both individuals.

VOCABULARY QUIZ: The Language of Conflict

Match the terms dealing with interpersonal conflict with their definitions. Record the number of the definition next to the appropriate term.

____ six hats technique (249)
____ accommodating (246)
____ argumentativeness (256)
____ gunnysacking (252)
____ beltline (255)
____ verbal aggressiveness (255)
____ compromising (246)
____ empathizing (248)
____ interpersonal conflict (241)
____ conflict resolution model (247)

1. A disagreement between connected individuals.
2. An unproductive conflict strategy of storing up grievances and holding these in readiness to dump on the person with whom one is in conflict.
3. A person's level of tolerance for absorbing a personal attack.
4. A tendency or willingness to argue for a point of view.
5. A conflict strategy designed to maintain peace and harmony in the relationship.
6. Understanding the conflict from the other person's point of view.
7. A tendency to defend your position even at the expense of another person's feelings.
8. A set of procedures for dealing with conflict consisting of five steps: define the conflict, examine possible solutions, test a solution, evaluate the solution, and accept or reject the solution.
9. Varied ways of looking at a particular issue to give you different perspectives.
10. A style of conflict management concerned with both the self and the other.

These ten terms and additional terms used in this chapter can be found in the glossary.

Study and **Review** the **Flashcards** at **MyCommunicationLab**

MyCommunicationLab

Visit MyCommunicationLab for a wealth of additional information on interpersonal communication. Flashcards, videos, skill building exercises, sample test questions, and additional exercises, examples, and discussions will help you continue your study of the fundamentals of interpersonal communication, its theory, and its skills.

GLOSSARY OF INTERPERSONAL COMMUNICATION CONCEPTS AND SKILLS

Listed here are definitions of the technical terms of interpersonal communication—the words that are peculiar or unique to this discipline—along with relevant skills where applicable (in *italic*). These definitions and skill statements should make new or difficult terms a bit easier to understand and should serve as reminders of the skills discussed throughout this text. All boldface terms within the definitions appear as separate entries in the glossary.

Abstract terms Words that refer to concepts and ideas that have no physical dimensions (friendship, value, fear). *See also* **concrete terms.** *Use both abstract and concrete language when describing or explaining.*

Accommodation The process of adjusting your communication patterns to those with whom you're interacting. *Accommodate to the speaking style of your listeners in moderation; too much mirroring of the other's style may appear manipulative.*

Acculturation The process by which one culture is modified or changed through contact with or exposure to another culture.

Active listening The process by which a listener expresses his or her understanding of the speaker's total message, including the verbal and nonverbal, the thoughts and feelings. *Be an active listener: Paraphrase the speaker's meaning, express understanding of the speaker's feelings, and ask questions when necessary.*

Adaptors Nonverbal behaviors that, when engaged in, either in private or in public, serve some kind of need and occur in their entirety—for example, scratching one's head until the itch is relieved. *Generally, avoid adaptors; they may make you appear uncomfortable or ill at ease.*

Adjustment, principle of The principle of verbal interaction that claims that effective communication depends on the extent to which communicators share the same system of signals.

Advice Messages that tell another person what he or she should do.

Affect displays Movements of the facial area that convey emotional meaning such as anger, fear, and surprise.

Affinity-seeking strategies Behaviors designed to increase interpersonal attractiveness.

Agapic love One of Lee's (1976) six types of love; compassionate and selfless love offered without concern for personal reward and without any expectation of reciprocation.

Ageism Discrimination based on age, usually against older people.

Allness The illogical assumption that all can be known or said about a given person, issue, object, or event. *Avoid allness statements; they invariably misstate the reality and will often offend the other person.*

Alter-adaptors Body movements you make in response to your current interactions—for example, crossing your arms over your chest when someone unpleasant approaches or moving closer to someone you like.

Altercasting Placing a person in a specific role for a specific purpose and asking that he or she assume the perspective of this specific role, for example, "As a professor of communication, what do you think of..."

Ambiguity The condition in which a message or relationship may be interpreted as having more than one meaning.

Anger management The methods and techniques by which anger is controlled and managed. *Calm down as best you can; then consider your communication options and the relevant communication skills for expressing your feelings.*

Anonymous messages Messages in which the author is not identified. Opposed to **onymous messages.**

Apology An expression of regret or sorrow for having done what you did or for what happened.

Apprehension *See* **communication apprehension.**

Argumentativeness A willingness to argue for a point of view, to speak one's mind. Distinguished from **verbal aggressiveness.** *Avoid aggressiveness (attacking the other person's self-concept); instead, focus logically on the issues, emphasize finding solutions, and work to ensure that what is said will result in positive self-feelings for both individuals.*

Artifactual messages Messages that are conveyed by objects that are made by human hands. Art, color, clothing, jewelry, hairstyle, and smell would be examples of artifactual messages. *Use artifacts to communicate desired messages and avoid those that may communicate negative or unwanted meanings.*

Assertive messages Messages in which you stand up for your rights but with respect for the rights of others. *Increase assertiveness by analyzing the assertive messages of others, rehearsing assertive messages, and communicating assertively. In communicating assertively: Describe the problem, say how the problem affects you, propose solutions, confirm your understanding, and reflect on your own assertiveness.*

Association A transitory type of friendship, often described as a friendly relationship.

Asynchronous communication Communication in which the individuals send and receive messages at different times (as in e-mail communication). Opposed to **synchronous communication.**

Attention The process of responding to a stimulus or stimuli; usually some consciousness of responding is implied.

Attitude A predisposition to respond for or against an object, person, or position.

Attraction The process by which one individual is emotionally drawn to another and finds that person satisfying to be with.

Attraction theory A theory holding that you develop relationships on the basis of three major factors: attractiveness (physical appearance and personality), proximity, and similarity.

Attractiveness A person's visual appeal and/or pleasantness in personality.

Attribution The processes by which we assign causation or motivation to a person's behavior.

Avoidance An unproductive conflict strategy in which you take mental or physical flight from the actual conflict.

Backchanneling cues Responses a listener makes to a speaker (while the speaker is speaking) but which do not ask for the speaking role, for example, interjections such as "I understand" or "You said what?" *Generally, give backchanneling cues to show that you're listening actively.*

Barriers to intercultural communication Physical or psychological factors that prevent or hinder effective communication.

Behavioral synchrony The similarity in the behavior, usually nonverbal (for example, postural stance or facial expressions) of two persons; generally taken as an indicator of liking.

Belief Confidence in the existence or truth of something; conviction.

Beltlining An unproductive conflict strategy in which one person hits the other at a vulnerable level—at the level at which the other person cannot withstand the blow.

Blame An unproductive conflict strategy in which we attribute the cause of the conflict to the other person or devote our energies to discovering who is the cause, avoiding talking about the issues at hand. *Avoid it; generally, it diverts attention from solving the problem and only serves to alienate the other person.*

Blended emotions Emotions that are combinations of the primary emotions, for example, disappointment is a blend of surprise and sadness.

Blind self In the Johari window model, this self represents all the things about yourself that others know but of which you're ignorant.

Boundary marker A marker that sets boundaries around or divides one person's territory from another's—for example, a fence.

Breadth The number of topics about which individuals in a relationship communicate.

Bullying Abusive acts repeatedly committed by one person (or a group) against another.

Captology The study of the ways in which electronic means of communication influence people's attitudes and behaviors.

Censorship Restrictions imposed on a person's right to produce, distribute, or receive various communications.

Central marker A marker or item that is placed in a territory to reserve it for a specific person—for example, the sweater thrown over a library chair to signal that the chair is taken.

Certainty An attitude of closed-mindedness that creates defensiveness among communicators. Opposed to **provisionalism.**

Channel The vehicle or medium through which signals are sent, for example, the vocal–auditory channel. *Assess your channel options (for example, face-to-face, e-mail, leaving a voicemail message) before communicating important messages.*

Cherishing behaviors Small behaviors you enjoy receiving from others, especially from your relational partner—for example, a kiss before you leave for work.

Chronemics The study of the communicative nature of time, of how a person's or a culture's treatment of time reveals something about the person or culture. Often divided into psychological and cultural time.

Civil inattention Polite ignoring of others (after a brief sign of awareness) so as not to invade their privacy.

Closed-mindedness An unwillingness to receive certain communication messages.

Code A set of symbols used to translate a message from one form to another.

Coercive power Power derived from an individual's ability to punish or to remove rewards from another person.

Cognitive labeling theory A theory of emotions that holds that emotional feelings begin with the occurrence of an event; you respond physiologically to the event, then you interpret the arousal (you in effect decide what it is you're feeling), and then you experience (give a name to) the emotion.

Collectivist culture A culture in which the group's goals are given greater importance than the individual's and in which, for example, benevolence, tradition, and conformity are given special emphasis. Opposed to **individualist culture.**

Color communication The use of color to communicate different meanings; each culture seems to define the meanings colors communicate somewhat differently.

Communication (1) The process or act of communicating; (2) the actual message or messages sent and received; (3) the study of the processes involved in the sending and receiving of messages.

Communication accommodation theory A theory of communication holding that conversationalists adjust to (or accommodate to) the speaking styles of each other.

Communication apprehension Fear or anxiety of communicating. *To reduce anxiety, acquire necessary communication skills and experiences, focus on prior successes, reduce unpredictability, and put apprehension in perspective.*

Communicology The study of communication, particularly the subsection concerned with human communication.

Competence "Language competence" is a speaker's ability to use the language; it is a knowledge of the elements and rules of the language. "Communication competence" generally refers both to the knowledge of communication and also to the ability to engage in communication effectively.

Complementarity A principle of attraction holding that you are attracted by qualities that you do not possess or wish to possess and to people who are opposite or different from yourself. Opposed to **similarity.**

Complementary relationship A relationship in which the behavior of one person serves as the stimulus for the complementary behavior of the other; in complementary relationships, behavioral differences are maximized.

Compliance-gaining strategies Behaviors designed to gain the agreement of others, to persuade others to do as you wish.

Compliance-resisting strategies Behaviors directed at resisting the persuasive attempts of others.

Compliment A message of praise, flattery, or congratulations.

Computer-mediated communication Communication between individuals that takes place through computer; usually refers to, for example, e-mail, chat groups, instant messaging, multiplayer video games.

Concrete terms Words that refer to objects, people, and happenings that you perceive with your senses of sight, smell, touch, hearing, or taste. *See also* **abstract terms.**

Confidence A quality of interpersonal effectiveness (and a factor in interpersonal power); a comfortable, at-ease feeling in interpersonal communication situations.

Confirmation A communication pattern that acknowledges another person's presence and indicates an acceptance of this person, this person's self-definition, and the relationship as defined or viewed by this other person. Opposed to **rejection** and **disconfirmation.** *When you wish to be confirming, acknowledge (verbally and/or nonverbally) others in your group and their contributions.*

Conflict A disagreement or difference of opinion; a form of competition in which one person tries to bring a rival to surrender; a situation in which one person's behaviors are directed at preventing something or at interfering with or harming another individual. *See also* **interpersonal conflict.** *Engage in interpersonal conflict actively; be appropriately revealing, see the situation from your partner's perspective, and listen to your partner. Approach conflict with an understanding of the cultural and gender differences in attitudes toward what constitutes conflict and toward how it should be pursued.*

Conflict styles The approach to conflict resolution, for example, competing, avoiding, accommodating, collaborating, and compromising. *Choose your conflict style carefully; each style has consequences. In relationship conflict, look for win–win (collaborating) solutions rather than solutions in which one person wins and the other loses (competing, avoiding, or accommodating).*

Congruence A condition in which both verbal and nonverbal behaviors reinforce each other.

Connotation The feeling or emotional aspect of a word's meaning; generally viewed as consisting of evaluation (for example, good–bad), potency (strong–weak), and activity (fast–slow) dimensions. Opposed to **denotation.** *Clarify your connotative meanings if you have any concern that your listeners might misunderstand you; as a listener, ask questions if you have doubts about the speaker's connotations.*

Consistency A tendency to maintain balance in your perception of messages or people; because of this process, you tend to see what you expect to see and to be uncomfortable when your perceptions run contrary to expectations.

Contact The first stage in relationship development, consisting of perceptual contact (you see or hear the person) and interactional contact (you talk with the person).

Content and relationship dimensions Two aspects to which messages may refer: the world external to both speaker and listener (content) and the connections existing between the individuals who are interacting (relationship). *Listen to both the content and the relationship aspects of messages, distinguish between them, and respond to both. Analyze conflict messages in terms of content and relationship dimensions, and respond to each accordingly.*

Context of communication The physical, psychological, social, and temporal environment in which communication takes place. *Adjust your messages to the physical, cultural, social–psychological, and temporal context.*

Contrast, principle of A principle of perception that holds that items that are very distinct from each other are seen as separate and not belonging to the same group.

Control An approach to interpersonal relationships in which one person tries to control what the other person does.

Conversation Two-person communication, usually following five stages: opening, feedforward, business, feedback, and closing.

Conversational management The management of the way in which messages are exchanged in conversation; consists of procedures for opening, maintaining, repairing, and closing conversations.

Conversational maxims Principles that participants in conversation follow to ensure that the goal of the conversation is achieved. *Follow (generally) the basic maxims of conversation, such as the maxims of quantity, quality, relations, manner, and politeness.*

Conversational rules The socially accepted ways of engaging in conversation. *Observe the general rules for conversation (for example, keeping speaking turns relatively short and avoiding interrupting), but break them when there seems logical reason to do so.*

Conversational turns The process of passing the speaker and listener roles back and forth during conversation. *Maintain relatively short conversational turns; after taking your turn, pass the speaker's turn to another person nonverbally or verbally. Respond to both the verbal and the nonverbal conversational turn-taking cues given you by others, and make your own cues clear to others.*

Cooperation An interpersonal process by which individuals work together for a common end; the pooling of efforts to produce a mutually desired outcome.

Cooperation, principle of In conversation, an implicit agreement between speaker and listener to cooperate in trying to understand each other.

Costs Anything that you normally try to avoid—things you consider unpleasant or difficult. *See also* **rewards.**

Credibility The degree to which people see a person as believable; competence, character, and charisma (dynamism) are major factors in credibility.

Credibility strategies Techniques by which you seek to establish your competence, character, and charisma. *Use these to establish your credibility but do so in moderation; too many will make you appear to be bragging.*

Critical thinking The process of logically evaluating reasons and evidence and reaching a judgment on the basis of this analysis.

Cultural assimilation The process by which people leave behind their culture of origin and take on the values and beliefs of another culture; as when, for example, immigrants give up their native culture to become members of their new adopted culture.

Cultural display Signs that communicate a person's cultural identification, such as clothing or religious jewelry.

Cultural display rules Rules that identify what are and what are not appropriate forms of expression for members of the culture.

Cultural evolution The theory, often called social Darwinism, that holds that much as the human species evolved from earlier life forms to Homo sapiens, cultures also evolve.

Cultural identifiers The terms used to talk about cultural identifications, for example, race or religion. *Use cultural* *identifiers that are sensitive to the desires of others; when appropriate, make clear the cultural identifiers you prefer.*

Cultural relativism The theory that all cultures are different but that no culture is either superior or inferior to any other.

Cultural rules Rules that are specific to a given culture.

Cultural sensitivity An attitude and way of behaving in which you're aware of and acknowledge cultural differences. *Cultivate cultural sensitivity by learning about other cultures and interacting with people who are culturally different.*

Cultural time The meanings given to the ways time is treated in a particular culture.

Culture The lifestyle of a group of people; their values, beliefs, artifacts, ways of behaving, and ways of communicating. Culture includes everything that members of a social group have produced and developed—their language, ways of thinking, art, laws, and religion—and that is transmitted from one generation to another through communication rather than genes. *Look at cultural differences not as deviations or deficiencies but as the differences they are. Recognizing different ways of doing things, however, does not necessarily mean accepting them. Communicate with an understanding that culture influences communication in all its forms. Increase your cultural sensitivity by learning about different cultures, recognizing and facing your fears, recognizing relevant differences, and becoming conscious of the cultural rules of other cultures.*

Culture shock The reactions people experience at being in a culture very different from their own and from what they are used to.

Date An extensional device used to emphasize the notion of constant change and symbolized by a subscript: For example, John Smith$_{2010}$ is not John Smith$_{2014}$. *Date your statements to avoid thinking of the world as static and unchanging. Reflect the inevitability of change in your messages.*

Decoder Something that takes a message in one form (for example, sound waves) and translates it into another form (for example, nerve impulses) from which meaning can be formulated. In human communication, the decoder is the auditory mechanism; in electronic communication, the decoder is, for example, the telephone earpiece. Decoding is the process of extracting a message from a code—for example, translating speech sounds into nerve impulses. *See also* **encoder.**

Defensiveness An attitude of an individual or an atmosphere in a group characterized by threats, fear, and domination; messages evidencing evaluation, control, strategy, neutrality, superiority, and certainty are thought to lead to defensiveness. Opposed to **supportiveness.**

Delayed reaction A reaction that a person consciously delays while analyzing the situation and evaluating possible choices for communication.

Denial One of the obstacles to the expression of emotion; the process by which you deny your emotions to yourself or to others.

Denotation The objective or descriptive aspect of a word's meaning; the meaning you'd find in a dictionary. Opposed to **connotation.**

Depenetration A reversal of penetration; a condition in which the breadth and depth of a relationship decrease.

Depth The degree to which the inner personality—the inner core of an individual—is penetrated in interpersonal interaction.

Deterioration In the stage model of relationships, the stage during which the connecting bonds between the partners weaken and the partners begin drifting apart.

Dialogue A form of communication in which each person is both speaker and listener; communication characterized by involvement, concern, and respect for the other person. Opposed to **monologue.**

Direct speech Speech in which the speaker's intentions are stated clearly and directly.

Disclaimer Statement that asks the listener to receive what you say without its reflecting negatively on you. *Use disclaimers if you feel you might be misunderstood. But avoid them when they're not necessary; too many disclaimers can make you appear unprepared or unwilling to state an opinion.*

Disconfirmation The process by which someone ignores or denies the right of another individual even to define himself or herself. Opposed to **rejection** and **confirmation.** *Generally, avoid disconfirmation along with sexist, heterosexist, racist, and ageist language, which is insulting and invariably creates communication barriers.*

Display rules Rules or customs (of a culture or an organization) that govern what is and what is not permissible communication.

Dissolution In the stage model of relationships, the termination or end of the relationship. *In dealing with relationship dissolution, break the loneliness–depression cycle, take time out, bolster self-esteem, seek support from nourishing others, and avoid repeating negative patterns.*

Downward communication Communication sent from the higher levels of a hierarchy to the lower levels—for example, messages sent by managers to workers or from deans to faculty members.

Dyadic coalition A two-person group formed from some larger group to achieve a particular goal.

Dyadic communication Two-person communication.

Dyadic consciousness An awareness on the part of the participants that an interpersonal relationship or pairing exists between them; distinguished from situations in which two individuals are together but do not see themselves as a unit or twosome.

Dyadic effect The tendency for the behaviors of one person to stimulate similar behaviors in the other interactant; often refers to the tendency of one person's self-disclosures to prompt the other also to self-disclose.

Dyadic primacy The significance or centrality of the two-person group, even when there are many more people interacting.

Dyssemia A condition in which an individual is unable to appropriately read the nonverbal messages of others or to communicate his or her own meanings nonverbally.

Earmarker A marker that identifies an item as belonging to a specific person—for example, a nameplate on a desk or initials on an attaché case. *Observe the markers of others; they often reveal a person's thinking about his or her territory.*

Effect The outcome or consequence of an action or behavior; communication is assumed always to have some effect.

Emblems Nonverbal behaviors that directly translate words or phrases—for example, the signs for OK and peace.

Emoticon Visual representation of emotion produced by a short sequence of keyboard characters.

Emotion The feelings we have—for example, our feelings of guilt, anger, or love.

Emotional abuse Behavior that is humiliating, isolating, or overly critical. *Avoid it.*

Emotional communication The expression of feelings—for example, feelings of guilt, happiness, or sorrow. *Identify and describe emotions (both positive and negative) clearly and specifically. Learn the vocabulary of emotional expression. Communicate emotions effectively: Confront the obstacles to emotional expression; describe your feelings, identifying the reasons behind them; anchor feelings to the present; and own your feelings and messages.*

Emotional contagion The process by which the strong emotions of one person are taken on by another person; the assumption that, like the flu, emotions may be contagious.

Emotional display Express emotions and interpret the emotions of others in light of the cultural rules dictating what is and what isn't "appropriate."

Emotionality in interpersonal communication Recognize the inevitable emotionality in your thoughts and feelings, and include emotion as appropriate in your verbal and nonverbal messages.

Empathy A quality of interpersonal effectiveness that involves sharing others' feelings; an ability to feel or perceive things from others' points of view. *Communicate empathy when appropriate: Resist evaluating the person, focus on the person, express active involvement through facial expressions and gestures, reflect back the feelings you think are being expressed, self-disclose, and address mixed messages.*

Encoder Something that takes a message in one form (for example, nerve impulses) and translates it into another form (for example, sound waves). In human communication, the encoder is the speaking mechanism; in electronic communication, the encoder is, for example, the telephone mouthpiece. Encoding is the process of putting a message into a code—for example, translating nerve impulses into speech sounds. *See also* **decoder.**

Enculturation The process by which culture is transmitted from one generation to another.

E-prime A form of the language that omits the verb "to be" except when used as an auxiliary or in statements of existence. *Be careful of the verb "to be"; use it with an understanding of how it might incorporate illogical assumptions.*

Equality An attitude that recognizes that each individual in a communication interaction is equal, that no one is superior to any other; encourages supportiveness. Opposed to **superiority.**

Equilibrium theory A theory of proxemics holding that intimacy and physical closeness are positively related; as a relationship becomes more intimate, the individuals will maintain shorter distances between themselves.

Equity theory A theory claiming that people experience relational satisfaction when there is an equal distribution of rewards and costs between the two persons in the relationship.

Equivocation A deceptive message that is purposely ambiguous and designed to lead people to think something different from your intention. *You sure made a statement* instead of *You made a complete fool of yourself!*

Eros love One of Lee's (1976) six types of love; seeks beauty and sensuality and focuses on physical attractiveness.

Et cetera (etc.) An extensional device used to emphasize the notion of infinite complexity; because you can never know all about anything, any statement about the world or an event must end with an explicit or implicit "etc." *Use an implicit, or sometimes an explicit, etc. to remind yourself and others that there is more to say.*

Ethics The branch of philosophy that deals with the rightness or wrongness of actions; the study of moral values; in communication, the morality of message behavior.

Ethnic identity The commitment to the beliefs and philosophy of one's culture; the degree to which a person identifies with his or her cultural group.

Ethnocentrism The tendency to see others and their behaviors through your own cultural filters, often as distortions of your own behaviors; the tendency to evaluate the values and beliefs of your own culture more positively than those of another culture. *Recognize your own ethnocentric thinking, and be aware of how it influences your verbal and nonverbal messages.*

Euphemism A polite word or phrase used to substitute for some taboo or less polite term or phrase.

Evaluation A process whereby we place a value on some person, object, or event.

Exaggeration A common deceptive message where you, for example, lead people to believe that, for example, you earn more money than you do or your grades are better than they are or your relationship is more satisfying than it really is.

Excuse An explanation designed to lessen the negative consequences of something done or said. *Repair conversational problems by offering excuses that demonstrate understanding, acknowledge your responsibility, acknowledge your regret, request forgiveness, and make clear that this will never happen again.*

Expectancy violations theory A theory of proxemics holding that people have a certain expectancy for space relationships. When that is violated (say, a person stands too close to you or a romantic partner maintains abnormally large distances from you), the relationship comes into clearer focus and you wonder why this "normal distance" is being violated.

Expert power Power that a person has because others believe the individual to have expertise or special knowledge.

Expressiveness A quality of interpersonal effectiveness that consists of genuine involvement in speaking and listening, conveyed verbally and nonverbally. *Communicate expressiveness and active involvement by using active listening, addressing mixed messages, using I-messages, and using appropriate variations in paralanguage and gestures.*

Extensional devices Linguistic devices proposed by Alfred Korzybski to make language a more accurate means for talking about the world. The extensional devices include et cetera, date, and index. *Use them; they help make language more descriptive of the world as we know it.*

Extensional orientation A point of view in which primary consideration is given to the world of experience and only secondary consideration is given to labels. Opposed to **intensional orientation.**

Face-saving messages Communications that preserve or even enhance a person's self-image and self-respect. *Use strategies that allow others, even your opponents in conflict, to save face.*

Facial feedback hypothesis The hypothesis or theory that your facial expressions can produce physiological and emotional effects via a feedback mechanism.

Facial management techniques Techniques used to mask certain emotions and to emphasize others; for example, intensifying your expression of happiness to make a friend feel good about a promotion. *Use these in moderation; too much excitement, for example, can appear phony.*

Fact–inference confusion A misevaluation in which a person makes an inference, regards it as a fact, and acts upon it as if it were a fact. *Distinguish facts (verifiably true past events) from inferences (guesses or hypotheses), and act on inferences with tentativeness.*

Factual statement A statement made by the observer after observation and limited to what is observed. Opposed to **inferential statement.**

Family A group of people with defined roles, recognition of mutual responsibilities, a shared history and future, shared living space (usually), and rules for communicating.

Fear appeal The appeal to fear to persuade an individual or group of individuals to believe or to act in a certain way.

Feedback Information that is given back to the source. Feedback may come from the source's own messages (as when you hear what you're saying) or from the receiver(s)—in forms such as applause, yawning, puzzled looks, questions, letters to the editor of a newspaper, or increased or decreased subscriptions to a magazine. *See also* **negative feedback, positive feedback.** *Listen to both verbal and nonverbal feedback—from yourself and from others—and use these cues to help you adjust your messages.*

Feedforward Information that is sent before a regular message, telling the listener something about what is to follow; messages that are prefatory to more central messages. *Use feedforward when you feel your listener needs background or when you want to ease into a particular topic, such as bad news.*

Feminine culture A culture that encourages both men and women to be modest, oriented to maintaining the quality of life, and tender. Feminine cultures emphasize the quality of life and so socialize their people to be modest and to emphasize close interpersonal relationships. Opposed to **masculine culture.**

Flexibility The ability to adjust communication strategies and skills on the basis of the unique situation. *Because no two communication situations are identical, because everything is in a state of flux, and because everyone is different, cultivate flexibility and adjust your communication to the unique situation.*

Flirting A type of communication in which you signal romantic interest.

Focus group An in-depth interview of a small group that aims to discover what people think about an issue or product.

Force An unproductive conflict strategy in which you try to win an argument by emotionally or physically overpowering the other person—either by threat or by actual behavior. *Avoid it; it attacks a person's negative face and almost invariably will create resentment.*

Formal time Temporal divisions that are measured objectively, such as seconds, minutes, hours, days, weeks, months, and years.

Friendship An interpersonal relationship between two persons that is mutually productive, established and maintained through perceived mutual free choice, and characterized by mutual positive regard. *Establish friendships to help serve such needs as utility, ego support, stimulation, and security. At the same time, seek to serve your friends' similar needs.*

Fundamental attribution error The tendency to overvalue and overweight the contribution of internal factors (i.e., a person's personality) to behavior and to undervalue and underweight the contribution of external factors (i.e., the situation the person is in or the surrounding events). *Avoid the fundamental attribution error, whereby you attribute someone's behavior solely to internal factors while minimizing or ignoring situational forces.*

Gender The cultural roles of "masculine" and "feminine" that are learned from one's culture. *See also* **sex.**

Gender display rules The cultural rules that identify what are appropriate and what are not appropriate forms of expression for men and for women.

General Semantics The study of the relationships among language, thought, and behavior.

Gobbledygook Overly complex language that fails to communicate meanings clearly and specifically. *When you suspect gobbledygook is being used to confuse rather than clarify, ask for simplification.*

Gossip Oral or written communication about someone not present, some third party, usually about matters that are private to this third party. *Generally, avoid it; it's likely to make others see you more negatively.*

Grapevine communication Organizational messages that don't follow any of the formal lines of communication established in an organization; rather, they cross organizational lines. *Listen carefully to these messages; they often contain crucial information.*

Gunnysacking An unproductive conflict strategy of storing up grievances—as if in a gunnysack—and holding them in readiness to dump on the other person in the conflict. *Avoid it; it leads you away from considering a workable solution to a problem.*

Halo effect The tendency to generalize a person's virtue or expertise from one area to other areas. *Beware of this tendency; it can lead you to misperceive a situation or person.*

Haptics The study of touch or tactile communication.

Heterosexism Negative attitudes and beliefs about gay men and lesbians; the belief that all sexual behavior that is not heterosexual is unnatural and deserving of criticism and condemnation.

Heterosexist language Language that denigrates lesbians and gay men. *Avoid it; it will make you appear a bigot or, at best, ill informed.*

Hidden self In the Johari window model, this self contains all that you know of yourself that you keep secret.

High-ambiguity tolerant cultures Cultures that are accepting of ambiguity and do not feel threatened by unknown situations; uncertainty is a normal part of life, and people accept it as it comes.

High-context culture A culture in which much of the information in communication messages is left implied; it's "understood." Much information is considered to be in the context or in the person rather than explicitly coded in the verbal messages. Collectivist cultures are generally high context. Opposed to **low-context culture.** *Adjust your messages and your listening in light of the differences between high- and low-context cultures.*

High-power distance culture Cultures in which power is concentrated in the hands of a few and there's a great difference between the power held by these people and the power of the ordinary citizen. *See* **low-power distance culture.**

Home field advantage The increased power that comes from being in your own territory.

Home territory Territory in which an individual has a sense of intimacy and over which he or she exercises control—for example, a teacher's office.

Hostile environment harassment A type of sexual harassment in which verbal and nonverbal messages about sex make a worker uncomfortable.

Identity management *See* **impression management.**

Illustrators Nonverbal behaviors that accompany and literally illustrate verbal messages—for example, upward movements of the head and hand that accompany the verbal "It's up there."

Image-confirming strategies Techniques you use to communicate or to confirm your self-image, the image you want others to see.

I-messages Messages in which the speaker accepts responsibility for personal thoughts and behaviors and states his or her point of view explicitly. Opposed to **you-messages.** *Use I-messages when communicating your feelings; take responsibility for your own feelings rather than attributing them to others.*

Immediacy A quality of interpersonal effectiveness that conveys a sense of contact and togetherness, a feeling of interest in and liking for the other person. *Maintain immediacy through close physical distances and eye contact and by smiling, using the other person's name, and focusing on the other's remarks.*

Impostor phenomenon The tendency to disregard outward signs of success and to consider yourself an "impostor," a fake, a fraud, one who doesn't really deserve to be considered successful.

Impression formation The process by which you perceive another person and ultimately come to some kind of evaluation or interpretation of this person.

Impression management The process you go through to communicate the impression you want the other person to have of you. Some writers use the term "self-presentation" or "identity management."

Inclusion, principle of The principle of verbal interaction holding that all members should be a part of (included in) the interaction.

Index An extensional device symbolized by a subscript and used to emphasize the assumption that no two things are the same; for example, even though two people may both be politicians, politician$1_{[Smith]}$ is not politician$2_{[Jones]}$. *Use the index to remind yourself that even though people are covered by the same label, they are each individuals.*

Indirect speech Speech that hides the speaker's true intentions; speech in which requests and observations are made indirectly. *Use indirect messages when a more direct style might prove insulting or offensive, but be aware that indirect messages also may create misunderstanding.*

Indiscrimination A misevaluation that results when you categorize people, events, or objects into a particular class and respond to them only as members of the class; a failure to recognize that each individual is unique. *Treat each situation and each person as unique (when possible) even when they're covered by the same label. Index key concepts.*

Individualist culture A culture in which the individual's rather than the group's goals and preferences are given greater importance. Opposed to **collectivist culture.** *Adjust your messages and your listening with an awareness of differences between individualist and collectivist cultures.*

Indulgence A cultural orientation that emphasizes the gratification of desires and a focus on having fun and enjoying life. Opposed to **restraint.**

Inevitability A principle of communication holding that communication cannot be avoided; all behavior in an interactional setting is communication.

Inferential statement A statement that can be made by anyone, is not limited to what is observed, and can be made at any time. Opposed to **factual statement.**

Influencing strategies Strategies designed to influence the attitudes or behaviors of others.

Informal time Temporal divisions that are approximate and that are referred to with such general terms as, for example, forever, immediately, soon, right away, as soon as possible. *Clarify your informal time terms; ask others for clarification when they use such terms, as appropriate.*

Information or persuasion power Power that a person has because others see that individual as having significant information and the ability to communicate logically and persuasively.

Information overload A condition in which the amount or complexity of information is too great to be dealt with effectively by an individual, group, or organization.

In-group talk Talk about a subject or in a vocabulary that some people present understand and others do not; has the effect of excluding those who don't understand.

Insulation A reaction to territorial encroachment in which you erect some sort of barrier between yourself and the invaders, such as a stone wall around your property, an unlisted phone number, or caller ID.

Intensional orientation A point of view in which primary consideration is given to the way things are labeled and only secondary consideration (if any) to the world of experience. Opposed to **extensional orientation.** *Avoid intensional orientation; look to people and things first and to labels second.*

Interaction management A quality of interpersonal effectiveness in which the interaction is controlled and managed to the satisfaction of both parties; effectively managing conversational turns, fluency, and message consistency. *Speak in relatively short conversational turns, avoid long and/or frequent pauses, and use verbal and nonverbal messages that are consistent.*

Intercultural communication Communication that takes place between persons of different cultures or between persons who have different cultural beliefs, values, or ways of behaving. *In communicating in intercultural situations, prepare yourself, reduce your ethnocentrism, confront your stereotypes, become mindful, avoid overattribution, reduce uncertainty, and recognize (1) differences between yourself and people who are culturally different, (2) differences within other cultural groups, and (3) cultural differences in meanings.*

Interpersonal communication Communication between two persons or among a small group of persons and distinguished from public or mass communication; communication of a personal nature and distinguished from impersonal communication; communication between or among connected persons or those involved in a close relationship.

Interpersonal competence The knowledge of and the ability to communicate effectively in interpersonal interactions.

Interpersonal conflict Disagreement between two connected persons.

Interpersonal effectiveness The ability to accomplish interpersonal goals; interpersonal communication that is satisfying to both individuals.

Interpersonal perception The perception of people; the processes through which you interpret and evaluate people and their behavior.

Interruptions Verbal and nonverbal attempts to take over the role of the speaker.

Intimacy The closest interpersonal relationship; usually characterizes close primary relationships.

Intimacy claims Obligations incurred by virtue of being in a close and intimate relationship.

Intimate distance The closest distance in proxemics, ranging from touching to 18 inches.

Intrapersonal communication Communication with oneself.

Involvement The second stage in relationship development, in which you further advance the relationship, first testing each other and then intensifying your interaction.

Irreversibility A principle of communication holding that communication cannot be reversed; once something has been communicated, it cannot be uncommunicated.

Jargon The technical language of any specialized group, often a professional class, which is unintelligible to individuals not belonging to the group; shop talk. This glossary is an example of the jargon of part of the communication field.

Jealousy A reaction (consisting of feelings, thoughts, and behaviors) to a physical or emotional threat to one or more of your significant relationships. *Be careful in displaying jealousy; it can be scary.*

Johari window A diagram of the four selves (open, blind, hidden, and unknown).

Just world hypothesis The belief that the world is just, that good things happen to good people (because they are good), and that bad things happen to bad people (because they are bad).

Kinesics The study of the communicative dimensions of facial and bodily movements.

Language The rules of syntax, semantics, and phonology by which sentences are created and understood; a language refers to the sentences that can be created in any language, such as English, Bantu, or Italian.

Lateral communication Messages between equals—manager to manager, worker to worker.

Leave-taking cues Verbal and nonverbal signals that indicate a desire to terminate a conversation. *Be especially alert to these types of cues, lest you be thought a conversational bore.*

Legitimate power Power a person possesses because others believe he or she has a right—by virtue of his or her position—to influence or control their behavior.

Lie bias The assumption that the person is most likely lying. Opposed to **truth bias.**

Linguistic collusion A response to territorial encroachment in which you speak in a language or jargon that the "invaders" don't understand and thus exclude them from the interaction. *See also* **withdrawal, turf defense,** and **insulation.**

Linguistic relativity hypothesis The theory that the language you speak influences your perceptions of the world and your behaviors and that therefore people speaking widely differing languages will perceive and behave differently.

Listening An active process of receiving aural stimuli consisting of five stages: receiving, understanding, remembering, evaluating, and responding. *Be especially flexible when listening in a multicultural setting, realizing that people from other cultures give different listening cues and may operate with different rules for listening.* The process of receiving, understanding, remembering, evaluating, and responding to verbal and/or nonverbal messages.

Long-term memory The memory that holds an unlimited amount of information indefinitely.

Long-term orientation A cultural orientation that promotes the importance of future rewards and so, for example, members of these cultures are more apt to save for the future and to prepare for the future academically. Opposed to **short-term orientation.**

Love A relationship with another person in which you feel closeness, caring, warmth, and excitement.

Low-ambiguity tolerant cultures Cultures that are uncomfortable with ambiguity, do much to avoid uncertainty, and have a great deal of anxiety about not knowing what will happen next.

Low-context culture A culture in which most of the information in communication is explicitly stated in the verbal message rather than being left implied or assumed to be "understood." Low-context cultures are usually individualist cultures. Opposed to **high-context culture.**

Low-power distance culture Culture in which power is relatively evenly distributed throughout the citizenry. *See* **high-power distance culture.**

Ludic love One of Lee's (1976) six types of love; based on entertainment and excitement, it is love as a game, not to be taken too seriously and with emotions held in check.

Lying The act of sending messages with the intention of giving another person information you believe to be false.

Machiavellianism The belief that people can be manipulated easily; also, manipulative techniques or tactics one person uses to control another.

Manic love One of Lee's (1976) six types of love; obsessive love, it is marked by a need for constant attention and affection, which when withheld leads to depression, jealousy, and self-doubt.

Manipulation An unproductive conflict strategy; a manipulative individual avoids engaging in open conflict but instead attempts to divert the conflict by being especially charming and getting the other person into a noncombative frame of mind.

Manner principle A principle of conversation that holds that speakers cooperate with listeners by being clear and by organizing their thoughts into meaningful and coherent patterns.

Markers Devices that signify that a certain territory belongs to a particular person. *See also* **boundary marker, central marker,** and **earmarker.**

Masculine culture A culture that views men as assertive, oriented to material success, and strong; such a culture views women, on the other hand, as modest, focused on the quality of life, and tender. Masculine cultures emphasize success and so socialize their people to be assertive, ambitious, and competitive. Opposed to **feminine culture.**

Matching hypothesis An assumption that you date and mate people who are comparable to yourself—who match you—in physical attractiveness.

Meaningfulness A principle of perception that assumes that the behavior of people is sensible, stems from some logical antecedent, and therefore is meaningful rather than meaningless.

Mentoring relationship A relationship in which an experienced individual helps train someone who is less experienced; for example, an accomplished teacher might mentor a younger teacher who is newly arrived or who has never taught before.

Mere exposure hypothesis The theory that repeated or prolonged exposure to a stimulus may result in a change in attitude toward the stimulus object, generally in the direction of increased positiveness.

Message Any signal or combination of signals that serves as a stimulus for a receiver. *See also* **stimulus.**

Meta-advice Advice about advice, for example, suggesting that they seek more expert advice.

Metacommunication Communication about communication. *Metacommunicate when you want to clarify the way you're talking or what you're talking about by, for example, giving clear feedforward and paraphrasing your complex messages.*

Metalanguage Language that refers to language.

Metamessage A message that makes reference to another message, such as "Did I make myself clear?" or "That's a lie."

Micromomentary expressions Extremely brief movements that are not consciously controlled or recognized and that are thought to be indicative of your true emotional state.

Mindfulness A state of awareness in which you are conscious of the logic and rationality of your behaviors and of the logical connections existing among elements.

Mindlessness A lack of conscious awareness of the logic or reasons behind your thoughts or behaviors. *Increase your mindfulness by creating and re-creating categories and being open to new information and points of view; also, beware of relying too heavily on first impressions.*

Minimization A deceptive message in which the facts or their importance are minimized.

Mixed message A message that communicates two different and often contradictory meanings—for example, a message that asks for two different (often incompatible) responses such as "leave me alone" and "show me more attention." Often, one meaning (usually the socially acceptable meaning) is communicated verbally and the other (usually the less socially acceptable meaning) nonverbally.

Model A representation of an object or process.

Monochronic time orientation A view of time in which things are done sequentially; one thing is scheduled at a time. Opposed to **polychronic time orientation.**

Monologue A form of communication in which one person speaks and the other listens; there's no real interaction among participants. Opposed to **dialogue.**

Negative face The desire to be autonomous, to have the right to do as you wish.

Negative face strategies Messages that recognize a person's right to autonomy. *Avoid messages that impose on others or otherwise encroach upon their independence and autonomy.*

Negative feedback Feedback that serves a corrective function by informing the source that his or her message is not being received in the way intended. Looks of boredom, shouts of disagreement, letters critical of newspaper policy, and teachers' instructions on how better to approach a problem are examples of negative feedback and will (ideally) serve to redirect behavior. *See also* **positive feedback.**

Netiquette Rules of politeness for online communication.

Network convergence The blending or sharing of one individual's circle of friends with another person's circle of friends.

Networking Connecting with people who can help you accomplish a goal or help you find information related to your goal, for example, to your search for a job. *Establish a network of relationships to provide insights into issues relevant to your personal and professional life, and be willing to lend your expertise to others.*

Neutrality A response pattern lacking in personal involvement; encourages defensiveness. Opposed to **empathy.**

Noise Anything that interferes with your receiving a message as the source intended the message to be received. Noise is present in communication to the extent that the message received is not the message sent. *In managing noise, reduce physical, physiological, psychological, and semantic noise as best you can; use repetition and restatement, and, when in doubt, ask if you're clear.*

Nonallness A point of view holding that you can never know all about anything and that what you know, say, or hear is only a part of what there is to know, say, or hear.

Nonnegotiation An unproductive conflict strategy in which an individual refuses to discuss the conflict or to listen to the other person.

Nonverbal communication Communication without words; communication by means of space, gestures, facial expressions, touching, vocal variation, or silence, for example.

Nonverbal dominance Nonverbal behavior through which one person achieves psychological dominance over another.

Object language Language used to communicate about objects, events, and relations in the world (rather than about words as in metalanguage).

Object-adaptors Movements that involve manipulation of some object; for example, punching holes in a Styrofoam coffee cup, clicking a ballpoint pen, or chewing on a pencil.

Oculesics The study of the messages communicated by the eyes.

Olfactory communication Communication by smell. *Become mindful of your own scent messages; they can serve as attractants and as repellants.*

Omission As a form of deception, omission occurs when you omit crucial details to hide the truth and to mislead the other person.

Online-only relationships Relationships that exist exclusively or primarily between social media users, for example, between "tweeter" and follower, blogger and reader, "friend" and contact on Facebook or LinkedIn.

Onymous messages Messages that are signed; messages for which the author is identified or known. Opposed to **anonymous messages.**

Open self In the Johari window model, this self represents all the information, behaviors, attitudes, feelings, desires, motivations, and ideas that you and others know.

Openness A quality of interpersonal effectiveness involving a person's willingness (1) to interact openly with others, self-disclosing as appropriate; (2) to react honestly to incoming stimuli; and (3) to own his or her own feelings and thoughts. *Increase openness when appropriate by self-disclosing, responding spontaneously and honestly to those with whom you're interacting, and owning your own feelings and thoughts.*

Other talk Talk about the listener or some third party. Opposed to **self talk.**

Other-orientation A quality of interpersonal effectiveness involving attentiveness, interest, and concern for the other person. *Acknowledge the importance of the other person: Use focused eye contact and appropriate facial expressions; smile, nod, and lean toward the other person.*

Outing The process whereby a person's affectional orientation is made public by another person without the gay man or lesbian's consent.

Overattribution The tendency to attribute to one or two characteristics most or even all of what a person does. *Avoid overattribution; rarely is any one factor an accurate explanation of complex human behavior.*

Owning feelings The process of taking responsibility for your own feelings instead of attributing them to others. *Do it.*

Paralanguage The vocal but nonverbal aspects of speech. Paralanguage consists of voice qualities (for example, pitch range, resonance, tempo); vocal characterizers (laughing or crying, yelling or whispering); vocal qualifiers (intensity, pitch height); and vocal segregates ("uh-uh" meaning "no," or "shh" meaning "silence"). *Vary paralinguistic features to communicate nuances of meaning and to add interest and color to your messages.*

Pauses Interruptions in the normally fluent stream of speech. Pauses are of two types: filled pauses (interruptions filled with such vocalizations as "er" or "um") and unfilled pauses (silences of unusually long duration).

Peaceful relations principle A principle of communication advising that you say only what preserves peaceful relationships with others.

Perception The process by which you become aware of objects and events through your senses. *Increase accuracy in interpersonal perception by identifying the influence of your physical and emotional states, making sure that you're not drawing conclusions from too little information, and checking your perceptions.*

Perception checking The process of verifying your understanding of some message, situation, or feeling. *Increase accuracy in perception by checking your perceptions: Describe what you see or hear and the meaning you assign to it, and ask the other person if your perceptions are accurate.*

Perceptual accentuation A process that leads you to see what you expect or want to see—for example, seeing people you like as better looking and smarter than people you don't like.

Personal distance The second closest distance in proxemics, ranging from 18 inches to 4 feet.

Personal rejection An unproductive conflict strategy in which you withhold love and affection and seek to win the argument by getting the other person to break down under this withdrawal. *Avoid it; it invariably creates more problems.*

Personality theory A theory of personality, complete with rules about what characteristics go with what other characteristics, that you maintain and through which you perceive others.

Persuasion The process of influencing attitudes and behavior.

Phatic communication Communication that is primarily social; communication designed to open the channels of communication rather than to communicate something about the external world. "Hello" and "How are you?" in everyday interaction are examples.

Physical abuse Behavior that involves threats of violence as well as pushing, hitting, slapping, kicking, choking, throwing things, and breaking things. *Avoid it; it will not only create relationship problems, it may have very unpleasant legal consequences.*

Physical noise Interference that is external to both speaker and listener and that interferes with the physical transmission of a signal or message.

Physiological noise Interference within the sender or receiver of a message, such as visual impairments, hearing loss, articulation problems, and memory loss.

Pitch In relation to voice qualities, the highness or lowness of the vocal tone.

Polarization A form of fallacious reasoning in which only two extremes are considered; also referred to as black-and-white or either/or thinking or as a two-valued orientation. *Avoid thinking and talking in extremes by using middle terms and qualifiers. But remember that too many qualifiers may make you appear unsure of yourself.*

Politeness Civility, consideration, refinement, respect, and regard for others as expressed verbally and nonverbally; interaction that follows the socially accepted rules for interpersonal interaction.

Politeness principle A principle advising that you treat others respectfully. *Communicate positiveness by expressing your own satisfaction with the interaction and by complimenting others.*

Polychronic time orientation A view of time in which several things may be scheduled or engaged in at the same time. Opposed to **monochronic time orientation.**

Positive face The desire to be viewed positively by others, to be thought of favorably.

Positive face strategies Messages that compliment and praise another. *Use these as appropriate.*

Positive feedback Feedback that supports or reinforces the continuation of behavior along the same lines in which it is already proceeding—for example, applause during a speech, which encourages the speaker to continue speaking the same way. *See also* **negative feedback.**

Positiveness A characteristic of interpersonal effectiveness involving positive attitudes and the use of positive messages expressing these attitudes (as in complimenting others) along with acceptance and approval.

Power The ability to influence or control the behavior of another person; A has power over B when A can influence or control B's behavior; an inevitable part of interpersonal relationships. *In communicating power: Avoid powerless message forms such as hesitations, excessive intensifiers, disqualifiers, tag questions, one-word answers, self-critical statements, overly polite statements, and vulgar and slang expressions.*

Power distance The degree to which differences in power exist among a people. *Adjust your messages and listening on the basis of the power-distance orientation of the culture in which you find yourself.*

Power play A consistent pattern of behavior in which one person tries to control the behavior of another. *Respond to power plays with cooperative strategies: Express your feelings, describe the behavior to which you object, and state a cooperative response.*

Pragma love One of Lee's (1976) six types of love; traditional approach to love, valuing social qualifications and family background and emphasizing logic and practicality over feelings.

Pragmatic implication An assumption that is logical (and therefore appears true) but is actually not necessarily true.

Pragmatics In interpersonal communication, an approach that focuses on communication behaviors and effects and on communication effectiveness.

Primacy and recency effects Giving more importance to that which occurs first (primacy) or to that which occurs last or more recently (recency).

Primary affect displays The communication of the six primary emotions: happiness, surprise, fear, anger, sadness, and disgust or contempt.

Primary emotions Basic emotions; usually identified are joy, acceptance, fear, surprise, sadness, disgust, anger, and anticipation.

Primary territory Areas that you consider your exclusive preserve—for example, your room or office.

Process Ongoing activity; communication is referred to as a process to emphasize that it's always changing, always in motion.

Protection theory A theory of proxemics holding that people establish a body-buffer zone to protect themselves from unwanted closeness, touching, or attack.

Provisionalism An attitude of open-mindedness that leads to the development of a supportive relationship and atmosphere. Opposed to **certainty.**

Proxemics The study of the communicative function of space; the study of how people unconsciously structure their space—the distance between people in their interactions, the organization of space in homes and offices, and even the design of cities. *Maintain distances that are comfortable and that are appropriate to the situation and to your relationship with the other person.*

Proximity As a principle of perception, the tendency to perceive people or events that are physically close as belonging together or representing some unit; physical closeness—one of the qualities influencing interpersonal attraction.

Psychological noise Mental interference in the speaker or listener, such as preconceived ideas, wandering thoughts, biases and prejudices, closed-mindedness, and extreme emotionalism.

Psychological time An emphasis on or orientation toward past, present, or future time; varies from person to person.

Public distance The farthest distance in proxemics, ranging from 12 feet to 25 feet or more.

Public territory Areas that are open to all people—for example, restaurants or parks.

Punctuation of communication The breaking up of continuous communication sequences into short sequences with identifiable beginnings and endings or stimuli and responses.

Pupil dilation The extent to which the pupil of the eye widens; generally, large pupils indicate positive reactions.

Pupillometrics The study of communication messages reflected by changes in the size of the pupils of the eyes.

Pygmalion effect The condition in which you make a prediction of success, act as if it is true, and thereby make it come true (as when, for example, acting toward students as if they'll be successful influences them to become successful); a type of self-fulfilling prophecy.

Quality principle A principle of conversation that holds that speakers cooperate with listeners by saying what they think is true and by not saying what they think is false.

Quantity principle A principle of conversation that holds that speakers cooperate with listeners by being only as informative as necessary to communicate their intended meanings.

Quid pro quo harassment A type of sexual harassment in which employment opportunities (as in hiring and promotion) are made dependent on the granting of sexual favors.

Racism Negative attitudes and beliefs that individuals or a society as a whole hold about specific ethnic groups.

Racist language Language that denigrates, demeans, or is derogatory toward members of a particular ethnic group.

Rate In relation to voice qualities, the speed at which you speak, generally measured in words per minute.

Receiver Any person or thing that takes in messages. Receivers may be individuals listening to or reading a message, a group of persons hearing a speech, a scattered television audience, or machines that store information.

Receptivity As a type of friendship, it is characterized by one person being the primary giver and the other the primary receiver.

Reciprocity As a type of friendship, it is characterized by loyalty, self-sacrifice, and generosity.

Referent power Power that a person possesses because others desire to identify with or be like that individual.

Rejection A response to an individual that acknowledges the person but expresses disagreement. Opposed to **confirmation** and **disconfirmation.**

Relation principle A principle of conversation that holds that speakers cooperate with listeners by talking about what is relevant and by not talking about what isn't.

Relational dialectics theory A theory that describes relationships as defined by a series of competing opposite desires or motivations, such as the desires for autonomy and belonging, for novelty and predictability, and for closedness and openness.

Relationship commitment A type of pledge to support and maintain a relationship because of a desire, an obligation, or some necessity.

Relationship communication Communication between or among intimates or those in close relationships; the term is used by some theorists as synonymous with interpersonal communication.

Relationship development The initial or beginning stage of a relationship; the stage at which two people begin to form an interpersonal relationship.

Relationship dialectics theory An explanation of the conflicting motives that people in close relationships often experience.

Relationship license Permission to violate some relationship expectation, custom, or rule.

Relationship maintenance A condition of relationship stability in which the relationship does not progress or deteriorate significantly; a continuation as opposed to a dissolution (or an intensification) of a relationship.

Relationship messages Messages that comment on the relationship between the speakers rather than on matters external to them.

Relationship rules theory A theory that holds that people maintain relationships with those who follow the rules the individuals have defined as essential to their relationship and dissolve relationships with those who don't follow the rules.

Relationship violence Generally considered to consist of verbal or emotional abuse, physical abuse, or sexual abuse.

Repair In the stage model of relationships, a stage in which one or both parties seek to improve the relationship. *In repairing relationships, recognize the problem, engage in productive conflict resolution, pose possible solutions, affirm each other, integrate solutions into normal behavior, and take risks as appropriate.*

Resemblance As a principle of perception, the tendency to perceive people or events that are similar in appearance as belonging together.

Response Any bit of overt or covert behavior.

Restraint A cultural orientation that fosters the curbing of immediate gratification and regulates it by social norms. Opposed to **indulgence.**

Reverse halo effect The tendency to judge a person you know to have several negative qualities to also have other negative qualities (that you have not observed); also known as the "horns" effect. *See also* **halo effect.**

Reward power Power derived from an individual's ability to give another person what that person wants or to remove what that person wants removed.

Rewards Anything that you want, that you enjoy, and that you'd be willing to incur costs to obtain.

Rhythm The recurring patterns of emphasis in a stream of speech.

Role The part an individual plays in a group; an individual's function or expected behavior.

Rules theory *See* **relationship rules theory.**

Schemata Ways of organizing perceptions; mental templates or structures that help you organize the millions of items of information you come into contact with every day as well as those you already have in memory; general ideas about groups of people or individuals, about yourself, or about types of social roles. The word *schemata* is the plural of *schema.*

Script A type of schema; an organized body of information about some action, event, or procedure. A script provides a general idea of how some event should play out or unfold, the rules governing the events and their sequence.

Secondary territory An area that does not belong to you but that you've occupied and that is therefore associated with you—for example, the seat you normally take in class.

Selective attention The tendency to attend to those things that you want to see or that you expect to see.

Selective exposure The tendency to expose your senses to certain things and not others, to actively seek out information that supports your beliefs and to actively avoid information that contradicts these beliefs.

Selective perception The tendency to perceive certain things and not others; includes selective attention and selective exposure.

Self-acceptance Being satisfied with yourself, your virtues and vices, your abilities and limitations.

Self-adaptors Movements that usually satisfy a physical need, especially to make you more comfortable, for example, scratching your head to relieve an itch, moistening your lips because they feel dry, or pushing your hair out of your eyes.

Self-attribution A process through which you seek to account for and understand the reasons and motivations for your own behaviors.

Self-awareness The degree to which you know yourself. *Increase self-awareness by listening to others, increasing your open self, and seeking out information to reduce blind spots.*

Self-concept Your self-image, the view you have of who you are. *To increase your understanding of self, try to see yourself, as objectively as you can, through the eyes of others; compare yourself to similar (and admired) others; examine the influences of culture; and observe and evaluate your own message behaviors.*

Self-denigration principle A principle of communication advising you to put the other person above yourself; to praise the other person rather than taking credit yourself.

Self-deprecating strategies Techniques you use to signal your inability to do some task or your incompetence to encourage another to help you out. *Avoid these or use in moderation; such strategies can easily backfire and simply make you seem incompetent.*

Self-disclosure The process of revealing something about yourself to another; usually refers to information that you'd normally keep hidden. *When thinking of disclosing, consider the legitimacy of your motives, the appropriateness of the disclosure, the listener's responses (is the dyadic effect operating?), and the potential burdens such disclosures might impose.*

Self-esteem The value (usually, the positive value) you place on yourself; your self-evaluation. *Increase your self-esteem by attacking self-destructive beliefs, seeking out nourishing people, working on projects that will result in success, and securing affirmation.*

Self-fulfilling prophecy The situation in which you make a prediction or prophecy and fulfill it yourself—for example, expecting a person to be hostile, you act in a hostile manner toward this person, and in doing so elicit hostile behavior in the person, thus confirming your prophecy that the person will be hostile. *Take a second look at your perceptions when they correspond very closely to your initial expectations; the self-fulfilling prophecy may be at work.*

Self-handicapping strategies Techniques you use to excuse possible failure, for example, setting up barriers or obstacles to make the task impossible and so when you fail, you won't be blamed or thought ineffective.

Self-monitoring Manipulating the image you present to others in interpersonal interactions so as to create the most favorable impression of yourself.

Self-monitoring strategies Techniques you use to carefully monitor (self-censor) what you say or do.

Self-presentation *See* **impression management.**

Self-serving bias A bias that operates in the self-attribution process, leading you to take credit for the positive consequences of your behaviors and to deny responsibility for the negative consequences. *Become mindful of giving too much weight to internal factors (when explaining your positives) and too little weight to external factors (when explaining your negatives).*

Semantic noise Interference created when a speaker and listener have different meaning systems; such noise can include language or dialectical differences, the use of jargon or overly complex terms, or ambiguous or overly abstract terms whose meanings can be easily misinterpreted.

Semantics The area of language study concerned with meaning.

Sex The biological distinction between males and females, the genetic distinction between men and women. *See also* **gender.**

Sexism Negative attitudes and beliefs about a particular gender; prejudicial attitudes and beliefs about men or women based on rigid beliefs about gender roles.

Sexist language Language derogatory to members of one gender, generally women.

Sexual abuse Behavior that is unwanted and directed at a person's sexuality, for example, touching, accusations of sexual infidelity without reason, forced sex, and references to a person by abusive sexual terms.

Sexual harassment Unsolicited and unwanted verbal or nonverbal sexual messages. *The first generally recommended option for dealing with sexual harassment is to talk to the harasser. If this doesn't stop the behavior, then consider collecting evidence, using appropriate channels within the organization, and filing a complaint.*

Sharpening A process of message distortion in which the details of messages, when repeated, are crystallized and heightened.

Short-term memory The memory you use to remember information you need immediately or temporarily, for example, remembering a phone number just long enough to dial it.

Short-term orientation A cultural dimension in which people look more to the past and the present; these cultural members spend their resources for the present and want quick results from their efforts. Opposed to **long-term orientation.**

Shyness A condition of discomfort and uneasiness in interpersonal situations.

Signal and noise, relativity of The principle of verbal interaction that holds that what is signal (meaningful) and what is noise (interference) is relative to the communication analyst, the participants, and the context.

Signal reaction A conditioned response to a signal; a response to some signal that is immediate rather than delayed. Opposed to **delayed reaction.**

Signal-to-noise ratio A measure of the relationship between meaningful information (signal) and interference (noise).

Silence The absence of vocal communication; often misunderstood to refer to the absence of communication. *Examine silence for meanings just as you would eye movements or body gestures.*

Silencers Unproductive conflict strategies (such as crying) that literally silence your opponent.

Similarity A principle of attraction holding that you're attracted to qualities similar to your own and to people who are similar to you. Opposed to **complementarity.**

Skills Proficiencies; interpersonal skills are those abilities and competencies for creating and responding to interpersonal messages effectively.

Slang Language used by special groups, often not considered standard in general society.

Small talk Noncontroversial talk that is usually short in duration and often serves as a polite way of introducing one's self or a topic. Talk that is brief and serves largely to pass a short amount of time in pleasant interaction. Sometimes, small talk is a preface to big talk.

Social clock An unwritten timetable for accomplishing a variety of tasks as established by an individual culture, for example, the "right" time to graduate or buy a home.

Social comparison The processes by which you compare yourself (for example, your abilities, opinions, and values) with others and then assess and evaluate yourself on the basis of the comparison; one of the sources of self-concept.

Social distance The next-to-farthest distance in proxemics, ranging from 4 feet to 12 feet; the distance at which business is usually conducted.

Social exchange theory A theory hypothesizing that you cultivate profitable relationships (those in which your rewards are greater than your costs) and that you avoid or terminate unprofitable relationships (those in which your costs exceed your rewards).

Social information processing theory A theory that claims, contrary to social presence theory, that whether you're communicating face to face or online, you can communicate the same degree of personal involvement and develop similar close relationships.

Social network An organizational structure that allows people to communicate, popularly used to refer to the online sites such as Facebook and MySpace, which enable people to communicate with others who share a common interest.

Social penetration theory A theory concerned with relationship development from the superficial to the intimate levels (depth) and from few to many areas of interpersonal interaction (breadth). *See also* **depenetration.**

Social presence theory A theory that argues that the bandwidth (the number of message cues exchanged) of communication influences the degree to which the communication is personal or impersonal. When lots of cues are exchanged (especially nonverbal cues) as in face-to-face communication, there is great social presence; when fewer cues are exchanged, as in e-mail, there is less social presence.

Source Any person or thing that creates messages—for example, an individual speaking, writing, or gesturing or a computer solving a problem.

Speech Messages conveyed via a vocal–auditory channel.

Spiral of silence A theory that argues that you're more likely to voice agreement than disagreement.

Spontaneity The communication pattern in which you say what you're thinking without attempting to develop strategies for control; encourages supportiveness. Opposed to **strategy.**

Stability Principle of perception that states that your perceptions of things and of people are relatively consistent with your previous conceptions.

Static evaluation An orientation that fails to recognize that the world is constantly changing; an attitude that sees people and events as fixed rather than as ever changing.

Status The level a person occupies in a hierarchy relative to the levels occupied by others. In the United States, occupation, financial position, age, and educational level are significant determinants of social status.

Stereotype In communication, a fixed impression of a group of people through which we then perceive specific individuals. Stereotypes are most often negative but may also be positive. *To avoid stereotypes, focus on the individual rather than on the individual's membership in one group or another.*

Stimulus Any external or internal change that impinges on or arouses an organism.

Stimulus–response models of communication Models of communication that assume that the process of communication is linear, beginning with a stimulus that then leads to a response.

Storge love One of Lee's (1976) six types of love; a gradually unfolding, peaceful, and tranquil love marked by companionability and shared interests and activities, sometimes difficult to distinguish from friendship.

Strategic emotionality A condition in which emotions are used to achieve some specific end (usually to control the behavior of another person) rather than to reveal one's true feelings.

Strategy The use of some plan for control of other members of a communication interaction, often through manipulation; often encourages defensiveness. Opposed to **spontaneity.**

Stress The relative emphasis that is put on a word in a sentence and that can often change the meaning of the sentence.

Subjectivity The principle of perception that refers to the fact that your perceptions are not objective but are influenced by your wants and needs, expectations, and predictions.

Substitution A deceptive message where you exchange the truth for a lie—for example, *I wasn't at Pat's, I was at my sister's.*

Superiority A point of view or attitude that assumes that others are not equal to yourself; encourages defensiveness. Opposed to **equality.**

Supportiveness An attitude of an individual or an atmosphere in a group that is characterized by openness, absence of fear, and a genuine feeling of equality. Opposed to **defensiveness.**

Symmetrical relationship A relation between two or more persons in which one person's behavior serves as a stimulus for the same type of behavior in the other person(s)—for example, a relationship in which anger in one person encourages anger in the other or in which a critical comment by one person leads the other to respond in kind.

Synchronous communication Communication that takes place in real time; sending and receiving take place at the same time (as in face-to-face communication). Opposed to **asynchronous communication.**

Taboo Forbidden; culturally censored; frowned upon by "polite society." Taboos may include entire topics as well as specific words—for example, death, sex, certain forms of illness, and various words denoting sexual activities and excretory functions.

Tactile communication Communication by touch; communication received by the skin.

Temporal communication The messages that your time orientation and treatment of time communicate.

Territorial encroachment The trespassing on, use of, or appropriation of one person's territory by another.

Territoriality A possessive or ownership reaction to an area of space or to particular objects.

Theory A general statement or principle applicable to related phenomena.

Tie signs Signals (generally nonverbal) that communicate your relationship status, the ways in which your relationship is tied together.

Touch avoidance The tendency to avoid touching and being touched by others.

Transactional view A view of communication as an ongoing process in which all elements are interdependent and influence one another.

Truth bias The assumption most people operate under that the messages they hear are truthful. Opposed to **lie bias.**

Turf defense A response to territorial encroachment in which you defend the territory against the invasion, sometimes with something as simple as saying "this is my seat," or you might start a fight as nations do. *See also* **withdrawal, insulation,** and **linguistic collusion.**

Turn-denying cues Signals (generally nonverbal) that indicate your reluctance to assume the role of speaker.

Turning points Significant relationship events that have important consequences for the individuals and the relationship and may turn its direction or trajectory.

Turn-maintaining cues Signals that help you maintain the speaker's role. You can do this with a variety of cues, for example, by continuing a gesture to show that you have not completed the thought, avoiding eye contact with the listener so there's no indication that you're passing on the speaking turn, or sustaining your intonation pattern to indicate that you intend to say more.

Turn-requesting cues Signals (generally nonverbal) that let the speaker know that you'd like to take a turn as speaker.

Turn-taking cues Signals (generally nonverbal) that indicate that you're ready to speak, to listen, or to comment on what the speaker just said.

Turn-yielding cues Signals (generally nonverbal) that tell the listener that you're finished and wish to exchange the role of speaker for that of listener.

Uncertainty reduction theory Theory that, as interpersonal relationships develop, uncertainty is reduced; relationship development is seen as a process of reducing uncertainty about each other. *To reduce uncertainty, use passive, active, and interactive strategies.*

Universal of interpersonal communication A feature of communication common to all interpersonal communication acts.

Unknown self In the Johari window model, this self represents truths about yourself that neither you nor others know.

Unproductive conflict strategies Ways of engaging in conflict that generally prove counterproductive—for example, avoidance, force, blame, silencers, gunnysacking, manipulation, personal rejection, and fighting below the belt.

Upward communication Communication sent from the lower levels of a hierarchy to the upper levels—for example, from line worker to manager or from faculty member to dean.

Value Relative worth of an object; a quality that makes something desirable or undesirable; ideal or custom about which we have emotional responses, whether positive or negative.

Ventilation hypothesis The assumption that expressing emotions (that is, giving vent to the emotions) lessens their intensity.

Verbal aggressiveness A method of arguing in which one person attacks the other person's self-concept.

Visual dominance The use of your eyes to maintain a superior or dominant position; for example, when making an especially important point, you might look intently at the other person.

Voice qualities Aspects of paralanguage—specifically, pitch range, lip control, glottis control, pitch control, articulation control, rhythm control, resonance, and tempo.

Volume In relation to voice qualities, the relative loudness of the voice.

Weasel words Words whose meanings are slippery and difficult to pin down to specifics. *Ask yourself exactly what the word means. Is someone (say, an advertiser) attempting to put something over on you?*

Withdrawal A response to territorial encroachment by which you leave the scene, country, home, office, or classroom. *See also* **turf defense, insulation,** and **linguistic collusion.**

You-messages Messages in which you deny responsibility for your own thoughts and behaviors; messages that attribute your perception to another person; messages of blame. Opposed to **I-messages.** *Avoid using you-messages that blame or accuse; invariably these will be resented and may easily cut off further communication.*

REFERENCES

Abel, G. G., & Harlow, N. (2001). *The stop child molestation book.* Philadelphia: Xlibris.

Adams-Price, C. E., Dalton, W. T., & Sumrall, R. (2004). Victim blaming in young, middle-aged, and older adults: Variations on the severity effect. *Journal of Adult Development, 11,* 289–295.

Afifi, W. A. (2007). Nonverbal communication. In B. B. Whaley, & W. Samter (Eds.), *Explaining communication: Contemporary theories and exemplars* (pp. 39–60). Mahwah, NJ: Lawrence Erlbaum.

Afifi, W. A., & Johnson, M. L. (2005). The nature and function of tie-signs. In V. Manusov (Ed.), *The sourcebook of nonverbal measures: Going beyond words* (pp. 189–198). Mahwah, NJ: Lawrence Erlbaum.

Albas, D. C., McCluskey, K. W., & Albas, C. A. (1976, December). Perception of the emotional content of speech: A comparison of two Canadian groups. *Journal of Cross-Cultural Psychology, 7,* 481–490.

Alberti, R. (Ed.). (1977). *Assertiveness: Innovations, applications, issues.* San Luis Obispo, CA: Impact.

Alessandra, T. (1986). How to listen effectively. *Speaking of success* [Videotape series]. San Diego, CA: Levitz Sommer Productions.

Allen, J. L., Long, K. M., O'Mara, J., & Judd, B. B. (2003, September–December). Verbal and nonverbal orientations toward communication and the development of intracultural and intercultural relationships. *Journal of Intercultural Communication Research, 32,* 129–160.

Alsop, R. (2004, September 22). How to get hired: We asked recruiters what M.B.A. graduates are doing wrong. Ignore their advice at your peril. *Wall Street Journal,* p. R8.

Amato, P. R. (1994). The impact of divorce on men and women in India and the United States. *Journal of Comparative Family Studies, 25,* 207–221.

Andersen, P. A. (1991). Explaining intercultural differences in nonverbal communication. In Andersen, P. A. (2004). *The complete idiot's guide to body language.* New York: Penguin Group.

Anderson, K. J. et al. (1998). Meta-analysis of gender effects on conversational interruption: Who, what, when, where, and how. *Sex Roles, 39 (August),* 225–252.

Angier, N. (1995, May 9). Scientists mull role of empathy in man and beast. *The New York Times,* pp. C1, C6.

Argyle, M. (1986). Rules for social relationships in four cultures. *Australian Journal of Psychology, 38,* 309–318.

Argyle, M. (1988). *Bodily communication* (2nd ed.). New York: Methuen.

Argyle, M., & Henderson, M. (1984). *The anatomy of relationships: And the rules and skills needed to manage them successfully.* London: Heinemann.

Argyle, M., & Ingham, R. (1972). Gaze, mutual gaze and distance. *Semiotica, 1,* 32–49.

Aries, E. (2006). Sex differences in interaction: A reexamination. In K. Dindia & D. J. Canary (Eds.), *Sex differences and similarities in communication,* (2nd ed., pp. 21–36). Mahwah, NJ: Erlbaum.

Arnold, L. B. (2008). *Family communication: Theory and research.* Boston: Allyn & Bacon.

Aronson, E., Wilson, T. D., & Akert, R. M. (2013). *Social psychology: The heart and the mind,* 8th ed. Boston: Pearson.

Aronson, J., Cohen, J., & Nail, P. (1998). Self-affirmation theory: An update and appraisal. In E. Harmon-Jones & J. S. Mills (Eds.), *Cognitive dissonance theory: Revival with revisions and controversies* (pp. 127–147). Washington, DC: American Psychological Association.

Asch, S. (1946). Forming impressions of personality. *Journal of Abnormal and Social Psychology, 41,* 258–290.

Ashcraft, M. H. (1998). *Fundamentals of cognition.* New York: Longman.

Ashkanasy, N. M., & Humphrey, R. H. (2011). Current emotion research in organizational behavior. *Emotion Review, 3,* 214–224.

Axtell, R. E. (1990). *Do's and taboos of hosting international visitors.* New York: Wiley.

Axtell, R. E. (1994). *Do's and taboos around the world* (3rd ed.). New York: Wiley.

Axtell, R. E. (2007). *Essential do's and taboos: The complete guide to international business and leisure travel.* Hoboken, NJ: Wiley.

Bach, G. R., & Wyden, P. (1968). *The intimate enemy.* New York: Avon.

Balswick, J. O., & Peck, C. (1971). The inexpressive male: A tragedy of American society? *The Family Coordinator, 20,* 363–368.

Barbato, C. A., & Perse, E. M. (1992). Interpersonal communication motives and the life position of elders. *Communication Research,* 19, 516–531.

Barker, L. L., & Gaut, D. (2002). *Communication* (8th ed.). Boston: Allyn & Bacon.

Barker, L., Edwards, R., Gaines, C., Gladney, K., & Holley, F. (1980). An investigation of proportional time spent in various communication activities by college students. *Journal of Applied Communication Research, 8,* 101–109.

Barna, L. M. (1997). Stumbling blocks in intercultural communication. In L. A. Samovar & R. E. Porter (Eds.), *Intercultural communication: A reader* (7th ed., pp. 337–346). Belmont, CA: Wadsworth.

Barnlund, D. C. (1975). Communicative styles in two cultures: Japan and the United States. In A. Kendon, R. M. Harris, & M. R. Key (Eds.), *Organization of behavior in face-to-face interaction* (pp. 427–456). The Hague, the Netherlands: Mouton.

Barnlund, D. C. (1989). *Communicative styles of Japanese and Americans: Images and realities.* Belmont, CA: Wadsworth.

Barrett, L., & Godfrey, T. (1988). Listening. *Person Centered Review, 3,* 410–425.

Baumeister, R. F., Zhang, L., & Vohs, K. D. (2004). Gossip as cultural learning. *Review of General Psychology, 8* (June), 111–121.

Baxter, L. A. (1983). Relationship disengagement: An examination of the reversal hypothesis. *Western Journal of Speech Communication, 47,* 85–98.

Baxter, L. A. (1986). Gender differences in the heterosexual relationship rules embedded in break-up accounts. *Journal of Social and Personal Relationships, 3,* 289–306.

Baxter, L. A. (2004). Relationships as dialogues. *Personal Relationships, 11* (March), 1–22.

Baxter, L. A., & Braithwaite, D. O. (2007). Social dialectics: The contradiction of relating. In B. B. Whaley & W. Samter (Eds.), *Explaining communication: Contemporary theories and exemplars* (pp. 275–292). Mahwah, NJ: Lawrence Erlbaum.

Baxter, L. A., & Braithwaite, D. O. (Eds.) (2008). *Engaging theories in interpersonal communication: Multiple perspectives.* Los Angeles: Sage.

Baxter, L. A., & Bullis, C. (1986). Turning points in developing romantic relationships. *Human Communication Research, 12,* 469–493.

Baxter, L. A., & Simon, E. P. (1993). Relationship maintenance strategies and dialectical contradictions in personal relationships. *Journal of Social and Personal Relationships, 10,* 225–242.

Bedford, V. H. (1996). Relationships between adult siblings. In A. E. Auhagen & M. von Salisch (Eds.), *The diversity of human relationships* (pp. 120–140). New York: Cambridge University Press.

Beier, E. (1974). How we send emotional messages. *Psychology Today, 8,* 53–56.

Bell, R. A., & Daly, J. A. (1984). The affinity-seeking function of communication. *Communication Monographs, 51,* 91–115.

Benoit, W. L., & Benoit, P. J. (1990). Memory for conversational behavior, *Southern Communication Journal, 55,* 17–23.

Berg, J. H., & Archer, R. L. (1983). The disclosure–liking relationship. *Human Communication Research, 10,* 269–281.

Berger, C. R., & Bradac, J. J. (1982). *Language and social knowledge: Uncertainty in interpersonal relations.* London: Edward Arnold.

Bernstein, W. M., Stephan, W. G., & Davis, M. H. (1979). Explaining attributions for achievement: A path analytic approach. *Journal of Personality and Social Psychology, 37,* 1810–1821.

Berry, J. W., Poortinga, Y. H., Segall, M. H., & Dasen, P. R. (1992). *Cross-cultural psychology: Research and applications.* New York: Cambridge University Press.

Berscheid, E., & Reis, H. T. (1998). Attraction and close relationships. In D. Gilbert, S. Fiske, & G. Lindzey (Eds.), *The handbook of social psychology* (4th ed., Vol. 2, pp. 193–281). New York: W. H. Freeman.

Bierhoff, H. W., & Klein, R. (1991). Dimensionen der Liebe: Entwicklung einer Deutschsprachigen Skala zur Erfassung von Liebesstilen. *Zeitschrift for Differentielle und Diagnostische Psychologie, 12,* 53–71.

Black, H. K. (1999). A sense of the sacred: Altering or enhancing the self-portrait in older age? *Narrative Inquiry, 9,* 327–345.

Blake, R. R., & Mouton, J. S. (1985). *The managerial grid III* (3rd ed.). Houston, TX: Gulf.

Blieszner, R., & Adams, R. G. (1992). *Adult friendship.* Newbury Park, CA: Sage.

Blumstein, P., & Schwartz, P. (1983). *American couples: Money, work, sex.* New York: Morrow.

Bochner, A. (1984). The functions of human communication in interpersonal bonding. In C. C. Arnold & J. W. Bowers (Eds.), *Handbook of rhetorical and communication theory* (pp. 544–621). Boston: Allyn & Bacon.

Bochner, S. (1994). Cross-cultural differences in the self-concept: A test of Hofstede's individualism/collectivism distinction. *Journal of Cross-Cultural Psychology, 25,* 273–283.

Bok, S. (1978). *Lying: Moral choice in public and private life.* New York: Pantheon.

Bok, S. (1983). *Secrets.* New York: Vintage.

Borden, G. A. (1991). *Cultural orientation: An approach to understanding intercultural communication.* Englewood Cliffs, NJ: Prentice Hall.

Brashers, D. E. (2007). A theory of communication and uncertainty management. In B. B. Whaley & W. Samter (Eds.), *Explaining communication: Contemporary theories and exemplars* (pp. 201–218). Mahwah, NJ: Lawrence Erlbaum.

Brody, L. R. (1985, June). Gender differences in emotional development: A review of theories and research. *Journal of Personality,* 53, 102–149.

Brown, P. (1980). How and why are women more polite: Some evidence from a Mayan community. In S. McConnell-Ginet, R. Borker, & M. Furman (Eds.), *Women and language in literature and society* (pp. 111–136). New York: Praeger.

Brown, P., & Levinson, S. C. (1987). *Politeness: Some universals of language usage.* Cambridge, UK: Cambridge University Press.

Brownell, J. (2006). *Listening: Attitudes, principles, and skills* (3rd ed). Boston: Allyn & Bacon.

Brownell, J. (2010). *Listening: Attitudes, principles, and skills* (5th ed.). Boston: Allyn & Bacon.

Bruneau, T. (1985). The time dimension in intercultural communication. In L. A. Samovar & R. E. Porter (Eds.), *Intercultural communication: A reader* (4th ed., pp. 280–289). Belmont, CA: Wadsworth.

Bruneau, T. (1990). Chronemics: The study of time in human interaction. In J. A. DeVito & M. L. Hecht (Eds.), *The nonverbal communication reader* (pp. 301–311). Prospect Heights, IL: Waveland Press.

Bruneau, T. (2009/2010). Chronemics: Time-binding and the construction of personal time. *General Semantics Bulletin, 76,* 82–94.

Buber, M. (1958). *I and thou* (2nd ed.). New York: Scribner's.

Bugental, J., & Zelen, S. (1950). Investigations into the "self-concept": I. The W–A–Y technique. *Journal of Personality,* 18, 483–498.

Bull, R., & Rumsey, N. (1988). *The social psychology of facial appearance.* New York: Springer-Verlag.

Buller, D. B., LePoire, B. A., Aune, K., & Eloy, S. (1992). Social perceptions as mediators of the effect of speech rate similarity on compliance. *Human Communication Research, 19,* 286–311.

Buller, D. J. (2005). *Adapting minds: Evolutionary psychology and the persistent quest for human nature.* Cambridge, MA: MIT Press.

Bunz, U., & Campbell, S. W. (2004). Politeness accommodation in electronic mail. *Communication Research Reports, 21*, 11–25.

Burgoon, J. K., & Bacue, A. E. (2003). Nonverbal communication skills. In J. O. Greene & B. R. Burleson (Eds.), *Handbook of communication and social interaction skills* (pp. 179–220). Mahwah, NJ: Erlbaum.

Burgoon, J. K., & Hoobler, G. D. (2002). Nonverbal signals. In M. L. Knapp & J. A. Daly (Eds.), *Handbook of interpersonal communication* (3rd ed., pp. 240–299). Thousand Oaks, CA: Sage.

Burgoon, J. K., Berger, C. R., & Waldron, V. R. (2000). Mindfulness and interpersonal communication. *Journal of Social Issues, 56*, 105–127.

Burgoon, J., Guerrero, L., & Floyd, K. (2010). *Nonverbal communication.* Boston: Allyn & Bacon.

Burgoon, J. K., Guerrero, L. K., & Manusov, V. (2011). In Knapp, M. L., & Daly, J. A. (Eds.), *The SAGE handbook of interpersonal communication* (4th ed., pp. 239–282). Los Angeles: Sage.

Burgstahler, S. (2007). Managing an e-mentoring community to support students with disabilities: A case study. *Distance Education Report 11* (July), 7–15.

Burleson, B. R. (2003). Emotional support skills. In J. O. Greene & B. R. Burleson (Eds.), *Handbook of communication and social interaction skills* (pp. 551–594). Mahwah, NJ: Erlbaum.

Buss, D. M. (1988). The evolution of human intrasexual competition: Tactics of mate attraction. *Journal of Personality and Social Psychology, 54*, 616–628.

Buss, D. M. (2000). *The dangerous passion: Why jealousy is as necessary as love and sex.* New York: Free Press.

Butler, P. E. (1981). *Talking to yourself: Learning the language of self-support.* New York: Harper & Row.

Buunk, B. P., & Dijkstra, P. (2004). Gender differences in rival characteristics that evoke jealousy in response to emotional versus sexual infidelity. *Personal Relationships, 11*(December), 395–408.

Cahn, D. D., & Abigail, R. A. (2007). *Managing conflict through communication* (3rd ed.). Boston: Allyn & Bacon.

Canary, D. J., & Hause, K. (1993). Is there any reason to research sex differences in communication? *Communication Quarterly, 41*, 129–144.

Canary, D. J., Cupach, W. R., & Messman, S. J. (1995). *Relationship conflict: Conflict in parent-child, friendship, and romantic relationships.* Thousand Oaks, CA: Sage.

Cannon, W. B. (1987). The James-Lange theory of emotions: A critical examination and an alternative theory. *The American Journal of Psychology, 100* (1987): 567–86.

Cappella, J. N. (1993). The facial feedback hypothesis in human interaction: Review and speculation. *Journal of Language and Social Psychology, 12*, 13–29.

Cappella, J. N., & Schreiber, D. M. (2006). The interaction management function of nonverbal cues. In V. Manusov & M. L. Patterson (Eds.), *The SAGE handbook of nonverbal communication* (pp. 361–379). Thousand Oaks, CA: Sage Publications.

Carey, B. (2005). Have you heard? Gossip turns out to serve a purpose. *New York Times* (August 16), F1, F6.

Carroll, D. W. (1994). *Psychology of language* (2nd ed.). Pacific Grove, CA: Brooks/Cole.

Caughlin, J. P., Koerner, A. F., Schrodt, P., & Fitzpatrick, M. A. (2011). Interpersonal communication in family relationships. In M. L. Knapp & J. A. Daly (Eds.), *The SAGE handbook of interpersonal communication* (4th ed., pp. 679–714). Los Angeles: Sage.

Chadwick-Jones, J. K. (1976). *Social exchange theory: Its structure and influence in social psychology.* New York: Academic Press.

Chang, H., & Holt, G. R. (1996, Winter). The changing Chinese interpersonal world: Popular themes in interpersonal communication books in modern Taiwan. *Communication Quarterly, 44*, 85–106.

Chanowitz, B., & Langer, E. (1981). Premature cognitive commitment. *Journal of Personality and Social Psychology, 41*, 1051–1063.

Cheney, G., & Tompkins, P. K. (1987). Coming to terms with organizational identification and commitment. *Central States Speech Journal, 38*, 1–15.

Cherulnik, P. D. (1979). Sex differences in the expression of emotion in a structured social encounter. *Sex Roles, 5*, 413–424.

Chung, L. C., & Ting-Toomey, S. (1999). Ethnic identity and relational expectations among Asian Americans. *Communication Research Reports, 16*, 157–166.

Ciccarelli, S. K., & White, J. N. (2012). *Psychology* (3rd ed.). Boston: Pearson.

Clance, P. (1985). *The Impostor Phenomenon: Overcoming the Fear That Haunts Your Success.* Atlanta: Peachtree Publishers.

Cline, M. G. (1956). The influence of social context on the perception of faces. *Journal of Personality, 2*, 142–185.

Cloud, J. (2008). Are gay relationships different? *Time* (January 28), 78–80.

Coates, J., & Sutton-Spence, R. (2001). Turn-taking patterns in deaf conversation. *Journal of Sociolinguistics, 5* (November), 507–529.

Coats, E. J., & Feldman, R. S. (1996). Gender differences in nonverbal correlates of social status. *Personality and Social Psychology Bulletin, 22*, 1014–1022.

Colley, A., Todd, Z., Bland, M., Holmes, M., Khanom, N., & Pike, H. (2004, September). Style and content in e-mails and letters to male and female friends. *Journal of Language and Social Psychology, 23*, 369–378.

Collins, N. L., & Miller, L. C. (1994). Self-disclosure and liking: A meta-analytic review. *Psychological Bulletin, 116* (November), 457–475.

Cooley, C. H. (1922). *Human nature and the social order* (Rev. ed.). New York: Scribner's.

Cooper, A., & Sportolari, L. (1997). Romance in cyberspace: Understanding online attraction. *Journal of Sex Education and Therapy, 22*, 7–14.

Cornwell, B., & Lundgren, D. C. (2001). Love on the Internet: Involvement and misrepresentation in romantic relationships in cyberspace vs. realspace. *Computers in Human Behavior, 17*, 197–211.

Cross, E. E., & Madson, L. (1997). Models of the self: Self-construals and gender. *Psychological Bulletin*, 122, 5–37.

Darwin, C. (1872). *The expression of the emotions in man and animals.* Chicago: University of Chicago Press (reprinted 1965).

Davis, M. S. (1973). *Intimate relations.* New York: Free Press.

deBono, E. (1985). *Six thinking hats.* Boston: Little, Brown.

DePaulo, B. M. (1992). Nonverbal behavior and self-presentation. *Psychological Bulletin, 111,* 203–212.

DePaulo, B. M., Lindsay, J. J., Malone, B. E., Muhlenbruck, L., Charlton, K., & Cooper, H. (2003). Cues to deception. *Psychological Bulletin, 129,* 74–118.

Derlega, V. J., Winstead, B. A., Greene, K., Serovich, J., & Elwood, W. N. (2004). Reasons for HIV disclosure/nondisclosure in close relationships: Testing a model of HIV-disclosure decision making. *Journal of Social and Clinical Psychology, 23* (December), 747–767.

Derlega, V. J., Winstead, B. A., Wong, P. T. P., & Greenspan, M. (1987). Self-disclosure and relationship development: An attributional analysis. In M. E. Roloff & G. R. Miller (Eds.), *Interpersonal processes: New directions in communication research* (pp. 172–187). Thousand Oaks, CA: Sage.

Derlega, V. J., Winstead, B. A., Wong, P. T. P., & Hunter, S. (1985). Gender effects in an initial encounter: A case where men exceed women in disclosure. *Journal of Social and Personal Relationships, 2,* 25–44.

DeVito, J. A. (1976). Relative ease in comprehending yes/no questions. In J. Blankenship & H. G. Stelzner (Eds.), *Rhetoric and communication* (pp. 143–154). Urbana, IL: University of Illinois Press.

DeVito, J. A. (1981). *The psychology of speech and language: An introduction to psycholinguistics.* Washington, DC: University Press of America.

DeVito, J. A. (1996). *Brainstorms: How to think more creatively about communication (or about anything else).* New York: Longman.

DeVito, J. A. (2003). SCREAM before you scream. *ETC: A Review of General Semantics, 60* (Spring), 42–45.

Dewey, J. (1910). *How we think.* Boston: Heath.

Dindia, K., & Allen, M. (1992). Sex differences in self-disclosure: A meta-analysis. *Psychological Bulletin, 112,* 106–124.

Dindia, K., & Canary, D. J. (Eds). *Sex differences and similarities in communication* (2nd ed.). Mahwah, NJ: Lawrence Erlbaum.

Dindia, K., & Timmerman, L. (2003). Accomplishing romantic relationships. In J. O. Greene & B. R. Burleson (Eds.), *Handbook of communication and social interaction skills* (pp. 685–722). Mahwah, NJ: Erlbaum.

Dion, K. K., & Dion, K. L. (1993a, Fall). Individualistic and collectivist perspectives on gender and the cultural context of love and intimacy. *Journal of Social Issues, 49,* 53–69.

Dion, K. L., & Dion, K. K. (1993b, December). Gender and ethnocultural comparisons in styles of love. *Psychology of Women Quarterly, 17,* 464–473.

Doherty, R. W., Orimoto, L., Singelis, T. M., Hatfield, E., & Hebb, J. (1995). Emotional contagion: Gender and occupational differences. *Psychology of Women Quarterly, 19,* 355–371.

Dolgin, K. G., Meyer, L., & Schwartz, J. (1991, September). Effects of gender, target's gender, topic, and self-esteem on disclosure to best and middling friends. *Sex Roles, 25,* 311–329.

Donohue, W. A., & Kolt, R. (1992). *Managing interpersonal conflict.* Thousand Oaks, CA: Sage.

Dovidio, J. F., Gaertner, S. E., Kawakami, K., & Hodson, G. (2002). Why can't we just get along? Interpersonal biases and interracial distrust. *Cultural Diversity and Ethnic Minority Psychology, 8,* 88–102.

Drass, K. A. (1986). The effect of gender identity on conversation. *Social Psychology Quarterly, 49,* 294–301.

Dresser, N. (1999). *Multicultural celebrations: Today's rules of etiquette for life's special occasions.* New York: Three Rivers Press.

Dresser, N. (2005). *Multicultural manners: Essential rules of etiquette for the 21st century* (Rev. ed.). New York: Wiley.

Dreyfuss, H. (1971). *Symbol sourcebook.* New York: McGraw-Hill.

Duke, M., & Nowicki, S. (2005). The Emory dyssemia index. In V. Manusov (Ed.), *The sourcebook of nonverbal measures: Going beyond words* (35–46). Mahwah, NJ: Lawrence Erlbaum.

Dunbar, N. E., & Burgoon, J. K. (2005). Measuring nonverbal dominance. In V. Manusov (Ed.), *The sourcebook of nonverbal measures: Going beyond words* (pp. 361–374). Mahwah, NJ: Lawrence Erlbaum.

Dunbar, R. I. M. (2004). Gossip in evolutionary perspective. *Review of General Psychology, 8,* 100–110.

Duncan, S. D., Jr. (1972). Some signals and rules for taking speaking turns in conversation. *Journal of Personality and Social Psychology, 23,* 283–292.

Duval, T. S., & Silva, P. J. (2002). Self-awareness, probability of improvement, and the self-serving bias. *Journal of Personality and Social Psychology, 82,* 49–61.

Eastwick, P. W. & Finkel, E. J. (2009). Reciprocity of liking. In Harry T. Reis & Susan Sprecher (Eds.), *Encyclopedia of human relationships* (pp. 1333–1336). Thousand Oaks, CA: Sage.

Eder, D., & Enke, J. L. (1991). The structure of gossip: Opportunities and constraints on collective expression among adolescents. *American Sociological Review, 56,* 494–508.

Egan, G. (1970). *Encounter: Group processes for Interpersonal growth.* Belmont, CA: Brooks/Cole.

Egan, K. G., & Moreno, M. A. (2011). Alcohol references on undergraduate male's Facebook profiles. *American Journal of Men's Health, 5,* 413–420.

Eggen, P., & Kauchak, D. (2013). *Educational psychology: Windows on classrooms* (9th ed.). Boston: Pearson.

Ehrenhaus, P. (1988). Silence and symbolic expression. *Communication Monographs, 55,* 41–57.

Einhorn, L. (2006). Using e-prime and English minus absolutisms to provide self-empathy. *ETC: A Review of General Semantics, 63,* 180–186.

Ekman, P. (1985). Communication through nonverbal behavior: A source of information about an interpersonal relationship. In S. S. Tomkins & C. E.Izard (Eds.), *Affect, cognition and personality.* New York: Springer.

Ekman, P. (2009). *Telling lies: Clues to deceit in the marketplace, politics, and marriage* (3rd ed.). New York: Norton.

Ekman, P., & Friesen, W. V. (1969). The repertoire of nonverbal behavior: Categories, origins, usage, and coding. *Semiotica, 1,* 49–98.

Elfenbein, H. A., & Ambady, N. (2002). Is there an in-group advantage in emotion recognition? *Psychological Bulletin, 128,* 243–249.

Ellis, A. (1988). *How to stubbornly refuse to make yourself miserable about anything, yes anything.* Secaucus, NJ: Lyle Stuart.

Ellis, A., & Dryden, W. (2007). *The practice of rational emotive therapy* (2nd ed.). New York: Springer.

Ellis, A., & Harper, R. A. (1975). *A new guide to rational living*. Hollywood, CA: Wilshire Books.

Elmes, M. B., & Gemmill, G. (1990). The psychodynamics of mindlessness and dissent in small groups. *Small Group Research, 21*, 28–44.

Epstein, R. (2005). The loose screw awards: Psychology's top 10 misguided ideas. *Psychology Today* (February), 55–62.

Epstein, R. M., & Hundert, E. M. (2002). Defining and assessing professional competence. *JAMA: Journal of the American Medical Association, 287*, 226–235.

Erber, R., & Erber, M. W. (2011). *Intimate relationships: Issues, theories, and research* (2nd ed.). Boston: Allyn and Bacon.

Faigley, L. (2009). *The Penguin handbook* (3rd ed.). New York: Longman.

Fengler, A. P. (1974). Romantic love in courtship: Divergent paths of male and female students. *Journal of Comparative Family Studies, 5*, 134–139.

Fesko, S. L. (2001, November). Disclosure of HIV status in the workplace: Considerations and strategies. *Health and Social Work, 26*, 235–244.

Fischer, A. H. (1993). Sex differences in emotionality: Fact or stereotype? *Feminism and Psychology, 3*, 303–318.

Fisher, C. D. (1997). Emotions at work: What do people feel and how should we measure it? http://epublications.bond.edu.au/business_pubs/1.

Fitzpatrick, M. A. (1983). Predicting couples' communication from couples' self-reports. In R. N. Bostrom (Ed.), *Communication yearbook 7* (pp. 49–82). Thousand Oaks, CA: Sage.

Fitzpatrick, M. A. (1988). *Between husbands and wives: Communication in marriage*. Thousand Oaks, CA: Sage.

Fitzpatrick, M. A. (1991). Sex differences in marital conflict: Social psychophysiological versus cognitive explanations. *Text, 11*, 341–364.

Fitzpatrick, M. A., & Caughlin, J. P. (2002). Interpersonal communication in family relationships. In M. L. Knapp & J. A. Daly. (Eds.), *Handbook of interpersonal communication* (3rd ed., pp. 726–777). Thousand Oaks, CA: Sage.

Fitzpatrick, M. A., Jandt, F. E., Myrick, F. L., & Edgar, T. (1994). Gay and lesbian couple relationships. In R. J. Ringer (Ed.), *Queer words, queer images: Communication and the construction of homosexuality* (pp. 265–285). New York: New York University Press.

Floyd, J. J. (1985). *Listening: A practical approach*. Glenview, IL: Scott, Foresman.

Floyd, K., & Mikkelson, A. C. (2005). In V. Manusov (Ed.), *The sourcebook of nonverbal measures: Going beyond words* (pp. 47–56). Mahwah, NJ: Lawrence Erlbaum.

Folger, J. P., Poole, M. S., & Stutman, R. K. (2013). *Working through conflict: A communication perspective* (7th ed.). New York: Longman.

Forbes, G. B. (2001). College students with tattoos and piercings: Motives, family experiences, personality factors, and perception by others. *Psychological Reports, 89*, 774–786.

Franklin, C. W., & Mizell, C. A. (1995). Some factors influencing success among African-American men: A preliminary study. *Journal of Men's Studies, 3*, 191–204.

French, J. R. P., Jr., & Raven, B. (1968). The bases of social power. In D. Cartwright & A. Zander (Eds.), *Group dynamics: Research and theory* (3rd ed., pp. 259–269). New York: Harper & Row.

Frentz, T. (1976). A general approach to episodic structure. Paper presented at the Western Speech Association Convention, San Francisco. Cited in Reardon (1987).

Fukushima, S. (2000). *Requests and culture: Politeness in British English and Japanese*. New York: Peter Lang.

Furlow, F. B. (1996). The smell of love. *Psychology Today, 29*, 38–45.

Furnham, A., & Bochner, S. (1986). *Culture shock: Psychological reactions to unfamiliar environments*. New York: Methuen.

Galvin, K., Bylund, C., & Brommel, B. J. (2012). *Family communication: Cohesion and change* (8th ed.). New York: Longman.

Gamble, T. K., & Gamble, M. W. (2003). *The gender communication connection*. Boston: Houghton Mifflin.

Gelles, R., & Cornell, C. (1985). *Intimate violence in families*. Newbury Park, CA: Sage.

Georgas, J., et al. (2001). Functional relationships in the nuclear and extended family: A 16-culture study. *International Journal of Psychology, 36*, 289–300.

Gergen, K. J., Greenberg, M. S., & Willis, R. H. (1980). *Social exchange: Advances in theory and research*. New York: Plenum Press.

Gibb, J. (1961). Defensive communication. *Journal of Communication, 11*, 141–148.

Giles, D. C. (2001). Parasocial interaction: A review of the literature and a model for future research. *Media Psychology, 4*, 279–305.

Giles, D. C., & Maltby, J. (2004). The role of media figures in adolescent development: Relations between autonomy, attachment, and interest in celebrities. *Personality and Individual Differences, 36* (March), 813–822.

Giles, H. (2009). Communication accommodation theory. In L. A. Baxter & D. O. Braithwaite (Eds.), *Engaging theories in interpersonal communication: Multiple perspectives* (pp. 161–173). Los Angeles: Sage.

Giles, H., Mulac, A., Bradac, J. J., & Johnson, P. (1987). Speech accommodation theory: The first decade and beyond. In M. L. McLaughlin (Ed.), *Communication Yearbook 10* (pp. 13–48). Thousand Oaks, CA: Sage.

Gladstone, G. L., & Parker, G. B. (2002, June). When you're smiling, does the whole world smile with you? *Australasian Psychiatry, 10*, 144–146.

Goffman, E. (1967). *Interaction ritual: Essays on face-to-face behavior.* New York: Pantheon.

Goffman, E. (1971). *Relations in public: Microstudies of the public order.* New York: HarperCollins.

Goldsmith, D. J. (2007). Brown and Levinson's politeness theory. In B. B. Whaley & W. Samter (Eds.), *Explaining communication: Contemporary theories and exemplars* (pp. 219–236). Mahwah, NJ: Lawrence Erlbaum.

Goleman, D. (1995a). *Emotional intelligence*. New York: Bantam.

Goleman, D. (1995b, February 14). For man and beast, language of love shares many traits. *The New York Times*, pp. C1, C9.

Gonzalez, A., & Zimbardo, P. G. (1985). Time in perspective. *Psychology Today, 19,* 20–26.

Gorden, W. I., & Nevins, R. J. (1993). *We mean business: Building communication competence in business and professions.* New York: HarperCollins.

Gordon, A. (2010). Facing up to fatigue. *Psychology Today, 43,* 29.

Gordon, T. (1975). *P.E.T.: Parent effectiveness training.* New York: New American Library.

Gottman, J. M., & Carrere, S. (1994). Why can't men and women get along? Developmental roots and marital inequities. In D. J. Canary and Laura Stafford (Eds.), *Communication and relational maintenance* (pp. 203–229). San Diego, CA: Academic Press.

Gottman, J. M., & Levenson, R. W. (1999). Dysfunctional marital conflict: Women are being unfairly blamed. *Journal of Divorce and Remarriage, 31,* 1–17.

Grace, S. L., & Cramer, K. L. (2003). The elusive nature of self-measurement: The self-construal scale versus the twenty statements test. *Journal of Social Psychology, 143* (October), 649–668.

Graham, J. A., & Argyle, M. (1975). The effects of different patterns of gaze combined with different facial expressions on impression formation. *Journal of Movement Studies, 1,* 178–182.

Graham, J. A., Bitti, P. R., & Argyle, M. (1975). A cross-cultural study of the communication of emotion by facial and gestural cues. *Journal of Human Movement Studies, 1,* 68–77.

Grandey, A. A. (2000). Emotion regulation in the workplace: A new way to conceptualize emotional labor. *Journal of Occupational Health and Psychology, 5,* 95–110.

Greengard, S. (2001). Gossip poisons business. HR can stop it. *Workforce, 80,* 24–28.

Greif, E. B. (1980). Sex differences in parent-child conversations. *Women's Studies International Quarterly, 3,* 253–258.

Greitemeyer, T. (2007). What do men and women want in a partner? Are educated partners always more desirable? *Journal of Experimental Social Psychology, 43* (March), 180–194.

Grice, H. P. (1975). Logic and conversation. In P. Cole & J. L. Morgan (Eds.), *Syntax and semantics: Vol. 3. Speech acts* (pp. 41–58). New York: Seminar Press.

Griffin, E., & Sparks, G. G. (1990). Friends forever: A longitudinal exploration of intimacy in same-sex friends and platonic pairs. *Journal of Social and Personal Relationships, 7,* 29–46.

Gu, Y. (1990). Polite phenomena in modern Chinese. *Journal of Pragmatics, 14,* 237–257.

Gudykunst, W. B. (1989). Culture and the development of interpersonal relationships. In J. A. Anderson (Ed.), *Communication yearbook 12* (pp. 315–354). Thousand Oaks, CA: Sage.

Gudykunst, W. B. (1993). Toward a theory of effective interpersonal and intergroup communication: An anxiety/uncertainty management (AUM) perspective. In R. L. Wiseman (Ed.), *Intercultural communication competence.* Thousand Oaks, CA: Sage.

Gudykunst, W. B. (1994). *Bridging differences: Effective intergroup communication* (2nd ed.). Newbury Park, CA: Sage.

Gudykunst, W. B. (Ed.). (1983). *Intercultural communication theory: Current perspectives.* Newbury Park, CA: Sage.

Gudykunst, W. B., & Kim, Y. Y. (Eds.). (1992). *Readings on communication with strangers: An approach to intercultural communication.* New York: McGraw-Hill.

Gudykunst, W. B., Nishida, T., & Chua, E. (1987). Perceptions of social penetration in Japanese–North American dyads. *International Journal of Intercultural Relations, 11,* 171–189.

Gueguen, N. (2003, Summer). Help on the Web: The effect of the same first name between the sender and the receptor in a request made by e-mail. *Psychological Record, 53,* 459–466.

Guerin, B. (2003). Combating prejudice and racism: New interventions from a fictional analysis of fictional racist language. *Journal of Community and Applied Social Psychology,* 13 (January), 29–45.

Guerrero, L. K., & Andersen, P. A. (1991). The waxing and waning of relational intimacy: Touch as a function of relational stage, gender and touch avoidance. *Journal of Social and Personal Relationships, 8,* 147–165.

Guerrero, L. K., & Andersen, P. A. (1994). Patterns of matching and initiation: Touch behavior and touch avoidance across romantic relationship stages. *Journal of Nonverbal Behavior 18,* 137–153.

Guerrero, L. K., & Hecht, M. L. (Eds.). (2008). *The nonverbal communication reader: Class and contemporary readings* (3rd ed.). Prospect Heights, IL: Waveland Press.

Guerrero, L. K., Andersen, P. A., & Afifi, W. A. (2007). *Close encounters: Communication in relationships* (2nd ed.). Thousand Oaks, CA: Sage.

Guerrero, L. K., Andersen, P. A., Jorgensen, P. F., Spitzberg, B. H., & Eloy, S. V. (1995). Coping with the green-eyed monster: Conceptualizing and measuring communicative response to romantic jealousy. *Western Journal of Communication, 59,* 270–304.

Guerrero, L. K., Jones, S. M., & Boburka, R. R. (2006). Sex differences in emotional communication. In K. Dindia & D. J. Canary (Eds.), *Sex differences and similarities in communication* (2nd ed., pp. 241–262). Mahwah, NJ: Erlbaum.

Hafen, S. (2004). Organizational gossip: A revolving door of regulation and resistance, *Southern Communication Journal, 69* (Spring), 223–240.

Haga, Y. (1988). Traits de langage et caractère Japonais. *Cahiers de Sociologie Economique et Culturelle, 9,* 105–109.

Hajek, C., & Giles, H. (2003). New directions in intercultural communication competence: The process model. In J. O. Greene & B. R. Burleson (Eds.), *Handbook of communication and social interaction skills* (pp. 935–957). Mahwah, NJ: Erlbaum.

Hall, E. T. (1959). *The silent language.* Garden City, NY: Doubleday.

Hall, E. T. (1963). A system for the notation of proxemic behavior. *American Anthropologist, 65,* 1003–1026.

Hall, E. T. (1966). *The hidden dimension.* Garden City, NY: Doubleday.

Hall, E. T. (1976). *Beyond culture.* Garden City, NY: Doubleday.

Hall, E. T. (1983). *The dance of life: The other dimension of time.* New York: Anchor Books/Doubleday.

Hall, E. T., & Hall, M. R. (1987). *Hidden differences: Doing business with the Japanese.* Garden City, NY: Doubleday.

Hall, J. A. (1996, Spring). Touch, status, and gender at professional meetings. *Journal of Nonverbal Behavior, 20,* 23–44.

Hall, J. A. (1998). How big are nonverbal sex differences? The case of smiling and sensitivity to nonverbal cues. In D. J. Canary & K. Dindia (Eds.), *Sex differences and similarities in communication: Critical essays and empirical investigations of sex and gender in interaction* (pp. 155–178). Mahwah, NJ: Erlbaum.

Hall, J. A. (1998). How big are nonverbal sex differences? The case of smiling and sensitivity to nonverbal cues. In D. J. Canary & K. Dindia (Eds.), *Sex differences and similarities in communication: Critical essays and empirical investigations of sex and gender in interaction* (pp. 155–178). Mahwah, NJ: Erlbaum.

Hampton, K., Goulet, L. S., Rainie, L., & Purcell, K. (2011). Social networking sites and our lives. Pew Internet & American Life Project (http://www.pewinternet.org/Reports/2011/Technology-and-social-networks/Summary.aspx).

Haney, W. (1973). *Communication and organizational behavior: Text and cases* (3rd ed.). Homewood, IL: Irwin.

Harris, C. R. (2003). A review of sex differences in sexual jealousy, including self-report data, psychophysiological responses, interpersonal violence, and morbid jealousy, *Personality and Social Psychology Review 7,* 102–128.

Harris, M. (1993). *Culture, people, nature: An introduction to general anthropology,* 6th ed. Boston: Allyn & Bacon.

Hart Research Associates. (2010). Raising the bar: Employers' views on college learning in the wake of the economic downturn: A survey among employers conducted on behalf of the Association of American Colleges and Universities. Washington, DC.

Harvey, J. C., & Katz, C. (1985). *If I'm So Successful, Why Do I Feel Like a Fake: The Impostor Phenomenon.* New York: St. Martin's Press.

Hatfield, E., & Rapson, R. L. (1992). Similarity and attraction in close relationships. *Communication Monographs, 59,* 209–212.

Hatfield, E., & Rapson, R. L. (1996). *Love and sex: Cross-cultural perspectives.* Boston: Allyn & Bacon.

Havlena, W. J., Holbrook, M. B., & Lehmann, D. R. (1989, Summer). Assessing the validity of emotional typologies. *Psychology and Marketing, 6,* 97–112.

Hayakawa, S. I., & Hayakawa, A. R. (1989). *Language in thought and action* (5th ed.). New York: Harcourt Brace Jovanovich.

Hays, R. B. (1989). The day-to-day functioning of close versus casual friendships. *Journal of Social and Personal Relationships, 6,* 21–37.

Heasley, J. B., Babbitt, C. E., & Burbach, H. J. (1995). Gender differences in college students' perceptions of "fighting words." *Sociological Viewpoints, 11* (Fall), 30–40.

Hecht, M. L., Jackson, R. L., & Ribeau, S. (2003). *African American communication: Exploring identity and culture* (2nd ed.). Mahwah, NJ: Erlbaum.

Heenehan, M. (1997). *Networking.* New York: Random House.

Helgeson, V. S. (2009). *Psychology of gender* (3rd ed.). Upper Saddle River, NJ: Prentice Hall.

Hendrick, C., & Hendrick, S. S. (Eds.). (2000). *Close relationships: A sourcebook.* Thousand Oaks, CA: Sage.

Hendrick, C., Hendrick, S., Foote, F. H., & Slapion-Foote, M. J. (1984). Do men and women love differently? *Journal of Social and Personal Relationships, 1,* 177–195.

Hensley, W. E. (1996). A theory of the valenced other: The intersection of the looking-glass-self and social penetration. *Social Behavior and Personality, 24,* 293–308.

Hess, U., Kappas, A., McHugo, G. J., Lanzetta, J. T., et al. (1992, May). The facilitative effect of facial expression on the self-generation of emotion. *International Journal of Psychophysiology, 12,* 251–265.

Hinduja, S., & Patchin, J. W. (2008). *Bullying: Beyond the schoolyard.* Thousand Oaks, CA: Corwin Press/Sage.

Hirofumi, A. (2003). Closeness and interpersonal outcomes in same-sex friendships: An improvement of the investment model and explanation of closeness. *Japanese Journal of Experimental Social Psychology, 42* (March), 131–145.

Hocker, J. L., & Wilmot, W. W. (2007). *Interpersonal conflict* (2nd ed.). Dubuque, IA: William C. Brown.

Hofstede, G., Hofstede, G. J., & Minkov, M. (2010). *Cultures and organizations: Software of the mind* (3rd ed.). New York: McGraw-Hill.

Hoft, N. L. (1995). *International technical communication: How to export information about high technology.* New York: Wiley.

Holmes, J. (1986). Compliments and compliment responses in New Zealand English. *Anthropological Linguistic, 28,* 485–508.

Holmes, J. (1995). *Women, men and politeness.* New York: Longman.

Hunt, M. O. (2000). Status, religion, and the "belief in a just world": Comparing African Americans, Latinos, and whites. *Social Science Quarterly, 81,* 325–343.

Iizuka, Y. (1993). Regulators in Japanese conversation. *Psychological Reports, 72,* 203–209.

Infante, D. A. (1988). *Arguing constructively.* Prospect Heights, IL: Waveland Press.

Infante, D. A., & Rancer, A. (1982). A conceptualization and measure of argumentativeness. *Journal of Personality Assessment, 46,* 72–80.

Infante, D. A., & Rancer, A. S. (1996). Argumentativeness and verbal aggressiveness: A review of recent theory and research. In B. R. Burleson (Ed.), *Communication yearbook, 19* (pp. 319–351). Thousand Oaks, CA: Sage.

Infante, D. A., & Wigley, C. J. (1986). Verbal aggressiveness: An interpersonal model and measure. *Communication Monographs, 53,* 61–69.

Infante, D. A., Rancer, A. S., & Avtgis, T. A. (2010). *Contemporary communication theory.* Dubuque, IA: Kendall Hunt.

Ingegneri, R. (2008). How should you handle tattoos and body piercing during a job interview. http://ezinearticles.com/?expert=Rachel_Ingegneri.

Jackson, L. A., & Ervin, K. S. (1992, August). Height stereotypes of women and men: The liabilities of shortness for both sexes. *Journal of Social Psychology, 132,* 433–445.

Jacobson, D. (1999). Impression formation in cyberspace: Online expectations and offline experiences in text-based virtual communities. *Journal of Computer Mediated Communication, 5.*

Jambor, E., & Elliott, M. (2005, Winter). Self-esteem and coping strategies among deaf students. *Journal of Deaf Studies and Deaf Education, 10,* 63–81.

James, W. (1884). What is emotion? *Mind, 9*, 188–205.

Jandt, F. E. (2009). *Intercultural communication* (6th ed.). Thousand Oaks, CA: Sage.

Janus, S. S., & Janus, C. L. (1993). *The Janus report on sexual behavior.* Hoboken, NJ: Wiley.

Jaworski, A. (1993). *The power of silence: Social and pragmatic perspectives.* Newbury Park, CA: Sage.

Johannesen, R. L. (1974, Winter). The functions of silence: A plea for communication research. *Western Speech, 38,* 25–35.

Johannesen, R. L. (2001). *Ethics in human communication* (6th ed.). Prospect Heights, IL: Waveland Press.

Johannesen, R. L., Valde, K. S., & Whedbee, K. E. (2007). *Ethics in human communication* (6th ed.). Prospect Heights, IL: Waveland.

Johnson, C. E. (1987). An introduction to powerful and powerless talk in the classroom. *Communication Education, 36,* 167–172.

Johnson, M. P. (1973). Commitment: A conceptual structure and empirical application. *Sociological Quarterly, 14,* 395–406.

Johnson, M. P. (1982). Social and cognitive features of the dissolution of commitment to relationships. In S. Duck (Ed.). *Personal relationships 4: Dissolving personal relationships* (pp. 51–73). New York: Academic Press.

Johnson, M. P. (1991). Commitment to personal relationships. In W. H. Jones & D. Perlman (Eds.). *Advances in personal relationships, Vol. 3* (pp. 117–143). London: Jessica Kingsley.

Johnson, S. M., & O'Connor, E. (2002). *The gay baby boom: The psychology of gay parenthood.* New York: New York University Press.

Joiner, T. E. (1994). Contagious depression: Existence, specificity to depressed symptoms, and the role of reassurance seeking. *Journal of Personality and Social Psychology, 67,* 287–296.

Joinson, A. N. (2001). Self-disclosure in computer-mediated communication: The role of self-awareness and visual anonymity. *European Journal of Social Psychology, 31,* 177–192.

Jones, C., Berry, L., & Stevens, C. (2007). Synthesized speech intelligibility and persuasion: Speech rate and non-native listeners. *Computer Speech and Language, 21*, 641–651.

Jones, Q., Ravid, G., & Rafaeli, S. (2004). Information overload and the message dynamics of online interaction spaces: A theoretical model and empirical exploration. *Information Systems Research, 15* (June), 194–210.

Jones, S. (2005). The touch-log record: A behavioral communication measure. In V. Manusov (Ed.), *The sourcebook of nonverbal measures: Going beyond words* (pp. 67–81). Mahwah, NJ: Lawrence Erlbaum.

Jones, S., & Yarbrough, A. E. (1985). A naturalistic study of the meanings of touch. *Communication Monographs, 52,* 19–56.

Jourard, S. M. (1968). *Disclosing man to himself.* New York: Van Nostrand Reinhold.

Jourard, S. M. (1971). *The transparent self* (Rev. ed.). New York: Van Nostrand Reinhold.

Judge, T. A., & Cable, D. M. (2004). The effect of physical height on workplace success and income. *Journal of Applied Psychology, 89,* 428–441.

Kanner, B. (1989, April 3). Color schemes. *New York Magazine,* pp. 22–23.

Kapoor, S., Hughes, P. C., Baldwin, J. R., & Blue, J. (2003). The relationship of individualism-collectivism and self-construals to communication styles in India and the United States. *International Journal of Intercultural Relations, 27*, 683–700.

Katz, S. (2003). The importance of being beautiful. In J. W. Henslin (Ed.), *Down to earth sociology: Introductory readings* (11th ed., pp. 313–320). New York: Free Press.

Kelley, H. H., & Thibaut, J. W. (1978). *Interpersonal relations: A theory of interdependence.* New York: Wiley/Interscience.

Kennedy, C. W., & Camden, C. T. (1988). A new look at interruptions. *Western Journal of Speech Communication, 47,* 45–58.

Kennedy-Moore, E., & Watson, J. C. (1999). *Expressing emotion: Myths, realities, and therapeutic strategies.* New York: Guilford Press.

Keyes, R. (1980). *The height of your life.* New York: Warner.

Kim, Y. Y. (1988). Communication and acculturation. In L. A. Samovar & R. E. Porter (Eds.), *Intercultural communication: A reader* (5th ed., pp. 344–354). Belmont, CA: Wadsworth.

Kindred, J., & Roper, S. L. (2004). Making connections via instant messenger (IM): Student use of IM to maintain personal relationships. *Qualitative Research Reports in Communication, 5,* 48–54.

Klineberg, O., & Hull, W. F. (1979). *At a foreign university: An international study of adaptation and coping.* New York: Praeger.

Kluger, J. (2005, January 9). The funny thing about laughter. *Time,* pp. A25–A29.

Knapp, M. L. (2008). *Lying and deception in human interaction.* Boston: Pearson.

Knapp, M. L., & Hall, J. (2010). *Nonverbal communication in human interaction* (7th ed.). Belmont, CA: Wadsworth.

Knapp, M. L., & Taylor, E. H. (1994). Commitment and its communication in romantic relationships. In Ann L. Weber & J. H. Harvey (Eds.), *Perspectives on close relationships* (pp. 153–175). Boston: Allyn & Bacon.

Knapp, M. L., & Vangelisti, A. (2009). *Interpersonal communication and human relationships* (6th ed.). Boston: Allyn & Bacon.

Knobloch, L. K., & Solomon, D. H. (1999). Measuring the sources and content of relational uncertainty. *Communication Studies, 50,* 261–278.

Koerner, A. F., & Fitzpatrick, M. A. (1997). Family type and conflict: The impact of conversation orientation and conformity orientation on conflict in the family. *Communication Studies, 48,* 59–76.

Koerner, A. F., & Fitzpatrick, M. A. (2002). You never leave your family in a fight: The impact of family of origin of conflict behavior in romantic relationships. *Communication Studies*, 53 (Fall), 234–252.

Koppelman, K. L., with Goodhart, R. L. (2005). *Understanding human differences: Multicultural education for a diverse America.* Boston: Allyn & Bacon.

Korda, M. (1975). *Power! How to get it, how to use it.* New York: Ballantine.

Koscriski, K. (2007). Facial attractiveness: General patterns of facial preferences. *Anthropological Review, 70,* 45–79.

Krebs, G. L. (1989). *Organizational communication* (2nd ed.). Boston: Allyn & Bacon.

Kurdek, L. A. (1995). Developmental changes in relationship quality in gay and lesbian cohabiting couples. *Developmental Psychology, 31,* 86–93.

Kurdek, L. A. (2000). Attractions and constraints as determinants of relationship commitment: Longitudinal evidence from gay, lesbian, and heterosexual couples. *Personal Relationships, 7,* 245–262.

Kurdek, L. A. (2004). Are gay and lesbian cohabitating couples really different from heterosexual married couples? *Journal of Marriage and Family, 66* (November), 880–900.

Lachnit, C. (2001). Giving up gossip. *Workforce, 80,* 8.

Langer, E. J. (1989). *Mindfulness.* Reading, MA: Addison-Wesley.

Larsen, R. J., Kasimatis, M., & Frey, K. (1992). Facilitating the furrowed brow: An unobtrusive test of the facial feedback hypothesis applied to unpleasant affect. *Cognition and Emotion, 6,* 321–338.

Lea, M., & Spears, R. (1995). Love at first byte? Building personal relationships over computer networks. In J. T. Wood & S. Duck (Eds.), *Understudied relationships: Off the beaten track* (pp. 197–233). Thousand Oaks, CA: Sage.

Lederer, W. J. (1984). *Creating a good relationship.* New York: Norton.

Lee, F. (1993). Being polite and keeping MUM: How bad news is communicated in organizational hierarchies. *Journal of Applied Social Psychology, 23,* 1124–1149.

Lee, H. O., & Boster, F. J. (1992). Collectivism–individualism in perceptions of speech rate: A cross-cultural comparison. *Journal of Cross-Cultural Psychology, 23,* 377–388.

Lee, J. A. (1976). *The colors of love.* New York: Bantam.

Lee, K. (2000). Information overload threatens employee productivity. *Employee Benefit News* (November 1), 1.

Lee, R. M. (2005). Resilience against discrimination: Ethnic identity and other-group orientation as protective factors for Korean Americans. *Journal of Counseling Psychology, 52* (January), 36–44.

Lee, T. M. C., Liu, H. L., Tan, L. H., Chan, C. C. H., Mahankali, S., Feng, C. M., et al. (2002). Lie detection by functional magnetic resonance imaging. *Human Brain Mapping, 15,* 157–164.

Leech, G. (1983). *Principles of pragmatics.* London: Longman.

Lenhart, A., Madden, M., Macgill, A. R., & Smith, A. (2007). Teens and social media: The use of social media gains a greater foothold in teen life as they embrace the conversational nature of interaction online media. *Pew Internet & American Life Project.* Retrieved from http://www.pewinternet.org.

Lenhart, A., Madden, M., Smith, A., Purcell, K., Zickuhr, K., & Rainie, L. (2011). Teens, kindness and cruelty on social network sites. Retrieved from http://pewinterest.org/Reports/2011/Teens-and-social-media.aspx.

Leung, K. (1988, March). Some determinants of conflict avoidance. *Journal of Cross-Cultural Psychology, 19,* 125–136.

Leung, S. A. (2001). Editor's introduction. *Asian Journal of Counseling, 8,* 107–109.

Lever, J. (1995). The 1995 Advocate survey of sexuality and relationships: The women, lesbian sex survey. *The Advocate, 687/688,* 22–30.

LeVine, R., & Bartlett, K. (1984). Pace of life, punctuality, and coronary heart disease in six countries. *Journal of Cross-Cultural Psychology, 15,* 233–255.

LeVine, R., Sato, S., Hashimoto, T., & Verma, J. (1994). Love and marriage in eleven cultures. Unpublished manuscript. California State University, Fresno. Cited in Hatfield & Rapson (1996).

Lindeman, M., Harakka, T., & Keltikangas-Jarvinen, L. (1997). Age and gender differences in adolescents' reactions to conflict situations: Aggression, prosociality, and withdrawal. *Journal of Youth and Adolescence, 26,* 339–351.

Lloyd, S. R. (2001). *Developing positive assertiveness* (3rd ed.). Menlo Park, CA: Crisp Publications.

Luft, J. (1984). *Group process: An introduction of group dynamics* (3rd ed.). Palo Alto, CA: Mayfield.

Lukens, J. (1978). Ethnocentric speech. *Ethnic Groups, 2,* 35–53.

Lustig, M. W., & Koester, J. (2010). *Intercultural competence: Interpersonal communication across cultures* (6th ed.). Boston: Allyn & Bacon.

Mackey, R. A., Diemer, M. A., & O'Brien, B. A. (2000). Psychological intimacy in the lasting relationships of heterosexual and same-gender couples. *Sex Roles, 43,* 201–227.

MacLachlan, J. (1979). What people really think of fast talkers. *Psychology Today, 13,* 113–117.

Madon, S., Guyll, M., & Spoth, R. L. (2004). The self-fulfilling prophecy as an intrafamily dynamic. *Journal of Family Psychology, 18,* 459–469.

Mahaffey, A. L., Bryan, A., & Hutchison, K. E. (2005, March). Using startle eye blink to measure the affective component of antigay bias. *Basic and Applied Social Psychology, 27,* 37–45.

Malandro, L. A., Barker, L., & Barker, D. A. (1989). *Nonverbal communication* (2nd ed.). New York: Random House.

Manes, J., & Wolfson, N. (1981). The compliment formula. In F. Coulmas (Ed.), *Conversational routine* (pp. 115–132). The Hague: Mouton.

Marsh, P. (1988). *Eye to eye: How people interact.* Topside, MA: Salem House.

Martin, G. N. (1998). Human electroencephalographic (EEG) response to olfactory stimulation: Two experiments using the aroma of food. *International Journal of Psychophysiology, 30,* 287–302.

Martin, M. M., & Rubin, R. B. (1994). A new measure of cognitive flexibility. *Psychological Reports, 76,* 623–626.

Masuda, T., Ellsworth, P. C., Mesquita, B., Leu, J., Tanida, S., & van de Veerdonk, E. (2008). Placing the face in context: Cultural differences in the perception of facial emotion. *Journal of Personality and Social Psychology, 94,* 365–381.

Matsumoto, D., & Kudoh, T. (1993). American-Japanese cultural differences in attributions of personality based on smiles. *Journal of Nonverbal Behavior, 17,* 231–243.

McBroom, W. H., & Reed, F. W. (1992). Toward a reconceptualization of attitude-behavior consistency. Special Issue. Theoretical advances in social psychology. *Social Psychology Quarterly, 55,* 205–216.

McCroskey, J. C., & Wheeless, L. (1976). *Introduction to human communication.* Boston: Allyn & Bacon.

McDonald, E. J., McCabe, K., Yeh, M., Lau, A., Garland, A., & Hough, R. L. (2005). Cultural affiliation and self-esteem as predictors of internalizing symptoms among Mexican American adolescents. *Journal of Clinical Child and Adolescent Psychology, 34,* 163–171.

McGinley, S. (2000). Children and lying. *The University of Arizona College of Agriculture and Life Sciences* (http://www.ag.arizona.edu/pubs/general/resrpt2000/childrenlying.pdf, accessed September 24, 2009).

McGlone, M. S., & Giles, H. (2011). Language and interpersonal communication. In M. L. Knapp & J. A. Daly (Eds.), *The SAGE handbook of interpersonal communication* (4th ed., pp. 201–238). Los Angeles: Sage.

McNamee, S., & Gergen, K. J. (Eds.). (1999). *Relational responsibility: Resources for sustainable dialogue.* Thousand Oaks, CA: Sage.

Mealy, M., Stephan, W., & Urrutia, C. (2007). The acceptability of lies: A comparison of Ecuadorians and Euro-Americans. *International Journal of Intercultural Relations, 31,* 689–702.

Meeks, B. S., Hendrick, S. S., & Hendrick, C. (1998). Communication, love and relationship satisfaction. *Journal of Social and Personal Relationships, 15,* 755–773.

Mehl, M. R., Vazire, S., Ramirez-Esparza, N., Slatcher, R. B., & Pennebaker, J. W. (2007, July). Are women really more talkative than men? *Science* 6, 82.

Merton, R. K. (1957). *Social theory and social structure.* New York: Free Press.

Messick, R. M., & Cook, K. S. (Eds.). (1983). *Equity theory: Psychological and sociological perspectives.* New York: Praeger.

Metts, S., & Planalp, S. (2002). Emotional communication. In M. L. Knapp & J. A. Daly (Eds.), *Handbook of interpersonal communication* (3rd ed., pp. 339–373). Thousand Oaks, CA: Sage.

Midooka, K. (1990). Characteristics of Japanese style communication. *Media Culture and Society, 12,* 47–49.

Miller, G. R. (1978). The current state of theory and research in interpersonal communication. *Human Communication Research, 4,* 164–178.

Miller, G. R. (1990). Interpersonal communication. In G. L. Dahnke & G. W. Clatterbuck (Eds.), *Human communication: Theory and research* (pp. 91–122). Belmont, CA: Wadsworth.

Miller, L. R. (1997, December). Better ways to think and communicate. *Association Management, 49,* 71– 73.

Moghaddam, F. M., Taylor, D. M., & Wright, S. C. (1993). *Social psychology in cross-cultural perspective.* New York: W. H. Freeman.

Molloy, J. (1977). *The woman's dress for success book.* Chicago: Follett.

Molloy, J. (1981). *Molloy's live for success.* New York: Bantam.

Montagu, A. (1971). *Touching: The human significance of the skin.* New York: Harper & Row.

Moon, D. G. (1996). Concepts of "culture": Implications for intercultural communication research. *Communication Quarterly, 44,* 70–84.

Morgan, R. (2008). A crash course in online gossip. *New York Times* (March 16), Styles, p. 7.

Morreale, S. P., & Pearson, J. C. (2008). Why communication education is important: The centrality of the discipline in the 21st century. *Communication Education, 57* (April), 224–240.

Morrison, R. (2004). Informal relationships in the workplace: Associations with job satisfaction, organizational commitment and turnover intentions. *New Zealand Journal of Psychology*, *33*, 114–128.

Mosteller, T. (2008). *Relativism: A guide for the perplexed.* London: Continuum International Publishing Group.

Mottet, T., & Richmond, V. P. (1998). Verbal approach and avoidance items. *Communication Quarterly, 46,* 25–40.

Mullen, B., Salas, E., & Driskell, J. (1989). Salience, motivation, and artifact as contributions to the relation between participation rate and leadership. *Journal of Experimental Social Psychology, 25,* 545–559.

Myers, K. K., Siebold, D. R., & Park, H. S. (2011). Interpersonal communication in the workplace. In M. L. Knapp & J. A. Daly (Eds.), *The SAGE handbook of interpersonal communication* (4th ed., pp. 527–562). Los Angeles: Sage.

Myers, S. A., & Zhong, M. (2004). Perceived Chinese instructor use of affinity-seeking strategies and Chinese college student motivation. *Journal of Intercultural Communication Research, 33* (September–December), 119–130.

Neher, W. W., & Sandin, P. J. (2007). *Communicating ethically: Character, duties, consequences, and relationships.* Boston: Allyn & Bacon.

Neugarten, B. (1979). Time, age, and the life cycle. *American Journal of Psychiatry, 136,* 887–894.

Neuliep, J. W., & McCroskey, J. C. (1997). The development of a U.S. and generalized ethnocentrism scale. *Communication Research Reports, 14,* 385–398.

Nichols, M. P. (1995). *The lost art of listening: How learning to listen can improve relationships.* New York: Guilford Press.

Nichols, R., & Stevens, L. (1957). *Are you listening?* New York: McGraw-Hill.

Noble, B. P. (1994, August 14). The gender wars: Talking peace. *New York Times,* p. 21.

Noelle-Neumann, E. (1991). The theory of public opinion: The concept of the spiral of silence. In J. A. Anderson (Ed.), *Communication Yearbook 14* (pp. 256–287). Thousand Oaks, CA: Sage.

Noller, P. (1993). Gender and emotional communication in marriage: Different cultures or differential social power? [Special issue: Emotional Communication, Culture, and Power.] *Journal of Language and Social Psychology, 12,* 132–152.

Noller, P., & Fitzpatrick, M. A. (1993). *Communication in family relationships.* Englewood Cliffs, NJ: Prentice Hall.

Norton, R., & Warnick, B. (1976). Assertiveness as a communication construct. *Human Communication Research, 3,* 62–66.

Oatley, K., & Duncan, E. (1994). The experience of emotions in everyday life. *Cognition and Emotion, 8,* 369–381.

Oberg, K. (1960). Cultural shock: Adjustment to new cultural environments. *Practical Anthropology, 7,* 177–182.

Onishi, N. (2005, April 27). In Japan crash, time obsession may be culprit. *The New York Times,* pp. A1, A9.

Owens, T. J., Stryker, S., & Goodman, N. (Eds.) (2002). *Extending self-esteem research: Sociological and psychological currents.* Cambridge, MA: Cambridge University Press.

Parker, J. G. (2004, September). Planning and communication crucial to preventing workplace violence. *Safety and Health, 170,* 58–61.

Parker, R. G., & Parrott, R. (1995). Patterns of self-disclosure across social support networks: Elderly, middle-aged, and young adults. *International Journal of Aging and Human Development, 41,* 281–297.

Parks, M. R. (1995). Webs of influence in interpersonal relationships. In C. R. Berger & M. E. Burgoon (Eds.), *Communication and social influence processes* (pp. 155–178). East Lansing: Michigan State University Press.

Parks, M. R. (2011). Social networks and the life of relationships. In M. L. Knapp & J. A. Daly (Eds.), *The SAGE handbook of interpersonal communication* (4th ed., pp. 355–388). Los Angeles: Sage.

Parks, M. R., & Floyd, K. (1996). Making friends in cyberspace. *Journal of Communication, 46,* 80–97.

Patterson, C. (2000). Family relationships of lesbians and gay men. *Journal of Marriage and the Family,* 62, 1052–1067.

Paul, A. M. (2001). Self-help: Shattering the myths. *Psychology Today, 34,* 60ff.

Pearson, J. C. (1993). *Communication in the family,* 2d ed. Boston: Allyn & Bacon.

Pearson, J. C., & Spitzberg, B. H. (1990). *Interpersonal communication: Concepts, components, and contexts* (2nd ed.). Dubuque, IA: William C. Brown.

Pearson, J. C., West, R., & Turner, L. H. (1995). *Gender and communication* (3rd ed.). Dubuque, IA: William C. Brown.

Penfield, J. (Ed.). (1987). *Women and language in transition.* Albany, NY: State University of New York Press.

Pennebacker, J. W. (1991). *Opening up: The healing power of confiding in others.* New York: Avon.

Peplau, L. A. (1988). Research on homosexual couples: An overview. In *Gay relationships,* J. DeCecco (Ed.). New York: Harrington Park Press, pp. 33–40.

Peterson, C. C. (1996). The ticking of the social clock: Adults' beliefs about the timing of transition events. *International Journal of Aging and Human Development, 42,* 189–203.

Pilkington, C. J., & Richardson, D. R. (1988). Perceptions of risk in intimacy. *Journal of Social and Personal Relationships, 5,* 503–508.

Pilkington, C. J., & Woods, S. P. (1999). Risk in intimacy as a chronically accessible schema. *Journal of Social and Personal Relationships, 16,* 249–263.

Pittenger, R. E., Hockett, C. F., & Danehy, J. J. (1960). *The first five minutes.* Ithaca, NY: Paul Martineau.

Placencia, M. E. (2004). The online disinhibition effect. *Journal of Sociolinguistics, 8,* 215–245.

Plaks, J. E., Grant, H., & Dweck, C. S. (2005). Violations of implicit theories and the sense of prediction and control: Implications for motivated person perception. *Journal of Personality and Social Psychology, 88,* 245–262.

Plutchik, R. (1980). *Emotion: A psychoevolutionary synthesis.* New York: Harper & Row.

Pornpitakpan, C. (2003). The effect of personality traits and perceived cultural similarity on attraction. *Journal of International Consumer Marketing, 15,* 5–30.

Porter, R. H., & Moore, J. D. (1981). Human kin recognition by olfactory cues. *Physiology and Behavior, 27,* 493–495.

Raby, M. (2012). Facebook access becoming mandatory part of job, college applications. http://www.slashgear.com/facebook-access-becoming-mandatory-part-of-job-college-applications-06217136/.

Ragins, B. R., & Kram, K. E. (2007). *The handbook of mentoring at work: Theory, research, and practice.* Thousand Oaks, CA: Sage.

Rancer, A. S., & Avtgis, T. A. (2006). *Argumentative and aggressive communication: Theory, research, and application.* Thousand Oaks, CA: Sage.

Rancer, A. S., Lin, Y., Durbin, J. M., & Faulkner, E. C. (2010). Nonverbal "verbal" aggression: Its forms and its relation to trait verbal aggressiveness. In T. A. Avtgis & A. S. Rancer (Eds.), *Arguments, aggression, and conflict: New directions in theory and research* (pp. 267–284). New York: Routledge/Taylor & Francis.

Rapsa, R., & Cusack, J. (1990). Psychiatric implications of tattoos. *American Family Physician, 41,* 1481–1486.

Raven, R., Centers, C., & Rodrigues, A. (1975). The bases of conjugal power. In R. E. Cromwell & D. H. Olson (Eds.), *Power in families* (pp. 217–234). New York: Halsted Press.

Rawlins, W. K. (1989). A dialectical analysis of the tensions, functions, and strategic challenges of communication in young adult friendships. In J. A. Andersen (Ed.), *Communication Yearbook, 12* (pp. 157–189). Thousand Oaks, CA: Sage.

Rawlins, W. K. (1992). *Friendship matters: Communication, dialectics, and the life course.* Hawthorne, NY: Aldine DeGruyter.

Read, A. W. (2004). Language revision by deletion of absolutisms. *ETC: A Review of General Semantics, 61* (December), 456–462.

Reardon, K. K. (1987). *Where minds meet: Interpersonal communication.* Belmont, CA: Wadsworth.

Rector, M., & Neiva, E. (1996). Communication and personal relationships in Brazil. In W. B. Gudykunst, S. Ting-Toomey, & T. Nishida (Eds.), *Communication in personal relationships across cultures* (pp. 156–173). Thousand Oaks, CA: Sage.

Reed, M. D. (1993, Fall). Sudden death and bereavement outcomes: The impact of resources on grief, symptomatology and detachment. *Suicide and Life-Threatening Behavior, 23,* 204–220.

Reiner, D., & Blanton, K. (1997). *Person to person on the Internet.* Boston: AP Professional.

Reis, H. T., Maniaci, M. R., Caprariello, P. A., Eastwick, P. W., & Finkel, E. J. (2011). Familiarity does indeed promote attractive in live interaction. *Journal of Personality and Social Psychology, 101,* 557–570.

Reisenzein, R. (1983). The Schachter theory of emotion: Two decades later. *Psychological Bulletin* 94, 239–264.

Reisman, J. M. (1979). *Anatomy of friendship.* Lexington, MA: Lewis.

Reisman, J. M. (1981). Adult friendships. In S. Duck & R. Gilmour (Eds.), *Personal relationships. 2: Developing personal relationships* (pp. 205–230). New York: Academic Press.

Rhee, K. Y., & Kim, W-B (2004). The adoption and use of the Internet in South Korea, *Journal of Computer Mediated Communication, 9.*

Rice, M. (2007). Domestic violence. *National Center for PTSD Fact Sheet.* http://www.ncptsd.va.gov/ncmain/ncdocs/fact_ shts/fs_domestic_violence.html. Accessed May 20, 2008.

Rich, A. L. (1974). *Interracial communication.* New York: Harper & Row.

Richmond, V. P., McCroskey, J. C., & Hickson, M. L. (2008). *Nonverbal behavior in interpersonal relations* (6th ed.). Boston: Allyn & Bacon.

Richmond, V., McCroskey, J. C., & Hickson, M. (2012). *Nonverbal behavior in interpersonal relations* (7th ed.). Boston: Allyn & Bacon.

Richmond, V. P., McCroskey, J. C., & McCroskey, L. L. (2005). *Organizational communication for survival: Making work, work.* Boston: Allyn & Bacon.

Riggio, R. E., & Feldman, R. S. (Eds.). (2005). *Applications of nonverbal communication.* Mahwah, NJ: Lawrence Erlbaum.

Rogers, C. (1970). *Carl Rogers on encounter groups.* New York: Harrow Books.

Rogers, C., & Farson, R. (1981). Active listening. In J. DeVito (Ed.), *Communication: Concepts and processes* (3rd ed., pp. 137–147). Upper Saddle River, NJ: Prentice Hall.

Rokach, A. (1998). The relation of cultural background to the causes of loneliness. *Journal of Social and Clinical Psychology, 17,* 75–88.

Rokach, A., & Brock, H. (1995). The effects of gender, marital status, and the chronicity and immediacy of loneliness. *Journal of Social Behavior and Personality, 19,* 833–848.

Roloff, M. E., & Chiles, B. W. (2011). Interpersonal conflict: Recent trends. In M. L. Knapp & J. A. Daly (Eds.), *The SAGE handbook of interpersonal communication* (4th ed., pp. 423–442). Los Angeles: Sage.

Roloff, M. E., & Solomon, D. H. (2002). Conditions under which relational commitment leads to expressing or withholding relational complaints. *International Journal of Conflict Management, 13,* 276–291.

Roper Starch (1999). How Americans Communicate. http://www.natcom.org/research/Roper/how_americans_communicate.htm.

Rosen, E. (1998, October). Think like a shrink. *Psychology Today,* pp. 54–59.

Rosengren, A., et al. (1993, October 19). Stressful life events, social support, and mortality in men born in 1933. *British Medical Journal.* Cited in Goleman (1995a).

Rosenthal, R. (2002). Covert communication in classrooms, clinics, courtroom, and cubicles. *American Psychologist, 57,* 839–849.

Ruben, B. D. (1985). Human communication and cross-cultural effectiveness. In L. A. Samovar & R. E. Porter (Eds.), *Intercultural communication: A reader* (4th ed., pp. 338–346). Belmont, CA: Wadsworth.

Rubin, R. B., & McHugh, M. (1987). Development of parasocial interaction relationships. *Journal of Broadcasting and Electronic Media,* 31, 279–292.

Rydell, R. J., McConnell, A. R., & Bringle, R. G. (2004). Jealousy and commitment: Perceived threat and the effect of relationship alternatives. *Personal Relationships, 11* (December), 451–468.

Sahlstein, E. M. (2004). Relating at a distance: Negotiating being together and being apart in long-distance relationships. *Journal of Social and Personal Relationships, 21* (October), 689–710.

Sanders, J. A., Wiseman, R. L., & Matz, S. I. (1991). Uncertainty reduction in acquaintance relationships in Ghana and the United States. In S. Ting-Toomey & F. Korzenny (Eds.), *Cross-cultural interpersonal communication* (pp. 79–98). Thousand Oaks, CA: Sage.

Satir, V. (1983). *Conjoint family therapy* (3rd ed.). Palo Alto, CA: Science and Behavior Books.

Savitsky, K., Epley, N., & Gilovich, T. (2001). Do others judge us as harshly as we think? Overestimating the impact of our failures, shortcomings, and mishaps. *Journal of Personality and Social Psychology 81* (July), 44–56.

Schaap, C., Buunk, B., & Kerkstra, A. (1988). Marital conflict resolution. In P. Noller & M. A. Fitzpatrick (Eds.), *Perspectives on marital interaction* (pp. 203–244). Philadelphia, PA: Multilingual Matters.

Schachter, S. (1971). *Emotion, obesity and crime.* New York: Academic Press.

Scherer, K. R. (1986). Vocal affect expression. *Psychological Bulletin, 99,* 143–165.

Schmidt, T. O., & Cornelius, R. R. (1987). Self-disclosure in everyday life. *Journal of Social and Personal Relationships, 4,* 365–373.

Schott, G., & Selwyn, N. (2000). Examining the "male, antisocial" stereotype of high computer users. *Journal of Educational Computing Research, 23,* 291–303.

Schutz, A. (1999). It was your fault! Self-serving biases in autobiographical accounts of conflicts in married couples. *Journal of Social and Personal Relationships, 16,* 193–208.

Schwartz, E. (2005, February 28). Watch what you say. *InfoWorld, 27,* 8.

Schwartz, M., & Task Force on Bias-Free Language of the Association of American University Presses. (1995). *Guidelines for bias-free writing.* Bloomington, IN: Indiana University Press.

Shaw, L. H., & Grant, L. M. (2002). Users divided? Exploring the gender gap in Internet use. *CyberPsychology & Behavior, 5* (December), 517–527.

Sheese, B. E., Brown, E. L, & Graziano, W. G. (2004, September). Emotional expression in cyberspace: Searching for moderators of the Pennebaker disclosure effect via e-mail. *Health Psychology, 23,* 457–464.

Shirley, J. A., Powers, W. G., & Sawyer, C. R. (2007). Psychologically abusive relationships and self-disclosure orientations. *Human Communication 10,* 289–302.

Sieter, J. S. (2007). Ingratiation and gratuity: The effect of complimenting customers on tipping behavior in restaurants. *Journal of Applied Social Psychology, 37,* 478–485.

Singh, N., & Pereira, A. (2005). *The culturally customized web site.* Oxford, UK: Elsevier Butterworth-Heinemann.

Smith, A. (2011). Why Americans use social media. Pew Research Center Publications. Retrieved from www.pewresearch.org.

Smith, M. H. (2003). Body adornment: Know the limits. *Nursing Management, 34,* 22–23.

Smith, R. (2004, April 10). The teaching of communication skills may be misguided. *British Medical Journal, 328,* 1–2.

Snyder, M. (1992). A gender-informed model of couple and family therapy: Relationship enhancement therapy. *Contemporary Family Therapy: An International Journal, 14,* 15–31.

Sorenson, P. S., Hawkins, K., & Sorenson, R. L. (1995). Gender, psychological type and conflict style preferences. *Management Communication Quarterly, 9,* 115–126.

Spence, C. (2008). Sensing the future. Retrieved from www.aqr.org.uk/inbrief/document.shtml?doc=charles.spence.28-02-2008.fut.

Spencer, T. (1993). A new approach to assessing self-disclosure in conversation. Paper presented at the Annual Convention of the Western Speech Communication Association, Albuquerque, New Mexico.

Spencer, T. (1994). Transforming relationships through everyday talk. In S. Duck (Ed.), *The dynamics of relationships: Vol. 4. Understanding relationships.* Thousand Oaks, CA: Sage.

Spett, M. (2004). Expressing negative emotions: Healthy catharsis or sign of pathology? www.nj-act.org/article2.html, accessed September 24, 2009.

Spitzberg, B. H. (1991). Intercultural communication competence. In L. A. Samovar & R. E. Porter (Eds.), *Intercultural communication: A reader* (pp. 353–365). Belmont, CA: Wadsworth.

Spitzberg, B. H., & Cupach, W. R. (1989). *Handbook of interpersonal competence research.* New York: Springer.

Spitzberg, B. H., & Cupach, W. R. (2002). Interpersonal skills. In M. L. Knapp & J. A. Daly (Eds.), *Handbook of interpersonal communication* (3rd ed., pp. 564–611). Thousand Oaks, CA: Sage.

Spitzberg, B. H., & Cupach, W. R. (2011). Interpersonal skills. In M. L. Knapp & J. A. Daly (Eds.), *The SAGE handbook of interpersonal communication* (4th ed., pp. 481–526). Los Angeles: Sage.

Spitzberg, B. H., & Hecht, M. L. (1984). A component model of relational competence. *Human Communication Research, 10,* 575–599.

Sprecher, S. (1987). The effects of self-disclosure given and received on affection for an intimate partner and stability of the relationship. *Journal of Social and Personal Relationships, 4,* 115–127.

Sprecher, S., & Hendrick, S. S. (2004). Self-disclosure in intimate relationships: Associations with individual and relationship characteristics over time. *Journal of Social and Clinical Psychology, 23* (December), 857–877.

Sprecher, S., & Metts, S. (1989). Development of the "romantic beliefs scale" and examination of the effects of gender and gender-role orientation. *Journal of Social and Personal Relationships, 6,* 387–411.

Sprecher, S., & Toro-Morn, M. (2002). A study of men and women from different sides of earth to determine if men are from Mars and women are from Venus in their beliefs about love and romantic relationships. *Sex Roles, 46* (March), 131–147.

Stafford, L. (2008). Social exchange theories. In L. A. Baxter & D. O. Braithwaite (Eds.), *Engaging theories in interpersonal communication: Multiple perspectives* (pp. 377–389). Los Angeles: Sage.

Steil, L. K., Barker, L. L., & Watson, K. W. (1983). *Effective listening: Key to your success.* Reading, MA: Addison-Wesley.

Stein, S. J., & Book, H. E. (2011). *The EQ edge: Emotional intelligence and your success.* Hoboken, NJ: Wiley.

Stephan, W. G., & Stephan, C. W. (1985). Intergroup anxiety. *Journal of Social Issues, 41,* 157–175.

Stewart, L. P., Cooper, P. J., & Stewart, A. D., with Friedley, S. A. (2003). *Communication and gender* (4th ed.). Boston: Allyn & Bacon.

Stewart, S. (2006). A pilot study of email in an e-mentoring relationship. *Journal of Telemedicine and Telecare 12* (October), 83–85.

Suler, J. (2004). The online disinhibition effect. *CyberPsychology and Behavior, 7,* 321–326.

Sutcliffe, K., Lewton, E., & Rosenthal, M. M. (2004, February). Communication failures: An insidious contributor to medical mishaps. *Academic Medicine, 79,* 186–194.

Swanbrow, D. (2011, May 16). Persuasive speech: The way we, um, talk sways our listeners. University of Michigan, Institute for Social Research, ISR Sampler. Retrieved from ns.umich.edu/new/releases/8404.

Tang, S., & Zuo, J. (2000). Dating attitudes and behaviors of American and Chinese college students. *The Social Science Journal, 37* (January), 67–78.

Tannen, D. (1990). *You just don't understand: Women and men in conversation.* New York: Morrow.

Tannen, D. (1994a). *Gender and discourse.* New York: Oxford University Press.

Tannen, D. (1994b). *Talking from 9 to 5: How women's and men's conversational styles affect who gets heard, who gets credit, and what gets done at work.* New York: Morrow.

Tannen, D. (2006). *You're wearing that? Understanding mothers and daughters in conversation.* New York: Random House.

Tavris, C. (1989). *Anger: The misunderstood emotion* (2nd ed.). New York: Simon & Schuster.

Teacher & Educational Development (2005). Effective use of performance objectives for learning and assessment. University of New Mexico School of Medicine (http://ccoe.umdnj.edu/forms/EffectiveUseofLearningObjectives.pdf).

Teven, J. J., Richmond, V. P., & McCroskey, J. C. (1998). Measuring tolerance for disagreement. *Communication Research Reports,* 15, 209-221.

Thibaut, J. W., & Kelley, H. H. (1959). *The social psychology of groups.* New York: Wiley. Reissued (1986). New Brunswick, NJ: Transaction Books.

Thorne, B., Kramarae, C., & Henley, N. (Eds.). (1983). *Language, gender and society.* Rowley, MA: Newbury House.

Tierney, P., & Farmer, S. M. (2004). The Pygmalion process and employee creativity. *Journal of Management, 30,* 413–432.

Timmerman, L. J. (2003). Comparing the production of power in language on the basis of sex. In M. Allen & R. W. Preiss (Eds.), *Interpersonal communication research: Advances through meta-analysis* (pp. 73–88). Mahwah, NJ: Erlbaum.

Ting-Toomey, S. (1981). Ethnic identity and close friendship in Chinese-American college students. *International Journal of Intercultural Relations, 5,* 383–406.

Ting-Toomey, S. (1985). Toward a theory of conflict and culture. *International and Intercultural Communication Annual, 9,* 71–86.

Tinsley, C. H., & Brett, J. M. (2001). Managing workplace conflict in the United States and Hong Kong. *Organizational Behavior and Human Decision Processes, 85,* 360–381.

Trager, G. L. (1958). Paralanguage: A first approximation. *Studies in Linguistics, 13,* 1–12.

Trager, G. L. (1961). The typology of paralanguage. *Anthropological Linguistics, 3,* 17–21.

Tyler, J. J., Feldman, R. S., & Reichert, A. (2006). The price of deceptive behavior: Disliking and lying to people who lie to us. *Journal of Experimental Social Psychology, 42,* 69–77.

Ueleke, W., et al. (1983). Inequity resolving behavior as a response to inequity in a hypothetical marital relationship. *Quarterly Journal of Human Behavior, 20,* 4–8.

Vainiomaki, T. (2004). Silence as a cultural sign. *Semiotica, 150,* 347–361.

Van Praagh, J. (2010). I am! I can! I will! (www.healyourlife.com).

Vangelisti, A. L. (2011). Interpersonal processes in romantic relationships. In M. L. Knapp & J. A. Daly (Eds.), *The SAGE handbook of interpersonal communication* (4th ed., pp. 597–622). Los Angeles: Sage.

Varenik, T. (2010). How tattoos and body piercing affect your career. http://www.resumark.com/blog/tatiana/how-tattoos-and-body-piercing-affect-your-career.

Varma, A., Toh, S. M, Pichler, S. (2006). Ingratiation in job applications: Impact on selection decisions. *Journal of Managerial Psychology, 21,* 200–210.

Victor, D. (1992). *International business communication.* New York: HarperCollins.

Vonk, R. (2002). Self-serving interpretations of flattery: Why ingratiation works. *Journal of Personality and Social Psychology, 82,* 515–526.

Waddington, K. (2004). Psst—spread the word—gossiping is good for you. *Practice Nurse, 27,* 7–10.

Wade, C., & Tavris, C. (1998). *Psychology* (5th ed.). New York: Longman.

Walster, E., Walster, G. W., & Berscheid, E. (1978). *Equity: Theory and research.* Boston: Allyn & Bacon.

Walther, J. B. (2011). Theories of computer-mediated communication and interpersonal relations. In M. L. Knapp & J. A. Daly (Eds.), *The SAGE handbook of interpersonal communication* (4th ed., pp. 443–480). Los Angeles: Sage.

Watzlawick, P. (1977). *How real is real? Confusion, disinformation, communication: An anecdotal introduction to communications theory.* New York: Vintage.

Watzlawick, P. (1978). *The language of change: Elements of therapeutic communication.* New York: Basic Books.

Watzlawick, P., Beavin, J., & Jackson, D. D. (1967). *Pragmatics of human communication: A study of interactional patterns, pathologies, and paradoxes.* New York: Norton.

Weathers, M. D., Frank, E. M., & Spell, L. A. (2002). Differences in the communication of affect: Members of the same race versus members of a different race. *Journal of Black Psychology, 28,* 66–77.

Weinberg, H. L. (1959). *Levels of knowing and existence.* New York: Harper & Row.

Wert, S. R., & Salovey, P. (2004). Introduction to the special issue on gossip. *Review of General Psychology, 8,* 76–77.

Wetzel, P. J. (1988). Are "powerless" communication strategies the Japanese norm? *Language in Society, 17,* 555–564.

Wheeless, L. R., & Grotz, J. (1977). The measurement of trust and its relationship to self-disclosure. *Human Communication Research, 3,* 250–257.

Whitty, M. (2003). Cyber-flirting. *Theory and Psychology, 13,* 339–355.

Whitty, M., & Gavin, J. (2001). Age/sex/location: Uncovering the social cues in the development of online relationships. *Cyber-Psychology and Behavior, 4,* 623–630.

Wigley, C. J., III. (1998). Verbal aggressiveness. In J. C. McCroskey, J. A. Daly, M. M. Martin, & M. J. Beatty (Eds.), *Communication and personality: Trait perspectives* (pp. 191–214). Cresskill, NJ: Hampton Press.

Wilkins, B. M., & Andersen, P. A. (1991). Gender differences and similarities in management communication: A meta-analysis. *Management Communication Quarterly, 5,* 6–35.

Willson, R., & Branch, R. (2006). *Cognitive behavioural therapy for dummies.* West Sussex, England: Wiley.

Wilson, S. R., & Sabee, C. M. (2003). Explicating communicative competence as a theoretical term. In J. O. Greene & B. R. Burleson (Eds.), *Handbook of communication and social interaction skills* (pp. 3–50). Mahwah, NJ: Erlbaum.

Winquist, L. A., Mohr, D., & Kenny, David A. (1998, September). The female positivity effect in the perception of others. *Journal of Research in Personality, 32,* 370–388.

Winters, J. (2009). Olfactory communication and mate choice. www.replicatedtypo.wordpress.com/2009/09/01/olfaction.

Wolak, J., Mitchell, K. J., & Finkelhor, D. (2003). Escaping or connecting? Characteristics of youth who form close online relationships. *Journal of Adolescence, 26,* 105–119.

Wood, J. T. (1994). *Gendered lives: Communication, gender, and culture.* Belmont, CA: Wadsworth.

Wrench, J. S., & McCroskey, J. C. (2003). A communibiological examination of ethnocentrism and homophobia. *Communication Research Reports, 20,* 24–33.

Wrench, J. S., McCroskey, J. C., & Richmond, V. P. (2008). *Human communication in everyday life: Explanations and applications.* Boston: Allyn & Bacon.

Wright, P. H. (1978). Toward a theory of friendship based on a conception of self. *Human Communication Research, 4,* 196–207.

Wright, P. H. (1984). Self-referent motivation and the intrinsic quality of friendship. *Journal of Social and Personal Relationships, 1,* 115–130.

Yau-fair Ho, D., Chan, S. F., Peng, S., & Ng, A. K. (2001). The dialogical self: Converging East–West constructions. *Culture and Psychology, 7,* 393–408.

Young, K. S., Griffin-Shelley, E., Cooper, A., O'Mara, J., & Buchanan, J. (2000). Online infidelity: A new dimension in couple relationships with implications for evaluation and treatment. *Sexual Addiction and Compulsivity, 7,* 59–74.

Yuki, M., Maddux, W. W., Masuda, T. (2007). Are the windows to the soul the same in the East and West? Cultural differences in using the eyes and mouth as cues to recognize emotions in Japan and the United States. *Journal of Experimental Social Psychology, 43,* 303–311.

Yun, H. (1976). The Korean personality and treatment considerations. *Social Casework, 57,* 173–178.

Zhang, S., & Merolla, A. (2006). Communicating dislike of close friends' romantic partners. *Communication Research Reports, 23 (3),* 179–186.

Zunin, L. M., & Zunin, N. B. (1972). *Contact: The first four minutes.* Los Angeles: Nash.

Zunin, L. M., & Zunin, N. B. (1991). *Contact: The first four minutes.* Los Angeles: Nash.

CREDITS

Photo Credits

page 1: Lewis Jacobs/NBC/NBCU Photo Bank/Getty Images; **page 2:** Claudiu Paizan/Fotolia; **page 10 (t):** OJO Images/SuperStock; **page 10 (b):** Tomas Del Amo/Alamy; **page 13:** Tyler Olson/Shutterstock; **page 14:** Tyler Olson/Shutterstock; **page 22:** The Everett Collection; **page 25:** Lewis Jacobs/NBC/NBCU Photo Bank/Getty Images; **page 28:** Jeff Greenberg/Alamy; **page 29:** Photos 12/Alamy; **page 32:** AP Photo/Robert E. Klein; **page 34:** White House Photo/Alamy; **page 36:** Digital Vision/Thinkstock; **page 39:** moodboard/Alamy; **page 43:** Giulio Andreini/MARKA/Alamy; **page 47:** Pearson; **page 50:** Jeff Greenberg/Alamy; **page 53:** Doug Hyun/ABC Studios via Getty Images; **page 56:** Nigel Hicks/Dorling Kindersley; **page 60:** Nigel Hicks/Dorling Kindersley; **page 63:** Ariel Skelley/Glow Images; **page 69:** MIXA/Alamy; **page 72:** Pearson; **page 75:** Stephen Coburn/Shutterstock; **page 76:** Doug Hyun/ABC Studios via Getty Images; **page 79:** White House Photo/Alamy; **page 81:** Dmitriy Shironosov/Shutterstock; **page 87:** Larry Williams/Corbis; **page 88:** Pearson; **page 89:** Trappe/Caro/Alamy; **page 93:** Alberto Ruggieri/Images.com/Corbis; **page 98:** Ryan McVay/Getty Images; **page 99:** White House Photo/Alamy; **page 101:** KPA Honorar & Belege/United Archives GmbH/Alamy; **page 103:** Digital Vision/Getty Images; **page 104:** Yuri Arcurs/Alamy; **page 105:** Pearson; **page 110:** Rostislav Glinsky/Shutterstock; **page 113:** ImagesBazaar/Alamy; **page 119:** Eric Audras/Onoky/Age Fotostock; **page 123:** KPA Honorar & Belege/United Archives GmbH/Alamy; **page 125:**Randy Tepper/© CBS/Courtesy: Everett Collection; **page 131:** joSon/Photodisc/Getty Images; **page 135:** David Mager/Pearson; **page 138:** NetPhotos/Alamy; **page 139:** Corbis Premium RF/Alamy; **page 143:** BAVARIA/Taxi/Getty Images; **page 148:** Pearson; **page 149:** Randy Tepper/© CBS/Courtesy: Everett Collection; **page 151:** Hector Vivas/Jam Media/LatinContent/Getty Images; **page 157:** Javier Pierini/Digital Vision/Getty Images; **page 161:** Vladimir Mucibabic/Shutterstock; **page 165:** isifa Image Service s.r.o./Alamy; **page 166:** Pearson; **page 168:** NetPhotos/Alamy; **page 170:** Hector Vivas/Jam Media/LatinContent/Getty Images; **page 172:** Eric Liebowitz/CBS via Getty Images; **page 174:** Pearson; **page 180:** CJG - Technology/Alamy; **page 182:** Big Cheese Photo/Big Cheese/AGE Fotostock; **page 186:** Pearson; **page 189 (b):** Corbis Cusp/Alamy; **page 191:** Dmitriy Shironosov/Shutterstock; **page 193:** Eric Liebowitz/CBS via Getty Images; **page 195:** AP Photo/Charles Sykes; **page 196:** allOver photography/Alamy; **page 197:** Angela Hampton Picture Library/Alamy; **page 201:** Pearson; **page 205:** Inmagine/Alamy; **page 206:** Martin Novak/Alamy; **page 210:** AF archive/Alamy; **page 214:** AP Photo/Charles Sykes; **page 216:** Peter "Hopper" Stone/Getty Images; **page 217:** Allford Trotman/Alamy; **page 219:** Radoslaw Korga/Shutterstock; **page 221:** Pearson; **page 222:** Michael Newman/PhotoEdit; **page 227:** Monkey Business Images/Shutterstock; **page 236:** Chad Ehlers/Alamy; **page 237:** Peter "Hopper" Stone/Getty Images; **page 240:** RIA Novosti/Alamy; **page 242:** Danny Feld/Disney ABC Television Group/Getty Images; **page 246:** Monkey Business Images/Shutterstock; **page 251:** Wavebreakmedia ltd/Shutterstock; **page 255:** DAJ/Amana Images inc./Alamy; **page 256 (t):** Warren Goldswain/Shutterstock; **page 256 (b):** Pearson; **page 259:**RIA Novosti/Alamy.

INDEX

Note: Italicized letters *f* and *t* following page numbers indicate figures and tables, respectively; italicized page numbers indicate glossary terms.

INTERPERSONAL MESSAGE SKILLS

Interpersonal Message Skills	Interpersonal Message Skills in Action	Interpersonal Messages Skills' Benefits
General Interpersonal Awareness Skills Chapter 1 and *Ethical Messages* boxes	• Communicating mindfully and ethically in face-to-face and computer-mediated situations • Adjusting your interpersonal messages to the situation	Increased satisfaction and greater effectiveness in accomplishing your interpersonal task
Cultural Skills Chapter 2 and throughout text	• Communicating cultural sensitivity by reducing your ethnocentrism, confronting your stereotypes, reducing uncertainty, and recognizing differences • Communicating effectively in intercultural communication situations	Profit from different cultural perspectives and avoid intercultural conflict and the perception of insensitivity
Self Skills Chapter 3	• Increasing perceptual accuracy by analyzing your own perceptions, reducing your uncertainty, checking your perceptions, and increasing your cultural sensitivity • Communicate desired and desirable impressions to others	Interact with greater confidence in a variety of interpersonal situations Perceive people and events more accurately Manage the impressions you communicate to others
Perception Skills Chapter 3	• Avoiding the pitfalls of perception, for example, creating self-fulfilling prophecies or giving inordinate attention to what comes first or last • Analyzing the bases of your perceptions, checking your perceptions, reducing your uncertainty, and increasing your cultural awareness	Perceive people and messages more accurately while avoiding the common obstacle that perceptual shortcuts can create
Listening Skills Chapter 4	• Listening effectively by avoiding the barriers to listening in receiving, understanding, remembering, evaluating, and responding • Adjusting your listening on the basis of the type of interpersonal interaction	Learn, relate, influence, play, and help more effectively through listening